CATAFALQUE

Other books by Peter Kingsley

Ancient Philosophy, Mystery and Magic

In the Dark Places of Wisdom

Reality

A Story Waiting to Pierce You

CATAFALQUE

BY PETER KINGSLEY

CARL JUNG AND THE END OF HUMANITY

First hardcover edition, in two volumes, 2018
First paperback edition, with minor revisions, 2021
Published by Catafalque Press, London
www.catafalquepress.com
contact@catafalquepress.com

ISBN 978-1-9996384-1-2

Painting on cover:
Cosmos by Neville Sattentau
www.nevart.co.uk

Book design by Leslie Bartlett
www.lesliebartlett.com

British Library Cataloguing in Publication Data
A catalogue record for this book is
available from the British Library

CONTENTS

ONE

1	MYSTICAL FOOL	3
2	BACK TO THE SOURCE	93
3	THE SUNSET WAY	209
4	CATAFALQUE	359

TWO

5	ABBREVIATIONS	451
6	NOTES	463
7	INDEX	801

Et ensi comme je sui oscurs et serai
enviers chiaus ou je ne me vaurrai esclairier,
ensi sera tous li livres celés
et peu avenra que ja nus en face bonté

1
MYSTICAL
FOOL

MYSTICAL FOOL

1

Something's beginning is always a particularly magical point, the opening into a world that's new.

There—this book has already begun, which means the magic has been done. And, now, all that's needed is to find the words to fill the abyss between beginning and end.

Probably it will be best to start with Eranos. Dreamed up during the early 1930s, the Eranos meetings began taking place each summer at Ascona in southern Switzerland and would soon become notorious.

Their original purpose was ambitious but simple—to create a supportive forum for openly and sincerely discussing spirituality, philosophy, the profoundest questions humans can ask about themselves or the world around them.

And over time the most influential figure at these meetings, due to his own presence as well as the people he drew to them, came to be Carl Jung.[1]

Because of my work on the origins of western civilization I was invited to speak at the Eranos gathering in August 2013. This book is an expanded version of the talks that, to the shocked surprise of many respectable people present, I delivered there.

Speaking at Eranos provided me with the opportunity to complete a certain circle in my life by acknowledging, and paying deep respects to, two people with whom I have the closest of ties. One of them is Henry Corbin; the other, Carl Jung.

It also gave me the chance to say a few things in public, for the first and perhaps the last time, about how my life's work has intersected with Jung's work as well as Corbin's. And it allowed me to complete a much larger circle by outlining what this all has to say about the nature of cultures—especially about the fate or destiny of our western civilization.

Both Carl Jung, somewhat ostentatiously, and Henry Corbin, a little more discreetly, played crucial roles at Eranos. Jung was one of the greatest and most original researchers in psychology the West has ever known. Corbin was welcomed into the Eranos circle as one of the greatest living experts on Sufi mystical tradition and as a scholar who, almost single-handedly, introduced the sophisticated realities of Persian spiritual wisdom to the West.

On the surface, the two of them could hardly have been more unlike each other in terms of training or formal interests. But inwardly it was a very different matter. And this can be rather difficult to grasp for people who never quite managed to learn what it means to look beneath the surface.

From one side we happen to have Jung's own words confirming in no ambiguous or uncertain terms that Henry Corbin was the one person who understood him far better than anybody else: that it was Corbin who had given him "not only the rarest of experiences, but the unique experience, of being completely understood".[2]

Such a meaningful statement should give us pause for thought—a very long pause.

And from the other side we have the striking words by Corbin, that he wrote to explain what became possible at

Eranos through the influence and inspiration of Carl Jung. He described how Jung's presence produced an "atmosphere of absolute spiritual freedom in which all individuals express themselves without the slightest concern for any official dogma and with just a single goal in mind: to be themselves, to be *true*".[3]

This, too, deserves pondering very carefully. To be true, not to be clever or entertaining or even inspiring but to be true, was no easy or casual matter in the eyes of Corbin. It meant far more for him than all the glib, superficial talk one tends to hear nowadays about me living my truth and you living yours—just as "truth" for him meant infinitely more than some arbitrary collection of facts.

To him truth, as well as the act of being genuinely true, are timeless and sacred realities that turn our whole illusory world of appearances upside down. They throw us off our comfortable chairs by showing us we are not the personalities we imagined we were: point us back to our true origin, our spiritual source.[4]

Of course words like this can sound very inspiring. But that, too, is just a part of the illusoriness—because we have managed even to turn spirituality into an illusion so we can protect ourselves from the reality of the spirit.

Our modern democratic age has manufactured a personal spirituality to meet everyone's needs which is absolutely guaranteed to be calm, sweet, peaceful, polite, positive, comfortable, reassuring, unthreatening. And instead of leaving the sacred well alone, which would have been the wisest thing to do, we domesticated it no less effectively than we managed to domesticate everything else; trivialized and thoroughly prettified it; agreed on making it into something politically correct.

But this happens to be almost the exact opposite of the ancient understanding—which is that spirituality and the sacred offer the profoundest challenge to our complacency, as well as presenting the most radical threat. The spirit is not only there to make us think deeply. It exists to take us into places where thinking becomes useless and even our cleverest ideas are left behind.

The story is just the same with regard to truth, or being true: they have come to mean more or less whatever we want them to mean. As a result we have lost any sense for the overarching, sacred reality of Truth that exists in virtually every culture except our own.

It can be helpful now to try and remember how according to ancient Greek tradition—which aside from being the tradition I feel closest to is also the source and seedbed of western culture—truth was seen as something extremely painful, even impossible, for most people to bear.

Truth, or *alêtheia*, had its own mythology that confronts humans with the grim but glorious reality of what they are "from the beginning": unimaginably glorious because of their boundless inner potential and unthinkably grim because of the overwhelming responsibilities such a forgotten potential brings.

This is why it—or she, because Truth often appears as a goddess—was always intimately involved in the superhuman effort to stop that process of forgetting. Her role, above all, was to preside over the supremely urgent task of remembering not what happened yesterday or even last month but what happened in the distant past that shaped this present moment and will also produce our future.[5]

So I am not going to be speaking very much about the past as the past. Neither do I plan on offering a view of ancient Greek spirituality as some pretty oasis: as one more fascinating distraction, yet another illusion.

I have been researching, writing, speaking, teaching about the distant past for over forty years; and to me the past as past is no longer relevant. Through writing more and more about the ancient world, about the origins of western civilization, I have ended up being forced—paradoxically but also quite logically—into the present time.

In other words, what I am going to be focusing on is the past as present: on how those aspects of the past we have been forced to forget have shaped and created the bizarre world that we live in.[6]

We are living through an extraordinarily difficult time now. The trouble is that most people, however intelligent they happen to be and however keen to keep up with the news, don't have the slightest wish to see with open eyes what really is happening in our world. Even if they sense or intuit or suspect something, they have an overwhelming urge to tune it all out and say "No, no: I don't want to know. I just want to go on as before."

Well, there is no going on as before. Maybe we'll think we can act in the same way for a few more years; but what we are leaving behind us is a totally different world. And we have a certain responsibility to wake up to the awareness of what that means.

I am going to be saying some disturbing things and there is no point in apologizing for that, because this is the truth of where western civilization has brought us. It has all been leading up to here.

Everything that was implicit in our civilization from the very beginning, everything that was already contained inside the seed of western culture, is being acted out now—in spite of us and regardless of our best intentions—because of what we have agreed to forget.

Our future is guaranteed, automatically determined, by the fundamental fact that we failed to honour our sacred source.

2

Talking at Eranos was the first time I'd spoken openly in two or three years.

It was a dream that, back at the start of 2011, bluntly and very directly instructed me to stop all the things I was doing: public speaking, teaching, meetings, interviews. Plenty of other dreams had also been pointing in the same direction, but this one was infinitely more explicit.

For a short time I found myself uncertain what to do—heavily leaning towards taking the radical actions needed, although only leaning. It goes without saying that one has to be a little crazy to pay too much attention to dreams.

In fact even most of the Jungians I have met, who literally make dreams their business, insist that no balanced person should ever obey messages or instructions given through a dream. Instead you have to argue with them; do some good negotiating; assert your conscious wishes; give all due weight to your own position.

But of course in this world everything ultimately becomes a question of picking one's preferred form of madness.

A couple of days later the matter was taken out of my hands. Two friends, living thousands of miles apart, called me almost at the same moment after having the most vivid dreams which very plainly were meant for me. And, just as plainly, both dreams were confirming the obvious and explicit message of my dream. Traditionally, in important matters one indication always needs to be considered with all due seriousness—but three indications are something that has to be acted on straight away.[7]

It became clear to me that everything had already been settled. I was being forced to obey and start carrying out the necessary changes.

One commitment which had become too late to cancel was an agreement I had made to speak at a large event near where my wife and I lived in North Carolina. I could never understand why I accepted the invitation in the first place, as the organizers were among the most difficult people imaginable. But just before the day of the event, that mystery was solved.

At the last moment an old Cherokee medicine woman in her eighties came down from the hills because she had been shown there was something she needed to do. When I arrived a little early on the morning of the gathering, she was there waiting; we went into a small room together to be alone. As we talked, I remembered my recent dream about stopping speaking and mentioned it to her.

Without a moment's hesitation she told me that the only reason she was there was because a bear had recently walked up her driveway, during the night, to wake her and announce that her presence and voice would be needed at this particular event. It had been years, she explained, since she had spoken in public because she had been living the life of silent solitude ever since a clear dream ordered her to stop any outer activity and put all her energy into going entirely inside herself.

Then, just before we stood up to go onto the stage and talk to the audience together, she leaned forward in her chair with the energy of a teenager and exclaimed: "Of course we obey these dreams! We *always* obey such dreams!"

There is no describing the refreshment of being able to see how intense and unpretentious, how simple and spontaneous, this wise woman was in responding with a whole heart to the call of life even when it disrupts all our tidy schemes and conscious plans.[8]

For myself, putting a complete end to any public speaking and sinking into inner silence led to the sudden realization that I had already finished planting the seeds of my work in North America. It also showed me what was needed next: to focus on creating a far stronger support for everything already seeded by returning, as close as humanly possible, to the original roots of this work in Europe.

And there is a certain edge of irony in the fact that a very dear friend—one of the few great indigenous medicine men still left in North America—was the person who summed up the whole matter most succinctly because he saw it with such clarity.

At the end of every civilization, he noted, the life of that civilization always returns to its source. In the case of western civilization that source is first and foremost the regions around the Mediterranean. And my particular medicine is needed to tend that source as long as such tending is needed; to stand watch over it for the sake of a distant future which will never be ours.

Wherever I am, the underlying support of Native Americans is very tangibly with me. Nothing can be more precious than the closeness of those encounters, which have always been so paradoxical; so unexpected; so surprising.

And essentially there is nothing more important to talk about because this is where we have come to. We are naked as westerners because we, too, have lost everything. We may seem more prosperous, but we are in exactly the same situation they have been squeezed into for hundreds of years.

We too are broken. All of us, not just some or a few, are addicts. We have lost any contact with our ancestral homes not because someone chased us out, but because we chase ourselves out. And there is not a single atrocity westerners can inflict on indigenous people that they have not also inflicted on themselves.[9]

We are no better than Native Americans—no better at all. In fact we are far worse, and worse off, because we no longer even remember what it is we lost.

3

For me personally one thing has been more extraordinary than any other about the Native American medicine women and medicine men, elders and chiefs I have been fortunate enough to meet.

This is their intuitive ability to understand immediately, and I mean instantly, what my work is before knowing a single factual detail about it or me—and before I even get the chance to say a single word. More than once I found myself being welcomed, and from the way events unfolded I could see that what they told me was true, with comments like: "As soon as I caught sight of you walking in, I knew from the way you walked that you work for the Ancestors."

These are people who because of how I walk, or because of what they see when they catch a glimpse of me for the first time from behind, are able to look straight into the heart of my work. They had no conscious interest in ancient Greeks, or the history of philosophy, or the origins of western civilization. Probably they'd never even heard, or ever would hear, peculiar words like "Presocratic". But intuitively, instantly, they knew the job I'm here to do.

And in each of their cultures, in every tribe, there is a name for what I do just as there is a name for what I am. In fact there is a whole host of names depending on whether one happens to be closest to the west coast of North America, or in the New Mexico desert, or nearer to the east coast.

Before I started meeting Native Americans, I could never understand why I was such a difficult person. I always tended to approach everything differently from other people. I would constantly do things back to front. People wanted to move forwards, I wanted to move backwards; they had to turn back, I had to keep going. I was what in many, many traditions—Cherokee, Lakota, Hopi—they have their own name for, their own particular word that means "the contrary".

And they said to me, one after another, in individual encounters: "Your work is tremendously important. Nobody in your supposedly civilized world will recognize what you do. No one will know the real reason. They'll assume you are being difficult. They'll just think you are complicating things unnecessarily.

"But we know; through our traditional wisdom we understand. Your work is crucial. Who you are is crucial, because you wake people up. You help them, force them, to face what they turned their backs on. Just through being who you are and without even having to say a word, you make people question everything on a deeper level than they are comfortable questioning things. You are Coyote, howling and calling from the outer edges of your society because you can see what they don't yet notice and because you remember what they already forgot.

"And that is your duty: to shock people into an awareness that all life comes from, and returns to, the sacred. That is your medicine: to remind people always of their source. That, as the contrary, is your unavoidable task: to dance in the open for the dead and, by walking backwards, turn people around to face their Ancestors whom they imagine they can do without."

So if I disturb you, and this is something I am guaranteed to do, try not to find ways of rejecting me and dismissing what I say—because maybe there is a reason for the disturbance.

Probably you are going to want to say: "OK, I agree with nine-tenths or three-tenths of what Peter Kingsley says. As for the rest, though: No, I don't want to go there."

But maybe, just maybe, it will be good for you to stop and pause and simply take another look.

Now of course, in Jungian terms, there is a name for what I have been referring to. In fact there are several names for what I am talking about.

This ties in with the archetype of the trickster, always on the fringes, turning everything upside down. This ties in with the shadow, bringing up what no one wants to see. And for the sake of completeness I should also add that it ties in with the archetype of the prophet who makes an utter fool of himself by claiming to present grand truths others are not aware of.

But, staying faithful to what I have just been saying, I am going to question all that and present everything from an altogether different point of view.

Anyone trained as a Jungian will almost certainly want to say: "Well, there we go! Peter Kingsley is identifying with the archetype of the trickster! Very dangerous! One should never, absolutely never, identify with an archetype."

And, true to my nature, I am going to say: "Yes, this is very correct and that danger is perfectly real. But in my own experience—and ultimately my experience is all I have to go by—there is a secret as well as a mystery that many people labouring in the world of Jung are unaware of."

The mystery is that we start off with the familiar image of an average, modest, serene human being: perhaps Swiss, perhaps Australian, French, American, it makes no difference. And here we have this ordinary person, this very down-to-earth and reasonable human being, unknowingly surrounded by all the invisible but dangerous archetypes. Swirling around and sometimes lurking threateningly near are the archetype of the trickster, maybe of a great goddess like Artemis or Aphrodite, perhaps the archetype of a prophet or someone else.

And you are told and warned, will read, are taught, that this ordinary human being must never ever identify with one of the divine archetypes. That way lies the danger of psychological inflation. That way, for any human, lies madness.

But the terrible secret which has been forgotten is that humanity, itself, is an archetype.

It can be quite amazing to watch how people will diligently observe, study, even become obsessed about everything else—and miss this. We are happy to recognize the archetypal reality of anything at all, except ourselves. There is really no excuse for forgetting that the ancient Greeks in their wisdom had a single word for us as humans: *anthropos*, which includes woman as well as man.

And you only have to look back to the Gnostics to find the plainest accounts and descriptions of *anthropos* in the fullness of its primordial, archetypal reality.[10]

This is the hidden, unspoken danger. Even the most enlightened of Jungians can avoid every other danger to the best of their ability—and forget the danger of identifying with being a human being.

The story happens to be just the same as it almost always turns out to be in the famous fairy tales or legends or myths. One fights so bravely and so hard against the threats and dangers coming from every possible direction but never manages to see the closest, and greatest, threat of all.

Jung himself of course was very quick to recognize the ever-present perils of psychological inflation—of identifying uncritically, unthinkingly, quite unconsciously with the divine archetypes—and to warn against them. He was only too aware of how deceptive the dangers are and how easily we trick ourselves: of how the pious, humble disciple is probably suffering from an even greater inflation and is even more puffed up than the spiritual master.[11]

One only needs to add that when we identify with ourselves as humans, when we accept our oneness with the collective human race, we are suffering the greatest inflation of them all.

And what happens when we identify with being a nice, modest, ordinary human being? The answer is very simple: We die. When we live like everyone else, we die like everyone else; start to lose our faculties as we turn sixty, seventy, eighty, ninety; drift off into trivialities and completely forget what life is all about.[12]

This, when everything has been taken into account and restored to its right place, is the price of identifying with the archetype of the human being.

In other words, as the great ancient Greek mystics and philosophers I often will be referring to understood so well, there is absolutely nowhere protected or secure. There is no safe ground anywhere—and precisely where we think is safest is the most dangerous place to be.

But the other side to this, as Jung was neither the first nor the last to realize, is that what seems to be far too risky is where our real salvation lies.[13]

4

There is an underlying problem here: a huge problem that can be summarized very easily.

In essence, it has to do with the progressive domestication of Jung's image, wisdom, discoveries. And this is where we have to get a few things straight because there are some facts many people would be only too happy to forget.

Carl Gustav Jung lived an extremely strange, not to mention crazy life behind the scenes. Because of who he was, as well as his active work and interests, he constantly found himself surrounded by archetypal energies. There were even times in his life when he deliberately invoked them.

For him, the need to hold on tight to at least some semblance of sanity when challenged from every side by just the opposite was much more than a theoretical requirement. It was the most urgent, pressing necessity.

And the threat of total madness was, to him, something palpably real.

Needless to say, there are plenty of Jung experts who collectively rally round to protect him—or, rather, protect themselves—by insisting that the wise man never came anywhere close to going mad. But the hollowness of their chorus speaks far louder than the reasoned implausibility of their words.

In fact all they manage to show is how little they really know. And over thirty years ago someone vastly more familiar than any of them with the actual, lived experience of insanity not only documented Jung's steady journey of descent to "the brink of madness". He also documented how carefully Jung's students, family, followers covered up what happened during the most intense and formative times of his life by creating a pious fiction that bears no resemblance to the reality.[14]

A lot has happened, though, in the period since R.D. Laing wrote down his observations. New evidence and documents have come to light—including the famous *Red book* Jung started working on while still in his thirties, straight after his break with Freud—which are so graphic that quite frankly one would have to be a little crazy to want to minimize the intensity of his intimate encounters with insanity.

We now have Jung's own account of how he literally had to cling on to the table in front of him to stop himself from falling apart. Of course anyone can read such details and forget them straight away: intellectuals will always have the marvellous ability to make anything mean no less, or more, than they want.

And perhaps only another person who also has been forced to hold on to reality by grabbing at a piece of furniture will appreciate exactly what kind of states Jung was grappling with.[15]

There are undeniably the best of personal, as well as professional, reasons for wanting to isolate Jung from the stigma of madness or near madness and keep him safe from both. After all, this kind of protectionism has had a long and active history.

Until the *Red book*, and other material, began becoming available people mainly had to resort to the sophisticated process of censoring Jung's own words behind the scenes. Now other methods of protecting him, just as sophisticated, have to be found.

But the truth is that to try and defend him like this is not to add to his stature at all—only to diminish it.[16]

Madness happens to be a primordial phenomenon very closely associated with those same ancient western philosophers and mystics I will be evoking throughout this book. At the same time, as Jung's English translator noted with rare insight, it happens to be no less closely associated with the traditional figure of the indigenous medicine man or shaman.

The unenviable discipline of first encountering, then finding ways of controlling, insanity is always essential for reconnecting the world of the human to the world of the sacred. But it also is a path fraught with risk and danger that demands superhuman strength.

And anyone is a fool who tries to emphasize the element of control at the expense of the insanity.[17]

Right at the core of Jung's life and experience, easily visible although tempting enough to ignore, lies an awareness that one comes face to face with the reality of the sacred not through sanity but in the terrifying depths of madness.

And there—in the confrontation with madness—is where our normal, collective sanity is seen for the even more horrifying insanity that it really is.

Then, every fixed idea one ever had about anything comes permanently crashing down; and the search begins to find some language that can say what everybody thirsts for but almost nobody wants to hear.[18]

The realizations involved here are something so pure they can never be duplicated in any paid-up system of training. Whatever one might like to believe, or make others believe, there is no imitating Jung's experiences; no faking them.

And this is what will always separate him even from the best-trained Jungian. To Jung himself, inner realities like the archetype of a man's feminine spirit or anima were not just handy concepts to appeal to or throw around whenever needed. They were direct, unmediated discoveries that at times almost cost him his life.

So in his raw encounters with the unconscious it meant something intensely real for him to have to keep repeating: "On absolutely no account must I identify with that archetype which is about to take me over." This happens to be quite different, though, from the situation where someone thinks: "Oh, there is not so much to worry about because I have in my pocket Jung's sensible warnings to keep a good distance from all those dangerous divine archetypes and not get anywhere too close. Everything will stay calm and professional because he gave us the basic guidelines we need to protect ourselves collectively in advance. We may have our thrills and moments of excitement, some victories, even a ruffled feather or two. But it will all be just fine because we are always moving forwards, progress after progress, on Jung's broadly reassuring shoulders."

Then—just like any other human being watching television or eating dinner—we sit comfortably in our archetypal mediocrity, our archetypal complacency, our archetypal conformity. Above all, we think we can magically confine the terrifying reality of the sacred to some separate place or room.

In other words we have divided ourselves off for a hundred good reasons, without even noticing it, from the divine.

And this is really what I would like to talk about: the hubris, the inflation, the insanity of separating ourselves from the sacred.

5

Earlier I mentioned the uncomfortable process of being stopped from speaking or appearing in public by nothing more solid than dreams.

There is a fair chance that anyone who has been forced to withdraw like this will have learned at least a little about what Henry Corbin, on the basis of his own experience, called "the inestimable virtues of silence". And included in those virtues is, rather paradoxically, the inestimable virtue of speech—because only an intimate familiarity with silence can allow us to touch, then become familiar with, the root of words.

In fact the first thing we forget when talking all the time is that speech is a privilege, not the right which our superficial minds so wrongly assume it to be. Speech, as every sacred tradition remembers, is among the purest of divine gifts.

That makes it extremely powerful. And this is where things become very serious because it means words have been entrusted to us as something to be extremely careful with.[19]

Like breaths, there is only a finite amount of words we are able to speak in a lifetime. We are not given enough that we can afford to waste them or play around, so we need to choose them with a great deal of care. Once they have been released, at a given moment and for a certain purpose, they are gone. The energy behind them will never be available for another purpose or another time.

And if we are going to use words to speak about the sacred—in other words, if we are going to make the special kind of effort needed to return them consciously to their source—then there is the constant question of exactly what to say as well as precisely how to say it.

One other aspect of the same process that has to be learned is how to suffer. This too can be immensely difficult to understand because, at least at first sight, it has nothing to do with the psychological or physical suffering each of us experiences as a person.

In today's world suffering has come to be treated as a highly individualized affair. You suffer, I suffer, for an endless list of theoretically specifiable reasons. And then civilization rushes in with its fixes, all its sanitizing cures.

But most people are far too frightened to ask—and ask with their whole being rather than out of rhetorical cleverness or curiosity—what kind of sanitization is possible in a world which itself is insane, is completely out of balance.

The truth is that beyond our personal sufferings lies another type of suffering: a suffering so horrific that anyone unfortunate, or fortunate, enough to encounter it would dearly love to be able to avoid it and be rid of it.

There is no explaining that suffering; neatly mapping it out; softening the sharpness of its edges which are enough to drive anyone crazy.

But to get rid of it would be the greatest possible disaster.

This is the suffering of experiencing how insanely and unsustainably selfish we have become as a culture, how unbearably forgetful—and of realizing that there always have to be a few people who through their conscious suffering are willing to balance the selfishness and foolishness and forgetfulness bearing down on the world we live in.

The fact that here lies a crucial aspect of Jung's own work can seem hard to believe nowadays, considering all the ways it supposedly has been developed and practised and carried forward. But this happens to be perfectly true. Even his insistence that, far from wanting to put a stop to people's suffering, his real wish was to help them suffer consciously can be easy enough to forget.

There is almost nobody, though, who cares to note the lengths Jung himself felt pulled to go to so that he could suffer consciously for the sake of the sacred—"because I wanted God to be alive and free from the suffering man has put on him by loving his own reason more than God's secret intentions". Of course he hardly expected anyone to take this kind of talk seriously, which to a certain extent explains why he qualified it straight away as just the words of a "mystical fool".[20]

What makes things so intensely troubling is that the selfishness and unconsciousness in question, the vanity of all the reasonableness Jung is referring to, are never only haunting the most likely places; the obvious places; the predictable ones.

That would be far too straightforward and easy.

They are everywhere but, above all, where you would least expect: in the brightest philosophical ideas, the noblest spiritual thoughts.

They tend to gather and flock around accepted concepts which sound so innocent and self-evident, so plausible and sensible, nobody thinks to question them. They attach themselves to the unshakeable convictions about ourselves that we picked up as children and keenly hold on to; the firmest of beliefs about our future, present, past.

And this applies also to our concepts of healing. In fact it applies even to the most basic language we use for healing—like the simple, familiar word "therapy".

Nowadays just the mention of therapy is enough to conjure up ideas of psychotherapy, physiotherapy, all the different ways I can be helped to get better. But this is not how things used to be.

Originally, *therapeia* in ancient Greek meant caring. And when you go back in time as far as you can, you come to one very specific and constant expression. *Therapeia theôn* meant attending to the divine, caring for the gods and serving them, doing what humans ought to do to make sure the gods are all right.[21]

Then something quite interesting happens.

There is a particular place where Plato focuses his thoughts on *therapeia theôn*, caring for the gods. And basically he argues: "Care for the gods? Why on earth would humans want to care for the gods when the gods are so much greater and better than us that there is absolutely nothing they could need? It might be nice for people, if they really want, to make a little gesture by paying the gods a bit of attention. But to feel one is doing something useful: that wouldn't just be pretty stupid. It would be utterly ridiculous."[22]

There is no need to say too much about the enlightened rationality here, which from any reasonable perspective all sounds exactly the way it should. And so far we have only come as far as Plato—his greatest disciple, Aristotle, is still waiting at the next turn in the road.

This is the way it works, though: one more milestone in the human mind's adventure of submitting everything to the criteria of its own reasoning, just another pace in separating people from the sacred.

As I mentioned earlier, words matter. In spite of all the ready justifications and superficial rationalizations, they have a significance and importance far beyond what our reasonable minds want to tell us. Always there are the consequences.

Once something like these thoughts of Plato, however original or unoriginal, has been put into words there is no going back. And from a deeper perspective nothing could be more disastrous because his argument is just another nail in the coffin of our relation to the sacred—is one more step in articulating the unconscious attitude that says "Let's make sure the divine takes good care of us. But as for finding what, in reality, the divine might possibly need: let it look after itself."

From here onwards one can sit back and watch how the idea of looking after the gods starts, almost as if by magic, vanishing from the western world. It gets pushed more and more to the fringes of ancient culture until even the notion of actually caring for the gods ends up being dismissed as something altogether alien and foreign: superstitious, barbaric.[23]

And those consequences extended far beyond Greece or Rome. For thousands of years Christians have flocked to church not to look after God; only to check that God is looking after them. The real motive is hardly to take care of Christ but to go on making quite sure every week he is still alive enough, suffering enough for our sins, to keep on attending to us in our absent-mindedness and self-absorption.

Of course there have always been the exceptions among Christian mystics. And I have seen for myself in rural Greece how old women go on caring for the icons inside the small churches as if they are caring for Christ and his mother in person. A sense still stays alive across different communities here and there, just before they are crushed by the ruthless forces of western progress, of what it means to care for the divine.

But in general the one thing civilized Christians have learned to care about is how God, at least what they think of as God, is going to care for humans.

And now it never for a moment occurs to us that the

divine might be suffering, aching from our neglect; that the sacred desperately longs for our attention far more than we in some occasional, unconscious spasm might feel a brief burst of embarrassed longing for it.

Rationality, spirituality, therapy of every possible shape and colour: the truth nowadays is very simple. They are all about me and me and me.

And the more tricks we create for helping to make some connection with the sacred—the flattering idea of co-thinking or co-creating with the divine, of looking to find the gods inside us, learning how to tame the divine archetypes so they will make us happier and more fulfilled—the less anyone understands what attitude and effort are really demanded if the divine is going to receive the help it needs from us.

The gods, if they still exist, are just here to give us our therapy because therapy is now for us. God forbid it would be for the gods.

The one tiny technicality we forgot is this: that whenever we take everything for ourselves we end up with absolutely nothing. First we have to know how to care for the gods if the gods are going to care for us.

6

There were other consequences to Plato's reasoning, too.

Whatever we like to think about our own intelligence, the gods are not fools; and even if nobody pays much attention to the events once set in motion, they do.

It needed a while—as always—for people to start noticing, but eventually the reports began flowing in. Plutarch, a famous Platonist from around the time of Christ and also a priest at the Delphic temple of Apollo, took the trouble to note how "oracles which once used to speak with many voices are now completely finished, like springs that have run dry".

He went on to talk about whole regions where "a great drought of prophecy has covered the land" because most of the old oracle sites "have been taken over either by silence or by utter devastation".

A couple of centuries later Porphyry, another well-known Platonist, quoted at length from two oracles essentially repeating the same message: it was already finished. One of them describes how the earth has swallowed back into her depths the thousands of oracle sites she had allowed to exist on her surface. The other says that now "there is no reviving the speaking voice" of the Delphic oracle which had become weaker, and dimmer, until finally it was locked up by "the keys of unprophesying silence".

And then there is the notorious "last oracle" ever given at Delphi which, with simple dignity, announces that for Apollo everything is over. "He no longer has a speaking spring: even the talking water has come to an end."[24]

Predictably it was militant Christians who helped shape the convenient narrative that all the old, primitive oracles had been silenced thanks to the welcome arrival of Christianity. But this is just religious opportunism at its best, and is completely to miss the larger picture—because the Platonists who so dutifully reported on the changes were much more than innocent witnesses.

With the flood of their words and writings, the endless stream of their philosophizing and theologizing, their constant theorizing and moralizing about the gods, they were intimately implicating themselves in what was happening. If the gods as living realities had mattered to them as much as they liked to believe, they might have done something genuinely noble: might have sunk into silence in sympathy and solidarity so they could be there together with the gods, could help them, support them.

Instead, they kept themselves busy papering over the cracks with cosmetic solutions while thinking and talking and writing without a break. And it never occurred to them that the gods might have had to go silent precisely because of all this human droning, because of so many people claiming to know more about the gods than the gods themselves.

It's a very common mistake and, psychologically, one of the easiest of all to make. We are so taken with the familiar sound of our voices that we much prefer to talk on and on about the sacred instead of allowing the sacred a chance to speak: instead of giving it the freedom to share, in its selfless ways, the secret of its own intentions.

I remember once, as a teenager on my own, walking across Tunisia. A car came along and the driver stopped to offer me a ride; he turned out to be the country's leading psychologist. He took me back to his family estate and, as the sun began to set, told me there would be a very rare gathering of Sufis starting soon out in the countryside that same evening.

He offered to take me: I said that would be wonderful. "And before we leave", he mentioned, "I have a home video I made of a similar gathering that I am going to show you." I explained, as politely and firmly as I could, that this sounded ever so fascinating but why spend time watching the video when we could be experiencing the actual reality?

He insisted, and by the time the film had finished the gathering was already over. The quality of the video had been so poor one could hardly see a thing.

This is how the human mind works: what we make, what we think, what we say, is far more important than any reality beyond or behind us. We were so busy with our flimsy substitutes that, before we can even register what happened, the moment of opportunity has passed.

That reality is already gone.

The Platonists had their very intelligent and reasonable strategies, then, for filling the void left by the departure of the gods. Now, naturally, we have ours—much more advanced, of course, far more sophisticated than theirs.

And no strategy can possibly be better suited for us westerners, more pampering of our egos, than the evolutionary one.

The gods left because we no longer need them: we have moved up and on. It was high time we were starting to stand on our own feet, take back responsibility for our lives. We had to begin making rational decisions for ourselves instead of depending on some oracle or divinity—although, needless to say, it's always in our power to bring back the gods at any stage if we ever want to.

As a matter of fact, so some stories go, these changes were overdue because the moment had arrived for everyone to grow more conscious. And all that's needed, now, is for intuitives to come along to console us with wonderful stories about where everything is heading: the fantastic human adventures in unfolding consciousness that lie ahead.[25]

The grim reality happens to be a little different, though.

As Jung saw, and often tried to emphasize, certainly we can look back and see changes or developments here and there across the last two thousand years. It would be incredible if we couldn't. But to suppose humanity, with all its pious hopes and illusions and aspirations, has made any real or fundamental progress: this is only another illusion because the problems we face now are just the same as they were two thousand years ago.

And we are just as unprepared to face them.[26]

Culturally, we are so obsessed with the restless myth of constant evolution—material progress, spiritual progress—that we fail to see what fools we make of ourselves or how blinded we are by our obsession. At times, to be sure, Jung could appear to be going along with this grand mythology. He could seem to be endorsing wholeheartedly our western "cult of progress"; reinforcing the "illusion" of our civilized triumphs.

But both "cult" and "illusion" are his own words. And often he acts exactly like the Presocratic philosophers, thousands of years before him, who realized that the only way to communicate anything at all to people was by speaking their illusory language and sharing their illusory words.[27]

The basic truth was that for him our much vaunted civilization and consciousness are the most fragile, delicate, ambiguous achievements. This is why—when confronted as a man of science with the infallible dogma, which somehow still finds a place in the popular imagination and even in the minds of prominent Jungians, that not only civilization but also consciousness must of course both be evolving—he continually found himself forced to hesitate.

And instead of agreeing, as any respectable scientist would automatically have been expected to do, he would use the sharp edge of irony or the darkest possible humour to question everything.[28]

Here, too, one could say he happened to be well ahead of his time. After all: in an essential sense he was only anticipating the growing awareness among leading-edge scientists today that our human species has been degenerating for thousands of years—physically, mentally, genetically.

But it does take time for facts to find some small place among all the paradigms and dreams of evolution.[29]

And there is also much more to the matter than that.

In fact it's only by going back far beyond the alchemists, even beyond the Gnostics who attracted so much of his interest, that one can really start to see why Jung's questionings and hesitations were so justified.

We still have the writings of the famous "Presocratic" philosophers who, two and a half thousand years ago, analyzed the human condition in searing and terrifying detail. But the way they described people then—hopelessly deaf and blind to reality, arrogant and confused, superficial and living their lives in a total dream, devoid of the slightest genuine consciousness and begging to be deceived, trapped by their own fantasies but imagining they are free—is not just some record of how things once used to be.

It's a perfectly accurate portrayal of the human condition right now.

Because they understood so well the timeless intricacies of the human mind, they not only were able to predict with the finest precision how their own teachings would be misunderstood and misinterpreted by intellectuals like Plato or Aristotle a century later. They were even able to anticipate the way their teachings would be twisted and distorted by the smartest of scholars down to the present day.

For them, real awareness was the rarest achievement imaginable. To them there was no greater miracle than how humans can manage to blunder through the whole of what they call life in utter unconsciousness while all the time dreaming that they are aware.

And their accounts of the human condition are uncannily accurate accounts of us, today, because there is no difference whatsoever between people's unconsciousness now and then.[30]

A lot appears to have happened in the last few thousand years. Great philosophers came. Christ came. Television came.

And nothing changed. We may have a few more tricks up our sleeves now along with some extra gadgets in our hands; but in terms of consciousness and conscience, hypocrisy and brutality, love and morality, at the very best we are just the same.

As for all our proud ideas about evolution—they are simply our best excuse for running from the reality of ourselves.

Of course we can go on thinking we are free to believe the lovely fantasies put out by people stuck in their throats and brains: their noble and bright ideas about where humanity is certainly going. The trouble is that intuitions and intuitives are sometimes right, often wrong.

And the only way of actually learning the truth about the past and the future for ourselves is when the spark of consciousness we are has been rammed, inch by painful inch, right down into the silent depths of our entrails.

7

In the darkest past it was traditional when starting to speak, or coming together with others, to invoke the presence of the sacred.

Perhaps you will be able to sense that this is what, in my own way, I have been making the effort to do. But I also need to make the point quite clear that invoking the sacred means invoking what's really sacred—not what might have been sacred for some other person or people hundreds, even thousands, of years ago.

We have to start by invoking what's sacred for us.

Of course we are free to complicate things and get into the messiest of arguments by insisting we are not at all sure what that would be. The simple truth is, though, that we all know perfectly well what's sacred to us; and have for a very long time.

Ever since we were children we have been able to sense what's sacred in a landscape—the sudden rush of birds in the morning, the smell and touch of a flower petal, watching sunlight make the trees or grass so luminously and shockingly green.

We all know what's sacred right from the beginning. No one ever has to teach it to a baby or child: they know just as we knew. They can find the sacred in a forgotten little back alley somewhere. They'll find it even in a weed, on a piece of moss.

But this leads straight to the real question that needs to be asked. I have to admit it's the last possible subject I would want to talk about, although at times like this there is no choice. And here is where things become really difficult because in terms of the West, in terms of this strange culture we have created and made our own, it's not enough to look inside ourselves and see what we can see of the sacred.

We also have to search ourselves and discover what it is inside each of us that—individually, but also collectively as a part of this western civilization—is hell-bent on destroying the sacred.

This is the question which has become so scary and also, for the sake of being truthful with ourselves as well as honest with each other, so necessary.

To be real about the sacred is to see not just what inside us is not sacred—but what it is inside us that's against the sacred. What is it in our civilization that's systematically, year after year and minute after minute, mile after mile and inch by inch, gutting everything sacred it touches: devouring it inside ourselves at the same time as irresistibly, inevitably, eating it up outside us in the beauty of landscape and nature?

When I was a teenager I often would hitchhike down from London to Stonehenge, sometimes in the middle of the night. And it was so simple there. I could creep in and sit quietly underneath the old stones, meditate, stay as long as I needed. Then, after I learned to drive and came back years later, aside from all the extra rows of barbed wire it was almost as if you had to buy a bunch of postcards just to be able to get somewhere close.

And this is simply a symbol of what we do.

Whatever hasn't already been wiped out—but by some miracle happens to have been preserved—now has to be preserved from us and put as far away as possible out of reach. There is no trusting ordinary human beings with the sacred, with what used to be sacred.

Then there are the times my wife and I have spent in North America. I can still vividly remember neighbours where we used to live, off the coast of Canada at the heart of what was once a sacred island, cutting down the enormous fir trees that held up the whole balance of nature for the sake of making a few dollars; the local government in New Mexico, bent on building a huge road right through the middle of inconceivably powerful petroglyphs that had been carved into the rocks tens of thousands of years ago; the magnificently brooding nature in North Carolina which had turned its face away from humans and hidden its deepest secrets because of what it had to witness the white man do to his black slaves, but above all to the Native Americans.

And Switzerland is where I used to come, together with my family, when I was a young boy—the exquisite houses with their beautiful façades and painted shutters, flowers outside, merging effortlessly into the landscape. Now, all you see everywhere is lumps of concrete because this is the only thing people know how to build in our progressive society: concrete blocks.

There is no end to the stories anybody could tell; and there is no need to ask if someone doesn't know what I mean, because everyone does.

But the question that does have to be asked is: what is it that's happening? What is this huge tide of so-called progress that's sweeping everywhere and pushing everything, everybody, on?

We walk and watch. We are bound to notice, maybe sadly as we get older, how much things keep changing from the ways they were before. And we just do our best to make do—to justify it all as livable, bearable.

Here and there we'll do our best to compensate: put a little Buddha statue in our garden, drive an environmentally friendly car, even join a protest. But each of us, deep down inside, realizes what we are up against and knows very well the tide will never be turned back like that.

Perhaps now and then, as we look around at the wrecking of nature and the sacred, we might be caught off guard and surprised by a tiny voice in our head that quietly asks: "But hasn't it all been done rather well?" Especially when we are tired, it can feel so much easier to rationalize everything rather than go on feeling at odds with the hard realities all around us; to do a few calculations and count up the new advantages, benefits, blessings.

And there is a certain calm reassurance that comes from joining in with the collective explanations—except that none of them ever comes anywhere close to being an explanation which is authentically real.

We can try blaming the population explosion. That's true to an extent, but barely scratching the surface. We can put the blame on technology. That's an effect of the tide, not its cause. We can feel justifiably horrified at the diabolical twistings of Christian doctrine that end up claiming Christ abolished the sacredness of land and nature when, by dying on the cross, he left the human heart as the only sanctified place on earth.[31]

There is an answer, though. It's the simplest of explanations that takes us back even beyond the beginnings of Christianity.

And its simplicity must be the reason why our infinitely complicated minds have overlooked it.

The answer is that every civilization has a sacred purpose. But we have forgotten ours.

And it's because of this forgetting that everything around—as well as inside—us has gone so terribly wrong.

8

It was a huge surprise for me, at age seventeen, being forced by some mysterious but irresistible impulse to go back to the ancient Greeks to find out where western philosophy began.

This was nothing at all, though, compared to the shock of being drawn to study in detail the surviving words of the earliest Greek philosophers—the so-called Presocratics—only to discover that the modern accounts of who they were and what they did are total fictions. Nothing, for the writers of those modern accounts, is sacred.

If mistranslation of the ancient texts is needed to bring them into line with present-day assumptions, then they'll be mistranslated. If mistranslation isn't enough, and the only trick guaranteed to silence their message is to change the ancient Greek texts themselves, that's exactly what will be done. But once you understand the motives and methods behind all this nonsense, the how as well as the why, it's not so hard to put that little bag of tricks aside.

The first of the early philosophers I encountered was called Empedocles. And over a period of time he demonstrated to me in every conceivable way that nothing could be further from the truth than to dismiss people like him as the primitive thinkers we imagine them to be.

These weren't some childish intellectuals, trying to pass themselves off as creators of the ridiculously complicated mental games later thinkers would soon start playing in their bizarre pursuits of wisdom. On the contrary: they happened to be great mystics already in possession of a simple wisdom that was as practical, and focused, as it was subtle. They included immensely powerful beings who—in harmony with others, in the deepest coordination—consciously worked together bringing a whole civilization into being.

These were people who laid the foundations of philosophy, of science, logic and cosmology, law and medicine, healing and education by fetching the seeds of all those disciplines from a different reality that the would-be guardians of our culture now don't even know exists.

They would go into another state of consciousness and bring their gifts into this world from the world of the sacred so that a fresh civilization could begin.

And yes, one of the many things this means is that even western science itself had a sacred source.

But don't think for a moment that what I am offering here is some kind of mystical interpretation. Quite to the contrary, it happens to be the only account capable of doing full justice—without any arbitrary distortions or wilful neglect—to the ancient evidence and documentation.

All those hard-headed rationalists who for centuries have looked down on mystics as foolish creatures, divorced from reality, have got everything wrong. It's they, themselves, who have lost any touch with the mystical reality that their science and their rationalism originally were meant to be.[32]

Simply to get a glimpse of this turns everything on its head and inside out. Then for the first time you start to observe and really understand the process of history, of culture, of civilizations, just the same as if you are watching a plant; a flower; any natural object.

After all, every culture is precisely what its name says it is: a part of nature, something organic needing to be tended and cultivated according to principles only planters and farmers know.

To the mind that tricks itself into thinking it sees everything in rational terms, nothing could sound more nonsensical. And this is a crucial part of the problem because we take our familiar ways of perceiving so much for granted that we completely forget what lies at the root of our own thoughts—not to mention our senses.

Perhaps it will be best if I just give the example of someone closely related to Empedocles. His name was Parmenides, and he is still remembered in the West as the inventor of reason or reasoning; as the ultimate founder and father of logic.

But in spite of his reputation, regardless of the hundreds of thousands of pages later philosophers have written around and about him, we have no idea any more of what logic for Parmenides really was.

Exactly the same as Empedocles, he put everything he had to say into poetry—into an incantatory text full of the strangest details and repetitions, a poem that used the ancient techniques of magic for carrying the listener or reader into another state of consciousness. And originally this was the purpose of logic in the West, just as it was the original purpose of philosophy and science and culture as a whole: to take us back to the sacred.

Parmenides paid the greatest attention, using all the appropriate language of his time, to explaining what happened when he was carried as an initiate along the path of the sun and down into the world of the dead; to describing how he had been given the gift of logic by the goddess Persephone, queen of the underworld, who greeted him down there in the darkness at the roots of existence.

And, in origin, this was the whole point of logic: to allow what had been received from the divine to complete its perfect circle by taking us straight back to the divine world it had come from.

That was how logic had been given. It wasn't logic as some dry discipline to tire our brains out and make us lose our ways in endless thinking. It was a logic given through visions and dreams, a gift to plunge us into the depths of ourselves and strip us of all our thoughts so it can train us to become conscious of the sacred reality at the heart of everything—ever-present, totally aware of itself without the slightest shading or distance, the living power behind the whole of existence.

There is nothing here even remotely similar to the kind of logic inflicted on children at school or whenever some person, far older and taller than ourselves, accused us of acting or talking illogically. Neither does it come anywhere close to the mechanistic accounts of it by writers like Nietzsche or Heidegger, who were only dressing up in brighter clothes the fashionable mistakes of their time.[33]

And the reason for this is very simple.

In our progressive sophistication and evolving civilization we have wiped out any trace of the truth that logic, along with everything else, once had its sacred place and purpose. And once the awareness of that has gone, everything else goes wrong.

As for all the learned mumbo jumbo which has been repeated century after century by academics, theologians, esotericists, about the existence of some fundamental contrast between limited human logic and the divine mystery of revelation—this is just one more sign of how completely and utterly we have forgotten that logic in its origin was the most perfect example of revelation.[34]

And anyone who looks closely at what this means will start to see it's far more than a question of history, or philosophy, or literature.

As a matter of fact this isn't even about ideas. It's about us; about the lives we live, or try to live; about the deepest purpose of our existence.

It also is a constant reminder that truth has to be found not by taking the easy route of flying off to heaven in some dazzlingly brilliant blaze of light but by following the path of the sun down into the depths of night where everything, including the darkest reaches of ourselves, is connected to the sacred.

These were the famous laws of logic that Parmenides inserted into the world as a seed, a gift for western culture, twenty-five hundred years ago. Like so many other lawgivers in that part of the world he belonged to, he made it quite clear none of these laws is to be changed.

Nothing should be altered. Nothing must be added. Nothing was meant to be taken away; and the reason for this, too, is very simple.

Just like other lawbringers—or prophets—of that time, he was bringing his laws as a message directly from another world.[35]

This all became as clear as day to me in the 1970s during my years of research at Cambridge University. For me, too, it was a lonely path as I followed the thread of Parmenides' own words that led far away from everything anyone would even remotely associate with logic.

Instead, to my growing amazement it plunged me straight into a world not of rational thought but of prophecy and inspiration; of ecstasy and other states of consciousness; of incantations and the use of repetition; of deliberately accessing the realm of visions and dreams through the practice of incubation or lying down to meditate in dark places.

It was only many years later that, all alone in a London library one Saturday afternoon, I happened to come across a large book that had just been published. When I opened it I realized, to my even greater amazement, it contained the results of archaeological work which without my knowledge had been going on for years at Parmenides' old hometown called Velia in southern Italy.

Whole series of inscriptions, including one for Parmenides himself, had been found along with a set of statues all carved out of blocks of marble. And together they were linking him with a tradition of inspired prophecy; with the mastery of ecstasy and different states of consciousness; with the use of incantations and deliberate repetition of words and sounds; with the practice of incubation by lying down in dark places to access the world of visions and dreams.[36]

Every detail I had deduced, one by one, from the surviving text of Parmenides' poem was confirmed with the most haunting and striking precision by physical pieces of stone hidden for centuries inside the earth. But of course to see the significance of that confirmation means having a pair of eyes—which is very far from common in a field where professional scholars dedicate themselves to the collective pursuit of blindness.

I remember once giving a lecture, to a group of international specialists who had gathered in All Souls College at Oxford University, about the self-evident links between these archaeological discoveries and Parmenides' own poem. After my talk, the most famous scholars in the room came up to me together and said indignantly: "But we are philosophers! We deal with ideas! Why on earth would we bother ourselves about lumps of stone?"

And that's fair enough, except when what was carved into the marble happens to be about ourselves—or rather is ourselves.

On an obvious level the inscriptions and statues are presenting a lineage of prophet–healers whose wisdom was transmitted, by adoptive father to adopted child, from the time of Parmenides down into the Christian era.

But on another level they are simply telling the story of our own origins—together with our destiny.

9

This was the original fragility of western logic and western science—as flexible as life itself, in their prophetic nature as delicate and frail as a flower.

To practise that logic, this science, meant learning how to work with the circlings of the sun and finding how to breathe. It was to sense when to think and when to go still; when to talk, when to go silent. It meant knowing when to lie down to rest, sink into sleep, do nothing.

But, naturally, that raises the question of what happened. And the simple answer is to look to the one place whose influence Parmenides and his successors struggled, to the point of death, to protect themselves from: all the questionable grandeur, the intellectual aspirations and military ambitions of ancient Athens.[37]

Aristotle lived not much more than a hundred years after Parmenides. Like Parmenides, he had what I guess one could call a professional interest in logic. He also showed a particular interest in the subject of prophetic dreams—of dreams said to be sent by gods to humans to give them the kind of knowledge or guidance they could never discover by themselves.

And that interest is, one could say, more than a little interesting considering how Parmenides himself had belonged to a prophetic tradition familiar with invoking as well as interpreting the divine guidance offered through visions or dreams.

A lot can change, though, in the course of a century—which helps to explain why Aristotle in Athens would choose to use his new-found logical powers to denounce prophetic dreams as fantasies, denounce people who claimed to have prophetic dreams as uneducated idiots, and above all denounce as absurd even the idea that dreams could be sent by the gods.

Of course this sounds, now, very modern and very familiar: so familiar, in fact, that there is no stopping academics from praising Aristotle to the heavens for his sophisticated reasoning as well as his brilliant insight on precisely this subject. After all, his reasoning is theirs and theirs is essentially still his.

But sometimes it can be useful to preserve a bit of balance—not to mention a little sanity. So I will give just one token example of Aristotle's brilliant, sophisticated demonstrations that prophetic dreams can't possibly have anything authentic about them.

To quote his own proof in his own unforgettable words: it's totally obvious that no gods are involved in sending dreams because, if they were, then "they would only communicate during the daytime and they would only communicate with the wise".[38]

As for the part here about communicating with the wise, it's best not to waste any precious breath on it—aside from noting that, in Aristotle's ever so slightly narcissistic mind, wisdom was the exclusive preserve of advanced philosophers like himself or his teacher Plato.

And if the gods refused to communicate straight with him, he could be perfectly sure they would never go near anybody else.

But as for the part where Aristotle imagines he can lay down some rigid rule about gods only communicating during the daytime: this is where anyone could wonder what on earth is going on.

To solve the riddle isn't so hard, though; and to follow the knotted thread of his logic needs no more than the slightest familiarity with the writings of his famous teacher.

Plato was very clear, especially near the end of his life, about what a wise person's attitude should be to night and night-time. According to him it would be wrong even to waste a moment's thought on describing night, or night's darkness, as something inferior to daytime. For him the fact of the matter was that they have absolutely no virtue at all, no presence, of their own because they are nothing but the absence of day.

And what this means in practice is that any conscious, responsible human wanting to live an intelligent life would be well advised to drown out each night with mental activities by squeezing into it as many daytime tasks as possible—because "while asleep no one is worth anything".

In other words: Parmenides' emphasis on the unique access offered to the heart of wisdom by letting oneself be carried into the darkest, most feminine, most unconscious depths of night is not only ignored. It's methodically, systematically excluded.[39]

And it's exactly the same story all over again when Plato finds himself having to explain why the supreme group of overseers or lawmakers he envisaged for his model state would need to meet, each single night, "from earliest dawn until sunrise".

In the eyes of the older mystics and philosophers whose tracks he is following very closely here—as he so often used to do—no other time of day could possibly be more logical because this was the most sacred moment of all.

It was that timeless, magical instant when the bringers of divine laws are able to fetch their gifts of justice and rightness out into the light from the darkest depths of the night.

But Plato was far too bright a thinker to accept light's dependence on night or its indebtedness to darkness. And so he came up with a reason of his own, the smartest justification he could think of, for deciding on such a highly unusual time. "This", he explains, "is the time that will allow everyone involved the greatest leisure and freedom from all their other activities and commitments."

Once again, Plato has worked his peculiar inverted alchemy. The choice had nothing to do with the sacredness of that dawning transition, so infinitely significant and subtle, out from darkness into day. And certainly it had nothing whatsoever to do with the fact that ancient tradition connected the source of prophetic wisdom—as well as lawgiving—with the ambiguous, feminine, hidden realms of darkness.

It was just about re-arranging one's hectic calendar to avoid scheduling conflicts.[40]

Simply to touch on such subjects is one of the most difficult things to do, because no sensible person is even meant to mention them. It's like scratching at the belly of reasonableness; systematically unravelling the myth of rationality that took hundreds and thousands of years to build up.

As for Plato, of course he has been turned into one of the greatest intellectual and spiritual heroes in the West. And it's understandable enough that people coming across his writings are often overwhelmed by their beauty. What's a little harder to understand is that their real beauty is above all the beauty of the landscape he had been allowed to wander through, crushing the plants and flowers in the process.

Appearances can be very deceptive. The more one grows familiar with what came before him, the more possible it is to appreciate that his magnificent myths aren't really his at all—except in the sense that he took them, without any formal acknowledgement, from the followers of Pythagoras who were gracious enough to host him on his visits to Italy and Sicily.

I should add, though, that this was hardly such a big deal for the Pythagoreans themselves. Evocative myths about the soul and its fate happened to be the most openly accessible, least valued or esoteric aspect of their teachings.[41]

But even in the process of taking these myths over Plato did a splendid job of misunderstanding them, rationalizing and trivializing essential details, gently jumbling things up.

Constantly in his artful writings he changed what wasn't meant to be changed, modified what ought to have been left alone; cleverly transferred to his own philosophy the language of mysteries and initiation which once had belonged to the sacred, to another world.[42]

Today, though, everything I have just described is fine and perfect: altogether commendable. That's progress. It's innovation. This is the way everyone does business in our restless, egoistic, well-trained culture of thieves.

But the fact is that, in mentioning these things, I am not talking as a part of the world Plato or Aristotle helped to create.

I am speaking on behalf of the world they almost destroyed.

10

We have slipped step by step into hell without ever noticing it, and should try to see why.

If Plato was an accomplished philosopher in the modern sense, he was far more accomplished as a producer of outright fictions. And this mattered in ways that, because we have made our nests and homes in those fictions, are a little hard to grasp.

Now we are perfectly used to being surrounded, even smothered, by facts and factuality. But, back then, reality hadn't quite detached itself yet from myth. And this meant that the process of making history was still a relatively simple matter of writing it—rather than having to go to the tedious trouble of trying to rewrite it.

All in all it was an extremely creative time, depending of course on how you chose to use or misuse the opportunities you had been given.[43]

In one of those imaginary dialogues that Plato became so famous for creating, he invented the fanciful character he refers to with deliberate vagueness as a stranger visiting from Velia.

Velia just so happened to be the name of Parmenides' home in southern Italy—of that very same town where the prophetic tradition flowing from him as founding father went on being quietly transmitted, generation to generation, adoptive father to adopted son, for over five hundred years.

And with the help of this background you'll be able to appreciate what Plato was doing when, in a flight of imagination, he decided to put into the mouth of his fictitious visitor from Velia the idea that it's time to murder "father Parmenides".

To state the situation with the crudeness needed: Plato is doing the very same thing with this Velian tradition that he also did to it in other fictional dialogues he wrote.

Deviously, insidiously, manipulatively, he insinuates himself into a role that isn't his; inserts himself uninvited into an initiatory lineage he doesn't belong to; systematically sets about sabotaging it by destroying it from within.

Certainly he puts on a good show of making his imaginary character sound ever so nervous about the whole matter, hesitant to carry through with the murder, reluctant. And the reason he does this is because he absolutely had to. At Athens, just to mention even the thought of committing patricide was considered one of the most atrocious crimes conceivable—the quintessential offence of inflicting violence on one's ancestors.[44]

But behind all the veils of literature, fiction, hesitation, that act of killing father Parmenides was carried out. The murder was done, only to be repeated time after time by scholars whose sole purpose and comfort lie in the world created by that murder.

And not many things in our culture are more important than to understand just what it is that Plato killed; how he killed it; why he killed it.

As the founder and father of his lineage in Velia, Parmenides had allowed himself to be taken on the most terrifying journey imaginable—straight down into the underworld, the bowels of all existence, to meet the queen of death.

From every normal or sane perspective it was the craziest thing anybody would be willing to do. And it was the most horrifically frightful place anyone would ever want to go. This is why, right down to the present day, there are scholars who instinctively try to keep the whole subject of the underworld hidden under wraps: who do anything they can to cover his destination up and pretend it doesn't matter at all where Parmenides might have arrived on his mythical journey.

But it could hardly have mattered more. If you were extremely lucky you might make it down in one piece, then even come back alive—and safe.

To anybody else, the underworld was deadly.[45]

Here, and nowhere else, is exactly where logic first came from. Logic in its purity, as originally introduced to the West, was the demonstration that nothing can ever change or die. Every single thought or feeling or perception that you imagine you ever thought or felt or perceived still exists, as a total reality, together with every other perception and feeling and thought—not in some restricted or abstract or qualified sense but in the fullest, most concrete sense imaginable.

Everything you thought you'd forgotten even including the thought itself, everything you had tried to push aside, every waking experience together with the most haunting or fondest of dreams, is still alive in this place where everything you thought of as life is already dead and where nothing ever dies.

In other words: western logic in its origin was the language, the experience, of the underworld.

But that means the only way to understand it is if you are able to go there, is to be taken to the realms of the dead, let yourself be dragged there—far away from what Parmenides poetically described as the beaten track of humans with all its obsessive distinctions between existent and non-existent, alive or dead. And this is precisely what, if you allow it, his logic still has the power to do.

This was Persephone's gift from her place beside the roots of all existence, beyond even life and death: a gift freshly delivered by Parmenides, as part of his prophetic message, at the dawn of our western world.

Plato, though, was an entirely different kind of fish. Of course he had heard about the Pythagorean discipline of learning to face death before you die; he would even write some inspiring words about it. He was extremely efficient, too, at publishing colourful myths about the underworld.

But as for going there—that was another story altogether.

And besides, in the figure of Parmenides he found himself confronted by an inhumanly gigantic problem.

Like any intellectual he felt the desperate pressure to think and discriminate and reason. The trouble is that Parmenides' logic in its craziness, its unbroken wholeness, its uncanny stillness, excludes those frantic human activities right from the start.

In other words, his logic was the end of everything we think of as logic—before logic as we know it had even begun.

So, if Plato was going to do what he wanted to do, he really had no choice at all. He would simply have to get rid of Parmenides before Parmenides got rid of him.

Through the fictitious voice of his visiting stranger from Velia, he describes exactly what kind of clever mental tricks would be needed to silence the message of the goddess: the tricks of insisting that yes but also no, no but in another sense yes. And he set about killing her message so effectively we don't even have any memory, now, of the fullness that was lost.

This is what led to the murder of Parmenides' divine logic, which through its utter stillness is beyond the reach or grasp of human thinking, and to the replacement of logic's sacred laws—in defiance of all the ancient warnings—by human reason, by the endless superficiality of its restlessness and questioning, its continuous need to qualify and argue about everything just like some petty lawyer.

The irony is that Plato was so fascinated with the power of his own thinking he actually believed he had invented something needed; something new.

In fact all he had done, though, was make the same old mistake that Parmenides himself had expressly warned against right from the start—the fatal mistake of constantly qualifying oneself, living as if something is true and real in one sense but in another sense not, just like any other human.[46]

This is what happens when you think you can improve on laws brought straight and fresh from another world.

But there is also a far greater irony than that. At the very beginning of his incantatory poem Parmenides had already described how people who keep on torturing reality like this, breaking it up into tiny pieces with their minds, aren't even living on the surface of the earth as they imagine they are.

In fact they are not alive at all. They are just wandering ghosts, drifting backwards and forwards and then around and around—"twin-heads, knowing nothing as they are carried along in a daze, deaf and blind at the same time"—down at some lonely but haunted crossroads in the underworld.[47]

And this is what happens when you think you can cut hell out of your little, well ordered life.

As soon as you believe you have conveniently removed the need to visit hell, the moment you decide you have the right to silence the voice that speaks from the depths of hell, you end up in hell yourself.

Or, in other words, one has to make the journey to the underworld to discover everybody is already there.

11

Then there is the madness.

Down in the underworld where western logic comes from, where the roots of earth and water and fire and sky merge into a single whole, the entire world as we think we know it with all its imaginary distinctions and divisions disappears. Everything we cling on to, everything we hold important, is gone.

And Aristotle was just being true to his usual sensible self when, with more than a little anxiety, he pointed out how utterly unreasonable Parmenides' logic happens to be. He complained that, if taken seriously, such a logic would lead any rational person straight to madness.

Or, as he liked to say, anyone refusing to distinguish between ice and fire is not just crazy like any other crazy person—but is even madder than a madman.

This wasn't only Aristotle speaking, though. Through his words you can still hear the kind of heated discussions about logic, or reason, that he along with Plato both found themselves being drawn into during the early days of the new Platonic Academy. The logic presented by Parmenides was a disaster from beginning to end because it wasn't just irrational. It was downright insane.[48]

But that's no more than half of the madness; and there is another side to it, too.

Plato himself exposes it only too well when he has his imaginary stranger from Velia express near panic at the insanity—the sheer madness—of being forced to commit patricide by killing "father Parmenides". And there was every good reason for fear considering how no crime was more polluting, or terrifying, in the Athens of Plato's time than the crime of murdering the father.

In short: we have all been tricked and deluded into believing that the birth of western reason was some virginally pure, immaculately rational creation.

On the contrary, it was the result of methodically killing off what Parmenides had brought into the world of the living as a divine gift from the realms of the dead. Right from the beginning, what we call reason came into existence with blood on its hands because it was just madness reacting to madness—the ludicrous human attempt to cover over the legacy of a divine ecstasy which sees straight through our world of illusions to its deepest source.[49]

To judge from the glibly dismissive statements made by Plato, then Aristotle, then any number of later scholars, the whole affair could seem nothing more than a joke. But this unswerving glibness is the single factor that makes the murder so appalling, so completely crazy: is what was already preparing an entire culture for the insanity of reason.

Here—not in some pretty picture postcard portrait of divine madness or prophetic frenzy—is the reality of what was done to the West to pollute the purity of sacred madness.[50]

And there is nothing coincidental about how, on his own tortured journey down into the world of the dead, Carl Jung came to see and record things which by now should be haunting in their familiarity.

From the very first moment he embarks on the account of his descent towards madness, which was to stay secret so long together with his *Red book*, he starts introducing the two spirits or beings who are crucial for understanding his entire work—and life. What he calls the spirit of this time is full of pride in its brash arrogance and reasonableness; blind and blinding; attached to cleverness and knowledge and science, or at least what it thinks of as science.

But the other spirit he meets there, down in "the dark underworld of the spirit of the depths", is the mystery that in a moment snatches that all away.

And few things could be more shocking as well as significant than the way that, almost at once, this spirit of the depths confronts Jung with the question: "Have you counted the murderers among the scholars?" Before he even has a chance to respond, though, the spirit of his time jumps straight in and sums up for Jung the totality of everything he will ever be able to write or say: "Whatever you say is madness."[51]

So, as soon as he comes near the halls and corridors of the underworld, the first things he is made to face are the murder committed by scholars and the inescapableness of madness—which is hardly surprising, considering how the crazy reality of that same underworld was just what scholars in their own madness had started murdering twenty-five hundred years ago.

Jung, however much or little he knew with his conscious understanding, was instinctively coming back home to where it all began.

And one other thing he is taught there, in a hundred different ways, is the utter madness hiding at every turn behind reasonableness and reason. He is even shown how reason is a poison that has slowly infected and destroyed us all.[52]

Lessons learned in the underworld, things seen and heard, don't go away. They leave their mark for the rest of one's life. They stay, unforgettable—and in the case of Jung, he was left with an indelible impression of what we usually call reason which is anything but usual.

For most people, anyone would have to be a little crazy to cast the slightest doubt on the value and usefulness of reasoning. It's a natural human faculty to take full advantage of and perhaps, in the case of an artist or mystic, put aside for a while when not actually needed.

But the fact is that, to him, it wasn't just an aspect of human nature available for us to use at any time we choose. Neither did he feel any pressing need to create some supposedly balanced picture by going out of his way to emphasize that reasoning has its good side alongside a bad one, is available to be used well as well as misused.

In his eyes it was something much more dangerous, potent and real—even when it might appear to be hopelessly ineffective. For him it was poison and murder, the thinnest of veneers on top of madness. It's a constant outrage against everything natural outside or inside us; an act of violence, almost apocalyptic in its intensity, aimed at the very essence of nature.

To be quite clear: it's not just that rationality in its laziness, or rigidity, sometimes accidentally allows these atrocities and abuses to happen. The cleverness of rationality is the atrocities and the abuses itself.

And all I can say is that his intuition was uncannily accurate.

Even though he wasn't familiar with the historical intricacies of how reason and reasoning came into being, he happened to be perfectly correct. He was right about the murder. And he was quite right about reason being the dully unconscious part of us that, thanks to its unnaturalness, forces the sacred to suffer—but also forces those few humans who know what they are doing to suffer, very consciously, so they can compensate for the reasonableness by restoring some balance between the human and the divine.[53]

To read Jung as he wanted and needs to be read seems, no less than in the case of reading ancient Greeks like Parmenides or

Empedocles, almost impossible. It stretches our fixed expectations too far; distorts beyond every tolerable limit the ways we struggle to keep some illusion of peace with the world around us.

Commentators are only too eager to leap on any comment he makes about reason that appears positive, or at least soothingly neutral. They don't hesitate to take isolated statements out of context without looking to left or right—creating the image of a Jung itching to condemn anyone with the nerve to speak negatively about reason for doing the damnable work of the devil, ready to denounce anybody crazy enough to deny that reason and science are humanity's crowning powers as nothing but deluded prophets.[54]

What they forget to mention is the way he goes straight on, without the slightest trace of apology or shame, to do the devil's work himself while playing to perfection the role of deluded prophet.

And what they somehow fail even to register is the heavy note of sarcasm that he constantly inserts into his remarks about reasoning: the ways he diabolically twists and turns the word, openly defies and mocks our reasonable assumptions, goes politely through the motions of praising it as humanity's highest power only to undermine it without a moment's mercy and unceremoniously tear it from its throne.[55]

In any normal world this gulf or abyss between what we expect and what Jung delivers, these assaults of his on what he can sometimes seem to treat as a virtual personification of reason, would raise an enormous question about what lies behind his persistent approach to our precious faculty of reasoning.

Here, though, I will just say what needs to be said—which is that this is the inevitable result of going to hell.

The underworld, as Jung understood very well, is the world of paradox: the paradox of darkness inside the light, of the sanity in madness.[56]

And of course paradoxes like these are anathema to reason because its chief purpose is to cover them over while making sure, at the same time, to hide its own true face.

But there is nothing more paradoxical than the fact that to get to see what it really looks like behind all its make-up—behind its apparent familiarity, the banality of its ordinariness, its everyday innocence and blandness—means having to make the journey into another world.

Our modern fascination with thinking and reading about mythology can make it easy to imagine that finding one's way down to hell is something extremely noble, even very reasonable. And I have encountered plenty of Jungians convinced that all it takes to be initiated personally into the mysteries of the underworld is a few well-regulated sessions of what's known in the trade as active imagination.

None of this, though, comes anywhere close to the reality. We each have our own hell—but, paradoxically, the underworld is the underworld because there is nothing personal inside it that hasn't been stripped out.

The underworld for Jung is the same as the underworld for Parmenides or the underworld now. It's just waiting for anyone crazy enough to be taken there. And there you are made to face the truth in its nakedness that can be almost too terrible to bear.

This is why on the most basic, instinctive level scholars have had such a hard time accepting that someone like Parmenides—founder of western logic—or Pythagoras would have been forced to visit the world of the dead while still alive. This also is why they try so desperately to intellectualize the terrifying, transformative power of Parmenides' logic.

And this is why until recently Jung's assistants, editors, publishers worked so hard to cut any mention of the underworld out of his writings: is why they tried to suppress the direct parallel he himself was so keen to insist on, between his own otherworldly journey and the traditional ancient Greek descents into the world of the dead.

It's why no one would allow him to place right at the start of his famous biography—in the original classical Greek, as he requested—the three words which, for him, were the most perfect motto to sum up his life's story as a whole.

Asmenos ek thanatoio are the words from Homer's *Odyssey* that expressed Jung's infinite relief at being allowed to return, alive and in one piece, from the underworld. They mean "Glad to have escaped from death".[57]

Now, of course, we have the published evidence of his *Red book* to offer some fuller flavour of where he went—and what it did to him.

We can read Jung's own words insisting that only he and nobody else really knew what happened during the three days Christ spent in the underworld, because he had experienced it. And we have his own account of how he came to realize that "travelling to hell means becoming hell oneself".

The trouble is that even being able to study what he said doesn't mean anyone is going to understand it, because these are hardly the easiest kind of words for people who are happy reading or writing about somebody else's journey to hell.[58]

In summer 1662 an Italian painter, Salvator Rosa, finished a portrait called *Pythagoras emerging from the underworld*. Down near the bottom right-hand corner of the painting is Pythagoras stepping out of the blackness, bent over with a twisted grin on his face: the infinitely ambiguous grin of someone who has come back to be of service to humanity but has seen through and past the crap of human illusions.

Filling the left half of the picture, in total contrast, are his enthusiastically devoted disciples—radiant with gladness and light. Women as well as men, some are raising their hands in thanks to heaven. Others are reaching down to help him up without any idea of what they might be touching.

And they don't have a clue what they will be doing in the next few years or generations to turn his whole teaching upside down.[59]

12

Then there is the embarrassing part—just a matter of names, anyone could say, except that sometimes names can matter.

Carl Jung insisted endlessly he was a man of science: a true scientist, empirical scientist. Those around him have, if possible, been even more devoted to promoting his scientific status and standing. But of course whenever there is such intense insistence, so much enthusiasm, one always has to look a little more deeply at what lies behind.[60]

And there is a lot that lies behind.

Documents keep emerging that show just how keen Jung was to conceal the realities of his work, his interests, himself behind the safe label of a scientist. He planned in advance what to hide and the best ways to hide it; busily manoeuvred behind the scenes to block anyone who tried questioning things he didn't want questioned or saying things he didn't want brought into the open; was far less concerned with any truth than with the often paper-thin impression of being a scientist that he chose to create.[61]

For every strong argument that he was a genuine and respectable scientist, there is just as strong an argument that he wasn't. But the strange thing is that—in all the pitched battles which keep being fought between those denying Jung was a man of science and those insisting he absolutely was—no one seems to pay any attention to the balanced statement of his position offered by Jung himself.

In perfect and exquisite alignment with the idea of two different spirits already introduced by him right at the start of his *Red book*, Jung liked to talk about himself as having two different personalities ever since he was a little child. What he called no. 1 personality, like his "spirit of this time", is not just filled with egoistic arrogance and pride.

It also loves parading as a master of dead systems, of sophisticated emptiness and glibness: hides its chronic uncertainty about itself as well as everything else behind the smiling face each of us presents to the world with all our vanity and illusions, pretence and confidence, our thirst for impressive learning and expertise, the craving for reputation or success.

And personality no. 2 is what has access to the spirit of the depths, to the realities of soul and meaning, to nature and to the life hidden away behind madness as well as death—is our "true self" living our "true life", is the dark root of our being.

Or as Jung expressed this difference on a different register: his no. 1 personality, with its unquestioning allegiance to the spirit of this time, is exactly what attracted him to science and reason. But the spirit of the depths, through his personality no. 2, is precisely what shattered that attachment; is what left him deeply humbled, an intensely lonely human being.[62]

For Jung himself these two contrasting personalities, along with the two spirits they correspond to, are fundamental facts of living in the world.

There is no merging of them, harmonizing of them, even any integrating of them. They balance each other as forces of nature, complement each other, struggle with each other in a conflict that never comes to an end.[63]

And if to our modern ears such a harshly irreducible dualism sounds disconcerting or downright bizarre, that's just another sign of how far we have drifted away from the roots of our own civilization—because this same basic idea of one spirit attracting and attaching us to our human world of appearances in constant conflict with a spirit of darkness and madness and the underworld that threatens to snatch us away from everything human goes back thousands of years.

To be more precise: it was absolutely central to the teaching of ancient prophet–healers such as Empedocles, or Parmenides. In fact it was, quite literally, the idea around which their entire teaching revolved. And when Jung turned to acknowledge those who had been the main inspiration for his own uncompromisingly dualistic view of the human psyche, it's no accident that he chose to mention Empedocles by name.[64]

The respectfulness expressed by Jung's surface personality towards the arts of science is perfectly plain to see.

It decorates and embellishes his work. Almost everywhere it's on the most brilliant and ostentatious display, just like the gaudiness of a loud brass band doing the best it possibly can to drown out the mysteries of silence.[65]

But that still leaves open the question of what his other personality wanted to say—even though the answer is equally plain.

For a long time it was known that Jung's *Red book* contained his deepest realizations as well as his most hostile statements about science. In fact that was one of the main factors always weighing against making it public.[66]

And now that the book has been published, this is exactly what we find.

Right at the start he spells out how his whole experience of descending into the underworld, along with his entire process of self-discovery, began from the moment when the spirit of the depths "took away my belief in science": how it took all his knowledge, all his rational understanding, and dedicated them instead to "the service of the inexplicable and paradoxical".

This is nothing, though, compared to what is still to come; is only a prelude to the point where Jung sets about describing with the most exhaustive attention to detail how, even more so than reason, western science in spite of its many great benefits and undeniable advantages is literally a poison.

To be more specific, it's a poison that only magic incantations can ever hope to counteract. And here, too, he is very careful to spell out how these magical incantations will need to be sung if they are going to have any effect at all.

They will have to be sung "in the ancient manner"—an unmistakable reference by Jung to those ancient mystical practices which, in their own time, were so intimately familiar to both Parmenides and Empedocles.[67]

13

It can be interesting to watch the reactions of those who at first were fullest of enthusiasm for the *Red book*—how unnerving they find these unscientific ideas, how embarrassing.

They have the best possible reasons for doing so. After all, Jung himself felt intensely self-conscious and embarrassed about them for as long as he lived.[68]

And it's only too easy for Jungians as well as Jung scholars to want to smoothe everything over by assuming that as he got older, became a little wiser, he snapped out of them and had realized the error of his ways.

He didn't. All he did was become a bit more guarded about what he knew—although you don't have to look very far to see what that was.

To be sure, it was an important part of Jung's mission to have his discoveries of the unconscious taken seriously and accepted by the scientific community. But at the same time he saw where science happened to be heading: straight into the abyss of destroying itself along with the rest of humanity.

From the time he wrote the *Red book* and for the rest of his life, one word that easily came to his lips whenever he found himself talking about the effects of western science or technology was the word "catastrophe". Another was "apocalypse". And when he decided to talk about what he was most afraid of, just a few years before he died, he stated without any hesitation: "modern science".[69]

But there are also two other words that never seemed too far from his tongue when the issue of modern science and its consequences came up.

Those words are "diabolical"; "devilish".[70]

And this is where we have to choose if we are just going to take from Jung whatever scraps attract our fancy while disposing of everything else—or if we are actually prepared to listen to what he says, pay attention to his language, follow where he goes.

Constantly he trumpets in every possible direction the announcement that, far from being a mystic, he is only a scientist. Family, entourage, associates join in as loudly as they can. Even the slightest taint of mysticism: that's something to be avoided like a plague.[71]

But then there is the reality of what was quietly going on inside him behind the brass band, without all the racket and noise.

For everyone—from his own family through professional colleagues to occasional visitors—it was an open secret that this is where the real Jung was to be found, but that he kept his mysticism well hidden for the sake of keeping his scientific reputation intact.

And if one were to ask why he didn't just go public and explain himself, instead, the answer is that he did. In fact he explained himself only too clearly, although it seems there are very few who have wanted to hear.

For example he once gave the whole game away when he complained how "people nowadays have such hopelessly muddled ideas about anything 'mystical', or else such a rationalistic fear of it, that if a mystical experience should ever come their way they are sure to misunderstand its true character and will do anything to protect themselves against, or just repress, its numinous reality." In other words: even to mention the word "mystical" in public is utterly futile because, as a direct result of people's "lack of insight and defective understanding", anything you say is guaranteed to be taken the wrong way. So for him the solution was quite simple.

Either don't talk about mystical matters at all, or talk about them in such a veiled way that only those with ears to understand will understand.

And then, as if this wasn't enough, there is the letter he wrote that comes as close as anything not just to giving the game away but to laying out the most basic rules of the game.

This is the same letter—excluded as if almost deliberately from the volumes of his published correspondence—where, humbly, intensely alone, he describes how in his life he had chosen the path of conscious suffering because he realized this is the only way to compensate for all the suffering inflicted on the divine by humanity's love affair with rationality. Immediately after stating that he saw it as his central role to help "God to be alive and free from the suffering man has put on him by loving his own reason more than God's secret intentions", he goes straight on in the very next sentence to state the truth quite bluntly:

"There is a mystical fool in me that proved to be stronger than all my science."[72]

Here we have everything Jung always seemed so determined to take his public stand and protest against. And what we can see is that, according to his own criteria, he is no longer just a man with all his delusions playing the role of prophet.

He is also a mystic together with all his foolishness.

He is no mystic and he is a mystic. He is exactly what he denies. And precisely what Jung would like to accuse others of he is guilty of, himself, just like the proverbial snake devouring its own tail.

You could say it's only a question of one single letter. And of course, in the most literal and obvious sense, that's true enough. But nothing is more important than to understand how these things really work.

Nowhere does he claim that the mystical fool in him is as powerful as the whole of his science—is equally strong. Instead he states, quite correctly, that it proved to be stronger.

And there is a very simple reason why.

The spirit of the depths will always be at odds with the spirit of our time, just as personality no. 2 will always be in conflict with the superficial wants and needs of personality no. 1. But at the end of the day, as he makes so clear in his *Red book*, the personality and spirit of the depths prove to be stronger.[73]

They are more powerful; more valid. You could call it a law of gravity: the logic of the underworld.

They are what truly matters. In spite of all the idiotic sound and short-lived fury, they are what has the last word.

14

In confronting the science of his time Jung was faced with quite a dilemma.

And ultimately there's only one honest or truthful solution to this dilemma—which is to face the fact that modern science in its existing forms, with its existing concerns and preoccupations, is no real science at all.

It's just a few broken, badly twisted fragments of what science should and could have been. In the most fundamental sense it's nothing but a "bastard of a science", as Jung once described the arrogant attitude that thinks it can block off access to the world of the unconscious: that believes it has the right to isolate and insulate humans from the living realms of the dead.[74]

Jung's own struggles to engage with science, to question science, redefine science, warn against science have kept people busy trying out every conceivable combination of engaging with his work or questioning it; redefining it; warning against it. But what's so easily forgotten in this battle of interpretations, personalities, words, is that on the deepest level there was never any need for Jung to set about redefining anything.

In spite of modernity's ruthless demands and its endless pressures, all he was doing was returning as a matter of instinct to what western science had been from the very start.

He was only finding his way back to what science, in the naturalness of its fragility, had originally been intended to be—a science already perfectly integrated with prophecy and healing, a science based on the arduous process of consciously descending into the unconscious, of going down into the world of the dead to bring back for the sake of others the gifts of wisdom and life.

This instinctive process of rediscovery has nothing to do with any familiar clichés about evolution or regression, least of all with any complicated intellectual schemes about regression and evolution at the same time.

On the contrary: it's just the simplest possible matter of genetics, of ancestry, of a reality forgotten by us on the surface of ourselves but remembered very well in our hidden depths.

We have to keep bearing in mind that for Jung—unlike Freud—the word "primordial" doesn't point to something we need to make a problem of or try to leave behind. "Rather, it is the solution to the problem of modernity."

And the solution to the problems of modern science lies in what science once used to be.[75]

That raises the question of how, or where, the primordial is to be found. It's perfectly true that Jung had the finest of libraries, full of books he studied and loved. But those books aren't what made him what he was or even gave him the knowledge that he had.

Assessing his wisdom by his books, inventing the fictional personality of a "textual Jung", is the height of academic absurdity—because he, better than anyone, knew there is no way of finding primordial reality in some library.

It has to be discovered inside oneself; can only be uncovered on the harrowing journey down into the world of the dead.

As for the process of reading, all the fuss about references and different texts: the best they can ever do is lend a helping and reassuring hand, offer a few timely echoes, give a bit of extra substance and form to what one already mysteriously knows, add some firmer outlines to the affiliations and lineages vaguely intuited inside.[76]

And as for where Jung's affiliations lie, I really don't have to say too much because just a few pointers should do.

For example, the ancient word that perhaps came closest in meaning to our "scientist" was *physikos*—a term often used to describe people like Parmenides or Empedocles. But not only is it the origin of our word "physicist". It was the source of our word "physician", as well; and Parmenides, together with Empedocles, happened to be healers too.

This is nowhere near the end of the story, though. Apart from being the common word for a physicist or scientist, a physician or healer, *physikos* was also the title given to alchemists alongside those prototypical scientists we like to call magicians.

And that brings us straight back to Jung's endless insistence on portraying himself as a pure empiricist who focused all his attention on the facts of experience—because the one specialist who used to concentrate more than anybody else on gathering and working with hard empirical facts was, as we can see so well with Empedocles, the ancient magician.[77]

But this working correspondence between Carl Jung and the earliest Greek philosophers isn't simply a matter of generalities. It also functions, as of course it should, even down to the kind of details so tempting to slip over or ignore.

Jung found himself using techniques for communicating, talking, writing, which would be extraordinary enough if used by anyone nowadays—not to mention a scientist. What those techniques lead towards is something almost completely submerged, something very different from the heady world of literary borrowings and theoretical ideas that tends to keep historians so frantically distracted.

Hardly visible any more, thanks to the efficiency with which it was stripped out of what he wrote or said, is his fondness for expressing himself through repetition: through circling with his words around the same subjects, time and time again.[78]

But that's exactly how Parmenides as well as Empedocles also used to express themselves—repeating and circling around themselves, from beginning to end, because it was the way they had been shown and inwardly trained how to speak.

After all, this was a time-honoured incantatory technique among magical healers: among the type of prophet–healer, or *iatromantis*, that they both really were in spite of the endless later attempts to dress them up as something else. These prophet–healers knew instinctively how to use their own words not only to keep focused, but for the sake of healing; were able to use repetition for opening the doors to the unconscious and easing the passage into the underworld.[79]

Just as surprising, by any modern standards, is Jung's very conscious policy of deliberately using ambiguity in his writings. "The language I speak must be ambiguous, must have two meanings."

He is careful to explain why for him this is so important. Intentional ambiguity is far superior to any other available form of communication. Ambiguity alone corresponds to the nature of reality, as well as the reality of nature; can do them both justice.[80]

There are some situations, though, where no amount of explaining is going to make any difference—will ever be enough.

For its own part, the bustling Jung industry has naturally or rather unnaturally done everything possible to sidestep any real consideration of the subject. In fact even the people who used to pride themselves on their personal closeness to Jung have shown how ill-equipped they are for understanding why he valued ambiguity so highly.[81]

But Parmenides and Empedocles, as well as other Greeks, were also very deliberate in their use of riddles and ambiguity. They, too, understood that only by being intentionally ambiguous can one evoke the fullness of reality and do it true justice.

And it was their welcoming of ambiguity that, more than anything else, brought Aristotle's mockery and fury down on their heads. As he irritably complained about Empedocles, who in his life was the perfect example of a prophet–healer:

"Avoid ambiguity! This is what people like to use when they have nothing to say but want to pretend they have something to say, like Empedocles for instance, who tricks and deceives with all his circlings and circumlocutions. And his listeners end up experiencing exactly what people in general tend to experience when listening to the words of prophets because, so long as prophets are speaking their riddling ambiguities, everyone just mindlessly nods along."[82]

Ambiguity has been well and truly excluded, drowned out by the voice of rationality—by what Jung liked to describe as the "petty reasoning mind, which cannot endure any paradoxes". Or at least this is what rationalists choose to think.

But what they forget is that originally ambiguity and paradox were an integral, essential feature of real logic: of the sacred logic which always stands untouched although savaged by their reasoning.[83]

Ambiguity is the voice of prophecy, and at the same time is like the wildness of nature. It plunges us into the streams of paradox, is a constant confrontation with our conscious need for control. And, strangely enough, ambiguity itself is not ambiguous at all.

On the contrary, it's perfectly clear; an endless invitation into the open landscape of reality. Paradoxically it's only the process of reasoning that, with each step it takes in trying to stamp out ambiguities, ends up creating new ambiguities instead—even while pretending to be on top of the very same situation it's simply making worse and worse.

The voices of Parmenides or Empedocles or Jung are so confusing to our conscious mind because they are calling us into places most people have lost the courage as well as the knowledge to go. Their ambiguities are total non-ambiguity: the confrontation of humans, then as now, with the truth of themselves.

But, at the same time, these ties linking Jung to the ancient world reach even further and far deeper than that.

Memories, dreams, reflections is the name of the famous book, published just after he had died, that he ended up ambiguously referring to as his "so-called autobiography". And certainly it contains his own voice—along with the voices of his secretary, his editors, his publishers.

Many expert hands came together to smooth over and set straight what he had said; domesticate it; "auntify" it by making it into something even the stuffiest of old maids would be happy to hear; and discreetly, when necessary, help it disappear.

Some of the things he wanted to say managed to get through. A lot of what he tried to communicate never did. And even though a more or less accurate record survives of the original memoirs that Jung himself dictated over a period of two years, it never was too easy for much information about them to trickle out.[84]

One of those things that has never seen the light of day was his reply when—during the first week of October 1957—he found himself being asked to speak out honestly about the real nature of his work. This is hardly a surprise. His reply is bound to sound so insignificant to any ordinary reader, so trivial, so devoid of any serious or meaningful content, that it would be a miracle if the passage had been allowed to stand in his published biography.

As he starts speaking, you can still hear him laugh. He declares that his entire work, all his presumed wisdom and grand achievement, boils down to this: that he fell into a gigantic hole from which he somehow, if he was going to survive, had to dig himself out.

Then—after quoting those words of Homer that always came to him whenever he pondered his luck in returning alive from the underworld, "Glad to have escaped from death", and making sure to recommend them as the best possible motto for the story of his life—he goes straight on to make the simplest of statements. His whole science, he explains, derived entirely from his visions and dreams.[85]

In just a couple of sentences, with the help of that free association he fell into when dictating his memoirs, he has spelled out a message which from any normal point of view is not just striking. It's incomprehensible, paradoxical, bizarre. And this is precisely why no one has paid it any attention.

Jung is saying that everything one could refer to as his science really came to him from the underworld; from visions; from dreams.

And this is exactly what Parmenides, master of incubation or entering other states of consciousness, lord of dreams, had demonstrated when he brought logic along with the freshest discoveries in western science straight back from his journey into the underworld.

Jung is simply reliving the way things used to be.

But just as Parmenides' teaching would soon be covered over, and its integrity broken by Plato along with so many other well-intentioned thinkers, the spirit of this time got to work very quickly and efficiently to cover over what Jung had wanted to say.

In fact it's essential to remember that the entity he chose to refer to as the spirit of our time isn't only obsessed and fascinated with all the trivial superficialities of life. Just thinking about it that way could hardly be more wrong.

On the contrary, there is nothing this spirit enjoys more than entertaining itself with what it doesn't understand—than fiddling and tinkering and interfering with the wisdom of the depths, subtly and imperceptibly rationalizing it, ever so cleverly making a mess of it by presenting it with a grand flourish as something of its own.[86]

And if you wanted, you could call our present understanding of Jung a masterpiece manufactured by the constantly bustling spirit of this time.

15

Just two days earlier, on the 1st of October 1957, Jung was at Bollingen: the stone tower and retreat he himself had designed, then helped to build, near the far upper edge of Lake Zurich.

Here too, as soon as he started talking, it was about his original dreams and visions—the visions and dreams from which all his later work would flow—that he wanted to speak.

His words, that day, were duly noted down as usual by his secretary. And eventually they would turn up, mauled, as one of the most thrilling climaxes in the published version of his biography.

Right at the end of the most central and crucial chapter called "Confrontation with the unconscious", Jung appears in grand style as hero of the depths: the hero whose whole life was transformed when he managed, more or less successfully, to work on the chaos of unconsciousness and against overwhelming odds hammer it into a shape and form he could present to his contemporary world.

Of course such a heroic role is something Jung himself delighted in playing when his no. 1 personality took the stage. And the myth of him striving valiantly with his "ordering mind" to inject some conscious arrangement into this unconscious chaos—just like the familiar notion of the unconscious as an incredibly destructive power that has to be worked with but mastered, organized, directed—is central to almost any appreciation of his work.[87]

There is only one problem. On that day at Bollingen, what he was saying could hardly have been more different.

He begins—not ends—with a comment about his more or less successful effort to impose some order on the seething material erupting out of the unconscious; compares his initial visions and dreams to the flow of fiery lava which, after a while, turns into solid stone so it can be worked on.

But only now does he explain where all his thoughts and comments have been leading: "It was the passion and intensity inside this fire, it was the stream of lava itself which is the force that compelled whatever happened to happen. And so, completely naturally, everything fell into its own proper place and order."

And this is where we need to pause before going on.

Jung's words move. On this particular day they were carrying him towards open acknowledgement of how the unconscious takes care of everything. We can have any number of anxieties about disorder; any amount of busy fantasies about imposing some order on it.

And the reality all the time is that the unconscious forces we are so frightened of are themselves, paradoxically, mysteriously, the true creators of order.

But for Jung's secretary, Aniela Jaffé, this was all moving in the wrong direction. She was writing a biography, almost an autobiography—and in her commendable devotion wanted to keep everyone focused on the virtues of the great man himself, not on the virtues of some unnameable unconscious.

So, with plenty of well-intentioned thoughtfulness, she scrupulously reversed the flow of his thinking; systematically inverted the sequence of his own sentences; ever so delicately turned everything on its head.[88]

If it was just a question here of Jung's own secretary dutifully tampering with the things he said, that would be significant enough. But it's only the start.

Almost as if he guessed that not everyone would understand what he had tried to say about the stream of lava taking care of everything, Jung goes straight on to repeat himself in even simpler and blunter terms. And now we no longer have to rely on Jaffé to educate, or entertain, us.

The one scholar who for years was able to study these unpublished interviews independently, and in far greater detail than anybody else, decided to make a translation of this very same passage available. And here, word for word, is his version of what Jung at the tower in Bollingen went on to say next:

"I wanted to achieve something in my science and then I was plunged in this stream of lava, and then had to classify everything."

The trouble is that, here too, Jung said nothing of the kind. What he really did say was very different: "I wanted to achieve something in my science, and then I bumped into this stream of lava, and then it brought everything into order."[89]

Here is perhaps the closest one could come to a confession from Jung as an old man about what, in his life, was really what.

The science he had tried to lay claim to, in spite of all his dashing dilettantism and amateur theatrics—on its own it came to nothing. All it did was bring him face to face with something infinitely vaster and more powerful than himself.

And, from then on, that power arranged and guided everything.

Of course you could say none of these distortions, these gross mistranslations, actually matter; and on a certain level you would be right. We are well past the stage where a couple more murders here or there are going to make much of a difference—and I am perfectly aware that, from any rational point of view, not one single detail in what I have mentioned is worth thinking or even reading about.

Besides, nothing would be easier than to say: We knew that anyway! It's common knowledge that, regardless of all his warnings and cautions about the dangers involved, Jung's whole work is based on his profoundest respect for the wisdom contained in our unconscious.

The fact is, though, that it never was or ever will be a question of what anybody knows intellectually. We can understand everything just wonderfully on the level of theory; of principle. But that's not the point.

The point is to watch how even the people closest to Jung alongside the brightest, most scientific of Jungian experts change him; rewrite him; silence him.

And we, too, might have the most brilliant knowledge lodged away in some drawer of our theoretical brain. But the only thing that counts is what each of us does in every moment with each thought of ours, every breath. All that matters is whether we can consciously stay with the mystery of the unconscious, helping it in its wisdom to arrange and order things, or whether we use our own accumulated wisdom to interfere.

Naturally one could call these misinterpretations and mistranslations sheer human error. Anybody determined to be uncharitable could even call them downright negligence, or worse. And in a sense they are both; but in another sense they are neither.

It's not just that they emerge independently, spontaneously, from some intelligent individual here or there. They are simply collective manifestations of the spirit of our time.

The trouble is that, in our superficially individualistic culture, we have no context for understanding this kind of mistranslation; no language; no frame of reference. For us, these misinterpretations are just accidents—if we ever notice them at all. It doesn't occur to us that there could be such a thing as a psychology of mistranslation, a pathology of rationalization.

And this is because those murders committed, so many centuries ago, by Plato and Aristotle have become the stream we all swim in. Our entire lives are a rationalization: one big mistranslation.

But that only ever becomes visible—if we can muster the courage to look—in the case where someone like Jung steps out of the stream.

Then, it's immediately the same old story as with Parmenides or Empedocles all over again. When Parmenides was taken down to the underworld only to be given everything he knew by the queen of the dead, she sent him back into the world of the living as a messenger: as a prophet whose job was essentially to do everything in her name.

Of course, in this world of illusions and deceptions, he had to appear to be a human like any other human—and, if possible, play the game of humanity better than anybody else. But for Parmenides himself, the underlying reality was that everything was being ordered; arranged; forcibly directed and guided by the divine power of the underworld inside him.

And, quite naturally, that's not the end of the parallels. Just as Jung's words were misinterpreted, mistranslated, altered, in exactly the same way Parmenides' words were manipulated and changed to make him say what others wanted him to say: what they needed him to say.[90]

Back then, as now, one had to do whatever it took to make Parmenides take the credit for his wisdom—not the sacred. It was simply a question of how best to tamper with his words to arrive at the desired result; and then that result becomes enshrined as history, the history in which we silently agree to bury reality.

16

A few days later, Jung gave another interview which his secretary quickly transcribed.

Vividly he describes what it was like as he started sinking into the underworld—having to learn how to find his way around in the world of the dead while still alive. This is where he mentions his unbearable aloneness because there was absolutely no one who could help or understand; tells about literally having to cling on to the table in front of him to prevent himself from falling apart; explains how he was terrified by the almost constant experience of feeling again and again he was being torn to pieces, ripped into shreds by the archetypal forces and powers inside him.[91]

And so we are brought back almost full circle to where we started, although now it should perhaps be a little easier to appreciate the true significance of what he goes on to say next.

He talks about how horrific the whole situation was. It was one endless storm; and through everything he had to pretend to be a normal father, play the role of husband, function as a doctor. That he was able to keep it all up was a matter of brute force.

Anyone else, he points out, would have been destroyed. "But there was a daimonic power in me."[92]

Amazingly, all it needs is Jung's mention of being a normal father and husband and doctor—and suddenly we know without the slightest doubt just what he is talking about. It's the same with the famous passage in *Memories, dreams, reflections* where he describes having to keep repeating the address where he lives, or reminding himself he has a wife and children, just to convince himself that he actually exists.

Jung is so normal, so like us! He is so grounded and balanced, so eminently human and sane: nothing could be clearer.[93]

And here, too, the significance of Jung's continuing ability to play the role of father and husband and doctor seems so obvious. Here is a man with an unbreakable ego who, through sheer conscious force or willpower, was always in command and knew how to keep everything under control. The fact that he managed to turn up for meals on time, even do his military service, is irrefutable testimony to the strength of the human ego and living proof of the fact that never for a single moment was his sanity in doubt.

This was a man consciously, triumphantly, taking his stand against the unconscious and winning out against it: an example to us all.[94]

But then there is the small matter of whether we care to pay attention to what Jung himself actually said.

Words, for him, mattered. He was only too conscious that the phrases and expressions he used had particular meanings, implications, innuendos which few people would ever care about or even notice; that it was a constant struggle, and losing battle, to try to preserve the "full value" of his words.[95]

And that final mention of a daimonic power or force, a "dämonische Kraft", happens to be far more than some throw-away statement.

On the contrary: the word "daimonic" meant something very specific, and perfectly consistent, for Jung. That's hardly surprising, because it also meant something very specific and consistent for Freud—and for Aristotle, and Empedocles and Parmenides and Homer.

Daimonic means what's divine in us, or as good as divine. It's what lies beyond or below or outside our human capacities, not to mention our human understanding. It has nothing to do with our own little conscious ego and the control we imagine we have, except for the fact that it's guaranteed to disrupt the flimsy stability of our egos and smash all our illusions of control.

It comes from somewhere else, is irresistible; mostly only shows itself in certain people who can be described as blessed, or cursed, depending on one's point of view. In Jung's own particular case, he saw it as an inheritance transmitted to him very specifically from his mother: an uncanny gift that has its source in the unconscious, belongs to the unconscious, points to the unconscious.[96]

And now—in the midst of the ordeal that during his interviews Jung kept using words like "terrifying" and "horrific" to describe, although his secretary very discreetly either erased or replaced the majority of them with nicer-sounding words—we can start to see the horrifying paradox unfolding in front of us.

Jung is not talking about his personal, conscious, human powers at all. Just the same as with the stream of lava: it's the power which is non-human and beyond human consciousness, or mastery or control, that takes care of everything.

Now for him, held between opposing worlds, nothing was simple any more.

Even to be human, or act human, involved a power that isn't human. Even the easiest and most trivial of things we all take for granted, like performing as a doctor or husband or father, literally required a superhuman force. Even the process of appearing to be normal was an act of magic.

As for his ego, its only real role was to mediate and witness and watch—watch the unconscious struggling to master the unconscious, power engaged with power, daimon against daimon.

And if you think I am making this up, that's simply because you are a stranger to the world of the ancient Greeks or the world Jung himself used to live in.

In such a world it goes without saying that only what's beyond human inside a human can stand up to the divine. It needs one divine force to come to grips with, or combat, or get the better of another. In the words of the famous old alchemical saying with which Jung was very familiar: Nature masters Nature, *Hê physis tên physin kratei*.[97]

In other words, it needs a non-human strength to become truly human. Even being the most ordinary human is, in reality, a superhuman task. And this superhuman task is what, for Jung, the process of seemingly human individuation happens to be.

To engage in it one has to be swept up into a battle of the gods, which is why the Jungian process of individuation will never be for wimps. It's not for those who are so terrified of being overwhelmed by the divine archetypes or of falling a helpless victim to their power that they think they can shrink away from them—as even the best trained Jungian analysts might try to do when they imagine it's safer to identify with being a poor, feeble, limited human being.

That, after all, is just to become hopelessly trapped in identifying with the dark side of the archetype of humanity.

In what can be numbered among the most important outlines of his whole psychology that he ever wrote, Jung described how "the strongest and best" are those who invoke danger deliberately; throw caution to the winds; "purposely expose themselves to the danger of being devoured by the monster of the maternal abyss". This is why true individuation is the rarest and most difficult thing. It's a path so hard it can be almost impossible to follow through to the end.

Or, as he would confess when hardly anyone was listening, it's only for the very few. After a certain stage most other people would be much better off just going back to church and living their collective lives like everyone else.[98]

The way is tough; immensely dangerous.

Nothing at all is guaranteed because this is the way of the magician. As for those apparently simple words about "a daimonic power inside me", so easy to slip over even for those who should have known better but didn't, Jung had already said everything that needs to be said—because possession of a daimonic power is, as he explains elsewhere, precisely the sign of a magician.[99]

And this is what, inescapably and regardless of anything we think or believe, it all comes down to.

An acquaintance of Jung's, Miguel Serrano, has left a few notes about their meetings and correspondence. To him it was self-evident that, as he would write to Jung a year before Jung's death, there are not many people who understand you—"not even your own disciples".

But he was also much more specific about what he realized made the man tick, kept him going; observed that "even though he fought against it, Jung condemned himself to be a magician who was willing to pass beyond the frontiers of official science in our time".

And as for this Jung he had encountered—"Jung, the magician"—only a poet or priest or magician would ever be "capable of propounding his message, interpreting the underlying language of his work, which is already there like a palimpsest".[100]

Perhaps you won't know what a palimpsest is. Not many people do.

It's an old Greek term: a word that describes the nature and fate of our western culture perfectly.

A palimpsest is a piece of writing material, like an ancient papyrus, on which what was written originally has been rubbed out and erased so that something else—often an entirely different kind of text—can now be written on top.

Sometimes the original text has been erased so completely that it's impossible to make out what it was, what it had said; or perhaps one never suspects there was anything else written underneath.

But mostly it's possible to make out the traces of a few words or isolated letters here and there—and even get a sense of what the obliterated text had been, of the deleted story it once wanted to tell.

2
BACK
TO THE
SOURCE

BACK TO THE SOURCE

1

I must have been about fourteen at the time.

The situation is still perfectly clear to my mind. A girlfriend in London invited me round to her family home. "My parents are out for the whole evening." And I remember thinking, "Well, maybe now I'm going to get lucky!"

When I arrived, the first thing she did was to take me straight into the living room. Quietly she said "There is something I'd like you to see", before switching on the television just as a documentary was starting about a man I had never heard of. There were some impressive views of a magic-looking castle that the peculiar man, called Jung, had built on the edge of a lake; and they awakened something in me, strangely moved me.

But for years all that stayed in my memory was the ghostly image of a tower beside a lake. And that was that. First I had to go through all my teens followed by every twenty: there are so many experiences we need to have.

Soon I was into my early thirties and confronted with what, back then, seemed the most impossibly difficult period in my life. One day a resolution took shape inside me that it was time to get away. I had only just learned to drive so I packed some things in a car, got up before dawn the next morning to go down to Dover and catch the first ferry for Calais.

Then I did the same thing I used to do so often as a teenager when I was searching, seeking, but didn't have even the remotest notion of what I was looking for. I would stand hitchhiking at the side of the road, any road, and take the next ride that came along: letting the road itself guide me. And now, in the car, I just drove without the slightest idea where I was going. I would stop to stretch my legs, have a bite to eat, keep an eye on the car's own needs for petrol and water and oil.

Otherwise, though, I simply allowed the road to take me—without a map, without even paying the least attention to any of the directional signs.

It was getting dark when I found myself at the French–Swiss border. But still I didn't have the tiniest interest in where this thoughtless experiment was taking me. Choicelessly I left the highway; watched myself driving along smaller roads, then streets; out into the cold December countryside. My only consolation was that I had a good sleeping bag and would be able to curl up comfortably on the back seat.

I was pulled onto a country lane, caught sight of a railway track running close by. At one point something beyond any conscious control unexpectedly told me to stop: I pulled over, with some difficulty, into the tall grass growing beside the road. And then it was as if I was being drawn physically out of the car, forced to cross the road, walk straight ahead into the pitch darkness without being able to see a thing in front of me. My only thought was that I hoped I'd be able to find my way back to the car.

After blindly groping forward and sometimes stumbling I started noticing a sharpness in the air, felt I heard a strange murmur, sensed I could glimpse a hint of something shifting in front of me. Suddenly I stopped—realizing I had come to the edge of water.

Then it was as if I was being yanked to my left, guided near the water's edge. There seemed to be some obstacles but nothing was clear except for a single white blur that appeared ahead of me. I came closer; saw, with difficulty, that it was some kind of stone; and experienced the abrupt, almost unceremonious need to sit down.

My last thought was how lucky I happened to be at least to be wearing a warm coat. And then any sense of myself was gone. I was no longer who I had been a minute ago, a lifetime ago. Without any warning or even the subtlest kind of transition I had turned into someone totally different—and yet no other than myself.

Just as sharp and clear as if I was meeting my own image right in front of me, I was a knight. My hair, I noticed, had become a pitch but shining black. I was a warrior in the fullest sense: immensely powerful and destructive but in a proper, not a vicious, way.

I was being confronted with myself as a destroyer. Even more, I was being shown the perils and dangers in this; the immensely difficult process of learning how to trust myself with this; how to discover, and keep discovering, its timeless essence which will always be beyond every positivity as well as negativity. But, at the same time, even to want to name this is to let it disappear.

And then, in a stunningly dramatic moment, the moon came out from behind the clouds—close to full.

Immediately everything was transformed. I glanced up and around and, to my amazement, I was right in front of the tower I had seen on television all those years ago: the tower built by that man called Jung. And the building itself was enough, straight away, to convince me of his greatness. On the one hand it was incredibly squat and strong, chthonic and rooted, a place that would never allow itself to be blown away; on the other, just like the place of a magical being or a structure from out of some fairy tale.

He has literally made a fairy-tale dream come true—on earth.

But it wasn't only my surroundings that had been transformed. Just as suddenly, looking towards the tower, I too had changed into the oldest and wisest of men. It wasn't some change I was imagining or thinking up. It was there in my body, in the sensation of my face and hands. I could feel it in the flowing grey hair, drooping grey moustache, trailing grey beard, and in the physical wisdom which is as ancient as time.

The wise old man is what he is because he has endured everything the earth can throw at him but, although he can seem so thoughtful to others, doesn't think or consider. This is the state he always abides in, which is the place of no abiding at all where spirit is united with earth. He just is the earth's suffering, made conscious; its beauty and pain; its humanity.

And then—I don't know how else to describe it—Jung came towards me, but not as a man although it was unmistakeably him. He came like a wind moving in a spiral, stirring everything but at the same time perfectly still. It was as if he was silently speaking from everywhere, but also from inside myself.

He carefully explained to me the real meaning of the word "home": where my true home is. At that time I had no way of knowing just how appropriate his advice would be, considering how I'd have to spend most of my adult existence moving from place to place without any fixed or ordinary home.

He went into telling me, through the silence, what I had to do; offered me guidance for the rest of my life. But finally this strangest of meetings was over and I knew it was the moment to go.

Before standing up I turned round in the moonlight to look at what, the whole while I had been sitting there, I'd been leaning against. The surface of the stone was flat but full of carefully carved inscriptions which, because of the shadows and the angle of the moon, were hard to read. But with patience

I could make out symbols for each of the inner planets—Sun, Moon, Saturn, Jupiter, Venus, Mars, with Mercury on a little figure in the middle—and was drawn straight to the word *kosmos*, which had been written in classical Greek.

So was all the rest of the inscribed text: a quotation at the top that I immediately recognized as coming from the ancient Greek philosopher Heraclitus and, at the bottom, a few famous words from Homer about being guided into the underworld "toward the gates of the sun and the land of dreams".

When I had managed to get up, I kissed Venus. As I walked down to the water's edge, the moon was shining above the lake but also reflected just as brightly in it.

There was the moon above, the moon below. And I was both.

2

Making my way back to the car was easy.

Inside I took out the little black notebook in my coat pocket and wrote down everything that had happened, starting with the date for title—night of 23 December 1985.

From that night on nothing for me would ever be quite the same. It was as if I had somewhere touched a consciousness of work to be done without having any conscious idea, yet, of what form that work would take. And I realize, needless to say, that in telling this I lay myself open to every kind of accusation.

Even the fact that Jung created a retreat for himself, here at Bollingen, where he spent most of his time alone is troubling enough for a lot of people. It's troubling for a very good reason. This is the place he was guided to withdraw to so that, over the years, he could nurture in solitude the prophetic secrets which had first been shown to him while he was working on his *Red book*.

And that happens to be a side of him which in spite of, or rather because of, the *Red book*'s publication not everyone wants to be reminded of.[1]

Of course I am also aware that for people nowadays who boast about how they have gone beyond Jung and left him far behind—who laugh at him for his horrific lack of rationality or truly evolutionary thought, who mock him for clinging to some quaint idea that life needs to have meaning instead of summoning the fortitude to embrace without any reservation our meaningless modern world—the tower he built at Bollingen is nothing but his "private psycho-Disneyland".

What they somehow fail to understand is that for certain individuals a base in nature away from the relentless pressures of such a wonderfully modern world, away from what Empedocles already referred to as "the ten thousand worthless things that exist among humans and blunt their cares", is an essential reference point of reality and sanity inside our collective psycho-Disneyland.[2]

But at the same time I am aware as well of how quick those who considered themselves the select few, privileged to be intimately acquainted with Jung himself, could be to complain that far "too many people live with an image of their relationship to Jung which is utterly unreal".

Needless to say, their point is unquestionably valid. The temptation can be irresistible to get caught up in some "fantasy relationship" with the man which has no grounding whatsoever in reality. And I will be the first to admit that everything I have said about my encounter with him at Bollingen is on any sensible assessment utterly, absurdly, unreal.

At the same time, though, it actually happened. I was drawn there, to his tower, to sit in the dark against his alchemical stone, driven blind.[3]

But I also found it very interesting to note as I wrote this book how—while Jung talks openly in his published memoirs about only being able to incarnate the living archetype of the wise old man at Bollingen, and nowhere else—the pages where he speaks out about the central importance for him of the archetype of the knight are locked up in what used to be a heavily guarded record of the interviews he gave just a few years before he died.

Hardly anyone had been allowed even to see that record, let alone read it, back in 1985. And, right down to this day, it has never been published.[4]

Naturally none of this does anything at all to change the fact that, from a rational point of view, everything I have described about my invitation to Bollingen—arriving as if by accident at that one particular place out of all the countless millions of possible places in Europe—is unbelievable.

Not to put too fine a point on the matter: practically speaking it's impossible.

But, again, it was only as I was writing this book that I came across a reference to the inscription Jung had carved in Latin just above his stone fireplace—right there at Bollingen. *Quaero quod impossibile*: "I seek what is impossible."

This is Jung himself in his own, carved words. He was never one more, pious believer in some ridiculously impossible dogma. On the contrary, he was a Gnostic who actively sought the impossible out.[5]

And as for what Jung was referring to, with these mysterious words of his about seeking the impossible, we can still say exactly what that was. He was referring to the courage of those who are prepared, regardless of risk or cost, to make the journey into the underworld so they will be able to encounter the queen of the dead—so they can come face to face with the goddess Persephone.

That, after all, is what Bollingen was for Jung. It was his point of entry to the underworld.[6]

On the other hand it would be easy enough to say, because it would be true, that what most of the people around him managed to do was simply to turn his great impossibility into their many little possibilities—their professional successes, satisfying achievements and especially their reassuring understandings.

But as the one person who had sat with him during some of the most intensely difficult times in his life, and heard him say things he couldn't tell anybody else, once stated: "no one, not even those closest to him, ever knew him as a whole".

In reality there was never an inner circle around him. There were only intensifying degrees of failure to understand the mystery and secret of what Jung was, or what his work was. As for those who would go on to explain how thoroughly and fully they understood him along with the most demanding of his writings, or congratulate each other on their complete and expert grasp of his ideas, it's only logical to consider them the biggest fools.

After all, one has to be infinitely careful in claiming to know anything about a person who often confessed he could never understand himself—and understood less and less of the mystery he was as he grew older.[7]

This is what happens when, every moment, one lives so closely with a mystery that one becomes it.

3

The question of what Jung's work was has been answered in a hundred different ways—and, in the most fundamental sense, never been answered at all.

At least it can seem safe to say that, underneath the endless shifting of trends and fashions and interpretations, there is one unquestionably stable point of certainty. This is the fact that he had an unflinching commitment to the individual: was selflessly dedicated to unlocking the secret inside each of us and helping everyone towards the goal of self-fulfilment.

After all, first and foremost he was a healer; a medical expert bent on treating people's problems and curing them of their personal suffering; a therapist of the human psyche, a carer for the individual's soul.[8]

And this line of thinking is just fine, so long as you avoid looking too closely at what he meant by the word "individual"—because then you will suddenly find yourself staring straight into a bottomless hole.

As for Jung the sensitive, intuitive healer: the stories told by people who visited him, only met him once or twice, stayed to be treated by him, are almost as extraordinary as fairy tales. With his magical insight he saw straight into their core; recognized them as an individual person in a way they had never felt recognized before.

And certainly that's one side of the coin. But there is the other side, too—which is that Jung couldn't have been less interested in what we think of as the individual.

It was only the impersonal realm beyond every personal undertone or overtone, the objective behind the subjective, that held his attention. Those around him were perfectly aware of the fact. His wife, always his strongest supporter and defender, could hardly have been blunter in her observation that he showed no interest in people at all "unless they exhibited archetypes": unless they allowed something larger than the human, something numinous, to show through.

And Jung's own language was just as plain. The people who came into his life only concerned him if they had something from the world of the sacred to convey to him, tell him, show him. "The moment I'd seen through them, the magic was gone." It was the daimonic power inside him, he explains, that ruthlessly and impersonally decided who would hold any interest for him—and for how long. He had little conscious power or choice in the matter; was forced by something far greater to keep constantly moving, hurting himself as well as others, destroying friendships, creating bitterness and resentment, leaving acquaintances far behind.[9]

To be sure, on a certain level the reality of the individual was always absolutely central for him. His whole view of life, especially as he got older, circled around the question of how individuals can find the inner courage to take a stand against "the spiritual and moral darkness" of governments which have grown far too powerful and seem destined to become even more intrusive in future.

But the trouble is that what Jung meant by warning against this moral and spiritual darkness, what he was pointing to in trying to shake people out of becoming just submissive and servile servants of the state, is something much more radical than most sensitive modern individualists might expect.

Constantly he kept trying to warn about the living presence everywhere of forces that are working all the time to trick us into staying asleep. Even when writing his most rarefied essays about alchemy he couldn't resist ending with a loud cry warning about Lucifer, the diabolical seducer, "the father of lies whose voice in our time, supported by press and radio, revels in orgies of propaganda and leads untold millions to ruin"—and is also perfectly capable of brainwashing us into believing we are individuals just because we think we can decide what colour car to buy, which television channel to watch, which spiritual practice to select for the coming week.

The fact is that, for Jung, nothing was more destructive of the individual than the collective western cult of the individual. And to be a true individual by becoming aware of the archetypal forces that, from moment to moment, are shaping even our most intimate and seductive thoughts: this is the coldest, loneliest thing for anyone to do.[10]

The real trouble here, perhaps the most crucial problem of all in approaching Jung, already begins from the time when he was making his way into and out of the underworld while starting work on the *Red book*.

On a superficial reading anyone could mistake this book of his for a celebration, even a gospel, of the individual: encouraging people to find their own truth and just live it regardless of anything or anyone else. It's only when one begins to read a little deeper that the underlying message starts making its way out—that the path towards becoming a true individual involves suffering and being tortured to a degree which is unimaginable, being ground down into nothing, having any and every illusion of ever being a genuine individual stripped away.

And it was out of Jung's almost ritualistic work in producing the *Red book* that the most essential aspect of his whole psychology, what he called the process of individuation, dramatically evolved.

But as for what he meant by this process of individuation: that's a fascinating story in itself.

Just the same as with the workings of alchemy, it's the most natural process in the world—although nothing could be rarer. It demands a certain consciousness, but our usual consciousness only gets in the way and blocks it; interferes.

Also, it has nothing at all to do with becoming some kind of individualist. As Jung himself tried to explain: "Individuation is not that you become an ego—you would then become an individualist. You know, an individualist is a man who did not succeed in individuating; he is a philosophically distilled egotist. Individuation is becoming that thing which is not the ego, and that is very strange. Therefore nobody understands what the self is, because the self is just the thing which you are not, which is not the ego ... something exceedingly impersonal, exceedingly objective."[11]

And please note that it's not I who am saying nobody understands this: it's Jung himself. And he is quite right, because in the process he is describing there is no one left to understand.

As for what he says here about the extreme objectivity and impersonality of the state involved, this is exceedingly important. It's a theme he sometimes weaves into and out of. But nowhere else does he mention it with as much power, or elegant simplicity, as during the course of a short talk he specifically dictated for his memoirs when he was already in his eighties—and that ended up being silently excluded from his published biography.

He describes the lonely, and solitary, process of individuation as this: as the inner process of dying "before surrendering oneself to the impersonal". His reference here is to the ancient mystical theme of dying before you die; to the mysterious process of being forced at some stage to withdraw from society, then being taken down into the underworld only to end up stripped of everything before being reborn, which in the history of western culture is associated especially with figures such as Empedocles or Parmenides. And this is why he would explain his particular kind of psychological training, the Jungian style of analysis, as a process of dying.[12]

But that's not all he has to say here.

On the contrary: he also presents individuation as a secret that has to remain a total mystery because, in approaching it, even the slightest possibility of human comprehension comes to a very abrupt and sudden end. By its very nature, the whole subject is such a secret that it's something no one will ever be able to grasp or understand. And he explains, in detail, how the mystery of individuation is the mystery of the Grail.

This, significantly enough, is the very same text I already mentioned earlier—the same talk where Jung speaks out about how centrally, how crucially, important for him the archetype of the knight happens to be because it's only by adhering to the unwritten laws of chivalry that the Grail can ever be won. The secret of individuation is that the one and only way to discover the Grail is by being it. It will forever remain undiscovered, and undiscoverable, except by simply becoming it.

And here is where he is able not just to state, as he so often does elsewhere, that individuation is always only for the very few. This is where, thanks to the ancient imagery and mythology of the Grail legend which he also shows he considers his own, he is able to explain why.

The quest demands everything. People can have as many romantic dreams, as many collective fantasies, as they want. The reality, though, is that the ordeal is far too hard. Almost no one can endure it. And those who think they are equipped to make sense of it or communicate it to others—they are the most unequipped of all.

This, as it were, is the quintessential myth behind Jung's psychology: the myth of individuation.[13]

But, needless to say, we are left with a very different picture nowadays.

Instead of individuation as a sacred mystery intended only for the unflinching eyes of the few, we are confronted with individuation democratized—thrown into the public sphere, open and free for all.

And of course this would be just wonderful, if anybody had the remotest idea what's really involved.

The most vocal of Jungians are quick to insist it was Jung himself who claimed that the fully individuated state is everybody's birthright: that, at least in theory, it ought to be capable of paving the way for a truly evolved humanity through "a Christification of many".

What they mysteriously agree to leave out, stay quite silent about, is how he would go straight on to add that there is not a hope in hell of this ever happening with humans the way they are. If most people were to get even the faintest taste of this Christification, the slightest whiff of this truly individuated state, they'd explode with uncontainable hubris and inflation; and then the world would end up even worse than it already is.

Time and again the identical phenomenon repeats itself like clockwork. Jung gives the clearest warnings. The warnings are ignored. He states how things could have been or should be—only to explain why, due to collective ignorance and unconsciousness, it's impossible for them to be that way. But his explanations are mutely, unceremoniously thrown aside.[14]

And if you were to ask why Jung's own direct warnings, explanations, qualifications are so blatantly pushed away I'd have to say: because of that very same ignorance and unconsciousness Jung was so persistent in warning about.

Here there is no mystery whatsoever. All we have is precisely that hubris he was describing, the identical inflation, acting itself out in front of our eyes.

But it's being acted out not by some ignorant members of the public—simply by very foolish Jungians.

4

Naturally the thrill, for fools, of ignoring warnings offered to fools is undeniable.

At the same time there is really nothing to compare with the sheer rush which comes from being able to stand up in public and beat the drum on behalf of what one Jungian describes, with pride, as "a psychology that purports to offer to all a more or less clear map of the territory of 'individuation'".

But the fact is that aside from his often contradictory hints, not to mention his outright warnings about the risks and dangers of even trying to walk a path so razor-sharp, Jung wasn't in the business of providing recipes or theories or rules.

The simple truth is that, whatever he appeared to do or say, he was no more offering a map "to all" than those ancient Hermetic teachers he admired so much who seemed to be doing such a fine job of offering people some concrete guidance—only to confuse their pupils stupid, almost drive their students crazy by systematically undoing everything they used to think they knew.[15]

And the even simpler reality is that what he was offering was completely off any map, modern or ancient. Just like the Hermetic writers he knew so well, what he was ultimately pointing to was life in God and through God.

To be more precise, he was offering immortality—opening a path to the experience of deification, of becoming a god.

This is not some fancy manner of speech, though. It may not have been something he wanted to make public, for obvious reasons. Even so, it was the inner world in which Jung lived and had his being. It was a world he might pull back the veil from, for those close to him. And it was the world out of which his most important work, the *Red book*, would emerge.[16]

There again, any serious player nowadays in the Jungian field is almost bound to feel embarrassed enough to insist there's no way he really meant any of these things. Heaven forbid that he ever intended such old-fashioned nonsense to be taken literally. After all, he was a modern psychologist—not some religious teacher or preacher of metaphysical truths.

But in saying that, the only thing they show is how totally they have misunderstood his message and meaning.[17]

To Jung, being a psychologist wasn't some magical entitlement to strip everything cynically down to a reductive explanation. On the contrary, it meant the incomparable privilege of being allowed to act humbly and without pretension as a servant in the one arena where the real drama of humanity's spirit is acting itself out: the human psyche.

As for the whole problem of religion or metaphysics, what he couldn't stand was the literalists and dogmatists who twist everything into some rigidly theoretical or moralizing formula. The only thing he was after was the living reality behind the fancy words; and all the struggling, forcing oneself, imitating, copying, inventing pious fictions is pointless when that reality is just another way of referring to nature.

For him it was simply a task of bringing the reality at the core of religion back from the realms of metaphysics and dogma to where it belongs, inside the human soul. As for the essential nature of his psychology, which so many influential religious figures would come to view with uncontrollable trembling and fear, he is very clear: "Psychology is concerned with the act of seeing and not with the construction of new religious truths".

And as for what he means here by seeing, he is even clearer. He means restoring what he calls our inner vision—which in most of us has been covered over and almost completely obliterated—because "we cannot understand a thing until we have experienced it inwardly".[18]

That was why he dared to infuriate people or hopelessly confuse others by describing the Christ as, in effect, a symbol of our own inner self. Only too often this is interpreted as meaning Christ was no longer a living reality for him but had just become a psychological symbol. In actual fact, that's the exact reverse of the truth.

To understand anything about Jung one first has to understand, and then remember, that for him there was no such thing as "just" a symbol. On the contrary, to him a true symbol was far more potent and intensely alive than the whole of our so-called reality.[19]

And when he comes to explain the Christ, symbol of our own self, this is how he defines it: as "an inner experience, an assimilation of Christ into the psychic matrix, a new realization of the divine Son" or, more simply, as "the 'Christ within'".

To make things even plainer, he described his role as being to shift our collective focus away from "the idea of the historical Christ" towards the reality of Christ as an "immediate and living presence". And the beauty of making this shift is that suddenly everything gets turned back to front; upside down. Instead of me seeking to imitate the Christ of history, it's the Christ of ancient stories and legends who starts imitating the changes that silently take place inside my soul.

Perhaps this will all sound very mystical. If it wasn't mystical, it wouldn't be so hard to understand. And besides, as Jung himself goes to great lengths to explain, that's just what it is.[20]

At the same time it has nothing whatsoever to do with the crony mysticism he so justifiably despised: the mysticism of superstitious people cluttered by their esoteric bibles and beliefs which he hated being accused of because, with everyone's muddled fears on the subject, nobody knows how to tell what's what or frankly even cares.

The reality is that, with his emphasis on direct seeing and immediate experience, Jung had pushed into a realm where any tidy or theoretical distinction between science and mysticism becomes impossible to make—in very much the same way that distinguishing between mysticism and science was utterly meaningless at the beginnings of our western world, with the great scientific pioneers such as Pythagoras or Parmenides or Empedocles.

For them, their science was an outgrowth of their mystical attitude and practice just as naturally as a flower is the outcome of a bud. For them, too, their emphasis was not on thinking or theorizing or speculating but on actually seeing: on seeing the obvious, on learning the obscure art of noticing what's right in front of one's nose.[21]

And from this point of view, where what Jung was trying to do is neither strictly mystical nor merely scientific and yet both at the same time, his psychology never offered even the remotest threat to religious experience. Instead, it was meant to be like a magnet pointing constantly to the secret at the heart of religion.

Its central aim, as he worked so hard to describe, is to explain how the natural inner work of transformation becomes "no longer a struggle, the very deliberate effort involved in imitation, but rather an involuntary experience of the reality depicted by sacred legend. This reality comes knocking"—it arrives by itself, spontaneous, uninvited, unannounced.

This is the actual, psychological experience of God in the human soul. And this, contrary to everything we are taught but as Jung himself insisted, is not just some subjective or purely personal experience.

It's the exact opposite. The experience of God is the first objective experience available to us in our lives. All the rest is subjective confusion and chaos. And to take this line of understanding one, little step further: the experience of God is the only real experience we humans can ever have.

This is the logic behind Jung's explicit statement—in the last major book he ever wrote—that even our most basic assumptions about the workings of a mystical, or alchemical, or psychological path are pure illusions. We like to think it's we who are treading the path; progressing; being transformed.

But that's not the case at all, because it's not our ego who walks the path.

It's our higher self: the hidden, divine reality inside us.

It never was about us. It was always about the sacred—only about the divine.[22]

5

Then there is the part inside each of us that's likely to be untouched and unconvinced by any of this.

Here is where you may say, with every good reason, that we have come a very long way from the day-to-day actuality of Jung as healer concerned with the ordinary drudgery of human suffering. And if you were to ask what all this has to do with psychotherapy, or the facts of sickness, the answer is—everything.

Jung was always looking through the personal in the people around him for a glimpse of the impersonal; looking past the individual to the archetypal. That's just a part of the story, though, because it wasn't only people who had to be transparent or serve as open windows into another world if they were going to catch his attention.

It was the same with their sicknesses, too. In one letter he wrote, which would soon become notorious because it captured his intentions so well, he stated very directly to an acquaintance:

"You are quite right, the main interest of my work is not concerned with the treatment of neuroses but rather with the approach to the numinous. But the fact is that the approach to the numinous is the real therapy and inasmuch as you attain to the numinous experiences you are released from the curse of pathology. Even the very disease takes on a numinous character."

In other words, even a neurosis only interested Jung if—hovering over its surface—he could see the shadow of the divine. For him everybody, everything, served its own proper purpose as an "approach to the numinous". Anyone who pointed in this direction was right: it's the numinous that happens to be real, not the neurosis.

And of course that means there is a tremendous danger, when trying to heal a person with any conventional therapy, of killing what's most precious; getting rid of what's most real. A magnificent success in terms of medicine could be the most tragic failure, a murder of the soul.

As for this expression, "numinous": it was a special favourite of Jung's. One could explain the word as serving to convey a sense of the sacred, or the presence of the divine—which would be fair enough. But there is a far better and more honest way of explaining what he meant.

The numinous is, very simply, the experience of the impossible in our lives. And that raw impossibility somehow never fits too well into human systems.[23]

At the same time, there is no limit to human resourcefulness in escaping the impossible. And this is why, today, whole books are being industriously published by Jungians about the numinous. In fact it's only too easy to forget that, with a subject as potent and elusive, intelligent discussion is the best possible way of persuading the reality behind the word to disappear.

Talking very learnedly and articulately about the numinous is what Jung himself used to refer to as an "apotropaic" form of language—attempting to speak nicely and politely and ever so welcomingly about something in the deep, unconscious hope it will go away. And if you care to look, you will see how far away it's gone.

As Jung himself prophetically warned: "You'll think up clever truisms, preventive measures, secret escape routes, excuses, potions capable of inducing forgetfulness". That's exactly what we have in the empty words invented for transforming the impossible into multiple opportunities and turning the numinous into something intended to serve the individual, instead of the other way around.

Domesticating the gods, taming the numinous by discreetly neutralizing it, has become all the rage. Jung, himself, had once called the actual practice of psychotherapy for what it almost always is: "a mere expedient, which prevents numinous experiences as much as possible". The only thing he perhaps was not aware of is how accurately he was describing the kinds of beneficent therapy that would soon be practised in his name—because the sacred never has been, or will be, a convenient stepping stone along our personal way to self-fulfilment.

On the contrary, it's our individuality together with all our problems as a person which is just a stone in the approach to the impossible.[24]

For Jung the numinous power of the sacred was something that always, whatever anyone might try to say, had him by the scruff of the neck. Its wildness and unpredictability ruthlessly drove him; ripped through his life and the lives of those around him even while providing him with the stability he needed; forced him especially at his very best to become a willing participant in its unfolding, "like it or not"; made him go out to fight like a knight, nature against nature, in a battle where the winners are losers and the victory is only given to those who surrender everything.

To Jung, himself, there never could be any escaping the fact that we are tools of the numinous whose only hope is to become conscious tools and wise ones. Nothing would be more foolish than to imagine we can turn the numinous into a tool of our own. But now the tables have all been turned.

Experience of the numinous has found itself converted into the tool of tools: been hammered and reshaped into a "therapeutic resource" to which Jungians alone can proudly lay claim. And it's so easy to forget the things that, not so long ago, Jung himself once said about Lucifer.

He explained how at the dawn of a civilization every spiritual truth only exists to point straight back to God, the creator. But towards the evening of any civilization just before it plunges into darkness—which for a culture that forgot itself is the time of Lucifer, diabolical seducer—spiritual truths are ever so subtly exploited until they end up "becoming no more than a tool in the hand of man".[25]

Really it's quite an achievement how in the space of a single generation, regardless of any effort to cling to Jung's original vision, Jungian psychology has already been dragged through every stage of a civilization: all the way from its beginning to its ultimate degradation.

Perhaps, though, you should forget I ever said that.

After all, it's more than a little awkward to have to listen to a grown man like Carl Jung talking about the power of Lucifer as if this was something real. And there is something just as uncomfortable about having to hear him describe his mystical foolery in agreeing to follow the path of Christ because he so much "wanted God to be alive and free from the suffering man has put on him by loving his own reason more than God's secret intentions".

But that's not even to mention the way he still, just a few months before he died, insisted on siding with a Native American elder who saw the light of the whole world right at the final edge of being extinguished by western rationalism—or the way Jung himself added that all he can do now in his old age is privately guard his own light and treasure because "it is most precious not only to me, but above all to the darkness of the creator".

Maybe it will be best if I simply stay silent about his absolute certainty that, in the people who came to him for healing, one thing was more essential than anything else: a deeply religious attitude, the sense that it's all for the sake of something far greater than ourselves. Otherwise, everything that in theory could go wrong is guaranteed to go wrong.

And no doubt I should avoid saying a single word about his absurd conviction that the best way of supporting a truly religious attitude is to help people step out of their personal dramas so they can find a place for themselves in history and at last experience a real "sense of historical continuity"—because without that sense of historical continuity no genuine or enduring healing is possible and, as a matter of fact, no escape from the threat of individual or collective inflation is even conceivable.

Or then again, it might just possibly be time to offer a brief reminder of what Jung himself described as authentic psychotherapy.

The situation he was faced with could hardly have been more paradoxical because, already early on, he had realized that the decisive question for every person is: Is that individual knowingly "related to something infinite or not?"

If not, that apparent individual's life is wasted; a dead end. This is what makes the personality as well as the work of Jung so numinously fascinating—the fact that every thought of his was centred on the divine.

And for him even the individual patients sitting inside his consulting room could fade into insignificance because, in spite of his meticulous attention to the incarnated details of this finite world, the main focus of his work lay somewhere else.

His fundamental concern was with the soul of humanity. It was with the great work of the alchemists, their *opus magnum*. It was with the most burdensome, but numinous, of undertakings that makes one consciously feel and often have to carry the whole weight of humanity's problems on one's shoulders.

This isn't just a job. It's a supreme responsibility: a divine responsibility, a sacred task.[26]

And perhaps here is where we are brought face to face with the greatest irony of all in Jung's psychology.

With incomparable intensity he worked at handing down a host of techniques and strategies of therapy, of potent aids along the mysterious path of individuation, which Jungians have busily applied to making their clients' lives more fulfilling as well as bearable—more personally enriching, far more humanly whole.

No one seems to have considered, though, that in the transmission something essential might have gone missing; got lost. And no amount of appropriate qualifications or lip service, of saying all the right words without the understanding of what they mean, can ever hope to make up for it.

As Jung himself made the effort to say: the mystery of individuation is the mystery of the Grail. But Grail legend speaks very plainly about the one crucial question that has to be asked—just like Jung's question about whether each individual is related to something infinite, or not—before the Grail itself can be won.

Until then, the whole earth remains desolate; wasted; dead.

You might suppose you know the general direction in which the Grail is to be found. You may even be ever so confident you have it in your grasp. But without that one question being asked, then answered, it's not just that all your own accomplished efforts are ultimately pointless—all your strivings for personal individuation utterly useless.

Even the world around you is going to be lifeless.

And for the real life to come back, nothing is more important than to know that magical question which has to be asked: Whom does the Grail serve?[27]

6

Jung visited India just once, in his early sixties.

The visit was filled with thrills and insights and excitements. But, as usual, when Jung needed to get sick he got sick—and was forced back inside himself.

Just after being released from hospital in the wildly bewildering city of Kolkata he had a dream that at first bewildered him too, and would end up leaving an enormous impression on him: as much as any other dream he would ever have.

For him, the geographical realities had a dramatically paradoxical effect. It was precisely through being so far away from Europe, so distant in Asia from the hearth and home of western culture, that Jung found himself confronted at last with the mystery of western civilization—and the secret of his role.

Instead of getting lost in the sights and smells and sounds of the East, he was simply using the whole experience as a chance to plunge into the depths of himself: exactly what the ancient Greek philosophers recommended.[28]

And this very same dream of his happens to be what, appropriately enough, would prompt him in his old age to start speaking out about the secret of individuation as well as about the archetype of the knight—because this was his dream of the Grail.

Physically in his Kolkata hotel room, he found himself on an island just off the coast of southern England. Together with a group of Swiss friends and colleagues he had come to a medieval castle at the southernmost tip of the island: the castle of the Grail. But Jung felt almost overwhelmingly alone in his awareness that the Grail and the home of the Grail and all the traditions about the Grail aren't only a matter of history or literature.

On the contrary, they are vitally meaningful; absolutely alive.

Then comes the main part of the dream—long, slow, brutally arduous. The Grail is missing and has to be found: needs to be brought back from such a small, nondescript house that no one would ever guess it had been hidden there. And it has to be brought back today, straight away.

Jung sets off, towards the north, still accompanied by people from his group. They march for hours. The land becomes more and more desolate; the sun sets and the darkness sets in instead. Finally they come to the sea and realize the island is split into two but there is not a single bridge, or boat, or road. Frozen, exhausted, everyone falls asleep one by one until only Jung is left awake.

And then he realizes that he, alone, is going to have to strip off his clothes and swim across the channel to fetch the Grail.

As a dream this has all the presence, and atmosphere, of something numinous. But just as striking as the dream itself is the way Jung chose to explain it.

If a psychologist was to want to help point the way towards an interpretation, it would be easy enough to suggest taking every single detail as simply an expression or reflection of the dreamer's internal state: as a comment from the unconscious on one person's private search for an inner meaning. But that's not at all how Jung read or saw it.

To him it wasn't just about some individual quest for psychological integration. It was about his work in—and for the sake of—the whole world. As his biography, with a sense of fatefulness, starts describing: "Myths that day has forgotten continue to be told by night, and powerful figures which consciousness turns into mere banalities and has reduced to ridiculous trivialities are resurrected by poets and prophetically revived."

And then it only takes a moment before we are hearing Jung begin to explain how, "imperiously, the dream wiped away all the intense daytime impressions of India and swept me back to the far too long neglected concerns of the West which had once expressed themselves in the quest for the Holy Grail as well as in the search for the philosophers' stone. I was taken out of the world of India and reminded, in the process, that India was not my task but only a part of the path—admittedly a significant one—which would bring me closer to my goal. It was as if the dream was asking me, 'What are you doing in India? It would be far better if you were to seek for yourself and for the sake of your fellow humans the healing vessel, the *servator mundi*, which you urgently need. For your state is perilous; you are all in imminent danger of destroying all that centuries have built up.'"[29]

I really wonder how many of the thousands of people who have read these words ever registered, on a conscious level, what they mean. In fact they are saying something extremely specific. To get to the place of understanding that specific something, though, almost inevitably involves the same kind of ordeal Jung himself was forced to go through in his dream.

Visiting India is all very nice and fine. Experiencing other cultures, getting a taste of the delicious East, being touched and even transformed by its spiritual traditions, can be very helpful in a certain round-about sort of way.

But none of this would have any value for Jung except in bringing him back to what truly matters and helping him remember what, on the deepest level, his entire life was about. Its only point was to return him to the realization of his real task and work, of his one duty and obligation and responsibility—to play the long-forgotten role of healer to the West.

For him, nothing could possibly be more important. The need is urgent: urgent beyond any words. The peril is all around us. The danger of total destruction is imminent.

But it's precisely when the need is most pressing and the peril is most immediate that people are least able to recognize the nature of the danger—let alone to explain to themselves, or others, the sense of urgency they feel.

To be sure, there are those who have struggled to convey the fact that Jung's task was cultural rather than individual. To earth these intuitions, though, to ground and locate them in space and time: that's a rather different matter.

And the trouble is that our culture has grown so sick there is not even a context or framework left for understanding what any of this actually means—because the awareness of what a culture is has just become a thing of the past.

This is why so many Jungians have flown off into grandiose fantasies about Jung as some culture hero personally inaugurating a glorious new age by leaving all the trash of Christianity and western materialism behind. But this insanely inflated nonsense has nothing whatsoever to do with the way Jung perceived his own task.

For him nothing new is possible without plunging back into the past—behind all of the dirt and materialism, the misunderstandings and corruptions, murders and perversions and distortions—in search of the secret at the heart of one's own culture. The core of his task was to rediscover the essential mystery of the West that so urgently needs to be treasured and guarded, protected and preserved, because only this can provide salvation: not some fantasies about an imaginary future.[30]

And here is where we find ourselves staring straight into the face of the major problem which has dogged students of Jung, as well as his critics, for years. That's the problem of his attitude to eastern religions and spiritual practices.

Certainly the seriousness of the problem is obvious enough. On the one hand, he praises to the heavens the insights offered by eastern traditions into the study of psychology and into the infinite intricacies of the human soul. On the other hand he felt an intense disgust for westerners taking up exotic practices of self-cultivation, or surrendering themselves to eastern forms of spirituality, which erupted into almost desperate bouts of impatience and irritability. And, only too predictably, scholars have reacted by picking at his arguments or trying to tear his reasoning apart with even more anger and irritation.[31]

If we take a look underneath the surface, though, it's so easy to see what Jung was really trying to say below all the things he did say.

Thanks to the utter bankruptcy of rampant materialism and modern Christianity, many sensitive westerners even as youngsters instinctively turn to the East—turn anywhere—to fill the terrible emptiness of meaning they have been brought up in. And the kind of nourishment they find in eastern spiritual teachings or teachers can help to a significant extent to provide what they, as individuals, need.

But we are not just the individuals we seem to be. And now, whether we know it or not, we have a collective obligation to rediscover western culture's original purpose: have an inescapable duty, as westerners, to face up to the full reality of what we lost.

Jung lays this out with a clarity, almost a savagery, that perfectly describes the situation we find ourselves in today. At the same time he effortlessly manages to undermine all our modern pretensions; our treasured assumptions and political correctnesses.

This is why in his memorial lecture for Richard Wilhelm, the Chinese scholar he had come to love and respect so much, he outlined a scenario that would have been more or less unimaginable when he was speaking almost a century ago—and with a darkly, almost perversely prophetic humour explained what others were far too pious to see.

Times were changing, he noted. Instead of western missionaries pouring out everywhere across the East to convert people with their gospel as energetically and methodically as they could, Christianity had become so exhausted that Buddhists were getting ready to seize their own opportunities because they realized now was the perfect moment for positioning themselves to start becoming missionaries to the West.

And in case some sincere listeners or readers were to wonder just where Carl Jung stood on such a delicate matter, he goes straight on to throw any doubt aside. For him, those westerners who would unhesitatingly open the gates of their own culture to the Buddhists weren't open-minded multiculturalists.

They were "spiritual beggars" who would blindly accept whatever handouts the East in its apparent generosity decided to offer—and in spite of all the talk about mindfulness, would practise the mindlessness of imitating other people's nobly spiritual truths.

"That is the danger about which it is impossible to give too many warnings", he added: as if, once again, anyone would have the slightest interest in heeding Jung's warnings.

Then he continues following the thread of his logic, so unfamiliar but so precise at the same time. "What the East has to give us should be merely a help in a work which we still have to do. Of what use to us is the wisdom of the Upanishads or the insights of Chinese yoga if we abandon the foundations of our own culture as though they were outlived errors and, like homeless pirates, settle with thievish intent on foreign shores?"

And for him it all points back to darkness, back to that darkness every westerner so desperately wants to escape from—not just our personal darkness, which is hard enough to confront, but the darkness of a whole corrupted culture and civilization.

This is where everything has to come back to, because the light of real wisdom "only shines in the dark": in the darkness of our own hell. If we want to experience the benefits of eastern wisdom, any wisdom, first we have to do the impossible work of coming to terms with the western truth about ourselves.

That's where the path really begins—with the realization that the only light which is going to be of any genuine use or value to us is the light we manage to bring, like a new sun, out from the darkness inside ourselves.

Without such an awareness, which still belongs shovelled away into some forgotten footnote, all the most potent meditation or yoga practices in the world are nothing but a recipe for even greater forgetfulness; are only going to delude us by leading us further and further astray.[32]

And these weren't just the thoughts of a man who was sad at the death of a friend.

Almost ten years earlier he had written what seems to have been a mysteriously poetic letter to an Englishwoman. As for the essence of what he evidently told her, it's summed up in the one direct statement that "Gnosis should be an experience of your own life, a plant grown on your own tree. Foreign gods are a sweet poison, but the vegetable gods you have raised in your own garden are nourishing. They are perhaps less beautiful, but they have stronger medicine."

There is an underlying principle here—just as there is in the warning at the start of the *Red book*, "Don't be greedy to gobble up the fruits of foreign fields." This is that real spirituality is not about gawking at exotic scenery: that's far too easy. It's about finding a way back to the sacred landscape, however horrifically desolate or abandoned it might feel, which somehow got lost and forgotten inside ourselves.

It's about learning to find one's own nourishment and medicine, however modest at first, as opposed to begging; starving; being made to swallow poison. And, above all, it's about rediscovering the ancient art of healing instead of joining the collective steady downward spiral into sickness and illusion and death.

Otherwise even one's best possible efforts to create, or try to enlighten, or be of help, simply hurry along the destruction.

But as to what that healing could be, what the healing vessel is which Jung had to labour so hard in his dream to search for, what the particular nutrition is which he struggled throughout his life just to make available: this is something utterly impossible to understand on the level of the rational mind.

Our rational mind is what hid it away in the first place. And reasoning will gladly either keep on trampling it underfoot in its ruthless march towards some global ideal of fulfilment, or go on twisting and distorting it beyond any recognition.

There is only one possible way to make any sense of this at all, and that's with what Jung referred to as the "plant-like naiveté" which intuitively realizes a culture is not just some theoretical abstraction. On the contrary, it's an organism that lives and dies; a plant; a tree.[33]

Our only real duty and purpose is to return far enough to the root of our civilization that we can remember—then help it remember—its sacred purpose and task.

And, naturally, the only question is how.

7

One of Jung's favourite themes was this: that the most precious of treasures lies ignored, totally neglected by people out in gutters and streets.

And true enough, there are things stated quite openly in his name which most of us prefer not to notice because we are far more comfortable picking up the little crumbs from here and there. As for the elusive mystery that always works to bring everything together, the mystery Empedocles simply called "the whole", it's so much easier just to pass it by.[34]

The published account of Jung's crucial Kolkata dream culminates in its pressing message to him to "seek for yourself and for the sake of your fellow humans the healing vessel, the *servator mundi*, which you urgently need". Of course his fondness for using Latin can be a little off-putting in a world where the language has been virtually forgotten.

But he had his good reasons for doing so, because this was how he could hint at the history of what he was trying to convey—a history stretching back hundreds and thousands of years into the depths of western culture.

Servator mundi is an older form of *salvator mundi* and means preserver or saviour of the world. In ancient and then medieval texts they were both standard ways of referring to Jesus Christ.

Inside the Latin alchemical literature Jung was so familiar with, it's exactly the same story.

And whenever Jung himself used one or the other, Christ is always either named explicitly or very present in the background. Needless to say, the healing vessel of the Grail was a symbol associated closely with the presence and the body of Christ. But by using this particular expression—*servator mundi,* cosmic protector or preserver—he was making the link that binds Christ to the central essence of his own work and duty and labour far tighter, stronger, closer.[35]

To associate Jung's work nowadays with religious ideas about saving the world is, it goes without saying, enough to get anyone crucified instantly. All sorts of theoretical disagreements about the details or practical meaning of his psychology are tolerated, even encouraged.

That doesn't include this, though. And there is more than a touch of irony about the fact that those progressive Jungians who feel terrified at the prospect of waking up one morning marked with the stigmata of religiosity are quite oblivious to how openly this theme of salvation is available for everybody to read, veiled by the lightest coating of Latin, in Jung's own authorized biography.[36]

There, it's no question of him just functioning as a good Christian. It was a matter of working directly with the innermost reality of the Christ—and especially with Christ's essential aspect as saviour of the world.

But all this is no more than the beginning.

The original record still survives of what Jung said to his secretary, during one of their interview sessions, about the dream he had in Kolkata. And it includes several details that, for more or less obvious reasons, never made their way into print.

First there is that mention of the Swiss friends and acquaintances who kept with him as far as the castle of the

Grail, then went on marching to the place where at last the land came to an end. Jung himself specifies, more than once, that in real life all these dream companions of his were members of the Psychological Club he had helped to create at Zurich as a meeting-place for people attracted to his work.

He also tells how he and they arrived at the castle as sight-seers, which suggests he was intensely aware on a certain level that the circle of early Jungians who gathered around him all shared the same basic attitude of psychological or spiritual tourists: were simply there for the view. They might be willing to make a certain effort, but were only prepared to go so far.

And then there is the most fascinating piece of information which the published version of Jung's biography made sure to leave out. The first spontaneous comment he offers as soon as he has finished telling his dream relates to the final scene, where all the people around him fall asleep and—completely on his own—he has to make the supreme effort to fetch the Grail.

There they all are, he exclaims: the young disciples at Gethsemane who have fallen asleep, leaving the Christ to face his destiny completely alone.

And here is where everything comes together, where the story completes itself—because in his alchemical studies Jung had been very careful to note that "Christ in the garden of Gethsemane" is none other than the *servator mundi*, "preserver of the cosmos".[37]

But now of course there is one entirely new complexion to this whole affair, which is that Jung is no longer just the brave knight dedicated to rediscovering at all costs the healing vessel of the *servator mundi*.

He has become the healing vessel himself: Christ the preserver, saviour of the world.

And here, too, is where all these interesting details become really fascinating—because it's as if suddenly a back door has sprung open into Jung's own scientific writings.

Often he would rail and thunder about people who were vain or ambitious or unconscious enough to set themselves up as self-proclaimed world saviours. And now we can see why this is an issue that would have concerned him so intensely: because he himself knew exactly what it meant, precisely what it felt like, to be faced with the task of saving the world.

Naturally we could just take a shallow breath and stop here: the same story as before. Nothing would be easier than to accuse Jung of blatant contradiction, even hypocrisy, and leave the matter at that.

But it takes a little more courage and effort to consider that there might just be a right way, as well as a wrong way, to set about saving the world.

As for the wrong way: there is no mystery about that at all. Jung makes it perfectly clear that the trap so many unprepared people fall into is to identify with the archetypal image of the saviour and then, through the sheer naivety of their identification, fall victim to a massive inflation—the almighty presumption of thinking they have literally become the one divine saviour themselves.

He is even kind enough to hint at simple but practical aids for disidentifying from the seductively archetypal energies of the unconscious. No better supplement exists for psychological insight or understanding than the true virtues of love and wisdom, not to mention the healthy ability to laugh heartily at one's god-almighty little ego.[38]

And just when all of a sudden everything seems so very clear, manageable, controllable, is the moment when those dangers of misunderstanding are far more present and palpable than ever before—because the even deeper trap people fall into is of assuming that as soon as you break the identification with something it dissolves automatically, magically vanishes, is gone.

This is why it's such a terrible mistake to equate the experience of becoming a god with the inflationary state of god-almightiness that always accompanies it. If there was no difference between them we could just sit safe at home; never bother to risk or learn a thing.

On the one hand, such inflatedness is nothing but the result of a tiny ego trying to identify itself with the imprint of the divine. Battling with these obnoxious manifestations of inflation is where any true psychology shows its worth because here—in the overwhelming encounter with the sacred—we only have the start of a psychological process, never the end.

And to help guard against the inflatedness of imagining Jungian psychology is alone in having access to such sophisticated ideas, I should add that there are mystical traditions which have been well equipped to deal with such very human problems for centuries. That's hardly surprising, though, in view of Jung's own constant fondness for appealing to "the great psychotherapeutic systems which we know as the religions".

But as for deification, on the other hand, this is an inexpressibly real experience that leaves its permanent mark on anybody touched by the fingers of the divine. It's what gave Jung much of his knowledge, as well as charisma; was a major initiation he had to pass through.

In fact he could hardly have been blunter about the matter: if you just identify with the experience and make no effort to come to terms with it as a human, you'll end up in a mental hospital.

Avoid the experience, though, and you are throwing the most valuable of gifts away.[39]

In short, try to walk away from it and it's sure to throw its shadow over you: haunt you for the rest of your meaningless nights and even emptier days. But if you learn the secret of how to relate to it consciously, then you'll find it settling as a new awareness halfway between you and the depths of your unconscious so that you are no longer overwhelmed by the forces which sweep over you—and no longer need to overwhelm them.

Instead, there is a new harmony of mutual respect; the primordial state of divine awareness hidden away inside a human body without any of the grabbing or inflation or identification; the life in God.

And there, protected from all our superficialities as well as stupidities, is where the world might just have to be saved each single moment with an urgency our egos could never come close to fathoming. In our collective human inflation we honestly think we can get away with fooling ourselves into assuming this world exists, and keeps existing, just for us to enjoy and exploit and destroy.

Quite possibly it doesn't, though. And maybe it doesn't even keep going by itself. Perhaps human consciousness has always been the miraculous magic that's needed for the moon and sun to rise; to sustain and preserve the cosmos; keep it safe.

But of course this would imply that to arrive at the place of discovering such a reality, deep inside, and being allowed to participate in it is the ultimate purpose of human existence—at the same time as being the hardest, most arduous thing possible for a woman or man to do.

It also would help to explain why mystical traditions such as Sufism, for example, are so keen to repeat that a few awakened people are always needed to keep this physical world connected to the world of reality; why they will sometimes even specify the exact number of truly conscious beings who have to live and stay alive at any time in any given country, for instance Syria. Without them and the quiet, invisible work they do "the cosmos would collapse".

In other words, there is no question or problem about having to save the world: there never was. The only problem is all the fuss and obstacles we put in the way.

The world needs saving. But it's precisely because we can't see this that the world is being destroyed.

So we are brought straight back to Jung himself—and his famous encounter with this very same understanding through his meeting, in New Mexico, with the Native American elder called Mountain Lake. It was a meeting of mind as well as heart which, aside from developing into a lasting friendship, would go on reverberating inside Jung for the rest of his life.[40]

And as he kept summing that basic understanding up: the only true dignity for a human lies in knowing that the sun would never be able to rise without the human's assistance.

It could never even set.

8

I suppose so much talk about Native Americans and Sufis could be starting to sound wonderfully, intoxicatingly exotic.

To be quite honest, though, there is nothing mysterious or mystical about it at all. The far greater mystery is how on earth people manage to forget that this is the way life exists, goes on existing: that the real work of saving the world has to be done, moment to moment, in a way hardly noticed or recognized by anyone.

And the truth is that it has to go unrecognized, unnoticed—most of the time even by oneself. The worst thing possible would be if the ego got to know about it, because then instantly it would be wanting to have a slice of the action; become implicated; get inflated; make a mess.

If you are going to have to identify with something, make quite sure never to identify with this. The greater part of the task is to keep it pure, uninterfered with, safe above all from yourself. So be sure to stay invisible, leave few or no traces of what really matters, cover your tracks.

The best solution is to learn how to trick everybody by gracefully putting your worst foot forward, playing to perfection the role of jovial bourgeois, even experimenting at being a reasonable scientist. And by the same token, the worst possible way of trying to carry Jung's real work forward would be by identifying oneself as a Jungian.

In short, the point of a psychology such as his is not to put a stop to the work of salvation but to put a stop to all the childish inflations so that the real work of saving the world can continue unimpeded; undisturbed.

It's to begin to discover and then live with the truth, which can sound so heretical from a conventionally therapeutic point of view, that the real reason for disidentifying from the archetypal energies is not so that we can be free from them but so that they can be free from us—free to move and work as they need in this physical world, assisted by our consciousness but uncontaminated by the unbecoming dramas of our human psychology.

Without the ego's inappropriate attentions and identifications, the archetypal reality doesn't fade away or disappear. Quite to the contrary, it flourishes. But to get to the point of understanding how these things work takes a lifetime of struggle; of battles fought and lost.

Jung called the mystery of individuation the secret of the Grail for a very good reason. There are all the sacrifices and hardships and heroics that come from going in quest of it, the noble chasing after even nobler causes—plus the added benefit of being able to fall asleep at any point one chooses.

At the same time, he also said what the secret of individuation is: explained that the one and only way to discover the vessel of the Grail, the *servator mundi*, is by becoming it. It will stay undiscovered, undiscoverable forever, except by simply being it. And such a simplicity usually only arrives, if one happens to be ever so lucky, in old age.

We still happen to have a record of the letters exchanged by Jung—it would be his last winter—with an Englishman just a few months before he died. He complains about the overwhelming impossibility of the difficulties he is faced with, about the depths of the darkness he finds himself immersed in, about how alone he feels in spite of the people he is surrounded by. The aloneness as he describes it is strangely reminiscent of that aloneness he had experienced years earlier, right at the end of his Kolkata dream, when he realized there was no one else beside him in his search for the Grail.

And the Englishman somehow finds it in himself to take a gamble, even at the obvious risk of provoking or antagonizing Jung.

I've heard you repeating endlessly, he plucks up the courage to write, that you are not some medicine man to your people—most certainly no world saviour. But in spite of all your public and consistent denials I am going to say this:

To me, personally, nothing could be clearer than that the reference in the Gospel of John to the light which "shineth in the darkness, and the darkness comprehendeth it not" is the most exact pointer possible to your own situation. While ordinary people can sometimes be forced against their will to take on the role of hero, your case could hardly be more different. Right from the start you were shaped out of "the stuff heroes are made of"; you have a heroic destiny, a heroic burden heavily weighing on your shoulders.

And just as the human Jesus had to die on the cross to bring light to other humans, it's the same with you. But "please forgive me for even suggesting this comparison".

Nothing could have prepared him for the surprise of reading Jung's reply:

"Your Biblical analogies are perfectly legitimate, as they are archetypic experiences, which are repeated again and again, whenever a new idea is born, or when a hero–child appears in the world. Time and again a light tries to pierce the darkness"—although it's a law that the bringer of the light will always have to pay a heavy price for the attempt. Then Jung touchingly goes on to admit just how naïve he was "in not expecting the darkness to be so dense".

But the one statement he makes which stands out from everything else could hardly be simpler, or more enigmatic. "To live an archetypic life is no reason for an inflation as it is the ordinary life of man."

To be sure, Jung was fond of emphasizing how ordinary a truly individuated person would seem to be: no loud individualism, no extravagant or fantastic claims. What he is saying here is much more than that, though.

Typically, in earlier years and days, the very questionable honour of living an "archetypic life" would have been reserved by him for the central archetypal figure of the West: Jesus Christ. But here the veil between Christ's life and Jung's life has been torn away. All the huff and puff of a whole life's work—the bitter struggle against inflation, the anguished warnings and tensions and denials—has vanished in a moment.

All the endless drama about needing for the sake of one's basic sanity to disidentify from the archetypal energies because of the inevitable inflation they cause is suddenly gone. To live an archetypic life is no reason, any more, to get inflated because "it is the ordinary life of man".[41]

Jung has finally managed to walk through the eye of the needle and find salvation through the danger he had always talked about. That's what it means to know how to keep moving with life; to be able to flow beyond oneself.

Where he ends up is a place of such simplicity that it's hard for anyone to understand. For him the totally extraordinary has become the utterly ordinary which, what's more, was the normal state of humanity right from the start.

And of course the other side to this—because there is always the other side—is that the apparent ordinariness of people who go about their disconnectedly meaningless lives is the most extraordinary violation of what we humans are meant to be. It's this very same abnormal normalness, always ready with its bright excuses, which makes the light-bringer's task even more excruciatingly difficult.

What Jung means here by an ordinary life is nothing like what we ordinarily think of as ordinary. For him, consciously living an archetypic life is the ordinary life of a human because ultimately the archetypes are all there is. To the extent that we are humans we participate in, we are, the archetype of humanity: the Anthropos, the Christ.

As would-be humans we love trying to find a rock to hide away under, where we think we can protect ourselves from the archetypes' dark glare—their impossible demands and strains. But as humans we are archetypes. And the stone is an archetype, too.

The irony is that to avoid the unbearable burden of living an archetypal life isn't a human option at all. Whatever we think of as personal is in fact profoundly inhuman, while it's only in the utter objectivity of the impersonal that we find our humanity.

And inside that entirely impersonal objectivity is where we can come to the point at which the Anthropos and the *anthropos*, the primordial and the ordinary human, are one and the same: the smallest equal to the largest and the largest inside the smallest.

Then you are not trying to illuminate people and save the world with your tedious possibilities in some ridiculously inflated fashion. Instead, you are allowing the impossibly simple energy of the saviour to do its work through you and finish whatever it needs to do.

As Jung liked to say, no one can ever see or know where the saviour will come from. It can arrive in the flash of a truly new idea. It can appear in the sudden, unbelievable movement of letting somebody somewhere be completely cleansed and healed of guilt—before vanishing as quickly as it came.

But to incarnate inside oneself that presence of the saviour, to embody it: that's a totally different matter.

And Jung makes himself very clear in his correspondence with the Englishman about the exact nature of that supposedly ordinary, but archetypal, life he has ended up being able to live without any inflation.

It's the archetypal life of the light-bringer—whom he has routinely equated in his other writings with Christ as *servator mundi*, "the Saviour and Preserver of the world".

But he also goes out of his way elsewhere to equate this figure of the light-bringer, who has to suffer for the ordinariness of other humans and whose burden as well as destiny Jung knew so well, with a reality that he notes has been completely suppressed and forgotten in the West.

That's the figure of the cosmic Christ as Saviour, described with such unparalleled wisdom by the Gnostics thousands of years ago, "who went forth from the Father in order to illuminate the stupidity, darkness, and unconsciousness of mankind".

The only thing to add is his own explanation—already suppressed and almost forgotten—that this benign movement of the Gnostic Christ into a darkened world precisely outlines, exactly defines, the real scope of Jungian psychology.[42]

9

Now, Jungian psychology exists in all sorts of shapes and forms and sizes for people to use—or let themselves be charmed by—as they choose.

Once, though, it was no more than a trembling fear. And that's where the real magic lies.

Through his initial confrontation with the depths of the unconscious—at those points where the borderline keeps shifting between insanity and sanity, then back again—all of a sudden Jung found himself terrifyingly alone.

Or at least that was how he felt to begin with, until he fell straight into the lap of the Gnostics.

With the help of surviving fragments from Gnostic writings—which for the most part happened to be passages hatefully quoted by early Christian saints just to prove how perverse and dangerous their teachings were—he came across people who had already experienced what he was experiencing. He recognized that he was in the presence of psychologists who managed to anticipate his psychology by two thousand years; found living friends, allies, companions; was no longer on his own.

And not only were they still alive, deep down inside him. He realized, to his even greater surprise, that a part of him was still alive inside them.[43]

The Greek word *gnôstikos* means "knower" or "realizer". And Jung was quite right to emphasize that the people presented as ancient Gnostics by our history books weren't Christian heretics, in the way most history books would have us believe. Instead, they were the real source of Christianity; were the carriers of a non-Christian knowledge out of which Christian creeds and beliefs and dogmas would all evolve.

In other words, it's not that the Gnostics were Christian heretics: it's that the Christians were Gnostic heretics. But, as Gnostics have always known, things do tend to get turned upside down and back to front inside our topsy-turvy world—which you may already have noticed is exactly what keeps on happening, at every conceivable opportunity, with Jung's psychology.[44]

At the same time, words like *gnôstikos* or *gnôsis* also have the strong underlying sense of being able to see directly; of inwardly perceiving, of intuitively recognizing as opposed to just believing or accepting what others say. And there is something almost tragic about the inability of people to see that this direct Gnostic seeing is what lies right at the heart of his entire psychology.

It's not for any lack of stating the case quite plainly. "Psychology is concerned with the act of seeing", as he patiently explains: with the immediate "inward experience" that depends on the "inner vision" which, itself, depends on our seriously atrophied "faculty of seeing".[45]

But actually to recognize what Jung is trying to say can somehow seem the most difficult thing in the world—in part because the naturalness of this direct perception he is referring to has perhaps become so painfully unnatural to us, and in part because so much of the evidence that spells out just what he meant has been unavailable for such a long time.

For instance there is the important letter he wrote to a close associate during March 1918, at a point when he was deeply involved in extracting some sense from those experiences that form the bedrock of his *Red book*. This colleague, Josef Lang, was one of the few people who had stayed on with Jung after the famous break with Sigmund Freud; had played a privileged role, as Hermann Hesse's therapist, in passing along from Jung many of the Gnostic ideas that appear in Hesse's novels; and was a person Jung would be keen to collaborate with in the very conscious labour of shaping, defining, even promoting his own psychology as something easy to tell apart from the psychology of Freud.

And in the letter he outlines two different sides to working with the unconscious.

On the one hand, he explains, we need to confront and experience the unconscious directly before trying to impose our usual views or ideas or opinions on it—have to face it in all the rawness of its essential reality without allowing any conscious influence or bias to interfere. But on the other hand we also have to come to grips with the essential meaning of the ancient Gnostic teachings, because only with the help that they provide will it be possible to create "the foundations for a theory of the unconscious spirit".

Once again, in his own way Jung could hardly have stated things plainer. We have to learn to look and see, not just outwardly into the physical world but straight into our own unconscious. And if we are going to do so we need the solid support, the grounding or foundation, that only the Gnostics' unique insights into the unconscious can provide.[46]

These, if you like, have to be the two wings on the bird of Jungian psychology.

And the most extraordinary thing here is not just that he is identifying the ancient tradition of the Gnostics as the only trustworthy source of knowledge available, anywhere in our conscious world, about how to confront the unconscious. It's that, while on the conscious side he looks for help in understanding the unconscious to the preserved writings of the Gnostics, the chief figures whom he meets deep down inside the unconscious are Gnostics.

In other words, on every possible side he is surrounded by Gnostic tradition—the same as in that famous image of the cosmic serpent swallowing its own tail. And more than one wing on this Jungian bird is Gnostic: they both are.

That's not all, though, by any means; and it's not just that Gnosticism would come to play such an absolutely central role, for the most part unnoticed, in Jung's work.

If possible, it would play an even more central role in his life—because by making his way to the underworld he didn't only meet friends and companions.

He also found his own teacher; or rather, his teacher found him.

From Jung's authorized biography we have the beautiful image of Philemon flying into his life as an old man who sails across the sky with the wings of a kingfisher. And we have the lovely picture of Jung himself strolling up, then down, his garden absorbed in silent dialogue with this same old man he called his inner guru—a pagan, we are told, with an exotic-sounding background as well as a certain "Gnostic coloration".

But while we can be ever so grateful to his secretary for lending her feminine touch to this charmingly pretty scene, it doesn't quite correspond to the whole story as Jung had wanted to tell it.

From the unpublished records of what he actually said, the first detail that leaps out is his raw fear. He can hardly stop repeating how scared he was to begin with, how terrified on realizing that what he had assumed was just some aspect of himself in fact was something else—was an immensely powerful and intelligent being in its own right.

But then comes the even greater panic of seeing the bottom fall straight out of his life; of realizing how completely alien this new reality is to everything he has always known; of recognizing what an utter catastrophe lies ahead if he can't find some way to come to grips with this craziness which, "once again", is staring him straight in the face.

In a sense he already gave the whole game away as soon as he chose to specify that Philemon has an "Egyptian–Gnostic–Hellenistic" background—because anyone familiar with those quintessentially Egyptian–Gnostic–Hellenistic texts known to us today as the *Hermetica* wouldn't only be unfazed by Jung's accounts of his panic and terror, but would expect them. These are simply the standard stages that have to be passed through in the process of discovering one's inner teacher.

Of course, though, Jung's secretary could hardly be supposed to have much interest in such historical curiosities. Her loyalty was strictly to him, not to what might or might not lie behind him. And that kind of sheer terror he describes would need a good deal of softening, massaging, toning down, because certainly it wouldn't be right in any way to create a bad impression of the man or his psychology.

As for managing, in the process, to obliterate any real continuity with those very same Gnostic traditions Jung was pointing to: that would be a trivial price to pay.[47]

And then there is the other point that jumps right out from the original record of what he, himself, said—which has to do with the question of Philemon's identity. In fact, far from making do with ambiguous comments about Gnostic colorations, Jung states point-blank and repeatedly: Philemon was a Gnostic.

Again, though, this straightforward identification of Jung's own teacher as a Gnostic was embarrassing enough either a century ago or half a century ago to justify simply leaving it out.

After all, he was walking on the thinnest ice by engaging even professionally with the topic of Gnosticism. Naturally one at least had to make the effort to maximize his distance from it, however small or large the cost.[48]

But, now, it wouldn't be so wise to think too much has changed—because this same attitude of needing, unconsciously even more than consciously, to keep him at arm's length from the Gnostics is still alive and well.

In the brand-new literature on the *Red book* there is already no end of commentaries explaining how Professor Jung saw it as his essential task to separate himself from Philemon: to bring about a "critical disidentification" between himself and this fantasy figure. His first and last obligation was to stand apart as the independent, rational, detached scientific observer engaged in his thought–experiments; his controlled, dispassionate exercises in ventriloquism.[49]

And it's purely a question of whether we choose to believe these explanations—or pay attention to Jung himself.

The picture that he painted of Philemon for his *Red book*, of his teacher with the kingfisher's wings, is already well-known enough from being splashed almost everywhere across books and magazines. But he also painted a very similar mural, upstairs at his own private retreat in Bollingen.

At the top of both paintings he formally addresses Philemon, in ancient Greek script, as "Father". And on the mural he has added, in the original Latin, an alchemical saying under Philemon's left wing. It's a beautiful text, known as a quotation from Hermes Trismegistus, that starts with the words *Protege me protegam te*: "Protect me—I will protect you." It continues with the statement "I give birth to the light even though my nature is darkness."

Then, though, it suddenly comes to an end with its climactic announcement. "Therefore nothing better, nothing more worthy of veneration, can come to pass in this world than the conjunction of myself and my son."[50]

That Jung addresses Philemon in both paintings as "Father" couldn't possibly be less surprising: repeatedly, inside the *Red book* and even during private discussions about the *Red book* with people he felt able to trust, he refers to his teacher as "Father" and has Philemon refer to Jung in turn as "son".

This, ever so simply, is how he defined the relationship between the two of them; or, even more simply, it's how the relationship between them defined itself. So nothing could be more significant than the fact that he has added, on the wall of his very private retreat, a Hermetic text which culminates in dramatically celebrating the conjoining—the alchemical conjunction—of father and son.

One would have to be rather blind or a little crazy not to see that there's no disidentifying from Philemon without the even more critical conjoining: that the whole point and purpose of any differentiation is to prepare the ground for the union.

That, after all, is what the *Mysterium coniunctionis* which Jung considered the summation of his whole life's work is about—the separation followed by synthesis, fission followed by the fusion.[51]

Probably this will sound very nice, at least in theory. But if we care to watch how the fusion of teacher and student actually manifests in practice, we just have to turn from Jung at his most private to Jung at his most public. A couple of years before he died he gave his most famous interview ever, to the BBC. And the single most famous point inside that interview arrives when, asked if he believes in God, he answers: "*I know.* I don't need to believe. I know."

Only fifty years later did it become clear that these words weren't really his at all. They were words that had been spoken to him by Philemon, his own teacher, another half-century before the interview ever took place.

What Philemon said to him silently, he spoke out loud. And now there is not the slightest room left for doubting what should never have been open to doubt in the first place—which is that whenever Jung insisted he was only interested in knowledge and not in beliefs, as he so often did, he wasn't really speaking as a typical modern scientist antagonistic to religious creeds or beliefs.

At heart he was speaking as a Gnostic whose one concern is with the knowledge, the absolutely terrifying knowledge, hidden away not only inside the root of every science but deep in the core of each religion.[52]

And at the same time, through pointing away from all the accumulated beliefs and dogmas of religions to that inner Gnostic knowledge, the Gnostic father and son were conjoined as one.

It can be quite a revealing experience to spend time in Jung's private library reading through the books about ancient Greek mystery traditions which he bought, and studied minutely, a century ago. Everything inside him springs to life as soon as he comes across any passages that touch on the initiatory process of discovering—or being discovered by—one's true father.

He underscores the printed words, adds lines or comments in the margin, inserts bookmarks when he stumbles on references to ancient Gnostic or Hermetic or magical texts which have been structured as dialogues between mystical father and mystical son; or to the esoteric practice, which reaches back to the Pythagoreans, of teachers adopting students as their own child; or to this adoption as an initiation into the mysteries of rebirth; or to such an adoption and initiation by the "spiritual father" as the most perfect merging, the sacred union, of father and son.

And there is one particular passage that he carefully has noted by leaving a clear mark in the margin. He has been reading the most Gnostic of the dialogues contained in the collection of sacred Hermetic texts known as the *Hermetica*, which again is not such a surprising choice when one considers how the *Red book* shows Philemon storing away his own sacred Hermetic texts inside a cupboard.

The dialogue is presented as an archetypal discussion between spiritual father and spiritual son. And at a certain point—after all the dramatic upheaval of the son suddenly realizing the horrific impossibilities he is confronted with and bravely stating how alienated he has become from everything once familiar to him and bitterly complaining about just how terrified he is of going crazy—the mood starts to change because it's time to move at last to the climax, to the mystery of rebirth.

Now Father, as the passage marked by Jung begins, "I see myself to be the All. I am in heaven and in earth, in water and in air; I am in beasts and plants; I am a babe in the womb, and one that is not yet conceived, and one that has been born; I am present everywhere." And as the Father replies: now you know what rebirth is.

Of course, for Jung, the one place that gave him unique access to the experience of rebirth was Bollingen—the place he had ritually dedicated as sacred to Philemon. And it's no coincidence that in his memoirs, right after describing this experience of rebirth there and just after mentioning Philemon by name, he goes straight on to say how easily he finds himself slipping into the state of feeling he is everywhere and present in everything; spread out across the whole landscape, in the water and in the clouds; alive in every animal and tree.[53]

It's not that he is copying or imitating anything. When you have the experience, you don't need to because you know. That's the whole point of the son being united with the Father.

In that union of the outside and inside, of the Gnostic or Hermetic readings and the Gnostic or Hermetic teacher, it's not a question of what one reads causing the experience—or even the other way around—but a question of something no longer remembered in the West.

It simply is a matter, as Jung would later apply himself in his scientific guise to trying to explain, of allowing them to exist together; independent but dependent; synchronous, simultaneous, side by side.

10

Philemon can take us straight to the heart of the truth about Carl Jung.

And he is also able to take us, if we are strong enough to go there, right to the heart of the lie. After all, any truth that doesn't stretch as far as to embrace the untruth is hardly a truth one could call complete. The only trouble is that, to get there, we are going to have to leave every leathered hypocrisy and imaginary honesty behind.

When Jung was at the point of turning eighty, he sent a note to an American woman about the being who had been his teacher. Early on, he wrote, it introduced itself as Philemon. And so, perfectly in line with ancient tradition, Jung was left to shoulder the task of understanding his teacher's name: what it really meant, what it meant for him.

The obvious step was to trace it back to the fictional character of Philemon who, together with his wife Baucis, features in Goethe's famous *Faust*. But naturally that raises the question of how Goethe himself had come by the name—and the only available answer is the abrupt reply he once gave a friend who asked him what his characters had to do with the Philemon and Baucis already well known in the ancient world.

Absolutely nothing!, Goethe snapped. They don't have anything to do with anything; I simply used the names to create "a good effect".

And, to be sure, this was a stunningly dismissive thing for him to say. But it was nowhere near as striking as Jung's own explanation of it: "a typical Goethean answer to Eckermann! trying to conceal his vestiges".

Here, in plunging into the mystery of Philemon and his wife which he once said he would give the entire world to be able to solve, Jung is adding his own comments—not Goethe's. With his reference to vestiges and concealment he is offering a faithful portrayal not just of someone else's situation, but of his own.[54]

And in case his statement needs any clarifying, I will explain it step by step.

Philemon's greatest gift to his adopted son was the direct knowledge or realization that everything we experience is not only alive, but real. Even all the thoughts that we unquestioningly think we have—they are independent realities like birds in the trees or animals running wild. Each idea or fantasy that comes to us isn't something we have imagined, fabricated, created: it's a living entity in its own right.

Just as Parmenides had said, everything you can perceive or even think about exists simply because it exists for you to perceive or think about. This is the basis of the underworld logic Parmenides had been told, two and a half thousand years earlier, to bring back to his fellow humans by the queen of the dead.

And this—as Jung himself would describe it after his own arduous descent into the so-called world of the dead where of course, unlike here in the world of the living, every single thing is still alive—is the gift of psychological objectivity. It's the gift of knowing without a shade of doubt that the psyche is real because it was a gift which had been handed to him, person to person, by the fantasy world itself; by his inner father and teacher.

But when he came to face the next challenge of handing on this gift to the world of humans, he realized he would never get very far if he offered it as something given to him by an imaginary being. So he presented it, instead, in a language that was bound to reassure and impress: the language of science.

This is how the groundwork came to be laid for his entire psychology; is the ultimate origin of techniques such as active imagination which trainees around the world would soon be busy copying, imitating, learning. And, at the same time, this predictable process of focusing on the gift while leaving the Gnostic giver in the shadows didn't just mark the stage of translating his experiences into a respectable scholarly idiom—or whatever high-sounding language we choose to use.

It also marked the start of Jung doing ever so precisely what he assumed Goethe was doing: hiding away the truth about Philemon through concealing his vestiges.

The funny thing is, though, that even the process of hiding or concealing always ends up taking on a life of its own. And there is more than a touch of humour about the situation Jung suddenly found himself in when, years later, he decided to fight back against Martin Buber's very public accusations that he was a Gnostic.

Buber, he complained, doesn't have the slightest right to accuse me of being a Gnostic because he doesn't have a clue about "the reality of the psyche"; is abysmally ignorant about my crucial discovery that there is an "*objective* psyche"; has no understanding at all about the complete independence and autonomy of every thought or entity inside it.

In other words, to prove to the public that he's not a Gnostic he appeals to the identical discoveries which were given to him as gifts by his Gnostic teacher.[55]

The paradox could hardly be more perfect, or complete. It's almost as if for a brief moment the whole forty years of fuss and drama spent claiming to be a faultless empiricist, the most impeccable scientist, blows away like spray to expose what was meant to stay unseen.

After all: no one was supposed to notice or know that the core principles he appeals to as showing how free his work is of any Gnostic taint had, each one of them, been revealed to him by a Gnostic.

But the paradoxical absurdity in this hidden irony offers just a taste of the other absurdities to come—because, as Jung already implies with his very knowing comment on Goethe's reply to Eckermann, concealing one's vestiges is never only a matter of concealing.

It's also a matter of pretending and denying; misdirecting and misleading; deceiving, simply lying.

And the reality is that this is exactly what Jung does best. He pretends beautifully, lies magnificently, all for the sake of concealing as much as possible the vestiges of his unrepentant inner affiliation with Gnosticism.

For instance there is the famous case of his *Seven sermons to the dead*, a mysteriously Gnostic text he had been circulating over the years among friends and colleagues as a quintessential extract from his work on the *Red book*. But as soon as Martin Buber dared to mention it in public, all hell broke loose. Instantly Jung swelled to the sublimest heights of self-righteousness—waving the *Seven sermons* away as nothing but a naively artful little poem he once had thrown together, long ago, during the briefest flurry of enthusiasm about some Gnostic writings he just so happened to stumble on way back at that distant point in time.

The unspoken truth, though, is that in private he had been keeping up his passionate readings and studies of Gnostic literature until the moment of Buber's attack. And even more important is the fact that secretly Jung always viewed these same *Seven sermons* as something altogether wonderful, embodying a wisdom "so much superior to my dull conscious mind"; as a very special gift to him from the unconscious, a unique source of light and hope, the ripest of fruits dropped into his lap; as the formal beginning of everything that would really matter to him, because through it he managed to express themes which would remain of the gravest importance to him for the rest of his work and the rest of his life.

Of course this is all a little awkward, not to mention stressful, for commentators to handle. Ever so nervously and politely—because it wouldn't do to offend anyone living or dead—they point out with the greatest of discretion that, here as well as elsewhere, he was not being altogether "candid" in his public statements or denials.

But just perhaps, faced with Jung's acknowledged and perfectly obvious lack of candour, a little more candour is called for from us. And that's not even to mention those cases where what he says and does is so shockingly shameless that, to be quite honest, it's almost as if no one can bear to look.[56]

He would do anything to cover his Gnostic tracks—not just fake or hide but commit what by any of our normal if hypocritical moral standards would be condemned as religious hypocrisy, intellectual fraud.

And it doesn't help at all to turn a blind eye. Even so, to keep watching certainly isn't easy.

Everything solid might seem as if it's being swept away. Any recognizable sense of ethics or integrity or consistency could feel as if it's being turned back to front and upside down. Jung himself, the brave man of science and wisdom, could appear to have sunk to become nothing more than the moral coward he once admitted he was.

But, in reality, everything is exactly where it should be. In fact we only have to listen for just a moment to his characteristic fury in denouncing his "medieval-minded critics" for daring to denounce him "as a mystic and Gnostic"—and immediately we are back on familiar ground.

Here we are, on firm land once more, with Jung's own dual view of the human psyche: a view inspired in no small part by the ancient philosophy of Empedocles. It's the old song-and-dance routine all over again of his two contradictory and conflicting personalities eternally at each other's throats, constantly struggling for the last word.[57]

This time around, though, we don't just have Jung the mystic loudly insisting he is not a mystic. We also have Jung the Gnostic shouting out even louder, as his no. 1 personality, that he's not the Gnostic he is as personality no. 2.

And there we have the definitive picture, able to satisfy everybody and nobody. Jung is a Gnostic but not a Gnostic—all in one.

11

To us, now, this talk of Jung as both a Gnostic and not a Gnostic is utter nonsense—and our heads simply spin.

But that makes it all the more interesting to note how, once, nothing would have been easier or more natural for people to understand. Trace Jung's own, very conscious alliance with Hermetic tradition back to its roots in the god Hermes and you will find even divinities proudly contradicting themselves by announcing the precise opposite of what everyone knows to be the case. Then there are the Popes who used to offer their full endorsement for the practice of stating, outwardly, the perfect contrary of the mysterious reality one knows inside.[58]

Today, though, this kind of deviousness is only appropriate for criminals and murderers. Each of us is so completely identified with our processed little truths that we don't even know what's happening just one level lower down in our own psyche. And our scholars—ultimate embodiments for Jung of personality no. 1, the most eloquent of spokespeople for the spirit of our time which pats itself on the back for its cleverness at getting rid of wisdom, mass murderers of everything profoundly real—destroy any slightest possibility of following him down into the depths of ourselves.

After all, our personality no. 1 isn't only interested in trivia or sport. It loves dabbling in whatever obscure subject it fancies misunderstanding; becomes a learned specialist in the world of personality no. 2, a leading expert on Jung and Gnostics and alchemy. This is why academics are so happy parroting Jung's own no. 1 personality every time he insists he's no Gnostic, because nothing can be more seductive than hearing the sound of our own superficiality bounced right back at us.[59]

But nothing, for Jung, is simple until one accepts that for him nothing is simple. And simply to listen to the voice of his personality no. 1 is a recipe for utter disaster because Jung's attitude to the Gnostics isn't just what it seems.

At the same time it's also Jung's attitude to Jung.

For example the defining characteristic, to him, of the no. 2 personality is quiet certainty: a certainty rooted in the experience of eternity. Aside from its fondness for lies the main characteristic of personality no. 1—fleeting creature of the moment, rooted in nothing outside itself—is its flipping and flopping, inconsistencies and uncertainties, the inner experience of being endlessly wracked with hesitations and doubts.

And we have to hold them both together if we want to appreciate why Jung sounds so undecided whenever he talks out about the Gnostics. He praises them for being so skilful at avoiding inflation only to accuse them of inflation, absolutely insists it's "clear beyond a doubt" that they were psychologists only to doubt that they were psychologists, accuses them of being primitive and childish only to admire them for being so sophisticated as well as two thousand years ahead of their time, denounces them for being metaphysicians only to admit that he isn't sure.

Of course the predictable reaction when confronted with these constant paradoxes, these blatant contradictions, is to try smoothing them over; is to do everything possible as a Jungian or Jung scholar to blunt the sharpness of their edges by fabricating some impossibly consistent account of his attitude to the Gnostics.

But this is completely to miss the point in every conceivable way.

First of all it's to overlook the fact that when Jung defines the basic method of communication adopted by ancient Gnostics, he states that they very deliberately spoke in paradoxes and used constant contradictions. In other words: even through the simple act of writing about the Gnostics just as he did, he was demonstrating to anyone with eyes and ears that he was a Gnostic.[60]

And then there is the other point—infinitely harder to swallow.

People love asking the question of what, exactly, Jung's attitude to the Gnostics happened to be. The only real answer, though, is to ask: Which of his two personalities are you asking about?

Just to ask that question spells death to every sentimental idea anyone might have about the man—and this reaches far deeper than the issue of his relationship to the Gnostics because it's a question even those closest to him were, very naturally, unable or unwilling to face.

In their lives as well as their writings they all created a benignly idealized image of him; found ways of relating to him day after day on a human level by smoothly blending his two personalities into one; hung on the master's every word unless he said something in an obvious moment of anger or it simply suited them not to.

But, as always, Jung was right in insisting that real wisdom or understanding only comes from the most unexpected and unappreciated source—because it was his English translator, frowned on as a mere intellectual and rejected as an outsider by most of Jung's inner circle, who stood alone in realizing how absolutely critical it was at any given moment to know if he was speaking from personality no. 1 or no. 2.

This, he explained, is what it means to face up to the shifting fullness of Jung's reality "with his 'two personalities' who invariably contradict each other" and who can switch places in the blink of an eye.[61]

Strip away the veils of familiarity and nothing can be taken for granted any more. We have to keep our wits constantly about us because there is always danger lurking under the surface of such a person's words. And in just the same spirit, not many people who read or study Jung would ever want to take the idea of him concealing his vestiges seriously because its implications are so terrifying.

It means we can never be sure if he means what he is saying or is saying what he is saying only to cover what he means. We can't even be certain who, or what, he is. But the most crucial point of all is that, with these two personalities, there is no question of right versus wrong. It's not that one of the two can be conveniently disregarded and only the other, the truth-teller, believed.

They both have to be listened to, ever so carefully, because they both have their own place: both have their role to play in the larger scheme of things.

The essential truth of Jung's Gnostic teacher Philemon belonged inside the sacred shrine he had made for him at Bollingen—which, uncoincidentally, happened to be the one place where Jung felt free to live from the depths of his personality no. 2. But the whole point of having a shrine is to contain the sacred, to protect it against contamination and profanation, keep it safe. And his cocky no. 1 personality with all its superficialities and deceptions and misdirections, its denials and lies, played an utterly indispensable part in misleading people; fooling and distracting the curious; keeping them well away.

This is why he hated talking in public about his relationship to the Gnostics, and is why the people who were near him amplified his fears even more. It's why he held his Gnostic "secrets" such as the *Seven sermons* so tight and close to his chest, which in turn explains the strength of his anger at Buber for trying to expose them.

Perhaps to talk about Jung and secrets might sound strange. But there is no reason at all why it should, because that comment of his about Goethe and vestiges is far from being the only place where he very plainly lays out the case for having to cover one's tracks; hide one's traces. In fact elsewhere he couldn't be clearer about the urgent psychological need, whenever touching on issues that matter most, to hide one's experiences by appearing to talk about things and people quite different from what one is really talking about—just as I am doing in this book.[62]

In the overall scheme of things everything has its place, even the deceptions and illusions. This is exactly what Empedocles was aiming to communicate with his teaching about the dual spirits behind the whole of existence: one of them a spirit of cheerful illusion, the other a spirit far too powerful for humans to bear. It's precisely why Parmenides, to the endless frustration and confusion of later thinkers, presented his own underworld teaching as having two halves.

One contains the goddess' revelation of the truth, but in her otherworldly wisdom she doesn't stop there. Instead she goes straight on to demonstrate how, alone, even the most perfect truth can never be complete by dedicating the second half of her teaching to deceptions and illusions; untruths and lies.

And it's well worth noting that Parmenides' cutting-edge contributions to the science of his time are all included in the second half of his poem, not the first. This is the way things used to be done in an age when the arts of trickery were still appreciated: still understood.

This also is why, again perfectly in line with ancient tradition, Jung states near the start of his *Red book* that the spirit of the depths is by itself as inadequate as the superficial spirit of our time—because it's only the ability to maintain a balance between the two, even at the cost of contradicting oneself, that ultimately matters. Then he goes straight into talking the strange language, so familiar already to Empedocles but so utterly alien to us, of not one but two madnesses.

One is the delusion of a human identifying completely with the wisdom spoken by the spirit of the depths; the other is the equal delusion of identifying unquestioningly with the spirit of our time to the point of seeing, just like almost everybody else, nothing but the surface of things. And one wonders how easy it would be nowadays to discover a single person who has experienced, through and through, the harrowing reality of what that truly means.

Recognizing the insanity of the unfortunate few who have been overwhelmed by their own unconscious is easy enough. Recognizing the collective madness of the many who are blindly and mindlessly led along by "the general spirit in which we think and act today" is, to say the least, a little rarer.

All of a sudden, we are being drawn back to that Gnostic vision of the Christ as a figure entering our world specifically "in order to illuminate the stupidity, darkness, and unconsciousness of mankind"; or to the insight of Jung himself when, just before he died, he stood amazed at how naïve he had been "in not expecting the darkness to be so dense".[63]

But there are some things that it's wiser by far not to mention out loud—and it's best simply to forget I ever said that.

12

In spite of his immense importance for Carl Jung, there is just one single scene where Philemon makes a physical appearance inside the main body of the *Red book*.

And that's not the only exceptional thing about this particular scene. The *Red book* is a seedbed bursting with significance for the rest of Jung's work. Whatever he would later discover or write about famously had its roots there, would flower from there.

But the fate of this one scene is unbroken silence. From it nothing visible flowers at all; and the central theme that emerges out of his encounter here with Philemon, Christ's friend, will never come to the surface even once in any other of his published writings.[64]

It could be quite tempting to assume that this is because Jung found nothing of any value in what happened between him and his teacher: nothing worth bringing into the collective world of personality no. 1. But for anyone at all familiar with how he really functioned, the alternative possibility is bound to spring to mind—which is that something here might have needed shielding from the spirit of our time, something much too fragile and precious to be made public.

And, as a matter of fact, soon we'll see the kind of unnatural disasters that instantly unfold from the very first moment even the most seasoned of Jungians lay eyes on this scene inside the freshly printed *Red book*.

There is also something else about the scene which is extremely odd. In it, Jung describes Philemon as "the magician". He goes searching for him because he realizes he, himself, is completely stuck and understands that—before he can take a single step forward into life—he is going to have to learn the secret of magic. And eventually he finds Philemon, tending his tulips, at the little cottage he shares with his wife Baucis out in the countryside.

But what's so odd about all this is that, as Jung knew very well, the cottage didn't even exist.

Ever since he was a teenager he had learned to live and breathe each scene of Goethe's *Faust* as if it was his own reality. Every single incident inside the drama happened to him; and one particular event affected him more deeply, shook him more personally, than any other.

It might come as something of a surprise to hear that in the second half of Goethe's play the character called Faust already appears—two hundred years ago—as the archetypal property developer. But nothing in this world is truly quite as new as we think it is. Already for Goethe, then for Jung, land development was the sign of the times: epitomized the great tide of so-called progress rising everywhere, sweeping away everything in its path, impossible to resist or even escape.

And because Faust felt he needed that little patch of land both Philemon and Baucis lived on, because he had the devil on his side, the humble old couple ended up being murdered and their cottage burned to the ground.[65]

In short, it could never be a question of Jung trying to convey the secret of his encounter with Philemon to our collective modern world because the encounter never had any place inside that world to begin with—had been obliterated, dramatically cut out of it, right from the start.

Instead, their magical meeting quietly took place in an alternate reality altogether unrelated to the spirit of our time. And meanwhile, up on the surface of himself, Jung dutifully went through the appropriate motions of insisting that of course it would be the absurdest thing in the world to suspect him of being an occultist or having anything at all to do with magic.[66]

The surface is only the surface, though. And he always found it difficult to keep entirely hidden what was bubbling underneath. For instance it's still easy to pick up on his excitement, as a young man in his thirties, bursting to tell Freud how he had found a perfect motto to encapsulate the message and purpose of the new psychoanalytic movement—a quotation he had discovered in the ancient Greek magical writings he was studying at the time.

Or to be more precise, the saying he had chosen came straight from the so-called Paris magical papyrus: a text which just so happens to preserve, more faithfully than any other document in existence, many of the most mysterious traditions surrounding that famous ancient magician called Empedocles.

But I wouldn't like to give the wrong impression that all Jung had done was to find, in this one magical saying, an ideal motto to define the emerging science of psychoanalysis. On the contrary, he also took it to heart as his own guide in the inexpressibly laborious process of starting to note down every single image or thought that came into his head—a process that led him straight into creating the *Black books* which, in turn, directly laid the groundwork for the *Red book* out of which the rest of his work would flow.[67]

And as Jung grew older, the magic didn't go further underground or just vanish. Instead it became far more apparent, although even more enigmatic.

Central to his whole work is the process of individuation; and central to the process of individuation is the unavoidable need for anyone or everyone to encounter at a certain stage, then integrate, the reality contained in the archetype of the magician. Like so much of what he tried to convey, this theme of encounter plus integration has been a cause of no small discomfort. There are more than just a handful of people who are only too eager to explain it as purely a matter of learning to disidentify from the primitive archetype of the magician and leave all that nonsense about magic far behind.

As usual, though, that's not quite what Jung himself had in mind. For him the first option, when confronted with this primordial power of magic, is to identify with it unthinkingly and in effect end up as the modern bourgeois version of what would once have been called a black magician.

The second is to become so scared of the magical power that one projects it as far away as possible into the safety of the heavens and turns into a grovelling, helpless little worm overshadowed by the omnipotent figure of God.

But the third way—according to Jung the correct way, what could well be called the only truly magical way of approaching magic—is to "assimilate" all the hidden contents of the magician archetype quite consciously inside oneself. And that could sound respectable, even scientific, enough if it didn't at the same time evoke with such uncanny precision the ancient mythical legends about gods swallowing magical divinities so they can absorb and incorporate their mysterious powers.[68]

For myself, I am going to steer well clear of any learned or scholarly discussion about the practicalities of swallowing and assimilating such a quintessential archetype of magic. After all, Jung knows what he is saying when he tells Philemon in the *Red book* that there are no professors left who know even the slightest thing about magic any more.

But it may be worth ever so quickly mentioning how there had already, by the time Jung was alive, been a lengthy tradition in the West of doctors as well as philosophers claiming that real magic only begins when one has left the whole external business of spells and rituals and ceremonies behind. In other words, it's not so much a matter of doing magic as of simply being the magic instead.

And we just so happen to meet with a strikingly similar picture of the magician who has left his magical doings behind in the *Red book*—right at the start of the scene where Jung manages to catch up with Philemon outside his cottage only to find what he jokingly, but also respectfully, refers to as an "old magician" who seems to have retired now from the business of magic and might at the very most just do an odd spell for someone now or then.

Naturally that's not all, though. With characters like Philemon, or Jung, it never is.

Almost as if deliberately to give the lie to the convenient image of Professor Jung as someone who left all his childish dabbling in the occult behind as he got older, and wiser, we also happen to have the reports of those who spent time alone with him during his final months—and would describe him, very specifically, as the "old magician".

And that's not even to mention the people who, after being allowed to visit him towards the end of his life, would come away with the unshakeable impression that they had not just been with an expert psychologist or scientist or scholar. They had been in the overwhelming presence of a living Gnostic; a living alchemist.[69]

But, as a true son of his father, the parallels between the two of them hardly stopped there.

Sometimes, just like Philemon, Jung too might find himself doing the odd spell for somebody now or then. And, almost as if purposely to frustrate anyone who would like to insist all these descriptions of him were only loose or humorous metaphors, we still have clear evidence of him performing traditional magic by following the exact procedures of ancient magical ritual right to the letter.[70]

Of course, here again, I am not speaking as I should. Everybody with even the slightest investment in defending Jung's reputation will be as appalled at the reality of Jung the magician as they are certain to be horrified at the prospect of Jung, saviour of the world.

Even so, the evidence can only be pushed away so far and people can only be fooled for so long. And, besides, the truth is that the world needs just a bit of saving—not from anybody else, but from ourselves.

It also needs a little magic, too, which is exactly why Jung sets out at the start of that exceptional scene in the *Red book* to find someone who will answer for him the central question of how magic is taught; how it can be learned.

When he finally meets up with the old magician himself, Philemon could hardly be more difficult or evasive—a grinding reminder of all the hardships and frustrations, humiliations and confusions, any would-be student would typically have been forced to submit to in the ancient world. And it's not that he hadn't been warned. Jung's own soul had already prepared him by predicting in the plainest possible terms that there was one thing he would have to sacrifice, and sacrifice completely, before he could even begin to learn magic.

That's the sacrifice of the slightest human desire for comfort; of any longing or craving for solace.

The words almost burn through the page as his soul keeps telling him, time and time again, about the darkly unconsolable future that lies ahead of him. Jung, for his part, never speaks again with more honesty or burning intensity than when he realizes what the gift of primordial magic actually is—what the proverbial magic wand is that he abruptly finds himself holding in his hand.

It's a black rod as crushingly heavy as iron and as comfortlessly cold as death: something of such piercingly terrible power it will tear his heart to pieces, nearly shatter his nerves.

And here, twisted and turned around Philemon's finger, he begins to experience what that means.

But at last, in this never-to-be-continued debate between student of magic and magical teacher, Philemon carefully allows the odd statements to slip out—statements which just so happen to define all that remains of Jung's published work far better than anyone might care to admit.

He explains, without explaining anything, that even to come within sniffing distance of real magic needs tremendous cunning because it can't be taught or learned; can't be known, certainly can't be understood; keeps silent and demands, ahead of anything else, the total unlearning of reason. As Jung himself comments after leaving, even the meeting that he just had with Philemon is magical and is thoroughly impossible to understand.

Then he goes on to add one crucial statement of his own: there can be no thinking about magic because "the practice of magic consists of making what is not understood understandable in a way and a manner which is not understandable."[71]

Now, if this whole episode in the *Red book* was respectfully left alone as it should, a certain balance could be preserved and things wouldn't be so bad. The problem is that it's not. In fact I have heard some of the most highly respected Jungian therapists lecturing not only about the *Red book*—but about this section in particular. And this is how they sum it up:

Magic, according to Carl Jung, is very easy to understand because it's just a way of dealing with the irrational. It's as simple as that, nothing more. It's nothing grand or special.

There is no great power, no magical wand or rod you can hold in your hand or anything like that. Magic is purely a matter of comfort; is nothing but a question of learning how to feel comfortable with the irrational, how to make it fully intelligible and understandable. That, if you want to know, is all that magic really is.

And if you don't see what's wrong with this—or, even worse, can't see anything wrong with it at all—perhaps I can humbly suggest that you should go back and start reading this book again from the first page.

That's what happens when anyone forgets Jung's constant warning never to explain anything away as "only" this or "nothing but" that. It's exactly what happens from the very first moment we ignore his nightmarish implication that, whenever we imagine we understand something he says, this is because we are unaware of the magical power he is using to manufacture such an illusory understanding.

Here is what happens when we have no real interest in the magic itself, let alone in paying the crushing price to be paid for learning it, but are only interested in shaping it into a tool to protect us from what it was meant to be. Above all, it's what happens when our desperate need for personal or professional comfort is so overwhelmingly strong it forces us to run far away from the depths as fast as our expert legs will take us: to put as much space as we possibly can between ourselves and the bewildering fact that "the thing that causes the greatest fear is the source of the greatest wisdom".

This is precisely why Jung realized that his own work was destined, just the same as Christ's, to become institutionalized—and, just like early Christianity, lose any of its real fire or spirit in a few short years. The high priests can never be stopped once they start to come.

As you can see, it would be superfluous for Jung's enemies or critics to try to destroy his work because those who speak and write in his name do a fine enough job on their own.[72]

This is how subtly, silently, invisibly the situation changes: is how easily, how surreptitiously, the intensity of direct experience slips and then slides unnoticed into something else. All of a sudden our no. 1 personality, with its cocksure ways of masquerading as master of the depths, has successfully invaded the domain of personality no. 2.

And this, it can be ever so important to understand, is its own magic. It's the very substance that our collective world is made of, a magic in reverse. It's a thing of the most amazing strangeness and gruesome beauty to watch—the perverted form of magic known as rationality.

For the rational part of us everything is reasonable and, even when we talk about magic, we are proving there is no such thing. But, for the magician, everything in existence is magic. Even trying to get rid of magic is among the most potent forms of magic: the magic of our age.

Here with our own inverted kind of magic, not anywhere else, is where we can start to discover for ourselves a bit about the power of magic. The real magic itself can never be learned, is impossible to teach or be trained in, because whatever we might glimpse of it would immediately get swallowed up by this magic we live and breathe in—the magic of our time.

This is the reasonable, progressive magic that invisibly destroys; the magic of a whole culture ripping itself up by its roots; of each of us celebrating new ways, just like the miniature Lucifers we are, of silently murdering our elders.

And if that sounds harsh, it's because none of us can claim to be miraculously exempt from the spirit of our time. We are all, without exception, being compromised and eaten away at every moment by the insatiably devouring appetite of "the spirit that runs through the masses".

Jungians or non-Jungians makes no difference. As Jung himself used to observe, those who go by the name of "Jungian" might like to think they are a little special but they are not. And there is no difference whatsoever between waving a magic wand now to get rid of Jung the magician and the centuries after centuries of industrious scholarship which, with impeccably irrational rationality, waved its own wand to get rid of Empedocles the magician; dispose of Parmenides the magician; obliterate any true trace of the primordial magic at the roots and source of our western world.

To approach Jung's magic is impossible without understanding that ancient magic, or what happened to it. I am not just referring to the irritating rituals or objectionable spells, but to the far deeper magic of how to create a whole culture—how to bring a new civilization into being.

For his part, he knew only too well why this magic had to be cut away completely from our modern world. As he explains in the *Red book*, "our time no longer needs magic" because now is the time of reason.[73]

And that's why the only future for Philemon's magic lies either in silence—or, with the inevitable circlings of time, in the even more silent destruction of what once destroyed it.

13

For anyone to suggest that the person who created perhaps the most liberating, most transformative psychology in the modern world devoted his life to penitence and repentance: this would hardly sound very reasonable.

But that's just what Carl Jung did. And its oddness is a strong hint at how many thousands of years we already have drifted away from him in the space of less than a century, just as it's a clear sign of how quickly we are sliding away from ourselves.

To be sure, he was never too open about what mattered most to him—as if that really made much difference. In fact he could be as direct and honest as he wanted and still, magician that he was, no one would quite register what he was saying.

Even so, he best felt able to be himself by himself at his private retreat in Bollingen; and, as if this wasn't secretive enough, carved a special text into the wall of the tower which he referred to as his "hidden inscription". Four words long, it summarized for him the whole purpose of Bollingen while at the same time telling a hidden story: *Philemonis sacrum Fausti poenitentia*, "Philemon's shrine—Faust's repentance".[74]

The first two words are straightforward enough. He had built the tower at Bollingen as a sacred place for his inner teacher. But the second are the riddle.

Ever since he read Goethe's *Faust* for the first time as a boy, Jung had come face to face with himself in the character of Faust; identified with him completely; felt as guilty, when Faust accidentally had Philemon and Baucis killed, as if he somehow had helped in the past to have them murdered; saw it as his personal responsibility to atone for the crime, or at least prevent it happening again, by confronting the Faust inside himself.

And the only way to understand this situation, humanly, is if we are willing to relate it to ourselves.

Faust is the classic example of a property developer who gets greedy, behaves badly, evicts some peace-loving people, even causes a death or two. And then what do we do? Most likely we sigh and do nothing, perhaps talk a bit about it with all the correct intonations of self-righteous superiority while inside ourselves accepting it as the terrible price to be paid for the blessings of living in such a convenient modern world.

There again, we might want to take legal action if we have the ways and means. Or more probably, in line with the energetic spirit of our age, we'll join up with the ranks of other activists to create innovative new ways of coming together to make the world a better place for everyone to live in.

But Jung repented.

To him all those outer solutions are the childish result of me believing I am a noble force of right and good while heroically projecting the violence of the problem somewhere else, anywhere else, as long as it's outside myself. This is why he backed out of cooperating with the United Nations in their grand plans for world peace—because he saw the arrogance and utter futility of rushing out to correct the world's wrongs in the firm belief that my own attitude is right and true. "It's a very long step from this conviction to the conclusion: the world is wrong and therefore I am wrong too."

And, as he immediately added: "To pronounce such words is easy, but to feel their truth in the marrow of one's bones is a very different proposition".

There, in the marrow of one's bones, is where things become serious; deadly serious. Here is where one has to choose whether to go out into the world or go in—all the way, not just dipping one's toes as spiritually or psychologically minded people like to do—into the depths of oneself. This is why Jung insisted "one virtually has to die" before being able to grasp the full reality of Faust's crime against Philemon or Baucis.

But it's also the reason why, right at the core of his *Red book* during the stage of his Christ-like descent into hell, he sees that nothing whatsoever can be done on any human or spiritual level until each one of us recognizes our own perfect "complicity in the act of evil".[75]

There is no forging such a recognition. None of the usual masks or masquerading will do—because whoever comes back with a direct awareness of that complicity has the haunting look, the unmistakable glance, of someone whose eyes have seen straight through hell into eternity.

And so we come to the part of this story about what that evil is. It's much the same story as before: Jung expressing himself ever so simply, ever so clearly, except that we don't notice because we are not allowed to. That's how powerful the magic is of this world we live in.

Plastered across his published biography is the plainest possible statement that this isn't the evil of some unscrupulous developer or businessman, as we would like to believe, but the evil in us all. And that's the ruthless search for improvement—for the newest, the newer, the new.

It's the gnawing sense of discontent and dissatisfaction that pushes us faster and faster into a non-existent future, the diabolical addiction to speed that robs us of our time and strips us of our lives while tricking us into leaving behind who we are and were meant to be, the wild violence of riding the torrents of progress that tear us away from our roots, the individual and collective stupidity of trading in something good for something promoted as much better which always magically ends up far worse, the increasing enslavement not only to technology and science but to government and the power of the state which promise greater freedoms only to take them all away.

Or, as Jung expressed himself in one of his interviews that never quite made its way into print, this is the evil of those who set themselves up as vicious innovators. And, by that, he is not just meaning what's technologically new but what's spiritually new; innovative ways of communication, interaction, education; better ways of doing good, more enlightened methods of waking up; every spiritual solution which seems to offer a fresh new alternative to our corrupt modern world of progress and materialism but is just a prettier part of it, a fancier extension.

In other words we are each of us, without even noticing it, vicious developers: are all Fausts carried along in our "hubris and inflation", murderers of Philemon and his wife every day. We are the ones who keep burning their cottage down with the intensity of our thoughts and the cleverness of our actions, because this is the way of the times.[76]

And this is why Jungians who are willing to listen to Jung are such a rare breed—because what he says is so utterly unreasonable, so absurdly and obviously unacceptable in our contemporary world. It would cost ever so much to look far enough inside ourselves to catch a glimpse of the bottomless truth that dismissing his message with such instant self-assurance is simply one more proof of our inflation and hubris.

After all, there is no need to go the whole way to hell just to discover everyone's complicity in an evil they are already quite happy admitting to.

The trouble is that we have arrived at a point where Jung is steering well away from what could seem to be the manageable problem of one, or two, individual patients' unhealthy inflation towards something far more terrifyingly real: collective inflation. And while nothing could be easier than to sit down and wisely discuss the collective inflation experienced by Germans during the lead-up to either of the first two world wars, we are never going to feel at all comfortable sitting down to confront the mass inflation of the culture we now live in—which is why a third world war is guaranteed.

Very pointedly, just as he is adding the final words to one of his most important works on alchemy, he comes straight back to the murder of Philemon and Baucis. As strongly as he can, he emphasizes that Faust's crazy inflation isn't the inflation of some real or fictitious individual. It's the inflation of the masses; and "the masses are blind brutes, as we know to our cost."

Then he goes on to say that a remedy exists for this collective inflation, which is discoverable in private. But such a remedy "is nothing that can be held up to the masses—only some hidden thing that we can hold up to ourselves in solitude and in silence. Very few people care to know anything about this; it is so much easier to preach the universal panacea to everybody else than to take it oneself" because then one might suddenly be forced to doubt everything.

And, naturally, "no doubts can exist in the herd; the bigger the crowd the better the truth—and the greater the catastrophe."[77]

This is the remedy of repentance: of Jung's penitence, the hidden thing that he held up to himself in solitude and silence. It's to perform the invisible, but unbelievably painful, penance of having to atone through the fabric of one's life for the collective crimes of humanity. And only inwardly can anybody guess how much appalling darkness and hardship someone might have to face and what gruesome sacrifices might have to be made in the sacred process of compensating for the unconsciousness and cruelty, the self-absorption and forgetfulness, of a whole country; of a continent; of the world we live in.

Of course this might sound almost as grim as it actually is. But the thing is that by turning away from the evil we don't make it disappear, and if we don't fully face the evil inside ourselves it follows us in everything. Then we can be going out and dancing and doing the most wonderfully stimulating things while tormenting Jung's spirit, haunted by the darkness inside us. And perhaps, just perhaps, it's only by going into the depths of ourselves that we will ever come to discover real joy.

Exactly the same as before, we are left with two magics. One, as Jung himself explains in an unpublished interview, belongs to the devil: is the vicious magic of ruthless innovation, of the new assassinating the old. The other is the magic of the solitary magician, of Philemon—or Merlin.

This, unlike the magic of the masses, is the secret and sacred task of protecting the past by leaving it undisturbed; by respecting one's ancestors, honouring the elders.

Or, as Jung's views on the subject have more publicly and politely been summed up: it means "recognition of 'the ancient'", means working inwardly to ensure the continuity of history and culture.[78]

To speak out like this about recognition of the ancient, about the continuity of history, can seem innocent enough. But actually to communicate something about it is a very different proposition—because the past he is referring to isn't some token history book, or a handy collection of myths and symbols on the bookshelf, or even a curious trip to some museum.

It's what once used to be the only logic, the logic of the dead, but now is laughably absurd. It's the dead themselves who call to us through the wind, sing to us through the birds, speak to us through children or our own visions and dreams. It's everything that eludes us as soon as we think a single thought, or just move to see it better, because there is no space at all for it in our ruthlessly functional world. And we can never be sure if what we really saw for such a brief moment was the magic of another world appearing in this, or the magic of this world erasing that.

That's why even to say these words, in our ever so reasonable existence which is falling apart as I speak, is almost impossibly difficult. Simply to be able to write them, arrange one word to follow another, is itself an act of magic—not to mention penitence. And to make any sense of them, to be able to follow them: that needs an act of magic, too.

Jung often noted he was such a complicated individual and had so many sides to him that no one person could ever hope to map them all, which is true enough because his life branched off into so many different outlets.

At the same time, this is only half of his story. What so mysteriously but predictably has been forgotten is the hidden root of Jung, from which all the other branches flowed. Repeatedly he tried to point to it as best he could; mentioned it here, there, often in the most unlikely of places. And through his whole adult life it always remained the same.

He already lays it out not in one of his later works on alchemy, or during some interview shortly before he died, but while he was still in his thirties and working away at the *Red book*:

"We are a blinded and deluded race." The only thing we know is how to exist on the surface of ourselves, live only for today, use our minds for thinking only of tomorrow. As for the past, "we behave towards it like brutes because we are not willing to receive the dead". Instead, we are only interested in doing the kind of work that brings visible results or success; and "above all we want to be paid." To do some hidden work that offers no one any visible benefit or service would probably strike anybody as insane.

But this insanity is just what's needed because "there is one indispensable, although strange and hidden work you have to do in secret: your most important work, your masterpiece". This is the inner work you have to do before you can ever discover your outer work in life. It's the work that you need to do, not for the sake of the people around you—but for the sake of the dead "who demand the work of atonement" and won't let you live until you do it.

So "don't look forward too much, but back and into yourself in case you fail to hear the dead."

In a strange but realistic way it's all for the best that most people do fail to hear the dead and do fail to hear Jung, because the past inside ourselves isn't just the source of life or purpose. It's also the ocean of the unconscious—infinitely fascinating, vastly treacherous and deceptive.[79]

Nothing is easier than to get lost there. And whoever wants to travel into it needs one thing as badly as a compass, which is the precision of focus.

What Jung found there—inside himself, deep in the past of his own culture—is something he often referred to throughout his life and tried to explain, as best he could. Again, though, almost as if by magic the image he conjures into view quickly mists over and keeps drifting off out of sight.

If you are not able to stay focused on it, you will lose your bearings and forget you ever saw anything. If you concentrate too much on some detail, you will end up trapped inside the limits of your psychology and the artificial structures of your mind.

But whoever is ready to keep it gently and firmly in focus will start, little by little, to make out the outlines of Jung's life—and, behind, of the hidden mystery at the heart of our western world.

14

There is a time when—reminiscing as an old man—Carl Jung relived in the sharpest detail his original experience of going back into history and sinking into the past.

He had been fascinated for years, when he was younger, with the legend of the Grail. Already he had started to ask himself: what is this Grail, this famous treasure so hard to attain? But Christianity gave no answer. In fact this is the one question Christianity is unable to answer.

Gradually he became aware of the huge gulf or gap in time dividing the medieval myth of the knights of the Grail from the far more distant past of antiquity. And he knew that to find his answer he was going to have to make his way beyond Christianity; get behind it.

Then he describes just what happened. To begin with, he let himself be carried back to the time of the knights in their quest for the Grail. But the only result was that he found himself plunged into total and utter darkness—not a single response or reply.

It wasn't until, like some inner archaeologist, he became able at last to descend all the way to the third century after Christ that he finally felt something change. Instead of nothing but darkness he began to notice things getting brighter, the beginning of light. He had the unmistakable sensation: here lives a part of myself.

And this was his discovery of the Gnostics, including Philemon. It was as if there was something of him in them and something of them in him, as if by reaching back through the past to his teacher in the figure of Philemon he had encountered his real self—had arrived at what, on the deepest level, he recognized to be his own truest shape and form. Here he was, home at last, not with his blood relatives or physical ancestors but together with his most intimate spiritual family where he belonged.[80]

So he had literally found himself, there as well as here at the same time: two Jungs, or two halves of one Jung, almost two thousand years apart. And, as always happens, from the first moment that he found himself he was lost.

He was with himself, reunited with his teacher, with those he belonged to and who belonged to him, in a period close to the time of Christ. He was in the twentieth century, too. The wisdom had started to flow from him, back then, into the newer him right now. But as for how he could consciously connect these two Jungs, make sense of their interaction, still he had no answer.

Once again there was the enormous gap, the hiatus, the unbridgeable distance between present and past. The Gnostics already had the basics of psychology; had confronted the archetypes in their lives and experiences; were up against the reality of a collective unconscious that powers our existence, defines and shapes our whole world. As for what lay between them then, though, and us now: "they lived in the first, second and third centuries. And what was in between? Nothing"—nothing but a gaping hole.

It was one of those riddles that could easily, to use his own expression, have made him lose his head. But, to his credit, he had the courage and integrity to avoid looking around outside himself for some cheap solution. And only eventually did he come to see that this nothing wasn't just nothing.

Only ever so slowly did he start to realize that the hole wasn't a hole. On the contrary, he began to become aware of an unbroken lineage linking and connecting the ancient Gnostics to our modern world: often hidden, sometimes persecuted, always to some degree or other submerged. That was the western tradition of alchemy, also known as Hermetic philosophy or the mythical golden chain.

Now he had the bridge from himself and his physical family back to himself, his teacher, his innermost family. And this is what alchemy would always be for him—a bridge, simply a bridge.[81]

But simple things are always the most difficult ones to understand: always the most elusive and the hardest to hold gently, as well as firmly, in view. It's so easy to forget what makes a bridge a bridge and that its whole purpose is to allow people to get across.

Instead, those who invest their minds and lives in busily helping to construct a bridge can soon end up itching to build their home on it and missing any larger sense of what exists on either side. All it takes is the slightest iota of self-importance or self-interest and the greater perspective, so subtle, so hard-won, is suddenly lost.

A bridge is about flow, as opposed to constriction or rigidity; about fluidity and movement; about the traffic of continuity. This is why, to Jung, there could never be any question of alchemy as opposed to Gnosticism. Quite to the contrary: for him the one flowed effortlessly into the other because alchemical tradition, itself, was Gnostic through and through.[82]

And even the separate phases of his life that he is supposed to have dedicated to studying Gnostic tradition first, only followed by alchemy much later, are largely a myth. Naturally the emphasis and apparent priorities had to shift with the passing of time.

The fact, though, which happens to be a fact particularly rich in significance is that he was already becoming acquainted with alchemy as soon as he started his studies of the Gnostics—in much the same way that he would continue working on Gnosticism for the rest of his days.[83]

But to see such a whole as the whole it is involves having to hold the completeness of it, its living reality, silently in the stillness of one's inner self.

Focus too much on this detail or that and you are lost because, paradoxically, the only way to keep one's clarity is by viewing everything from the perspective of the surrounding blackness. This, after all, is the reason why Jung tried the best he could to emphasize that the sense of historical continuity which was so crucial for him belongs to the world of personality no. 2—and can only be appreciated by someone attuned to the vast regions "of inner darkness".

Of course, judged by the spirit of our age, in saying such things he was stepping way out of line. To conventional historians, or at least those few scholars prepared to waste time in studying him, history is strictly their domain and Jung with his amateurish fantasies about historical continuity was just an imposter. But the joke is on them because, very simply, he understood the all-important materials far better than them; had laboured for years to become fluent in the ancient languages which they, if they bothered to read any of the texts at all, could mostly only approach through poor translations; knew his way around the subtleties of the evidence with an openness and an attentiveness even the greatest experts couldn't match because, like his friend as well as colleague Henry Corbin, he understood that the so-called facts of history will always remain a closed book without entering the mystery which lies behind them.

And he did these things, outstripped scholars in their scholarship to a degree they were hardly able to notice, because for him much more was at stake than they could ever imagine.[84]

Many academics tend to feel quite free to come up with whatever new theories or crazy hypotheses they want—in fact often the crazier the better. But for Jung it was never about needing to be clever, although this can seem almost impossible to understand.

Instead, it was about the most serious and solemn of obligations: about his responsibilities towards the living and, above all, his duties towards the dead.

The thing about the dead, which should only rarely be said because one never knows who is saying it, is that they are not just dead. Whether approached correctly or wrongly, respected or forgotten, acknowledged or ignored, they are far more alive than we are.

In one way or another they live with us, through us, as us. "They still live on."

A second thing about the dead is that, in whatever matters to them, they demand the most uncompromising precision. And a third is that whenever life happens to be viewed from their perspective, everything looks back to front like in some kind of mirror—appearing as just the opposite of what we are pleasantly ready to expect. What from our side of the bridge seems perfectly solid and real is the purest fantasy to them while what, to us, seems nothing but fantasy is the firmest of foundations on the other side.

This is the reason why, far from boasting that through his masterful scientific work he had managed at last to place the bizarrely fantastic world of Gnostics and alchemists on a solid foundation, Jung stated the exact reverse: that only the solid foundation offered by Gnosticism, and by alchemy in leading back to the Gnostics, had managed to stop his whole psychology from remaining the emptiest and hollowest "phantasmagoria".[85]

It was only the historical continuity they were able to provide that had the power to bring him, along with his work, back into the real world. And this reality lies not in the hectic rush of ephemeral present moments that keep tearing, dragging us further away from ourselves; not even in the meditative stillness of the present moment which becomes just another excuse for escaping our primordial nature.

On the contrary, it lies in the depths of a living past which every present moment exists to serve—because that's where our true root and purpose are waiting to be found.[86]

Noticed, or unnoticed, this historical continuity is the bedrock of his work and his psychology. But, as so often, we can stand watching him repeat the same statements only to see them immediately being washed away by the tides of time.

For example, there is the one rare talk he grudgingly agreed to give about the Gnostics in which he explained that "if we seek genuine psychological understanding of the human being of our own time, we must know his spiritual history absolutely." By spiritual history he meant, very specifically, the two thousand years connecting us back through the past of western culture to the time of the Gnostics.

To him this recognition of the ancient, as he called it, wasn't a matter of theory or academic speculation. It was a question of the most urgent practice. Jung was speaking as a healer, a psychiatrist, a clinician when he kept insisting there can be no real cure of a human being without understanding that person's true history. And he wasn't just talking about childhood history or even parental history, because "we are not of today or of yesterday; we are of an immense age."

Or as I once wrote: "We're ancient, incredibly ancient. We hold the history of the stars in our pockets."

It was as a caring doctor trying to help his patients deal with their apparent sufferings, their everyday neuroses, that he claimed the only genuine treatment often lies in drawing them out from the little world of their personal troubles into an awareness of the "supra-personal connections" behind what they are experiencing—into "a supra-personal consciousness with a sense of historical continuity".

The only healing for them exists in taking them beyond themselves. The only attitude or state of mind that can help them is a truly religious attitude: not religion as dogmas or creeds, but "the religious attitude *per se*". And it's precisely for allowing this religious attitude to emerge "that the sense of historical continuity is indispensable".

This is what the ancient Greeks and Romans meant by the process of being reborn, the mystical process of rebirth out of the personal into the impersonal. Otherwise, everything in an individual's attitude will be "obviously wrong". This is how one single person's seeming neurosis can be undone, because what manifests as private neuroses is for the most part simply a lack of history—the collective neurosis of a culture that abandoned its ancestors and, in the process, forgot itself.

What feels so wrong inside us is what already went wrong in history, and of course the other way around. Our modern-day neuroses aren't just one person's problem, your problem, mine. They are the delayed result, postponed but perfectly inevitable, of what happened to the Gnostics two thousand years ago at the point in time when orthodox Christianity suppressed and crushed their truth: obliterated their wisdom.

And the message from the heart of Jung's psychology is that unless we understand inside ourselves what happened then, we are never going to be free now.

It's exactly the same, again, with Aristotle—and the way he forced the western mind to deviate "from its original basis" by making it leave the psyche, our one true source of direct experience, behind. Only when we start turning back to where we come from, back to what in spite of all our modernities we still are, can any real or lasting healing occur. And that's the labour of repentance for the crimes of the unrepentant; recognition of the ancient in the maintenance of continuity; restoration of the bridge.

This is the reason why Jung's famous biography announces that without history there can be absolutely no psychology. But such a provocative statement is so open to misinterpretation that it can also be helpful to look at some of the much more specific things he said which were never allowed into print.

For instance there is his unpublished, forgotten statement about just how crucially important the ability to read ancient Greek or Latin texts had been to him; and to be able to read them not in translation, but direct in the original language. Without a thorough working knowledge of those languages, he claims, it's impossible to come to any real insight into western culture—or arrive at any authentic understanding of psychology.[87]

One could probably count on the fingers of a single hand the number of Jungian theorists and practitioners who have taken this advice to heart, or would ever be prepared to do so. It's far more profitable to rush off and, while claiming to be working in his name, build even more Faustian bridges across to nowhere.

And that's quite a shame, because then one throws away the chance of discovering what Jung discovered or seeing what he saw.

One of the greatest miracles in existence is the way that, for us as humans to begin with, this material world becomes our only foundation and basis. If we ever have the courage to turn and steal a glance into the world of the unconscious, the only thing we can see is bottomless chaos and an infinitely swirling abyss without any firm basis or foundation at all.

But if we are able to muster the far greater courage needed to throw ourselves into that abyss, after falling and losing sight of anything solid for what feels like an eternity we finally arrive at the reality familiar to alchemists as the "everlasting foundation"—or referred to by Jung as the "indestructible foundation".

Naturally, for the sake of our sanity as human beings, we always keep that longing to have a strong and stable foothold in the physical world. This is simply a symbol, though, of that other foundation; and nothing is ever the same after at last finding the real foothold somewhere else.[88]

That's where we are confronted with the primordial precision, the incalculable fineness of detail and structure, beyond anything imaginable in this ephemeral world of the living. That's the uncanny exactness and compactness of Parmenides' otherworldly logic which he was instructed to bring straight back from the realms of the dead.

And, in the case of Carl Jung, what he was shown was the precisest outlines of a structure spanning two thousand years—the vast structure reaching back from our present day through all the whirling mists and darkness past alchemists, then Gnostics, to the dawn of western culture.

15

Once someone has been taken into another world and given a vision of reality, the whole game of personal existence is over.

There have never been any people who were presented with such visions for themselves. The primordial law states that whatever is provided in the underworld is only given so it can be carried back, unchanged, intact, to the world of the living. That's the sacred contract, signed at the beginning of time, between the living and the dead.

This is why, as Jung duly noted, at a specific point he no longer belonged to himself alone and no longer even had the right to do so. From then on, his life belonged to the living as well as the dead: existed for the "generality", for the sake of the whole.

And Jung himself understood that when you truly no longer live for yourself or belong to yourself then you become, just like Christ, a source of life for others.[89]

Only then, when the personal inside a person gracefully or reluctantly gives way to what lies beyond the personal, is when one starts being able to grasp the true meaning of urgency—the nearly unbearable, burning urgency of eternity pressing onto and right into time.

This was the urgency that, at the start of 1938 in Kolkata, burst through Jung's dream about the Grail and forced him back with a jolt from India to the West: back to its desperate need for the healing vessel or *servator mundi* which is the only thing capable of protecting and saving the western world. "For your state is perilous; you are all in imminent danger of destroying all that centuries have built up."

There is a sad inevitability about the way that, with the particular rigidity and dogmatism only a dutiful disciple can provide, such a momentous statement would end up being embellished with the usual half-truths or half-untruths. As perhaps the most influential Jungian went on to note in commenting on this dream, inside the healing vessel of the Grail lies "the answer to the spiritual problem of our cultural tradition"—which is true enough. But then she has to add that "this secret, however, is contained nowhere save in the symbolism of alchemy" which Jung was focusing most of his conscious attention on at the time.[90]

It can be such an irresistible temptation to divide a person's life into separate phases of work; into new fields of discovery and understanding. We don't even realize that this, too, is the Faustian solution: getting sucked along by the illusions and seductions of progress. In fact the pull is so strong that one can howl and cry and warn but there is nobody, not even those close by who could or should, who will ever notice.

And it's precisely the same in our own lives. Wisdom's beginning is to give up on the endless fuss of looking hopefully into the future for some final solution to our ignorance, some perfect correction to the mess we've made so far.

It starts in the same way it ends—with looking back, exactly as Jung recommended, and into oneself. Instead of stepping forwards we have to walk backwards into the place inside us all where the answers already lie and have always been waiting.[91]

That, in a simple word or two, is the essence of this whole book.

Dreams, especially the big dreams, never tell our lives in a straight line. They dance around, then back on themselves in circles or spirals. And when Jung was reminded inside his Kolkata hotel of the crucial need to find the healing vessel of the Grail he was just being reminded, in the way only dreams can do, of what he already knew.

For a long time before visiting India he had been writing, lecturing, teaching that the symbolism of the Grail reaches back past the medieval alchemists into the Gnostic and Hermetic traditions of antiquity. To be a little more specific: he traced it straight back to the magical symbol of the *kratêr*, an old Greek word for the mysterious mixing-bowl that initiates threw themselves into so they could be baptized into rebirth and immortality and salvation.

As it so happens, almost ten years earlier than that dramatic Kolkata dream he was half-jokingly talking with students about how anyone nowadays wanting to find the *kratêr* of the Gnostics—the healing vessel of rebirth and salvation—shouldn't look for it any more in the ancient alchemical centres of Egypt. Instead it could be found, quite simply, in Zurich.

And to make things even clearer he playfully if unsubtly hinted that not only was this *kratêr* the psychological work he did with his patients, but he himself was the living *kratêr*. He, Carl Jung, was the eternal fountain of youth: the saviour offering humans the *pharmakon athanasias*, "the medicine of immortality which makes the new man".

This was far more than some joke, though. On the contrary, the logic behind it all was impeccable. Just as the only way for a knight to discover the Grail was by becoming it, and just as the only way to serve the *servator mundi* is inwardly to be the saviour and protector of the world, so the one and only way to make the *kratêr* work is by becoming the *kratêr* oneself.

And to get a sense of how profoundly serious this whole matter was for him, nothing can be better than to remember that he envisaged the entire "prehistory of his psychology"—meaning the history of Jungian psychology before any Carl Jung appeared on the scene—as embodied in one single symbol.

Needless to say, that was the symbol of the *kratêr*. So, in just the same way that he came to equate the mystery of the Grail with the secret of individuation and would see it as his central task to recover the abandoned Grail vessel for the sake of the West, he had discovered in the Gnostic vessel of the *kratêr* the primordial symbol of his own psychology.[92]

But strange as it might seem, to be watching Jung trace his psychology back beyond himself, there is one other factor we have to bear in mind.

In his published writings, as well as his lectures, he made sure to track this quintessential symbol of the *kratêr* even further than the Gnostic and Hermetic circles of antiquity. In fact already from the very first time that he ever refers to the *kratêr* of rebirth, he specifically connects it with the name of one particular person: Empedocles.

Since the time when he was still a young student he had never managed to shake off his fascination with the ancient legends about how Empedocles died in Sicily by climbing the crater of Mount Etna—then throwing himself into the volcano so he could become immortal, be reborn as a god. And here, as Jung was quick to recognize with his fine eye for the sense of words, is where the old Greek term *kratêr* no longer just meant some pretty mixing-bowl or carefully fabricated vessel.

Instead, it was the crater of a magnificent volcano seething with lava and water and fire—one of the most terrifying examples on earth of nature's utterly inhuman power to destroy, transform, give birth.

Here, with these legends about Empedocles predating not only medieval alchemy but even Gnosticism by centuries, he realized he had got back as far as it was possible to go to the source and origin of all those traditions about a *kratêr* as well as a Grail: to the earliest prehistory of his own psychology.

As you may have guessed, though, there is much more to the matter than that. For Jung, history was the diametrical opposite of what we've come to think of as history. Actually to go back into the past wasn't a question of wandering off into the blank irrelevance of hundreds or thousands of years—but of returning to the primordial source of one's life, one's inspiration, one's existence.

And from the time of his work on the *Red book* right through to the end of his life he was perfectly clear about the nature, as well as the identity, of his own primordial source. The single point of origin for all his later work and understanding was the experiences he laboured first to endure, then embody, then make sense of, through his *Red book*. But the source of those visionary experiences themselves was the overwhelming outflows of lava he had happened to bump into at the scene of a massive volcanic crater: the crater that gave him access to the underworld.

So, with the ancient Greek philosopher who is known as Empedocles, Jung had arrived at the root of his psychology in every meaningful sense. Historically, he had reached the ultimate source of its lineage and pedigree. And symbolically, energetically, psychologically, he was all the way back again at the primordial origin of its unstoppable vitality: right at the source of its raw, transformative power.[93]

Of course even to think of linking Jung and his psychology to some ancient philosopher is bound, nowadays, to sound like a blatant example of stretching the evidence too far. But, quite to the contrary: it's only by allowing the evidence to speak for itself, without any pulling or stretching or concealing, that we can help what Jung called the real "historical pattern" to emerge.

For him the all-important point of historical reference was the ancient Gnostics. And he was as familiar as anyone, far more familiar than most, with the complex multiplicity of influences that had constantly fed into both Gnostic and Hermetic traditions—from Egypt, Mesopotamia, Judaism, Christianity, Greek religions or philosophies.

As a matter of fact without any appreciation on our part for such complexities, for the so-called syncretism of such different influences, there are details and aspects of Jung's writings we will never be able to understand.[94]

But this makes it even more striking that, when he came to explain how he viewed the phenomenon of Gnosticism, he described it as first and foremost a philosophical tradition firmly planted in the lineage of Greek philosophy. And it's exactly the same story, which ought to be no cause at all for surprise, when he turns to alchemy.

In a letter he once sent to his Jewish friend, Erich Neumann, he stated without any hesitation that not only his own psychology but also western alchemy "is deeply rooted in Europe, in the Christian Middle Ages and ultimately in Greek philosophy". This has disappointed, even angered, some commentators who would much rather that Jung had kept silent about philosophy and said almost anything else instead.

The simple truth is, though, that here we have him being perfectly clear about how he views and experiences his own work—because here, especially in the statement about Greek philosophy, we have "his explicit confession as to his own tradition".

And there is a double logic hidden behind that statement of his.

On the one hand, while well aware of Egyptian and other elements that contributed to alchemical tradition in the West, he had the profoundest respect for the alchemists' own insistence on describing themselves as "philosophers".

Over time he learned to live and breathe with the countless references they make throughout their texts to the philosophers' stone, the philosophers' vessel, the philosophical fire; to the philosophical art and work and task which is the true philosophy, as opposed to the philosophy of Aristotle; to the garden of philosophers with its philosophical tree, the riddles of the philosophers, the ancient gatherings and assemblies of philosophers. He was only too familiar with the fact that Greek, then Arab, then Latin alchemical literature often makes a point of looking back in particular to the great Presocratic philosophers as supreme masters of the art. And he was finely attuned to the exquisite subtleties of a situation where, two thousand years after Parmenides' death, an alchemical writer in Italy could describe how it was Parmenides who had saved him from his errors by guiding him onto the right path—just as there happen to have been Arab alchemists and mystics who gathered together into "Empedocles circles" because they had found in Empedocles a greater authority, a truer source of prophecy and revelation, than even Muhammad himself.[95]

But as usual that's just a part of the story because, on the other hand, there is Carl Jung's own connection to philosophy.

For modern philosophy, which "never says anything of the slightest practical value" with its hollow theorizing and useless jargon, he felt little aside from disappointment or downright contempt. This makes it all the more remarkable, though, that when asked if his psychology was just another religion he would say no: Don't compare my psychology to the established religions with their lumbering pretensions and dogmas and creeds. The truth is that, far from being a missionary or founder of some new religion, "I am speaking just as a philosopher" because we psychologists "are philosophers in the old sense of the word, lovers of wisdom".

And the best way of all to understand this psychology of mine, he would add, is to compare it to ancient philosophy.

Of course that raises an obvious question about what kind of ancient philosophy Jung was referring to. He was hardly thinking of Plato, who to him had always been the classic example of a theorist so full of smart ideas he was never able to apply them in practice. He certainly wasn't thinking of Aristotle, either, who in his mind was more responsible than anyone else for forcing western consciousness to deviate from its natural course.

But as for what existed before this Aristotelian deviation or diversion, the most striking thing is that he goes almost completely silent.[96]

And there is a very good reason for that silence because, in spite of all his intuitions and inner affinities and well-founded suspicions, something far more powerful was governing his understanding of Presocratic philosophy: sheer, unfettered prejudice.

He already lays his cards on the table when he states that, right from its formal start with Pythagoras, western philosophy had never been anything more than the densest kind of intellectualism and rationalism "as moulded by the Greeks". But that's because he is just parroting the bastard wisdom endlessly churned out by the German textbooks of philosophy he had been devouring since he was a child—textbooks which mindlessly projected the rampant rationalism of the eighteenth, nineteenth, twentieth centuries back onto the ancient world.

It's exactly the same when he declares that the Presocratic philosophers were concerned with physical objects, instead of consciousness. And this was especially true of "the nature philosophers like Empedocles" who had the most "marvellous naiveté" with regard to the objects of nature, or nature herself, because at their stage in history they had not yet been graced with the opportunity for self-reflection and inner awareness which would only be made available to humanity through Socrates or Plato.

But that, too, is simply the inflated evolutionary nonsense which would lead the collective western mind into two world wars and which Jung as an intelligent European of his own time was forced to live and breathe.

And it's the same all over again with his almost laughably disjointed description of Empedocles as "one of the very early Greek philosophers and a sort of saviour"—because this is how every single handbook of ancient philosophy would introduce the man, as a hopelessly divided character who tried to live the respectable life of a philosopher and scientist on the one hand while falling into all sorts of religious quackery on the other.

Still, while there is nothing very virtuous in this rehashing by Jung of the wisdom of his time, there is nothing particularly unvirtuous about it either.

After all, it was Jung himself who had the rare humility and deep self-knowledge needed to admit that no one alive is "immune to the spirit of his own epoch"—and that "regardless of our conscious convictions, we are all without exception, in so far as we are particles in the mass, gnawed at and undermined by the spirit that runs through the masses." Or as Empedocles had tried to say almost two and a half thousand years earlier, even those who go out of their way to speak the most uncomfortable truths are forced to accept that mostly they are just going to have to play along with the normal conventions like anyone else.

To be sure, there were times when Jung thoroughly enjoyed performing the role of sophisticated modern scientist: when he absolutely loved spouting the usual clichés about primitiveness and naivety and cultural evolution even though he knew inside himself, far more than any of his proud disciples, just how superficial and deceptive they happen to be.

And this is because he also knew when to leave things well alone. So many signs and pointers were leading him back to the ancient, Presocratic philosophers. But the essential point is that it was never his duty or his job to follow them.

There are some things that one has to be either a total fool or a helpless victim to get involved in. Jung understood the truth of this better than anybody, which is why he put off getting involved in the intricacies of alchemical tradition for as long as he possibly could. And when eventually he realized he was going to have to surrender almost a half of his adult life to unravelling the mysteries surrounding western alchemy, he saw it as his unavoidable curse and damnation.

That was his task: not to make his way back even further, past the Gnostics into the collective darkness surrounding the origins of western civilization, but to make his way forward from them into the modern world.[97]

And this is where my work comes in.

It took the better part of half a lifetime to discover, then document, that the Presocratics weren't the primitive rationalists they have been made out to be by hundreds and thousands of years of accumulated prejudice; to trace out every detail of the paths that led back from the Gnostic or Hermetic circles of Egypt to Empedocles, Parmenides, the Pythagoreans in Sicily as well as southern Italy; to show that western alchemical literature did derive in the most meaningful way from Presocratic tradition and that, when alchemists put what seemed to be sayings of their own into the mouths of their ancestors, they were often preserving genuine elements of Presocratic teaching which the more intellectualizing lineages of Aristotle or Plato had already stripped away; to explain how the stale rubbish we have been fed for centuries about rational Greeks versus prophetic Hebrews and about the cold intellect of Athens versus the passion of Jerusalem was meant to cover over the fact that both Greeks and Jews had their prophetic traditions which were linked to each other even geographically, physically; and that the truest successors of figures like Parmenides or Empedocles weren't later Greek philosophers but the greatest of Gnostic prophets.

Strangely enough, in the process I found myself documenting how the symbolism of the Gnostic or Hermetic *kratêr* does reach back to the volcanic craters of Sicily and Italy. But I was also able to demonstrate that the stories of Empedocles' death weren't about his physical death at all. That was the crudest of misunderstandings.

The legends of him throwing himself into the crater of Mount Etna were, in origin, coded accounts of his ritual descent into the world of the dead. In fact this massive volcano happened to be a major, very ancient centre of prophecy. Temples had been built out of lava on its slopes; families of prophets, referred to as "dream–prophets" because they specialized in the interpretation of people's dreams, were living surrounded by bubbling craters of water and mud right beside the volcano's edge.

And considering Empedocles' famous role as a prophet himself—not to mention the intimate connections between those legends of his leap into Etna and the biblical figure of Elijah in particular—it was more than a little peculiar to find Jung describing in his *Red book* how when he arrived at the bottom of the great crater inside the underworld he happened to be standing right beside "the house of the prophet", the prophet Elijah.

But as for the silliness about Empedocles being one of the earliest Greek philosophers plus "a sort of saviour" on the side: that wasn't the case at all. In fact it would be hard to state the truth of the matter more incorrectly, because Empedocles the philosopher was Empedocles the saviour. His philosophical teaching was his unnoticed work of salvation and his saving work was his philosophy.[98]

The personal dimension, for Empedocles just as much as for Jung, of making a jump into the underworld through a volcano was ruthlessly simple. Ritual or no ritual, it was to risk insanity if not outright death.

First it meant being totally melted down into the most basic elements of what one is; recast and re-fused into one's own primordial origin. Then it's a matter of watching yourself being fused with the primordial, elemental origins of the entire physical world.[99]

That, of course, is the point where you no longer live for yourself because inwardly you no longer are yourself as a person. And the streaming lava, for Empedocles, wasn't just the flow of his own poetry or creativity. It was the molten lava that threw up the shape and form of an entire culture, that erupted into time so it could bring our western civilization into being—because new cultures don't just happen by themselves.

On the contrary, they are born when the right people in the right place at the right moment have the ferocious courage to leave all the dead crustings of civilization behind and leap into the volcano of themselves.

It never quite made sense that Jung would only want to trace the source of his own psychology back to a bunch of solitary alchemists or some ragtag group of Gnostic heretics. But here we have what lies behind them all: the founders of a new civilization, the burning purpose at the heart of our western world.

16

Ever since that blind visit I unwittingly paid to Bollingen over thirty years ago, I have kept seeing the same image of a tunnel being dug through an enormous mountain.

The hole was being bored by two men who started at opposite ends and were going to complete their work by meeting, halfway, in the middle. One of them was Jung; I was the other.

It was only much later that, well into the process of writing this book, I began to discover how important for him the imagery of digging or boring had happened to be.

From the first moment I sat down to write I had the physical, constant, almost eviscerating experience of not simply reaching down into some unconscious depths. Instead I was being forced to describe, then keep reporting, what I found as I quite literally scraped the very bottom of the unconscious.

Nothing could be more deeply, impossibly inhuman; closer at every moment to insanity; nearer to physical death. But it was no surprise eventually to come across Jung's own mention of those who manage to "touch the black bottom of human existence"—while everyone else flits around as flat and tepid phantoms ecstatic at the shallowness of their coastlines, at the tedious mediocrity of their wide and busy roads.

As for that process of cutting and scraping a hole through the mountain of stone: this is where you learn the darker meaning of eternity because it's so infinitely slow.

Of course you could say how absurdly arrogant I'm sounding, to dare set myself on a level with Jung—let alone to talk about helping to complete what he left undone. But that would only show you haven't understood a thing. All the excruciating boring is eventually so painful that there is nothing of a person left.

Then one day one wakes up to discover what it means to be faceless. There are no masks there, no personalities, because if there were you wouldn't survive a minute.

And this is the biggest problem of all with wanting to approach someone like Carl Jung—a problem that usually gets larger the closer you get. It's so tempting to see him as a personality and then like him, hate him, love him; be amazed at his creativity or threatened by it; assiduously ignore him or turn him into the cornerstone, the foundation, of your life.

That's all an illusion and utter self-deception, though, because there is no understanding him without understanding what lies behind him. If Jung had just been a scientist, his life and work would never have become such eternal objects of fascination. If he had simply been a mystic, no one would ever have cared so much.

But his science coupled with his mysticism is what's so irresistible because it pulls us straight back past him, way beyond his personality, to the impersonal reality that lies buried at the roots of our western world and contains the secret of what our culture was meant to be.

This is the reason why his published biography begins with a single statement which has probably been read a million times and, perhaps, been understood once or twice in any blue moon:

"My life is a story of the self-realization of the unconscious."

In other words, there is no Jung. His life wasn't the story of Jung realizing himself. It was a story of the unconscious realizing itself through the passing appearance of a conscious Jung.

And when you come to that point of awareness there is no one there: just a darkly mysterious substance. There is a body and a voice and hands, but only the primordial power of the unconscious emerging through a human form.

Then there is nobody at all—only the carved stone inscriptions once left behind for Parmenides in his old hometown, or the inscriptions carved by Jung as he worked away on his own stone tablets at Bollingen.

That's what happens when you carve yourself into living stone through the words you write, the breaths you take, until the stone is all that's left.[100]

THE
SUNSET
WAY
3

THE SUNSET WAY

1

I have visited Parmenides' hometown of Velia—where the inscriptions carved out of marble for him as well as other prophet–healers were found; where his logic was given to him along with all his science—just once in my life.

It was the spring of 1999 and the archaeologist in charge of the area allowed me to stay at a large house she owned, within walking distance of the site where I could inspect the inscriptions and statues every day. I became friends with a local couple who invited me to dinner one evening.

But a strange, inner prompting told me not to accept: simply to go to bed early instead. And almost as if it had been waiting to see if I would accept its invitation, I was visited by an intensely vivid dream.

I am a small boy but a grown man at the same time. My parents—these were my "real" parents as opposed to my physical parents—own land, beautiful fields, fields of my heart. But one day I arrive home to find that they have given the go-ahead for people to come in and cut most of the trees down; make everything respectable, domestic, lined up in neat rows.

The trees have been cut down here, there, all chopped back. The wildness, the primitive power and magic, are ruined: gone.

I stand there in total shock, alone. My parents aren't home yet. It's as if they have deliberately left, or just pretended to go out, so they won't be there when I come back. The horror has reverberated through the depths of my being.

It's totally gone: that magic, wonder, power, that being which had been mine, which I used to be part of. Now it's just docked, domesticated garden land.

And a man comes up to me in a slighty shabby business raincoat, beige or grey. He starts speaking to me very affably, ever so shrewdly. He says that of course I know what it's all about because I, like he, understand the importance of legal assessment work. I know what's what. I know why such things need to be done for insurance purposes—realistically, and so on, and so on.

And I start to cry. I don't mean cry in the sense of weeping, but cry in the sense of gently howling. I am absolutely inconsolable. Nothing, nobody, could ever console me for what has been done; what has been lost; taken away forever by this so-justified action of my parents.

I am set to leave, go, do anything, go anywhere: God knows what. The pain is through my whole being, is my whole being.

My sister—even though she was older than me in physical reality, we always have been almost as close as twins—comes up to me. She tries to reason with me; says it's really not that bad; that I'm exaggerating; mustn't make a fuss; shouldn't be so upset. And to her horror I start to howl out loud.

I howl with primordial pain, grief, rage: the howl of the trees that don't live any more, have been killed. It's the howling of wild nature.

But suddenly, or rather gradually, my sister hears the howl; acknowledges it, responds to it. To everyone's civilized horror we howl together. She has heard the call of the trees, the wildness of nature, in and through me. And she has answered.

We realize we could possibly be locked away as insane. But we don't care, don't consider. We ourselves are that wildness at last, again—beyond reason or reasoning, argument or justification, fear or respectability and social or family ties.

They were my beloved trees; my heart. And the lawyer, the assessment man in his shabby coat, had tried to say: "Well, to tell you the truth, I think it's been done very well and looks rather good."

As a dream, it shook me to the core. Of course it was telling me some intensely personal things about myself. But even before I had fully awoken I knew that the ancient spirit of this place—Parmenides' place—was speaking through it and saying much, much more.

On the most obvious level it was simply about the agonizing pain of growing up; about the loss of innocence, of oneness with nature and beauty. Soon we are doing just the same as everybody else: gritting our teeth and getting over it, moving on, learning how to look fondly at all the concrete blocks around us so we can develop an admiring eye for their wonderful storage capacities and insulation.

Then, before we know what's happened, we are no longer listening to the lawyer's voice speaking with its constant drone of authority everywhere in the society that surrounds us.

We are the lawyer ourselves, because this is what our mind has become. And wherever we look, even inside our most private self, even at spirituality or what feels most sacred, we are quietly assessing everything with the cold calculating eyes of a lawyer in his shabby raincoat: weighing each detail up, converting whatever we once hoped might bring us back to life into another shrewd trick for escaping it.

Way beyond even that and behind it all, though, the wild spirit of Velia was blowing through the dream—the prophetic spirit of our ancestors, the breath of a reality far wiser and more evolved than the supposedly sensible world we stroll around in as would-be adults.

That reality, forgotten now because it was so neatly chopped down and nicely rationalized long ago, had been and still is a world of laws: true laws, the kind of laws genuinely worthy of a human being. In fact before leaving Velia I was shown those laws one after another, each of them inscribed on its own block of marble, during the course of a dream that lasted the whole night and still continued after I woke up.

But there couldn't possibly be any greater distance or difference between those timeless laws and the sliding, makeshift legalities of our shabby lawyers. And gradually I came to realize that this was the real message of the dream.

In our society we tend just to see what seems in front of us, no more, because we have been trained to accept it all without question. What we don't understand, though, or even feel any need to understand is where everything comes from.

Nothing simply appears out of nowhere; and the lawyer in my dream didn't spring out of nowhere, either. He is nothing but the inescapable consequence of killing off our sacred laws—of carefully interfering with the gifts which had been brought back from another world.

And this applies to all those things we find ourselves surrounded by, whether we think we want them or not. They are just the end product of nature being cut off and destroyed; of a primordial energy being twisted, forcibly diverted from its original course; of manipulating the sacred.

We honestly tend to believe nowadays that we can choose to leave the sacred behind, forget about it and get on with living our modern lives. What we have forgotten, though, is that when the sacred is no longer honoured or valued it doesn't go away. It doesn't vanish into some vacuum, some void.[1]

The ancient blessings don't just disappear. Instead, the law is for them to turn straight into a curse that chases and hounds us. And perhaps I should give another example of how this works.

Different religions have all sorts of ideas and beliefs about the nature of God. But none of those dogmas or doctrines will ever do anything to change the simplest and most intimately human experience of encountering face to face—inside a doorway, a kitchen, out in the garden—the crushing reality that you realize can kill you in an instant. And, once you have glimpsed this, it will never leave you the same again.

I am referring to the reality of God as omniscient and omnipresent and omnipotent: as knowing everything because of being everywhere and the power behind the whole of existence.

Traditionally there have always been the people who are strong enough to endure such an experience and—most often as prophets—play the role of intermediaries between the human and the divine. But this raises a very obvious question.

That's the question of what happens when those people fade out of the picture because we no longer care as a culture for any contact with the overwhelming reality of the sacred and because, instead, we suppose we can maintain the laughable illusion of ourselves being the ones in control.

The answer is that when we no longer respect or acknowledge the living qualities of divine consciousness and presence and power, they find themselves forced to adapt to our parody of a reality.

And they do so by adjusting their shape and form to become the nightmare of a big-brother surveillance state which is blatantly omniscient and omnipresent and omnipotent—and will be living up to its divine attributes with even greater faithfulness and accuracy during the years to come, all because we thought we could abandon the sacred.

Naturally this is no laughing matter. As they say, it's not some ordinary walk in the park. It's a matter of neglecting and misusing divine energy, the most powerful energy there is; and that never ends well.

Divine laws get twisted into human laws which end up becoming absurdly inhuman. Divine attributes are distorted into mechanisms of human control that become even more inhuman. And it's no coincidence that the most fanatical extremes of legalism, with someone new rushing to sue someone else roughly every second, as well as the most fantastic ingenuity in pushing towards a technological ideal of total global surveillance both have their home in modern America.

On the contrary: these straightforward facts spell out the secret of America in its simplest possible form.

As a nation it always thought it could claim for itself the mantle, the mystique, of exceptionalism; of being totally unique and different from any other nation on earth. But the United States of America is not exceptional at all, except in one sense— that it's the perfectly inevitable and unavoidable culmination of the course western culture has been on for thousands of years.

Its dreams, its ideals, even its proudest ambitions, are not its own. America's famous manifest destiny is nothing but the end result of the West throwing out what could have been its true destiny.

And as for the steady, unconscious descent into technological hell: this is exactly what happens when a society forgets that even its science has a sacred source deep inside the underworld.

It's only logical.

2

It's interesting to watch Jung's initial impressions of the United States at the time of his very first visit.

The year was 1909 and he was being welcomed as an international celebrity—encountering even more interest in his work than Freud who had come with him. But when he wrote back to his wife Emma about this "wonderland" he had found himself plunged into, he made a comment of such oracular simplicity that hardly anyone seems to have paid much attention to it:

"As far as technological culture is concerned, we lag miles behind America. But all that is frightfully costly and already carries the germ of the end in itself."[2]

The prophetic tone of this comment is, just as much as the surgical precision of the warning, unmistakable. It's a world apart, though, from the extravagant prophecies about America's uniquely privileged future that were circulating during, as well as before and after, his lifetime. American occultists pulled back any veil covering the true nature of their country's celebrated exceptionalism when, sometimes with the blessing of presidential approval, they revealed how the United States was at last destined to fulfil the ambitious Platonic and Aristotelian dream of seeing an empire ruled by advanced philosopher–kings.

Even the ancient Egyptian priests, people were asked to believe, had already been longing to create this philosophical empire in America. The famous golden fleece, searched for by ancient Greek heroes somewhere in the ocean to the west, was really the American Declaration of Independence. And here was the perfect soil for producing the next stage in human evolution: "here was a virgin continent populated only by nomadic Indian tribes, a vast territory suitable in every way for the great human experiment" which simply involves following the "Universal plan" for humanity "until the Platonic empire is established on the earth, and the towers of the new Atlantis rise from the ruins of a materialistic and selfish world."[3]

Most foreign spiritual teachers who came visiting from Asia were understandably stunned by the grandness and beauty, the rawness and undeveloped potency of the land.

America was a wonderfully inviting place to create new centres for their work, and it was easy to become almost intoxicated by the country's apparently endless possibilities.[4]

But Jung, to his credit, managed to keep his feet firmly planted on the ground and never forget the realities of human psychology. On a return visit in 1912 he gave an interview to the *New York Times* which was published under the title: "America facing its most tragic moment". In it he warns, as directly and urgently as possible, about the tremendous danger threatening Americans—not from outside themselves but from the darkly unconscious forces inside them that they are unwilling or just unable to face.

He doesn't only point to the qualities of murderous savagery and cruelty that allowed them to conquer a whole continent with such sophisticated efficiency. Above all he points to the expansive ruthlessness of their reasoning; to the extreme brutality of their coldly abstract logic. He explains as a physician that, although he would be glad to help in the painful process of becoming conscious, there's very little he can do without the full cooperation of the patient.

And this is where the real problem lies. "America does not see that it is in any danger. It does not understand that it is facing its most tragic moment: a moment in which it must make a choice to master its machines or to be devoured by them—and since it does not know this I would not want to hurt it."[5]

Perhaps, because Jung is trying so hard to be tactful as well as truthful, I should emphasize the obvious here. What he found himself warning about was the immediately looming danger of Americans being taken over and destroyed by their machines, their technology, their gadgets—over a hundred years ago. But even more important is his ominous addition: because the consciousness of Americans "does not know this I would not want to hurt it".

Everything, here, has to be read with the greatest scrutiny and care. Jung is very plainly calling attention to a present danger while hinting, just as plainly, that the American psyche not only doesn't know. It doesn't want to know. It doesn't want to wake up; doesn't actually want, in spite of the eager words about transformation, to be transformed.

And there is not the slightest good reason why it should. Jung never had any real passion for urging Americans to set off on some grand heroic search so they could discover their higher selves and wake up to their spiritual destiny—which of course is what most Americans who aren't ruthlessly pursuing material success are already doing in their brutal quest for self-improvement and self-discovery.

Instead, they have to discover what they least want to face or confront: the ruthlessness of their mechanical thinking and rationality. Of course it's much easier to export that brutality, or hide it behind a hundred shades of lipstick. But to come face to face with it, directly, is something almost no one is willing to do.

Far more attractive is to go on believing what Jung himself refused to believe; to hope optimistically, confidently, desperately that if enough people can come together and wake up then all of us will enter a new age. And the entire world will be transformed.

It's so much simpler not to notice how every collective movement towards raising the awareness of humanity gobbles up what tiny remnant of consciousness people still have only to throw them even deeper into unconsciousness—or how overwhelmingly tempting it can be, in the intensity of one's enthusiasm, to snatch at the fragments of wisdom intended to offer access to a reality beyond the ego and use them to strengthen the ego instead.[6]

None of this offers any form of a solution. There is no graceful or painless exit into some glamorous new age, even newer than all the other new things Americans already are used to, out of the tragic situation in which America finds itself. And it should be no surprise at all that, when towards the end of his life Jung listed the things he was most afraid of, he chose to mention the ones he did.

He was not just afraid of unconsciousness in general. He wasn't only afraid of modern science. In spite of his very genuine fondness for Americans with their remarkable openness and intuitiveness, for American cars, for American slang, he was afraid above all of America.

Communism, for him, wasn't anywhere close to being such a threat. Even in a flattening, repressive regime at least a real individuality can survive somewhere underneath the surface. But in a society where every American is mass-educated to turn into an individual, when each single girl and boy is collectively injected with the skills of self-empowerment, then—in spite of all the song and dance, all the countless choices and therapies, all the magnificent illusions—deep down inside there is going to be a deadly emptiness.[7]

And then there is the danger of one day having to confront, behind its mask of individualism, the real face of collective

America: an America that crushes human beings underfoot like specks of dirt unless they agree, each single one of them, to pledge themselves to the machine.

It was a little over ten years after his 1912 interview with the *New York Times* that, again, Jung found himself speaking in America about America.

This time it was in private, to a special group of people he felt he could trust. And he was talking about the ruthlessness of the American psyche—as well as about Americans' disrespect, their total disregard, for the "ancestors".

To him the two went hand in hand. On one hand ruthlessness is the inhumanly mechanical, unconscious attitude that stands in the way of any real access to the ancestors. On the other, once we are cut off from our ancestors we are also brutally cut off from ourselves.

There was nothing he considered more important. The ancestors, the dead, are the only true source of life in our world of the living. But this fragile world of ours is linked by such an infinitely slender thread with the reality beyond our reality that to block off the realm of ancestors by refusing to value or acknowledge or respect it, as the modern psyche with its ruthless rationality tries to do, is the perfect recipe for disaster.

Of course to most people writing nowadays about Jung, in fact even most Jungians, this is little more than words. And that helps to explain why no one has noted how deeply he was influenced, in the things he said about ruthlessness as well as the ancestors on this particular occasion, by Mountain Lake—the elder he had just met in the New Mexico desert during his first conversation ever with Native Americans.[8]

To be sure, on one level Mountain Lake was only confirming and reinforcing the conclusions Carl Jung had already arrived at by himself. At the same time Jung was doing quite a bit more, at this small New York gathering, than talking theoretically about Americans or the unsolved problem of the ancestors still present in their land: much more.

To anyone attending the meeting it might have sounded as if he was leading a rather interesting discussion on some somewhat delicate subjects. But the fact is that Jung himself, along with one friend in the audience who just so happened to be the woman responsible for introducing him to Mountain Lake a few days earlier, had an entirely different experience of what was taking place.

To him, far from being a simple seminar or lecture, what happened was something quite extraordinary. It was as if he had literally been caught up in performing "a ceremonial for the Dead". And even more striking is his awareness that, in spite of such a carefully controlled environment with its hand-picked participants, the after-effects of this ceremony were on the edge of becoming explosive and evoking what would have been dangerously negative reactions.

Obviously one could skate around on the surface just like anybody else; but there were unforeseeable risks involved, even among friends, in engaging on a serious level with the American psyche.[9]

In public, needless to say, it was an altogether different matter.

Jung always had at least one eye closely watching the workings of the unconscious, inside himself but also in others, and went out of his way to pay attention to its particular wishes or needs. He was respectfully aware of how distant as well as tenuous the connection tends to be between the egos of Americans and their unconscious shadows, and felt more than a little wary of treading "on the tiger's tail that is the American unconscious". To him it was a part of his duty as a physician only to say what was strictly appropriate or needed on any occasion; and, as a human being, there might be times when he preferred being just a little economical with the truth.[10]

In what's perhaps the most entertaining as well as famous presentation of American psychology that he ever offered an American audience, Jung brought his colourful repertoire of comments and anecdotes to a close by homing in on what he described as the collective attitude of America.

And he defined this central characteristic, very simply, as the "heroic ideal"—the delightfully refreshing can-do mentality already drummed into Americans as children that pushes them on until they drop and tells them everybody has the makings of a hero, the sky is the limit, there is nothing I can't achieve once I set my mind on it.[11]

This all sounds absolutely wonderful, provided nobody ever pauses to wonder what such a "heroic ideal" might mean in terms of Jung's psychology as a whole.

But the moment one does ask that question, things rather rapidly fall into place.

For Jung, when a whole country identifies collectively with the kind of heroic ideal that sets no limit on what its people are able to achieve—that not only allows but encourages them "heroically to impose their will, have their own way" and cry out loudly "Where there is a will there is a way!"—everything might look fine for a while on the outside. But inwardly such a country is already in the grip of the same psychological disease, referred to by Jung as the sickness of god-almightiness, that dragged Germany into the First World War before plunging it straight into the ultimate chaos of Fascism and the Nazis.[12]

This is only on the collective level, though. And of course for Jung everything always has to come back to the individual, which explains why he put so much intensity into describing the sphinx's riddle he encountered on his own path into the depths of himself.

It was a riddle so essential for him as a human to solve, so crucial, that he realized there could be no dodging or escaping it. He was faced with the simplest possible choice. Either he would have to find the answer, whatever it cost him, or he would have to kill himself.

And he came to understand that the unbearable question confronting him was the riddle of why he had to kill his own heroic ideal—why in spite of his overwhelming grief and remorse he was being forced to destroy all those personal qualities he had learned to value most, everything he considered noble and was most attached to, his dominant sense of efficiency and power and force but above all the power of his own intellect.

There was no way around it. There is no short cut. All these conscious or unconscious attitudes have to be destroyed and left behind on the path out of unconsciousness into a real consciousness, because even what we proudly think of as our consciousness is only an obstacle. Ideals are the ultimate temptation; and to think I can do what I want is the greatest delusion.

"My heroic idealism had to be abandoned, for there are higher things than the ego's will, and to these one must bow."[13]

Here we end up at the heart of Jung's hard-earned understanding about what really is involved in coming face to face with the truth of oneself as a human. And to anyone reading what he says about having to abandon one's heroic idealism at all costs, it would be easy enough to suppose this is no more than Jung at his finest—as well as his most eccentric. This is simply Jung, the questionable psychologist, veering off into the mystical by discussing his own private experience in the vainest of hopes it might have some greater application.

Then one would have to think a little deeper.

What Jung is trying to convey here might sound strange, rather extreme, certainly quite optional in our modern world—

especially in the world of modern spirituality with its countless choices and heroic possibilities. But that only goes to show, once again, how far we have drifted away from any trace of collective sanity in the West.

Jung in his struggles, his apparently solitary realizations, is not at all alone; far from it. We still have fragments of ancient texts recording the voices of Babylonian wisdom which, thousands of years ago, were saying much the same thing that ancient Greek prophetic tradition would still be saying centuries later.

If somebody says "I am a hero"
That person will end up humiliated.
If someone claims "I can do it!"
Then that person will end up a nobody.[14]

There is nothing exceptional about this in the least: nothing mysterious or unusual, certainly nothing to feel surprised or troubled or defensive about.

On the contrary, this is the most basic reality of human psychology. There are no exceptions at all because the laws—not the ones made by humans but the laws that make humans—are quite clear.

There never are.

And this is simply the voice of wisdom calling out from the dawn, the roots, the source, of our western civilization to that civilization's ultimate manifestation.

3

The wonder is how everything, absolutely everything, anyone can name that makes our so-called civilization unique has a sacred source—a sacred purpose.

The awareness of that sacred purpose, just the simplest act of awareness, is what shapes our culture's sacred geography: is what creates its sacred landscape. And as we lose any sense of that inner landscape inside ourselves we lose, automatically, a sense of the sacredness all around us.

When we watch the trees inside us being chopped back and down, let the sacred source of our western world be cut off for any number of extremely sensible reasons, here is where we end up. There is a hidden reality we all share—in which every slightest thing has its proper place, its beauty, function, integrity.

It's the landscape of our own true nature that contains the most detailed instructions and guidance for just what's needed. And the loss of that sacred landscape, which once had been our culture's life force, is the initial ecological disaster from which every other environmental catastrophe outside us follows inevitably: as a matter of course.

Now there are all sorts of opportunities for positioning oneself as pro-progress or anti-progress, pro-technology or anti-science. But these imaginary choices are total nonsense. It's utter futility to be for technology or against it without glimpsing, knowing, understanding what western science was from the very beginning—a gift offered by the gods with a sacred purpose.

Once science has forgotten that purpose, everything is already lost. And this isn't a modern problem at all. Plato as well as Aristotle were already blazing a trail in genetically modifying the seeds of our western culture, stripping them of their natural power, thousands of years ago: squeezing themselves into the picture and taking credit where none was due.

That sacred potency refuses to go away, though. It never disappears. If only it had, things might not have turned out quite so bad—because it stays but changes shape, becomes the power that haunts us by feeding on the chaos, slowly but ever so steadily destroys our world along with us.

There is no expert or specialist left who holds the key to western science, or to logic, or to the human mind; let alone to our humble senses. And it's so difficult now to say a word about this, because even the sense of how to listen has been lost.

To be sure, we may think we are willing to listen. But as for the genuine willingness to change, rather than just going through the inescapable motions of change, there is far too much already at stake.

We have all gone a long way down this road—have forgotten what it means to want something truly essential for ourselves. It's so much simpler to go on listening to the lawyers outside and inside us, believing in the reasonableness of existence, compromising here and then there and then back here.

And rather than starting to take real responsibility for ourselves, it's far easier picking up the crumbs from under the tables of other cultures: doing a touch of shamanism or Hinduism, a little Zen meditation, a tasty bit of Tibetan Buddhism or an exciting mixture of them all, going away on some vacation before coming back again to the brutality of our western society with its normality and triviality as well as the hollow emptiness of its surveillance.

Honestly to want to face, then keep facing, the darkness of our western culture—where we are, are heading, have come from—one would have to be mad.

The funny thing is that here I am, waving my hands; making a fuss about the origins and dawn of our western culture, sharing this guarded secret hidden by the West from the West that the West has a sacred source. It can all sound so extraordinary, so strange.

But what I am saying is the last thing anybody could actually call extraordinary—because nowhere on this planet are you going to find one single traditional culture that doesn't remember, down to the finest detail, having its sacred purpose and source.

Without even realizing it, we are completely on our own. It was we ourselves who manufactured this peculiar myth called progress, where things are meant to get better. Of course there is no reason at all for bothering about origins when we are supposed to be managing so much more effectively, more efficiently, every day. From the first moment a baby becomes able to gurgle, this is what's trumpeted in its ears; and the trouble is that, with our imaginary sense of superiority inside our adult bodies, we never grew beyond the stage of being those little babies.

Leaving aside the influence of western civilization, nothing could be more intuitive—the most natural thing in the world—than for any culture or tribe that still survives to remember and celebrate its sacred origin. One only has to think of the beautiful saying by Rumi, most famous of Persian Sufis:

Look into the source of every skill or invention and
There you'll find that its root and origin was revelation.
Humans learned them all, each single one, from the prophets.

It sounds so nice, so pretty. Not quite so nice, though, is the realization that this applies not only to everyone else: not just to people living in some foreign, exotic country.

It also applies to us westerners because, as inheritors from the ancient Greeks, we too have our own prophets who were closely connected in their time to the prophets of Israel and the Middle East.[15]

But to let that fact sink in would really never do, because then we would have to start taking complete responsibility for the secret at the root of our own culture rather than picking away whenever we feel like it at other cultures' fruits.

This is why there can be such an excruciating suffering simply in the act of discovering that western civilization, just like any other, came into being out of prophecy; from revelation. It's why there is such a crushing weight of aloneness in holding such a secret, because the price of taking it seriously has become so great.

Mostly, the best one can do is watch as the prophecies that gave life to other cultures are puffed up into pretty stories while the prophets who gave their lives for ours go on being taunted and ignored. Historians love nothing more than to jeer at those ancient western prophets, laugh at the extravagant fools they made of themselves, poke fun at Parmenides and Empedocles for their grandiose revelations—for "condescending to lighten the darkness in which, as they thought, the rest of mankind was stumbling".

The fact that these prophetic figures had the apparent arrogance to question our own unquestionable arrogance, that they dared to challenge the integrity of our collective wisdom by claiming we are all asleep and even our fantasies of waking up are just another form of sleep, offers every possible justification for dismissing them as absurdly irrelevant or downright mad while tucking their teachings away inside some drawer.[16]

And so we manage to forget that traditionally prophets didn't only come with their pressing messages, their edifying recommendations—which of course everyone is at liberty either to accept or rather reject.

They also came to cry.

Beyond their attempts to communicate in ways our intelligent minds can at least pretend to make some sense of, they also came to convey the rawest pain of humans' separateness from the sacred. And they cried at people's blank refusal in spite of their solemn pretence, all their vacant piety, to understand—because, ironically, the anguish in the cry is justified by the response the cry evokes.

But, curiously, Carl Jung didn't forget. On the contrary: he knew that cry only too well. It was what kept pushing him on against the odds, regardless of all the opposition and misunderstanding.

He was familiar with it through the teachings of the notorious Gnostic prophet and saviour, Mani, whose final shriek or cry will announce the ending of the whole world. Above all, though, he knew it as the famous "cry of Merlin".

This is the cry not just of Merlin the magician but of Merlin the great prophet who, Jung came to realize, contains inside himself the essential secret and central significance of the Grail; who ends up, in spite of all his magic, being inwardly forced to give up on people because their stupidity causes him so much suffering they make him mad; the same Merlin who finally withdraws from the world into the silence of the forest and, a bird himself, can only be heard through his cry which is no different from the crying of the birds.

And during his last years Jung had the shock of his life when he suddenly realized that, through withdrawing more and more into his tower by the lake at Bollingen, he had been living the legend of Merlin down even to the smallest details.

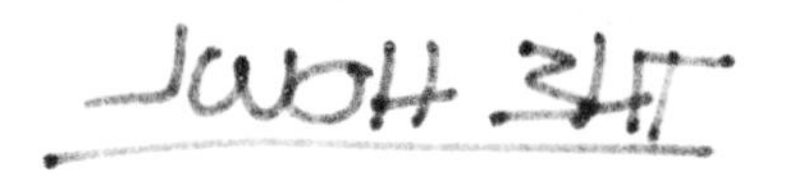

He was Merlin. The whole of his work, everything he ever published, was that ancient prophetic cry. And, exactly like Merlin, he was doomed never to be understood by humans.[17]

After all, if humans don't know how to decipher the crying of the birds it's not very likely they will be able to understand the cries of Carl Jung.

THE HOWL

4

There is something about the dream I had at Velia that took me a long time to start to understand.

It had to do with the howl that came out of me, louder and then louder, before spreading to my sister.

I am not saying I didn't intuit immediately in the rawness of my own direct experience what this is—because even while I was still asleep I did. It's the shrieking of animals, the wailing and crying of birds, shockingly articulated through a human. It's the sound of the sacred shouting to itself; the voice of life welling up inside us that denies the rightness of everything wrong outside us.

It's the only response strong enough, primordial enough, to take a stand when even our most meditative versions of tranquillity have become nothing but the subtlest forms of complicity.

It's the roaring stream of endless emotion flowing below all our reasonableness and respectableness—way underneath our tidy and nicely domesticated spiritual paths—that we have no end of trouble reconciling ourselves with, that we don't even have the agility to let ourselves hear. It's the unbearable awareness that none of our clever strategies is ever going to work because they only make things worse, carefully layering more levels of illusion on top of every other illusion.

It's the call bursting out from one's depths that has no self-conscious purpose; no stated or unstated motive; no wise wish or hope to change, improve, bring about some better understanding. And it's not just the pain at the loss of our inner nature, or the grief at remembering what we've lost.

It's also what makes that nature alive again.

It's what Jung so perfectly described as nature's outrage against all the ruthless artificialities and sophisticated rationalities trying to crush her. And in terms of our own western culture nothing could possibly be less reasonable. Nothing could be less justifiable or acceptable, less appropriate or tolerable.

On the contrary, to howl is utter madness because it's the one and only thing that cuts straight through our shabby little fittingnesses until there is nothing left that fits.

But what took me so long to realize was that—although it can feel the loneliest thing on earth to do—in being shown how to howl on that cold night at Velia I couldn't have been further from alone. Instead, I had just been introduced to the reality of the prophets.

We do a fine job, the most splendid one imaginable, of forgetting. It wasn't at all easy to erase the awkward truth that Hebrew prophets were constantly howling and, what's even worse, had come to instruct others in how to howl. Greek prophets, too, like Empedocles: they howled, they wailed. The cities of Mesopotamia which kept such close ties to Hebrew traditions and the Hebrew language had their own name for one particular kind of prophet. It meant "wailer" or "howler".

And when ancient Greeks came into contact, as they most definitely did, with shamans bringing their wisdom and power from Central Asia they used just a single word to describe them.

They called them *goês*, which means the "howler".

Shamans and healers and prophets, Hebrew prophets, Greek prophets, Babylonian prophets: they all used to be howlers. Often "howler" was the only title or name they were known by. And they happen to have far more in common than meets the eye.

Whatever the occasion, regardless of the reason why they seemed to be howling, they were howling for the sake of the dead. They howled over the death of individuals, of a people; of a culture, of humanity. They would howl for all those who imagine they are still alive—but are already dead too.[18]

Prophets are never just talking to someone over there, or me, or you. They are prophets because they howl to the whole world. Even if the words they're made to speak are for one audience only, their howling has no limits. It's heard by people; it's heard by nature. It wakes the living. It stirs the dead.

This is all a little bit too big for most of us, though. So we cut out the howl and ignore it; turn prophets into preachers and reformers and the kind of petty moralizers we can so easily relate to; reshape them in our image, bend their figure to our will, reinvent them as nothing but reflections of our own egoic ambitions.

And of course we love to suppose that the one and only thing they are concerned about is reaching us—although we'll make sure to move heaven and earth to prevent them coming anywhere near us.

It can sound grating but ever so amusing when our politicians and forecasters and gurus set themselves up as prophets, pose as prophets, do business as prophets; and we wrongly assume this is what prophets always used to do. We can't even grasp the simple fact that whatever egos those people once had were ground into the earth. Real prophets are never proud of being prophets because they are too busy being bent over sideways by the weight of our unconsciousness together with the overwhelming vision of our past, where we are headed, what we've become.

Most of them, and not just Jonah, would beg to be freed from the need to say or do anything. They fight their role as much as they can. They would run from it if they could.[19]

It may seem strange, very strange, that to return to the beginnings of western philosophy could bring us not to the beauties and clarities of abstract thinking. It brings us to this: to the sheer horror of what we have forgotten and collectively agree to go on forgetting for the common good.

And underneath all the new–age platitudes being politely piled nowadays a mile high above the centuries of Christian platitudes, the pulsing heart of religion is what it always has been—the howl. Don't think you will ever arrive at any real stillness except through the howl; and don't imagine there is any hearing the howling of the cosmos without sinking into the deepest possible stillness.

The prophets howl to knock down the cardboard of our reasoning, howl at the damage we can't help inflicting on ourselves and the world around us, howl to give a voice to the sadnesses and depressions of a whole culture that everyone else has been left either to suffer or exploit in silence.

They howl at the eternal inconsolableness buried under all the brutal consolations offered by religion, philosophy, spirituality. They howl at the pointlessness of waking people up just so they can watch them fall straight asleep again, howl at the utter futility of even hoping to make anyone understand.

And they howl, not because nobody understands but because no one can tolerate their howl.

After all: there is not the slightest reason why anyone in her or his right mind would want to hear it, let alone listen to what lies behind it, because the sound of that cry turns one's whole life upside down.[20]

This explains why, over the centuries, it came to be agreed that the most sensible thing possible is not just to silence the howl. A much more effective solution, not to mention far more economical, is simply to get rid of prophecy instead.

And so the history of the West, along with the Middle East, turned into a tedious story of drowning prophecy in mockery and streams of meaningless words. It was systematically silenced in Greece; neatly finished off in Judaism, too; banished as much as possible from Christianity; and removed, most elegantly of all, from Islam thanks to the dogma of Muhammad as the final prophet.[21]

There is always the little trick, though, that those who think they have everything under control try to pretend they can forget.

We may be ruthless enough to destroy ourselves, but we just don't have the ability to cut off the root of prophecy. And the moment people finally fancy they got rid of it, that's when they are likely to discover it hadn't disappeared at all.

It was simply driven underground. In other words it went where it belonged, went where reason so desperately wants and needs it to stay: hopefully safe and sealed off in the mental asylum.

This is how the lineage of ancient prophets ended up passing, as it were, through Allen Ginsberg in the 1950s. He started working at his poem called "Howl" during 1954. Its very first line announces that it will be all about madness—and eventually leads through to the final chorus "I'm with you in Rockland", roaring with Ginsberg's undying sympathy and empathy for the mental patients at the notorious Rockland State Hospital near New York.

So we have a specific year: 1954. We have a particular place: Rockland State Hospital. And very soon we'll see how uncanny these stories of madness can really be with their sweet irony; with their strange exactness of detail that somehow no amount of reasoning can ever match.

Ginsberg, himself, was no stranger to mental hospitals. He would later describe how the howling enshrined in his title was inspired by the poetic, ecstatic cries he heard inside an asylum. But, for him, that's not where the real madness lies.

Seen through his eyes the entire world has gone mad. The whole of western culture is insane, which is exactly why it needs to lock up the only ones who are sane: who have managed to glimpse what we really are, where we have come from, where we are going.

And to him that madness was, above all, the mechanical insanity of America. It was the sanctified monstrosity of robotic efficiency methodically exuded from Reason—the same machine-like reasoning that makes even the gentlest, most sensitive people crazy. But of course it's never easy for anyone, whether Ginsberg or Jung, to say such things; and it's no big surprise that he faced quite some challenges in saying them.[22]

Through his own lengthy process of trial and error Ginsberg would eventually find there was only one way for him to portray this collective insanity, convey it in a medium that would keep its terrifying actuality alive. That wasn't through ordinary poems but through poetry envisioned, very consciously, as a work of magic: as a deliberate act of healing, a science of incantation and repetition based on the pattern and rhythm of breathing.

In other words he spontaneously, naturally, found his way back to the poetry of the old Greek prophet–healers who once helped to give birth to our western world.[23]

But that's not to say he didn't have his own very particular sources of inspiration.

Night and day he immersed himself in the world of the Old Testament prophets. As well as hearing the howling with his own ears inside the madhouse, he saw it preserved in writing across the centuries by Hebrew prophets. He found the beat and metre he used, his incantatory and hypnotic style, already present in the rhythmic language of Hebrew prophecy.

Even inside a federal court of law he was presented, and defended, as a Hebrew prophet. He cried and howled over the fate of everyone around him like the Hebrew prophets. He, too, had overpowering visions that forced him to talk about the past and present realities people in their "drear consciousness" are chronically incapable of seeing—not to mention about America's demise.

Just like the Hebrew prophets he understood that there is no escaping into God to get away from all the destruction here, because God *is* the destruction.

And like them he appreciated that having to play the role of a prophet isn't some egoic satisfaction or glorious honour. On the contrary, it's a "terrible fucking situation to be confronted with".[24]

But even prophecy has its tender compensations. And in the outer world Allen Ginsberg became aware of one reality that, through its infinite delicateness, brings with it "the prophetic image beyond our present strength of flesh to bear".

This is the reality of birds—above all when they fly down. That's when they have the power to transfigure time, almost destroy it, as suddenly they embody the simple presence of the prophetic word.

Whether we notice them or not, they are always here; now. They are never gone for long while we are alive.

And they will be there at our graves to swoop and cry and mourn for us—shrieking and calling and remembering God's name, the God we kept forgetting to care about, when we are gone.[25]

5

One of the finest prophetic howls dates back a long time: close to three thousand years.

The Hebrew prophet Micah perfectly manages to sum up the prophet's role by bringing everything back to its barest basics.

I will wail and howl.
I will go stripped and naked.
I will howl like a jackal and wail like an owl.

And there is something here in the comparison with owls and jackals that—thanks to the miracle of erudition—every biblical scholar and translator and commentator manages to slide over because it's so downright simple, so totally irreducible to anything else.[26]

In wailing like an owl and howling like a jackal, the prophet is crying with the voice of nature. Or to say it another way: a prophet is the purest, rawest nature talking and calling as a human.

That's likely to sound, to us sophisticated westerners, the ultimate in absurdity. We mostly tend to think of prophets as pitiful, almost ridiculous figures—utterly unnatural, otherworldly, twisted, crabbed. But this is just the result of all our unnatural, otherworldly, crabby, twisted conditioning reversing the truth completely and blinding us to what each of us needs to see.

From beginning to end, prophecy is simply about what's natural. As a matter of fact nothing in our human experience could be more natural because the reality of prophecy is all about the nature, inner and outer, we left behind.

And the one thing we somehow manage to miss is that, above everything else, it's about life.

As a culture we are collectively quite happy pretending to show a bit of respect for prophecy while continuing to mock it and prostitute it, attack it, commodify it. But that's exactly what we do to nature. And we do it because we forgot, long ago, that prophets are the guardians of creation.

They are the preservers and protectors of life.

This is why it's always prophets who, in sacred traditions, know the language of the birds. And they don't just understand it. They know, the same as shamans, how to speak it—how to talk and call and cry along with the birds.

Inside their prophetic bones they carry the memory of older days when birds and animals and humans all spoke the same language; when humans could turn into birds and birds would change into humans.

But they don't only remember those days. They bring them back to life again.

These were the most ancient forms of prophecy in the West: watching the swooping of birds, constantly listening to their sounds, paying attention to the meaning of the breeze stirring the leaves in the trees.

Everything works perfectly together. Hearing what the birds say leads, automatically, into deciphering the message of the breeze. And it's the same story in Jewish tradition, as well as Islam. When the prophet Solomon became king he was able "to rely on the birds and the winds to rule wisely"—because as soon as he learned the language spoken by the birds they explained to him, straight away, the language of the winds.

This is what it is not just to live in nature, or work with it, or enjoy it, or do one's noble and sentimental best as a human to protect it. This is what it is to be a part of nature; to see and hear with nature's own ears and eyes; to speak out with nature's crackling, cackling voice.[27]

But—and there aren't many bigger buts—most of these legends about birds communicating with humans are placed in another time, another age, for a reason.

We have come a long, tortuous way from any naturalness since then. And whoever feels moved nowadays to cry out how marvellous this mythical material all sounds, how romantic, no longer has any idea of what's actually involved because to hear a bird speaking and also understand it isn't going to be nice or lovely at all.

Instead, it's likely to be one of the most terrifying shocks in a person's life.

To get a genuine feel for where we are now, some true sense of what's happened, we have to get back down on solid ground and turn around to face the past. And it will be enough just to start by looking back to Porphyry—the chatty Platonist who fondly enjoyed writing obituaries for oracles and was so pleased with his reasoning he didn't even notice, except perhaps in a moment of depression, how his own talkativeness was contributing to the end of anything real.

There is one rather interesting place where he finds himself speaking quite openly about ancient myths, even recent stories, of people being allowed to understand the language of the birds.

But then—in a sudden bout of self-consciousness—he remembers what it means to be a civilized, intelligent human being. “Let’s leave those things aside and be done with them”, he writes, “because of our natural, inborn inclination to disbelieve.”

And this was closing in on eighteen hundred years ago. Even back then, nothing could be more “natural” than to disbelieve in what’s most natural. Already then the innate naturalness of understanding nature’s language was something to dismiss as embarrassingly unnatural because the unnaturalness of disbelieving in our naturalness had become our second nature.

Of course, in saying this, Porphyry was dutifully doing his job as a faithful Platonist. After all, it was Plato himself who hundreds of years earlier had brought up the old myth of a golden age—when humans could talk the same language as any animal—just so he could ask a clever question. Was humanity better off then, or are we better off in our modern society now?

And his ironic, abrasive answer could well prove one of the dumbest statements ever made in history. The whole question boils down, he says, to whether the people of that age used their familiarity with the language of animals to engage them at length in rational discussions about philosophy.

If they did, he explains, they were better off; if not, not. But until someone comes along with a reliable account of exactly what discussions humans used to have with the animals and birds back then, “let’s leave those things aside and be done with them.”

It might seem incredible that intelligent people over the centuries have taken this pretentious silliness seriously. But really it’s quite understandable—because we have nothing else left.

Living on the surface of ourselves, all we have is these clevernesses to give us some sense of self-value or worth; and very few of us will feel comfortable hearing a prophetic voice like William Blake’s express anything near the full depth of fury at Plato’s “pompous ignorance” that the philosopher, for all his apparent wisdom, so amply deserves.[28]

To put those things aside and be done with them: that's exactly what we did. And what happened over the past two thousand years—the silencing of nature, the mutilating of a whole culture—has been far more thorough than we can guess.

This is why even many of the greatest modern sages, experts on spirituality, authorities in the esoteric, manage to stamp out the power of nature precisely when they seem to be doing the opposite. We only have to look at the best known of the so-called Traditionalists, René Guénon, and the way he opens his famous treatise about "The Language of the Birds":

"The expression is clearly a symbolic one, since the very importance that is attached to the knowledge of the language—it is considered to be the prerogative of a high initiation—precludes a literal interpretation."

In other words, heaven forbid that such a mysterious language involving such a high initiation would have anything to do with dirty physical birds. Far from it: the "birds" here don't refer to birds at all.

Instead they "symbolize the angels, who precisely stand for the higher states of being."

As for all those fluffy creatures we can notice flitting outside our window and even, if we are able to stop our constant thinking long enough, hear when we step out for a breath of fresh air—we would be wise to leave those things aside and be done with them while, in the top-heavy fantasies of our intellect, imagining we can communicate straight with the world of angels.[29]

That's not the way it ever worked, though, or ever will. Learning the language of the birds is done just as the prophets do: out in the open, crying and calling with longing from the depths of one's belly, crawling with clawed feet along the earth while eyeing every single detail, because it's the birds chanting and howling around us that have the power to snatch us out of our reasoning minds into eternity.

Finding people who are able to explain this isn't easy. In fact everything else about our lifeless world seems to deserve explaining—aside from this.

But it's possible. And I will just quote a few sentences from my friend Stéphane Ruspoli, who was also a close friend of Henry Corbin until the day Corbin died, where he describes the personal experiences recorded by the great Persian Sufi Najm al–Dîn Kubrâ.

"Kubrâ begins with these striking words of praise: 'Glory be to God who has taught us the language of the birds.' And his masterpiece of mystical theology goes on to offer the most extraordinary details about asceticism, about withdrawing into retreat from the world—as well as about the practice of *dhikr*, or prayer of the heart, which Kubrâ connects directly with the crying and moaning of birds.

"And here is one particularly impressive passage about the 'spontaneous cry' that bursts from the heart of lovers when they become one with God through invoking his supreme name:

"'The wailing and moaning of lovers keeps growing stronger with every single mouthful as they drink to the full from the cup of sadness and quench their thirst—eventually getting used to it and finding the greatest pleasure in its taste. Then the cry they utter, quite involuntarily, becomes a natural expression of coming closer and closer to God: the Beloved.

"'Just as all the sounds emerging out of a bird's throat stem from a groaning deep down inside its entrails, in exactly the same way pilgrims too reach a particular state of mystical emotion where bird cries start escaping from them. This is the result of so much inner pressure being released. It's the result of their familiarity with God. It's a result of the joy that this familiarity brings them'."

Then Kubrâ goes on to explain how all this started becoming real for him.

"I heard these cries when I encountered a dervish, emptied of everything except for God, along the road. What he was doing met with my strong disapproval. I questioned him about it and he answered: 'It's all for the good if God so wishes, and nothing but a blessing.' He didn't go into any more details because in his clairvoyance he saw that I hadn't yet attained the appropriate station.

"But later—when the time came for me, too, to reach this station and experience for myself the extreme power of bird cries—I at last understood that the crying of a dervish is, indeed, really a cry.

"And I chewed and bit my fingertips in remorse. And I praised the glory of God just like someone who has been overcome by amazement; who is dumbfounded, stunned."

Here, right from the start, Kubrâ does nothing to make matters smooth or tidy or easy. On the contrary, even with his opening praise of God "who has taught us the language of the birds" he is simply speaking the truth in the deepest possible sense straight as he experiences it—flouting the conventions of Islam, breaking one of its greatest taboos in presenting himself as a prophet.

But what he says has nothing to do with prim or proper fantasies about prophets and angels. It's not some sweet, otherworldly experience because it's quite literally something that grabs you by the entrails.

And it should be no surprise at all to read what Kubrâ goes on to add—right after describing that state of wildly crying like a bird which he, as well as the dervish he'd met, both found themselves overpowered by.

"Those are the times when everyone, except for the rare individual who knows and understands, will assume you have gone mad."[30]

6

You may well suppose that—with so much talk about madness and prophets, language of winds and language of birds—I have completely lost my bearings.

That would be reasonable enough; but the fact is that I am intimately familiar with every inch of this route. I know exactly where these access corridors lead because they are the back entrance to something you will never be able to make any sense of by approaching, the way people so often want to do, from the front.

If you were to look honestly at the hypocrisy behind the pious enshrining of prophetic books in the Jewish and Christian bibles, you would have to laugh. Embalmed, preferably unread, in sacred text they are safe enough. But if you were to encounter the reality of the prophets: God help you.

Hebrew prophets, just like Greek prophets, already knew from the very start all the absurdities and impossibilities they were meant to contend with. And the truth is that it wasn't enough for one religion or culture after another to silence prophecy by attempting to cut it off at the source. That was fair enough, as far as it went—one more technique for trying to insulate ourselves from those who warn and howl and cry.

But the single defence against prophecy which, over the centuries, proved far more effective than any other has been the accusation of madness.

It can be quite surprising to realize that, already in their own time, the sanctified Hebrew prophets were being mocked and dismissed as insane. They certainly weren't alone, though.

Greeks and Romans, too, almost made a business of dismissing their own prophets as mad. And this intimate habit of closely associating the prophet—whose job it was to bring a little sanity and balance back into the world—with insanity still clings tight to the roots of western culture.[31]

Along with the evolution of psychology as a fledgling discipline in the nineteenth century came the urgent need, interestingly, not to change any of these assumptions or associations but just to create an updated language for them instead. Learned experiments got underway and soon experts were playing with impressive-sounding terms, like hysterical catalepsy, to account for the peculiar forms of insanity supposedly so characteristic of prophets.

It was only during the twentieth century, though, that the real industry of diagnosing prophecy began kicking into action. Streams of scientific expressions started flooding the literature and manuals and textbooks. There was "psychosis"; there was "schizophrenia", not to mention the ever-popular label of "pathology"; and, to lend an extra flourish, "paranoid schizophrenia" was added as well.

Of course nothing betrayed the illness, the trauma, the psychosis of prophets more obviously than their howling. The trouble is that, logically, this might mean wolves and jackals and coyotes are all in pressing need of treatment—while Native Americans performing their sacred ceremonies must be crying out for medication. But it's best not to be too logical. After all, we are only dealing with madness: finding the right-sounding label is the thing that counts.

And it didn't take too long before even those flimsy scientific labels were sounding a little out of date. So, almost as if to honour the new millennium, psychologists as well as biblical scholars hatched an even better language for explaining prophecy away.

With the help of the American Psychiatric Association they found the perfect term for a fresh generation. Those tragically unfortunate ancient prophets had been suffering all along, undiagnosed, from "post-traumatic stress disorder".[32]

There is one specific feature well worth noting in this steady march of progress: how quick and eager modern Jungian writers tend to be to fall obediently into step, in particular across North America.

As a matter of fact there are those who have been extremely happy making the most gracious contributions of their own—citing Jonah, for example, as a classic case of obsessive-compulsive disorder or oppositional defiant disorder.[33]

But in contributing their own pathologies to the psychological interpretation of prophecy, Jungian authorities went a great deal further than that.

One only has to look at the case of a very dynamic and highly reputed Jungian practitioner, James Kirsch, who for years maintained a close professional relationship with Jung himself. In fact his position on the matter, stated with the unmistakable certainty of religious dogma, could hardly have been clearer.

Would-be prophets, he explained, are guilty of the most fundamental misunderstanding. Anyone throughout the last two thousand years who made the grave mistake of stepping into the shoes of prophecy was heading straight for psychosis, paranoia, schizophrenia, insanity, catastrophe. And the single greatest tragedy is that all those figures who so sadly either almost fell, or did fall, into a massive psychological inflation by imagining they could act out the role of prophet were never even aware of the fact they had been born too early.

It was absolutely unavoidable that they would just become helpless "victims" of the process of individuation, rather than conscious participants in it, because each of them happened to be living "before the time was ready". They were unfortunate enough to have lived before Dr. Jung came into the world—before the decisive turning point in history when his psychology was created to help them, to save all the would-be saviours by saving them from themselves.

Of course the irony is that the real person suffering from a state of inflatedness here is the faithful Jungian who wrote such statements and so fervently believed them. But there is a still greater irony in the fact that Jung himself, even up until the year before he died, didn't stop warning this man as forcefully as he could: kept trying to make him realize the massive psychological inflation he had become a victim of through identifying so closely, so ruinously, with Jung's own work and psychology.[34]

Words falter here, come to a stop, turn around and back on themselves because it's not just ideas or theories that are on the line. It's people's lives, as well—the lives of prophets, of therapists, and above all of the so-called ordinary people caught in between.

And if you were to suspect this isn't the end of the story you would be right, because there is the other case I would be very glad to step around if I only could. That's the case of Edward Edinger.

Edinger has come to be described as the single most influential Jungian in America during the second half of the twentieth century—not to mention the finest spokesperson for Jung himself that North America has had the good fortune to know. He never met him; had no personal contact with him. But it was the man's ideas that captured him.

Soon he was completely convinced that Jung's psychology offered a new, post-Christian path of salvation. He also felt sure Jung was the most important person who had walked the earth since Jesus Christ, a relatively tame belief compared to the claims of other Jungians.

And in the humblest contrast Edinger saw himself as a perfectly modest, utterly ordinary missionary dedicated to spreading the wisdom of an extraordinarily magnificent master: always a truly terrifying combination. In other words, everything that Jung throughout his life had strained to keep out of public view and away especially from his own eyes was all of a sudden being put on grand display by this self-effacing disciple for the whole world to be able to see.

But it's not his views and theories that interest me, or his unwrapping of Jung's ideas while often managing to turn them discreetly inside out, or his rather mediocre erudition. What concerns me is Edinger's actions; what he did.

Quite late in his life he gave a series of lectures about prophecy. And rather predictably, in tune with the spirit of the times he lived in, he came to explain that the whole business of being a prophet was sheer psychosis from beginning to end. But, in his particular case, this made him start fondly reminiscing about an incident that happened when he was still a young man.

At the time of that incident he was working as a psychiatrist in a mental hospital near New York. He had also been immersed, as a patient, in Jungian analysis for several years. But far more significant than the relative newness to him of Jung's psychology at that earlier point in his career is the undisguised pride, the total lack of reflexivity or self-questioning, with which as a venerable teacher and authority in his sixties he still derives pleasure from reliving the details of what he had done.

And for those details he mentions a specific year: 1954. And he also mentions a particular place: Rockland State Hospital.[35]

“Indeed”, he explains, “the whole archetype of the prophet is a common content of the psychoses. I can give you a personal example of that. This comes from a patient I saw when I was working at Rockland State Hospital many years ago, in 1954 as a matter of fact. Here is the way I described the patient upon admission.

“‘Twenty-four-year-old slender blond man. He was a minister. The story was that his difficulties began about three weeks ago when he was serving as a minister for three rural churches in upstate New York. At this time he began hearing auditory hallucinations of God, telling him that he was the Messiah, the second coming of Christ. He states that he fought against this message and carried on conversations with God, insisting that this could not be. God, however, told him that at the very least he must take this information to the churches and convey it to them. And while describing this he is rather apologetic and sheepish, knowing perfectly well that this is an insane idea.’”

With mounting condescension Edinger takes a moment to document this twenty-four-year-old’s doubts, his conflicts, his uncertainties—as well as the strikingly thoughtful ways in which he was trying to explain his own situation to himself. And with the magnificent arrogance of a man who thinks he knows everything but perhaps knows nothing, who doesn’t even pause to consider how desperate the young minister must have been to find some way back to the freedom of nature, impatiently he goes straight on to explain:

“Well, he wasn’t really as good as this sounds. He was delusional and assaultive, so he had to be confined on the violent ward. I made a record some days later from that ward:

"'He is quite confused in thinking, still receiving messages from God that he is the second coming of Christ. Sometimes he wants to march out of the hospital and start preaching the message. The messages come from the wind and from the birds when they fly down and flutter their feathers ...'"

"That's an example", as our doctor expertly sums up the whole case, "of being overcome by the prophet archetype and falling into an overt psychosis."

It's rather hard to believe that Edward Edinger, a well-read man, had no knowledge of the fact that observing and listening to the wind and the birds was the cornerstone of ancient prophecy—or that those who knew how to hear as well as see the messages contained in the sounds of the wind and the movement of birds were once considered the closest of people to the divine.

But the question is not whether, as a matter of intellectual book knowledge, he was aware of this or not. The only question is why on earth, whether as a young doctor or a much older lecturer, he should ever care.

For any psychologist, even any orthodox Jungian, prophecy is the last possible thing to entertain as something serious. And in the case of Edinger we can glimpse just what this means: can see how literally he took his conviction that prophecy is never an issue to be taken literally.

As soon as he has finished revisiting those old case records from Rockland, he goes straight on to compare his blond minister with the ancient prophet Jeremiah point by point. Jeremiah and the minister not only were exactly the same in imagining they were prophets. They even shared the identical doubts and conflicts; struggles and fears.

But above all they both made the same fatal mistake of acting out the role of prophet, because that's the purest psychosis. "Then one *is* crazy".

In other words, with all his learned lecturing and writing about the prophets, Edinger himself "wasn't really as good as this sounds"—because if he had come across Jeremiah he would have done his job without a moment's thought and locked him up in Rockland, too.

And naturally he had to. There is nobody alive who wants to be challenged by the reality, as opposed to the fakery, of prophecy. No one in any truly civilized culture can be expected to tolerate the brutal violence of a man who hears the sacred speaking in the breeze or in the gentle fluttering of a bird's wings as it flies low and close to the ground.

Edinger has a fascinating passage about just how bad being a prophet is for one's social life. He notes how bitterly Jeremiah complained about his harmonious relationship to other people being destroyed when he came bringing messages from another world; how he was locked up and humiliated in public for howling. "Even at the very best, even at the most careful, it can be very dangerous to be a prophet—if one tells all that one sees or intuits." And so only fools would say what they intuit or see.

He even, along with other Jungians, leans on a false etymology of the word "prophet" so he can pretend that the true job of someone like Jeremiah should have been "to adapt his message, to mediate it to the psychological reality of those he is talking to". Otherwise, everything goes wrong. "He loses his relatedness to other people; he fails to take into account their reality."

The simple truth is, though, that the meaning of the ancient word "prophet" has nothing whatsoever to do with adapting one's message to a human audience. The word means "to speak on behalf of" the divine. It means just to serve as a mouthpiece: to say whatever the sacred is needing to say.[36]

And one can talk until the cows come home about prophets failing to take into account everybody's reality. But then who, aside from prophets, is going to talk about everyone failing to take into account the divine reality?

Instead we go on living out our therapeutically self-serving lives, assured that whoever threatens to disturb us will get whatever's coming to them: be labelled appropriately, put away.

And so there is no one brave enough left even to ask about the collective craziness—the total psychosis—of a world that has silenced its prophets.

7

So we come back at last to Jung.

If one stops just to look and listen, it can be remarkable to note what starts quietly stepping out from the shadows—because while still alive he was surrounded on every side by voices accusing him, reprimanding him, mocking him for wanting to be a prophet.

But these weren't only the voices of fools. Included among them was the voice of his old friend and colleague Sigmund Freud who at times also had the nerve to describe him as a mystic, not to mention crazy.

And, even more strikingly, some of them were the voices crying out inside Jung himself: taunting, tormenting, torturing him.

There is nothing here to worry about, though; nothing at all.

The most devoted of Jungians, those people who happened to be closest to him, were of a single mind and voice in rejecting the slightest murmur of any nonsense about him being a prophet. The same goes for the best and finest minds, apparently, in the world of Jungian scholarship.

It's all such a silly mistake: the crudest of misunderstandings. There is nothing to see here, not a single doubt to linger on; the facts of the matter couldn't be simpler; the case is closed.

And anyone stubborn enough still to feel unsatisfied by these collective assurances is sooner or later going to be faced with something far more decisive—Jung's own unfailing habit of stridently insisting, time and time and then time again, that he wasn't a prophet.

The case is not just closed. It's already sealed and disposed of.[37]

The trouble here, the awkward little problem we are so quick to overlook, is that in reality things rarely are quite so simple. As the saying goes: where there's smoke there is often fire, and if you notice dentists rushing around intensely denying they are astronauts you are bound to ask the reason why.

Also, there is the need for a healthy dose or two of common sense. It can be interesting to watch how, whenever Jung raised the question of whether Freud deserved the title of prophet, he would innocently use the term as an expression of praise. But when Freud, or others, raised the spectre of Jung wanting to become a prophet there was nothing nice intended at all. And why, with this word being bandied around as a term of such outright mockery or abuse, Jung would have cared to add to his troubles by heaping such an obvious insult on his own head is beyond any sane person's understanding.

Add to this the fact that he very shrewdly used to note how any "real prophet or saviour" who decided to go public would be destroyed by our modern world of television and media within a few short weeks, and one can appreciate why even if Jung knew he was a prophet he would have been the last person ever to admit it.[38]

Then, of course, there is that matter of his constant denials which any number of people have been gullible enough to point to as the ultimate criterion of truth. But we have already seen more than enough examples of his public denials—Jung the

Gnostic denying he is a Gnostic, Jung the mystic insisting he is not a mystic, Jung the magician waving his wand and solemnly declaring he is no magician—to get a visceral sense of exactly what he meant by "concealing one's vestiges".

I do appreciate, though, that this can all be a little hard to accept. And so, if it still seems difficult really to believe that he could have condoned the blatant act of saying things which are downright deceitful or false, I will just mention one other passage which should put everybody's doubts to rest.

In those green and innocent days when he hadn't yet learned the full price that has to be paid for openly revealing one's enthusiasms, Jung gave Freud quite a shock by telling him their new psychology of the unconscious was a religion: in fact was destined to be the new religion, even complete with its own saviour probably waiting somewhere in the wings.

But soon he would also be offering Freud a warning. Especially among friends or colleagues, he explained, one has to be careful. All the gossip, the backbiting, the murmurs of rebellion are nothing but normal reactions to something that behaves and performs and looks just like a religion. So we have to take the necessary steps to model ourselves on the esoteric traditions of antiquity. Concealment is the key. Our psychology will only grow and thrive inside the atmosphere of a secret religious conclave that meets in private, behind closed doors.

What's more, though, we need to make sure to protect all this from our own impatient ambitions to go public with everything we have discovered—because our psychology "is much too true to be acknowledged or recognized, yet, in public. First and foremost, this is what we have to do: we have to restrict ourselves to handing out masses of falsified, adulterated extracts and passing round nothing but watered-down versions of it."

And if you plan on looking the passage up inside the authorized English translation of Jung's letters to Freud, you may as well give up because all you will find is a crudely diluted and falsified version of what Jung once wrote.[39]

So perhaps, as most people do, you too enjoy your own drinks adulterated; completely watered down. And there is nothing wrong with that at all.

But if you happen not to, and have a strong enough longing for the truth as well as the internal fortitude to handle it, then it might be time to think twice before swallowing the masses of palatable denials that Jung was a prophet—and look, instead, at what he actually said about the subject of prophecy when he chose to touch on it.

The obvious place to start is with a piece he once wrote which very understandably, because it seems to come so close to mapping the unmappable territory of the psyche, has almost assumed the status of an introductory textbook for Jungian psychology.

The original version dates back to 1916, when he was still struggling intensely to come to terms with the experiences documented by his *Red book*. In it he directly takes aim at the ambitiousness of people who are so weak-minded they give way to the temptation of believing they are prophets. Then he ends with an even more pointed comment about the danger of "setting oneself up" as a prophet: of rushing to become a missionary to others rather than quietly watching over oneself, silently integrating one's psychological discoveries into ordinary everyday life.

And, now that the *Red book* has been published, nothing could be plainer than the full extent to which these general warnings are based on Jung's very personal struggles and bitter experiences at the time—while he was battling in private with what he specifically describes as his own prophetic ambition, fighting against the almost overwhelming temptation to accept the role of prophet for himself.[40]

But twelve years later, with the even greater experience of a man in his fifties, he went back to his original text and rewrote it. In addition to his initial warning about ambition and temptation, which he left intact, he included a whole new section on prophecy and the problem of inflation. And to judge from those who for the better part of a century have been either loudly insisting or at least silently implying that according to Jung prophecy is the direct equivalent of inflation and psychosis and delusion, that to him all prophets are false prophets by their very nature, anybody would assume he must have been very clear about the matter himself.

In fact, whoever those commentators think they have been reading or listening to or learning from, one thing can be said for sure. It certainly isn't Jung.

The most surprising thing about this revision is how extremely brief his comments are about prophecy itself:

"In general, I wouldn't want to deny that real prophets do appear. But, by way of precaution, I would prefer as a very first step to question each individual case—because to accept someone as genuine is far too serious a matter to be decided flippantly or offhandedly. Every true prophet defends himself valiantly against the unconscious demands and expectations of this role. So, when a prophet just springs out of nowhere on the spur of the moment, it's better to suspect a psychic loss of equilibrium."

Of course, to the sceptically minded this is the plainest confirmation of Jung's sceptical-mindedness. Nothing could be easier than to join him in brushing off the whole topic of prophecy, flippantly, offhandedly, as pathological or very dubious at best.

But the fact is that in the space of this short half-paragraph he has mentioned the possibility of real prophets, genuine prophets, true prophets no less than three times—quite consistently with the way he often mentions the same possibility elsewhere. And all that's needed is simply to step through the door he is holding open.[41]

Jung's statement that "every true prophet defends himself valiantly against the unconscious demands and expectations of this role" belongs in a very specific context. It refers straight back to what he has just been saying a moment before about how only the rarest and best among people are strong enough in their longing that they are willing to expose themselves, on purpose, to the incalculable danger of being devoured by the primordial unconscious; about how only the truest heroes ever manage to defeat the monster of the depths not just once, in some instant glorious battle, but time and time again; about how the only way to win the mythical treasure, the secret power, the hidden magic contained inside those depths is by absolutely refusing to identify with their collective force.

And if one cares to put together everything Jung says or hints at here about this figure of the true prophet, the resulting picture couldn't be clearer.

Real prophets have the strength and virtue to do what no one else is willing, or able, to do. They struggle with all their might against their own ambitions and vanity; manage to maintain their psychological balance by knowing, in particular, how to laugh at the fools they are and never take themselves too seriously. They fight against the constant temptation to display themselves as prophets in public, together with the usual dramas that involves.

Above all, though, they refuse to identify with the intoxicating role of prophet even inwardly or in private. And this plays itself out not just invisibly—because, in the hard-won battle to become a real prophet, there is nobody there to make a claim about anything or parade some prophetic status—but also with immense patience over a long period of time.

That's precisely the reason why, in his few fleeting comments about prophecy, Jung makes everything revolve around slowness and perseverance as opposed to speed. Becoming a prophet isn't a matter of becoming an overnight sensation: it takes time, because first one has to become the prophet and saviour of one's own being. And judging whether someone really is a prophet isn't an issue of making instant, spur-of-the-moment decisions either.

That, too, needs time.

But you may notice, now I've spelled all this out, that he doesn't say any of it openly. And the name for that is magic.

He says it all without seeming to say anything; touches on the subject of prophets for the briefest moment or two only to let himself be distracted almost immediately and, before you notice what's happened, rush off into talking about something else. He cleverly uses double negatives—"I wouldn't want to deny"—rather than committing himself by stating anything directly in a positive way.

And the whole time he is counting on you not only not to notice what he is actually pointing to, which would require an active attention not many people have, but to project your own unconscious prejudices onto his words and assume he is saying the precise opposite of what he is.

In other words: it's not enough for him to speak theoretically about prophecy. Instead, even when he is talking about prophets he instinctively follows the hallowed and time-honoured tradition of speaking as a prophet.

He hints and hides rather than talking openly; conveys his meaning to the very few who are willing and patient enough to listen; but to everybody else he gives just enough rope to let them hang themselves, because all they really want is to go on being deceived.

This prophetic language is in essence no different from the prophetic language used by Empedocles, or Parmenides, or anyone else who has to communicate after coming back from the world of the dead. Underneath its veil of apparent vagueness it contains an uncanny exactness—a mathematical precision which we ignore at our peril.

That preciseness is the reality of the timeless need for true, authentic prophets to serve their culture or community in ways they alone are ready to do.[42]

And, if one cares to consider Jung's other writings, it's only too obvious there was nothing else he could possibly hint at or say. But even though there are so many more words one could add to his, and no doubt should, I'll simply cut things short.

While Jungians like Edward Edinger were cheerfully psychoanalyzing and classifying and diagnosing prophets in their books, their lectures, their practices, Jung for his own part kept crying out: Keep your hands off our prophets and leave them alone! Stop trying to analyze or classify them from an individual point of view because it's the stupidest thing to do. They are acting, speaking, urgently communicating as representatives of the collective unconscious and burrowing into the details of their personal psychology is futile.

While a Jungian like James Kirsch was insisting that any prophet who hasn't had the benefit of a Jungian analysis will automatically become an unconscious "victim of the process of individuation", Jung himself was stating on the contrary that throughout the whole of history prophets have always served their people as supreme models of individuation.

And, far from being unconscious, they are the most conscious guides and leaders of their people; lone beacons of psychological health.

While Edinger makes such a fuss about prophets' greatest weakness lying in the fact that they are not able to adapt to the people or the world around them, Jung himself hints that the greatest strength of prophets—just like artists—lies precisely in their failure to adapt, because this is the one way they can help bring the collective imbalance back again into balance.

While Jungians in general mostly tend to see prophets as perfect models of inflation, miniature psychological disasters waiting to happen, Jung took the extraordinary step of portraying them as their people's best protection against the supreme psychological disaster: as the only ones strong enough to take a stand against the devastating ravages of collective, not to mention individual, inflation.

And while there is no denying that anyone seeing visions or hearing messages straight from God is running an obvious psychological risk, there is also no denying that nothing could be more dangerous for a culture than ignoring the true prophets who—in spite of all their own struggles to stop hearing or to prevent themselves seeing—still end up bringing messages and visions from another world because they are the only ones able to perceive the real needs of their times.[43]

For most of these points Jung would refer to the Hebrew prophets and the Jewish people. This might make it seem ever so easy nowadays to dismiss what he says as only appropriate in a specific historical context; only relevant to some other time or place. But that would be to ignore the absolutely fundamental importance he ascribed to the Bible in his own psychology.

As he tried to explain, for a westerner there is no psychology without the Bible. "We must read the Bible or we shall not understand psychology. Our psychology, our whole lives, our language and imagery, are built upon the Bible." And there is a significant warning here: of course we can use Jung's work however we want, convert it into a handy tool to suit our own purposes.

But unless we know the Bible almost as well as he did, can pick up on his subtle references and hints, we are never in a thousand years going to understand his real meaning.

If prophets were essential for the psychological health of the Jewish people, they are essential for ours. If they were the few individuals among the Jews who could be called most individuated, least inflated, most sane, then perhaps they are the only figures available to us in our sophisticated civilized existence who are not completely crazy.

And if such suggestions sound more than a little strange, it can help to remember that for Jung the most perfectly ordinary people in our modern western culture aren't anywhere near as perfect as they seem. Quite to the contrary: every such person nowadays "suffers from a hubris of consciousness that borders on the pathological".

But the most telling thing of all is that in his eyes even the most extreme, most psychotic, most impossibly deluded case of a religious inflation due to someone acting out the grand role of prophet is no worse than "the rationalistic and political psychosis that is the affliction of our day"—the collective psychosis of our world.[44]

8

And so Jung's few quick pointers to the true, real, genuine prophet simply disappear; vanish, ignored, back into the silence where they belong.

But these brief comments were only the start of what he would end up contributing to his textbook account of prophecy and the problem of inflation. And the most important thing to note about his final version of the text is an extremely simple one: the number of his words.

For every word he uses, in that space of half a small paragraph, to touch on the dangers of becoming a prophet he goes straight on to use four or five words—in the longer paragraphs that follow—to illustrate the dangers of becoming a prophet's disciple. And here we suddenly encounter a very different face of Jung.

The entire passage turns into a delightfully relaxed but scornful parody of all those devoted followers who find no end of sweetness and lazy joy in sitting at the Master's feet, laying all the liability and responsibility for their lives at Master's door, guarding against having a single thought or idea of their own, scooping the great truth straight from their Master's hands so they can mindlessly repeat it as if this somehow makes it their own truth: their own answer, their own discovery.

For them it's an ideal situation. Somebody else is there to carry all the burden and responsibilities, the real-life dangers and risks, while they creep about cowering behind their false modesty; gloating over the magnificent treasury of wisdom they claim for themselves although it isn't even theirs; bursting onto the world scene to proclaim themselves proud guardians of an exclusive truth denied to everyone else, flushed and swollen with their own borrowed importance. At the same time, through their boundless adulation and deification of the Master they are able to enjoy the supreme pleasure of also feeling themselves grow in size.

Even while outwardly appearing to be ever so ordinary, all of a sudden they are filling the skies—because it never dawns on them that to try hiding away in modesty and humility from the imagined dangers of inflation is among the greatest possible forms of inflation.

Naturally the most striking thing about this meticulous description is the way Jung has managed to shift the whole focus away from what by any ordinary logic he ought to be explaining, which is a prophet's inflation, onto the inflation of a prophet's disciples. And if what he describes with such intensity sounds strangely reminiscent of the dedicated Jungian Edward Edinger, proclaiming Jung's unparalleled greatness of stature while deriving enormous satisfaction from his own modesty and smallness, that's no accident.

In fact Edinger was well known for speaking of himself as, very precisely, "an ordinary man in most respects except for my ability to see Jung's size". One could truthfully say that—with a prophetic clarity—Jung had already managed to see what kind of things were going to be unfolding for his work inside the space of a single generation.[45]

But, just as naturally, nothing would be worse than to exaggerate.

The best experts insist they have already fully accounted for Jung's intimate insight into a pupil's inflation, and state with utmost confidence that—although in theory there might always be one or two bad apples among the very lowest grade of Jungians who perhaps could fit his image of inflated disciples—this passage has no bearing at all on the Jungian community as a whole. On the contrary, his acute sensitivity towards the dynamics of inflation shows how infinitely careful he was to keep any such nonsense well away from the world of Jungians. In fact, we are told, he shaped and formed his Jungian community ever so consciously as a deliberate defence and antidote against such childish dynamics; a perfect model of how to avoid them.

As for what could possibly have prompted such a passionate portrayal of the prophet's inflated disciples: maybe he was thinking about a couple of lost Theosophists or other cultists who, by some unaccountable twist of fate, had once washed up in his consulting room.[46]

And this is what happens when those who write about Jung have no idea of what he meant by the power of the unconscious.

If we really want to understand what Jung was getting at, with his textbook account of a prophet's disciples, it can be helpful to start by looking back at the *Red book*—and at what he was actually saying behind the scenes.

On the surface it can all sound perfectly splendid. With his message from the underworld he is coming to set everyone free, clapping everybody on the back and encouraging them to follow their own way; find their own truth to live by which is true only for them. But, underneath that glitzy surface, Jung is also saying something slightly different:

Stop trying to copy me. Leave me alone. I am sick to death of everyone imitating everything I say or do. For God's sake find your own way and stop leaning on me as if I am going to fill your emptiness, answer your questions for you, miraculously give you the truth to replace all your lies. Stop sucking me dry, as if my life is what you need to live your life.

And don't try taking my mysteries or stealing my secrets, because they are not yours—they are mine. Have the guts to face your darkness and jump into the crater of your own volcano because that's the only way you are ever going to find what's yours.

The truth is, though, that being imitated was one thing he soon learned he would have to put up with even from the Jungian men and women who seemed closest to him. There would be imitation of his deepest secrets, of his teachings, of his smallest tics and mannerisms too. Absolutely the last thing that the people around him were going to do, he realized, was to leave him alone.[47]

And this is where we come back, again, to his peculiarly close sense of affinity with Empedocles.

It was around twenty-five years after the huge struggles he documented in the *Red book* that Jung revisited one of his favourite topics: the descent into hell through a volcanic crater and, much more specifically, the legends of Empedocles dying by throwing himself into Mount Etna. But, this time, he couldn't resist cracking one of those trademark jokes that somehow manage to reveal as much about him as any of his most serious scientific texts.

Of course he could never quite get to the bottom of why Empedocles would have killed himself in such a way, for the simple reason that the legends were no more talking about Empedocles' physical or literal death than Jung had physically died when he made his own journeys to the underworld. Even so, that didn't stop him from trying—and driving home a point or two in the process.

I often wonder, he said during a famous seminar in 1938, why he did it. Ancient writers had their own kinds of theories and explanations. "But in the biography of old Empedocles we get the real clue! You know, he was very popular: wherever he appeared, large crowds of people came to hear him talk, and when he left town about ten thousand people followed him to the next one where he had to talk again. I assume he was human, so what could he do?"

And Jung has the answer. Empedocles had to find some place where no one could run after him: somewhere "to escape his ten thousand lovely followers". So he jumped into the volcano.

Here, in this hilariously simple story, we almost have it all: crowds upon crowds of devoted followers doing just what inflated disciples do best, pursuing Empedocles everywhere to scoop out his wisdom and suck up his every word as if it holds the secret of life, transferring their hopes and expectations and fantasies onto the Master while laying their burdens and responsibilities at his door until he simply couldn't stand it any more.

At the same time it doesn't need much of a sixth sense to be able to detect in Jung's ridiculously forced explanation not only a major vein of sympathy for old Empedocles, but an even greater trace of autobiographical self-reference. By telling the story this way, he is hardly just telling the story of a famous ancient prophet and saviour called Empedocles.

He is saying something essential about himself. And, as it happens, there is no need at all for any special senses here—because we also have the most explicit of statements from someone who, for years, fiercely treasured her role as one of Jung's most trusted confidantes.

Barbara Hannah has left a very convenient note explaining that, whenever she heard Empedocles' name being mentioned, she couldn't help thinking back to what Jung had said about him. Immediately, she would be reminded of the way he used to describe the wise old man as throwing himself into a volcano because of all the people who "flocked around him wanting to hear about things of life. Transferences drove him there, said Dr. Jung, and added: 'and if you are not careful, I shall land there too!'"

So, all of a sudden, those "ten thousand lovely followers" devotedly chasing their Master everywhere are no longer Theosophists. And they are no longer Empedocles' disciples, either—because they are also Jung's.

What's more: they are not just some low-grade would-be Jungians living at a distant remove from his faithful inner circle. They even include, or perhaps one would have to say especially include, those very Jungians who considered themselves his nearest and dearest.

And the one most unavoidable consequence of all this is that the person playing the role of prophet to these prophet's disciples is no longer only Empedocles. On his own admission, it's Carl Jung himself.[48]

But in case anyone has an illusion that the resulting picture of Jung as the great prophet figure surrounded by inflated, unconscious disciples is just due to a temporary lapse of judgement or seriousness on his part I'll quickly shift the focus forward by another twenty years—to one of the last sets of interviews he ever gave before he died.

In June 1958 he sat down with his secretary to talk for a bit about death and the dead. We all, he explained, have a particular task or burden which is to find an answer through the living of our own lives to the questions left unanswered by our ancestors: by the dead. This is what it really means to find one's myth.

To do that, though, one has to learn to live very close to the dead; one's own dead.

And for him, he adds, little by little that burden has become less and less because through his life he has answered them. He has done everything he needed to, or could. To his own dead he gave his own answer, and that has nothing whatsoever to do with anyone else. It's nobody else's business! The trouble is that the only thing people want to know is what my answer is so they can mindlessly rattle it off and make my answer appear to be their answer. Of course this means they are leaving their own dead completely unanswered, but they couldn't care less—because to set about discovering their own living answer to their own dead through their own effort would be far too uncomfortable, much too risky and stressful.

Let's just go ahead and project all our burdens onto old Jung, they say, because he knows how to make everything fine and good.

Here it is again: lazy followers laying all their burdens at the Master's feet, dodging the inconvenience of having to search for an answer themselves because it's so much easier imitating and impressively parroting the Master's own answer instead. After all, isn't it an unquestionable fact that the prophet's disciple possesses "the great truth—not his own discovery, of course, but received straight from the Master's hands?"

And inwardly he was just as sick of the situation as he had been forty, almost fifty, years before.

There is one other thing, too, that he bitterly adds in the middle of complaining about the living while explaining about the dead. Who on earth, he asks, really understands anything about this at all? Where, he wants to know, is there anyone who in all honesty understands the slightest part of what this actually means?[49]

It sounds an insignificant enough thing to say—the kind of comment to excuse as a purely rhetorical question and put aside.

But that would be a major mistake.

Often Jung used to mention the one sure, telltale sign of a saviour figure or prophet or magician: the utter conviction such people hold that there's no one in the world who understands them. So the irony is that, in making precisely this point while lamenting his inflated followers' inability to understand him, he is offering the most archetypal confirmation of his own role as a prophet.

In fact the older he got, the more insistently he kept asking himself who understood what he had been trying to do. The answer was always the same. Someone might understand a bit about this or that, then make a big meal of it. As for who understands the whole, though, how it all hangs together—to be perfectly frank, there is no one at all.

It's an answer that runs like a painful refrain through the interviews he gave towards the end of his life. But at the same time, in those interviews he also happened to give a very particular name to this cry of incomprehension. He called it the cry of Merlin: the prophet's cry that no one understands and that makes the prophet cry even louder because no one understands it.

This is the cry that Jung identified as his own, in just the same way he identified himself with Merlin. And so we have Empedocles the prophet, with whose predicament Jung identified so strongly; we have Merlin the prophet, too; lastly we have Jung. But rather than just lumping all three of these figures together as prophets, which would be the laziest of things to do, the crucial point to note is that each of them is a prophet with a difference because of the one characteristic they share in common.

They all renounced the role of prophet. Empedocles renounced it by dying because he couldn't take the nonsense any more, Merlin by withdrawing into the forest and crying because he couldn't put up with it either. Jung renounced it, as well, by absolutely refusing to identify with being a prophet—or let himself get trapped in the golden cage where prophets end up imprisoned together with their disciples.

The paradox for him was that, in spite of all the exotic trappings and fancy trimmings, really there is nothing mysterious whatsoever about the unconscious relationship between a prophet and a prophet's disciple. From a psychological point of view the whole saga is "so humanly understandable that it would be a matter for astonishment if it led to any further destination whatever". And when something potentially so sacred is turned into the dullest example of business as usual, the only mystery left is the one of not knowing whether it would be better just to laugh or cry.

The true mystery, which is the mystery of entering a world no human can hope to understand, begins with simply renouncing everything. It starts at the moment when, like the sun at midheaven, we have reached our own highest point and are faced with the great choice in our life. Either we go on struggling pointlessly to keep climbing higher and higher; automatically repeat whatever strategies we are used to until at last there is nothing left to do except accept the final pleasures of a graceful retirement; become stiffer and drier only to end up unconsciously sinking down, like everybody else, into the waters of death.

Or else we die before we die and make that descent quite consciously: "No one should deny the danger of the descent, but it *can* be risked. No one *need* risk it, but it is certain that some one will. And let those who go down the sunset way do so with open eyes, for it is a sacrifice which daunts even the gods."[50]

After such a sacrifice the bird, at least the prophet bird, is no longer in the cage. But don't imagine this is the end of Jung the prophet. It's only the end of his soaring public ambitions to become a prophet—so that he can sink back into his own primordial depths, and the real work of the prophet can begin.

9

For Jung it was perfectly clear: the descent he made into the crater of the underworld, his major encounter with the unconscious, that immense labour and love he devoted year after year to creating the *Red book*, are what marked the start of his real work because everything he would do later came from here.

One can understand the wisdom of those intellectuals who have had the courage to speak out against the *Red book*—to denounce it as utter rubbish that belongs in the garbage can of history and should never have been published. The truth is that it's loaded with such grossness, so much of the disgusting crudity characteristic of the unconscious, even Jung himself was thoroughly embarrassed and discomforted by what it contains.

But the trick is that unless you embrace all the crudeness of the unconscious reality wholeheartedly, unless you know like Jung that the pearl is only found in the filth, you are going to end up empty-handed with nothing aside from a cheap necklace of dried theories; of hollow concepts. It would have been best if you had never begun.[51]

As for the scholars who have been wise enough to embrace the *Red book* and make it an object of study, the question remains whether they have understood much better than those who just reject it. Even its editor has insisted that of course this is a text to be understood psychologically—a word that can mean a million things to a thousand people—instead of religiously, let alone mystically.

Or as another scholar has explained: at the start of the *Red book* Jung sets off in quest of his soul, not in search of God. And that proves this is not some religious text but simply a work of psychology, a book for the analytical mind.[52]

All I can say is that, if this was true, it would be very strange indeed.

Right from the start of his career, years before the *Red book* was even a glimmer in his eye, Jung had always seen the work he did as religious through and through. As he said to Freud, quite frankly, back in 1910: the organized religions have lost their instinctive power, our psychology alone can replace them, but "religion can only be replaced by religion".

It's a statement that would echo, more and more refined although just as distinctly, down through the rest of his days. To be sure, many conscientious efforts have been made over the years to blur or simply obliterate the religious dimensions of his work; to silence, as effectively as possible, his own emphasis on the religious nature of what happened to him during his descent into the underworld. But such acts of suppression change nothing, at least nothing that counts.[53]

And as for this question of psychology's connection to religion—we may as well deal with the issue once and for all.

It can be almost a religious experience to realize how few people even in the Jungian community have taken the trouble to come to terms with one of Jung's most important writings, where he states just what psychology is and why it matters to him so much.

With crystal clarity he explains that, far from being a replacement or substitute for religion, it's the very essence of religion—because the central concern of psychology is, by definition, the mystery of the soul:

"So long as religion is only belief and outward form, and the religious function is not experienced in our own souls, nothing profound or radical has happened. It still remains to be understood that the *mysterium magnum*", life's great mystery, "is first and foremost rooted in the human psyche. Whoever doesn't know this from inner experience may be a most learned theologian, but doesn't have a clue about religion".

Then Jung simply moves from provocative to even more provocative. "If it was not a fact of experience that supreme values reside in the soul", he goes straight on to add, "psychology would not interest me in the least ... I have been accused of 'deifying the soul'. But it's not I—it's God himself who deified it! It's not I who assigned a religious function to the soul, I merely presented the facts." And so he arrives at the heart of psychology, as well as the core of people's resistance to it:

"If the theologian really believes in the almighty power of God on the one hand and in the validity of dogma on the other, why then does he not trust God to speak in the soul? Why this fear of psychology?" In other words, here we have his own statement of what psychology is—as well as why it matters so much.

It's the art or science of learning to listen to the voice of God speaking in the human soul.

Far from the soul existing in Jung's mind as some psychological alternative to religion, or God, it's the only possible pathway to both. This is why for him Soul is Wisdom—Sophia in Greek, Sapientia in Latin. Inside the *Red book* itself he painted this spirit of Wisdom just as he wanted her to be seen: standing tall, veiled but magnificent, in a crowded church.

And later he would comment on what he had painted:

In all her ambiguity and ambivalence she—Soul, Sophia—appears with her veiled face as an extraordinary, utterly mysterious feminine being "in a church, taking the place of the altar". This is how the reality of the soul will eventually be restored "to the Christian church, not as an icon but as the altar itself".

But to understand the significance of his painting we also need to go back a bit in time. To be more specific, we have to go back to another of those letters Jung wrote to Freud when he was still trying to convince him that the real future of psychology lies in gradually pulling away the veil from the secret at the heart of religion while making sure to keep its essential mystery hidden:

"I have the feeling that this is a time full of wonders. And, if the omens from the gods do not deceive, I dare say you are quite correct that thanks to your discoveries we indeed find ourselves on the threshold of something truly glorious—something I can't think of any name for aside from the Gnostic notion of *Sophia*, which is an Alexandrian expression perfectly suited for the reincarnation of ancient wisdom in psychoanalysis."

The only thing to add is that Jung was never able to help along this process of Sophia's reincarnation while he stayed with Freud. To do that, he first had to make the journey to hell all on his own. And if we want to know what the *Red book* really is, this is it: the physical reincarnation of ancient wisdom which he already had predicted to Freud.[54]

But with the publication, now, of that veiled wisdom we are faced with a problem. People are notoriously adept at making as much or as little as they want out of words, even images—at stripping religion of its religiousness, ignoring anything they dislike, inserting all their pet political correctnesses.

So if we care to understand a little about the birthing of that private and hidden and secret wisdom, about what the process of creating the *Red book* involved at around the time it was actually being created, we are going to have to be able to look back at it from a fresh perspective.

And there are probably no better eyes to choose than Cary de Angulo's. A well-educated American, she came to Zurich in 1921. Soon she caught Jung's attention not because of her devotion but, on the contrary, because of her rigorous impartiality; because of her critical objectivity which he would learn to value more and more over the years; on account of her ability to stand beside him always ready to challenge, tease, call his bluff, when everyone else was too terrified to say a word.

Even so, during the first year after she arrived she was explaining to him that "Every hour I spend with you has holiness in it for me"—not, she adds, in the sense that she is worshipping him but in the sense that his simple presence inspires her to strain and reach towards something only Jung has managed to express so potently. And this sensation of a holiness in his presence was something far from unique to her alone.

But it was well over another year later before he found himself guided to invite her to help him with his work on the *Red book*. Immediately she realized what this meant: that he was expecting her to keep her spirit so pure, her physical body so unintrusive, her mind filled with so much tenderness that she would be incapable of causing him any harm because "you are taking me into the inner dwelling house of your soul".

Before she ever had a chance to see the *Red book* for herself, she was already aware—obviously because of what Jung had communicated to her—that it was a being, a personality, in its own right. Instinctively she felt she would far rather never see or touch it than approach it in a way that could come across as disrespectful, aggressive, brusque.

And when she arrived at his home for her first day of work, she found it open in his study. Even so, something inside her prevented her from getting too close.

The book, for her, was "so full of magic" that she couldn't even bring herself to sit down right in front of it. And she felt so unworthy of leaning over it that she would twist her body as well as her eyes almost beyond what was physically possible, like someone trying to bend over to look round a corner.

The very last thing she wished was to impose on it in any way—as she gently allowed the pregnant atmosphere of his library to fold her back into the vast "shadows of past ages".[55]

Nothing comes even close, though, to the importance of another passage in Cary de Angulo's personal records. She has been acknowledging how she is not always able to follow Jung or agree with him intellectually about this and that; how there are some important truths which for him are self-evident facts that she doesn't have the evidence, and maybe never will, to accept. But strangely and quite mysteriously, as she admits to him, none of this changes a thing.

In spite of every apparent pointer to the contrary, she simply knows that as a living and embodied human being he is *right*—and the reason she knows this is because "Your personality is that 'Kleinod' that reappears in the world only now and then. I know that to be so and why it is so."

What she is claiming to know, here, with such certainty can seem so obscure it's hardly worth pausing for. But, as with so many details surrounding Jung, if we ignore it we'll throw something infinitely significant away.

"Kleinod", in German, means a precious jewel. And there is no doubting at all what Cary de Angulo is referring to. One of Jung's most important works, *Psychological types*, had been published only the year before; and a central thread running through that book is, precisely, the theme of the "Kleinod" or precious jewel.

This jewel, as he explains there, is the only thing truly capable of easing humanity's sufferings. Even more than that, though, it's the renewer of life and of the sacred. In fact, it's the creator of the new God.

The trouble is that, thanks to the rationalism of our conscious human world, it gets completely lost. The jewel is divine; is the irrational, impossible solution to humanity's problems which had been foretold by the prophets long ago. It represents the birth of the redeemer, the saviour.

And as Jung goes to the special trouble of pointing out while evoking his own, tireless quest for the impossible: "The saviour is always a figure endowed with magical power who makes the impossible possible".

But for exactly this reason the jewel is rejected by everyone who thinks only in terms of the possible, the rational. Even the simplest of people are completely dumbfounded by it, are left suspicious as well as troubled. To any conventional sense of conscience it's utterly disgusting. The high priests, too, not only see nothing divine in it. On the contrary, they consider it the most insolent violation of God and just shudder at the sight of it in their total disgust—because even the priests are rationalists through and through. The academics of course dismiss it as lacking any of the qualities that would make it worth studying. The jewellers throw it out as a fake. The worst absurdity of all, though, is that you can't even try to get rid of it because the police will catch you for possession of illegal goods.

And this jewel represents not just the freedom, but also the duty, to be what one is. That's the reason why people are so frightened of it, so quick to hurl it into the streets and even attack anyone who happens to find it.

All that's left, then, is for it to do its impossible and transformative and seemingly destructive work deep in the collective unconscious. It can be buried, almost forgotten. Or it can be rationalized, which in its way amounts to the very same thing. But it can't be stopped because this precious jewel is the incarnate Bodhisattva, the Buddha, the Enlightened One; the jewel in the lotus. And as Jung goes on to add:

"The saviour–nature of the jewel is made perfectly clear by the fact that it appears only once in every thousand years. It's a rare event—this appearance of a saviour, a Saoshyant, a Buddha."[56]

So when Cary de Angulo speaks quietly about him being the precious jewel that "reappears in the world only now and then", she is not shouting from the rooftops but just talking in private to herself or Jung. And she is describing him as the great saviour. He is the Christ-like cornerstone predicted by the ancient prophets such as Isaiah, before being rejected by the builders in precisely the way Isaiah had foretold; he is a Buddha of the West. Or he is the Saoshyant, an expression Jung himself would later explain by placing it in its proper context of ancient Zoroastrian religion:

"It is in the Zoroastrian teaching that every thousand years—which simply means an indefinite world period, about half of a month of the great platonic year—a Saoshyant appears (that is a reaper, a saviour), who teaches people a new revelation, a new truth, or renews old truths, a mediator between god and man."

This timeless figure of the Saoshyant is always "called out through the need of the time, the emergencies of the actual epoch". Or in other words, each Saoshyant is invariably summoned by a very specific situation which Jung himself defines as a situation of enormous unconsciousness; massive confusion; a collective sense of disorientation when people are at a loss because they don't have a clue any more what to do. And so these Saoshyants, these wisest of "prophets, appear in times of trouble, when mankind is in a state of confusion, when an old orientation has been lost and a new one is needed".

It's the simplest of logics: "when God dies, man needs a new orientation. In that moment the father of all prophets, the old wise man, ought to appear to give a new revelation, to give birth to a new truth."

And nothing might seem easier than to believe that when Cary de Angulo describes Jung himself as one of these saviours or Saoshyants bringing their latest revelation, "the father of all prophets" reborn, this is just the result of her own unbalanced imagination gone wild—except for the fact that it was her rigorous ability to keep a firm grip on her feelings and imaginings which allowed him to trust her in the first place.

For all its comforting appealingness, soon we'll see that to dismiss in this way what she is trying to say would be a complete and utter dead end: a very reasonable dead end but, still, a dead end.

As Jung makes sure to emphasize halfway through his detailed account of the "Kleinod" or saving jewel, any normal and reasonable attitude is totally incapable of understanding what the jewel means because there is nothing normal about it at all. "Reason must always seek the solution in some rational, consistent, logical way, which is certainly justifiable enough in all normal situations but is entirely inadequate when it comes to the really great and decisive questions." We can go along fooling ourselves for a while that our collective reasonableness and rationality will safely carry us through.

But "when the rational way proves to be a *cul de sac*—as it always does after a time—the solution comes from the side it was least expected". This is the unfailing law of psychology which even psychologists often fail to take the time, or immense trouble, to learn: that eventually the rational solution always fails.

And as for the alternative, Jung goes straight on to explain that the other side—the side which is least expected to provide any kind of solution when all else fails, but always does—is the side of the prophets.[57]

After all: it was bound to be the case that the only possible approach to the reality of the prophets would always be from the scorned side, the silenced side, the disgusting side of prophecy. At the end of the day the only lasting good is going to come from the side openly mocked by rationalists, disposed of by Jung scholars, rejected by Jungians, even repulsive to Jung himself.

10

And here is where we finally arrive—whether in what could be called, quite rightly but very impolitely, our blindness we realize it or not—at what really matters.

It's best not to dabble in the *Red book*, because one thing is absolutely certain: whatever we believe, whatever we proudly imagine, we're not going to be allowed to leave with our respectability intact. Of course we can try to fool ourselves individually and collectively, but nothing is going to change that unconscious fact.

If we think such a book is meant to help us process new ideas in our busy brains, put out thoughtful words through our busy mouths, we are mightily mistaken. We have to go down much further than that—past even the feelings in our chest, right down to our entrails. As Cary de Angulo understood perfectly well, she was nowhere with the *Red book* until she was able to experience it forever twisting her bowels.

Some things are just too self-evident to be denied. And one of them is that the *Red book* is a book of prophecy.

Commentators have flocked to comment on the undeniable. For instance, it was only when the First World War broke out that Jung started work on what would turn into his *Red book*—because only then did he realize that the stream of horrific visions and dreams he had been experiencing during the months, then weeks, leading up to the beginning of war weren't just a sign he was going mad as he originally feared.

They had been prophetic. In other words: the *Red book*'s creation was based, from the very start, on the prophetic power of his own unconscious and on the intensity of his need to explore what this means.

Then there is the solemn sequence of quotations from the prophet Isaiah that he chose to write out on its opening page; as its opening page. After he'd finished carefully copying them he made sure to add his own name alongside the precise place, and year, when he wrote them—with the unmistakable implication that he, his work, this book he was just starting, were fulfilments of the ancient prophecies.

This is not to mention, at least not yet, the prophetic tone running through the book as a whole.

And there is even the title he formally gave it: *Liber novus* or "The new book", indicating with all due clarity that a replacement for the New Testament of Christianity had arrived. "Thus", as its first editor has been bound to admit, "it was presented as a prophetic work".[58]

But then the only thing to do is simply to hold one's breath—and wait for the inevitable.

The three quotations from the prophet Isaiah that fill out the first page of Jung's *Red book* are also cited by him elsewhere: in *Psychological types*, the text he was writing at roughly the same time as his much more private work on the *Red book*.

That's not all, though, because both *Psychological types* and the *Red book* quote each of the three passages in exactly the same sequence even though this is different from their original sequence inside the book of Isaiah itself.

Quite obviously what he has to say about them there, in *Psychological types*, will have a bearing on why he is using them here. And the fact is that, there, he quotes these passages from

Isaiah ever so specifically to show what happens when people are brought face to face with the "Kleinod" or precious jewel—that very same jewel Cary de Angulo had come to see inside the person of Jung himself.

The three quotations talk about the saviour opening a path through the middle of the desert, about the opening of the eyes of the blind. But first they raise the question of who in the world of humans is going to believe this, or to whom this divine secret could possibly be revealed, because there is nothing about the saviour figure that seems worth respecting or valuing at all.

Everyone tries to find some way of hiding from it: sooner or later ends up scorning and despising it, instead.

For his own part Jung takes the time to explain, in modern terms as plainly as he can, just what Isaiah means. This rejection that the prophet describes is precisely what happens when people in their total blindness manage to get rid of the impossible saviour or Saoshyant—the father of all prophets—by pushing aside the unexpected and rejecting everything they consider unsuitable, unacceptable, inappropriate.

And he warns, in fact prophesies, that the way people nowadays will keep on doing this is by retreating into their collective rationality or rationalistic collectivity. They'll do it by huddling in the reassuring warmth of their mutual reasonableness and protecting each other, but especially themselves, from the irrational mystery at the heart of the unknown.[59]

One might have hoped that some intelligent person, somewhere, would have managed to put two and two together and realize what this all means. But nobody has noticed how Jung's prophecy has already been fulfilled to the letter.

Perhaps the most obvious example of what he was predicting is a fifty-page review of the *Red book*, published by one of the most highly reputed Jungians alive today and instructing the Jungian collectivity in what to think and do. The discipline of psychology, it insists, "belongs to the generality" because psychology's only real concern is with "universal reason". This is why each psychologist is not just some private individual but above all is "a member of the scientific community"—and it's why every psychologist's solemn duty is to reject the *Red book*'s appalling irrationality. "We are well advised to dissociate ourselves from the *Red book* and instead base our work on Jung's published psychology", his firmly established body of scientific writings, because "we have not become psychologists in order to listen to revelations".

Not every Jungian, though, has the strength or weakness of character needed to dismiss the *Red book* out of hand; and this is the point where the real power of that rational collectivity Jung was referring to comes into play, as the irresistible spirit of our time.

Also, it's the point where our own minds become incomparably clever at tricking themselves—because the best way to reject something one finds embarrassing is to make a big fuss about accepting it first before coming up with a fine, long list of reasons for rejecting it later.

And so, thanks to the slow growth of consensus, an eminently sensible compromise has already been reached. Jung's *Red book* may seem prophetic at first glance, but really it's not. He can be excused to an extent for believing that those dreams and visions he had were prophetic of the great war to come, but there are far more respectable and rational ways to explain them away instead. The *Red book*'s tone and language might sound sincerely prophetic to an untrained ear.

But in fact they are just rhetorical flourishes: nothing of the slightest substance or significance. As for the fanfare about a "new book", it certainly does convey a sense of something religious—but the less said about that, inside our progressively secular world, the better.

And to set all these unfortunate issues to rest comes the most indispensable, most decisive argument of all. Jung himself was no prophet but, on the contrary, an anti-prophet because he did the very opposite of meekly accepting a prophetic role as any genuine prophet would or should.

Instead, he courageously displays his freethinking modernity by questioning and doubting the whole business of prophecy; arguing with it; fighting it with every fibre of his being. As for the resulting tension, the extraordinary conflict pitting prophet against anti-prophet, it runs through the veins of the *Red book*—and only goes to prove how completely removed this is from any simple, traditional, old-fashioned prophetic text.[60]

And the only question left is how low it's possible to hold one's head in shame at the unfathomable ignorance, demonstrated by these statements, about the reality not only of prophecy but also of Jung.

First there is that little matter of his prophetic visions and dreams.

On top of the very sensible commentators who instinctively know—just like Porphyry—that any talk about prophecy is something for us to leave aside as irrational rubbish and be done with, there is also another much more specific phenomenon involved. This is the new orthodoxy rapidly springing up in Jungian circles which insists on abolishing the word "prophetic", whenever discussing Jung's visions or dreams, and replacing it with the far safer-sounding term "synchronistic" so there will be no more unpleasant overtones of prophecy or of mysterious glimpses into the future.

Those experiences of his during the lead-up to war and the start of his work on the *Red book* are something we can comfortably explain away now, by turning his own scientific language against him, as synchronicity. And everyone can sigh a breath of relief at not only getting rid of the disturbance but, in the process, getting rid of Jung.[61]

More than two thousand years before his time, Aristotle had already done a fine job of killing off all that superstitious silliness about inspired insights into the future and forcing it into a virtual underworld of its own. Since then, intellectuals have lined up through the centuries to hand him "the palm of honour" for being the person who "first entirely denied the existence of prophetic dreams". Even Sigmund Freud ended up glad to accept the reality of telepathy along with any number of other things but, whenever faced with the question of whether dreams might be prophetic, couldn't resist kneeling to the rational authority of Aristotle.

With Jung things couldn't have been more different. Along with a handful of equally rebellious predecessors whose memory he treasured, he not only insisted on accepting the existence of prophetic visions and dreams. He even reserved for them pride of place inside his worldview; and this is a position from which, with his instinctive underworld sensitivities, he never budged or changed.[62]

Of course he was extra-cautious about the ways he actually talked about such things. There was always the most delicate balance in what he chose to say or not say, or to whom. But it's another matter entirely when even the most devoted Jungians end up reverting to the role of little Aristotles.

And at the very least, if they do find themselves needing to settle back into that habitual attitude of rational murder which Jung had almost killed himself trying to break, one could at least expect them to be conscious of just what they are doing.

Then there is that other issue of Jung struggling so visibly, and tensely, with the role of prophet.

The idea that becoming a prophet is some simple-minded affair of flying off into ecstasy by escaping the burdens of humanity is one of the biggest delusions imaginable. Prophets—real prophets, genuine prophets—have always been among the most conflicted, burdened people walking the earth. The Old Testament prophets in particular were notorious for opposing rather than meekly accepting their role; for doubting, fighting, resisting, challenging it; for arguing with God.

The unbearable tensions between prophetic and anti-prophetic aren't the signs of a failed prophet, or of rejecting the prophetic task. They are among the best proofs of the presence of a true prophet. We may not know this any more, let alone understand it, with our reasonable modern educations or possible Sunday-school brainwashings.

But Jung did. As so often, Cary de Angulo hit the nail straight on the head when she wrote to him about the strangely human poignancy in the turmoil of his having tried to the fullest extent possible "to avoid the task the Spirit of the Deep laid upon you, and then when you accepted it" is when the grace finally came.

This drama of rejection followed by an always reluctant, if inevitable, acceptance is exactly the reality portrayed and conveyed by the *Red book*. It's also precisely the reality of prophecy.[63]

And as for the result of that acceptance: it could hardly be more obvious.

It's Jung's "new book" itself.

Strange to say, in all the growing discussions about the purpose of his *Red book*, no one yet seems to have noticed that he stated exactly what he meant by the idea of a "new book" within the last couple of years before he died. He did so in the context of frankly explaining what, throughout his life, had mattered to him most; talking about the battles he was still engaged in from the core of his being because, behind all the scientific appearances and rhetoric, they defined everything in his existence.

Those battles weren't with other so-called scientists, or even with people working in the field of psychology. They were religious battles against the identical forces of repression that almost two thousand years earlier, with their allegiance to blind faith and belief and dogma, had crushed the Gnostics into non-existence.

And it was not as a scientist that he found himself fighting to the very end of his days for the cause of authentic religious experience. Instead it was as an ancient but resurrected Gnostic that, already an old man getting ready to die, he still had the fire in him to challenge the Christian church which mindlessly keeps insisting: "no religious experience please, as the truth has been revealed for all times and God is not supposed to be able to produce a new book after the original edition 2,000 years ago".

Defiantly, almost half a century earlier, Jung had played his part in writing that "new book"—that revised edition, produced by God, of the Holy Bible—even though he never quite saw the possibility or the rightness of making it public. And as for the crucial question of how on earth such a new book is produced by God, the answer couldn't be simpler.

God produces it through his prophets, who do and say not what they want as humans but what the God inside them commands.

And so we are brought back to the most basic meaning of the word "prophet"—which doesn't have anything to do with telling the future. What the word was meant to describe is the person who at any moment in history speaks or writes or communicates faithfully, accurately, without interfering with the process, on behalf of the divine; serves as a mouthpiece to record exactly what the sacred is needing to convey.

This is why it's so important to note what happens right at the heart of Jung's "new book", straight after he has been allowed to witness the great *Mysterium* or mystery of his own deification. He walks up to the prophet Elijah, kneels at his feet, and Elijah for his part tells him precisely what he has to do: "Above all, write exactly what you see".

Here we have one prophet telling another just what he needs to do as the necessary consequence of accepting his prophetic role. Like any other prophet, he has to write exactly what he has been shown or told. But it also helps to be aware of the way that here, in this scene which just so happens to take place in front of the prophet's house at the base of the volcano leading down to the underworld, Jung is taking his own place inside a much more specific tradition—one leading back past Dante, past Plato, even past Parmenides to the dimmest beginnings of visionary literature about journeys into the realms of the dead.

That's the tradition about the solitary person who manages to go down all the way to the underworld while still alive, only to be told to return as a messenger or prophet to the world of the living so as to report "exactly what you have seen".

And, naturally, this has a rather uncomfortable implication. On the surface, nothing could be more reasonable than to assume that Jung's immense labours in accurately documenting every single thing he witnessed or experienced during his archetypal journeys are a living proof of his commendable devotion to the principles of experimental science.

Underneath these modern considerations, though, is the very different reality that his commitment to writing everything out with such scrupulous care had nothing to do with science as we understand science.

It was simply the result of him accepting his prophetic task, just as it had been accepted by Zoroastrians and Greeks and Gnostics for centuries before his time.[64]

Of course that means nothing could be less surprising than the way Jung's language and tone, in his "new book", are already prophetic right from the start. But what's likely to be a little more surprising is the perfectly logical consequence of this simple fact, provided one cares to look it straight in the eye.

For instance, there could be no better or more blatant example of a prophet's language than his scathing denunciation of people—not just some small group of people but humanity at large, the entire human race—as "blind and deluded". They "behave like brutes", ignoring what's hidden; trampling the past, neglecting the dead.

This sweeping condemnation, this blanket denunciation of humanity as a whole, is the classic style of prophetic revelation. Parmenides in his own time, over two thousand years earlier, spoke exactly the same way. And it's not a question here of rhetorical flourish: the only rhetorical flourish is the ungrounded attempt by commentators to dismiss such revelatory language as no more than a rhetorical flourish.

The best one perhaps could hope for would be to find ways of sealing off this *Red book* from the public, even from the unseasoned eyes of Jungian therapists; of insulating it from his supposedly scientific work. But here is where we come to the heart of the problem—because Jung's prophetic language isn't restricted to the *Red book*. It never was.

On the contrary: he cries and complains repeatedly about the blindness of humanity throughout his scientific work. And at the conclusion to one of his maturest achievements in the field of psychology he goes well beyond the language of his "new book", portraying the whole of humanity as literally crazy with inflation. But it's still the same basic message, the same intensely urgent tone, the same choice of words. "The masses are blind brutes". The inflated collective consciousness of humanity "is incapable of learning from the past, incapable of understanding contemporary events, and incapable of drawing right conclusions about the future".

As for trying to reason with that collective consciousness—to work together in a constructive fashion on some healthy rational approach—nothing could be more futile. Nothing for Jung could be more pointless, because it actually hypnotizes itself "and therefore cannot be argued with. It inevitably dooms itself to calamities that must strike it dead".[65]

Up until the *Red book*'s publication it was easy enough to skip quickly over such passages, in spite of their desperate tone or rather because of it, and turn a blind eye. But the reality is that if you scratch away the scientific façade of his psychological work, behind the veneer you will find Jung the prophet everywhere.

And this is not even to take into account the things he chose to keep out of sight or deliberately hide away—such as the extent of his indebtedness to the prophetic works of William Blake.[66]

But what matters most is the disturbance caused by this book's undesirability, regardless of whether people rush out excitedly to welcome it with open arms or not. It's a deadly virus; a massive earthquake capable of shaking every rational edifice built up on the work of Jung to the ground; the eruption of something way down inside us which is incalculably destructive of all the tricks we use not only for understanding Jung but to understand ourselves.

This is the honest reason why so many people sense his *Red book* as a danger, however they try to negotiate their fear. What really scares them is not that it reveals a side of Jung quite unrelated to his accepted psychology or science—even at odds with them.

The truly frightening thing is that it forces us to view the task of doing science, or being a psychologist, with the eyes of a prophet.

11

When the corn disappears is when the disaster and the rage arrive—and this is just what has happened, will happen, with the losses of our knowledge about prophecy.

We have come to believe it's all about telling the future. But that's the least part of prophecy because the most important function of prophets, the function from which everything else springs, has always been their ability to tell the past.

Even the best-known texts of the Bible show how a prophet is someone with miraculous insight into what has happened already—not what will happen. And in ancient Greek tradition, too, nothing could possibly be plainer. For a prophet like Empedocles, prototypical psychologist, the first and foremost task was to find the answer to what originally went wrong with humanity that made everything the way it is. The business of prophecy was to enter an ecstatic state of reality that lays bare the "ancient crimes" for which, in our supposedly normal existence, we are still being punished and tormented today.

Already at the very start of Homer's *Iliad* the prophet stands out as the one indispensable figure who can look into the unseen and see who offended the sacred, when, how; what's behind all the sickness and suffering and death unleashed because someone, somewhere, violated divine law. It's the same again with Cassandra, the crazy seer. She was instantly recognized as a prophetess not because she was able to say what's going to come in the future, but because her prophetic insight exposed her to the horror of the murders hidden in the past.

And one of life's ironies is that sometimes, in spite of himself, even a rationalistic fool like Aristotle will end up getting something right. About the famous prophet Epimenides—who in a state of incubation used to enter a kind of awareness that was neither sleep nor waking so he could make his way down, just like Jung, to the underworld and have encounters there with divine beings—he managed to report the essential. "He didn't prophesy about things that will happen in the future but about things that already happened in the past and are unseen, unknown".[67]

This primordial past is the domain of the prophet as guardian of creation: preserver of nature and protector of life. It's where prophets may have to stick their heads out of now and then, so they can offer some prophecy about the future, because there is no knowing the future without the most intimate knowledge about the past; without first learning how to move freely among the creatures of the past with their untold stories of beauties and horrors, creatures which most people even in their wildest dreams would never imagine are still alive.

As a prophet Jung intuited this perfectly, which is why he describes in the *Red book* what made a prophet of him by using just the words he did: "And so I became a prophet because I found delight in the primordial, in the forest and the wild animals".

Gently and so eloquently he says it all—that to become a prophet means returning deep into the past until you are brushing against the root of yourself, your primordial beginning and ultimate point of origin. But a prophet whose words are noticed and understood is not much of a prophet, because the role of prophets is always to state what the collective awareness of people is not yet able to grasp.

And sure enough, Jung's own statements don't stand a chance because they run so completely contrary to the modern horror of us progressive little Fausts rushing to throw ourselves off the nearest cliff into another non-existent future.

It seems only too obvious: his "new book" or testament must be all about the dramatically new and radically improved psychological future we can now look forward to at the solemn dawning of a new age. But so much obviousness can be quite a hindrance to seeing what the *Red book* is really about.

The wonders and terrors it contains are the terror and wonder of our own past, with the dead hanging round our necks. As for the future, at times he is willing to bring us to its brink so we can contemplate the horrors that lie ahead if we can't face the horror that lies behind us; in us.

And he also states as clearly as he can: leave the future alone. It's none of your business, never was.

As for what our business is then, if we are not in the rationally acceptable position of being able to improve our own future and interfere with the future of others by creating the world we want—this is the question that propels Jung into one of the most desperate sections of the *Red book.*

His answer is that our only business now as true humans is to give up all our reasoning and rationalizing and go searching, instead, for magic. It's to sacrifice our cravings for comfort, to abandon our illusions of science and submit to the incomprehensible, to become Christs by letting ourselves be crucified all alone. It's to face the need to return, in full consciousness, to the primordial point of origin where our own will is suddenly suspended and the mind stops still; to accept the unbearable tension of being transformed, inside the thoughtless awareness of this present moment, into what we always have been.

And there is one magical ending to that tension—although you can count on it coming, absurdly, irrationally, from the one place you would have least expected. As for what that resolution is, that saving release: Jung explains it in the most deceptively simple of terms.

"Always it's something primordially ancient, and for that very reason it's something new—because whenever something left behind long ago comes back again into the changed world of today, then it's new. To give birth, inside an age, to the primordially ancient is creation. This is what it means to produce the new; and that's what saves me. Salvation is the solution of the problem, the resolution of the task. The task is to give birth to the old in a new time."

In other words: contrary to every single assumption injected into our forward-looking minds, the only thing that's new is what's most ancient. Everything else is nothing but a bluff, a distraction, a waste of time.

And far worse, every time we very reasonably fool ourselves into believing we know the future we need, we are blocking our true future and wrecking what needs to be.

From any normal or rational point of view, we look into the past to lose ourselves in nostalgia and sentimentality; look into the future to create what's new. But, in reality, we lose ourselves by chasing the future and create what's new by returning into the past.

And without the prophets who are willing to take us back to the primordial reality of what we are, we have no future left.

Everything else is just a fake, an illusion, a waste of life, because the only real and lasting creation consists of consciously reincarnating what's most ancient—not even of having to update or streamline or modernize it but of importing it exactly as its essence dictates. Our modern, updated, streamlined world will take care of the rest.

That's how our ancestors, whom we may have forgotten although they haven't forgotten us, are respected and welcomed;

is how a genuine historical continuity is assured; is how we stop being passive victims of history but, on the contrary, can consciously bring the past into the present for the sake of the future.

And it's the shock of that direct encounter between modern and old which, like the shock of cold water meeting molten iron, creates the new.[68]

This is one of the most revealing parts of the *Red book*—created with its archaic script, its Latin quotations, its phrases taken from ancient Greek—not just because it tells the secret of prophecy but because it states what Jung's "new book" is.

As he already tried telling Sigmund Freud a few years earlier, the only way to describe the birth of psychology at the dawn of the twentieth century was in terms of reincarnation: as the act of reincarnating the ancient Gnostic wisdom, Sophia, in a modern age.

As it happens, even the act of giving birth to the ancient in the new is a Gnostic process. And that act of reincarnation was devotedly inscribed in, portrayed inside, respectfully embodied as the *Red book* itself.

But, of course, if we wanted to limit this process of reincarnation to some unusual writing inside a single book we once again would be sadly mistaken. And if we wanted to believe that Cary de Angulo was just indulging her personal imagination when she looked on Jung himself as the precious jewel—the Saoshyant or saviour, the father of all prophets who appears in the world by reincarnating now and then for the sake of humanity—this would be because we haven't yet understood how to read Carl Jung.

Prophets are quite used to hiding their truth out in the open, like some priceless jewel at the marketplace, because they know that our reasonable expectations will make us brush it aside. And this is precisely what Jung does in his *Red book*, unobserved.

Time and time again, in the text itself, he addresses Philemon as his father; time after time, Philemon refers to him as his son. But at the top of the single most famous picture in the *Red book*—of Philemon with his kingfisher wings spread out—Jung has clearly written out an explanation of the painting in ancient Greek.

Prophêtôn patêr polyphilos Philêmôn means "Father of prophets, beloved Philemon".

Again, on the beautiful mural displaying the same image which he painted upstairs at his private retreat in Bollingen, he added almost the same dedication: also in Greek, also at the top. This time, though, his wording was a little more specific.

Instead of the familiar word *patêr* or "father" he used the much rarer expression *propatôr*—a technical term for the primordial principle hovering behind the whole of creation, the incomprehensible spirit of the depths, which appropriately enough he had taken straight from the ancient Gnostic texts he studied and loved so much. *Philêmôn tôn prophêtôn propatôr* means "Philemon, primordial father of the prophets".

And just below Philemon's left wing Jung has conveniently added the Latin alchemical text in which the spiritual father insists that he and his son are one.

Jung is Philemon's son, Philemon is his father, and Philemon is the beloved father of the prophets. There is no need to be some mathematical genius to see where this is leading. In public, Jung could deny he was a prophet as much as he wanted for the sake of keeping his secret secret. But that's only because, in the privacy of his own retreat as well as in the mystery of his unpublished "new book", he was able to state silently and ever so plainly who he was: a prophet, son of the prophets' beloved father.[69]

After all, this is exactly how prophets speak for those who have eyes to see and ears to hear—openly stating without seeming to state a thing. And what separates those who take note of the obvious from those who miss it is what distinguishes those who read Jung with their expectations from those who read him.

You will note that he doesn't describe Philemon as "father of the prophet" but is very careful to call him "father of the prophets". And as for who those other prophets are, often in future years he will list the names of his elder brothers.

They are Zarathustra, Buddha, Christ, Mani, Muhammad. Or rather, because father and son are really one, it would be better to say that the primordial saviour incarnated three thousand years ago as Zarathustra and since then "he has been Christ, he has been Muhammad, he has been Mani. He went and he came, he died and was born again."

He—the most ancient father of all prophets who reincarnates whenever needed in the shape of the son—is "the one that goes and the one that comes", returning "only now and then". Periodically he arrives again in the world of today, a "rare phenomenon", the old reappearing in the new.

Or according to the language of a passage from the *Bhagavad gita* which Jung inscribed in his *Red book* right alongside the picture he had painted of Philemon, as a miniature commentary on it: "Whenever there is a decline of the law and an increase of iniquity, then I put forth myself. For the rescue of the pious and for the destruction of the evildoers, for the establishment of the law I am born in every age."

That's not even to mention the different lineages of brothers, sisters too—the rest of the prophets and saviours, Bodhisattvas and Buddhas, avatars and Saoshyants, all inwardly supporting and reinforcing each other down through the ages.[70]

And among them, prophetic son of his prophetic father, Jung discreetly lived with the secret suffering of knowing that he was one.

12

Ten years or so went by from the time when Jung was snatched down into the underworld.

Conventional wisdom would have it that everything in his life had returned pretty much to normal. He had regained his balance, nicely integrated the experience, and was back to being a model of serenity: solid rock and example to all.

The reality was a little different. Years earlier he had gone in search of his soul, then found her. Now she wouldn't leave him alone.

During the first week of 1922 he was noting down the discussions between them. She is explaining that she is totally in charge now. She rules him because she serves him. Or rather, she doesn't serve him personally but serves his calling; his mission.

And when he nervously asks what that mission is, her answer is simple. It's to bring a new religion into the world—then proclaim it.

All Jung can do, for his part, is complain. The one issue he complains about more than anything else is, very humanly, his inability to sleep: he works during the day but can't get any rest at night. And she is open enough to admit that already for a long while she deliberately has been keeping him awake, interfering with his sleep, because there are far more important things he needs to be attending to than his day-to-day chores.

Of course myths have to exist, in particular around a personality as commanding as Jung's. People close to him were keen on maintaining the soporific notion that his sleep was blessedly sound, miraculously deep, because no one could be more at peace with the unconscious than he was.

That's only a part of the truth, though. The fact is that as soon as he started writing, young or old, the first thing likely to go out of the window was his sleep. When he was meant to write but didn't, he got sick to the point where he couldn't get any rest; when he did write, the process was often so intense that he couldn't sleep either. From the moment that the daimon inside him took over, whatever its name, his nights were no longer his own.[71]

One of the blessings that did stay with him during those early years of the 1920s was the chance to talk about his experiences honestly, directly, intelligently with the woman he had come to trust so much—Cary de Angulo. On a winter's day in January 1924 they sat together. And this is what, based on her memory of their discussion, she would later write down with that quality of preciseness he valued her for so highly:

Jung, she noted, informed her he had just dreamed the previous night that she was to help him with the *Red book*. Faithful to his dream, he already had decided to hand everything over and explain the entire material to her as completely as he could so that she and she alone would be able to understand each of his ideas from "the foundation". He described how painful the process of writing, even of painting, was; how mad it all seemed; the difficulties he found himself surrounded by.

And in her meticulous style she went on to record his account of what was really happening with the *Red book*, reciting his own explanations back to him.

"There were various figures speaking, Elias, Father Philemon, etc. but all appeared to be phases of what you thought ought to be called 'the master'. You were sure that this latter was the same who inspired Buddha, Mani, Christ, Mahomet—all those in fact who may be said to have communed with God. But the others had identified with him. You absolutely refused to. It could not be for you, you said, you had to remain the psychologist—the person who understood the process. I said then that the thing to be done was to enable the world to understand the process also without their getting the notion that they had the master caged as it were at their beck & call. They had to think of him as a pillar of fire perpetually moving on, and forever out of human grasp. Yes, you said it was something like that. Perhaps it cannot yet be done. As you talked I grew more and more aware of the immensity of the ideas which are filling you. You said they had the shadow of eternity upon them and I could feel the truth of it."

Overwhelmed, she added that she didn't see herself as being in any way capable of really helping him with the gigantic task he had taken on.[72]

Of the various names here, many will already be more or less familiar: Philemon father of prophets, the prophet Elias or Elijah, the other prophet Mahomet or Muhammad, Buddha and Christ. But the one name that, strangely enough, may sound strange is the name of Mani.

I say "strangely enough" because, of all these names, in a way his almost deserves to be known best. Jung, for sure, knew perfectly well who Mani was. He had been an extraordinary prophet and healer and painter, born in Babylonia about two hundred years after Christ, who founded an immensely sophisticated world religion known as the Manichaean religion which was to take root from the western edges of Europe right across Asia into China—before being systematically wiped out by Christians, Buddhists, Zoroastrians as perhaps the most potent and terrifying form of Gnosticism that ever existed.

Coming on for two thousand years before the new-age movement even saw the light of day, Mani had not only claimed he was bringing together in his own mission the most essential teachings of Buddha; of Christ; of every other prophet, including Zarathustra, who had lived before him. He also proclaimed himself as the fulfiller and completer, as the one true successor and superseder of all their wisdoms: as the Seal of Prophets.

At the same time, and very consciously in the mould of older figures like Empedocles, Mani presented himself not just as a saviour and prophet and healer—but as a scientist, too, with a detailed insight into the workings of the world and of the human psyche which only the direct experience granted through revelation can ever hope to provide.

Carl Jung, for his own part, was fascinated by Mani's amazingly intricate explanations of the physical world; followed the unearthing of Manichaean manuscripts, by German archaeologists at Turfan in Central Asia, with riveted attention; warmly praised Mani for his skills not just as the founder of a world religion but as a wonderful painter.[73]

And here he is, late on a January afternoon in Zurich, comparing himself to a series of these prophets and saviours.

Understandably enough, for a minute you might have started wondering what on earth he is up to—referring to himself in one and the same breath right alongside an entire list of redeemers, prophets, fathers of prophets.

Then comes the word to conjure with, the golden key to our peace of mind: identify. And it only takes a moment for everything to fall neatly into place. All those prophets whom Jung might seem at first glance to be comparing himself to had made the crucial mistake of identifying themselves with "the master". He, on the other hand, "absolutely refused to. It could not be for you, you said, you had to remain the psychologist—the person who understood the process."

The magic spell has been broken. Once again, with his grand gesture of disidentification we can breathe easily and sleep even easier.

Here he is, once more, the man we know and trust and feel safe with: the pragmatic psychologist, the sensible scientist who with a sceptical wave of his hand can leave all that prophetic nonsense behind.

But of course, if you pay attention, you will see that no spell was broken. And Jung has left absolutely nothing behind.

That act of disidentification has done nothing whatsoever to get rid of "the master". On the contrary, it brings us up very close to a man aching to help people understand how much they needed to get rid of any notion that "they had the master caged as it were at their beck and call". What he wanted was for them to let him be free, allow him to move freely—which is why Jung and Cary de Angulo both found themselves discussing this same master a week later and agreeing to describe him as a titanic being who, striding across the universe, transcends the whole world.

And here, it's all about learning to see him "as a pillar of fire perpetually moving on" just outside of human reach. Needless to say, this pillar of fire isn't some image arbitrarily picked out of nowhere. Biblically, it was the mystery of the divine presence itself: the living God who, every night, would appear to the chosen people to guide them through the desolation of the wilderness.

But, significantly enough, the pillar of light or fire also happens to have been a symbol of immense importance in Manichaean tradition as well as for Jung—symbol of the complete human being, of the perfected prophet.[74]

And as for Jung himself, what we are left with is not the reductive theorizing of some calculating psychologist. Instead, nothing remains except for the image of a man left face to face with the sheer immensity of living directly underneath the shadow of eternity; and in those eternal darknesses there are so many impossible things just waiting to be done by the being who, as Cary de Angulo realized, is a jewel precisely because he doesn't identify with being a jewel.

In other words: if you care to look at what was happening, are interested enough to read sentence by sentence what our text is saying, you will see what the effect of Jung's psychological disidentification actually is.

It's the same story as before—all over again. It's not about disposing of the archetypes and making them vanish. It's about consciously setting them free; about helping them as only a human can, through the non-inflation of non-identification, to carry on with doing their real work in the world.

What might have sounded such utter heresy, because it flies straight in the face of every reasonable therapeutic mentality, is no heresy at all. Disidentifying from the archetypal realities was never just about keeping our human psychology uncontaminated and pure. It's also about keeping the archetypal realities pure and uncontaminated by us.

Mani, Christ, Muhammad, Buddha, Zarathustra: they all did the best they possibly could. The only problem is that even to accept and identify with the role of prophet or saviour is to corrupt it. And if you still want to think I am talking heresy I'll simply have to prove you wrong by quoting from one of Jung's most famous seminars.

"Zarathustra was a saviour, the great teacher, just as good as Christ or Mani or Muhammad or any of the great prophets. But if a human being identifies with that figure, there is an admixture of human psychology, and it is due to this mixture with human imperfection that the face of Zarathustra appears like the face of a devil … is no longer pure."[75]

This, if you like, is Jungian psychology not from the merely human but from the sacred point of view. And now, if we dare to watch, we can start to see the grand trick being played out behind all the fine-sounding talk about being a humble psychologist; nothing but a scientist.

The human work of learning how to disidentify from the archetypes was always inspired by something more than purely human. From the very start, Jungian therapy was never meant to be just another therapy in the modern sense of being about me and me and me: it was about the *therapeia* of serving, and caring for, the divine.

Behind their exterior there is far more to Jung's professional role as a psychologist, his respectable scientific job, than meets the eye. They stop him from identifying, getting inflated, puffed up. They allow him to stay grounded in this world, modest, objective, critical especially of himself—and do the work of a true mystic.

This is a paradox we have been forbidden in the West to remember, hardly allowed even to understand. It's a paradox that his friend Henry Corbin was to become well acquainted with, thanks to those Sufis who had kept the teachings of Empedocles and other Presocratics alive in the East. Mysticism alone is just useless gush; but, trained to work together, mystical experience and a scientific attitude become the two wings of a single bird.

Someone full of mystical beliefs can perhaps at best be considered a third-rate mystic, just as a scientist full of reasonable assumptions and firm convictions is a scientific fool. Real mysticism is to abandon any possible identification and, from moment to moment, surrender everything—which is why scepticism is the most mystical attitude of all.

One has to be infinitely cautious, though; be endlessly sceptical about one's scepticism; constantly remember to doubt one's own doubt. People who like to call themselves sceptics are mostly just superficial compromisers who settle on a little patch of scepticism that attracts them because they are afraid of going further. But true scepticism, followed to its logical conclusion, grows into what Jung himself called the "greatest doubt" and leads straight to the secret of life.[76]

In other words his famous psychology, his much vaunted science, had a mystical goal all along. Here, more than anywhere else, is where the scientist son is reunited and perfectly conjoined with the mystical father.

Or to state the matter just a little less discreetly, his science and psychology are serving a prophetic purpose—carrying the great work of prophecy forward, leading the lineage of prophets and saviours one step further into the future.

And that brings us right back again to his discussion with Cary de Angulo.

There happens to be something in what he tells her that anybody nowadays is almost bound to skip over without noting its significance. In fact only someone as familiar with Gnostic or Manichaean literature as Jung himself was would ever recognize it. But it's not just a question of what he says.

It's even a matter of the subtleties inside the way he says it.

At a certain point he makes the impressive claim that the supreme master inspiring his work on the *Red book* "was the same who inspired Buddha, Mani, Christ, Mahomet—all those in fact who may be said to have communed with God". He was unlike all those older prophets, though, because in one crucial respect he has left them behind: has learned the absolute need no longer to identify.

In other words he is just like them on one fundamental level and on another, equally important level has gone beyond them.

But what's not nearly so obvious is that this very same double claim lies right at the heart of Manichaean as well as Gnostic traditions. In a certain sense it even defines them.

First, the newest prophet in the latest generation takes care to list the names of his major predecessors: there was a general fondness for listing the names of prophets in groups of four. He also has to make sure to state that the source of his own inspiration is the same as, is identical to, the source that inspired all those who came before.

And then he is confronted with the need to explain how he has gone beyond every one of his distinguished predecessors—how he is not just continuing their work but taking it to another level altogether by adding his own, unique contribution.

That's what it means to be carrying the lineage of prophets to the next stage, to fulfil and complete their work at the same time as totally transforming it: to become, in oneself, the Seal of Prophecy.

This is just what Mani did, for his own time and age. Perhaps I should mention that two of the ways he chose to advance beyond those who had gone before him were by deciding to paint his revelations, as well as write them; and by consciously coming to grips with the fact that the major culprits always responsible for destroying any revealed religion by already subverting it within the space of a single generation are not, as one might suppose, its obvious competitors or enemies.

It's the devoted apostles, followers, disciples.[77]

And in repeating the identical formality this is exactly what Jung does, too. Even while outwardly he is presenting himself as a psychologist, inwardly he is doing something else. At the same precise moment as he seems to be announcing how modern he is, he is revealing how ancient he is in his deepest mode of thought.

He is talking just the same way Mani did. He is speaking as a Gnostic.

It still might sound a little strange to hear someone pointing to such an intimate connection between one of the most influential figures in the twentieth century and a forgotten heretic called Mani. But the fact is that, whether we want to notice or not in this record of a winter's conversation, the early 1920s would find Jung taking the pages right out of Mani's book: reading straight from Mani's script.

And it's no coincidence that four years earlier, at the start of the year 1920, he had a major dream in Tunisia about one particular book—the book which he came to realize would be "absolutely essential" in giving him the power to confront, and ultimately master, the overwhelming daimonic forces of the unconscious.

It was a book which, in his dream, gave him the extraordinary sense that "this was '*my* book', that I had written it". If he could only hold on to that sense, he knew he would find inside its pages whatever strength he needed for commanding and befriending the archetypal realities beyond his conscious reach.

But as for what this book, Jung's own book, looked like: with its magnificent calligraphy on milky–white parchment it wasn't written in a European script, not even in Arabic. "Rather, it looked to me like the Uigurian script of West Turkestan, which was familiar to me from the Manichaean fragments from Turfan."[78]

This book of his, so uniquely written not just for him alone but by him alone—the book of his own psychology which would allow him to understand and even make friends with the unconscious—is at the same time the writing produced by Mani and Mani's followers. Once again, the language of Jung is the language of Mani.

As for that intricate script he has been shown, the script of the unconscious so many others will soon be trying so hard to decipher: it isn't European or Arab or African.

In its quintessential form it's the script of ancient heretics; the calligraphy of the Manichees.

Exactly the same as emerges with such revealing detail in that discussion between him and Cary de Angulo, the prophet Mani with his searing teaching about light and darkness has got deep underneath his skin. And in spite of every appearance to the contrary, Jung's magnificently scripted psychology wasn't some solitary creation.

On the contrary, it was simply the new religion that his soul once hinted he would be bringing to the world—the latest, most updated, most freshly reincarnated method of salvation.

For us today, in spite of his earlier comments to Freud about creating a religion which would replace Christianity, nothing could be more tempting than to dodge or reject outright that terrifying statement by Jung's soul about a new religion and its proclamation. But while this may be the way we treat our souls, it's not the way he treated his; and, in reality, some things don't ever go away or become unsaid.[79]

He definitely might, almost certainly would, reject the literal and crude interpretation of what she does say—because the entire point of his psychology was to work towards finding its innermost meaning. This is precisely the reason why, in line with his Gnostic dedication to direct experience, he would never be the founder of some cult with set dogmas or creeds. After all, even Christ never had any intention of creating an outer religion.

But it's also why he would repeatedly tell those who worked with him that they and he belonged to an "invisible church": to a "secret church", free of any outer rules, which exists behind and beyond every visible or formal institution.[80]

And so Jung would present himself to the world as a man with a mission but no mission; as a mystic without being a mystic. He would be the bringer of a message but no message, in the same way that he was both a prophet and a saviour without being either.

As for his whole psychology, far from serving to dispose of prophetic traditions it was itself the purest of offerings at the altar of prophecy. And, although he felt unable to say very much except to the closest or most trusted of colleagues, in reality his science was exactly the same as Mani's science—or Empedocles' science.

It, too, was prophecy and revelation through and through: a science designed to let the presence of God become even more present by allowing the prophetic role to fulfil itself, without any contamination or identification, in the modern world.

13

Right at the start of the *Red book* Jung states that according to the spirit of this time there can be no justification, or defence, for the things he is going to say.

No, that's not good enough and I need to be more precise. In the very first sentence of the *Red book* he admits that—if he was to speak in the spirit of this time—nothing whatsoever and absolutely no one would be able to justify the message he has to proclaim. "Verkünden" is his word for proclaim; but it's also a word that means, as it most certainly does here, both preach and prophesy.

And so, from the opening sentence, Jung is presenting himself as a prophet with a mission and a message to convey.

In the same spirit, according to the same logic, I realize there can be no possible justification for documenting his unadorned experience of the relationship between prophecy and science—because this is the very last thing that on the surface of our collective existence we want to hear.

But here, based on his own exquisitely consistent accounts which stretch across almost fifty years, is what he said:

The spirit of the depths wanted him. Even though he had the personal and overpowering sense of needing to keep going deeper inside himself, the reality is that it was needing him.

It tore him away from everything including any reassurance of sanity—shattered all his childish attachment to worldly wisdom and science. Next, it forced him to serve as its mouthpiece and speak on its behalf; overcame his resistance through the mystery of its grace; compelled him to write what it was so urgently and timelessly needing to convey to the world of humans.

"Glad" every day "to have escaped from death", he was helpless in the face of this primordial spirit's overwhelming power: amazed it hadn't crushed him already. And he had absolutely no choice.

If he held off on writing down what needed recording, refused to say what had to be said, automatically he'd be robbed of his ability to speak on behalf of anything or anybody else; robbed of any joy; robbed of any life. His one and only hope was that just by obeying, by writing down exactly everything he had been shown and whatever he'd been told, he would be released from his ordeal—freed from the prophetic task.

But he wasn't freed at all. And slowly he learned the central lesson already learned by that favourite figure he was always glad to keep in mind: Odysseus. After each ordeal comes the next ordeal.

There was a part of him, the human part we all know so well, that simply couldn't stand what he was being forced to do. The crude, raw reality of having a prophetic mission turned his stomach; revolted him with its repulsive aura of unconscious pretentiousness. As for the grand prophetic language of what he was being made to write, its bombastic archetypal style, working with it was like sheer agony and torture.

He knew very well he had his message and mission, his "Botschaft" as he called it in German, which he was needing to bring to the world: the prophetic task he had been given by the spirit of the depths and that he soon came to realize, beyond any doubt or question, would never be taken away. He was perfectly aware that trying to abandon it wouldn't just make his life worthless.

It would kill him. But he also knew the language he was using for this message wasn't the right one—and he was going to have to find another.

So, gradually, he started understanding that to stand any chance at all of getting the message across he was going to have to make his way back from the world of the depths to the human side of reality. He would need to find solid ground again under his feet, which in his case would mean returning to the world of science with its seemingly solid methods; its firm conclusions.

In other words, the next ordeal was to be a task of translation: was to set about translating his prophetic message into the language of science.[81]

Of course he wasn't the first person to have to complete this archetypal return from the realms of the gods, and the dead, to the land of the living. Two and a half thousand years earlier both Parmenides and Empedocles found themselves having to adapt, after their own underworld journeys, to living and speaking again as more or less ordinary people by very consciously re-adopting the normal human conventions—above all to translating their experiences of a reality beyond anything human into a familiar, everyday language which anyone could understand and which would contribute to the science of their times.

But one of the points most worth noting about their returns from the world of the gods to what Jung would later describe as the "human side" is that this wasn't something they had to try and work out by themselves. Quite to the contrary: very visibly, in Parmenides' case, it was the divine that took care of everything.

And for Empedocles, together with Parmenides, the one decisive factor that made it possible for them to return effectively as prophets to the world of humans was the divine reality called *mêtis*.

Mêtis is the ability to adapt, translate, shift shape; is the instinctive inner wisdom that can steer a consistent course for us across the constantly changing waters of existence; is the infinite subtlety and alertness that's needed to make the impossible transition successfully, faithfully, exactly from one level of reality to another; is the cunning of knowing how to keep concealed and disguised while revealing no more than is appropriate at any moment.

Above all, though, *mêtis* is the supreme art of trickery and deception in a world that's full of deceit and tricks.

Naturally to us modern, well-adapted humans nothing could sound more absurd than to think of someone's successful return to the warm and safe and solid world of humans as a deception. But that's only because in our collective, inflated, unquestioning identification with the human condition we never experience what it actually means to fall under the archetypal spell of becoming human. Neither have we probably ever experienced what it feels like to be snatched away from all that's human by a power far greater than oneself and forced to leave the world of humanity behind—before eventually being forced to return.

This return is never an easy matter. And to understand just a little of what the process involves, it's enough to think of that mythical figure who already was so familiar even before the time of Parmenides or Empedocles.

When Odysseus finds his exhausted way back, at long last, to the seemingly safe and solid world of his own home he doesn't rush straight ahead to embrace his wife. Every single detail is going to need a great deal of calculation. And the first thing he does after his enormous sufferings and losses, his horrific aloneness, his journey into the underworld as well as all his other magical ordeals, is to face the next ordeal.

Now he has to disguise himself and, of course with divine assistance, pretend to be a beggar.

For Empedocles, as well as Parmenides, the situation is just the same. As they both keep emphasizing, and as somehow keeps slipping the keen minds of their modern commentators, the use they are going to have to make of human language will be sheer cloaking and deception and disguise. It couldn't possibly be otherwise—because as soon as you come back to the human side and start talking to people in their own language, the only thing they are going to hear is the hum of their familiar words and concepts.

All they are going to see when they look at you is their own humanness and mundanity reflected back to them, which is simply to say that your translation was a great success.

You have translated so well from the language of the dead into its mirror opposite, the language of the living, it never once occurs to them that all the time you are actively translating from something else. You don't have to trick or mislead anyone, because people are so excited at the sight of their own reflection that they are delighted to deceive themselves.

And this, unnoticed, is just what happened with Carl Jung.

Almost the funniest part of it all is that there have been several times when popular writers suggested he was no ordinary scientist but—on the contrary—nothing but a prophet in disguise masquerading as a scientist. Of course the reactions haven't been nearly as amusing, or amused, and those who claim to know and understand most about Jung will have absolutely none of it. If he says he is a scientist then he is simply a scientist and that's the end of the story.

What's even funnier, though, is the way Jung lays his own cards so plainly on the table but so few people care to look.

It's not just a matter, either, of those explicit comments he makes towards the end of his life about how the whole of his work consisted of one single need: the need to translate the prophetic message he had been given by the spirit of the depths into the language of science. There are also the equally clear statements he made when he was far younger, going out of his way to explain that “today the voice of one crying in the wilderness must necessarily strike a scientific tone if the ear of the multitude is to be reached”.

Needless to say, this voice of one crying in the wilderness is a direct appeal to language once used by the prophet Isaiah—and this comment of Jung’s could hardly be more to the point, considering his own awareness that today any real prophets or saviours who announce themselves to the public as prophets or saviours will be destroyed by our modern world in a matter of weeks.[82]

In other words: the prophet who puts on the princely, or beggarly, disguise of being a scientist isn’t a failed prophet but an extremely intelligent prophet. And so at long last we arrive again at the same passage I already touched on earlier, which has been buried under more than its fair share of random misunderstandings; wilful misinterpretations; arbitrary mistranslations.

But, as Empedocles already said a long while ago, what’s worth mentioning once is worth mentioning twice.

This is the passage dating from the 1st of October 1957, when Jung was talking openly at Bollingen about those original experiences of his from which first the *Red book* and then all his later work would flow.

A question had happened to come up about the enormous difference in style between his published works—which of course didn’t include the *Red book* at that time—and the spontaneous accounts he was willing to offer of his dreams or inner life. And his answer, as recorded by his secretary, was to talk about lava.

Those dreams and inner experiences, he explains, are the primordial substance underlying everything. But to describe his published books he evokes the image of a creator god busy producing order out of chaos and explains them as simply an attempt to shape this primordial material, this seething volcanic lava, into some kind of orderly cosmos.

Then he goes straight on to add that "it was the passion and intensity inside this fire, it was the stream of lava itself which is the force that compelled whatever happened to happen. And so, completely naturally, everything fell into its own proper place and order." But almost as if he knows he won't be heard, and in the dim hope of preventing any misunderstanding, he takes the trouble a moment later to repeat himself:

"I wanted to achieve something in my science, and then I bumped into this stream of lava, and then it brought everything into order."

We have already seen how well that attempt to avoid any misunderstandings worked out—and how the only two people who took it upon themselves to translate this passage both totally distorted its meaning.

But, again, nothing is more important than to understand that these mistranslations aren't just a matter of accidents or technical errors. And it's time now to be a little clearer about what's really involved.

What Jung is actually doing is, in one fell swoop, cancelling out our human language as well as all our normal understandings of ourselves or the world around us. We assume we are the ones who shape and create some order out of the primitive lava. Always we talk not only to others, but also to ourselves, as if we are the ones responsible for making something out of the rough rock and stone of existence.

But it's all done through us, for us. In fact we don't do a thing because, thanks to a divine process we can't or won't acknowledge, it's the sacred that takes care of everything.

And in case you want to argue with this as any normal human has to, in case you feel the need to misinterpret it as any rational person is obliged to do, I will quote another passage—from a seminar Jung had given over twenty years earlier—to show how far I am from making anything up.

He had been talking, in the seminar, about the archetypal reality of the unconscious and how ambiguous it is. It's the source of life but also the source of all destruction and death. And our own skill as humans is what determines, or at least seems to determine, whether we are able successfully to navigate a course for ourselves over the turbulent waters of the unconscious.

This—he explains—is why every single religious system in existence has been built, with such care, as a ship which will offer people the specific kind of wisdom they so deeply need for navigating a path through the elementary dangers of life. But then, sure enough, he comes to the crux at the heart of the paradox.

Quite obviously, unquestionably, it's the skill of humans that brings everything together and creates such sophisticated systems. And yet the very obviousness of this is, precisely, the biggest trap. To believe that we, ourselves, bring anything together is just a delusion. To claim that our own skills are responsible for producing such systems, or creating anything else, is to make the most hopelessly inadequate statement.

It's nothing but our thoughtlessly conventional human language—"the ordinary language" we use in assuming that we are the inventors of things, that Moses invented the laws he brought, that Christ and the Old Testament prophets were kind and good-hearted folk who came up on their own initiative with suitable ways for helping their people.

But the problem with this whole grand narrative, Jung insists, is that it doesn't come anywhere near to explaining the real facts. And the real facts are that all these methods and techniques for building ships are not human "inventions, but are revelations". They are "a revealed truth or a perceived truth which has been thought before man has thought. Before I had that thought it had already been thought, and I merely happened to perceive it once in time; it has been there since eternity, is always there, has always lived, and I just happened in a certain moment to perceive it."

Of course that briefest moment of perception, that little glimpse we are allowed to have as humans into the thinnest slice of reality without ever managing to see the whole, is what leads straight into inflation. Suddenly the little human is saying: Look what I saw, look what I invented and discovered, look at all the things I can do and know!

And then, needless to say, you are behaving exactly the same as any other unconscious person. Inwardly, though, "you are absolutely done for"—because in your ordinary arrogance you have wiped out any trace of "the revelation of the thought that existed before man had the thought".

Now you just have perfectly human religion, completely human science. And the reality of that revelation is gone.[83]

So, here again, Jung is moving in a direction few people are even able to notice; let alone are willing to go. Most of us are, quite frankly, desperate to rescue him from his early days of prophecy and revelation: to restore him to the role of a respectable scientist tinkering with his human remedies for this problem or that.

But here he is, again, pointing everything back to the reality of revelation—to that timeless, primordial revelation which has existed "since eternity". The trouble is, though, that this reality isn't a theoretical concept or something to understand with the mind.

On the contrary: there is only one possible way to approach it which is when it's directly seen, and experienced, as a reality. And the direct vision of this pre-existent eternity is the one thing able to save us from drowning in the impossible paradox that even our skill at navigating the waters of the unconscious is, itself, a skill given to us by the unconscious.

As for what this means, the implications are very simple. Whenever you hear Jung talking about himself, or read him offering his human assurances about this and that, make sure you have enough *mêtis* or alertness not to believe him. Whenever he discusses the things we have to do and achieve to become conscious, avoid problems, grow up, don't believe that either because he is only using a convenient kind of shorthand.

He is just using the conventional human language which, he is quick to admit, is totally inadequate.

This is the problem with returning to the human side—because to become a whole human means having to learn how to deceive and be deceived. As he states the matter with such clarity, to create the possibility of being understood by humans means using "the ordinary language" which automatically pulls down a veil over eternal truth; hides the revelation.

Or as Empedocles, for his part, had already gone to such lengths to explain: the ordinary language used by humans turns reality upside down and back to front, magically obliterates the timeless truth of what we are. But, just like Jung, he had absolutely no choice and was forced to add *nomôi d' epiphêmi kai autos*. "I, too, conform to convention."[84]

For anyone involved in this process of return to the human side it's a completely hopeless situation—from the human point of view. You have to take a stand against human conventions and refuse to conform because this is the only way to balance or correct the massive ignorance they contain. But if you blindly refuse to conform, you are lost.

You have to be ready and flexible enough to adapt. But if you make a deliberate attempt to adapt by consciously compromising, as any sane or reasonable person would recommend, again you are lost because you sacrificed your own integrity together with the essential wildness of your message.

And then, as always, there is the forgotten third alternative—which in this particular case is to stand back and let the unconscious itself do the adapting, is to allow the flowing lava with its own divine *mêtis* to do precisely what's right.

The result will be completely baffling to any human observer: a riddle that defies every attempt at some sensible understanding and for which, ultimately, there can be no rational defence or justification at all.

Still, whether in the middle of people or alone, you will be impossibly lonely. At least you will have the satisfaction, though, of knowing that your real work is being done for you.

And in the case of Jung, all his apparently conscious choices had been made for him already by the unconscious—even the choice of scientific language for translating his prophetic message into, even the particular design of the disguise or costume he was going to have to put on.

Even the cloak he would use to cover the raw power of the unconscious was selected for him by the unconscious itself. And everything his ego would so normally, so effortlessly but so foolishly take the credit for had already been taken care of on his behalf.

14

But then there is the rest of what he said on October the 1st, 1957.

Just before emphasizing for the second time that he doesn't deserve any personal credit for his life's achievements, that everything fell naturally and quite spontaneously into place thanks to the unconscious flow of lava inside him, Jung makes a sudden confession about himself:

"I'm the damnedest dilettante who ever lived. I wanted to achieve something in my science, and then I bumped into this stream of lava, and then it brought everything into order."

And here, as so often, we are faced with a simple choice. We either go on fabricating our collective fantasies, keep weaving our reasonable myths about what he meant—or we work our way down with him to the truth of what he actually said.[85]

As it happens, Jung goes straight on to explain why he has just dismissively called himself a damned dilettante.

By this, he says, he means he has spent the whole of his life borrowing other people's knowledge. To be sure, a little of what he did was original. But in everything else, the material he used for creating and building up his psychology didn't come from his own being; didn't have its source in the raw primal substance, the primordial prophetic material, flowing deep inside him.

Instead he took it all from outside, grabbed pieces from here, snatched bits from there. Regardless of every appearance to the contrary, he didn't really create anything himself but just dabbled in this or that like any other dilettante.

And that, he adds while being interviewed by his secretary at the Bollingen tower, is exactly what happened in the case of his involvement with alchemy. His work on alchemical tradition was never an inner experience for him: he simply snatched and grabbed whatever he happened to find outside. Year after year he read books, then more books, searching for some kind of material that would allow him to cloak and cover the "primordial revelation" he had received—the "Uroffenbarung", as he called it—which by himself he was completely unable to master or cope with.[86]

As far as Jung is concerned, there aren't many things that are more important to understand. A few weeks later he would also mention to his secretary how extraordinary it was to discover that his experiences, during the time of his critical descent into the unconscious, were the same as the experiences of the alchemists and the other way around. But the fact of this simple correspondence, stated by him here so clearly, isn't what mattered most.

What's even more significant is the fact that in writing about their experiences he was actually covering over and hiding his own.

Jung loved complaining as well as exaggerating. And when the sheer amount of work involved in tracking all the intricate details of alchemical tradition weighed him down, he enjoyed groaning to the people around him that this ordeal of researching and writing about alchemy was causing him far more pain and trouble than anything he'd had to suffer during his earlier ordeal of descending alive into the underworld. Of course to those helpers of his who hadn't made the journey to hell—and were happy for the most part to see with his eyes, live through his experiences—it was irresistibly tempting to take him at his word.

But, at the same time, there is an element of truth in his complaint. His terrifying ordeal of travelling down into his innermost depths was a task of stripping everything away so as to open himself to his own naked, primordial, eternally solitary, prophetic reality. Then his enormous, years-long ordeal of studying alchemy was the task of covering that reality over once again.

As a covering, it couldn't have been more appropriate—because one aspect of alchemical tradition which has strangely been overlooked, although Jung himself was well aware of the fact, is that from the very beginning western alchemists viewed their tradition as prophetic. So even when he was translating his prophetic message, cloaking his prophetic mission, he made sure to select a prophetic tradition to complete the task; or, rather, let it be chosen for him.

Still, though, that precious alchemy of his was no more than a covering: a disguise.[87]

And this is just what his science would be for him. It's what he himself called a "Bekleidungsstoff"—a cloaking material to cover and disguise what was most important. Many people feel a huge sense of victory, not to mention relief, because he finally grew up; slammed the door shut on his immature silliness about prophecy; managed to "find his true life's work" by shaking that nonsense off and abandoning it definitively in favour of science.

But while these explanations might seem valid enough if you are just looking at the reflective surface of things, the reality is that Jung didn't abandon anything. He simply covered it over, decked it out, disguised what was most essential.

In the early days of his naïve ambition, when he still wanted to achieve something for himself through science and hadn't yet bumped into that stream of lava, he already had plenty of doubts and reservations about becoming a scientist. Even so, he immersed himself wholeheartedly in the scientific world and began to see it as his future and destiny.

And his encounter with the lava took all that away: took away his belief in science, took away his heart. From then on, it was just a matter of snatch and grab—of playing the role of dilettante not because he enjoyed being a dilettante or wanted to become a better dilettante, but because now his heart was somewhere else.

In fact, on the most obvious level, a dilettante is precisely what Jung became. He turned here, drifted there; let himself get dragged into grand new projects and schemes only to abandon them, often causing the other people involved a vast amount of trouble and frustration, in midstream. All the time through the science he had his eye on something beyond the science, and everyone who didn't share his vision simply couldn't see what was going on.[88]

For instance, there is what now has become one of his most famous scientific ideas: the theory of synchronicity. After he had died, the leading British Jungian Michael Fordham proudly presented it to the English-speaking world as Jung's successful attempt "to strip off the fantasy, magic and superstition which surround and are provoked by unpredictable, startling and impressive events" and show that "they are simply 'meaningful coincidences'".

But the fact is that Jung's theory of synchronicity wasn't aimed at "simply" anything; and certainly, whatever anyone might like to think, it wasn't aimed at stripping out magic. Quite to the contrary, Jung himself had made it abundantly clear what he was wanting to offer with his idea of synchronicity. He was presenting to the world an updated, reincarnated version of the ancient magical theory known as *sympatheia*—the occult western tradition of "sympathies" or correspondences which happens to be traceable back all the way to Empedocles and was always understood as revealing the mysterious hand of God, the magical insertion of the timeless into time.

And rather than wanting to strip such mumbo jumbo away so as to make synchronicity scientifically respectable, his real aim was to achieve almost the exact reverse through the most elegant act of sabotage: to plant a bombshell inside the scientific consciousness that would shake it to the core, to strip away scientists' pretensions by rupturing the fabric not just of time but of contemporary science itself, to drag the modern rational mind right to the border of what's acceptable or possible only to push it into the unknown.

Beyond everything else, though, his central concern was not to create and then promote one more scientific theory. Instead, it was to shock people out of their mental complacency into a direct experience of the fullness—the Gnostic *plêrôma*—that lies at the root of our being.

This primordial experience, as he passionately explained to those who were willing to listen, is where his idea came from. And this is where it was supposed to lead back to again.[89]

So everything comes back to what lies behind his science; what hides below it. In other words, there is not the slightest chance of understanding what Jung actually means when he talks about his scientific dilettantism without relating it straight to what he calls his "Uroffenbarung": the "primordial revelation", so overwhelmingly real and powerful and alive, that was flowing deep inside him at the core of his whole being.

There is nothing at all accidental about his choice of such a striking expression. "Uroffenbarung" is a word that already had been used in the German language for years to describe the existence of direct divine revelation outside of Christianity, or before Christianity—a kind of revelation open and accessible to prophets anywhere, everywhere, since the beginning of time.

Of course anyone can talk about such primordial revelation as a matter of theory. But the actual access to that timeless reality belongs to prophets alone while the only traces of it, as a direct experience, are to be found in prophets' lives. And thanks to the markings he left inside his books we can still see how closely Jung associated this notion of primeval revelation, as well as the word "Uroffenbarung" itself, with one prophetic lineage in particular.

That was the lineage of the Gnostics—and especially of the prophet Mani.[90]

Once again, everything fits perfectly into place on every possible level. Jung not only saw himself, inwardly, as a prophet. He was also able to situate that prophetic role in a far broader perspective not just spiritually, but historically too.

And then there is the coherence, equally perfect, of the picture that emerges from those late interviews he gave—as duly noted and recorded, day after day, by his devoted secretary—during the proverbial winter of his life.

Every word and expression Jung used, towards the end of 1957, has its proper place and function and logic. The unique access he was given to primordial revelation, to "Uroffenbarung", is the crucial factor that unavoidably forced on him his "Botschaft": his prophetic mission and message to the world which had already been announced from the very first sentence of his *Red book*.

Or to rephrase that in slightly more human terms, he was unable to master or manage or cope with the sheer wild power of this "Uroffenbarung"—which he ended up having to wrap inside the cloak of science—in exactly the same way and for precisely the same reasons that he was unable to tolerate the raw prophetic message he had been handed, and which he ended up having to translate into the language of science.

Now it should be ever so easy to understand why the point had to come when Jung would give up his work on the *Red book* so that he could start working away at the study of alchemy instead.

And at the same time we can understand why he never published the *Red book* as long as he stayed alive—because it contained the raw, prophetic material he couldn't handle by himself but worked so skilfully to cover over and disguise.

Of course that wild destructive power is something no human can ever manage or cope with, which is why Jung couldn't hope to master it on his own. Instead, it has to manage and cope with us. But this brings us straight back again, as yet another demonstration of how perfectly everything holds together, to the prophetic lineage of Mani.

Back in 1920, when he had his dream at Tunis about the extraordinary book which would allow him to master the overwhelming daimonic power of the unconscious, he realized that this mysterious book of his—his own book, the book he already had somehow written himself—happened to be a Manichaean text. The book of his own psychology turned out to be a book of Mani.

And this is how it has to work, because the only power strong enough to master the primordial prophetic revelation is the prophetic power of the primordial revelation itself.

That revelation or "Uroffenbarung" is always the same in its primordial timelessness. But the infinitely subtle wisdom of the unconscious as it manifests through a prophetic lineage creates the paradox that, in the lives of the prophets, this revelation is always changing. Like each new wave as it crashes on the shore of our human existence, it's fresh; reborn.

It's the wave of revelation that, in mastering us, sets us free. Or to say this in other words: the unconscious is the problem and the unconscious, if we can consciously watch and humbly wait as only a real prophet knows how to, is its own solution. Mani's book is a gift from the unconscious, so generous, so inexpressibly intimate and personal, which will allow Jung to master the impersonal power of the unconscious because the unconscious is the key to itself.

Everything else, the scientific posturing along with all the dilettantism, is just a distraction from the real work being accomplished in the depths of silence; an elaborate ruse for throwing everyone, including oneself, off the scent; a totally faithful translation into the ordinary human language which can never get anything right; the most complex dissimulation which at the same time is the simplest possible method, thrown up by the unconscious itself, for keeping one's vestiges well concealed.

And here, too, the consistency in Jung's understanding could hardly be more perfect.

Over forty years before sitting down to tell his secretary how he had once been forced to translate his mission and message into the language of science, he was still deeply immersed in his work on the *Red book*. And that's when he recorded the details, taking care to note down every expression and turn of phrase, of what suddenly happened during a heated debate he found himself engaged in with his soul.

Now, an old man abruptly interrupts him, is the time for you to grow up and leave science behind. Your destiny lies in the depths and, for that, science is hopelessly superficial and shallow—is "mere language", nothing but a tool for you to use. Although it might look and sound impressive enough, it's just the latest edition of scholasticism.

That's all. You had better get over it; be done with it, once and for all.

But here is where the confrontation becomes even more interesting. Jung is getting worried and objects that, if he renounces the whole of science, this will surely be a failing on his part: a blatant offence against the spirit of the time. No, the old man says back to him, you don't understand.

That's not what I am saying at all, because "you shouldn't renounce it completely but should consider science merely your language". From now on, it's nothing more than the language you need to use.

And that's all it would ever be for Jung. But we do love to be fooled, which means we miss out on noting the exquisite agreement between what he stated so clearly in his eighties—about having had to translate his prophetic message into the language of science—and what he already had been told no less clearly, almost half a century earlier in a talk with his soul, about having to use the language of science as a simple tool.

There is a popular Faustian pastime nowadays, which is to discuss all the ways in which Jung's concepts and theories kept evolving over the course of his career. And to be sure, that's a fair enough insight into the shallow surface of his dilettantism; into what can quite accurately be described as his "many unfinished beginnings". But if we look far enough down underneath the shifting tides of scientific language and terminology, absolutely nothing changed at all.[91]

Of course it's altogether natural to be wanting as humans, just like Jung himself in a certain way, to leave the prophetic revelation behind for the sake of science: for the science which ideally, as Parmenides or Empedocles already acknowledged, represents the very best any human intelligence is capable of. But actually to do that isn't too easy when even the science, as we've seen from so many different angles, is just a part of the inescapable revelation.

In fact the essential nature of this primordial revelation which exists, as Jung says, since eternity and can only be glimpsed with the eyes of eternity is its timelessness. It's behind and ahead of us, was there before either we or our culture were born and will still be there long after we are gone.

You don't ever leave it behind because, far deeper and greater than any science of ours, it's what endures—what, once again, has the last word.

15

And so we are brought back, one last time, to that letter Jung once wrote about the mystical fool; about the mystical fool inside him always being stronger than all his science; and about what as a mystical fool he knew he had to do.

We can trick and delude ourselves, as his letter explains, about the future evolution of consciousness if that's what we want. But the only way forward for humanity doesn't lie through sweetness and hope. It lies in crucifixion, along "a path of blood and suffering". And who really cares for such an excruciating increase in awareness, consciousness, responsibility? Who can stand or endure it?

Who on earth would find the deliberate, and willing, embrace of such suffering worthwhile? That, he says, is the question; and naturally he would never force his own answer on anybody else. "But I confess that I submitted to the divine power of this apparently unsurmountable problem and I consciously and intentionally made my life miserable, because I wanted God to be alive and free from the suffering man has put on him by loving his own reason more than God's secret intentions. There is a mystical fool in me that proved to be stronger than all my science."

There is no way, now, not to come back to this letter because only now is it possible to appreciate what Jung is saying. And the place to start is obviously with his deliberate, conscious, intentional acceptance of suffering—suffering to compensate for the ignorance of humans while, at the same time, suffering for the sake of freeing and healing God.

One of the absurdities that Jungians and Jung scholars have silently come to live with is the unspoken need to keep certain aspects of his life and work well apart because, if one was just to let them fit together into a natural whole, the results would be too horrific to bear. And that's exactly the present situation with regard to the theme of psychological compensation.

On the one hand we can see very clearly how, an old man in his eighties, he would look back over his entire existence and explain it all as a process of compensation. Everything he had spoken or written, everything he was as the being called Carl Jung, had essentially been nothing but a compensation for our modern times; a counterweight to our rational world; a conscious remembering of what in our reasonableness everyone has chosen to neglect and forget; a coherent unveiling of the things that, in spite of any apparent interest and fascination, nobody really wants to see or hear.

On the other hand, he used to explain that this work of compensation is precisely the work of a prophet. As he would say about any great beings, anywhere in the world, who appear as modern prophets: they are going to play "the same compensatory role in relation to their people as the Old Testament prophets did in relation to the 'faithless' children of Israel. Not only do they urge their compatriots to remember their thousand-year-old spiritual culture. They actually embody it and, by doing so, serve as an impressive warning never to forget the claims of the soul even in the midst of all the novelties of western civilization with its materialistic acquisitiveness and its technological and commercial worldliness." And of course in this passage he is exactly portraying himself—his own inexhaustible efforts at urging westerners to remember their cultural continuity and spiritual past, at bringing a little sanity into the "lunatic asylum" of western rationalism, even at warning about how the modern disease of acquisitiveness spreads like wildfire out from our material into our spiritual worlds.

God forbid, though, if anyone was to connect these two streams and suggest he himself was playing a prophetic role; if anybody was even to hint that this one hand belongs alongside the other hand because they are the two hands of a single being, Jung the prophet.

But this little letter ever so conveniently brings everything together, once and for all.

What Jung is saying here about being prepared to suffer for God, about wanting to set God free, make God whole, takes us straight back to a crucial passage in the *Red book* where he is saying exactly the same things at the same time as peppering each statement he makes with quotations from the prophet Isaiah—including the very same quotations he already had placed, so prominently, at the beginning of the *Red book* itself.

It's the norm nowadays in our post-modern, post-structural world to note those opening quotations from Isaiah for half a second or perhaps even for two and rapidly move on to the rest of the text before leaving that behind as well. But nothing could be more naïve than to suppose those quotations were put there by Jung just for the sake of superficial sightseers and intended to be left behind as soon as possible.

On the contrary: they are there not only to set the tone for the rest of his "new book" but, at the same time, to set the tone and serve as model for the rest of his life.

Everything that needs to be known about the thankless existence of a compensator is stated, so completely, so compactly, inside the very first passage Jung quotes from Isaiah right at the start of the *Red book*: "Truly, he himself has borne our sicknesses and he himself has carried our pains."

For Jung, just as for Isaiah, the role of prophet is never—even for a moment—what it seems. As he constantly keeps warning, it never is going to be what one expects. Humanly, nothing could be more tempting than to think of saviours or prophets as missionaries arriving to lecture and preach.

But for him that's the worst conceivable kind of caricature alongside the ridiculous image of a saviour as someone sent to help us escape from life, because a true saviour will only be able to extricate us from our illusions by incarnating the wisdom of life itself.

Real prophets or saviours don't set themselves up for anything except to labour and suffer, often silently or alone, for the sake of what the collective consciousness of humanity doesn't have the strength to face. Here is where the task of prophet merges without the slightest effort into the task of saviour, because the prophet's job isn't just to announce some future saviour but to embody the saviour's presence by consciously embracing suffering.

And here is where we come straight to the heart of western psychology's problem with prophecy. That hunger the prophets have for suffering, for making themselves miserable in the name of what they consider some higher cause, is to our modern minds the most blatant symptom of obsessive masochism; psychotic perversion; mental sickness. But this is where we are also brought straight to the hard core of Jung's stubbornness in so strenuously refusing to subject ancient or modern prophets to psychological analysis.

Prophets may suffer terribly: inevitably do. They often have to suffer intentionally and consciously, too. The crucial point is, though, that the suffering is not their own. And neither, for that matter, is the psychotic perversion.

Instead they are simply the ones who have to hold, through suffering, the unbearable tension of balancing inside their consciousness the unconsciousness of humanity as a whole—who are called to carry the weight of humanity's psychosis in the remote hope that a few other individuals, here or there, might take enough responsibility to share the dark burden of learning how to suffer rightly.

When Jung used to mention no longer belonging to himself, this is a large part of what he was referring to: the harshly humbling reality of discovering how to balance, inside oneself, not just one's own individual psychology but everyone else's. The healthy focus in Jungian circles on leading a personally full and balanced life is all very fine and good.

At the same time, though, it has to be viewed in another light entirely if for a few people it might need to take the back seat to discovering a quite different kind of balance; if it's no more than a prelude to the vastly harder, and riskier, task of compensating not only one's own imbalances but the imbalances of the world.

Then the rules of the game are changed completely. All the bets are off and the best anybody can hope to do is to live the most balanced life possible in an outer sense by acting—to the maximum capacity of one's human powers—as a seemingly ordinary human being.

But as for the rest: whatever guidance and wisdom are needed will have to come from a far deeper place than anything human, as the ancient prophets explained and as Jung knew just as well.

So when he talks in his letter about consciously and intentionally making his life miserable—"because I wanted God to be alive and free from the suffering man has put on him"—Carl Jung is taking his place, very knowingly and deliberately, inside a long tradition of prophecy.[92]

And then there is the other detail he goes straight on to add: "I wanted God to be alive and free from the suffering man has put on him by loving his own reason more than God's secret intentions." But, here too, we can't afford to skip a single word.

To hold up our faculty of reason as the one thing that makes God suffer, then to perform the intentional act of quite consciously compensating for the damage done by this reason, is something impossible to understand through reasoning.

In fact each normal, plausible, perfectly justifiable and ever so reasonable thought anyone has without paying any attention to the divine mystery behind it: that's exactly what a prophet has to suffer, and compensate, for.

Or to state the matter a little more bluntly, reason has become God's enemy. What Jung is saying is that not just every minute but every moment of our compulsive reasoning, every obsessively reasonable act or word or thought, each tolerably scholarly murder, is a direct offence against the sacred. And don't imagine you are going to understand, even notice, what he is really thinking and saying and doing if you are identifying with your daylight rational faculty—because he is simply having to compensate for you.

That's not all, though. There are other places, too, where he states with equal intensity that the human faculty of reason is the greatest violator and chief enemy of nature. And what may seem almost impossible to register any more in the massive ocean of collective reasonableness is that to present our human power of reasoning as the enemy, not just of nature but of God, isn't the teaching of a psychologist; let alone a scientist.

There is something totally different involved here.

But we only have to look towards the prophetic tradition William Blake belonged to, and which Jung knew so well, to see that it's the teaching of prophecy. Or rather, it's the primordial roar of suffering that we can hardly tell how to recognize any more. It's the silent howl of prophets working with the full weight and force of nature behind them to neutralize all our politely murderous rationalizations of life, of God, of the unconscious.

And—behind even that—it's the need deep inside each of us to reach back prophetically to the forgotten logic which has been murdered, which keeps being murdered, by reason itself.

Unnoticed because there is such a heavy cost for noticing, each statement Jung is making in this letter is the statement of a prophet; then, again, of a prophet. And so we come to the next comment of his, offered almost as a gentle explanation for the things he has just said:

"There is a mystical fool in me that proved to be stronger than all my science."

As we already have seen, these are the words of someone instinctively attuned to the spirit of the depths—which, for all its hiddenness, has far more strength and endurance than the shifting trends of science or the spirit of our time.

There is also something else, though, contained in this seemingly straightforward comment. But it's something that will only become apparent if you know the Bible as well as Jung did: in fact as well as he insisted any genuine student of psychology would have to know it.

This expression "mystical fool" was his own, shorthand way of using standard prophetic language to describe the prophet who goes unrecognized; unacknowledged; unheard.[93]

Everything he says here in his letter is the perfectly consistent confession of a modern prophet—a real prophet in both his life and work, not the absurd caricature of inflated prophets which we with our inflated rationalism mistake for the reality behind it.

And the substance of what he says couldn't be truer. Jung the prophet would always prove stronger than Jung the scientist; outlast his own science; not only have the last word but the last silence, as well.

In the autumn of 1959, just a year or two before he died, as he was getting weaker he decided to go back to the *Red book* so he could finally bring it to completion.

But he couldn't. He tried to finish off the last, unfinished, painting. He wasn't able.

As he told his secretary—who was better at noting down his words than at daring to ask what they meant—it was death that stopped him. And we can still see why.

His last painting was of over a hundred human faces: most of them vividly alive, some of them nothing but ancient skeletons. For him, though, evoking people's faces was far from being some casual or innocent process. On the contrary, it was an almost magical act.

As a matter of fact there is one passage in his published biography where he explains how—throughout his whole life from childhood into old age—he kept experiencing visions of human faces that would appear to him while he was falling asleep. Often these were the faces of people he knew who, after they had presented themselves to him in this way, would soon die.

And then there is the other detail that never made its way into print.

This is the detail of what he, himself, originally wanted to say—which is that those visions of faces actually revealed the future to him by predicting people's coming deaths. But his immediate family was none too happy at the thought of such intimately mystical confessions getting out; and so the mention of Jung's prophetic powers was deleted, ever so discreetly, from the published text.

Being shown the faces of people before they die is one thing. Making the effort to paint such human faces, not just the way they appear alive but already as ancient skulls, is another. And so even when Jung made the final effort to return from what he called the "human side" to his prophetic *Red book*, even when he tried as an old man to complete at long last what he'd started almost half a century earlier, it would seem his prophetic powers are precisely what stopped him.

Theoretically there was no end even then to the possibilities of what he could have gone on writing, or painting, just as there is no limit to what I could keep saying here. But Jung wasn't interested in chattering on about the realms of possibility or possibilities. His quest was for the impossible.

And as soon as he had magically managed, just like the prophets he wrote about, to make the impossible possible it was already time to be moving on.[94]

From our superficial and altogether legitimate point of view, the problematic failing or inadequacy of the *Red book* is that it didn't include the human perspective—the perspective that brings us all together, with our ordinary language and ordinary thoughts, to get almost everything wrong. But underneath this, its problem has nothing to do with incompleteness or lack.

On the contrary, its only problem is the overwhelming power as well as the indescribable fullness and perfection of that other reality it was meant to convey: a reality in the face of which every human effort is inadequate, in which the end is already tucked up inside the beginning.

And just as the *Red book* had begun with prophecy, it was prophecy that would abruptly bring it to an end.

16

Everything he had written, Jung explained towards the end of his life, was the result of what he'd inwardly been instructed to say and do.

He couldn't escape any of it, evade it, avoid it; couldn't write anything else, either, aside from what he was commanded to write. Each book he started working on soon shaped up to be another unique attempt at introducing the utter ineffability of a completely different reality—the "unsayable" always lurking in the background of our collective existence—into the familiar, objective world of science and learning.

The process had a beginning, a middle, and then an end in the last major book he ever wrote. When he finished *Mysterium coniunctionis* he realized he also had finished the underpinning, the solid grounding, of his entire work. This is when he was released, at last, from his post; acquitted of his task. And in the very same instant that he arrived at the ultimate foundation of his whole psychology, he simultaneously bumped up against the remotest boundaries of what can be known: against the transcendent, where everything and everyone goes silent.

Of course this is hardly the confession of a scientist or psychologist—but of a religious, and profoundly mystical, person. At heart Jung wasn't placing the study of religion, of what sometimes is referred to very professionally nowadays as the "religion–making process", in the context of science or of psychology. On the contrary: the many commentators who claim this have made a little mistake, because at root he was placing his whole science and psychology in the context of religion.

After all, he was the first to admit that even his psychology itself happened to be nothing but "a movement of the spirit"; a movement rising out of the depths which, far from him owning or possessing it, had taken complete possession of him and his life. His only role was to submit, and serve.[95]

While he was still in his sixties this process of submission rapidly intensified after he got so ill, during 1944, that he almost died. The unspeakable experience of ecstatic mystical union in coming face to face with death started pulling him away again from the "human side" and back, unavoidably, inescapably, towards the world he already had sunk into while being worked on by the *Red book*: that other reality to which the death we all run from is always the key.

And if we are going to understand the published works he produced during the final years of his life, we will have to do better than view them as individual islands of creativity. We are going to have to understand the sea.

The first major book to emerge, with irresistible force, from his ordeal in 1944 was called *Aion*. But its title isn't just the ancient Greek word for an age in the history of the world, or even for eternity. It's also an extremely deliberate reference by Jung to the name of the great god who ruled over time in the ancient mysteries—the very same god he had found himself dramatically merging and uniting with during his crucial experience of deification in December 1913, right at the start of what would become his engagement with the *Red book*.

And to avoid any misunderstandings about the importance of *Aion* as a written work, it will be enough just to quote his own way of connecting it back to the illness that almost killed him in 1944:

"Before my illness I had often asked myself if I were permitted to publish or even speak of my secret knowledge. I later set it all down in *Aion*. I realized it was my duty to communicate these thoughts, yet I doubted whether I was allowed to give expression to them. During my illness I received confirmation and I now knew that everything had meaning and that everything was perfect."

The problem, though, with secret knowledge is that it still remains secret even after it's been written down. You can labour over it; analyze each word; intellectualize or wax lyrical about them all. But the secret is never available to the mind because what appear as intellectual ideas and theories are just a cloaking for something else. So I will restrict myself to mentioning a single detail about *Aion*, which is that one particular figure happens to be absolutely central to the structure and content of the book as a whole.

This is Joachim of Fiore, a twelfth-century mystic and heretic who for many reasons—with the famous teaching of past, present and future world ages that was revealed to him—can be considered one of the most influential prophets in the course of Christian history. The entire structure of *Aion* is masterfully designed as Jung's continuation or extension, his updating or renewal of the "vision" given to Joachim almost eight hundred years earlier.

And to prevent any misunderstandings about the importance for him of Joachim, or Gioacchino as he sometimes called him, I will just quote something Jung wrote to a trusted friend.

He has been explaining that we are very close to the end of what Joachim called the Christian age, or aeon, at the critical point of transition into the post-Christian aeon due to come next. But the trouble is that almost nobody, including among so-called Christians, has learned yet what it means to be a real Christian; has learned to walk what he calls elsewhere the voluntary "path of blood and suffering". There is hardly anyone who has done the inner work that was needed and is even remotely prepared. "The vast majority of people is still in such an unconscious state, that one should almost protect them from the full shock of the real *imitatio Christi*. Moreover we are still in the Christian aeon, threatened with a complete annihilation of our world."

Then Jung goes straight on to hint at his own role in this situation, at the particular nature of his "job": "As there are not only the many but also the few, somebody is trusted with the task to look ahead and talk of the things to be." Or as he moves into stating the matter even more clearly, "Thus I am approaching the end of the Christian aeon and I am to take up Gioacchino's anticipation and Christ's prediction of the coming of the paraclete. This drama is at the same time exquisitely psychological and historical. We are actually living in the time of the splitting of the world."

In other words, Jung was voluntarily stepping into the role of prophet who has been entrusted with extending and renewing Joachim's prophetic vision for the present age.

Learned commentators have been duly horrified. Expecting for some reason that his one and only concern would be to act the respectable part of objective psychologist, or detached historian, they stand amazed at the "remarkable leap" he unpredictably makes from cold textual analysis into playing such an engaged and unexpected role. But the sense of such remarkable leaps might simply be due to the fact that Jung was never, even to begin with, in the place we imagine he was leaping from. And others have been a little quicker to admit that here he is presenting himself, quite plainly, as a contemporary prophet: "as a modern Joachim di Fiore ushering in a new age of the Spirit".

That's only the start, though.

When he talks about "taking up" Joachim's work and vision, Jung is using the identical language he also uses elsewhere for describing his relationship to Merlin—whose prophetic role he had very specifically "taken up again" in his psychology. This language of taking up, through or rather as one's lifetime, an unfinished task that needs renewing and completing in our present age was his way of hinting at the essential mystery of what he called karma or rebirth.

And so we see Jung karmically linking himself, as well as his psychology, to two of the most potent prophetic figures in the western world.

But even this is only a part of the story—because it just so happens that the prophetic traditions stemming from Joachim became inextricably intertwined with the prophetic traditions ascribed to Merlin. Prophecies of Merlin merged through the centuries with prophecies of Joachim to the point where, in practice, one could often hardly tell them apart. And it's this dual but single tradition of prophecy that Jung found himself inescapably carrying on.[96]

As for Merlin, with his solitude and craziness and haunting cry: we have already seen how wholeheartedly he identified with this mythical predecessor of his. As for Joachim: there is just one point I will mention because, if it's grasped, it's enough to show how hopelessly with our modern naivety we doom ourselves to misunderstanding Carl Jung.

Time after time Jung used to deny he was a prophet and, fools that we are, there is something so gullible inside us we just want to go on taking him each single time at his word. I can keep pirouetting around myself citing all the details of his statements about needing to lie, his references to the practice of concealing one's vestiges, his own endless dancing between personalities no. 1 and no. 2, and it probably won't change a thing. Ever since we were children we have been trained to believe obediently almost everything we are told and—in spite of our headstrong opinions which aren't even our own—that's precisely what we do.

But there is one point I didn't yet have a chance to mention, which is that in the history of our western culture nothing is more standard or routine than for prophets to deny they are prophets.

One of the most notorious cases of a prophet denying he is a prophet was none other than Joachim of Fiore. It's not only a question of Joachim, though, or of the different prophetic figures in and around his time who also wisely pretended not to be prophets—because prophetic visions are all very well and good provided they come from a distant past but are apt to cause no end of problems when they come from someone you happen to know.

Quite to the contrary: the denials have been going on for thousands of years in a tradition that reaches back all the way to the world of the Old Testament itself. And in fact the Hebrew prophet Amos perfectly managed to create the template for whoever came later with his most straightforward of declarations that "I am not a prophet".

In other words, just as to resist and challenge and struggle with and even rebel against becoming a prophet isn't the proof of not being a true prophet but only an indication of the opposite, to deny outright that one is a prophet is the mark of an authentic prophet too.

It's simply part and parcel of the prophetic job. And by "taking up" the work of Joachim, Jung was finding himself at home with a long line of individuals who were like him in many more ways than one.

When he insisted so adamantly that there is no understanding him or his psychology without knowing and understanding the

Bible, he was being far more serious than one might think. But we are so contaminated with the inflation of modernity, we don't even realize how great a problem our ignorance has become. And this ignorance of prophetic tradition, in particular, isn't limited to Jungians by any means—because we live in a world where even most Jews nowadays hardly have the slightest clue about their prophets any more.

With Jung, things were rather different.

His father was a tragic but very talented man who not only studied every corner of the Hebrew Bible, including the ancient prophets. He even became an expert on biblical commentaries written, centuries before his time, at Jerusalem in Arabic. And Jung's poor opinion of him as a human being would only strengthen the extraordinary influence that his father's interests kept exerting on him, at a subterranean level, for the rest of his life.

But it wasn't just a matter of the subjects his father had studied. There is something else about these subjects that mattered far more—the infinite subtleties and refinements of the culture behind them, an intuitive sense for intricacies which comes from studying them but is as distant from anything offered by a modern education as an oriental carpet from a doormat.

Perhaps you still want to think such quaintly biblical sophistications are details we can easily afford to ignore when approaching Jung. The truth is, though, that these subtleties don't just exist to add to the finer resonances of his message or offer a touch of richer colour here and there.

They change absolutely everything: convert the most categorical no into a resounding yes, transform every yes of ours into a no. But, today, the mention of such subtleties might give us a moment's shock; even a split second of disorientation.

Then, the chances are we'll just spring straight back into taking everything at face value—into trusting what shouldn't be trusted while making sure to ignore what should—with the result that our cats or dogs would probably understand Jung far better than we do.[97]

And so we come to that other book he wrote which, as things turned out, would be his ultimate gesture of reconciliation with his father.

From the point of view of his superficial everyday personality, *Answer to Job* was a damnable piece of work: the words of an "unspeakable fool" who was stupid enough to disrupt the wishes of the bourgeois coward inside him and disturb his own longing to go on sleeping peacefully like everyone else.

From the point of view of his deeper personality, at home in eternity, it was the greatest gift; the fisherman who magically catches a whale, or the whale who catches the fisher; a magnificent piece of music; something so perfect that, after the initial revisions he made to remove the worst and craziest of his apparent blasphemies, it was the one piece of work he would never dream of modifying or changing.

As for how exactly it related to *Aion*, Jung's answer was simple. In theme and topic the two books were intimately linked. At the same time, though, *Aion* had been far too polite—much too civilized and "man-made".

Now was the time to go wild. And that's literally what happened.

For forty years, since the time of his work on the *Red book*, the material that would erupt into *Answer to Job* had been bottled up inside him. And the only way it could come out, as so often with Jung, was through sickness. He became ill, the fever itself is what forced him to write, and only when he had finished did the sickness leave him.

All sorts of wonderful fantasies have been spun, half-true, about Jungian psychology as an eminent method for avoiding extremes; for finding internal balance and equilibrium, true groundedness, the seamlessly accomplished integration of each function and faculty inside a human being. Then there are the well-manicured notions about Jung himself as the perfect model of a serene, fully balanced, equilibriated wise old man. But sometimes the humble reality tended to be a little different.

And when the daimon of Jung's creativity erupted, all hell broke loose.

Writing *Aion*, which had caused him more and more sleeplessness the deeper he went, was difficult enough. But *Answer to Job* swept through him, along with his home and household, like a storm. Although his fragile health obviously wasn't up to it, as always he had no choice. For the months that he was writing, then revising, the text there were times when he not only hardly slept but hardly shaved; hardly washed.

People in his immediate circle were terrified of what might happen to him as well as what he might do to them. He shut himself away for hours and worked until he was exhausted. Then he became moody and often furious, lashed out for no reason, was crude and rude. The greatest fear of all was what would happen if journalists turned up unexpectedly to interview him—and the secret hope was that they just might end up interviewing the gardener instead, because at least he was much "closer to reality. Jung lived now in another world."[98]

As for what the book itself was about, what he was being driven so hard to say: it was about the darkness of God and the suffering the divine darkness causes in our human world.

But just as important as its main topic and theme is the fact that, in spite of any appearances hinting otherwise, Jung wasn't going to be talking theoretically or historically or theologically about this darkness—about the darkness of Job's God, the God of the Old Testament. On the contrary, he made himself perfectly clear that through his little book he wouldn't be debating or arguing about God.

He would be arguing with God, directly, instead. What he was being forced so overwhelmingly to do, and what his father would come back from the dead to thank him for, was to stand up and confront God; challenge God face to face; speak to God, argue with God, as only a human can. And that meant being as incapable of distancing himself from God with the help of the usual nice theories, polite abstractions, as Job with his excruciating suffering had been unable to remove himself.

It meant consciously and intentionally suffering just as Job had chosen to suffer—and not only as Job had nobly suffered but as Christ, the archetypal suffering servant, would suffer too. It involved deliberately taking God's darkness on himself by entering so deep inside it that, from there, he could compensate for humans' ridiculous obsession with the deceptive light of reason.

It also involved, needless to say, having to accept all the misunderstandings and abuse that would be hurled his way. But those were hardly going to make any difference because, as he answered when asked what the writing of *Answer to Job* really entailed: thanks to it "I live in my deepest hell, and from there I cannot fall any further".

And if this sounds very familiar, it should—because we are back in the place we never even left, which is the land of prophecy.

I do understand that any memory of such a long-forgotten place, of our own indigenous land and earth and nature, is far too painful now to recognize. That's why for the most part all we allow ourselves to appreciate in Jung is the person, the inventive man, the self-willed character: never, God forbid, the force he himself pointed to time and time again as the reality responsible for overpowering and compelling him to do the things he did.

A large part inside each of us refuses, to the bitter end, honestly to acknowledge that he was serving as the mouthpiece and spokesperson for something far beyond him—to recognize his indispensable role in what he called the "tragic self-contradiction" of being forced from the depths of the unconscious to challenge God's unconsciousness, of having to help the power of the unconscious take a stand against the power of the unconscious, of making it possible for God to argue with God.

That's all, in its purest form, a little too disconcerting to admit. And so it could only be a matter of time before Jung had to face the full impact of the abuse, not to mention misunderstandings; before everything would be reduced, very rationally and systematically, to the petty and personal and biographical; before he would even be accused of anti-Semitism for his tasteless attacks on the Jewish God, or at the very least of bad timing because he'd dared to produce *Answer to Job* so soon after the horrors of the Holocaust.

But what's almost never noticed is how strange it is, for a supposedly anti-Semitic text, that *Answer to Job* contains such respectful references to Jewish sacred literature and traditions. And even when these references are occasionally pointed out, what's even stranger is the failure to realize that it's not just a question of the Jewish material contained inside the book.

What's far more important is the book's essential form, because—according to Jewish sacred traditions—there is only one kind of person who has the ability, the authority, the audacity to challenge or argue with God face to face.

And that, naturally, is a prophet.

One rare bird who, even before the book's official release, realized the truth of what Jung was doing through *Answer to Job* just so happened to be his closest Jewish friend: Erich Neumann. The very first message he sent to Jung after reading an early copy of the text was to say how intensely this book, the finest and deepest Jung had ever written, was gripping him.

As a matter of fact, he added, it's so much more than a book that it can hardly be called a book at all—because "in a very real sense it's an argument with God, similar to what Abraham found himself involved in when he argued with God".

And just as Abraham was the very first person in the Bible to be described as a prophet, he was also the earliest of the biblical prophets to challenge or argue with God. With the passing of time an entire lineage of argumentative prophets would follow on from him: a lineage culminating in the most notorious disputer with his own maker, and crier against the violence of the divine, who was the prophet known as Habakkuk.[99]

Of course, though, there should be no need to state the obvious which is that most of us are sensible enough for our tolerance to have its limits. Nowadays, to hear Jung mentioned in the same breath as Isaiah or Abraham or even Amos is hard enough. But to hear his name coupled with an obscure prophet like Habakkuk—that's pushing things much too far.

And I am not going to argue with that. Instead, I'll just leave the matter to others who are far more capable of arguing than me.

One very odd characteristic that Jung became famous for was seeing everything, even the most ordinary of everyday objects, as alive; as a conscious, individual, often nameable being. It's a tendency that his followers weren't quite sure whether to laugh at, imitate, or generalize into impressive theories and dogmas—without ever realizing or admitting to themselves that this strange quality of seeing everything as timelessly and interconnectedly alive is, itself, a unique feature of a prophet.

But in Jung's particular case there is yet another factor to consider, which is that this gift of seeing all objects and even thoughts as conscious living beings had been given to him directly by his own beloved teacher Philemon: the *prophêtôn patêr*, "father of prophets".

And of all the objects that surrounded Jung through his later life, there is one specific set which in a sense mattered to him more than anything else.

His smoking didn't just give him pleasure; make his physical existence tolerable; his work and efforts bearable. It also symbolized what held him to the earth—his identity and most basic existence as an utterly simple, very lonely human being.

As for the pipes he used: they came and went. But the one object that didn't go or come was his bronze tobacco pot which he used for filling each different pipe. It had been handed down to him, obviously through his father, from his grandfather. And you will already have guessed its name.

It was Habakkuk.[100]

CATAFALQUE
4

CATAFALQUE

1

I prefer to say little about Henry Corbin not because there is little to say, but because what does have to be said is best surrounded by silence.

From my teens through to my early thirties I was held fast in an awareness that the oldest western philosophers—the so-called Presocratics—weren't just the rationalists they are usually claimed to be.

They also included mystics and prophets. This might sound like a matter of purely historical or antiquarian interest, except that it was nothing of the kind. The awareness weighed on me with an inhuman, inescapable, almost crushing burden. And at the same time it penetrated every aspect of my very human daily life with the sense of something not only immensely ancient but, in particular through the presence of Empedocles, infinitely alive.

Nowhere in the whole of western literature was there any serious tradition that made the slightest effort to come to grips with this. It was a secret which had been so effectively sealed off from our collective western nightmare that nowhere in the world around me was there the slightest reflection of any such reality—until one day the proverbial book flew off a shelf as I was walking across the floor of a London bookstore and landed, already open, right in front of me.

When I stopped to see what peculiar message was lying at my feet, I noticed that the book was by someone called Henry Corbin. As for the passage staring up at me: it was a quotation from a seventeenth-century Persian Sufi stating that the oldest western philosophers, back before the time of Aristotle, included the greatest of mystics. It added that they'd given their whole lives to the "effort of spiritual struggle" and, very far from being devoted to reasoning or rationality, "one might even say that they are frankly hostile to them".

Just like that, with Henry Corbin's abrupt eruption into my life, the aloneness I had been suffering from was over. Through slowly searching the rest of his work I soon discovered that, according to Persian Sufis, the Presocratic philosophers were crucial early links in what Corbin himself came to call "prophetic philosophy". And so I was brought face to face with the ridiculous paradox that Persian Sufism had rescued and preserved the secret of the West which the West itself had forgotten—the secret understanding that western philosophy, logic, science, even the apparent arts of reason, all had their origin in the experience of another world.[1]

Then, as such things happen, I was introduced to Henry Corbin's widow. The deepest and most mysterious of friendships began, with her revealing details about her husband which he had always hesitated to put in print. But now there was a constant intensity and urgency in what she told me because things had already got so out of hand, with all the misunderstandings and misinterpretations of what he'd written, that she felt the crushing burden of needing to set matters straight.

One of the many key points she kept coming back to during the hours we spent together was the question of her husband's real identity and purpose—not as a scholar with some minor mystical leanings but as a mystic, inwardly directed to play the role of academic. And she loved talking about the time she and he spent together in Iran; describing how the great spiritual teachers or *sheikhs* often offered to initiate him as a Sufi on condition that he converted to Islam; and how he always politely refused. "Thank you for your invitation but there is no need, because I already have my inner *sheikh* inside me."

Even so, although there seemed almost no end to the personal and intimate details she confided to me, it's not as if the whole of what she told me had simply been kept unsaid. Instead, some of it already had been publicly mentioned by him in such an elusive and allusive way that nothing would be easier than not even to notice.

Once for instance, in the context of an unusual interview shortly before he died, he explained just what his view was on the subject of conversion. In it Corbin recalls his experience at an international conference about twenty years earlier, when "one colleague from a distant country" heard him talking about Persian spiritual tradition the way he normally used to do and "whispered to his neighbour: 'How can anyone talk like that about a religion that isn't your own?'

"But what does it mean", Corbin stops his story to ask, "to make a religion or a philosophy 'one's own'? Unfortunately, there are people who are only capable of thinking in terms of 'conversion' because that's what allows them to attach a collective label to who you are. No way! Anyone who talks about 'conversion' hasn't understood anything about the 'esoteric'."

Then he goes on to describe what real esotericism, or inwardness, actually implies for a person—by citing the prophet Isaiah. Such an individual "is forced to keep his secret. *Secretum meum mihi*, 'My secret is for me'. The secret of the castle of the soul." And he makes sure to add that "the community, the *ummah*, of esotericists from all places and all times is that 'inner church' which demands no outer act or gesture of belonging as a requirement for being allowed to take part. But this inner connecting link is the true link because no one can remove it or take it away, it can't be damaged or destroyed, and because only thanks to it is there any truth in the saying that 'the mouth speaks from the fullness of the heart'."[2]

Here, of course, we are brought straight back to the essence of what Henry Corbin meant by that "absolute spiritual freedom" he encountered at Eranos in the presence of Carl Jung.

Helped along by his biblical quotations, he arrives right at the heart of Jung's whole psychology with its overriding emphasis on the devastating effects of every external collectivity. At the same time, what he says here about the reality of an "inner church" corresponds exactly to what had already been said by someone over half a century earlier.

That was when Jung himself appealed to the example of Christ by quoting from the Bible, just like Corbin, and for the sake of those around him explained how "if we belong to the secret church, then we belong, and we need not worry about it, but can go our own way. If we do not belong, no amount of teaching or organization can bring us there."[3]

2

There is always another side to everything, and on the other side of outer spiritual freedom lies something else.

That other side is freedom's darker half: the reality of the inner teacher or *sheikh*. Here, too, Corbin explained the essential quite plainly—although there is no saying for certain if what he allowed to be published was far too brief or, on the contrary, not nearly brief enough.

Again just a few months before dying he had taken the greatest care to record how in October 1939 he left Paris, with his wife, for Istanbul. It was meant to be a three-month mission to gather manuscripts containing texts by a Persian Sufi called Suhrawardî. But that was just life's excuse or pretence.

Thanks, outwardly, to the war those three months turned into six years; and during this time of freedom from any outer distractions "I learned the inestimable virtues of silence, of what initiates call 'the discipline of the arcane' (*ketmân* in Persian). One of the virtues of this silence is that I found myself placed, I alone together with him alone, in the company of my invisible *sheikh*: Shihâb al-Dîn Yahyâ Suhrawardî, who died a martyr in 1191 at the age of thirty-six which happened to be my own age at the time."

Day and night, Corbin describes, he worked on translating Suhrawardî's writings—and "when those years of retreat finally came to an end I had become an *Ishrâqî*".[4]

Probably there is no point at all in spelling out the obvious. But this deceptively simple passage, with its passing reference to the quintessential mystical experience of encountering one's invisible teacher, contains the most secret kernel of his life as well as his work.

For him Suhrawardî would always be his single, innermost orientation: his central point of focus. And Suhrawardî's own inner focus and orientation would always be on the *ishrâq*—on the point of dawn in the East. This *Ishrâqî* tradition he gave rise to wasn't, as people in the West are lazily inclined to suppose, a tradition of pure enlightenment or illumination.

It was, much more specifically, the tradition of those who appear with the dawn; who belong to the moment of dawning; who tirelessly and timelessly work at fetching the gifts of the sacred into the light of day.

And as for Corbin himself: on his frank admission he wasn't just some scholar studying or reporting on the intricacies of this antique tradition. He was now an initiated *Ishrâqî* in his own right.[5]

There is one important detail, though, which is missing from this published account of his—but which his wife made sure to discuss with me a number of times. This is the fact that he realized Suhrawardî was invisibly, silently, overwhelmingly, even geographically, holding him fast. He had the very distinct, quite physical awareness that he wasn't holding the strings of his life because his teacher was; using outer circumstances to corner him; trap him and trick him; keep him, for whatever time was needed, all to himself.

And from then on, his life was no longer his own.

But even this had been noted and mentioned by Corbin in his published writings, for anyone willing to look.

Ten years before he died, he briefly described to an academic audience in France how his fateful introduction to Suhrawardî's writings is the single event that sealed his destiny. "I was drawn (*entraîné*) into becoming publisher of the works of Suhrawardî and Suhrawardî drew me (*m'entraîna*) far, far away from the peaceful tasks entrusted to me at the National Library."

It would be so easy to ignore the repetition here of the word *entraîner*, "drawn … drew", except that there is nothing accidental about it at all. On the contrary, this kind of repetition is literally a signature. For ages it's been the standard sign of initiation into the sacred mysteries, just like Jung's announcement at the start of the *Red book* about how he had been forced, forced, taken, taken by the spirit of the depths—or Parmenides' account right at the start of his poem evoking how he had been carried, carried, carried, carried into the realities of another world.

This is how Corbin and Jung and Parmenides were pulled into meeting with their superiors, as Empedocles called them. And the point of this pulling, in Corbin's case, could hardly be clearer.

It was to show that our ideas of truth, or reality, are just an upside-down illusion. We, among the so-called living, are not in charge of our lives as we think. The real fingers around our necks or on our pulses are not our own. As a matter of fact we are hardly alive at all, here, because the real truth is that we are held fast in the grip of the dead.[6]

This is why Suhrawardî's tradition is, itself, so dangerously alive. It's able to reach out through and across the centuries, secretly, silently, whenever someone is ready—whoever, wherever, you are. And that aliveness explains the name he gave his *Ishrâqî* tradition: the "eternal leaven".

Just like leaven or yeast it contains its own living germ, its transformative enzyme, inside. But that also makes it a perpetual source of ferment; of disorder and disturbance, agitation, unpredictable change. And this in turn is exactly why Suhrawardî was killed at the age of thirty-six, put to death by the rigid powers of dogmatism for opening the door to too much life.

Instead of admitting as expected to the Islamic clergy that prophecy was dead, that it had come to an end with Muhammad, when interrogated he gently indicated it was still alive inside him.

But even more threateningly, and offensively, he allowed prophecy to spread unchecked not just forward into the present or future. He also followed it far into the past—openly announcing that his own tradition of the dawn reached back way beyond Muhammad to the earliest Greeks and Persians. That was one of the main reasons for his execution: that he made the mistake of treading in the footsteps of the Ancients.

In fact aside from describing this troublesome leaven or restless ferment as eternal, he had another name for it too. At times he also called it "the leaven of the Pythagoreans".

And he traced this livingness back not just to the sacred figure of Hermes but very specifically, very explicitly, to somebody else in particular—the philosopher and prophet Empedocles.[7]

3

Just like some cosmic cycle, the prophetic impulse to find life in death is always going to be met by the deceptive need to turn life into death.

Even through his final role as a martyr, not to mention many of the details in his teachings, Suhrawardî was following the traces of one very particular prophetic tradition: the lineage stemming from the great Gnostic known as Seal of the Prophets, Mani. And as is bound to be the case with such sacred traditions, that heretically challenge every cherished collective belief, the most potent threat to the threats it poses is never going to come only from outside.

On the contrary, it's going to come from the innermost circle—in exactly the same way that it also comes from inside us.

As a twentieth-century *Ishrâqî* Corbin lived, for the most part unnoticed, the life of a knight: a spiritual knight entrusted with upholding the laws of chivalry. And in his case this meant, especially, always looking for the absolute best inside the people around him.

That was his protection but also his vulnerability, even naivety. This is why during the times he spent in Iran forming collaborations, forging friendships, creating alliances, he learned to expect the highest and finest among his closest colleagues; assumed they too, like him, understood the mystery of that invisible bond which comes from belonging to the inner church beyond any empty formalities of external religion or conversion. It was this inner bond, this direct link between heart and heart, that he believed would let "my Iranian friends feel perfectly at ease" with him as they all laboured together in "a friendship free from any mental reservation or ulterior motive".[8]

But, needless to say, things didn't quite work out that way.

It was the same story whether Henry Corbin was present or absent; still alive or already dead. His most intimate and influential Iranian colleagues just couldn't resist, whenever the opportunity presented itself, criticizing him sharply for failing to take a physical teacher by converting to Islam.

The irony is that they were perfectly familiar with the altogether legitimate tradition, inside Islam, of the so-called Uwaisîs: Sufis who happen to have no outer teacher because they have been initiated, all alone with their teacher alone, by an invisible *sheikh*. They also knew very well how these rare Uwaisîs are supposed to be guided and sustained by the spirit of Khidr—a mysterious figure often identified with the prophet Elijah.

At times they were even tempted to cite the Uwaisîs as a direct and obvious parallel to the case of Corbin, only to dismiss such a parallel straight away. After all, Corbin's appeal to the reality of an inner teacher was plainly little more than the fantasy of a dreamer; the product of too active an imagination.

And what was equally significant was their eagerness to dispose of the inescapable awareness that gripped Corbin of being held fast by an invisible *sheikh*—the physical and gut-wrenching experience Corbin's wife Stella and I were often drawn to discuss of being pulled in one direction as opposed to another, dragged by the finest intelligence away from every distraction, forced without the slightest choice into the depths of oneself.

But, upstanding men of religion that they were, to them this was basically all just words. For them nothing could be simpler than to turn the ruthless reality of faceless force into some pretty image of Suhrawardî taking Henry Corbin, "almost literally", by the hand and kindly guiding him from place to place. At the same time, for them such images were only fancy metaphors meant to gloss over the fact that everything Corbin had done was purely the result of his own conscious choices and wishes and decisions.

And in saying all this they were just as much rationalists as every one of those upstanding Jungians who benignly imply that Jung himself was only talking the language of metaphor when he reported being forced and dragged away from everything familiar by the invisible spirit of the depths—because his dedication to plumbing the abyss of the unconscious was, of course, the result of his own very conscious decision and wish and choice.[9]

That's only the first half of this little tale, though. And even more significant than the treatment of Corbin by his so-called colleagues is the way they treated Suhrawardî.

In the eyes of Corbin, one of the most striking things about Suhrawardî's vision of sacred history is that it valued ancient Greek sages just as highly as Islamic mystics. It was a vision that saw both West and East as ultimately, not to mention primordially, one. The timeless energy inside the leaven moves through time wherever it wishes and chooses—not where we choose or decide.

But for Corbin's closest Iranian friend and collaborator, who even worked with him in editing the actual texts of Suhrawardî, that was totally unacceptable. So he did what anyone in his shoes would be bound to do; cut off, ever so subtly, the flow of life through Suhrawardî's tradition of dawning; did what he could to kill off the living leaven inside it. And instead of mentioning the idea of an "eternal leaven" he silently, absurdly, replaced it with something else: the notion of an "eternal dough".

Suddenly the mystery so alive in this ferment had been downgraded to some passive substance waiting, inert, to be activated by the right people at the right time—especially by orthodox forces inside the tradition of Islam. Everything was back again under human supervision and conscious control, the borders of orthodoxy not only protected but tightly closed.[10]

And, needless to say, it's the same story as Carl Jung's lava all over again. When Jung made the mistake of talking about the living stream of volcanic lava spontaneously taking care of everything, bringing everything into its right place, that wouldn't do at all. We can very comfortably state with perfect assurance what he had been meaning and wanting to say, which is that he himself took good care of everything; put it all in its appropriate place.

In other words: the only sensible, dependable solution is to mistranslate.

Now everything has been fixed with Suhrawardî, too. To any casual eye, Corbin's work is being faithfully continued—but, in reality, discreetly undermined. It's so simple, so subtle. Everything seems and sounds the same, but nothing is. Just the slightest twist is needed, the tiniest hint of dogmatism or excess rigidity, and the entire dynamic has changed; just one speck of impurity and the original, prophetic vision is lost.

And this isn't only a matter of how some person, here or there, translates a text. It's a question of how each of us lives, at every moment of any day or night. Whenever we let go of ourselves because we don't trust enough, or there is something deep inside we are desperate to forget, then we have missed our chance.

But if we hold on too tight—convince ourselves we've mastered what our little minds can never grasp—the betrayal is complete and the damage has already been done.

4

The tenderness in Carl Jung's confession of his "extraordinary joy" at being completely understood by Henry Corbin, while the rest of his life was a more or less total "intellectual vacuum", is like the intimacy of horses recognizing each other by their scent.

And, needless to say, an equal tenderness is called for if we are going to understand the nature of this understanding. But, instead, it's been sucked up and away into the vacuum of total incomprehension.

Nowadays the authoritative account of Corbin's relationship to Jung has it that, after meeting him, he got terribly excited; had a wonderful intellectual honeymoon with Jung's ideas; was quick to assert his freedom and sooner or later had left any Jungian influence behind. And this had to happen, we are told, because Jung and Corbin were different. Jung carved in stone and Corbin didn't, so it would be absurd to imagine there could be any enduring empathies or profound similarities between them. These encounters of independent-minded thinkers are always just a flash in the pan.[11]

In fact, though, that's not how things happened at all—for a very good reason.

This archetypally American story of excitement and instant thrills only touches on the outermost surface, the external, the exoteric: on what Jung called the world of personality no. 1. And such a superficial approach is bound to end up utterly clueless in the face of what Henry Corbin, for his part, referred to as the true inwardness of esotericism or the esoteric.

The first time that Corbin and Jung ever met was during the late summer of 1949.

After the Eranos conference in southern Switzerland Jung invited Corbin back to his home on the outskirts of Zurich for a discussion that, "so warm and open, so full of promise for the future", lasted for hours. And they had plenty to talk about—not, as one might naively think, by butting heads over this particular issue or that but by exploring together the kinds of awareness which are needed for gaining access to the inner truth behind every external issue.

For instance it's no coincidence that they both, quite independently of each other, had been absorbed in uncovering and evoking the *cognitio matutina* or "dawn consciousness" buried inside us all: the selfless awareness which, still inspired by the wisdoms of the night, hasn't yet been contaminated by the irresistible urge at the sunset of a civilization to exploit any spiritual truth until it becomes one more diabolical tool in our all-too-human hands.[12]

Then, three years later, came the great encounter for which Corbin would say all their previous meetings had been just a preparation—their encounter over Jung's *Answer to Job*. Henry Corbin's enormous review of the book is what prompted Jung to write that it was Corbin who had given him not only "the rarest of experiences, but the unique experience, of being completely understood". And it might seem tempting to dismiss this statement as no more than the enthusiastic acceptance of the enthusiastic review of one, particular book.

But that would be to miss the point entirely.

For Jung *Answer to Job* was the one, and only, book he ever published that was brought directly into existence from the depths of the sacred inside him. It, not he, had done the writing as it swept like a hurricane right through him. At the same time he described hearing it as music: the same music Corbin, too, would hear when he sat down to read it. Everyone else was panicking about the book's acceptability; desperately doubting or attacking it; nobly trying to rationalize it; justify it.

But Corbin and Jung were the two people who silently listened.[13]

The acuteness of the situation was perfectly clear to Jung. Writing this one book brought him face to face with the most essential aspect of his whole work, of his real task. And the entire medical profession—psychiatrists, healers, clinicians—didn't have the slightest idea what that work or that book was about.

This doesn't mean he just gave other professionals the cold shoulder, though, or dismissed them for their total lack of understanding. On the contrary, with striking humility and the rarest honesty he realized that their attitude of defensive mockery and aggressive stupidity was also his; that the typically dumb medical point of view which had infected them had infected him, as well; that their resistance to the numinous reality of the sacred was, at the same time, the stubborn resistance and idiocy of his own "dull conscious mind" which will always claim it knows what it never can.

Now, of course, everything works exactly in reverse. We all have Jung's wisdom implanted like some clever little computer in our dull conscious minds and our understanding is crystal clear even when we don't understand a thing.[14]

But that's not the whole story, either, because he didn't just find himself confronted with the incomprehension of independent scientific experts or of the expert scientist inside him. He also found himself face to face with the incomprehension of his well-intentioned followers. And from their initial reactions to the book, even before it was officially published, he realized that the Jungians too are no different from anyone else.

It was the same situation, all over again, as with Christ's disciples falling asleep in the garden at Gethsemane. Far from Jungians being able to fill the abysmal void in which he was so accustomed to living, that intellectual vacuum also consisted of them.[15]

This was the vacuum, the terrible aloneness, that Henry Corbin stepped into. And as for what it was that made his response to *Answer to Job* so special, the answer could hardly be plainer.

His long review of the book, which Jung considered not only so rare but so completely unique in its understanding, presented *Answer to Job* from start to end as a work of prophecy—and Jung, himself, as a prophet in the truest sense of the word.[16]

Of course Jung's closest Jewish colleagues would also try to say as much, in their own ways. Erich Neumann, for his part, would compare the Jung of *Answer to Job* with Abraham in his typically focused but suggestive style. James Kirsch, shortly before he died, would devote a passionate lecture to painting the Jung who wrote *Answer to Job* as the greatest prophet of our age.

And it's to Kirsch, too, that we owe one of those vivid details which lend an altogether new complexion to our understanding of the time when Jung was working on his *Red book*: "He, himself, told me that during the years in which he received the revelations, i.e., from 1912 to 1916, his face became quite luminous, radiant, like that of Moses, and that people were afraid to look at him."

But Kirsch, as Jung's friend, was afflicted with an insight that psychologically he couldn't handle. And what made Henry Corbin's extended discussion of Jung as creator of *Answer to Job* so exceptional is that—because of his own immersion in a living prophetic lineage stretching all the way from Persian Sufis back even beyond the ancient Greeks—he lived what he wrote.

That's why he could not just describe, but also recognize, the most intimate tastes and smells of prophecy so well.[17]

5

The discussions over *Answer to Job* continued between Jung and Corbin during visits, by both Corbins, to Jung's home in the Zurich suburb of Küsnacht; also at Bollingen.

But there is one particular meeting they had, in September 1955, which is worth mentioning. Years later, after Jung was already dead, Corbin would look back at it with special fondness as well as regret because—"alas!"—it was the last in-depth encounter they ever managed to have. And it just so happens that the handwritten notes he made of that discussion, straight after the meeting had taken place, still survive.

The notes are full of "yes, but"; of agreements followed by subtler points of disagreement. And anyone who skimmed through them without paying attention could even imagine Corbin wanting to complain because Jung wouldn't simply accept, or submit to, his personal point of view.

Again, though, that would be to misunderstand the situation completely.

Corbin lists, from memory, the subjects they discussed: music, God and soul and devil, therapy and revelation, vision and visionary consciousness, psychological integration and the sacred, going beyond the profane and leaving the rational intellect behind, Ibn al-'Arabî and the mystical identity with God, true individuation as becoming God or God's secret.

But at the same time he also lists the subtleties of movement from subject onto subject, with the conversation gracefully shifting through the most delicate and esoteric aspects of Sufi teaching. In fact just to follow that movement, step by step, is to realize what this conversation really was—not some clumsy rough-and-tumble of different ideas, but a dance.[18]

And anyone at all familiar with the practices of Sufism will recognize this dance for what it is.

In Persian as well as Turkish its name is *sohbet*—the traditional name for the inexplicable closeness and pleasure and joy felt by the pure-hearted in each other's company. This is the reason why "Sufis say there are three ways of being with the mystery: prayer, then a step up from that, meditation, and a step up from that," *sohbet* or the supreme joy of mystical dialogue.

To be drawn into the reality of *sohbet* is suddenly to have the direct experience that, instead of just talking to some other human, you are speaking with "a person like the dawn". And the funny thing is that, right at the climax of noting down this conversation with Jung, Corbin even states explicitly what's going on.

"Suprême joie du dialogue", he carefully records: the supreme joy of dialogue. But he's not just noting down some theoretical idea they discussed, one more passing subject of conversation. He is also recording what actually took place in that space between him and Jung—as an immediate continuation and confirmation of the "joie extraordinaire" or "extraordinary joy" Carl Jung had already experienced on being so uniquely, so completely, understood by Henry Corbin.

In other words, what they were talking about and what they were doing were one and the same thing. Their discussion was, itself, the experiences they were discussing.[19]

And to have left their interaction there, in the borderless formlessness of infinite mystical union, would psychologically have been a total disaster.

But Corbin was no fool—which is why, at the end of his notes, he marks the stage of bringing everything back again into a world of separation. There is Jung, and there is Corbin, and there is a healthy reminder of the differences between them because Jung will always be the psychologist and healer; Corbin will never stop being the mystic and metaphysician. Or as Corbin himself explains, Jung's main focus will always be on the case of some sick patient needing help while mine will always be on the ideal case of a mystic.

And then he adds the three words, in ancient Greek, which bring everything to a close: *monos pros monon*, "alone to alone".

This, originally magical and mystical, expression was a key theme for Corbin because it conveys so well the nature of our invisible bond with the divine reality inside us. For him it captures the infinitely simple, but endlessly mysterious, essence of true individuation—of the process which allows would-be humans to grow up to become real individuated humans, genuinely "solitary, authentically alone, freed from every collective norm" because they just let themselves be held in a constant alignment with the eternal aloneness of their higher self.

Here is that same inner secret, again, for which Corbin liked quoting the prophet Isaiah's *Secretum meum mihi*; "My secret is for me". And it's a secret which always will be *monos pros monon*, alone to alone, "in the sense that no one else is present to such intimacy".

But this, too, isn't all.

Behind that mystical sense of connection to one's own divine reality there is another, even more ancient meaning of those words. *Monos pros monon* also can refer to the most intimate conversation and dialogue between two human beings. And as a matter of fact this particular meaning features right at the start of that review Corbin wrote for *Answer to Job*.

Or to be more precise: this is how he introduces not just his review, or the book, but Jung himself. Jung, he launches straight into explaining, is one of those very few rarest of people who have become genuinely and authentically alone inside themselves with the divine mystery; have managed to do what's almost unheard of by separating from every ready-made opinion or collective idea. And "it's because we find ourselves, here, in the presence of this man *alone* that I would like to invite all those who are *alone* to meditate on this book and to listen to this message if they truly are *alone*."

Of course the terrifying consequence of what he is saying is that hardly anyone is alone because most people are surrounded all the time by their collective projections, cluttered by ghostly illusions, crowded out by constant expectations and aspirations wherever they go.

Even so, his conclusion is remorseless. Whoever hasn't discovered this total inner aloneness is doomed to fail from the very outset in any attempt at understanding Jung, or Jung's work—because only the alone can understand the alone, *monos pros monon*.

And just how accurate he was in his estimate of Jung, not to mention Jung's work, is perfectly evident from what we know about the period when Jung himself was being worked on by his *Red book*. Now we can see in its naked clarity how he conceived of the individuation process: as the way to become God, for sure, but as a way that's closed off completely from everyone not able to tolerate the cosmic aloneness of their own almost unbearable singleness and uniqueness.

To be individuated, as Jung understood, is to become a single distant star—is to have to learn how to live far out in the coldest and most solitary spaces, beyond even the experience of death. And to fail in this process of individuation, which is also the process of becoming a real human, means being sent to join the swarming masses of the collectively unsatisfied dead.

Once again, then, Corbin with his *monos pros monon* isn't just listing another quick topic of conversation between him and Jung on one September day in 1955.

On the contrary, he is describing the secret dynamic of the conversation itself; the innermost nature of their interaction; the spirit instructing the dance.

To anyone else the dance is, naturally, bound to be as inscrutable as the spirit behind it is invisible. Exoterically, people can't stop themselves obsessing over the obvious differences between Corbin and Jung without ever glimpsing what lies beyond. When Corbin describes coming to a place where formally he had to separate from Jung, the last thing they will guess is that he is just noting what two knights will always have to do at the crossroads—follow their own, lonely path in the search for what both Jung and Corbin knew to be the ultimate mystery of the Grail.

Even then the separation is only outer, never inner. But it would never once occur to them that all the outer differences are simply what guarantees the inner aloneness which allows the divine aloneness to flower.

And, just as naturally, they'll fail even to register the comment made by Corbin in his review about "the ultimate, the unforgivable, truth of the *alone to alone*". That, as he explains in the obvious hope of not being noticed by anyone unable to understand, is the inexcusable truth of the solitary prophet who is forced to speak out and bear witness to the ultimate aloneness of God.[20]

Only now is it possible to make out the real thread connecting this meeting, in 1955, to the original creation of Jung's *Answer to Job*. When Corbin looked back at that particular meeting, years later, with such affection and regret there was one specific feature of the encounter which still struck him forcefully.

This was the way that the theme of music, which is how they'd begun their dialogue, led back even further to Jung's original experience of hearing the book playing itself as if it was music.

Right at the start of their discussion, Corbin had taken the initiative of asking Jung how he experienced the real power and virtue of music: its therapeutic virtues, its spiritual power. And what touched him most of all was Jung's reply—which is that "music only has any purificatory virtue if it leads us into an inner *visionary* experience, using that word in its strongest and prophetic sense".[21]

Again, for Corbin, every single road he travelled with Jung started and ended with prophecy. This could hardly be less surprising, though, when we consider the main themes and interests that held both men together.

One simply has to think of Khidr: the mysterious prophet and inner guide, more real than any outer teacher, who only appears in all his modest greenness to those he allows to see him. And nothing could be less unexpected than the fascination with him these two men shared—considering that for both of them their teachers happened to be, just like Khidr, invisible prophets of the most special kind.[22]

It would be easy to add other examples such as their shared passion for Joachim of Fiore, the Christian prophet who pretended not to be a prophet, and their shared awareness of his crucial importance for any true understanding of the West. But then there are the less obvious cases, like the importance of imagination, which take us straight into the powerhouse of their ideas.

Jung's work is famous for the central role it gives to "active imagination"; Corbin's, for the central role it ascribes to what he would call the "imaginal" as opposed to the merely imaginary. And with one, as well as the other, a kind of complacency can make it easy to imagine one knows exactly what each of them means.

The reality is, though, that at the back of their ideas about imagination lies one ancient notion known to both of them by its Latin name. That's the idea of *imaginatio vera*: of real or true imagination.

This profoundly paradoxical idea, which derives from ancient Hermetic and mystical traditions, is like the hidden heart beating at the core of everything else they said or did. For both of them alike, and in this they were perfectly at one, it's the forgotten principle that divides reality from all our usual self-indulgent fantasies; our constant imaginary thinking.

At the same time this true or real imagination is the power responsible for creating everything around and inside us, from our inner thoughts right out to the stars. It's also the power that can bring us back into the productive, functioning centre of ourselves—because, as Jung states the matter so succinctly, "the real is what works".

And historically, as Corbin knew only too well, this aptitude for "true imagination" is the rare faculty that belongs to one particular kind of person.

It always has been reserved, above all, for prophets.[23]

6

Henry Corbin arrived back in Paris from Tehran, for the very last time, at the beginning of 1978: his final return to the West from the place he had come to consider his spiritual home.

Inwardly, during the months leading up to his death that October, he was living more and more in a world of prophets—and of the mysterious inner music he already had discussed with Jung a quarter of a century earlier. Outwardly, right to the end there were people yapping at his heels from every corner wanting their meal; their little pound of flesh.

Even so, in the West just as much as anywhere else, his chivalrous ethic held him back from objecting when they twisted or manipulated his writings and ideas to suit their own self-centred ends.

His policy was crystal clear. He felt duty bound never to criticize colleagues openly or disagree with them in public; only to emphasize the points on which they agreed; even, if necessary, to invent the points of agreement; and, especially when disappointed or betrayed, to keep addressing individuals as his dear colleague and friend.[24]

And among the worst problems he had to face, back in the West, were the Jungians. On one level, in the spirit of collegiality he was happy to offer them his fullest encouragement and support. On another level he was exhausted by them, along with any number of other people or things: sick to death of the way they kept psychologically pushing him over the edge by trying to convert the Sufi ideas he had been introducing to the West into a tool they could exploit with their all-too-human hands.

For instance there was the case of James Hillman. Jimmy from New Jersey had a truly brilliant, scintillating, fearless mind. And in a very public move he decided to make not just Carl Jung but also Henry Corbin the two "immediate fathers" of what, eventually, he would choose to refer to as his imaginal psychology. What was kept much less public, and what Stella described to me in the greatest detail on more than one occasion, is how things turned out when Hillman made his pilgrimage to Paris to ask Corbin's blessing for this "imaginal psychology" of his.

With only Stella present, Corbin yelled at Hillman for misusing and abusing the language of the Sufis; denounced his appropriation of the word "imaginal" as totally illegitimate; and left the room in a storm after asking his wife to show him out.

After that, of course, Corbin's chivalry prevented him from openly offering any criticisms or even the slightest hint of disagreement. And in public Hillman would remain, to the end, his dearest colleague and friend.[25]

But this isn't to say that when he felt the full burden of the situation weighing down on him, as it did just a few months before he died, he didn't issue warnings: the clearest, strongest warnings about reducing spiritual truths to the level of trivial intellectualizing and cheap psychologizing. Naturally, though, Hillman paid no notice and neither did anyone else.

Or to be a little more precise, American intellectuals would come out in force to criticize Corbin severely for even daring to issue warnings. Everyone, we are told, has the right to make anything out of anything—and for elders to warn their juniors is nothing but stuffy, old-fashioned, patriarchal authoritarianism.

And in one of those strange ironies it's safer not to notice, Corbin happened to be more familiar than almost anybody else with the old Persian sacred traditions that vividly depict young people's disrespectful refusal to heed the warnings of their elders as the surest pointer to the dissolution and destruction of a culture; to the death and ending of an age. For him it was an indescribable pain to watch what's most sacred being turned into a plaything and to witness the powerful ancient prophecies being fulfilled right in front of his eyes.[26]

Nothing could be wider of the mark, though, than to think that the Jungians he encountered would only be a problem for Corbin in his old age.

Since first coming into contact with them he had always found their collective unconscious fondness for imitation and clever clichés and second-hand, warmed-over ideas a total travesty of what Jung himself valued above anything else: the fullness of individuation, a total inner aloneness, the willingness to be guided inwardly wherever that guidance leads and "with all the consequences this entails".[27]

But, by the end of Corbin's life, Jung had already been gone for over fifteen years—which was a long enough time that, under the pressure of constant bombardment from Jungians, he sometimes mentally forgot what it had all been about. On a certain level, the meetings between the two of them had drifted into almost a distant memory.

Even so, the essence never changed. The love and affection, respect and inner gratitude he felt towards Jung ran just as deep.[28]

And so did his loyalty.

It can be easy to miss the significance of the way that Corbin's closest Iranian collaborator, Seyyed Hossein Nasr, used to keep on taunting and needling him by denouncing Carl Jung as a misguided fraud. Nasr belonged to a band of intellectuals and would-be esotericists who called themselves Traditionalists. Mostly, aside from Nasr himself, these Traditionalists were Europeans who had become converts to Islam and somehow believed this entitled them to speak with authority about all the world's religions—not to mention everything else, including Jung's psychology.

To begin with, some of them had an undeniable quality of piety; even saintliness. And a fair amount of what they said could be a little banal, to be sure, but wise enough. The most noticeable thing was not so much the rigid orthodoxy of their intellectualism as their tendency to pontificate about subjects they simply couldn't understand.[29]

In a peculiarly unconscious re-enactment of the full-scale assault by ancient Platonists, almost two thousand years earlier, on the Gnostics they launched the most vicious attacks against Jung—making all the same mistakes as the Platonists of substituting their supposedly valid beliefs for the immediacy of direct experience, of laying claim to the possession of some "primordial tradition" which was nothing but a manufactured fantasy.

They would write at length with the greatest apparent learning about esotericism but without realizing that when you talk like this about the esoteric you turn it, just like Jung's spirit of our time nicely dressing up as the spirit of the depths, into its exact exoteric opposite.

And even though many of these Traditionalists were Muslims, the fact had mysteriously escaped them that with all their theorizing they were violating the essential spirit of Islam. In laying out their grand systems and mental schemes they'd forgotten how, according to the Qur'an, every human structure is just another speck of dust waiting to be swept away from the Face of God.[30]

As a young man, Henry Corbin's initial approach to them had been open-handed as well as diplomatic; but when he came up against the full force of their hidebound righteousness that didn't last for long. And, much later, every time that Nasr chose to lash out at Jung it was Corbin who passionately sprang to his defence.

By standing up for Jung he was fighting in support of what, to him, would always be most precious. The truth is that it was Jung, as spokesperson for the unknown spirit of the depths, who had turned into a living embodiment of Khidr—and it was the so-called Traditionalists who "really hit the roof" when Jung as Khidr appeared on the scene out of nowhere to point people back again towards the source of life.

Any superficial differences in opinion between Jung and Corbin faded into insignificance compared to this. That's why, even when Corbin was trying to describe to westerners the realities of spiritual experience in ancient Persia or among Persian Sufis, he found himself being brought straight back to Jung. Or as he explained: we are dealing here with realities which are so subtle and so archetypally powerful but "so alien to our normal modern consciousness that, without the teaching of C.G. Jung, it would be difficult to get any sense of what they mean as a lived experience".

And as he also expressed himself far more personally, trying to convey in public his infinite gratitude to Jung: "It was at Eranos that the pilgrim who had arrived from Iran was destined to encounter the one who, through his *Answer to Job*, made him understand the answer he was bringing inside himself from Iran. The path towards the eternal Sophia"—the same Sophia painted by Jung for his *Red book* as the lived experience of the soul who snatches you away into eternity before helping you, or at least some part of you, to return.[31]

But then there is the even more significant fact that Corbin wrote what almost amounted to a whole book, which has just been published recently, about Jung.

He wrote it with one key purpose in mind which was to show how, when understood as it should be, Jungian psychology is the only real equivalent for westerners of Zen or Tibetan Buddhism in the East. And it's the only real equivalent because, beyond the dogmatism of Traditionalists as well as the dogmatism of Jungians, it offers direct access to the essence of spiritual experience—the original "primordial experience", potentially available to all of us in the West but rejected for so long as heretical, which has been banished century after century by the dogmatism of the Christian Church.[32]

Naturally there is the strangest paradox here—that an orientalist who spent the whole of his adult life specializing in Persian traditions and spent half of it feeling at home outside of Europe would point back, so emphatically, to his own western culture.

But this is exactly what Corbin did. And it's also why he felt so little sympathy for the western Traditionalists who took what they thought were new identities by converting to Islam and, in some cases, abandoned their own original culture for dead.

To him, everything he did in the East was intended as an act of service to the West. He knew he would always, first and foremost, be a westerner; that his ultimate duty was to contribute to the West; to help heal it, rescue it from its forgetfulness, return it to its spiritual source.[33]

And it's important to understand just what he saw when, as a westerner, he looked at Jung and Jung's psychology—which for him as an outsider was far more than some specialized technique. It was Jung's knowledge, his real science, of the soul.

In the work he wrote about Jung, and about Jung's teaching of individuation, he describes exactly what he found himself looking at. I see, he says, the arrival of the dawn. I see the sun rising in the east. But by this he didn't mean the physical east.

He meant the inner east: the east inside us all.

To reject our western culture by looking to the geographical east for one's identity and true self, for teaching and guidance, is the perfect way to end up lost; to get ripped up, as Corbin quotes directly from Jung, by our roots; or as Jung also says, to forget we ever had a garden and try to feed ourselves by gobbling up foreign fruits.

And Corbin explains that this point of the sun rising at a new dawn which he encounters in the work of Jung is the same as the moment of dawn or *ishrâq* in the Sufi teaching of Suhrawardî. It's strange to see how not only did Corbin understand Jung in the light of this Sufi tradition but Jung only felt completely understood by a Sufi.[34]

This could all sound very pretty, except that prettiness is not at all what it's about. What it is about is the last thing we want to know about, which is the responsibility we have as westerners to face the darkness of our own culture without looking away. And nothing could be more wrong than to imagine that Corbin was too spiritual to face this inner darkness.

He didn't talk too much about it because he saw that as Jung's job; but he knew perfectly well when to face the darkness, and how. It can be very useful to study and learn from eastern teachings—except when you try to use them to cover over the darkness and emptiness you feel inside. They may be able to throw some light on your problem, but they are never going to solve it.

And they aren't going to solve it because the only real solution ever comes from the problem itself.

When Corbin wanted to illustrate this he turned back, appropriately enough, to western legends of the Grail. The best way he knew of making his point was to quote the beautiful saying: *Seule guérit la blessure la lance qui la fît*, "The wound is only healed by the lance that made it."

Jung, too, was intimately familiar with this same situation in the Grail legend—this impossible task of healing the wound through the instrument that caused it. On one hand, of course, this was precisely his task.

On the other, when he talked about it in objective terms, he described this work of returning to heal the gaping wound caused so long ago as the impossible work of the equally impossible saviour or Saoshyant; of the precious jewel, father of all prophets, who comes back after thousands of years bringing a completely new revelation.

And just how impossible this task is starts to become clear when one finds the courage, if only for a moment, to face that individual but also collective emptiness and darkness inside oneself—without trying to do anything, such as thinking good thoughts or inventing childish schemes, to fill the hole.[35]

7

Shortly before he died, Jung recalled a prophecy his soul had told him—predicting his future when, almost half a century earlier, he still was immersed in the work he was doing on the *Red book*.

She had prophesied that first he would be drawn and quartered; then the different parts of him would be thrown onto scales to be weighed before being sold off. Like so many shamanic realities, this prophecy had the profoundest significance along with the crudest of implications.

And helped along by everyone who has no time for the reality of the soul, or the mysteries of prophecy, what she described is precisely what happened.

As soon as somebody turned up, especially from America, with the exciting news that another organization had been created for training potential future Jungians he'd feel crushed: devastated. Also, far closer to home, it was only thanks to a great deal of artful blackmail and trickery that people were finally able to persuade him to accept the inevitability of an institute being founded at Zurich in his name. But even at the grand opening in 1948 he had trouble concealing his grudgingness or reluctance about the whole affair.

Somehow the words managed to slip out that "My grandfather, Carl Gustav Jung once founded a home for retarded children. Now I am founding one for retarded adults." And behind what he said was the implication, as always, that people wanting to understand his work simply had themselves to blame if they tried consulting those who claim to act or speak in his name. They should go straight to his books, instead.

Occasionally he did decide to turn up at the new institute, but not often. In line with his usual philosophy of non-interference he deliberately, and very humorously, kept aloof; left everybody to do the kinds of things they were going to do anyway, make fools of themselves according to their choosing, draw their own conclusions, cause all the usual confusions.[36]

There was just one single condition he insisted on when agreeing to so much hocus-pocus, because it was the only thing that to him really counted. This was that the primary aim and focus of the Zurich institute would be to pursue interdisciplinary research into a whole range of subjects he took great care to list and name. That it would become a place for training therapists was the last possible purpose he had in mind.

In fact even the institute's director stated, right from the start, that to create training courses for would-be Jungians would be a total absurdity because the individuation process for every individual person is so utterly unique.

Soon enough, though, the institute had been turned into a training centre for producing future Jungians while any plans for in-depth research were abandoned. And, thanks to that peculiar inverting of reality one so often encounters in such situations, it didn't take long before people were looking back amazed at Jung's failure to grasp the true aim of the institute or understand what its purpose was meant to be.[37]

This is how delicately, but persistently and insidiously, history is rewritten. In Jung's own name, officially and very efficiently, Jungians were managing to get rid of Jung. Naturally there could and still can be any number of plausible excuses, round-about reasonings, in-depth defences to justify the ongoing march of evolution. But the result was described with horrifying simplicity by Wolfgang Pauli—the famous physicist, and collaborator with Jung in their work on synchronicity, who had been invited to serve as scientific patron before threatening to resign because the institute had totally betrayed its principles.

According to him the grandly named C.G. Jung Institute had already devolved into a conveyor belt aimed at the mass production of what can never be reproduced; into some kind of Faustian assembly-line mentality although, of course, inbuilt in this mentality is a refusal to see the truth about itself. And there is more than a little irony in the fact that it was Pauli as a scientist who felt he had to defend the unconscious against therapists who were professional experts at ruining their patients' dreams.[38]

But it wasn't only Wolfgang Pauli who happened to see things this way.

Henry Corbin, too, stood appalled as he watched those who called themselves Jungians taking the discoveries made by Jung in the depths of the unconscious and then converting them into mechanical tools—into little instruments or some kind of automatic apparatus they can conveniently switch on in any and every situation regardless of how appropriate, or inappropriate, the device might happen to be.

For him, as for Pauli, it was a horror to see people with their collective fantasies about individuation turning discoveries of such profundity into such mechanical and even destructive clichés.

In the case of Corbin, though, what astonished him most of all wasn't the Jungians. It was the fact that, when he mentioned his very negative impressions to Jung, Jung immediately and from the core of his whole being agreed.[39]

There is no real need to say that actually there was no need to be so surprised. Jung himself had made it only too clear in his writings how painfully aware he was of the tendency for well-meaning followers and disciples to get everything back to front by confusing discoveries with dogmas; by never learning truly to explore or discover for themselves; by snatching at the end result of someone else's learning experience "in the hope of making the process repeat itself" and, in so doing, "turning the whole process upside down".

"This", as Jung adds, is how it happened in the past "and how it still happens today."

Then there are all the times he used to write about the endless rubbish his pupils loved fabricating and inventing on the basis of things he himself had said, or published; about all the people who claim to speak as legitimate representatives in his name but essentially don't have a clue "what it's all about". And that's not even to mention his own observations of how, at those moments which matter most, the so-called "Jungian gang" were neither better nor wiser than any other perfectly ordinary humans—let alone the observations made by others about how quickly Jungians could turn into little more than monsters.[40]

But as for what it is that Henry Corbin found most surprising in Jung's full-bodied response: Jungians have already enjoyed for years playing around with the report that once, in an exasperated although humorous mood, Jung had announced to a group of his followers "Thank God I am Jung and not a Jungian." What they apparently are not aware of is that this was much more than some kind of in-joke intended for Jungians alone.

As a matter of fact Stella Corbin used to describe to me how Jung physically came alive from tip to toe at the exact same moment he would say these words, to her and her husband, each time they met in private. And she remembered in particular when the two Corbins were leaving Jung's Zurich home one evening and, still standing on the doorstep, he boomed out at them through the night: "Thank God I'm not a Jungian!"[41]

This problem of Jungians was inseparable, to his mind, from the problem of institutes created in his name as well as from the even bigger problem of the future that lay ahead for his work. And it's no accident at all that—when he spoke about the Zurich institute, in particular, to people he trusted—his forecast was rather bleak.

At times he would describe it as coming along well enough, only to add what a danger there is of professional teachers and teaching systematically killing off every true idea. That, he adds, is the sad fate one can hardly escape; but with a great deal of care it should be possible, at best, to keep the boat "afloat for a while" and help those archetypal ideas to live out their destiny whether inside the institute or outside it.

And then he notes that no real truth can ever be destroyed, however desperately people try to wipe it out.

He also could be even more specific, though, about all the problems of followers and disciples—insisting that "the Institute would be lucky if it did not outlive its creative uses within a generation".

With other teachers and teachings sprouting up everywhere, all of them bursting to promote themselves into eternity, Jung's grim view about the future of any organization created in his name might sound like an extraordinary testimony to his scientific modesty. But to understand his statements that way would be to misinterpret them entirely, because he wasn't comparing his own work to the work of some modern scientist.

He was comparing it to the work of Christ. For him, everything he said about living ideas and the impossibility of keeping them alive in an institutional organization was based directly on his understanding of what happened to Christ's teaching as it was absorbed; totally transformed; killed off bit by bit by the Christian Church.

Everything, naturally, has its place in the grand scheme of things. As he used to say: the spirit and fire of the Christ had to vanish, be stamped out, so that the lovers of institutionalism could exist. The birth of the Church was simply Christ's second crucifixion and death.

And, after that, the only way the spirit of Christ could stay alive was inside the heart of a few hidden heretics and mystics. Aside from them, the institutions of Christianity would turn into exactly what he predicted would happen to the world of Jungians as soon as he died.

Both of them, the one just like the other, would be taken over by the official quackery of priestly posers enthusiastically peddling their fake remedies and dead imitations.

But there is one other detail in this picture which can be easy to miss—because even Jung's virtual prophecy that the institute in Zurich was unlikely to stay alive for more than a single generation is nowhere near as arbitrary as it might seem.

That great predecessor of his in the lineage of heretics and Gnostics he belonged to was the prophet Mani; and it was Mani who stated, very specifically, that only the words preserved inside the prophets' own books are capable of keeping their teaching alive.

For all those prophets who failed to take due precautions by either not writing any books, or writing too few, the corruption of their teachings was guaranteed. "Their first disciples already had misunderstood them, and the misunderstandings had multiplied from generation to generation ... so that in the end the kernel of truth was completely lost in the medley of error."

And that effortlessly brings us to the same point where we started because, "from the Manichaean point of view, the traditional enemies of the other religions were not greater sinners than their apostles, teachers, and propagators. All of them were equally guilty of leading mankind astray from the path of the truth."[42]

8

It's not a very welcome surprise nowadays to hear Jung placed back, again, in his own spiritual context because suddenly everything risks making too much sense.

And none of this is very good news for any of those many Jungians who have made a business of modernizing and streamlining him; of adapting his psychology to the realities of the twenty-first century by efficiently arranging its exit from the claptrap of disreputable texts such as his *Red book*.

The greatest trouble with such attempts at modernization was always going to be that, to arrange a successful exit from something, one first has to understand what's being exited—but really to understand that, in this case, is to realize there can be no possible exit at all.

And the neglected reality this all comes back to is, for Jung, the fact that everything meaningful or worthwhile depends absolutely on the divine will.

Each book he ever wrote came to him as a divine task, commissioned by the unconscious. At the same time each genuine contact that he or his books ever happened to have, with anybody anywhere in the world, was the direct result of a divine "grace" working mysteriously beyond the understanding of any human.

He was aware of being able to make himself immediately present through his published words to individuals living in different places, other countries; and this unmediated contact has nothing to do with the structures of institutions or organizations because, as he explains, it has nothing to do with space and nothing to do with time.

In fact a person doesn't even need to read a word Jung has written, but just hear something about him, to be given instant access to the innermost secret of his being: to what he calls "the divine cause of my existence". And as he adds, sounding strangely like Christ, "Conforming to the divine will I live for mankind, not only for myself, and whoever understands this message contained in and conveyed by my writing will also live for me."

Everything else—including any other book written about him or even by him—is a total waste of time unless it, too, is produced in conformity with the will of the divine. And as for the forming of Jungian institutes or organizations, certainly anyone could claim that these also have been willed by the divine.

But, just as definitely, that won't be the same divine will which Jung himself had in mind.[43]

Of course his pessimistic prophesying is not going to be the best of news, either, for the many Jungians who are more spiritually inclined—who look up to him as ushering in the glorious new age of Aquarius, who believe the Christification of the many is well underway and are ready to come together to celebrate an unprecedented new era of learning how to co-create with the divine, who recognize in the *Red book*'s publication a wonderfully synchronistic sign of our collective advancement to the stage where the whole of his teaching can at last be absorbed and understood.

It would be too much to hope such people might realize that all this speculative frenzy is nothing but a transposition of the brutal modern fantasy about material progress from an economic onto a spiritual plane. It's exactly the same euphoria; the same insane manipulation of facts and figures; the identical dishonesty and self-deception.

The reality is that fifty *Red books* can be discovered or published, a hundred, and if we don't know how to read them they will make no difference at all. Each time we clap ourselves on the back for our increasing familiarity with Jung we walk in exactly the opposite direction from Jung himself, who had the terrible modesty to stand face to face with his idiocy and came to understand less and less about anything as he grew older.

As for the *Red book* itself, it's about our own blood. The true synchronicity has nothing to do with flushed egos but with the fact that, when he started work on it, the world was being faced with a major calamity—while when the book came to be published, almost a century later, the world would be facing calamities far greater. And unless we are prepared to go even deeper into the darkness of the unconscious than Jung went, unless we are willing to find the superhuman strength it takes to laugh as he did at the prospect of total destruction, we don't stand a chance of getting close to the real spirit and fire.

As for that Christification of the many: Jung gave good reasons why it luckily hasn't happened yet, which means the Christ is still free to come and go with the breeze. As for co-creating with the divine, or becoming divine, the only divinity Jung could find the honesty to speak about was the superhumanly divine power we together now have to destroy ourselves.[44]

And that just leaves the age of Aquarius.

To be sure, Jung was able to speak as a visionary of a "new religion" which finally will emerge six hundred years in the future—of the gigantic temple already starting to be built invisibly by countless people "in India and China and in Russia and all over the world".

But there are some essential aspects of such a vision that we owe it to ourselves to take note of. First, it's quite clear from Jung's account that this vast temple whose foundation and pillars are already being built by any number of people everywhere around the world isn't just the work of Jungians. Its structure, and nature, reach far beyond that.

Second, those few people involved with him who here or there are truly working for the future are helping in their small way to build not the new psychology but what he refers to as "the new religion"—one more sign out of a thousand that for Jung his work was always, first and foremost, a matter of religion. And third, this isn't the only place where he happens to talk about a period six hundred years in the future.

Quite to the contrary: he also used to explain that he was perfectly resigned to the prospect of his own work not being recognized or acknowledged for a very long time. In fact he anticipated a future where it simply would disappear, along with pretty much everything else, due to war or an age of "barbarian disintegration". His one slender hope was that "*if* our civilization survives or somewhere mankind survives, perhaps in Australia or God knows where", then his work might somewhere or somehow be dug up once more.

And in that case he would share the fate of Meister Eckhart whose work was buried and forgotten for six hundred years, then suddenly got dug up again so people could realize he was one of the most important mystics who had ever lived.

Here, too, there are some crucial points to take note of. Once again, nowhere is there the smallest trace of him wanting to be remembered as a famous scientist because again it's all a matter of religion: of comparing himself, a lonely figure in the modern world, to one of the few greatest mystics from the Middle Ages.

But that's only the least of what Jung here is actually saying.

For him the most likely future lying ahead of us all is global annihilation, massive war, the catastrophic descent into barbarism on the part of a civilization which had existed for thousands of years. And if—only "*if*"—some tiny remnant of that civilization still happens to survive after the coming period of utter destruction, then there is a distant chance of his work being dug up somewhere so it can be a part of the new world.

Of course, on the large scale, that doesn't speak well for the survival of our own world or for the continuity of everything we have come to consider ours. On a vastly smaller scale it's also another little dent in the self-importance of organized Jungians, because none of their busyness is going to make the tiniest real difference; isn't going to change the inevitable outcome in the slightest. If six hundred years in the future Jung's work is dug up, just as Meister Eckhart's had been dug up, that will be due to the grace inherent in his work itself and won't have anything to do with the interpretations or misinterpretations imposed by followers.

For a long while, Tibet has had its tradition of *terma*: spiritual treasures which are buried and forgotten during the darkest of times only to get dug up by someone, or spontaneously reveal themselves, when the time is due.

But the West has its own tradition of these buried treasures, too.[45]

Now it should be clear why, in the greater scheme of things, Jung had so little energy for helping Jungians along with their institutional dreams. It should be even clearer, though, that what lies ahead for humanity in Jung's own mind is much more than just a speed bump or two.

Instead, what he inwardly foresaw was the darkest period of forgetfulness. And this brings us straight to the most important point of all.

Always Jung would emphasize that the future is totally alien and incomprehensible to us in the present. Any life and earth and new humanity will be so completely different in the age of Aquarius that it's a waste of time to speculate about them in our old, dying age. He explained how one aeon always provides the seeds and the seedbed for the aeon to come.

But, as the ancient Gnostics pointed out, no one tries to sow in summer or harvest in winter. And as Jung pointed out, what the seeds planted now will sprout into is none of our business to be sticking our noses into; is none of our concern. What is our concern is what none of us, rushing towards our doom, has too much time left for—which is to learn about our real culture and psychology by learning, naturally with the help of Latin or Greek, about our past.

The first thing to appreciate is that times of transition from one age into another are always intensely difficult. Then the second is that any transition becomes not just difficult, but more or less impossible, when the lessons of the age being left behind haven't been fully learned. This is why Jung as prophet placed so much internal emphasis on his private life of voluntary suffering and conscious sacrifice, and is why those commentators and interpreters who quaintly claim his psychology was aimed at transcending all the Christian values couldn't be more wrong.

It's why he also emphasized that, sinking as we are into a state of darkness, we are still living inside the Christian aeon of Pisces which means "we shall need Christian virtues *to the utmost*"; and it's why, far from abandoning those close to him, he kept supporting and encouraging them.

After all, a little encouragement in the face of the impossible is always welcome. We have to understand that prophets involved in the impossible work of saving the world from itself aren't interested in profit and loss. They don't do what they do for the sake of failure, or success.

They do it because they have to.

But, needless to say, that doesn't in any way lighten the abysmal darkness lying ahead. To fantasize about a new world or a new humanity hundreds of years away is utter futility because the only thing worthy of us as conscious humans is to confront, with all our strength and honesty, our own present along with its immediate future.

What he saw in this particular transition was something far worse than the usual affair, at such times, of mass melancholy and despair. "Now we are coming to Aquarius", as he wrote to a friend, "and we are standing only at the very beginning of this apocalyptic development!"

And, as he would do more than once, he quoted a Latin text from the ancient Sibylline oracles that contains an old visionary prophecy not exactly in line with the new–age celebrations of an Aquarian age:

Luciferi vires accendit Aquarius acres, "Aquarius sets on fire the savage powers of Lucifer."[46]

9

During the last year of his life, the man who had helped so many people through their depression fell into the deepest depression.

In November 1960 Jung wrote some words of explanation to the same Englishman to whom he also wrote, with such simplicity, about the utter ordinariness of living an archetypal life—and about never suspecting the darkness of the modern world could be so dense.

He described, for Eugene Rolfe, how a disease which had just almost killed him is what forced him "to understand, that I was unable to make the people see, what I am after. I am practically alone. There are a few, who understand this and that, but almost nobody, that sees the whole."

And he asked: "Why should I live any longer? My wife is dead, my children are all away and married. I have failed in my foremost task, to open people's eyes to the fact, that man has a soul and that there is a buried treasure in the field and that our religion and philosophy is in a lamentable state. Why indeed should I continue to exist?"[47]

But he wouldn't be left alone with his questionings for long. Rolfe was so touched by the letter, he shared it with leading Jungians in London. News about it spread and soon people were flocking around, as they still are, to convince themselves his sense of failure was nothing real; just a momentary lapse; that he didn't stay depressed for long and soon was fully back to normal.

Also, they've been quick to answer his questions for him—more firmly and intensely as time goes by.

Of course, they tell him, you didn't fail! If only you could look at us now, fifty years on, you would see that we are the ones you were waiting for. You have no idea how fast humanity has moved forward since you died. Thanks to you there has been such a collective awakening, so much progress in making the unconscious conscious, that what people couldn't dream of understanding while you were alive we understand quite easily now. You sowed the seeds. We are the fruit.

Needless to say, no one with the exception of Rolfe was very much concerned about Jung: only about themselves, their reputations, especially their self-justification. And in that, they showed themselves incapable either of seeing the whole or of understanding what he was after.

Also, they don't seem to have realized that in making their grand claims to be just the ones he was dreaming of—in warming up the fake Native American prophecy that we are the ones we have been waiting for or, according to the latest popular Jungian jargon, "we are the leaders we have been waiting for"—they might be precisely the reason why, looking ahead, Jung became so depressed in the first place.[48]

Failure, for true prophets, is absolutely guaranteed. It's also why, to the extent that their message is left alone, they will always be unpopular. And the eagerness to see the seeds sown by Jung already bearing fruit might sound ever so humanly natural except that, in the greater scheme of things, it's to miss the most essential purpose of his work.

The real fruit lies, if anywhere, hundreds of years down the line—even though in our own world of instant self-gratification it can seem inconceivable to think of anything taking so long.

And as for that modern cliché about making the unconscious conscious: it can sound immensely impressive when talked about this way.

Sometimes a little reality check is helpful, though. Jung, himself, was so concerned with maintaining the balance between consciousness and unconsciousness that he tended to view this exclusive emphasis on making the unconscious conscious as a summary of Freud's intentions rather than his own.

The law is that, from generation to generation, some things can be made conscious only for others to slip back into unconsciousness; new virtues come into play while old ones fall away on the spinning wheel of time. And where Jung is concerned, few things could matter more right now than to note how—during his last months alive—his ideas about consciousness profoundly changed.

There had always been a lingering hint of ambiguity in the importance and value he attached to consciousness. But finally, through his meditations, he was taken into states where he left any trace of conscious awareness far behind and admitted that at the end of the day "he does not trust consciousness in the usual sense any more".[49]

Eventually he managed, in a manner of speaking, towards the end of 1960 to snap out of his depression—even if not straight away. That, in a nutshell, was the beauty of his two personalities. He was, just like Henry Corbin, a master of appearances and disguises; accomplished showman; prodigious diplomat.

Right to the end he knew how to smile radiantly for group photographs, enjoy tasting the best of wines. His personality no.1, with its expansive worldliness and joviality, had all the massive grandeur of the swankiest American hotel in Chicago or New York.

It was positively presidential.[50]

But, underneath, there was something even more massive going on: something no amount of showmanship could manage to hide. And, if you wanted, you could call it war.

War was, literally, the ultimate source of his most creative and significant work. It had been the prophetic dreams and visions which kept haunting him during the months before the start of the First World War that would lead him to begin the work on his *Red book* from which so much else would come. Still, though, it's not just that Jung was already aware of impending disaster before war ever broke out.

He stayed aware of war's dark reality even after the worst seemed over. When the Second World War at last gave way to peace, most people in Europe were only too happy to begin breathing again; throw themselves into the process of restoration and starting anew; optimistically get back to living life as usual.

But Jung couldn't, because he knew western culture was over. To him Europe was nothing more than a "rotting carcass", and he could clearly see the same things that anyone whose eyes were open at the time would have seen towards the end of the Roman Empire.

For him the nightmare of war had brought the world not to peace, but to "the precincts of hell". And although it can feel wonderful to go on enjoying what little still survives of a great civilization, deep inside themselves the people know that it's just "a remnant and that its days are counted".

To Jung, in his awareness, there was no snapping out of the grimness of war; no return to normal. And he was simply forced to stay immersed in that awareness all the time—because if you are concerned in the real sense with saving and preserving the world, that's exactly what you have to do.

If you can't stop people from acting out their need to go to war, there is ultimately no point in fighting the inevitable. Then at least you have to salvage, and protect, the secret essence of their culture so that its seeds or embers can be kept alive for some distant future through all the destruction which is still to come.[51]

10

Jung had been trained very well as a lord of war by the spirits of war.

His job was to go where no one else will; do and say what others will do their best to forget. While everyone else tries as well as possible to get on with their little business, swallow the fabricated news they are fed and then regurgitate it as verdicts that are never theirs, he would have none of it.

As he explained in the *Red book*, the real reason he could see war coming was because he carried the war inside him. But then, of course, there is no avoidance or escape. Then you are forced to breathe with the inhuman as well as the human, to heave with the sea. And it's no coincidence that the alchemists described this inner fight to perfection—the immensity of the internal struggle, the "fighting and violence and war".

Appreciating the ways Jung loved living in harmony and sympathy with nature can seem relatively easy. At the same time, though, he was so completely committed to what alchemy calls the work opposed to nature that it can be hard to notice its markers or signs.

One of the simplest examples is the fact that the deeper he had to sink into the unconscious for the sake of his writing, the worse his sleep would be disturbed. Over the span of a human lifetime, this all takes its toll so that what for others is sleep and normalcy is never quite normal any more.

And it's touching to see how, up until the month before he died, he kept struggling and fighting with his weakened body just so he could bring the writing to an end.[52]

But then there is also what happened in 1944, seventeen years before his death when he nearly died. People love reading as well as writing about the mystical experiences he had at the time, out on the boundary line between living and dying. Even so, almost no one cares about what he described as happening next—because for us humans even the greatest experiences of blissful ecstasy or mystical union take their toll, ruin us just a little more.

He described the torment and torture of being forced back into this flat, grey, box-like material world. He talked about the unbearable restrictedness and clumsiness and crudeness of physical existence which, of course, is the existence we humans happily run around in with all our subjective dramas of suffering and aspirations and illusions. He explained what an agony it was, literally, to leave the inexpressible fullness of objective reality behind and exchange it for such hollowness; to be separated from the objective world of true imagination beyond our rational fantasies and crazy imaginings.

With an honesty that can hardly be appreciated except by those who have experienced what he is referring to, he admits how infuriating and irritating he found everything on his return—making a mockery of every easy cliché about psychological integration. And one devastating implication of what he is saying is that the famous experience of mystical union, the tremendous secret of the *mysterium coniunctionis* kept hidden from us so well, doesn't take place on the physical level of existence at all.

It doesn't take place here for the simple reason that, just as the Gnostics used to say, this material world is nothing but the crudest of illusions. The real mystery of union belongs to another reality, not ours; and compared to that reality our physical world, for all its importance, is impossibly empty and pale.

He also makes a point of not only saying but repeating like the ancient Gnostics, just like Mani, just like Persian Sufis such as Suhrawardî, that this physical existence he had to return to is a prison. The trouble is that, once you have experienced it as a prison, you don't wake up one day and—because the sun just so happens to be shining—the bars and the cage are suddenly gone. As Jung himself points out: even though he managed to find his way around again inside his hideous little box and objectively accept it with all its idiotic limitations, for the rest of his life he would always remember it was nothing more than a box.

True freedom, once tasted, is something we never forget; and the fact is that, after such an experience, the greater part of us never comes back because it simply couldn't fit inside the prison. Then there is only a little bit of us left here while the rest of us remains behind. And this is why, especially when he was writing, it became more and more obvious to the people near him that he was living in another world.

It's why, in finishing his last major book, he came up against the experience of transcendence—because to arrive at such a paradoxical place of being impersonally present while, at the same time, profoundly absent you need to be more inhuman than human. It's also why, during the last few months before actually dying, he spent so much time immersed "in an 'in between' state" where our human feelings tend to count for very little and all our normalcies become just a distant memory: a state he had always known about but never had the chance to sink into so deeply.[53]

Of course, though, most of the people around him were far too well adapted to a life behind bars to know anything about existence beyond the prison or about the inner realities of war. And there is more than a little to learn from the story of Michael

Fordham, who in many respects was the most influential of the British Jungians; a chief editor of Jung's collected works; and who has been described as being, together with James Hillman, one of the "two major original figures following in the wake of Jung".

The letter that Jung had ended up writing to Eugene Rolfe, describing his sense of total failure and the inability of anyone to understand his work as a whole, fell into Fordham's hands. Reading Jung's confession to his sense of total failure, not to mention his lament about no one understanding his work as a whole, he was none too pleased—and jumped on a plane to Zurich.

"I believe that I was, if not the last visitor to Küsnacht, very nearly so, before Jung's death", Fordham explained. "When I arrived he was in his dressing-gown looking very frail. I told him about the letter and how distressed I was about it. I then went on to say how we in England were in a strong position to rebut open misunderstandings and were striving to further recognition of his work. As I talked I started to realize that Jung did not want to hear such reassurances. He seemed to become weaker and weaker, looking at me as if I were a poor fool who did not know a thing. He did not reply but, after a short time, he rose from his chair and I thought he was going to have a fit. All he said was: 'Fordham, you had better go' and I walked out of the room feeling sad and a failure. I think he died, if not the next day, at least in the next few days."

That feeling of failure, not only Jung's but now also his, lingered with Fordham for the rest of his own life. He supposed it must have been Jung's concern for the survival of humanity, as he went on to speculate, and his intense engagement with such "profound matters that had made him feel that he had not succeeded in his mission. When I came to see him I did not touch on these matters but spoke superficially. If I had not done that I would have had to convey my thought that it was the delusion of being a world saviour that made him feel a failure."[54]

Here was one of the greatest Jungians, editor of his published works, who never noticed Jung's delicate insistence that behind the delusion of being a world saviour lies the true inner work of selflessly safeguarding the world—just as behind the delusion of being a prophet lie the agonizingly timeless realities of prophecy.

And this just goes to show that you can get on as many planes as you like without ever taking the first step.

11

At the end of his life in 1961, Jung had visions no one wants to know about.

For the few details that still survive we are dependent on his closest collaborator, Marie–Louise von Franz—and an interview she gave in her rough-and-ready English almost twenty years after Jung had died.

When she was asked by her interviewer for the truth about what had happened, her answer was edgy and abrupt:

"I don't want to speak much about it. But he tried to convey to his family some things when he was right dying, and they didn't get the point, so he called for me. But they wouldn't let me be called. But one of his daughters took notes, and after his death she gave them to me. There is a drawing with a line going up and down, and underneath is 'The last fifty years of humanity' and some remarks about the final catastrophe being ahead. But I have only those notes."

The interviewer asked her to say how such a prospect made her feel. "One's whole feeling revolts against this idea!", she answered. "But since I have those notes in a drawer, I don't allow myself to be too optimistic."

Even so, she adds, she does try to pray that the catastrophe of humanity being destroyed along with the rest of life on our planet won't happen—that a miracle will happen instead, because

"I think one shouldn't give up. If you think of *Answer to Job*: if man would wrestle with God, if man would tell God that He shouldn't do it, if we would reflect more, we might just sneak round the corner with not too big a catastrophe."

And on that more hopeful note, relaxing ever so slightly, she brings the subject to a close by offering one final detail. "When I saw Jung last, he also had a vision while I was with him. But there he said, 'I see enormous stretches devastated, enormous stretches of the earth. But, thank God, it's not the whole planet.' So, perhaps, *that* is what lies ahead."

There are just a few points here, after everything said in this book, that perhaps still need to be made; and the first has to do with Jung's family refusing to call von Franz.

There is something remarkable about how consistent families can be in denying the requests of the dying. I know of a man whose one, final wish while still in his own home was to call for the family cat to be brought and placed on his belly. But his wife and daughter would have none of such nonsense. And it's not that the business of dying is far too frantic, or serious, to allow for any distractions.

It's that the wishes of the dying have to be denied as a matter of principle, for the sake of control, because to give in to them would be to give in to death itself: to end up getting sucked into its chaotic swirl.

By refusing to grant what a dying person asks for, the family stubbornly holds on; unconsciously ensures that the wishes of the living win out over the wishes of death. And often this is only the beginning of an even more unconscious process that keeps dragging everyone downwards, generation after generation. Family members can take control of the dead person's memory, money, reputation, books—but they have absolutely nothing because the spirit is already gone.

And only by consciously, collectively, allowing such a spirit to go free can they ever free themselves.

The second point has to do with that vision von Franz mentions at the end: the vision he had in her presence, the last time she ever saw him, when he was shown vast stretches of the earth altogether devastated and supposedly said to her "thank God it's not the whole planet".

In theory and on paper, to anybody with little direct experience of visionary realities, that probably sounds just fine. Psychologically, though—and we do happen to be talking here about psychologists—it's totally wrong.

Even blissful visions of mystical union can be powerful enough, in their sheer rawness, to wreck a human being. But visions of catastrophe are far more devastating for any healthy person, let alone for a sick and weakened old man on the edge of death.

You don't just jump out of such a vision so you can announce with your conscious mind "thank God that's not too bad", and calmly assess it from outside. You are physically held inside it; caught in its lingering aura.

And if Jung was really the one who said "thank God it's not the whole planet"—rather than von Franz letting her memory impose the comment on him—this will have been the result of her insistently questioning him, as he struggled the best he could to communicate, and dragging out of him some reassurance because that's what she wanted to hear.

Of course this already adds a little wrinkle to the smooth continuity of Jungian tradition which not everyone might be glad to accept. In 2013 I brought up the subject with von Franz's interviewer and suggested that perhaps her instinctive need to soften the harshness of Jung's prophecies might have helped to throw a cloak over his own experiences.

But, with a commendable firmness, the lady who had interviewed her stated she would have absolutely none of that. Such speculation, she insisted, would be completely meaningless and lead to utter confusion. Marie–Louise von Franz, with her unfailing thoroughness and carefulness, makes it quite clear that after Jung's vision of total destruction she visited him on a quite separate occasion and during this visit he had a second vision—a vision of far less devastation.

To be sure, she admitted, this second vision indicated that the devastation would be enormous; but the prospect now was nowhere near as bad because, unlike with the first vision, there would be no destruction of humanity or end to life on our planet.

And it would be so nice to end the discussion here, except that what she was telling me so firmly and forcefully is wrong.

That second, and supposedly softer, vision is the one Jung had in von Franz's presence when she saw him last. But according to her partner and housemate, Barbara Hannah, the last time she ever saw Jung was eight days before he died. And on the other hand nothing could be easier than to understand what von Franz meant by her odd statement that he had his, supposedly first, vision about the terrifying end of humanity "when he was right dying".

"Right", here, is clearly the best she could do in English to find a direct equivalent for the German word—"gerade"—which means "just", "exactly", "at precisely the same moment".

In other words, the vision Jung is supposed to have seen first was experienced by him right at the moment of death; and the vision that supposedly came afterwards had in fact come to him a week earlier. The second vision is the first and the first is the last.

As the Gnostics knew, as Empedocles understood so well, we humans can't help inverting the logic and sequence of reality. Every time we come up against something important, our minds infallibly end up getting everything back to front and upside down. Through her very understandable reluctance to discuss such a horrible subject, or confront it directly, von Franz has created a perfect example of the ancient phenomenon known as "ring composition"—starting by complaining that she doesn't want to speak about it, ending by trying as hard as she can to sound some optimistic note, while tucking away what mattered most of all in the middle.

And the absurdest part of this magical drama, this modern-day re-enactment of the avoidance rituals surrounding what used to be considered taboo, is that it's totally unnecessary. It completely misses the point because the contrast imagined by von Franz between ultimate destruction and a destruction that "only" devastates enormous stretches of the earth, between Jung's first vision and the second, is no real contrast at all.

Traditionally it has always been understood that—in those gigantic catastrophes which wipe out virtually every last remnant of humanity—somehow and somewhere a few tiny seeds or embers will manage to survive. A part of the prophetic design, just as much for ancient Greeks as ancient Sumerians or Babylonians or Jews, is that there has to be some Noah.

Naturally, though, that doesn't help everyone else very much. And with her optimistic version of only enormous stretches of our planet being destroyed, Marie–Louise von Franz was just clutching at straws.

But that's exactly what we are reduced to when we end up hiding someone's final vision away in a drawer.[55]

12

At death the rules change, and all of a sudden you are entering another domain: the domain of the contrary.

What used to be valid no longer is. What once was important no longer matters, which is why dying means having to learn how to live in a totally different way. And someone with Jung's natural intelligence would instinctively do what he did in the months before—start dying before dying by withdrawing more and more from our normal consciousness, dive deeper and then deeper into the unknown.

That's what, traditionally, has always been understood as the preparation for death: needing to develop a new organ as if one suddenly is having to discover how to function in water or a fish is being forced to adapt to breathing on dry land.

But what's often even tougher than the ordeals of learning how to die is the challenge of facing the utter incomprehension of the people one is leaving behind.

At the time of Jung's final vision about the last fifty years of humanity, in June 1961, his immediate family not only didn't get the point or have the slightest clue what he was going through. They even refused to call the one person who, theoretically, might have. Then she in turn—instead of passing on to others what he'd gone to so much effort to have recorded when he hardly could use his voice to speak, his hands to gesture or draw—just shut it away for the rest of her life inside a drawer.

Of course you could say she was within her rights to do so, which she definitely was; that her decision was eminently sensible for the sake of keeping the Jungian enterprise optimistic, credible, afloat. In fact you could claim that, in shutting the evidence away inside a drawer, she was doing no more than repeating what Jung had done when he shut the *Red book* away from the public inside his home.

And, at the same time, she had just knocked the last nail into the coffin of Jung as a prophet.

There were plenty of other nails. His own family would also act quickly and promptly to knock all such gruesome rumours on the head: take every necessary step to erase any hint at Jung's prophetic powers from his biography. Marie–Louise von Franz, too, would play her dutifully reasonable part in squashing his reputation as a prophet—along with a fair amount of the truth, as well.[56]

But that was the least of it.

Jung's secretary, Aniela Jaffé, has led any number of people astray by silencing his own confession that he was forced to put the work on his *Red book* aside because of its wildly prophetic nature—and by creating, in spite of his urgent warnings, the total fiction that he ended up having to lay it aside because he found it too "aesthetic".[57]

Then there has been the steady rush of Jungians ever since, stamping out any manifestation of Jung the prophet as fast as they can. Just in the last few years, since the *Red book* was published, they have had a field day discrediting or disposing of every single reference to prophecy they possibly could.

And in doing so they have managed to justify all his doubts about allowing the book to be published: have demonstrated, to perfection, why for the rest of his life he chose to keep it hidden away.

Jung himself had always been immensely sensitive to how much, or little, he could openly say about prophetic matters. People since then no longer have any need for such sensitivity, though, because they throw everything to do with prophecy straight out of the window.[58]

The great reluctance expressed by von Franz to speak out about his final, prophetic visions fits only too well into a vastly larger picture. Even so, there is something very particular about them; very special.

And that has to do with the way Jung's last vision, about the end of humanity, took place "when he was right dying": precisely at the point of his death.

All the staking of claims to his inheritance and legacy, the excitement about carrying his work forward into the future, has completely obscured and covered over one crucial consideration which would be obvious to anyone with a genuine understanding of history; a true respect for the past. This is the fact that for thousands of years western culture has valued the visions and words of the dying at the moment of their death even more than anything they ever happened to see, or say, while alive.

Malista anthrôpoi chrêsmôidousin, hotan mellôsin apothaneisthai. "People prophesy especially", as Socrates is supposed to have said, "just before they die." This tradition of *divinare morientes*—of the dying being able to see as prophets, speak as prophets, during their crucial last moments alive—has been massively important throughout western literature as well as inside the physical texture of people's lives.[59]

And beyond this vital element of prophecy at the moment of leaving the body, of being given the insight that's needed to see accurately the future lying ahead, other more humanistic elements also came into play in a way that would define the essential aspects of *ars vivendi*—or the art of living—and *ars moriendi*—or the art of dying—during the centuries before Jung's own time.

One was the understanding that, at the moment of death, the masks are finally stripped away. All the faking and posturing and hiding, all the fancy ambiguities and double-talk, give way to naked honesty. "There is no more pretending", as Montaigne said in the sixteenth century: you just show what's "at the bottom of the pot".

And another had to do with the attitudes and responsiveness of the living. There was a perfectly intuitive understanding that the real function of family members is to stand by in full sensitivity and support during this critical moment of transition because what the dying person experiences and sees and tries to convey at the *hora mortis*, the hour of death, is like a condensed biography—a summary of the whole life just lived.

But even more critically urgent in certain circles was the importance of a close and trusted friend being present, as "the essential intermediary between a dying speaker and the public", to record the person's final words and gestures; faithfully to preserve each single detail of them; and, above all, to transmit them fully and selflessly to the people at large for the sake of generations to come.[60]

Of course, thanks to the unrelenting rationalism of the twentieth century, when it was Jung's turn to die in the summer of 1961 all these ancient and humanistic traditions were already in tatters. At the same time, though, not only did he happen to be intimately familiar with the details of this centuries-old wisdom about how to live: how to die.

In fact that was the very least of it, because ever since the time of the work he was forced to do on the *Red book*—which would be little more than his formal invitation into the world of the dead—he had found himself becoming an integral part of those traditions.

For the rest of his life, as the rest of his life, he would be inwardly living them; dying them.

And considering not only his profound respect for our history as westerners, but above all the uniquely high value he ascribed to prophetic visions as well as dreams, the very least one could have done would have been to restore his final terrifying visions to their rightful place in his life.

But for the sake of propriety, and the usual fakery of trying to continue with business as normal, they have been completely suffocated instead. Rather than seeing this as a positive sign of progress and evolution for Jung's psychology, though, it would be far more accurate to see it as a sign of radical regression to an infantile state; as showing how immature the psychology still is of those who, as Jung contemptuously used to comment, "mouth my name" without any idea of "what it's all about".

After all, he did repeatedly insist that the ultimate goal of his psychology—just like the ultimate purpose of ancient philosophy—is simply to prepare for the moment of death. But as he also explained to someone close to him, only a couple of years before he died: my psychology, to be sure, like any real psychology is purely a preparation for an end. Or to be more precise, it can be considered a preparation for *the* end.

And he makes it quite clear, here as well as elsewhere, that he is not only referring to the end of an individual. He is referring to the end of our culture.

Then he adds that there is only one real question left, which is the question of what precisely we are going to end up killing. And the choice for him was very straightforward.

Either we all manage to kill our collectively "infantile psychology" by going through the painful process of growing up—or we just kill ourselves.[61]

Two years on, it was exactly the same story for Jung: simply a later chapter. And now we, too, are left with a choice.

Either we hide the evidence of his life and death away so we can shuffle on with our own, because we don't understand what's needed. Or we do the right thing and look at the bottom of our pot.

13

It was one night just at the start of 2011.

I had no idea, at the time, of Jung's final vision fifty years earlier about the final fifty years of humanity. My wife and I were living up in the mountains of North Carolina and, halfway through that night, it was like a call I could no longer resist. I knew I had to sink deep down inside myself to see what's happening in my life; with my work; in the world.

And then there is the shock of being shown, all of a sudden, what already has happened—not just in my own little life, my private world.

In the intense quiet which sometimes comes at the middle of the night I see that everything has stopped. But the stillness is full of terror because this isn't the stillness of nature resting for the night.

This is the stillness at the end of a civilization. Quite literally, our western world has come to an end.

When I looked more closely I could see how each culture has a momentum, just like the spiral movements described by Empedocles that lie behind any cosmic cycle. In a cycle everything spins in one direction—before eventually coming to a stop.

For an indefinable moment, neither inside nor outside of time, there is the stillness between two contrary motions. Then everything begins rotating in the opposite direction. And this is the point we've come to: that torn poise of utter stillness at the end of one movement, one cycle, one directional thrust, before everything turns into reverse.[62]

As it is in the cosmos, so it is in any animal or human but also in the life of a civilization. And this civilization has come to an end. The movement has stopped. The energy behind its momentum is over; spent.

Anyone sensitive enough to the depths can recognize this instinctively, physically, deep inside. But to feel it needs a certain courage because the stillness at the end is horrifying. It's not the beauty of nature's silence with the birds and animals tucked up, asleep, and the sun's loudness concealed for a while from the earth. This is another silence.

It's the silence of everything you know coming to an end, just like that. But of course to realize this consciously would be too big a shock. And so what happens is that—like a wheel or a disk still spinning even after it's been switched off—people keep on rushing around because they don't want to realize anything has stopped.

Just the same as those cartoon characters who race out into the void and don't notice they are right above the abyss, we go on trying to think everything is normal. For a few unreal moments we are running above empty space although there is nothing any more, no foundation or support, to hold or take us forward. We are simply being carried by the ghostlike residue of that original movement which is nothing more, now, than the momentum of our own unconscious habits.

But even that will fizzle out: come to a stop until everything drops, which is when there is chaos. And this is the reason why all the familiar structures around us are having to crash and collapse. It's not because of corruption, or because the wrong people got into power, or to make way for something fairer and stronger and better that we can build.

It's because the energy needed to prop up our collective existence is exhausted—and there is the undertow, ever so imperceptible, of the opposite movement stirring.

The trouble is, though, that this new direction has nothing to do with anything our minds are familiar with. It's nothing those minds of ours can be a part of, because it's completely contrary to whatever they think they know.

It's so new we can only even possibly start to intuit it by going deep into the nothingness inside ourselves where we become free from every pattern of thinking, every single thought form, any memory of the way things have been along with any expectation or fantasy or noble ideal or hope of how things should be—because that's all still the momentum of the old. First comes the silent call to die totally into the stillness, so as to be able to become a part of what the new movement will be.

First one has to experience the ending, not only of oneself but of a whole civilization: has to realize that it's all already finished. And then it becomes clear that, although everyone can appear not to be aware of how nothing is real any more, secretly most people already are. They are just too confused, or afraid, to say anything about what they sense inside themselves.

It's only a process of nature: nothing to be scared of. Our own culture, like any other culture in the past or future, is simply a natural organism—just as the word, itself, implies. And every organism happens to be finite, which means it dies.

The big problem is that, humanly, this is almost impossible to accept. It's so hard not to want to hide our deepest intuitions away somewhere inside a drawer; so undignified to go ahead and hide them.

But certainly sentimentality isn't going to help. Neither, for that matter, is hope.

Neither is the technology that brought us here, because we lost the keys to its sacred dimension long ago. Consciously we just don't have the wisdom or knowledge needed, although with our tricks and toys we do like to fool ourselves that we do.

We have forgotten what it means truly to miss that wisdom: to howl for its loss.

And right to the edge of the precipice we go on trying to deceive ourselves it will all work out just fine.

14

Five months before March 2011, which is when the earthquake and tsunami struck Fukushima, I was taken high above the earth in a dream and allowed to look down over the north-east coast of Japan.

There, I was told, is where a major disaster will happen. Populations will be forced to leave. But the entire world is going to be affected—and that will only be the first in a whole string of catastrophes.

I was even shown the dimple on the cheek of the very feminine being, serious but with the faintest trace of a smile around her face, who had been empowered to carry the effects of the catastrophe over sea and land on the winds. And I understood that this will be the work of the mythological Harpies brought back to life all over again: the female spirits, part human and part bird, who are responsible for snatching away half the food of their blinded victims and making whatever they leave behind inedible by taking care to shit on it.

Their most famous victim in myth was a prophet who had given the gods' secrets away. But, strange as it might sound, we have all become prophets now with our pride in predicting the little things as well as the big—and in thinking we can take the gods' secrets for free. In our modern, rational age we despise the idea of prophecy or prophesying not because we have gone beyond it.

We hate it because we long to be even better prophets than the prophets once were, by cutting out any dependence on the divine. It's not that we look down on them because we dislike what they did but because we crave to have their divine powers for ourselves. This is the wanting that makes us so special; so extraordinary; and will bring us down.

As for the reality of prophecy: it's so simple and ordinary, nothing special at all. As this example of Fukushima shows, it's still quite possible to see things clearly in advance. And that's because everything first appears inside us, then takes months or even much longer to work its way out.

Considering that fifty years on from Jung's final prophecy in 1961 brings us to 2011, you could say he was wrong about the end of humanity. After all, no pictures of us being destroyed were ever shown on the television.

But that's not how these things are measured—because the real endings, the ones that matter, don't happen outside.

They take place far down inside us, where the living and the dead rub shoulders and pass each other on their way to work.

When my wife and I were still living in New Mexico I often had to fly to California. And one afternoon, returning to Albuquerque, the flight crew started their usual announcement over the speaker system as we were preparing for our descent.

Everything was just the same as normal except that, this time, it was totally different. Although the woman's voice churned out the standard statements she had made hundreds of times before, there was something in her tone that sank straight into my being. And I realized that when a culture forces a human to act so automatically, talk so robotically, the humanity inside the person is lost—lost first in that individual, then in the world.

But what's lost, this way, is never recovered; it's gone for good.

It's exactly the same with the fancy invention of phone menus that came from America. First, it was enough to press this button or that. After a while, pressing a button was no longer acceptable and now you had to start talking into the phone.

There is one minor problem, though: a little catch. Every traditional culture or society in the world has known that the power of the spoken word is sacred. Humans were given the tools of language or speech by the divine so that they could communicate, and honour, the divine. And when we end up using that sacred gift of voice to talk to machines, then we have crossed an uncrossable line.

Everything can seem to go on working and functioning, for a while. But our role in existence has been hollowed out; our human purpose on this planet turned completely upside down. There are divine laws we are no longer aware of that are non-negotiable, because they are there for a reason. And when certain violations progress from accidental, to repeated, to deliberate, there are consequences from which there is no coming back.

Humanity isn't something we have a right to. It's the finest possible commodity that has to be cultivated, treasured, protected: otherwise it just slips away through our fingers and, before we even know what happened, is gone.

The haunting question is who is left to know it—because it needs humanity to tell the difference between humanity and the lack of it. This is such a delicate matter that we can glimpse it only to lose sight of it in the next moment; drift close to it, only to slip away.[63]

Needless to say, we can recite from memory and parrot and mimic as much as we want. But we don't prove we are human by patting ourselves down and reassuring each other we have two arms and legs and a head. This just proves we are animals in human bodies, which is easy enough to confirm if we honestly are ready to look.

And once that germ of humanity is gone, nobody will ever be the wiser.

15

At the end of January 2012, I was staying with friends in the south of Switzerland.

One afternoon I went up to my room at the top of the house and lay down to incubate in the old way—the ancient western method of meditation used for entering into the depths inside oneself.

And almost straight away I came to the strangest place I had ever been before. There I was brought face to face with the reality of this present age, not as it's seen from our world of the living but as it's viewed from the world of the dead.

What I was shown was like a huge picture book, but continuous and without any pages. It contained all the smallest details of each aeon and stage in life on earth, including the great periods of human civilization: explained in images how they actually function, are made possible, what their real purpose is from the perspective of eternity.

At the far left of every period was a vertical line separating it from the age before, with another at the far right marking it off from the age to come. Stretching out from the line on the left was something that looked like half of a horizontal belt or band, with the other half reaching towards it from the line on the right. And the aim of each age is to link the half of the belt on the left to the half on the right to create a single chain connecting its point of origin to its point of destiny.

This is the continuous band, running from the distant past into the distant future, that humanity is asked and expected to travel together with the rest of life on earth.

But the one section I was being encouraged to see, inside that pageless book, is the section corresponding to this period we now are in. And what was most extraordinary about it, when I looked, was that we are not at the end of an age at all. On the contrary, we are right in the middle of it—and totally lost.

A voice coming from beside me explained that because of our collective "forgetfulness and laziness" we abandoned any path, which means we've broken the essential link between our future and our past. We are so hopelessly disoriented, so sure when there is nothing to be sure of and so uncertain where certainty is the one thing needed, that we can no longer tell left from right or down from up.

And I started to understand the exquisite logic of what I was being shown: the quintessentially underworld logic which, as always, is so much more rigorous than the ridiculous attempts we make at pretending to be reasonable.

We like to think of each age as a single unit, with its beginning and end. But the dead are far more cunning than us, and strap the second half of what we call an age to the first half of the next so they can see exactly what's happening—what really works. It's the transitions between ages, as Jung understood so well, that truly matter; have such a central importance. And if we can carry the essence of one age, unbroken, into the beginning of another we have achieved something genuinely worth recording.

The trouble is that in our case nothing is being carried forward.

Halfway through this period of life on earth which was meant to count for something in the eyes of eternity we lost our bearings and, thanks to the laziness of our forgetfulness, let the crucial link between past and future fly apart. The result is that we are left wandering and spinning in a void, searching for remedies perfectly designed to make the situation worse, incapablc of gctting back on track.

The faster we spin, the more desperate the solutions; and instead of realizing that we are lost at some insignificant point out in the middle of nowhere, we prefer to dream about some grandly critical climax. To compensate for the overwhelming sense of confusion and utter uselessness that keeps rising inside, we conjure up illusions of some global awakening even while steadily falling further asleep—try to console ourselves with fantasies about being at the cusp of something magnificent, about edging to the threshold of a glorious renaissance, to the dawn of a great rebirth.

The reality is, though, that now isn't the time for giving birth to anything truly new. Instead, it's just a question of how little or much of the initial impulse that originally gave rise to our culture we are able to carry through the coming maelstrom.

And to be quite clear: if that forgotten sacred impulse at the root of our world is simply allowed to fizzle out because of our laziness, this doesn't mean our present age will finish early so as to make way for something new.

It will just drag on into eternity for its allocated time—a blank, an empty nothingness that counts for nothing. And whether that happens to be a time of brute barbarism or technological annihilation or technological perfection doesn't matter at all, because in terms of humanity there will be nothing doing.

From the point of view of the dead, that will be the futile and inglorious ending of our current aeon. From the point of view of the living, it will be the first few centuries of what we prefer to think of as a new age: completely fallow, static, dead. And as I was coming close to writing this, it was quite a shock to find how Joachim of Fiore used to describe the first six hundred years or so of every new period or age.

He mentioned being shown how "each age must be preceded by a period of incubation": a time of enormous outer changes and disturbances during which any remaining seeds of humanity are quietly left to incubate, latent, inactive, fallow.[64]

If we had only learned what it means to beat our way back all the way past our inhumanity to our primordial nature, we could have discovered how to move straight through the eye of the storm. It would have been possible with the tiny light of our individual awareness to incubate in the depths of the darkness during the far greater incubation of the world—and consciously nurture those seeds for the future.

But that's not going to happen this time, at least hardly at all, because we lost the link to our primordial past.

16

Halfway through the night, in the middle of March 2013, I woke abruptly with a dream.

The dream was as simple as it was insistent—one single word being displayed in front of me, spelled out for me with perfect clarity. It was a word that I somehow knew, in my sleep, I had never known the meaning of or even heard of in my waking life: Catafalque.

When I did wake up, I was still repeating the word time and time again so I wouldn't forget. I was almost certain it must just be an imagined invention of my subconscious mind that doesn't actually exist.

But as soon as I managed to look it up in a dictionary I found to my great surprise that, down to the very last letter, it does. And whether or not I, personally, had come across the word already at some forgotten point in my daily life couldn't have mattered less—because the unexpected experience of a word or expression presenting itself so forcefully is always, if you watch the process, nothing short of magic.

It didn't take a long time of reading the dictionary definitions before the meaning of the dream started sinking in. I took and told it to a very holy old man who always welcomes me ever so politely when I visit him at his tiny home, the walls all covered with paintings, on the rocks beside the sea. And he explained to me not only that, but also how, I need to write this book.

"Catafalque" comes from an old Italian word used to describe the decorated, elegantly embroidered, wooden structure that would be erected as the base on which a famous or important person's coffin could be placed. It stood there as a basic framework, supporting whoever had died, in the middle of all the funeral ceremonies; the processions; the paying of final respects.

And that, in a word, is the purpose of my work: to provide a catafalque for our western world.

If such a statement sounds strange to you, it's because you don't understand that this world of ours is already dead. It existed for a while, did the best it could, but is nothing more than a lifeless remnant of what it was meant to be. And while the optimistic consciousness of our mass media, our education system, our collective hysteria keeps trying to practise some weird necrophilia on the body of our culture there is something else completely different that needs to be done.

The correct attitude right now is to come together to raise a ritual lament. You could call this the most basic hygiene, as well as sanity. We need to grieve; need to celebrate the ending before a clean new beginning can ever take place. As indigenous people instinctively know, but we've forgotten in our cold-heartedness, when the time comes for weeping one has to weep.

And this is the moment for marking, and honouring, the passing of our culture. It's the time to tie up the loose ends and tidy up; finish off with nobility and dignity; clear everything away and put one's house in order.

There is no need now for optimism or hope. On the contrary, we have entered a place where every hope has to be abandoned and to keep on indulging in optimism is a shameless dereliction of our duty. The one thing needed is the exact opposite of our manufactured hoping, which is the divine reality of faith—because faith is the most extraordinary flower, as alive and intelligent as it's beautiful, which you can meet out on the street in the dark or alone back home if your vision isn't stunted by hope.

As for optimism, it's just as devastating as pessimism in preventing us from seeing the realities everywhere around us.

Of course even to talk about the possibility of some magical middle ground, hidden between hope and despair, is almost pointless when confronted with the collective pressure to rush off the cliff out of sheer expectant greed for more and more. And as for the foolishness of claiming everything is over: nothing could sound as rationally or blatantly absurd.

But this is simply the impossible nature of the situation we are faced with.

As Jung once noted, in pointing to the realities of the soul "I am refuted all along the line, just like someone prophesying a thunderstorm when there isn't a single cloud in the sky." There is nothing that could seem more crazy. "The truth is, though, that questions of the soul always lie below the horizon of consciousness. And in addressing this problem of the soul we are talking about things right at the boundary of what's visible; about the most intimate and fragile things; about flowers that open only in the night."

There are times, as he said, when you don't go on trying to fix or solve—when, not just with a difficult patient but with a whole age, you acknowledge there is nothing left to be done. Then, as great Sufis and alchemists have realized, even to pray is to interfere: is an act of disrespect.

Naturally that doesn't mean you don't submit to accepting with humility, with a genuine sense of ethics and responsibility, whatever duties are imposed on you by life. But it's only what Jung called the "small and fragmentary people" who always need to occupy themselves with doing something, improving something.

And that could even include psychologists, so busy with their bag of tricks they completely miss the crucial atmosphere or essential spirit out of which every trick emerges and into which it will also disappear.

All the inner work of exploration and integration is nothing but the first very tentative, preliminary steps: little more than the crudest of ruses for distracting people long enough from their superficial selves that perhaps, for a moment or two and even three, they'll really start facing their depths. But the ultimate purpose, as he made very clear, is not to integrate.

It's to die—consciously leave ourselves behind, shed absolutely everything, strip every trace of identification or attachment away.

As for the existence of some future: to me it was quite revealing, after years of telling people we belong here in the present and should leave the future alone because it belongs to the people of the future, to open the *Red book* when it came out and find Jung saying the same thing in just the same words. "The future should be left to those who belong to the future."

And as he paradoxically adds, this is "the great way—the way of what is to come".[65]

Just as there have to be people who consciously help to bring a culture into being, there have to be those who consciously help to bring it to an end. And this is the moment for the catafalque, when we need to be brave enough to focus on just what's needed because the catafalque is also for us.

It's the time for learning our primordial or original instructions, as Native Americans have referred to them for centuries, all over again; the time to turn around and face our ancestors, to dance for the dead.

As for this book: you are welcome to take it seriously if that will help you not to take yourself seriously. But the worst thing would be to take it seriously only for it to trouble you or weigh you down. Its style is likely to feel strangely unfamiliar—because this is the ancient style we've forgotten, along with the modern.

It's the choiceless rhythm of the winds and rain. I would never want you to know even a thousandth of what its writing involved. And you can try your best to criticize it if you are an expert at judging how the weather should be assessed.

The enormous notes are a joke, grotesque monuments to a culture that abandoned itself. But if you ever care to dip into them, you might find some of them are like a miniature book offering an opening to another world.

As for the point behind it all: that's very simple. The point is to leave us stripped of everything—even of Jung who so badly needs to be set free, even of this book.

It's only by shedding everything, including ourselves, that we sow the seeds of the future.

TWO

ABBREVI-
ATIONS
5

ABBREVIATIONS

ACU	C.G. Jung, *Archetypes and the collective unconscious* (Collected works, vol. 9/I; 2nd ed., London 1968)
AE	H. Corbin, *L'archange empourpré* (Paris 1976)
Aion	C.G. Jung, *Aion* (Collected works, vol. 9/II; London 1959)
AJ	H. Corbin, *Autour de Jung*, ed. M. Cazenave and D. Proulx (Paris 2014)
AN	C.G. Jung's unpublished alchemy notebooks (1935–1953), held by the Foundation of the Works of C.G. Jung in Zurich
APMM	P. Kingsley, *Ancient philosophy, mystery and magic* (Oxford 1995)
ARV	H. Corbin, *Avicenne et le récit visionnaire* (3 vols. Tehran 1952–54)

AS	C.G. Jung, *Alchemical studies* (Collected works, vol. 13; London 1967)
AWA	H. Corbin, *Alone with the alone* (Princeton 1998); first published as *Creative imagination in the Sûfism of Ibn 'Arabî* (Princeton 1969)
BB	C.G. Jung, *The black books*, cited according to the original volume and page numbers of Jung's journals
CBA	The archive of Cary Baynes (born Cary Fink and, from 1910 to 1927, Cary de Angulo), held in the Wellcome Library, London
CD	C.G. Jung, *Children's dreams*, ed. L. Jung and M. Meyer–Grass (Princeton 2008)
CS	Esther Harding's unpublished notes on the "Cornwall seminar" given by Jung at Polzeath in July 1923 (Beinecke Library, Yale University)
CT	C.G. Jung, *Civilization in transition* (Collected works, vol. 10; 2nd ed., London 1970)
DA	C.G. Jung, *Dream analysis*, ed. W. McGuire (London 1984)
DP	C.G. Jung, *The development of personality* (Collected works, vol. 17; 3rd ed., London 1970)
EII	H. Corbin, *En Islam iranien* (4 vols., Paris 1971–72)

EJ	*Eranos–Jahrbücher*
Empedocles	cited according to the fragment (fr.) numbers in H. Diels, *Poetarum philosophorum fragmenta* (Berlin 1901) 74–168 and L. Gemelli Marciano, *Die Vorsokratiker* ii (2nd ed., Berlin 2013) 138–438
ENM	P. Kingsley, "Empedocles for the new millennium", *Ancient philosophy* 22 (2002) 333–413
ETG	C.G. Jung, *Erinnerungen, Träume, Gedanken*, ed. A. Jaffé (Zurich 1962)
FC	The *Fonds Henry et Stella Corbin*, held in the École pratique des hautes études, Paris
FJ	Sigmund Freud / C.G. Jung, *Briefwechsel*, ed. W. McGuire and W. Sauerländer (Frankfurt 1974)
FP	C.G. Jung, *Freud and psychoanalysis* (Collected works, vol. 4; 2nd ed., London 1970)
fr./frs.	fragment(s)
FRJ	*Remembering Jung*, two conversations with Marie–Louise von Franz during March 1977 and September 1979, produced by George Wagner and directed by Suzanne Wagner (3 DVDs, C.G. Jung Institute of Los Angeles, Los Angeles 1991)

HC — *Henry Corbin*, ed. C. Jambet (L'Herne, vol. 39; Paris 1981)

HJ — *Carl Gustav Jung*, ed. M. Cazenave (L'Herne, vol. 46; Paris 1984)

IDPW — P. Kingsley, *In the dark places of wisdom* (Inverness, CA 1999)

IJJS — *International journal of Jungian studies*

IJP — C.G. Jung, *Introduction to Jungian psychology*, ed. W. McGuire and S. Shamdasani (Princeton 2012)

JAP — *Journal of analytical psychology*

JB — C.G. Jung, *Briefe*, ed. A. Jaffé and G. Adler (3 vols., Olten 1972–73)

JBA — C.G. Jung biographical archive, Countway Library of Medicine, Boston

JH — *Jung history*

JJ — *Jung journal*

JJTP — *Journal of Jungian theory and practice*

JJW — *C.G. Jung, Emma Jung and Toni Wolff*, ed. F. Jensen (San Francisco 1982)

JK	*The Jung–Kirsch letters*, ed. A.C. Lammers (2nd ed., Abingdon 2016)
JL	C.G. Jung, *Letters*, ed. G. Adler and A. Jaffé (2 vols., London 1973–76)
JM	S. Shamdasani, *Jung and the making of modern psychology* (Cambridge 2003)
JN	*C.G. Jung und Erich Neumann: Die Briefe 1933–1959*, ed. M. Liebscher (Ostfildern 2015)
JP	The Jaffé Protocols, being Aniela Jaffé's initial transcript of the biographical material she noted down in shorthand during her interviews with Carl Jung between September 1956 and October 1958 (C.G. Jung Papers, Manuscript Division, Library of Congress, Washington D.C.)
JPPF	*Jahrbuch für psychoanalytische und psychopathologische Forschungen*
JS	*C.G. Jung speaking*, ed. W. McGuire and R.F.C. Hull (Princeton 1977)
JSB	S. Shamdasani, *Jung stripped bare by his biographers, even* (London 2005)
JV	C.G. Jung, *Visions*, ed. C. Douglas (2 vols., Princeton 1997)

JW — *The Jung–White letters*, ed. A.C. Lammers and A. Cunningham (Hove 2007)

JWCI — *Journal of the Warburg and Courtauld Institutes*

KI — James Kirsch, "C.G. Jung's individuation as shown especially in *Answer to Job*"; unpublished transcript of a lecture given in the 1980s and cited with the permission of Thomas Kirsch

KY — C.G. Jung, *The psychology of kundalini yoga*, ed. S. Shamdasani (Princeton 1996)

MC — C.G. Jung, *Mysterium coniunctionis* (Collected works, vol. 14; 2nd ed., London 1970)

MDR — C.G. Jung, *Memories, dreams, reflections*, ed. A. Jaffé (London 1963/New York 1973)

MDRC — The original English-language typescript for *Memories, dreams, reflections*, held at the Countway Library of Medicine in Boston

MH — *Matter of heart*: a documentary film directed, produced and written by Mark Whitney, Michael Whitney and Suzanne Wagner (C.G. Jung Institute of Los Angeles, Los Angeles 1983)

NL — G.F. Nameche and R.D. Laing, *Jung and persons: a study in genius and madness* (University of Glasgow special collections, MS Laing A3);

	for the origins and composition of this unpublished typescript see Nameche, *On the origins of this book* (ibid., MS Laing A6)
NZ	C.G. Jung, *Nietzsche's 'Zarathustra'*, ed. J.L. Jarrett (2 vols., Princeton 1988)
OMM	Shihâb al–Dîn Yahyâ al–Suhrawardî, *Opera metaphysica et mystica*, ed. H. Corbin (i, Istanbul 1945; ii, Tehran 1952)
PA	C.G. Jung, *Psychology and alchemy* (Collected works, vol. 12; 2nd ed., London 1968)
Parmenides	cited according to the fragment (fr.) numbers in H. Diels, *Poetarum philosophorum fragmenta* (Berlin 1901) 48–73 and L. Gemelli Marciano, *Die Vorsokratiker* ii (2nd ed., Berlin 2013) 6–95
PB	W. Pauli, *Wissenschaftlicher Briefwechsel mit Bohr, Einstein, Heisenberg u.a.*, ed. K. von Meyenn (Berlin 1979–2005)
PJB	*From Poimandres to Jacob Boehme*, ed. R. van den Broek and C. van Heertum (Amsterdam 2000). 17–40 = P. Kingsley, "An introduction to the *Hermetica*"; 41–76 = Kingsley, "Poimandres: the etymology of the name and the origins of the *Hermetica*"
PP	*Psychological perspectives*

PPT	C.G. Jung, *The practice of psychotherapy* (Collected works, vol. 16; 2nd ed., London 1966)
PR	C.G. Jung, *Psychology and religion* (Collected works, vol. 11; 2nd ed., London 1969)
PSIE	L. Gemelli Marciano, *Parmenide: suoni, immagini, esperienza* (Sankt Augustin 2013)
PT	C.G. Jung, *Psychological types* (Collected works, vol. 6; London 1971)
QPT	*The question of psychological types: the correspondence of C.G. Jung and Hans Schmid–Guisan*, ed. J. Beebe and E. Falzeder (Princeton 2013)
RB	C.G. Jung, *The red book*, ed. S. Shamdasani (New York 2009); in cases where my English translation differs from the published one, I refer to Jung's original text according to the German edition (*RBu*) or the folio and page numbers of his illuminated manuscript
RBu	C.G. Jung, *Das Rote Buch*, ed. S. Shamdasani (Düsseldorf 2009)
Reality	P. Kingsley, *Reality* (Inverness, CA 2003)
SB	H. Corbin, *Spiritual body and celestial earth* (2nd ed., Princeton 1989)

SD	C.G. Jung, *The structure and dynamics of the psyche* (Collected works, vol. 8; 2nd ed., London 1972)
SFJI	*San Francisco Jung Institute library journal*
SL	C.G. Jung, *The symbolic life* (Collected works, vol. 18; 2nd ed., Princeton 1980)
SM	C.G. Jung, *The spirit in man, art and literature* (Collected works, vol. 15; London 1966)
SNZ	*Jung's seminar on Nietzsche's 'Zarathustra'*, ed. and abridged by J.L. Jarrett (Princeton 1998)
SSO	H. Corbin, *Sohravardi: Le livre de la sagesse orientale* (Lagrasse 1986)
ST	C.G. Jung, *Symbols of transformation* (Collected works, vol. 5; 2nd ed., London 1967)
SW	P. Kingsley, *A story waiting to pierce you* (Inverness, CA 2010)
TE	C.G. Jung, *Two essays on analytical psychology* (Collected works, vol. 7; 2nd ed., London 1966)
ZL	C.G. Jung, *The Zofingia lectures* (Collected works, supplementary volume A; London 1983)

6

NOTES

NOTES TO PART I

[1] The Eranos gatherings have recently become a subject of intense interest for academics. See e.g. R. Bernardini, *Jung a Eranos* (Milan 2011) and in *Spring* 92 (2015) 1–26, H.T. Hakl, *Eranos* (Sheffield 2013), and that strange masterpiece of modern prejudice and pseudo-learning—*Religion after religion* by S.M. Wasserstrom (Princeton 1999)—together with Maria Subtelny's patient response, *Iranian studies* 36 (2003) 91–101.

[2] "C'était pour moi une joie extraordinaire et une expérience pas seulement des plus rares, mais plutôt unique, d'être compris complètement. Je suis accoutumé de vivre dans un vacuum intellectuel plus ou moins complet ...": letter from Jung to Corbin dated 4 May 1953 (*FC*). For the French original see *HC* 328 = *AJ* 156; for an English translation, *JL* ii 115. This letter is ignored by Tom Cheetham, who wastes his time listing all the theoretical points on which Jung and Corbin *would* and *should* have disagreed while—as a true follower of James Hillman—missing what is most essential (*Green man, earth angel*, Albany 2005, 47–54; *After prophecy*, New Orleans 2007, 103–12; *All the world an icon*, Berkeley 2012).

[3] "… cette atmosphère de liberté spirituelle absolue, où chacun s'exprime sans souci d'aucun dogme officiel et en ne s'efforçant qu'à être soi-même, à être *vrai*": *Revue de culture européenne* 5 (1953) 12. Compare also Corbin's comments, recorded 25 years later just before he died, on the lasting legacy of Eranos: "… une liberté spirituelle intégrale. Chacun découvrait peu à peu et laissait parler le tréfonds de lui-même. … Cet entraînement à être franchement et intégralement soi-même devient une habitude que l'on ne perd plus …" (*HC* 48).

[4] See e.g. his *Avicenna and the visionary recital* (London 1960) 27–32 (*ARV* ii 31–7). When Jung found himself being drawn to say that the only truth there can be for you is your truth (*RB* 231 n.27), he was warning against the psychological dangers of trying to imitate someone else's truth (ibid. 231b)—which ironically is where the superficial attempt to live one's own truth always tends to end up—and, similarly, was speaking out of a depth of experience far removed from the level of the conscious personality. On the weighty implications for Jung of living "my truth", and the essential requirement that it embrace the sacred reality of the timeless as well as all the dramas of time, see the prologue to *Memories, dreams, reflections* (*MDR* 17/3) with P. Bishop's comments, *Carl Jung* (London 2014) 10–13.

[5] On the undesirability and painfulness of truth see e.g. Empedocles fr. 114.1–3 Diels = fr. 159 Gemelli Marciano; *Reality* 313. T.S. Eliot, with his "human kind / Cannot bear very much reality" (*Burnt Norton* I), speaks as a perfect student of the Greeks. Truth and remembering "from the beginning" (*ex archês*): cf. especially J.–P. Vernant, *Journal de psychologie*

normale et pathologique 56 (1959) 6–7 with M. Detienne, *Les maîtres de vérité dans la Grèce archaïque* (Paris 1967) 47; also G. Nagy, *Homeric questions* (Austin 1996) 122–6.

[6] It was some time after writing this that for the first time I came across these words by Henry Corbin: "… The past must be 'put in the present' … The genuine transcending the past can only be 'putting it in the present' … And I believe it can be said that the entire work of Eranos is, in this sense, a *putting in the present …*" (*Man and time*, ed. J. Campbell, London 1958, xvii).

[7] See e.g. M. Lings, *Muhammad* (London 1983) 105–6.

[8] Significantly, Jung himself had little patience with those who made an issue of doubting whether the so-called "primitive medicine man" could in any true psychological sense be called conscious or individuated. "'Well, I don't know about that', he said. 'They may not be conscious but they hear the inner voice, they *act* on it, they do not go against it—that is what counts'" (*JS* 211).

[9] On Hitler's heartfelt gratitude to the British and especially Americans for inspiring his concept of concentration camps, and how he "often praised to his inner circle the efficiency of America's extermination—by starvation and uneven combat—of the red savages who could not be tamed by captivity", see J. Toland, *Adolf Hitler* (Garden City, NY 1976) 702. For the venerable ancestry of the term "final solution" in the nineteenth-century history of the American military, and more specifically in the "final solution of the Indian problem" devised

by General William T. Sherman, see M. Fellman, *Citizen Sherman* (New York 1995) 260, 274, 452; J.A. Emison, *Lincoln über alles* (Gretna, LA 2009) 21, 67, 269–70.

[10] Jung felt it important to emphasize almost exclusively the transcendent aspect of *Anthropos*, with the paradoxical result that he separated this archetypal "human" from ordinary human reality and experience. See especially *Aion* 198 §310 (Anthropos as "*homo maximus*", the king figure in direct contrast to "the anonymous individual of the populace"), 204 §318 (Anthropos as "empirically the most important archetype"), 231 figure A (distinguishing "Anthropos the higher Adam" from "Man the lower Adam"), 246 §388 (Anthropos as transcendent), 257 §406 ("the archetype of the Anthropos"); *JL* ii 619 (questioning the ability of our self-conscious egos "to establish a conscious relationship with the Anthropos, i.e., the natural self. For, as you rightly point out, it would mean extending ego-consciousness into the realm of the transcendent"). This is all fair enough from a certain point of view; but it also is only one side of the coin. The other side is the perspective that Gnostics themselves were much more inclined to emphasize. According to that perspective, we ordinary humans are absolutely nothing outside of or without this archetypal reality. We are literally shapeless: unable not only to think or talk but even to stand or walk. See e.g. Clement of Alexandria, *Stromata* 2.8.36.4 (Adam was created "in the name of *Anthropos*" when the primordial *Anthropos* "was established inside man") and 2.8.38.5 ("the *Anthropos* in the pleroma and the man 'according to his image' who received the archetype inside him") with F.-M.-M. Sagnard, *La gnose valentinienne et le témoignage de saint Irénée* (Paris 1947) 121–2 and 137–8; *Extracts from Theodotus* 50.1–51.1 ("... the

Man inside man ..."; cf. R.P. Casey, *The 'Excerpta ex Theodoto' of Clement of Alexandria*, London 1934, 72–5, 143); *Corpus hermeticum* 1.12–17 (W. Barnstone and M. Meyer, *The Gnostic bible*, Boston 2003, 505–7); J. Lacarrière, *The Gnostics* (London 1977) 31–2; G. Quispel, *Gnostica, Judaica, Catholica* (Leiden 2008) 157–60. Ironically, on this particular issue Jung turns out to be more of a dualist than many of the so-called Gnostics—although the relationship between them is usually described as being the exact opposite.

[11] *TE* 170–1 §§263–5; J. Hopkins, *Chung-Hwa Buddhist journal* 21 (2008) 163, who wisely points out (ibid. 163–4) that even to believe in finding real solutions through politics or economics or social change is for Jung an unfailing sign of psychological inflation. Of course one would need to include most Jungians nowadays in the category of pious disciples. For a recent attempt at summarizing Jung's ideas about inflation see L. Schlamm in *Encyclopedia of psychology and religion* (2nd ed., New York 2014), ed. D.A. Leeming, 870–3.

[12] Some time after writing this, I came across these words by Jung and Marie-Louise von Franz: "Old age is ... the gradual breaking down of the bodily machine, with which foolishness identifies ourselves. It is indeed a major effort—the *magnum opus* in fact—to escape in time from the narrowness of its embrace and to liberate our mind..." (*Spring* 1971, 135, cf. *JL* ii 580); "... at the end of life there is the big showdown. Have you frittered away your life in superficiality, or as Jung said about a woman once, 'Five minutes after her death, she'll not remember this life any more'. Or have you built something eternal ...?" (von Franz, *PP* 38, 1998, 16).

[13] This is one of the most constant, and central, themes in my book *Reality*: on the dangers of identifying with being a human see especially 347–495. Jung himself became familiar with the ancient linkage between danger and salvation especially through the work of Friedrich Hölderlin, and his poem "Patmos": *JPPF* 4/1 (1912) 432–4 = *Psychology of the unconscious* (New York 1916) 445–7 (cf. *ST* 407–10 §§630–5), a passage that already connects Hölderlin's words "Where danger is, there lies salvation" with descent into the underworld; *RB* 300 n.205; *PT* 264 §446; *CT* 94 §195; *JL* i 65 with n.5 and ii 193 with n.1; *MDR* 231/245; P. Bishop, *The Dionysian self* (Berlin 1995) 100–1; S. Shamdasani, *C.G. Jung: a biography in books* (New York 2012) 12–19, 215 n.19.

[14] R.D. Laing in *NL* 99–103. One recent example of the valiant Jungian protectors is Marvin Spiegelman with his insistence that, far from ever coming close to being schizophrenic or schizoid, "Jung, of course, was nothing of the sort; he braved immersing himself in the unconscious without succumbing to it, providing an example for many of us to do the same and find our own myth" (*PP* 49, 2006, 317). Recent attempts to squash "the familiar myth of Jung's madness" have been spearheaded by the editor of the *Red book* itself (*JSB* 72–5, 80, 95); but despite Sonu Shamdasani's unique access to original documents, he together with James Hillman both reveal themselves as ungrounded intellectuals in their lighthearted tiptoeing around the topic of madness and in Shamdasani's quaint denial that Jung was "at any point on the verge of tipping over" (*Lament of the dead*, New York 2013, 69–71). Compare also L.S. Owens, *The Gnostic* 3 (2010) 23–4, 30, who relies a little too heavily on Shamdasani; and T. Kawai, *JAP* 57 (2012) 380, who argues quite sincerely that Jung's most overwhelming experiences are far removed from schizophrenia

or psychosis because he happened to see things "very clearly" (not the wisest of diagnostic criteria) and because he had visionary rather than acoustic hallucinations. In fact the material preserved, thanks to the *Red book*, is just as much acoustic as visionary; and Jung himself remembered the entire process as an experience of hearing rather than seeing (*JP* 145, 170).

[15] For Jung grasping at furniture see S. Corbett, *New York Times magazine* (20 September 2009) 36—"'I often had to cling to the table', he recalled, 'so as not to fall apart'"—together with the famous original Protocols on which Jung's *Memories, dreams, reflections* was based but that were held back from publication. There he describes in his own words how he often had to cling on desperately to the table in front of him to prevent himself from falling apart; and during those times experienced the most terrifying of moments, again and again having the constant feeling of being torn to shreds (*JP* 174, a passage badly rationalized and miscontextualized by S. Shamdasani, *Spring* 57, 1995, 125). For madness in the *Red book* see Jung's patently authentic musings at *RB* 238, 295–8; also the touchingly honest appraisals by V.W. Odajnyk, *PP* 53 (2010) 448–451 and M. Stein, *JJ* 4/4 (2010) 96 as well as Tina Keller's important eyewitness testimony that Jung "would now and then say how close he had felt to insanity" (W.K. Swan, *JAP* 51, 2006, 503 and *The memoir of Tina Keller–Jenny*, New Orleans 2011, 27 §68). For the even earlier threats of "delusion and madness" that already confronted Jung years before he started work on the *Red book*, cf. A. Carotenuto, *A secret symmetry* (New York 1982) 190 with A.C. Elms, *Uncovering lives* (New York 1994) 67–8. In light of all this it would seem more than a little simplistic of Shamdasani to claim that Freud's repeated complaints during both 1912 and 1913 about

Jung being downright "crazy" are nothing but "psychoanalytic character assassination", carried out by Freud purely "as a way of discrediting" Jung's ideas (*JSB* 72). As for the relation between going mad and being afraid of going mad, which is a fear Jung experienced far more than once: Shamdasani again argues with the same simplistic reasonableness that there is a world of difference between the two because "in some sense, the fear of losing one's mind is a mark of one's sanity" (*Lament of the dead*, New York 2013, 70). What he fails to mention is Jung's own insistence, based on vastly more intimate as well as professional experience, that the transition from a fear of going mad into becoming mad is the slipperiest slope imaginable (*IJP* 105–6). Also worth noting is Jung's inner conviction as a medical student that actually to go mad and experience madness for himself would be the best way of understanding, and helping, his patients (*JP* 252).

[16] Prior to publication of the *Red book* in 2009, one had to make do with Jung's warning that the book "will strike any superficial observer as sheer insanity. And this is exactly how it would have ended up if I had not been able to contain the overwhelming power of the original experience" (*ETG* 387; cf. *RB* 360). But even this comment was restricted to the German text of *Memories, dreams, reflections*: for the English version, Jung was only allowed to note in passing that the experience could theoretically "have driven me out of my wits" (*MDR* 181/189). On the saga of control and censorship surrounding the editing and eventual publication of his so-called autobiography, see A.C. Elms, *Uncovering lives* (New York 1994) 51–70; S. Shamdasani, *Spring* 57 (1995) 115–37 and *JSB* 22–45; also D. Bair's account, *Jung* (Boston 2003) 585–617. One of the main editors of Jung's collected works in English, Michael Fordham, has quaintly commented on

the madness ("far madder") contaminating original drafts of *Memories, dreams, reflections* before the text had been subjected to an appropriate editing process (*Spring* 57, 1995, 122–3: his use of the comparative form of the word "mad" is very eloquent). For the so-called "subtleties" silently introduced into the text by Fordham and his secretary see e.g. Bair 614, and contrast Jung's own desperate plea: "I *want* the book to look crazy!" (ibid. 613).

[17] For madness and mastery of madness in early Greek philosophy see *Reality* 430–53, 479–80; for the continuation of the theme, *RB* 238 n.89, 321 n.313. One of the first people to recognize Jung—"a walking asylum in himself, as well as its head physician", "a lunatic" who "went through everything an insane person goes through"—as someone whose achievement is that he belonged "in a long line of 'shamans' who understood 'madness, and can heal it, because at periods they are half-mad themselves'" was his own translator, R.F.C. Hull. See D. Bair, *Jung* (Boston 2003) 292–3, 616–17. I trust I will be excused for laughing at the irony of modern-day scholars denouncing Hull as a "rationalist" (*JSB* 50; cf. N. Pilard, *Jung and intuition*, London 2015, 10, 117–18), or of prominent Jungian intellectuals dismissing him as an intellectual (*JSB* 51 n.136). On Jung's immense, lifelong regard for Hull and for the "aliveness" of his translations see Bair 583–4 together with the copies of their correspondence held at the Library of Congress (especially Jung's letter to Hull dated 27 December 1958). For shamanism and madness cf. e.g. M. Eliade, *Myths, dreams and mysteries* (New York 1961) 225; M. Hoppál, *Shamans and traditions* (Budapest 2007) 35; C. Pratt, *An encyclopedia of shamanism* (New York 2007) 4, 91, 116, 304, 436, 513; *Reality* 440.

[18] Madness as the place where one encounters the sacred: see e.g. M. Stein, *JJ* 4/4 (2010) 96 on Jung's "transformed view of sickness and health. In the Red Book, he advocates embracing one's madness on the grounds that God is to be found there precisely. … Just how deeply Jung carried out this project in his own case is amply demonstrated in the text. He gives very convincing impressions of pushing the mental envelope to the edge of insanity …". Ordinary sanity as insanity: *RB* 238b (when talking about delusion and sickness, don't forget to include the insanely obsessive influence exerted on us by the spirit of our time which never stops forcing us to view only the most superficial surface of things), 298a (our everyday existence, even more so than all our noble philosophies and great words of wisdom, is not only illogical but totally mad). Of course this raises in passing the question of just what madness is and what possible usefulness the term can really have, aside from denoting states of unusual psychological intensity: cf. J. Custance, *Wisdom, madness and folly* (New York 1952) with C.G. Jung, *SL* 349–52; J.W. Perry, *The far side of madness* (Englewood Cliffs 1974) and *Trials of the visionary mind* (Albany 1999); J. Hart, *The way of madness* (London 1997); P. Williams, *Rethinking madness* (San Rafael 2012).

[19] For Corbin's very brief autobiographical comments, recorded just before he died, about the process of being taught "les vertus inestimables du Silence" directly by his inner teacher or *sheikh* see *HC* 46. For Empedocles' exquisitely beautiful comments on the nature of words see *ENM* 353, 399–404; *Reality* 518–33. To him, as well as other so-called Presocratic philosophers (for Parmenides note e.g. Theophrastus, *On the senses* 4 = Parmenides fr. 33.21 Gemelli Marciano = A.H. Coxon, *The fragments of Parmenides*, 2nd ed., Las Vegas 2009, 142–3 §45),

absolutely everything in existence is full of consciousness and life—even right down to the words we humans speak. Marie-Louise von Franz has claimed that what makes the "alchemical myth" the only one worth living in the West, and the only one capable of reviving western civilization, is the alchemists' appreciation of matter as alive and conscious; their deep understanding of the feminine; and their willingness to face the problem of opposites (*PP* 38, 1998, 16). What von Franz fails to note is that all these understandings were quintessential aspects of the Presocratics' teachings (for the feminine see *IDPW*; for the opposites, *Reality* 29–30, 85–6, 212–13). No doubt this is because she held the faultlessly rationalistic and commendably evolutionary-minded view of Presocratic philosophy as nothing but a youthful and naïve "kind of springtime of the spirit" (*Puer aeternus*, Santa Monica 1981, 101).

[20] Jung was quite open in stating that his work was never intended to help people escape their suffering but was meant to give them the strength they needed to suffer consciously (cf. e.g. *PPT* 81 §185; also R. Aziz's comments, *C.G. Jung's psychology of religion and synchronicity*, Albany 1990, 42–4 and M. Stein's, *JJ* 4/4, 2010, 96). Only in private, though, did he indicate just how far he took the practice of conscious suffering: see especially the letter published by G. Adler in *PP* 6 (1975) 12 ("… I consciously and intentionally made my life miserable, because I wanted God to be alive and free from the suffering man has put on him by loving his own reason more than God's secret intentions. … Try to apply seriously what I have told you, not that you might escape suffering—nobody can escape it—but that you may avoid the worst—*blind* suffering"). On God, for Jung, as a directly experienced reality rather than a theological belief cf. e.g. *JS* 251, 427–8; for his protest at the

utter superfluousness of mere belief in the presence of such experience, which thanks to its directness is naturally the greatest possible threat to believers and disbelievers alike, *JL* i 141–2.

[21] On this absolutely fundamental idea of offering *therapeia* to the gods see e.g. Hesiod, *Theogony* 100 and *Works and days* 135; *Homeric hymns* 3.390 and 32.20; Pindar, *Olympian odes* 3.16; Herodotus, *Histories* 2.37; Euripides, *Electra* 744 and *Ion* 187. *Therapeia* and cognates were also used to describe the process of tending the sick or wounded, and this was the sense that helped Plato to shape our exclusive modern preoccupation with providing *therapeia* for body and soul (*Gorgias* 464b, 513d; *Laches* 185e). It should perhaps be added that James Hillman's favourite etymologizing of the word *therapeia* (*A blue fire*, New York 1989, 73: "… the chair of the therapist is indeed a mighty throne …") is complete self-serving fantasy.

[22] See Plato, *Euthyphro* 12e–15c; F.-G. Herrmann in *A companion to Greek religion*, ed. D. Ogden (Oxford 2007) 390. One of the many dark ironies here is the way Aristotle—along with a steady lineage of later thinkers—managed to convince himself that, if anybody is to be capable of offering real *therapeia* to the gods, it can only be by becoming the purest of rationalists (Aristotle, *Eudemian ethics* 1249b13–23; M.L. McPherran, *Journal of the history of philosophy* 23, 1985, 287–309). This is nothing but a mockery of Socrates' sacred service to the god Apollo (Plato, *Apology* 23b–c, 30a), which had led him to heal people of their illusions by destroying all their proud concepts instead of helping to build them up (cf. *PJB* 29–31 and *Reality* 129, 150–6; for Apollo as both healer and destroyer see *IDPW*). But it also is a shining example

of how easily perceived realities can become distorted and even inverted within the space of just a single generation or two, although we soon will be encountering many more such examples in the case of Jung and his successors.

[23] A. de Jong, *Traditions of the Magi* (Leiden 1997) 213–22, 399–400; H. Remus in *Text and artifact in the religions of Mediterranean antiquity*, ed. S.G. Wilson and M. Desjardins (Waterloo 2000) 535–6.

[24] Plutarch: *On the ending of the oracles* 411e–f. Porphyry: G. Wolff, *Porphyrii de philosophia ex oraculis haurienda librorum reliquiae* (Berlin 1856) 172–4; K. Buresch, *Klaros* (Leipzig 1889) 41–2 n.8; B. Haussoullier, *Études sur l'histoire de Milet et du Didymeion* (Paris 1902) xxviii–xxix §XLIII; J.J. O'Meara, *Porphyry's 'Philosophy from oracles' in Augustine* (Paris 1959) 70 n.1; J. Fontenrose, *Didyma* (Berkeley 1988) 219–222; *Porphyrii philosophi fragmenta*, ed. A. Smith (Stuttgart 1993) 370 §322F (the reductionist explanations of the second oracle by A. Busine, *Paroles d'Apollon*, Leiden 2005, 350 are quite absurd); for the background cf. A.P. Johnson, *Religion and identity in Porphyry of Tyre* (Cambridge 2013) 172–8. On the famous "last oracle" see T.E. Gregory, *Greek, Roman & Byzantine studies* 24 (1983) 355–66; to explain the oracle as prompted by an earthquake blocking a physical spring (M. Henry, *Phoenix* 39, 1985, 50–2; P. Athanassiadi, *Deltion tês Christianikês Archaiologikês Etaireias* 15, 1989–90, 277 and n.65) is to overlook the centuries-old prophetic language about the drying up of prophecy's flow.

[25] For a modern example of this fashionably half-rational, half-intuitive view see J. Naydler, *The future of the ancient*

world (Rochester, VT 2009) 168–204. With unshakeable confidence Naydler declares, on the basis of so much growing interest among people today in divination and different forms of spirituality, that "for us the gods and spirits are returning" (179)—evoking the new-age naivety which leads contemporary pagans from California to visit Delphi for a few days, interfere with the earth there by burying a few crystals, and then claim they have re-activated the ancient oracle. Re-activating sacred sites or gods or goddesses is the new craze: it seems never to occur to anyone that they might have no interest whatsoever in being re-activated or playing our little games. For his broad view of history Naydler follows in the footsteps of Rudolf Steiner, who during his life was given some beautifully fruitful intuitions; but one only has to look back at what Steiner said about the ancient world to see how utterly unintuitive his ideas about the history of western culture happened to be, or how deeply contaminated his understanding was by the collective prejudices of the time he lived in. As for his supposedly revealed knowledge of forgotten civilizations, Carl Jung's drily humorous earthiness says it all: So long as "Herr Steiner" claims to understand the language of Atlantis but can't understand the Hittite inscriptions recently discovered in the Near East, there is no good reason to get too "excited" about any of the great things he has to say (*JL* i 203–4). For the pervasive ignorance of history underpinning most modern ideas about both material, and spiritual, evolution see e.g. *SW* 172–3; for the actual source of our mythologies about Atlantis, ibid. 127–8.

[26] Note for example Jung's finely balanced statement from a few years before he died that—while it was only his extended and solitary study of Gnostic as well as alchemical tradition which at last had shown him something real about "the development

of our unconscious relations to the collective unconscious and the variations our consciousness has undergone"—we westerners are totally lost without any understanding of the alchemical or Hermetic wisdom which bridges the gap between ancient Gnostics and our modern world. "The Gnostics lived in the first, second, and third centuries. And what was in between? Nothing. And now, today, we suddenly fall into that hole and are confronted with the problems of the collective unconscious which were the same then two thousand years ago—and we are not prepared to meet that problem" (R.I. Evans, *Jung on elementary psychology*, New York 1976, 232; cf. *JS* 350–1).

[27] "Our cult of progress": *MDR* 230/244. The "illusion" of our triumphs: ibid. 227/240. For the Presocratics, their self-evident self-contradictions, and their immensely subtle uses of language see *Reality* 415–25; *ENM* 382–4. Failure to approach Jung's work as a whole in the fullness of its ambiguity leads to the ridiculous situation where he is condemned for not being enough of an evolutionist by scientifically-minded thinkers and for being too much of an evolutionist by "traditionalist" authorities on religion (P. Pietikainen, *Utopian studies* 12/1, 2001, 51–4; R.P. Coomaraswamy in *The betrayal of tradition*, ed. H. Oldmeadow, Bloomington, IN 2005, 61 with W. Smith, ibid. 266): cf. G.–F. Calian's timely comment, *Annual of medieval studies at CEU* 16 (2010) 176.

[28] Note e.g. his published comments in 1936: "I would call it progress that in the 2,000,000 years that we have existed on earth, we have developed a chin and a decent sort of brain. Historically what we call progress is, after all, just a mushroom growth of coal and oil. Otherwise we are not any more intelligent than the old Greeks or Romans" (*New York Times* for 4 October 1936; cf. *JS* 89). Compare also his

climactic, and equally sarcastic, warning against imagining one is "infinitely cleverer than all the benighted heads of the Middle Ages" (*PR* 200 §294); *JV* i 148–9 (on the Middle Ages as a period when "the idea of any real improvement did not exist ... Real belief in any kind of progress is an absolutely modern invention") with ii 1047–50 (where Jung is forced by the insistently optimistic attitude of a prominent Jungian, Barbara Hannah, to address his "more or less temperamental" tendency to question whether there is "any movement for the better in the world ... one could say things have become better. But in another sense that is most questionable. I don't know whether our life is happier than the life of the primitive man, or whether life today is better than life in the Middle Ages ... it is quite doubtful whether things have become better ... don't forget that we have very limited knowledge ... we simply do not know ..."); *RB* 330b (on the question of returning to, and slowly working towards completing, the Middle Ages) with n.354 and *MDR* 223/236; *Man and his symbols* (New York 1964) 52. And for Jung's demonstration, not only through his writings but also through his way of living, that what haunted him more than anything was the "deplorable shortcoming in modern humanity" due to our complete loss of ancient and medieval sensibilities cf. A. Haaning's comments: *JAP* 59 (2014) 22 and ("Back to the Middle Ages") 27–8.

[29] There are some good lessons in human psychology to be learned from observing how those same scientists who used to relish equating increases in relative brain size with an increase in intelligence—so long as it supported the thesis of our superiority to our ancestors as well as other animals—are now busy chasing their own tails after discovering that the brain size of humans has been shrinking for thousands of

years. See e.g. B. Hood, *The domesticated brain* (London 2014) 3–4: "The finding that the human brain has been getting smaller over our recent evolution runs counter to the generally held view that bigger brains equal more intelligence, and that we are smarter than our prehistoric ancestors ... Nobody knows exactly why the human brain has been shrinking, but it does raise some provocative questions about the relationship between the brain, behaviour and intelligence. First, we make lots of unfounded assumptions about the progress of human intelligence. We assume our Stone Age ancestors must have been backward because the technologies they produced seem so primitive by modern standards. But what if raw human intelligence has not changed so much over the past 20,000 years? What if they were just as smart as modern man, only without the benefit of thousands of generations of accumulated knowledge? We should not assume that we are fundamentally more intelligent than an individual born 20,000 years ago ..." For brain shrinkage and other signs of degeneration cf. also K. McAuliffe, *Discover* 31/7 (September 2010) 54–9; C.N Shaw and J.T. Stock, *Journal of human evolution* 30 (2013) 1–8; A.A. Macintosh, R. Pinhasi and J.T. Stock, *American journal of physical anthropology* 153 (2014) 173 and *Journal of archaeological science* 52 (2014) 376–90. As for the Darwinian theory of evolution itself, together with the huge number of noble or savage lies which since the time of Darwin have been needed to defend it, see e.g. M. Baigent, *Ancient traces* (London 1998) 23–39, 100–116.

[30] See Parmenides fr. 6.4–9 and Empedocles fr. 2 Diels = Parmenides fr. 13.5–10 and Empedocles fr. 7 Gemelli Marciano; *IDPW* 221–3 and *Reality*, especially 83–125, 326–41. "What they call life": Empedocles fr. 15.2 Diels = fr. 15B.6 Gemelli Marciano (*to dê bioton kaleousi*); cf. *ENM* 360 with

Reality 404–5, 419. For the language used to describe humans by Empedocles as well as Parmenides compare the Aeschylean *Prometheus bound* 447–50—a passage which eloquently underlines the fact that, for both of them, any real process of human evolution has not yet even begun.

[31] See e.g. R. Williams, *Open to judgement* (London 1994) 103; D. Brown, *God and enchantment of place* (Oxford 2004) 154–5. And for the continuing vitality of this theme, which is so much favoured by property developers across the very same region of southern Switzerland where the Eranos gatherings have always taken place, see M. Caratti's editorial in *La regione Ticino*, 12 June 2013, 1 ("Dal momento in cui Gesù muore su una croce … non esiste più nessun luogo sacro sulla terra. Sacro è l'uomo …").

[32] See *APMM*; *IDPW*; *Reality*, together with my comments in *ENM*, especially 354–6; *Works and conversations* 22 (2011) 22–37; *PSIE* with L. Gemelli Marciano, *Die Vorsokratiker* ii (2nd ed., Berlin 2013). One would hope there is no need to emphasize how different this is from the familiar scholarly practice of picking out the religious, mystical and even shamanic ideas inadvertently "inherited" by Presocratic philosophers from their ancestors—only to claim that the unique feature of Presocratic thought was its constant efforts to rationalize these older traditions. See for example H. Diels, *Parmenides: Lehrgedicht* (Berlin 1897) 3–27; K. Joël, *Der Ursprung der Natur-Philosophie aus dem Geiste der Mystik* (Jena 1906); F.M. Cornford, *Classical quarterly* 16 (1922) 137–50, 17 (1923) 1–12, and *Principium sapientiae* (Cambridge 1952); W. Jaeger, *The theology of the early Greek philosophers* (Oxford 1947); E.R. Dodds, *The Greeks and the irrational* (Berkeley 1951); and, on the concept of "inheritance", G. Vlastos, *Gnomon* 27 (1955) 70.

[33] On the nature of Parmenides' logic see especially *Reality* 11–306, 563–85 with *ENM* 369–81; *PSIE* 43–126, 215–87 with *Ancient philosophy* 28 (2008) 21–48. For Friedrich Nietzsche's fantasies about the icy coldness and "rigor mortis" of the goddess' teachings, see his *Philosophy in the tragic age of the Greeks* (South Bend 1962) 69–90. Martin Heidegger's even clumsier misunderstandings of the poetic language and style so exquisitely, and deliberately, used by Parmenides are on full display in his *Parmenides* (Bloomington, IN 1992). As for Rudolf Steiner's quaintly patronizing words about the role played by Parmenides "in the progress of human development toward the stage of thought experience", these too are utter nonsense—partly due to the numerous mistakes and inaccuracies in Steiner's account of Presocratic philosophy, most of them imported by him without any question or discrimination from the textbooks of his time, and partly due to his insistence on forcing everything into a naïve evolutionary mould (so e.g. *The riddles of philosophy*, Spring Valley, NY 1973, 28–30). Much the same as with the crude misreadings of Heraclitus by the great yogi Sri Aurobindo (*Essays in philosophy and yoga* = *The complete works of Sri Aurobindo* xiii, Pondicherry 1998, 215–54; for Heraclitus' so-called "*logos* doctrine" see *Reality* 566–7), the lesson waiting to be learned is that spiritual teachers are all well and good but to mistake their intuitive insights for divine omniscience is a little childish. Even the most genuine spiritual realizations have little power by themselves, regardless of all the rhetoric and wishful thinking, to correct the prejudice and collective misunderstandings embedded in the human brain.

[34] Altogether typical in this regard is the so-called Traditionalist, Frithjof Schuon, whose writings on the subject demonstrate just how far removed he is from representing

any authentically "primordial" tradition—or even from being able to convey some genuine understanding of the impulses that gave rise to our western world (*Logic and transcendence*, Bloomington, IN 2009, 42–6, 95–6). Schuon's "logic" is simply the humanized reasoning of Plato and Aristotle which, as the last head of the ancient Platonic school emphasized with appropriate finality, is altogether incapable of accessing reality. For Damascius' elaborate contrast between the apparatus of human reasoning (*apodeixeis anthrôpikai*) and the simplicity of divine intuition, which is precisely what logic once used to be, see e.g. his *Questions and answers about first principles* 1.5 (*Traité des premiers principes* i, ed. L.G. Westerink and J. Combès, Paris 1986, 9–11; *Problems and solutions concerning first principles*, trans. S. Ahbel-Rappe, New York 2010, 72–4) with P. Athanassiadi's comments in *Damascius: The philosophical history* (Athens 1999) 55. And for some timely help in exploding the mythical notion that rationality and reasoning are somehow designed to help us arrive at the truth, see the recent research published by H. Mercier and D. Sperber, *Behavioral and brain sciences* 34 (2011) 57–74.

[35] For Parmenides as a lawgiver, for the extremely real sense in which his entire logic was given as laws, and for the intimate links connecting this lawgiving with prophecy as well as with the practice of incubation, see *IDPW*; *Reality* 15–178, 563–76. On the absolutely fundamental importance of not changing anything in these laws see *IDPW* 209–10 and *Reality* 55–9, 563 plus the further references cited; Deuteronomy 4:2 with e.g. D.I. Block, *How I love your Torah, o Lord!* (Eugene 2011) 6 n.3; and the usual rationalizing modern discussions such as G. Camassa's in *Les savoirs de l'écriture*, ed. M. Detienne (Lille 1988) 147–50, in *Le législateur et la loi dans l'Antiquité*, ed. P.

Sineux (Caen 2005) 29–36 and in *Scrittura e mutamento delle leggi nel mondo antico* (Rome 2011).

[36] The book I had come across was M. Fabbri and A. Trotta, *Una scuola–collegio di età augustea* (Rome 1989). I integrated the archaeological discoveries with Parmenides' own poetry in *IDPW*; cf. *ENM* 375–80, *Reality* 578 and more recent discussions such as L. Bergemann, *Kraftmetaphysik und Mysterienkult im Neuplatonismus* (Munich 2006) 19, 301–25. For the discoveries in Parmenides' hometown of Velia and their crucial links with prophetic tradition note also G. Pugliese Carratelli in *Magna Grecia*, ed. Pugliese Carratelli (Milan 1988) 233, G. Camassa in *Magna Grecia e Oriente mediterraneo* (Atti del trentanovesimo convegno di studi sulla Magna Grecia, Taranto 2000) 348, L. Vecchio, *Le iscrizioni greche di Velia* (Vienna 2003) 74–6, 91 and *Filosofi e medici* (Pozzuoli 2004) 38, 40, 46, *PSIE* 64 (cf. L. Rossetti and M. Pulpito, ibid. 16); for their links with the practice of incubation, S. Musitelli, *La parola del passato* 35 (1980) 241–55, G. Sacco, *Rivista di filologia e di istruzione classica* 109 (1981) 36–40, Pugliese Carratelli 230, Camassa 347 and G. Costa, *La sirena di Archimede* (Alessandria 2008) 168–81.

[37] For Parmenides, his successor Zeno, and the modesty of their hometown in southern Italy versus the imperialist "arrogance" of Athens, cf. e.g. *IDPW* 197–203, 225–6 and *Reality* 301–6; *PSIE* 108–110. On the issue of relations with Athens see also *APMM* 155–6, 339–41; *SW* 114–16, 127–8, 148. I documented at length the traditional practices of learning how to breathe, be silent, use one's senses to the full, in *Reality*. One sign of how completely out of touch modern intellectuals, including so-called experts on Jung, are from such realities is provided

by the ridiculous statements of Wolfgang Giegerich: "It has been said about Pythagoras, who believed in the transmigration of souls, that when he erected himself and craned his neck with all his mental powers he was effortlessly able to view every detail in his ten or even twenty former lives" (*JJTP* 6/1, 2004, 23, supposedly citing Empedocles). In fact what Empedocles had said about Pythagoras is that he was able to see back into previous lifetimes not by craning his neck but through conscious breathing, when he stretched his lungs and diaphragm a certain way (Empedocles fr. 129 Diels = fr. 186 Gemelli Marciano; *ENM* 355, 400–1). Giegerich should perhaps think twice before criticizing Jungians, as well as Jung, for the fundamentally amateurish and unscholarly nature of their publications (*JJTP* 6/1, 2004, 41–2, A. Casement, *JAP* 56, 2011, 542).

[38] Aristotle, *On prophesying in dreams* 464a20–22. For the praises still heaped on him because of this text see e.g. E.R. Dodds, *The Greeks and the irrational* (Berkeley 1951) 120 ("coolly rational without being superficial, and he shows at times a brilliant insight"); P.J. van der Eijk, *Medicine and philosophy in classical antiquity* (Cambridge 2005) 189 ("intriguing … sophisticated"); W.V. Harris, *Dreams and experience in classical antiquity* (Cambridge, MA 2009) 233.

[39] "… While asleep no one is worth anything …": Plato, *Laws* 807d–808c; the continuation, where Plato specifies that all children absolutely have to be supervised each single moment of every day because otherwise they are no better than beasts, is also worth reading. The difference between this attitude and the great "nocturnal work" imposed on Jung by his soul (*RB* 211b; L.S. Owens, *The Gnostic* 3, 2010, 30, 41) is as plain as

the difference between night and day. For Parmenides' own approach to the unconsciousness of darkness and night—which to him is no reason to avoid them but, on the contrary, an invitation to penetrate and explore them—see *IDPW* 64–5 with *ENM* 377–8 n.108 and also R. Padel, *In and out of the mind* (Princeton 1992) 71. The traditional mystical view of the soul's prophetic powers while the body sleeps at night (so e.g. Pindar, fr. 131b Maehler) would of course be subjected to the usual rationalizing treatment by Plato (*Republic* 571d–572b, *Timaeus* 70d–72b) and was still acceptable to Aristotle right at the start of his philosophical career (fr. 10 Rose = *On philosophy* fr. 12a Untersteiner). But for the disparagement of night, as opposed to daytime, in Aristotle's own later writings cf. P.J. van der Eijk, *De insomniis, de divinatione per somnum* (Berlin 1994) 319; and note how different the attitude to sleep and dreams held by Plato in his "mature" old age has become from what was clearly the attitude of the historical Socrates (W.V. Harris, *Dreams and experience in classical antiquity*, Cambridge, MA 2009, 25, 55, 161, 250–2).

[40] "From earliest dawn until sunrise" and "this is the time ...": see Plato, *Laws* 951d, 961b with, for the traditions he followed and then obscured, *IDPW* 207–13. It will be noted that Jung, too, was drawn to an awareness of the unique importance associated with "the sun at the moment of rising": with "the moment", "the moment of dawn" (*JAP* 58, 2013, 165 with n.6, cf. also *JL* i 44). On the depths of darkness and night as the ultimate source of laws see *IDPW* 213–19; and on the crucial linkage in ancient Greece betweeen prophecy and darkness cf. R. Padel's fine observations, *In and out of the mind* (Princeton 1992) 69–77. As for Arthur Versluis' claim that, with its exclusive focus on a spirituality of light, "Platonism represents

the original intellectual inheritance of the West"—few assertions could be more misleading or misinformed (*Religion of light*, Minneapolis 2013, 26; cf. 83, "the essential wisdom tradition of the West").

[41] W. Burkert, *Lore and science in ancient Pythagoreanism* (Cambridge, MA 1972) 121–3; *APMM* 368. In other respects, though, Plato must certainly have worn the patience of his Pythagorean hosts rather thin—for instance when, after sending messages begging them to find a practical way to break him out of prison because the man he had naively wanted to train to become a philosopher–king had locked him up, he went on to criticize them for being too practical. See *SW* 155–7.

[42] On the extent of Plato's indebtedness to earlier mystical as well as mythical traditions, and his failure to grasp their subtleties, see *APMM*; on his rationalizations of those earlier traditions, *IDPW*; and on his inability to hold or transmit the reality they contained, *SW*. Neither can Plato in all honesty even be credited with discovering the famous Platonic archetypes or "ideas" (cf. *APMM* 88–93, 103–7 for Pythagoreans; J. Broackes, *Classical quarterly* 59, 2009, 46–59 for Socrates): basically he just tried to make sense of them with his reasoning mind, which is quite impossible, and ended up creating a terrible mess. For his transpositions of initiatory and mystery terminology see e.g. C. Riedweg, *Mysterienterminologie bei Platon, Philon und Klemens von Alexandrien* (Berlin 1987); A. Bernabé in *Plato's 'Sophist' revisited*, ed. B. Bossi and T.M. Robinson (Berlin 2013) 41–56; B. Sattler in *Philosophy and salvation in Greek religion*, ed. V. Adluri (Berlin 2013) 151–90.

[43] For the general situation see *IDPW* 39–43 and also, on the nature of facts, *Reality* 17–22. One example of flesh-and-blood

figures reacting to Plato's inclusion of them as characters inside his published fantasies is offered in Athenaeus' *Deipnosophists* 505d (Gorgias 82A15a Diels–Kranz; *Reality* 483).

[44] On killing "father Parmenides", the details about the Velian background, and the related discrediting of Parmenides' adopted son Zeno by Plato in his other fictitious dialogue called *Parmenides*, see *Sophist* 241d–242a with *IDPW* 39–45, 150–62; *Reality* 303–5; *PSIE* 107–113, 232, 275–84. As for "Elea", the crude form of the name Velia which was to become popular in the West largely thanks to Plato, see *ENM* 375 n.101. It will be noted that the word "father" or *patêr*, applied by him here to Parmenides, also had the much broader sense of "ancestor": G. Nagy, *Pindar's Homer* (Baltimore 1990) 177 §58, 195 §88. On the enormity of patricide for ancient Greeks see e.g. J.N. Bremmer's comments in *Interpretations of Greek mythology*, ed. Bremmer (London 1987) 49: "An ever-present possibility, parricide was considered to be one of the most appalling of crimes … Imputation of parricide was one of the 'unspeakable things' which could result in legal action; even the word 'parricide' was only mentioned with reluctance, if at all"; and note also Plato's own strictures, *Laws* 869a–c, 880e–881e. For the quite insanely foolish lengths to which some contemporary academics are still willing to go in the remote hope of being able to distance Plato from any accusation of committing patricide, see e.g. J.A. Palmer, *Plato's reception of Parmenides* (Oxford 1999) 145–7; D. O'Brien in *Plato's 'Sophist' revisited*, ed. B. Bossi and T.M. Robinson (Berlin 2013) 117–55. And for the repeated murders of Parmenides committed ever since Plato's time by not only distorting his teaching, but also violating and changing his own words, see especially *Reality* 117–44, 566–9; *PSIE* 217–29.

[45] See e.g. Strabo, *Geography* 14.1.44 (*tois d' allois adytos estin ho topos kai olethrios*, of an incubation shrine offering access to the underworld), *IDPW* 81–3; and for the full implications of Parmenides' *outi se moira kakê proupempe* (Parmenides fr. 1.26 Diels = fr. 8A.32 Gemelli Marciano) see ibid. 61–5, 101–5. On the perfectly specific and coherent geography of Parmenides' descent into the underworld cf., aside from *IDPW*, W. Burkert, *Phronesis* 14 (1969) 1–30 = *Kleine Schriften* viii (Göttingen 2008) 1–27; G. Cerri, *La parola del passato* 50 (1995) 458–67 and *Parmenide di Elea* (Milan 1999) 98–109, 172–83; *ENM* 369–81 and *Reality* 23–272, 563–70; L. Gemelli Marciano, *Ancient philosophy* 28 (2008) 21–46 and *PSIE* 65–81, plus the further references at *IDPW* 239–40 and *ENM* 373 n.94. Those brave academics who try to cast doubt on Parmenides' destination (e.g. M. Miller, *Oxford studies in ancient philosophy* 30, 2006, 1–47) no longer have the remotest understanding of how to approach, or read with respect, ancient mystical texts.

[46] For Plato's murder of Parmenides together with his paternal logic as stemming from the desperate need to qualify what Parmenides himself had left dangerously and, for all the busy thinking of our "wandering minds", very frustratingly unqualified see the plain statement he puts into the mouth of the "stranger from Velia" at *Sophist* 241d (... *patraloian* ... *biazesthai to te mê on hôs esti kata ti kai to on au palin hôs ouk esti pêi* ...); *Reality* 83–8, 97, 304–6. The whole point and purpose behind Parmenides' most basic law of logic—that reality as well as everything in it "either is or is not", without the slightest possibility of compromise or qualification—was that anyone willing to take the risk of meditating on it will sooner or later be brought to a direct awareness of the timeless reality beyond all existence (*IDPW* 162–223, *Reality* 44–8). The whole point and purpose behind Plato's explicit violation of this law was

to restore the possibility that what is not also "in one sense" (*kata ti*) is and that what is also, "in a certain respect" (*pêi*), is not. By violating Parmenides' laws with his patricidal little "in one sense" and innocent-sounding "in a certain respect", with his endless need to qualify, his constant ifs and buts, Plato was able to lay the ground for all the complicated theorizing of later western thought. At the same time, he also ended up walking straight down the path of "is but also is not" which the goddess in Parmenides' poem had already mocked as being the quintessence of human futility (Parmenides fr. 6.4–9 Diels = fr. 13.5–10 Gemelli Marciano).

[47] Parmenides fr. 6.4–7 Diels = fr. 13.5–8 Gemelli Marciano; *Reality* 83–110.

[48] The roots and source of every element: Hesiod, *Theogony* 736–45, 807–10; M.E. Pellikaan–Engel, *Hesiod and Parmenides* (Amsterdam 1974) 19–30, 49; *IDPW* 51–3, 125–6. Parmenides' logic as madness: Aristotle, *On generation and corruption* 325a13–23 (… *maniai paraplêsion einai* … *oudena gar tôn mainomenôn exestanai tosouton* … *dia tên manian*); cf. *Reality* 212, 479 and, for some crucial remarks on the Academic as well as sophistic background to Aristotle's statement, L. Gemelli Marciano, *Democrito e l'Accademia* (Berlin 2007), especially 120–1.

[49] For the stranger from Velia on the madness involved in deciding to kill Parmenides see Plato, *Sophist* 242a (*manikos einai*). Aside from being obvious to Plato himself (*maniais orgês tôn gennêtorôn tolmêsai kteinai tina*: *Laws* 869a), the connection between patricide and madness is deeply embedded in the unconsciousness of western culture (cf. e.g. A.N. Pfau, *Madness in the realm*, PhD thesis, University of Michigan 2008, 152–3);

and Jacques Derrida does well to note the potent presence of this connection here in Plato's *Sophist* (*On hospitality*, Stanford 2000, 3–11). But otherwise Derrida's analysis of the passage is invalidated by his strange failure to realize that the stranger is not just a stranger, any stranger—but an *Eleatês xenos*, a stranger who quite specifically has come from Velia.

[50] The most famous discussion of sacred madness or prophetic frenzy in western literature is, inappropriately but predictably, the iconic passage where Plato posits the existence of "divine" or good kinds of madness which are quite separate and distinct from any other kind of craziness (*Phaedrus* 244a–245b, 249c–d, 265a, 266a). Certainly this rationalizing, even sophistical, attempt at separating good types of madness from bad ones can make for some pretty literature—but its popularity shows how, as a culture, we always will prefer empty rhetoric over reality. The truth is that any such distinction is completely artificial (E.R. Dodds, *The Greeks and the irrational*, Berkeley 1951, 68; for the ambiguities involved cf. also *IDPW* 55–92), ignoring all the paradoxical and chaotic and hellish aspects of madness as an actual reality. On the deceptiveness, and dangerousness, of such superficial distinctions see *Reality* 438–41; and note how, in spite of his high-flown insistence that we shouldn't be afraid of madness (*Phaedrus* 245b), when it came down to daily life Plato wanted to have as little to do with mad people as possible (A. Gocer, *Apeiron* 32/4, 1999, 32).

[51] *RBu* 230 (cf. *RB* 230b). For the two spirits see *RB* 207–8, 229–30, 238–9 n.91 ("… the dark underworld of the spirit of the depths …"); and, for Jung's initiation into the mysteries of the underworld by the spirit of the depths, 246 n.162. It will be noted that, although Jung formally dedicates some sections of the *Red book* to the theme of descending into the

underworld (*RB* 237b, 288b), the presence of the underworld is constant almost throughout; and the "technique of descent" that he employed corresponds, even down to the smallest details, to ancient methods for the practice of incubation (*IJP* 68; *MDR* 174/181; *RB* 246 n.161). Also worth noting is the fact that Jung's two favourite terms for describing his descents, *katabasis* and *nekyia*, both derive straight from ancient Greece. For *katabasis* see already *FJ* 540 §300J (25 February 1912) and, as an early indicator of his enthusiasm for the word, the handwritten note he tucked away at the back of his own copy of Albrecht Dieterich's *Nekyia* ("*katábasis* ...!"); also *ST* 365 §572, *KY* 18, 86, *SM* 139–40 §213, *RB* 239 n.96, *SL* 38 §80, 120 §264, *NZ* i 694, ii 1194, *PA* 329 §436 (compare M. Stein's comments, *JAP* 57, 2012, 281), *PR* 508 §828, *MC* 350 §493, *CT* 355 §674. *Nekyia*: see especially *ETG* 103–4 and *PA* 53 n.2; also *SM* 138–9 §§210–13, *SL* 38 §80, 107 §239, *PA* 120 §156, 141 §178, *ACU* 184 §311, *Aion* 209 §327, *ST* 431 §671, *MC* 73 n.211.

[52] On the madness constantly standing behind the thin façade of reasoning, see for example *RB* 298a. For reason as poison, note especially his powerful account of how not only have we all been poisoned but we then proceed to "spread poison and paralysis around us by wanting to train all the world around us to be rational" (*RBu* 280a; cf. *RB* 280b). On a superficial level one could compare the hostile attitude to rationality that manifested in the circles surrounding Stefan George and Ludwig Klages: see e.g. R.E. Norton, *Secret Germany* (Ithaca, NY 2002) 226–8 and, for Jung's relation and reaction to both men, *CT* 181 n.3 (cf. 347 §657) with P. Bishop, *The Dionysian self* (Berlin 1995) 197 n.26, 291, 302–3 and n.7, 309–11. But Gemelli Marciano makes the essential point that what we are confronted with in the *Red book* is far less a question of literary

concepts, or even attitudes, than of hard inner experience (*PSIE* 231–3, 280).

[53] For Jung on "outraged Nature" seeking revenge against "the individual and his rationally ordered world ... for the violence his reason has done to her" see especially *PR* 344 §531 together with the commentaries of bewildered scholars such as L.O. Gómez in *Curators of the Buddha*, ed. D.S. Lopez (Chicago 1995) 199–200. And note also Jung's concluding words to the same paragraph, "Man is never helped in his suffering by what he thinks of for himself; only suprahuman, revealed truth lifts him out of his distress" (an expression of the purest Gnostic sentiment: W.C. Grese, *Corpus hermeticum XIII and early Christian literature*, Leiden 1979, 72, 84). On the apocalyptically destructive powers of reason, cf. e.g. *JL* ii 209 (January 1955); and compare his much earlier comments in the *Red book* contrasting the living experience of God with the "ashes of rationality" (*RBu* 337a, cf. *RB* 339a). As for the passage already cited earlier, where Jung describes embarking on the path of conscious suffering to save the divine from having to suffer "because I wanted God to be alive and free from the suffering man has put on him by loving his own reason more than God's secret intentions", see *PP* 6 (1975) 12; and on his personal sense of needing to balance, or compensate for, everyone else's reasonableness cf. *SL* 704 §1585. Without any doubt, as Walter Odajnyk has been honest enough to point out, nowadays that would include the need to compensate for the reasonableness of many Jungians. Compare his frank comment on Jung's words about all the murderers among the scholars: "Unfortunately, one could add, the same can be said of psychotherapists and psychoanalysts whose rational reductive explanations kill the living spirit and undermine any creative

resolution of the problems they are asked to address" (*PP* 53, 2010, 449).

[54] In a strange monument to lopsided scholarship Sonu Shamdasani cites part of an unpublished letter that Jung wrote to his colleague Josef Lang on 17 January 1918, where he warns Lang about the risks of working with the unconscious, as a plain illustration of Jung's absolute refusal to be dismissive of reason or science (cf. *RBu* 209a and *RB* 207a, unwisely followed by S.L. Drob, *Reading the Red book*, New Orleans 2012, 181). "The danger lies in the delusion of being a prophet which often is the result of working with the unconscious. *It is the devil* who says: 'Be disdainful of reason and science, humanity's supreme power'. This is something we must *never* forget." Shamdasani correctly notes that Jung here is quoting Mephistopheles, the devil in Goethe's *Faust* ("Verachte nur Vernunft und Wissenschaft, Des Menschen allerhöchste Kraft", 1.1851–2: in the original letter Jung writes out these words as verse). But he completely fails to take into account the intense and enduring sympathy Jung felt for Goethe's Mephistopheles (*MDR* 68–9/60–1, 85/80, 221–2/234–5, *JP* 212), not to mention the intimacy of his relationship with the devil (*RB* 259–61). He also omits the previous paragraph of this same letter which, aside from showing how eager Jung was to enlist Lang in the project of presenting a solid scientific foundation for his psychology (cf. *SL* 825), helps as well to highlight how little Jung's own unconscious was ultimately committed to such a project. The multiple mistakes in Shamdasani's English translation at *RB* 207a ("prophet's delusion" instead of "delusion of being a prophet" for "Prophetenwahn", "That is never appropriate" for "Das ist *nie* zu vergessen") are—especially from someone

claiming to be alone in setting true scholarly standards for the study of Jung (*Cult fictions*, London 1998, 112; *JAP* 45, 2000, 469)—inexcusable.

[55] For instance M.H. Barreto makes a noble effort to challenge "the misunderstanding" of Jung as someone who "discards or undervalues reason", and to correct it by quoting Jung's own assurance that "I am far from wishing to belittle the divine gift of reason, man's highest faculty" (*JJ* 9/1, 2015, 37, citing *ACU* 94 §174). But if Barreto had turned back just one page, and taken the trouble to read such a reassuring statement in its context, he would have realized that this apparent exaltation of reason as humanity's divine and highest faculty is dripping with irony. In fact, despite his propitiatory claim to be "far from wishing to belittle the divine gift of reason, man's highest faculty", Jung has just done precisely that—describing how the attachment to rationality derives its power from an "infantile parental complex" which always "turns into sheer intellectuality", and painting the most gruesome picture of reason as emitting "a deceptive light" that "spreads a darkness over all those things which it would be most needful for us to know" (ibid. 93–4 §§173–4; compare his scornful rejection of the worshipful attitude towards reason as "our overwhelming illusion", *SL* 261 §598, as well as his horror at the "rationalistic darkness which will yet extinguish the little lamps of understanding", *JAP* 46, 2001, 194). With equal determination Jung also goes on to do the exact same thing elsewhere, disdainfully mocking the authority of reason while openly dethroning it from its usurped position as humanity's "supreme arbiter" (*PR* 452 §735). Barreto continues to argue for the idea of Jung as a defender of rationalism by quoting his statement that "a relativation of rationalism is needed, but not an abandonment of reason, for the reasonable thing

for us is to turn to the inner man and his vital needs" (*JJ* 9/1, 2015, 37, citing *JL* ii 286). Here too he fails to note the deviousness of Jung's dark subtlety as he twists the very essence of reason inside out and outside in, ironically insisting that the only reasonable course of action is to pursue the one thing reasonableness resists more than anything else: the impulse to turn inside (compare his abrupt use of the same strategy in *QPT* 76; *SD* 380–1 §§738–9). And it's the identical story again when, in one of his seminars, Jung not only praises animals for their reasonableness but sweetly insists that we humans can only become reasonable if we make the effort to imitate them: "for it is very difficult to be reasonable" (*JV* i 168; cf. *JL* i 119). This of course is Jung skilfully and systematically undermining the very basis of rationality by standing on its head the standard western doctrine that animals are *aloga*, beasts deprived of reason.

[56] For underworld as place of paradox in antiquity see e.g. *APMM* 77 with n.27, *IDPW* 67–8; compare Jung's comments linking the spirit of the depths with paradox, *RB* 229b; and on his appreciation for the deliberate ambiguity and multiple meanings of "the ancients" see *RBu* 244 n.144.

[57] The suppression of Jung's strong desire to express a parallelism between his own destiny and the fate of Odysseus in descending to the underworld is, itself, a sorry story. The German edition of *Memories, dreams, reflections* does permit him to reflect broodingly on the solitary destiny that had been assigned to him of performing, "like Odysseus, a *nekyia*, the descent into dark Hades"; but in the American and British versions this has been surgically removed (*ETG* 103–4, cf. *NL* 102 with *RB* 304 n.223 and S. Muramoto, *Spring*, 1987, 166–7). Shamdasani has also dug up an unpublished note,

short but poignant, by Jung's secretary about the central chapter of *Memories, dreams, reflections* called "Confrontation with the unconscious": it states that "The strong excitement Jung underwent still reverberates when he tells of these matters. He proposes as the epigraph for this chapter the quotation from the *Odyssey*, 'Happily escaped from death'" (*JAP* 45, 2000, 465, citing *MDRC* 120 n.1). This comment by Aniela Jaffé is certainly very significant—although Shamdasani seems to be unaware here not only that ever since 1962 it has been included in the published German edition of Jung's biography (*ETG* 180 n.4), but also that the unpublished Protocols on which the biography is based contain Jung's explicit statement recommending these same words from the *Odyssey* be used as an opening quote or motto for the entire book rather than one chapter alone. See *JP* 147 where, straight after being invited to speak openly about the whole scope of his life's work, Jung is recorded as quoting the Homeric saying "Glad to have escaped from death" and noting that in its original Greek wording it would make the most perfect epigram or motto if it could be printed right at the beginning of his autobiography. And yet all these details only add extra force to Shamdasani's conclusion that "with the complete omission of all these statements in the English edition, the Homeric echoes of Jung's confrontation with the unconscious were lost, together with the connection to his numerous references to Odysseus' *nekyia* in the *Collected Works*" (470 n.5). For the source of the Greek words Jung so much wanted to quote from Homer see *Odyssey* 9.63, 9.566, 10.134. On the ancient background to the traditions about Pythagoras' descent into the underworld see W. Burkert, *Phronesis* 14 (1969) 1–30 = *Kleine Schriften* viii (Göttingen 2008) 1–27 and *Lore and science in ancient Pythagoreanism* (Cambridge, MA 1972) 151–61; *APMM*; S. Schorn in *A history of Pythagoreanism*, ed. C.A. Huffman (Cambridge 2014) 300–1; and as a typical example of the persistent attempts by "rational" scholars to keep suppressing any traces of these traditions see now L. Zhmud, *Pythagoras and the early Pythagoreans* (Oxford 2012) 216–18.

[58] Experiencing what happened to Christ in the underworld: *RB* 243b, cf. 304b; L.S. Owens and S.A. Hoeller in *Encyclopedia of psychology and religion* (2nd ed., New York 2014), ed. D.A. Leeming, 979. "Travelling to hell means becoming hell oneself": *RBu* 240a, 244a (cf. *RB* 240b, 244a). Christ, too, became Hell: *RB* 242b. Toshio Kawai offers a frightening example of orthodox Jungian reactions to such statements when he notes that, although Jung's descent into hell was "surely terrible", his account of it shows he "has never lost sight of the position of the ego. This was not a total loss" (*JAP* 57, 2012, 381).

[59] For Rosa's own delightfully caustic comments on the scene see *Lettere inedite di Salvator Rosa a G.B. Ricciardi*, ed. A. de Rinaldis (Rome 1939) 141 §107; also X.F. Salomon in *Salvator Rosa*, ed. H. Langdon (London 2010) 87. Quite predictably the archetypal modern scholar, Carl Huffman, inverts the entire symbolism of the painting: "Pythagoras himself is an obscure figure … What is at the center of the painting and takes up the bulk of the space is the reaction to Pythagoras by the other figures. Thus, the historical Pythagoras may not be as important as the reactions to him" (*A history of Pythagoreanism*, Cambridge 2014, 2). For Huffman's unfailing ability to turn Pythagorean tradition on its head and, regardless of any real cost, sacrifice the most important evidence in the name of some illusory rationality see e.g. *Reading ancient texts*, ed. S.

Stern-Gillet and K. Corrigan (Leiden 2007) i 57–94 and *The Continuum companion to Plato*, ed. G.A. Press (London 2012) 26 together with my warnings in *Classical review* 44 (1994) 294–6 and *SW* 155–8.

[60] For Jung as scientist, and psychology as science, see e.g. S. Shamdasani, *JM* 29–99 along with the surreally one-dimensional essays in *Jung and the question of science*, ed. R.A. Jones (Hove 2014). R. Main in his book *The rupture of time* (Hove 2004) not only was unable to take advantage of the *Red book*'s publication, but also downplayed the complexity of many statements by Jung about science which had already been published. And although he is to be commended for noting Jung's "bold attempt to return to the kind of unitary world-view that had prevailed before the emergence of modern science" (123), his belief that this just involves skipping "two or three centuries of the dominance of reason and science" (2) is more than a little wide of the mark.

[61] See e.g. Jung's letter of 4 December 1931 to Gustav Heyer, carefully insisting on the strategic need to distance Jungian psychology "for quite a long time" from any association with mysticism or parapsychology (H.T. Hakl, *Eranos*, Sheffield 2013, 66), or the angry letter he wrote to Rascher Verlag on 27 July 1957 "claiming that it had been the responsibility of Rascher, as his publisher, to ensure that his psychology was not presented as unscientific, or even alchemical" (P. Bishop, *Seminar* 34, 1998, 381). Bishop goes on to describe not only how Jung's "disciples were manoeuvring in the background to influence the reception of his psychology" but also what a significant role Jung happened to play "in establishing his public image", constantly promoting himself "as a scientist who nonetheless managed to go beyond the boundaries of

conventional science" (381, 384). For more of his perpetual shufflings behind the scenes see D. Bair, *Jung* (Boston 2003) 550–5—as well as independent reports about the lengths Jung would go to and the concealments he would keep operating "in order to preserve his scientific reputation" (P. Brunton, *Reflections on my life and writings* = *The notebooks of Paul Brunton* viii, Burdett, NY 1987, 214).

[62] For personalities no. 1 and no. 2 see *MDR* with *JP* 297–303; also D. Bair, *Jung* (Boston 2003) 15–16. On the correlation of personalities no. 1 and no. 2 with the spirit of this time and the spirit of the depths see S. Shamdasani, *RB* 207–8. Dead systems: *RB* 232b. "True self": *MDR* 55/45. "True life": ibid. 18/4, 214/225. For the spirit of the depths, the spirit of this time, science and reason cf. e.g. *RB* 229b, 234a.

[63] Mark Saban well emphasizes the fundamentally "dual nature of the human personality" according to Jung, a duality which regardless of every Jungian cliché will never in a human's lifetime be outgrown or integrated into a homogenous whole: a dualism of two "radically incompatible" personalities which, although perceived and noticed "only by the very few" (*MDR* 55/45), presents a constant threat to the psyche's unity and sustains a tension that will never be resolved (*How and why we still read Jung*, ed. J. Kirsch and M. Stein, Hove 2013, 17–20). This is the underlying reason why Jung himself always stressed how complicated he was and how full of contradictions he, as well as his work, happened to be. See e.g. *JL* i 441; his letter to E.A. Bennet dated 10 October 1956 (*JAP* 45, 2000, 466); T. Keller, *Inward light* 35 (1972) 11 (cf. *The memoir of Tina Keller-Jenny*, ed. W.K. Swan, New Orleans 2011, 20 §47); D. Bair, *Jung* (Boston 2003) 300.

[64] For the fundamental conflict in Empedocles between two opposing spirits or "daimonic" beings, Aphrodite versus "mad Strife", see *Reality* 345–461; for Aphrodite against Persephone in Parmenides, ibid. 205–20. It will be noted that the competing claims of both spirits have to be balanced in our human awareness and consciously given their places in our lives, just as Jung himself emphasized (*Reality* 215–30, 255–94, 377–487; *RB* 238b). For Jung's early acknowledgement of Empedocles see *ZL* 79 §203 with P. Bishop, *The Dionysian self* (Berlin 1995) 37–8. In the same text he had just evoked Empedocles as a prime example of the "ardent desire for truth" (*ZL* 70 §179), although anyone familiar with Empedocles' writings will realize that his presence and influence on Jung also extend far beyond these two mentions of his name. See e.g. *ZL* 83 §217 ("The elements began to love and hate each other, and multiplicity was born out of their opposition") and even 83 §218 on "the roots of dualism" (for Jung on Empedocles' "roots" cf. *PR* 38 n.9, 167 n.5; *AS* 195 §242). Tellingly, Freud too was very glad to acknowledge Empedocles as anticipating his own most fundamental views about the essential polarity and duality of the human psyche: see G. Tourney, *Bulletin of the history of medicine* 30 (1956) 109–17.

[65] For the imagery of the brass band as symbolic of Jung's superficial and worldly personality no. 1 see his finely accurate self-characterization: *MDR* 204/214. The real-life brass bands that evoked this striking dream image are listed by him in the still unpublished Protocols for his autobiography (*JP* 83–4).

[66] See, for example, Paul Bishop's comments in 1998 (*Seminar* 34, 384) on the active suppression of the *Red book* specifically because it questions the conventional image of Jung as a scientist. Cary de Angulo's personal notes about Jung and his

Red book, dating from the early 1920s, are especially precious in this regard. Note, in particular, her mention of how certain he was that he would totally "lose out" as a scientist if the book was ever published; her reference, again, to his conviction that by publishing it he would permanently exclude himself from being able to enter into battle in "the world of rational science"; and her own wish that there was some way he could make the book available to all the people who need it while at the same time protecting himself against the "stupidity" of those who would reject it (*RB* 212b, 214a; *CBA*). In an excellent demonstration of this stupidity, soon after its publication the Jungian scholar Robert Segal dramatically cursed the *Red book* for expressing "a shocking hatred by Jung of science *per se*" and dismissed it as "an embarrassment" that "should have been kept locked away forever". He even, irony of ironies, cites Aristotle as an eminent example of what Jung should have aspired to be (*IJJS* 6, 2014, 74–9). But in fact all Segal has done is revive, quite unconsciously, the age-old game already played by Aristotle of trying to salvage the respectable parts of Presocratic wisdom while trashing whatever seems "unscientific" or mystical. See *APMM* with my further comments in *ENM* 350–6.

[67] "Took away my belief in science … the inexplicable and paradoxical": *Red book*, folio i verso = *RB* 229b; cf. 238a (Jung begs his soul to protect him from science and keep him far away from the bondage of its cleverness), 267 n.44, 307–8, 313a, 336b. Science as a poison in spite of its advantages: *RB* 278–83. The magical incantations sung "in the ancient manner" ("nach uralter Weise"): 283–6. It will be noted that for ancient Greeks, and especially in the magical or Orphic circles associated with healers like Empedocles, the single word *pharmakon* meant both poison and incantation; remedy as well

as spell. See e.g. D. Collins, *Magic in the ancient world* (Oxford 2008); F. Jourdan, *Revue de l'histoire des religions* 225 (2008) 5–36. Murray Stein has, correctly and very appropriately, connected this dramatic passage in the *Red book* about magical incantations to ancient Orphic traditions (*JAP* 57, 2012, 291–3). For Jung's fascination with these traditions see *JPPF* 4/1 (1912) 167–8, 178, 370–3, 398 = *Psychology of the unconscious* (New York 1916) 133–4, 147, 373–7, 406; *RB* 237 n.83, 301–2 n.211, 327 n.340, 364; Stein 291–4 plus G. Quispel, *Gnostica, Judaica, Catholica* (Leiden 2008) 249–50, 255–60. And note, too, his crucial quotation from Goethe's poem "Urworte. Orphisch" near the start of the *Red book* which has been pointed out by Paul Bishop (*How and why we still read Jung*, ed. J. Kirsch and M. Stein, Hove 2013, 69, citing *RB* 233–4). Jung's own pencil markings inside the books belonging to his personal library (e.g. W. Schultz, *Dokumente der Gnosis*, Jena 1910, lxxxv–lxxxvii; H. Leisegang, *Die Gnosis*, Leipzig 1924, 99; cf. *AN* vii 118) also show his very specific interest in the influence of Orphic lore, particularly relating to the god Phanes, on later Gnosticism. For the direct links between Orphic magical traditions, Parmenides and Empedocles see *APMM*; *IDPW* 62–8, 89–94, 121–3, 132, 212–14; *ENM* 373–80. Empedocles and magical incantations: *APMM* 222, 247–8, 342; *ENM* 395. Parmenides and magic incantations: *IDPW* 119, 141, 170; G. Pugliese Carratelli in *Magna Grecia*, ed. Pugliese Carratelli (Milan 1988) 234–6.

[68] On 3 October 1957 Aniela Jaffé triggered a spirited monologue by Jung about the very same passage in his *Red book*—the Izdubar episode—where the poison and incantations are mentioned (*JP* 147–8). He vividly relives the experience of being forced against his conscious will to write such ridiculous nonsense; complains bitterly about just how much this cost

him; and insists that no one could possibly understand what he had to endure.

[69] For Jung's overriding fear of science see e.g. *JJW* 92: "I am not afraid of communism; I am afraid of unconsciousness and of modern science … The atom bomb is in the hands of unconscious people. It is like giving a baby a kilo of gelignite, it eventually blows itself up" (spoken in 1955). It can be disconcerting to watch how even the most reputable Jung experts assume that, whenever he describes western cultural history as culminating in "modern science", he must be telling a nice "linear narrative of history" based on an optimistic model of evolution which automatically excludes any possible "apocalyptic" ending (cf. e.g. P. Bishop, *Jung's 'Answer to Job'*, Hove 2002, 132: "… although he is deeply attracted to the apocalyptic convictions of some of the texts he is analysing, ultimately he remains committed to a linear narrative of history … 'via alchemy to modern science'"). What they completely, and one could say conveniently, forget is that modern science for Jung had its own apocalyptic as well as catastrophic connotations. See e.g. *PR* 450–1 §§733–4 (modern science's creations "eclipse even the horrors described in the Apocalypse"), 461 §747, 463 §749, and especially the "evolutionary" picture sketched by him in *Modern man in search of a soul*: we as humanity are now "the disappointment of the hopes and expectations of the ages. Think of nearly two thousand years of Christian ideals followed, not by the return of the Messiah and the heavenly millennium, but by the World War among Christian nations with its barbed wire and poison gas. What a catastrophe in heaven and on earth! In the face of such a picture we may well grow humble again. It is true that modern man is a culmination, but tomorrow he will be surpassed. He is indeed the end-product of an age-old

development, but he is at the same time the worst conceivable disappointment of the hopes of mankind. The modern man is conscious of this. He has seen how beneficent are science, technology and organization, but also how catastrophic ..." (London 1933, 230; cf. *CT* 77 §§154–5).

[70] On the diabolical consequences of modern science and technology see e.g. *SL* 567 §1306, ironically addressing "the benevolent god of science" who has "produced the most diabolical war machinery" (spoken in 1936); *PR* 48 §85, "Look at the devilish engines of destruction. They are invented by completely innocuous gentlemen" (1937); M. Serrano, *C.G. Jung and Hermann Hesse* (London 1966) 53 = *JS* 397, "The more successful we become in science and technology, the more diabolical are the uses to which we put our inventions and discoveries" (1959).

[71] See e.g. R.I. Evans, *Jung on elementary psychology* (New York 1976) 147, 217 = *JS* 333 ("Everyone who says I am a mystic is just an idiot"), *JL* ii 290, *JJW* 46; A. Jaffé, *Was C.G. Jung a mystic?* (Einsiedeln 1989) 1; M.–L. von Franz, *PP* 38 (1998) 15; S. Shamdasani, *JM* 1, 101. Freud had already worked hard to make Jung sensitive to the slightest accusation of being a mystic. See his letter to him dated 12 May 1911 about "dem Schimpf 'Mystiker'", the ultimate insult of being called a mystic (*FJ* 466 §255F), as well as his letters to Alphonse Maeder dated 21 September 1913 (*Schweizerische Zeitschrift für Psychologie* 15, 1956, 117) and to Ernest Jones dated 19 May 1921 (*The complete correspondence of Sigmund Freud and Ernest Jones, 1908–1939*, ed. R.A. Paskauskas, Cambridge, MA 1993, 424). Last, but not least, see Jung himself: *IJP* 25 and *FP* 339 §781, where he humorously sticks the label of "mystic" back onto Freud.

[72] Letter written in 1926 and, as Gerhard Adler calmly notes, "not published in the selections now available": *PP* 6 (1975) 12. For the common knowledge during Jung's lifetime that he kept his mystical side a secret, note e.g. Paul Brunton's record of the time Jung privately admitted to him in his home at Küsnacht "that he kept his mystical belief and experience secret in order to preserve his scientific reputation" (*Reflections on my life and writings* = *The notebooks of Paul Brunton* viii, Burdett, NY 1987, 214; for Brunton's visit cf. *JL* i 236 n.); and compare the similar admissions by colleagues and family as recorded in *The fountain of the love of wisdom*, ed. E. Kennedy–Xypolitas (Wilmette 2006) 318 (von Franz), 321 (Jung's son Franz). "People nowadays … defective understanding": C.G. Jung, *Symbolik des Geistes* (Zurich 1948) 422–3, cf. *PR* 184 §274; and compare the wording of his letter to J.B. Rhine in 1935 (*JL* i 190).

[73] See already the opening paragraph of the *Red book* where the spirit of the depths is introduced as possessing a "greater power", throughout all time, than the spirit of this time (*RB* 229b: "höhere Macht"); *RB* 233b (the spirit of the depths surpasses and dominates the spirit of this time, which in comparison is ineffective and invalid), 239 n.91. For no. 2 personality as far more valid and powerful than no. 1 see especially Jung's crucial explanation at *JP* 302 of how, while no. 1 personality keeps rushing towards one thing or craving another, no. 2 will say something altogether different but that's what matters ("aber das gilt"); and while anybody identifying with personality no. 1 is bound to be haunted by constant feelings of uncertainty due to living in an unpredictable and relative world, what counts ("was gilt") is the world of no. 2. Mark Saban is only very partly correct in claiming that, of Jung's two personalities, "neither is more 'real' nor more

fundamental than the other"; and from a practical point of view he is altogether wrong in denying that Jung considered personality no. 1 "in any way inferior or subservient to personality No. 2" (*How and why we still read Jung*, ed. J. Kirsch and M. Stein, Hove 2013, 20–1). Significantly, just as with Jung, the story is the same with Empedocles: the hidden principle of Strife, his spirit of the depths, is what will ultimately always have the final word on every level by returning each part of existence to its primordial nature or "root" (*ENM* 384–6, 392–4; *Reality* 347–453).

[74] For Jung's fiery denunciation of Freudian rationalism, in particular, as a "bastard of a science" because it's simply a very respectable attempt at "blocking off and protecting oneself" from the huge dangers of making the journey into the unconscious see *JB* i 185 (cf. *JL* i 141). Note here, in the contrast he draws between the illegitimacy of modern rational science and the journey of medieval knights on their sacred quest, his obvious allusion to the legends of the Grail. For the genealogy of his vivid bastard imagery see the opening to Otto Rank's famous June 1924 lecture at the University of Pennsylvania (*A psychology of difference*, Princeton 1996, 51–2; E.J. Lieberman, *Acts of will*, New York 1985, xxvii).

[75] "Rather, it is the solution …": P. Bishop, *Carl Jung* (London 2014) 15. And compare S. Shamdasani's tentative comment, referring to the episode in the *Red book* where western science is described as a poison that has to be counteracted by incantations: "Jung tries to construct a new science that will no longer wound or lame Izdubar. He's trying to construct a new science that redeems or provides new access to the ancient" (*JAP* 57, 2012, 375).

[76] See Jung's classic comments on the role of "primordial experience" in art: *SM* 90–8 §§141–52; and for his own, inner experience of returning to the "primordial beginning" see *RB* 247a, 251a. The fashionable attempt to reduce him to a "textual Jung", conveniently cutting away the raw dimension of experience from his life and work, is made by P. Bishop: *Carl Jung* (London 2014) 18–21. But Sonu Shamdasani too—aside from his gratuitous and irrelevant mention of a "primal scream"—sadly shows how little he understands of Jung when he claims that in the "depths, we do not find pure experience as such, no 'primal scream', but biblical and classical figures" (*C.G. Jung: a biography in books*, New York 2012, 100). If only he had read carefully the passage from Jung that he himself cites, he would have found him saying just the opposite: "the primordial experience … is so dark and amorphous that it requires the related mythological imagery to give it form. In itself it is wordless and imageless ... It is nothing but a tremendous intuition striving for expression. It is like a whirlwind that seizes everything within reach and assumes visible form as it swirls upward …" (*SM* 96–7 §151, cf. 91–2 §143). For the process of discovering the words and the imagery needed to convey a primordial experience of the depths see also *Red book*, folio i verso (poorly translated at *RB* 230b) with *PSIE* 231.

[77] On the word *physikos*, its particular meanings and applications, see Marcel Mauss' simple but elegant comments in *A general theory of magic* (London 1972) 143; A. Dieterich, *Abraxas* (Leipzig 1891) 51 n.2 (a book unique in its importance for Jung: *RB* 349 n.93); *APMM* 229; *IDPW* 140–6 (for the significance of Parmenides being called *physikos*) with the detailed bibliography on the word at 248. For Jung's repeated, and emphatic, declaration that his own interests were purely

empirical as opposed to metaphysical—"I observe, I classify, I establish relations and sequences between the observed data" (*JL* ii 567)—see e.g. B. Hannah, *Jung, his life and work* (New York 1976) 78, S. Shamdasani, *JM* 99. No one in this connection stops to consider that, for centuries and millennia, those experts who specialized in empirical as opposed to metaphysical issues were traditionally the magicians (Mauss 139–44; *APMM* 227–32).

[78] Aniela Jaffé had initially wanted her biography of Jung to start with him explaining how much he valued repetition because "My thinking is circular; I circle around questions repeatedly. That method is congenial to me …". But, as Shamdasani has noted, the passage was omitted and this means "something rather central to Jung's self-understanding landed up on the cutting floor" (*Spring* 57, 1995, 124, referring to *MDRC* v). For the German original of Jung's comments here on repetition and circularity see *JP* 260/275; and for Jung on the importance of "circular thinking" especially in Gnostic or alchemical tradition compare e.g. *PR* 96 n.59, *AS* 84 §§110–11, *MC* 102 §123 with n.54.

[79] Repetition and circularity in the writings of Parmenides and Empedocles: Parmenides fr. 3 Diels = fr. 12 Gemelli Marciano; Empedocles frs. 24–5 Diels; J.P. Hershbell, *Classical journal* 63 (1968) 351–7; L. Ballew, *Phronesis* 19 (1974) 190–6; D.W. Graham, *Classical quarterly* 38 (1988) 305; G.M. De Rubeis, *Studi classici e orientali* 41 (1991) 87–93; *ENM* 334 with n.2, 358–9, 363, 370–1. On their underlying role and function see *IDPW* 118–27, 246, *ENM* 379–80 with n.111, *Reality* 34–6; L. Gemelli Marciano, *Ancient philosophy* 28 (2008) 32–45 and *PSIE* 58–9, 71–103, 267–70; also M. Detienne and J.-P.

Vernant, *Les ruses de l'intelligence* (Paris 1974) 51–6, 261–304 with J.M. Rahm, *Deconstructing the western worldview* (PhD thesis, University of Alaska Fairbanks 2014) 12, 26, 44, 62, 86, 118. For scholars' brutish impatience with repetition as used, especially, by Parmenides cf. H. Diels, *Parmenides: Lehrgedicht* (Berlin 1897) 23–5 ("careless … naïve … amateurish"), A.P.D. Mourelatos, *The route of Parmenides* (2nd ed., Las Vegas 2008) 35 ("almost puerile … awkward and pointless … expressive failure"); and on repetition's altogether unhealthy associations with "archaic thought" see B.A. van Groningen, *Mnemosyne* 24 (1971) 179. Parmenides as a *iatromantis*: *IDPW* 101–230; and for the healing power of a *iatromantis'* words cf. e.g. *euêkea baxin* at Empedocles fr. 112.11 Diels = fr. 157.16 Gemelli Marciano with *APMM* 220 n.7. One other aspect of repetition which may become familiar to readers of this book is the ancient habit of touching on a theme or subject very briefly to begin with, only to return to it later—each time filling in more of the missing details and helping to make the implicit just a little bit more explicit (Diels, *Parmenides* 22–4; *ENM* 371).

[80] See especially his letter to Zwi Werblowsky dated 17 June 1952 (*JL* ii 69–71); also *RB* 244b with n.142, 268–70, 302 n.211, *AS* 162–3 §199, *PA* 15–16 §18. With characteristic earthiness Jung emphasizes that real ambiguity involves far more than verbal games—note his comment in the *Red book* on how easy it is to play at ambiguity, but how hard to live it (*RB* 244b)—although of course his warning has done nothing whatsoever to stop modern Jungians from engaging in the soulless mental gymnastics of post-structuralist "indeterminacy" (M. Saban in *How and why we still read Jung*, ed. J. Kirsch and M. Stein, Hove 2013, 6–25).

[81] Gerhard Adler, for example, cites the words Jung wrote to Werblowsky about ambiguity in June 1952 simply so that he can distinguish his attitude from the "clear, systematic, technical way of thinking" of Freud (*Selected letters of C.G. Jung*, Princeton 1984, vii–viii)—as if the significance of Jung's writing style can only be grasped in the context of a relationship ended forty years earlier. Otherwise there is more than a little tension between Jung's own emphasis on the crucial importance of ambiguity and the predictable rush by Jungians, especially in North America, to make his message as clear and plain and simple to digest as possible. No one stops to ponder the dangers posed by Edward Edinger's altogether commendable efforts ("Many people compare his writings to those of Jung but find him much easier to read") to strip Jung's ideas of their ambiguities and transform them into something "more accessible to the general reader", "easier to grasp" (T.B. Kirsch, *The Jungians*, London 2000, 71, 101). And meanwhile Jung's explicit statements about the vital need for ambiguity are conveniently forgotten by scholars so that they can turn back undisturbed to their task of criticizing him for the confused, murky, nebulous and unsystematic nature of his writing (so e.g. P. Bishop, *Jung's 'Answer to Job'*, Hove 2002, 132; R. Main, *The rupture of time*, Hove 2004; J. Mills, *IJJS* 5, 2013, 19–43).

[82] For intentional ambiguity in Presocratic philosophy see e.g. P. Merlan, *Kleine philosophische Schriften* (Hildesheim 1976) 4–5; *APMM* and *ENM* 362–81; G. Costa in *Linguistica è storia*, ed. S. Marchesini and P. Poccetti (Pisa 2003) 73 and *Ainigma e griphos*, ed. S. Monda (Pisa 2012) 56–68. On unsolvable riddles, ambiguity and initiation into the mysteries of the underworld cf. *IDPW*; *ENM* 378. This is of course worlds apart from the mentality of most later Platonists, who

spent their time "ferreting out" the ambiguities of much older philosophers and claiming to be able to unravel them in the brilliant light of reasoning (J.M. Dillon and W. Polleichtner, *Iamblichus of Chalcis: The letters*, Atlanta 2009, 14–15, 70). "Avoid ambiguity! ...": Aristotle, *Rhetoric* 1407a32–7 (abbreviated); cf. H. Diels, *Kleine Schriften zur Geschichte der antiken Philosophie* (Hildesheim 1969) 177 with n.3, *APMM* 43–4 and *ENM* 370 n.85. The passage is, naturally, very valuable in showing that ambiguity as well as repetition was linked with circularity. For Empedocles as prophet and *iatromantis* see especially frs. 112.10–11 and 146 Diels = frs. 157.15–16 and 184 Gemelli Marciano with *APMM* 220 n.7, 344–5, 382–3, *IDPW* 206–7 and *ENM* 343 with n.19, 380, plus e.g. M. Garani, *Empedocles redivivus* (New York 2007) 3–4. In deciding to question whether Empedocles considered himself a prophet, M.A. Flower (*The seer in ancient Greece*, Berkeley 2008, 81 n.23) inexplicably forgets to read the texts he himself refers to (*mantosunai* belong by definition to a *mantis*). Far more reliable guidance is offered by James Olney, who astutely bestows the title of *iatromantis* on both Empedocles and Jung: *The rhizome and the flower* (Berkeley 1980) 155–7.

[83] On the quintessential role of ambiguity in Parmenides' logic see *Reality* 15–306, 401, 565, 577 with *ENM* 369–81. Jung on "this petty reasoning mind, which cannot endure any paradoxes": *PA* 16 §19. It should be remembered that Jung specifically praised the "ancients" for their mastery of ambiguity and multiple meanings (*RBu* 244 n.144, cf. *RB* 244 n.143).

[84] Jung on the "so-called autobiography": *JL* ii 550; D. Bair, *Jung* (Boston 2003) 606, 639–40; S. Shamdasani, *JSB* 35. And for Jung's protests at the "auntification" of his own words

see A.C. Elms, *Uncovering lives* (New York 1994) 51–70; Shamdasani, *Spring* 57 (1995) 129–31; Bair 611–15, 632–6. With regard to the still unpublished Protocols, Jung's secretary and editor Aniela Jaffé would later go out of her way to deny that they correspond exactly or word for word to what he himself had said while being questioned and interviewed by her: see her letter of 26 November 1981 to William McGuire as well as her covering letter to the Library of Congress dated October 1983, both filed on open access with the library's copy of the Protocols. But one has to realize that she had the strongest legal reasons for asserting at least some degree of creativity in producing them because—throughout her extended battle with Jung's family to claim copyright of this original autobiographical material for herself—she had to maximize in every possible way the importance and extent of her own contributions while paradoxically minimizing the extent and importance of his. This is not even to mention the psychological difficulties she clearly ran into through her work on Jung's biography, suffering a "gigantic inflation of the ego" and ending up as confused as "a hypnotized bunny" (Bair 599, 606). At any rate her later reminiscence, in the letter to McGuire, of how Jung had talked to her by following a kind of "Freudian line of associations" (cf. Shamdasani, *Spring* 57, 1995, 123) agrees down to the smallest detail with what one still finds in the Protocols; and there is Ximena de Angulo Roelli's significant comment, too, that reading them for the first time was just like hearing Jung himself talk again. In fact, as she notes, his characteristic rhythms are so intact that Jaffé must have been extremely accurate and careful in preserving what he had said (letter to William McGuire dated 1 October 1979, held in the same files).

[85] *JP* 147. For Jung's method of free association here in replying to Aniela Jaffé's question, see her letter to William McGuire dated 26 November 1981 (Library of Congress); S. Shamdasani, *Spring* 57 (1995) 123–4.

[86] Note, for example, how the enormous metallic volumes containing the entirety of Jung's knowledge are presented to him not by the spirit of the depths—but by the spirit of his time. See *Red book*, folio i verso (*RB* 230b); and compare folio ii verso (*RB* 233b) on all learning and scholarly erudition belonging, by definition, to the spirit of this time.

[87] For a fine recent discussion of Jung's "ordering mind", and its role in converting the chaotic contents of the unconscious into their opposite, see M. Stein, *Minding the self* (Hove 2014) 64–75. Stein's study also has the virtue of showing how easy it can be to choose between opposing perspectives when explaining what happened to Jung during his period of descent into the underworld. Very humanly Stein describes how Jung "decided to follow what he called 'the Spirit of the Depths'" (66), even though Jung himself explains that he never had any choice in the matter at all (cf. e.g. *JP* 145, 173). Or as he says right at the start of the *Red book*, he has "no choice" because the spirit of the depths "forces … possesses a greater power … subjugated … took away … robbed … forced … took …" (*RB* 229b)—in just the same way that Parmenides emphasizes right at the start of his own account how he was irresistibly taken into the underworld, "carried … carried … carried …" (Parmenides fr. 1.1–4 Diels = fr. 8A.7–10 Gemelli Marciano; *IDPW* 53–4, 119–20, *ENM* 370–9, *Reality* 26–7, 34–6, *SW* 90, 103–7). All due respect and acknowledgement absolutely have to be

paid to Jung's classic statement that "a real settlement with the unconscious demands a firmly opposed conscious standpoint" (*TE* 213 §342), although in reality there are various different levels involved. And when (e.g. *JP* 169) he warns against overvaluing the unconscious he is referring, very specifically, to the dangers of identifying with it or being devoured by it.

[88] The crucial sentence here in the Protocols is "Das ist die Leidenschaft, die in diesem Feuer lag, dieser Lavastrom, der hat's erzwungen und alles hat sich dann ganz natürlicherweise eingeordnet" (*JP* 149; Jaffé had started typing the words "was ich dann" after "und alles" and before "hat sich dann", but crossed them out). Jaffé has completely missed the point of this sentence in rewriting it for the published German version of Jung's biography ("und die Leidenschaft, die in seinem Feuer lag, hat mein Leben umgeformt und angeordnet", *ETG* 203), while the English version only carries her misunderstanding a step further: "and the heat of its fires reshaped my life" (*MDR* 190/199, cf. *MDRC* 145). Of course these are beautifully inspiring new–age sentiments; but they are not what Jung had meant, or said. Otherwise, comparing this page of the Protocols with the corresponding pages of the published German or English biographies offers a valuable insight into Aniela Jaffé's working method. She inverts the order and sequence of more or less every single sentence, almost systematically reversing Jung's own flow. Also—a major exhibit for anyone studying the arts of mistranslation—she replaces Jung's mention of his initial wish to bring the seething material of the unconscious together into a coherent and orderly world ("in eine Welt einzuordnen": clearly he meant "world" here in the ancient Greek sense of an ordered *kosmos*) with the altogether different idea that he had wanted to incorporate it

"into the contemporary picture of the world" (*MDR* 190/199; cf. *JP* 144, 169). And she personalizes what for Jung was a statement of principle, that out of the fiery lava emerges solid stone and then out of the solid stone it becomes possible to create something, by replacing it with the simple declaration that he himself was able to work on the stone (this sentence has been struck out of the English text). With regard to Jung's principle, and how it actually works for someone who stays conscious of all three phases during this process of creating something out of stone, we have his own account of what happened when he worked on carving the famous stone at Bollingen. First he became aware that the stone was looking at him; and from then on, in the inscriptions he carved, he just allowed the stone to speak (*MDR* 214–16/226–8; cf. *JL* ii 290: without thinking "I just brought into shape what I saw on its face"). On the other hand, regarding the destructive effects of Jaffé's often arbitrary and chaotic method in reworking for publication the original statements made by Jung, see already S. Shamdasani, *JAP* 45 (2000) 465–6 and *JSB* 29; D. Bair, *Jung* (Boston 2003) 778 n.87.

[89] "Ich wollte etwas leisten in meiner Wissenschaft und bin dann auf diesen Lavastrom gestossen, und der hat dann alles angeordnet" (*JP* 149); Jung expresses himself in more conventional language at *JP* 177, *RB* 190/360. The mistranslation is Shamdasani's (*JM* 22), who ironically on the very same page—as often elsewhere—criticizes the English *Collected works* for the shoddy quality of their translations from Jung's German.

[90] For Parmenides, illusions and deceptions, his role as prophet along with the game of being human, and the manipulations

as well as mistranslations of his words, see *Reality* 9–306. Well worth mentioning in this context is the process by which the goddess' original demand that Parmenides should yield, without a moment's doubt or hesitation, to the irresistible force of her persuasion became corrupted into the philosophically far more acceptable command to "judge for yourself by reason"—even though this corrupted version of the text is impossible to justify on any rational or philological grounds. But, as usual, scholars will still go to the most ridiculously irrational lengths in the effort to support their rationalistic misreadings. See *Reality* 117–44, 566–9; *PSIE* 84–90, 215–29; and for similar examples of specialists falsifying ancient texts and other evidence in the name of some spurious "rationality", repeating their predecessors' flagrant mistakes from century to century simply because they are unable to face what that ancient evidence was wanting to say, compare e.g. *ENM* 353–6, 399–401.

[91] *JP* 174 (12 October 1957). Shamdasani mentions this fear of being torn apart, very misleadingly, right at the end of a paragraph about Jung's "problem of what to do with Toni Wolff"—implying to any casual reader that it stemmed from the internal conflicts and tensions in their relationship (*Spring* 57, 1995, 125). But Jung makes it perfectly clear that what he is afraid of is of being torn apart by the overwhelming power of the many archetypal forces or voices, such as Philemon, who are rising up and speaking through him: in other words, the various beings who appear throughout the *Red book*. See especially *JP* 144–5 and 174–5 (Philemon); also Cary de Angulo's draft letter to Jung dated 30 January 1924, recording how Jung told her he had been "very nearly torn asunder" in the battle between the world of physical reality and the world

of spirit (*RB* 213b; *CBA*). As for Toni Wolff: at this stage, with her "bird-fluttering", she was little more than a helpless and disoriented bystander who was unable to guide or reassure him in any meaningful way (draft letter from de Angulo to Jung dated 26 January 1924: *RB* 213b, *CBA*; cf. *JP* 171–1). Well worth noting, in this context, is Jung's own association of lava imagery with insanity: *JV* i 594–5; compare also Virginia Woolf's "Madness is terrific I can assure you … and in its lava I still find most of the things I write about" (*The letters of Virginia Woolf* iv, ed. N. Nicolson, London 1978, 180; C. MacKenna in *Insanity and divinity*, ed. J. Gale, M. Robson and G. Rapsomatioti, Hove 2014, 72).

[92] "… Aber es war eine dämonische Kraft in mir": *JP* 174. The sentence, as well as Jung's immediate thought process, ends abruptly here. Once again, Aniela Jaffé shows her true colours in the version she helps to cook up for the published biography (*ETG* 180; *MDR* 171/177). Naturally she leaves out any mention of Jung clinging to tables. From elsewhere she introduces comparisons to Nietzsche and Hölderlin (cf. e.g. *JP* 149, 227), shifting onto a literary and philosophical level his grimly raw account of the day-to-day struggle for sheer survival. Then she becomes Jung's cheerleader-in-chief, replacing his statements of fear and terror with the bold assertion that he had never entertained a single doubt; has him affirm his "unswerving conviction that I was obeying a higher will" which offers a notable contrast to his own confession that everything for him had seemed impossible until, immersed in a horrific darkness, he realized his only hope was to obey a higher will and endure even though he didn't understand one single thing (*JP* 171); and ends her paragraph with his dramatic celebration that he "had mastered the task", "der

Bewältigung der Aufgabe", which is something Jung himself at the time considered unachievable ("die ich selber nicht bewältigen konnte", *JP* 149). But none of this comes even close to the way in which she inserts a comma right at the end of Jung's crucial statement that "there was a daimonic power in me", before making him go straight on to add "and from the beginning there was no doubt in my mind that I must find the meaning of what I was experiencing in these fantasies" (cf. *JP* 175)—demonstrating with her busy "improvements" that she didn't have a clue what Jung had meant by daimonic power. In fine collegial spirit Gerhard Adler praises Aniela Jaffé for "her complete grasp" of Jung's theoretical ideas (*JL* i and ii xviii); but predictably he says nothing about her far-from-complete grasp of the realities behind those ideas.

[93] See for this *MDR* 181–2/189 and *JP* 226–7. Of course not many of us will want to consider in any depth what the snapshot of a man who has to recite his own address just to convince himself that he exists, or the fact of having a wife and five children, really tells us about his state of mind at the time. It will be noted that, although Jung refers throughout the whole passage to his family alone, three times this has been changed by his editors and publishers to "my family and my professional work" or "my family and my profession". Aside from that, calling his family a "joyful reality" in the English version of his biography (*MDR* 182/189, repeated by Shamdasani: *Lament of the dead*, New York 2013, 72) is not only rather too strong a translation of Jung's own "beglückende Realität" but is hardly a true description of his family life at the time (*NL* 100–1, 110).

[94] This explanatory stance is best exemplified nowadays by the discussion held between Sonu Shamdasani and James

Hillman: *Lament of the dead* (New York 2013) 69–72. Of course it has been aided immensely by the heroic spin Aniela Jaffé introduced into the published biography.

[95] See for example Jung's letter to Michael Fordham dated 18 April 1946 and published now in *JSB* 48–9.

[96] The classic definitions of *daimonios* offered by S. Tromp de Ruiter are still a good starting-point for understanding the daimonic in Homer: *De vocis quae est 'Daimôn' apud Homerum significatione atque usu* (Amsterdam 1918) 169 ("whoever is led or carried along by some divine or numinous power … and whose character and abilities exceed the limits of humanity due to the working of an occult power"), 169 n.1 ("only as a result of divine influence"; "'Daimonic', ever since the time of Homer, means any individual who seems to draw on an inexplicable source and every influence which is experienced as superhuman"), 171 ("not of one's own will but due to a certain hidden power"). The daimonic in Parmenides: O. Gilbert, *Archiv für Geschichte der Philosophie* 20 (1907) 25–45 with *ENM* 370–1. In Empedocles: M. Detienne, *La notion de 'daïmôn' dans le pythagorisme ancien* (Paris 1963) with W. Burkert, *Gnomon* 36 (1964) 563–7; L. Gemelli Marciano, *Aevum antiquum* 1 (2001) 205–35; *Reality* 358–65. In Aristotle: P.J. van der Eijk, *Medicine and philosophy in classical antiquity* (Cambridge 2005) 145 n.27 ("The 'daemonic' … consists in the fact that it escapes rational control"), 191–2 ("'beyond human control', the opposite, so to speak, of 'human'"), 247 n.30. In Freud: D. Kalsched, *The inner world of trauma* (Hove 1996). For the daimonic in Jung see *RB* 264b (the daimonic lies beyond all the pretty appearances of our visible world), *JV* i 257, *JL* i 344 (defining it as "an unconscious content of seemingly overwhelming power" linked

to "possession") and ii 487 ("compelling"; ever since "ancient times" it has been understood that "no amount of reason can conjure" it magically away), 531–2 ("To hell with the Ego–world!"), *MDR* 328/356 ("There was a daimon in me ... it overpowered me") and 387–9 = *RB* 352–3. On the daimonic inheritance, the mysterious nature that Jung inherited from his mother in all its primordial ruthlessness and power, see *MDR* 59–60/50 with J. Sherry, *Carl Gustav Jung: avant-garde conservative* (New York 2010) 19; and contrast James Hillman's predictably kitsch rendering of Jung's "daimonic inheritance" for the American spirit of our time (*Sphinx* 1, 1988, 9–19).

[97] Compare especially *MC* 350 §493, where Jung cites the Latin version of the saying—*natura naturam vincit*—in describing the primordial "conflict of opposites" that acts itself out when the adept is "drawn involuntarily into the drama" of the unconscious as the direct result of a *katabasis*, or descent into the underworld. See also ibid. 29 n.152, 79 §86, 264 n.23; *AS* 77 §102, 161 §198, 321 §426; *PPT* 262 §469; *ACU* 130 §234; *Aion* 159 §244. Basic references for the original Greek saying are *Physici et medici graeci minores*, ed. I.L. Ideler ii (Berlin 1842) 214.15–215.14; *Collection des anciens alchimistes grecs*, ed. M. Berthelot (Texte grec, Paris 1887–88) 20.6, 43.20–1, 57.14–15; H. Diels, *Antike Technik* (2nd ed., Leipzig 1920) 131 and *Die Fragmente der Vorsokratiker*, ed. Diels and W. Kranz, ii (6th ed., Berlin 1952) 219.20–1; J. Bidez and F. Cumont, *Les mages hellénisés* (Paris 1938) i 203–4, 244–6, ii 313–21; A.-J. Festugière, *La révélation d'Hermès Trismégiste* i (2nd ed., Paris 1950) 228–37, 433–4; J.P. Hershbell, *Ambix* 34 (1987) 12–14 = *Alchemy and early modern chemistry*, ed. A.G. Debus (London 2004) 70–2; M. Martelli, *The 'four books' of pseudo-Democritus* (Leeds 2013).

[98] See e.g. Jung's comments to Miguel Serrano in May 1959 about someone who "worked with me for a while, but he was unable to follow through to the end. The path is very difficult ..." (*C.G. Jung and Hermann Hesse*, London 1966, 61); or to Esther Harding in May 1960, "People may have to go back to the Church when they reach a certain stage of analysis. Individuation is only for the few ..." (*Quadrant* 8/2, Winter 1975, 17). "The strongest and best ... the maternal abyss": *TE* 169–70 §261 = 287 §477.

[99] With the "dämonische Kraft" at *JP* 174 compare especially the "ursprünglichen und darum dämonisch wirkenden Kraft" of the medieval magician, *Psychologische Typen* (17th ed., Solothurn 1994) 197 §316; cf. 219 §347 and 239 §383 ("als dämonischer Mächte ... als Zauber, als mit magischer Kraft geladen"). For the intimate connection between the "daimonic" and magic see also *RB* 240b; *TE* 96–7 §§153–5; *JL* ii 82. The idea of a special magical, or non-human, power accessible to certain humans is one of the main themes that drew Jung to ancient Gnosticism: note e.g. his deliberate underlining of the word "Kraft" in the copy he owned of Hans Leisegang's *Die Gnosis*, at the point where Leisegang is explaining the extraordinary powers of Simon Magus (Leipzig 1924, 61). And note, too, Jung's dramatic description of the magician as a being of pure mystery who is "superior in strength to all men" ("an Stärke allen Männern überlegen"): *RB* 328–9. Of course the mistake of rendering "dämonische Kraft" as "demonic strength" in the published English version of his biography (*MDR* 171/177: contrast the original and more accurate rendering at *MDRC* 120) is, considering all the modern nuances of the word "demonic", an even worse distortion of what Jung had meant by these words; but the verbal landscape

has already been so scarred and disfigured here that a bit more damage makes little difference.

[100] *C.G. Jung and Hermann Hesse* (London 1966) 82, 61, 64.

NOTES TO PART 2

[1] See Walter Odajnyk's finely perceptive comments on how—in service to the spirit of the depths and also in a movement directly parallel to the traditional withdrawal of mystics into monasteries or deserts—Jung himself "would have to withdraw into the desert, into a monastery. In time, Jung's need for a withdrawal from the world so as to nurture the terrible secret he carried was realized with the construction of his hermitage at Bollingen" (*PP* 53, 2010, 450–1). It will be noted, too, that the highly unusual living arrangements which were to make such a powerful impression on Jung as a child when he visited the hermitage of the famous Swiss mystic Brother Klaus or Nicholas of Flüe were also the first and most obvious inspiration for the living arrangements he would later recreate at Bollingen. What a good idea, Jung was already thinking as a young boy, to have one's family in one house and live the life of a saintly hermit in another building which would be somewhat distant but not too far away—"with a pile of books, and a table for writing, and an open fire …" (*ETG* 84; cf. *MDR* 84–5/78–9).

[2] Bollingen as Jung's "tiny private psycho–Disneyland": Wolfgang Giegerich, *JJTP* 6/1 (2004) 48, reiterated years later

by his claim that in reality Bollingen for Jung was nothing but a false "simulation" or "cloud-cuckoo-land" (*IJJS* 4, 2012, 14–15). For the hollowness of Giegerich's theorizing see, aside from his own writings, Sophia Heller's *The absence of myth* (Albany 2006); and for a pithy reply to Giegerich, Murray Stein's comments in *Initiation*, ed. T. Kirsch, V.B. Rutter and T. Singer (Hove 2007) 87–91. There are few greater ironies than Giegerich's own failure to realize that the imaginary "logic" on which he bases his entire posturing—the narrative of an evolutionary push from *mythos* into *logos*, from myth into rationality—is itself an outdated myth which has become completely obsolete. See e.g. *APMM* with G.W. Most in *From myth to reason?*, ed. R. Buxton (Oxford 1999) 25–47. "The ten thousand worthless things ...": Empedocles fr. 110.6–7 Diels = fr. 156.8–9 Gemelli Marciano; *ENM* 353.

[3] "Too many people live with an image ..." and "fantasy relationships": Gerhard Adler in *JSB* 65. Only after speaking at Eranos did I come across my notebook from 1985 containing the full details exactly as I had recorded them. Needless to say, in describing what happened on that night I have absolutely no intention of condoning—let alone encouraging—trespassers. Even Jung himself had more than enough trouble with unwanted visitors at Bollingen while he was still alive (D. Bair, *Jung*, Boston 2003, 324). But it seems that whoever, or whatever, wanted me there had some very different concerns.

[4] *JP* 308–9. The published biography does allow Jung to mention twice, in passing, the dream image of a knight (*MDR* 160–1/164–5, 167/172–3). But here, in the unpublished Protocols, he brings both of those dream occurrences together during the course of an extended commentary on that very same dream about his search for the Grail which—

uncoincidentally—we soon will come to. In the process of doing so, he explains that this dream figure of the knight represents his own ancient forefather or ancestor; describes how the Grail is a reward for living the life of a true knight and how one can only set off in quest of the Grail after inwardly being accepted as abiding by the rules for becoming a knight; and emphasizes in no uncertain terms that the mysterious gift of the Grail received by a knight is the deepest secret possible for a human which is the true secret, or mystery, of individuation. Neither is there anything coincidental about the fact that the archetypal figure of the knight, along with the equally archetypal rules of chivalry bound up with traditions surrounding the Grail, were also of the most fundamental importance for Henry Corbin in both his life and his work. See e.g. *Face de Dieu, face de l'homme* (Paris 1983) 31, 208–31; *EJ* 39 (1970) 87 with nn.32–3, 92, 140; ibid., 40 (1971) 311–56 with *IDPW* 217–19; *EII* iv 178, 390–460; Corbin and M. Sarraf, *Traités des compagnons–chevaliers* (Tehran 1973); *Cahiers de l'Université Saint Jean de Jérusalem* 1 (1974) 8–9, 25–51 with R. de Châteaubriant, ibid. 13–23, 5 (1978) 166–9, and C. Jambet, ibid. 10 (1983) 49–67; R. Bosnak, *SFJI* 7/1 (Winter 1987) 26. As a matter of fact one could say that the entire encounter and friendship between Corbin and Jung was governed by their ancestral values of chivalry, about which most people nowadays who try to discuss Jung's relationship with Corbin sadly no longer have the remotest understanding.

[5] For the inscription *Quaero quod impossibile* at Bollingen see the unique report by Fowler McCormick in *Carl Gustav Jung, 1875–1961: a memorial meeting* (New York 1962) 13, who rightly calls attention to its "challenging words"; also *MH* 1:16:05–22. About the forgotten art of working with the impossible I already wrote a little treatise several years ago

(*SW*). Interestingly, the identical Latin saying is quoted by Victor White in a letter he wrote to Jung during June 1948 (*JW* 125). White's mention here of this very same saying, which is unattested anywhere in classical Latin literature, implies that he had come face to face with the carved inscription during one of his earliest visits—he was first invited in 1946—to Jung's retreat at Bollingen. There is an obvious and fundamental contrast between "I seek the impossible" and the famous statement *Credo quia impossibile*, "I believe because it's impossible", often attributed to Tertullian although in fact just a popular paraphrase of Tertullian's own words at *On the flesh of Christ* 5.4. This is why White in his letter quotes the two Latin sayings together, *Credo quia impossibile* as summarizing the attitude of Pistis or belief and *Quaero quod impossibile* as embodying the attitude of Gnosis or the thirst for direct knowledge. This, also, is why Father White has just stated in the same paragraph how profoundly moved he was by Jung's definition of his own lifework as "essentially an attempt to understand what others apparently can believe" (*JW* 125; cf. ibid. 119 = *JL* i 502 and e.g. *PA* 15–17 §§18–19). In his eyes Jung would always be, whether for better or worse, a perfect spokesperson for the way of the Gnostic.

[6] As for what lies behind the Latin saying that Jung chose to inscribe above his fireplace at Bollingen, I am deeply grateful to Jung's grandson Ulrich Hoerni who has pointed me to its obvious source of inspiration. In Goethe's play, Faust is encouraged by the prophet Manto to descend into the underworld to meet Persephone herself with these words: "Den lieb' ich, der Unmögliches begehrt", "Him I love, who seeks the impossible" (*Faust* 2.7488; these words have, indeed, been specially underlined by Jung in his personal reading copy of *Faust*: *Goethes Faust*, ed. H.G. Gräf, Leipzig 1913,

353). Manto, daughter of Asclepius and greatest of healer–prophets, then continues (and Jung has marked these words, too, in his text): "Enter, bold spirit! Joy will be yours! The dark passage leads to Persephone who … lurks waiting for the secret, forbidden greeting. Here I once smuggled Orpheus in …". Meanwhile, just outside the tower, the bottom of the inscription I had been leaning against directly quotes Homer's words about being led by Hermes past the gates of the sun and the land of dreams into the underworld (*Odyssey* 24.12). Even the lake beside which Jung built his tower was intimately associated, in his mind, with the Homeric portrayal of journeying into the world of the dead (*ETG* 103–4); he was perfectly explicit about the direct connections between the Bollingen tower itself and the world of the dead (*MDR* 213–24/225–37: cf. T. Ziolkowski, *The view from the tower*, Princeton 1998, 144); and just before he died he dreamed that he was going to live in an "other", otherworldly, Bollingen (B. Hannah, *Jung, his life and work*, New York 1976, 344). I have devoted a book (*APMM*; cf. *IDPW*) to the ancient Greek idea of sacred places as points of access to the underworld.

[7] "No one, not even those closest to him …": Cary Baynes in *JSB* 64; for the sentiment cf. 39–42. Just how intimate and important a role Cary Baynes had played as Jung's confidante is shown by the ease with which he spoke to her about things his own lover and supposed source of inspiration, Toni Wolff, was unable or unwilling to understand (draft letter from Cary de Angulo to Jung dated 26 January 1924, *CBA*; cf. ibid., 13 February 1924; *RB* 213–14). On Jung as not able even to understand himself because he remained a total mystery to himself, see especially the famous closing words in his published biography: *MDR* 329–30/358–9. The frequent remarks he makes, whenever he has an opportunity, about

the abysmal inferiority of his "dull conscious mind" (letter to Henry Murray dated 2 May 1925, Papers of Henry A. Murray, Harvard University Archives; cf. *JL* i 42, *RB* 215a) are comments that should always be taken seriously.

[8] For Jung's axiomatic concern with the individual see e.g. *TE* 3–5; *CT* 148–9 §315 and 153–4 §§326–9 with ibid. 247–305 = *The undiscovered self* (London 1958); *SL* 609 §1392 with 261 §599; *JL* ii 461–2; and the programmatic statement about his whole life being devoted to the goal of finding a way to penetrate the "secret of the personality" (*MDR* 197/206, *JP* 14). Wolfgang Giegerich comments on some of these passages but, with his brittle rationalism, draws the strangest conclusions (*JJTP* 6/1, 2004, 39–40).

[9] For some general observations see Aniela Jaffé, *From the life and work of C.G. Jung* (2nd ed., Einsiedeln 1989) 132–3; *NL* 120–2, 157–8; P. Pietikainen, *Alchemists of human nature* (London 2007) 124–5. For Emma Jung's protest to her husband, that "you are not interested in anybody unless they exhibit archetypes", see M. Fordham, *The making of an analyst* (London 1993) 117; W. Colman, *JAP* 47 (2002) 493. And for Jung's own comments on the matter see especially *MDR* 328–9/356–8; also *JL* i 49, *JV* i 7. "The moment I'd seen through them ...": *ETG* 359, cf. *MDR* 328/357.

[10] For Jung on "the spiritual and moral darkness of State absolutism" see especially *The undiscovered self* (London 1958) 2 = *CT* 247 §488; and R. Main, *The rupture of time* (Hove 2004) 120, who takes note of Jung's concern that the most vulnerable country in this regard is America. On Lucifer as "the father of lies ..." see *AS* 250 §303 and, for Jung's intense sensitivity—

unmatched by many supposedly conscious people nowadays—to the powers of propaganda or mass suggestion, *SL* 605 §1386, 609–10 §§1392–3, *JM* 340–4.

[11] On the *Red book* as a template for Jung's developed understanding of "individuation" see Shamdasani, *RB* 207b; *JAP* 55 (2010) 38–9; *JM* 322; and for some very brief comments on the history of the word cf. ibid. 306 n.41 with R. Noll, *The Jung cult* (2nd ed., New York 1997) 367 n.42. On the absolutely central significance of the individuation process in Jung's later work see *MDR* 200/209; *JAP* 57 (2012) 366–7. For individuation as an entirely natural process that may require a kind of consciousness but often does not, see e.g. *JS* 210–12 and *JL* ii 583 = *JAP* 46 (2001) 482; these statements by Jung about the total naturalness of the process are something that a conscientious modern Jungian can, of course, hardly be expected to accept (B. Stephens, ibid. 482–3). "Individuation is not that you become an ego …": *KY* 39–40. On that "which is not the ego" cf. e.g. *JL* ii 258–9, and for Jung's sharp distinction between individuation and individualism see especially *TE* 173–4 §§267–8; *PPT* 108 §227 (on extreme individualism as "essentially no more than a morbid reaction against an equally futile collectivism"). James Hillman once again reveals his ostentatious flair for trivializing Jung when he defines individuation as "the realization of innate idiosyncrasy … It appears phenomenally, in any odd moment of differentness" (*Sphinx* 1, 1988, 14). For the utter objectivity—as well as impersonality—of the individuated state according to Jung see *MDR* 270–7/289–98, together with Paul Bishop's comments on the close correlation in Jung's mind between objectivity and eternity (*Carl Jung*, London 2014, 187–8). And as for why the word "self" happens to be spelled with a small or lower-case

"s" in the standard English editions of Jung, it can be helpful to recall the simple explanation that "lower case is used in the *Collected Works* to avoid the appearance of esotericism" (A. Samuels, *Jung and the post-Jungians*, London 1985, 73).

[12] Individuation as the inner process of dying "before surrendering oneself …": *JP* 309 ("… bevor man sich dem Unpersönlichen überlässt"). For the terminology of surrender, or "sich überlassen", in German mystical literature see e.g. *Semantik der Gelassenheit*, ed. B. Hasebrink, S. Bernhardt and I. Früh (Göttingen 2012); Jung's use of it here raises major doubts about the truth of any blanket statement to the effect that "the mystic's unconditional and permanent surrender of his whole being, even his consciousness, to God, cannot be identified with the individuation process" (L. Schlamm, *European journal of psychotherapy and counselling* 9, 2007, 412 n.3). But it also raises additional questions about the validity of attempts to differentiate categorically between the process of individuation and mystical processes in general. On this important issue see now F. Bower, *JAP* 44 (1999) 567–9; Schlamm, *Harvest* 46/2 (2000) 108–28 and 52/1 (2006) 7–37; J.M. Spiegelman, *PP* 52 (2009) 260; J.P. Dourley, *Jung and his mystics* (Hove 2014); and note Jung's clear tendency to model the individuation process on mystical traditions while also formulating it, wherever possible, as a further refinement of spiritual norms (e.g. *SD* 225–6 §431, *PPT* 234 §448: for surrender cf. 82 §§186–7; and compare S. Shamdasani's comment that "Individuation only means something in a soteriological context", *JJ* 4/1, 2010, 172). On Jungian analysis as preparing to die see *RB* 266–7, 273–5; the letter from Jung to Cary Baynes dated 2 November 1945 (*CBA*; cf. Shamdasani, *Quadrant* 38/1, 2008, 23–4); *Spring* (1970) 178 = *JS* 360; and note, too, Jung's pithy portrayal of

the individuation process as what happens to a person when "outwardly he plunges into solitude, but inwardly into hell" (*SL* 453 §1103). Unfortunately there are scholars now who enjoy comparing such statements by Jung with Pierre Hadot's research into the tired theme of philosophy as preparation for death among ancient Platonic and post-Platonic intellectuals (cf. e.g. R. Màdera, *Spring* 92, 2015, 235–54). But what Jung found himself involved in has very little, if anything, to do with the trivializations and rationalizations by later Greek or Roman philosophers that Hadot has done such a skilful job of popularizing: on Hadot's own obsession with rationalizing and "rational control" see *SW* 111, 171. The experience of dying before one dies according to Parmenides, Empedocles and ancient mysteries: *IDPW* 61–76; *Reality* 29–43.

[13] *JP* 308–9. When Jung calls individuation a "mystery", he also intends this word to be understood in the much stronger and more literal sense that the individuation process is a re-enactment of ancient initiation mysteries (cf. e.g. *SL* 486 §1162, *JL* i 141). His extended use of the Grail mythology here, just a few years before he died, in explaining the real meaning of individuation gives the lie to the very rational and unfortunately very fashionable idea nowadays that Jung saw his evolutionary task as being to leave the antiquated world of mythology behind so he could introduce people instead to a scientific or "post–mythic" world of psychology. On the contrary: his psychological work was aimed specifically at renewing forgotten myths and mysteries by restoring them, as a true scientist, to life. Note also his statement in 1934 that "individuation is now our mythology … It is a great mystery … we don't *know* what it is …" (*NZ* i 208; cf. P. Pietikainen, *Alchemists of human nature*, London 2007, 127). In the sharpest

contrast to contemporary Jungians, who are often inclined to present individuation as a "system" which "is commonly nurtured in a consulting room in the presence of a therapist" (J. Weldon, *Platonic Jung*, Asheville 2017, 184), Jung himself emphasized that by no means does Jungian therapy lead to individuation except in the remote sense of being just one small step along the way towards the distant and elusive goal of a potential individuation (*JL* ii 469). On the reality of individuation as only for the very few see—aside from *JP* 308–9, spoken by Jung in 1958—*SL* 453 §1099 (written in 1916) with R. Noll, *The Jung cult* (2nd ed., New York 1997) 249; M. Serrano, *C.G. Jung and Hermann Hesse* (London 1966) 61 (spoken by Jung in 1959); M.E. Harding, *Quadrant* 8/2 (Winter 1975) 17 (spoken by him in 1960). In the 1940s Jung drew the quite logical conclusion that the vast majority of people are beyond being helped directly, and can only be influenced at all by a handful of individuated leaders who are not afraid to exert complete control through the power of "suggestibility" (*SL* 609–10 §§1392–3, cf. *CT* 221 §451). Pietikainen (*Utopian studies* 12/1, 2001, 48–9) is quite right to compare this scenario with the familiar Platonic, and ultimately Pythagorean, notion of philosopher–kings; but he is altogether wrong in suggesting that these leaders' purpose would be to "divine the psychological processes in the deep recesses of the human mind and explain to other, less privileged individuals what is wrong with them and how to right the wrong and to become true personalities". On the contrary: their role is not to deepen people's understanding or even change their attitudes, but simply to change their behaviour by exploiting their gullibility (*SL* 610 §§1393). That, as Empedocles would say, is as much as can be humanly accomplished (*ENM* 360–9; *Reality* 326–37).

[14] On the democratizing of individuation see A. Samuels' dry analysis, *Jung and the post-Jungians* (London 1985) 110–13. The words "a Christification of many" occur inside the crucial final paragraph of Jung's *Answer to Job* but, if they are to be understood, they have to be read in their proper context: "The indwelling of the Holy Ghost, the third Divine Person, in man, brings about a Christification of many, and the question then arises whether these many are all complete God–men. Such a transformation would lead to insufferable collisions between them, to say nothing of the unavoidable inflation to which the ordinary mortal, who is not freed from original sin, would instantly succumb …" (*Answer to Job*, London 1954, 180; cf. *PR* 470 §758). In other words the "Christification of many" is logical enough as a theoretical or potential next step for humanity, if individual humans would only take on themselves the enormous burdens and sufferings involved without any trace of self-deception (*RB* 234b), but practically is unrealizable. As Paul Bishop sums the situation up: "From this conclusion, as logical as it might seem, Jung retreats, for various reasons. How would they all get on? Very badly … What would the consequences for each of them, as an individual, be? Equally devastating … Here—in the very final paragraph of his *Answer to Job*—Jung himself shifted the moment of total integration from the here-and-now into the Gnostic wastes of infinite time" (*Jung's 'Answer to Job'*, Hove 2002, 161–2). But for the famous American Jungian Edward Edinger, and any number of later writers who have been fooled by him, these were all irrelevant niceties to be dispensed with. He abruptly stops quoting Jung at the catchy "Christification of many", forgets about the rest, and declares: "That is the relevant phrase '… the indwelling of the Holy Ghost, the third divine person in man, brings about a Christification of many' … That is what

is meant by the imagery of the incarnation of God in many through the agency of the Holy Ghost" (*PP* 25, 1991, 44). As for pinning down the source of such evangelical strategies and infectious zeal, it may help to consider that Edinger's parents were both Jehovah's Witnesses (*JJTP* 1/1, 1999, 58; *PP* 39, 1999, 42). John Dourley also shows the irresistibility of such interpretative tactics when he quotes Jung's rough sketch of how the ancient gods turned into one god, then the god became man—and now "even the God–man seems to have descended from his throne and to be dissolving himself in ordinary people". Dourley swiftly announces that this means humanity itself is now "encouraged by the unconscious" to "pursue the emergence of its native divinity into consciousness", but somehow forgets to mention what Jung went on to say: "in our day even the God–man seems to have descended from his throne and to be dissolving himself in ordinary people. That, no doubt, is the reason why his seat is empty. Instead, modern man suffers from a hubris of consciousness that borders on the pathological. This psychic state in individuals corresponds to what, on a larger scale, is the hypertrophy and totalitarian pretensions of the ideal State ..." (*Psychologie und Religion*, 4th ed., Zurich 1962, 99, cf. *PR* 84 §141; Dourley in *Psychology and religion at the millennium and beyond*, ed. J.M. Spiegelman, Tempe 1998, 24).

[15] For the comment about "a psychology that purports to offer to all ..." see M. Saban in *How and why we still read Jung*, ed. J. Kirsch and M. Stein (Hove 2013) 10. On the razor-sharp path which will cut you to pieces and is so full of suffering that only very few are capable of walking it, see *TE* 239 §401 where Jung makes sure to quote the biblical and ancient initiatory saying "Many are called but few are chosen" (Matthew 22:14; cf.

Plato, *Phaedo* 69c). On the inadequacy of all theories, routine rules or recipes cf. e.g. *SL* 493 §1172; C.G. Jung, *Entretiens* (Paris 2010) 173; *JP* B27 (13 June 1958). For the methodology and techniques of ancient Hermetic teachers see P. Kingsley, *Parabola* 22/1 (Spring 1997) 21–5 and in *PJB* 17–40. Jung was very conscious of the debt owed by his theory of individuation to "Hermetic" philosophy in the broadest sense of the word (*SL* 486 §1162, cf. *PR* 468 §755).

[16] Hermetic immortalization and deification: J.–P. Mahé, *Vigiliae Christianae* 45 (1991) 347–75; M.D. Litwa, *Becoming divine* (Eugene 2013) 94–101. For individuation as life in God see *SL* 719 §1624, where Jung can still be heard crying out that "*Individuation is the life in God*" because a person "is obviously not whole without God" and this wholeness is the only conceivable meaning of either divine incarnation or individuation. Individuation as deification: "Whoever does not follow the *principium individuationis* to its end does not become a god, because he is not able to endure the singleness" (*BB* v 168, deliberately presented by Jung as a commentary on John 10:34). For immortality see e.g. *IJP* 154 ("when we obtain a complete realization of self, there comes with it the feeling of immortality ... a feeling of eternity on this earth"); G. Lachman, *Jung the mystic* (New York 2010) 145. As for the "certainty of immortality" that comes from being initiated into the "mystery of deification", one of the most telling passages is Jung's autobiographical account of what happened in December 1913 when he experienced being transformed into the lion-headed god Aion of the ancient Mithraic mysteries. See *IJP* 103–7; *RB* 252; R. Noll, *Spring* 53 (1994) 12–60 and *The Jung cult* (2nd ed., New York 1997) 209–15; M. Stein, *Transformation* (College Station 1998) 43–6 and in *Initiation*, ed. T. Kirsch,

V.B. Rutter and T. Singer (Hove 2007) 91–4 (although Stein's attempt to distinguish between "deliberate" and "spontaneous" initiation has little basis in fact); C. MacKenna in *Insanity and divinity*, ed. J. Gale, M. Robson and G. Rapsomatioti (Hove 2014) 64–6. Many things could be said about the blatantly false claim that this "mystery of deification" and the resulting "certainty of immortality" were, according to Jung's account at *IJP* 106, only experienced by ancient initiates and not by Jung himself (A. Stevens, *JAP* 42, 1997, 673) but none of them is polite; and the rational insistence on distinguishing in such a context between "actual transformation" and merely "symbolic" experience (L. Corbett, *JJ* 5/3, 2011, 73) reveals, as we will see, a complete misunderstanding of what Jung meant by symbolic reality. There are two points about this experience of deification that need mentioning here. First, Cary de Angulo's visualization of Jung as a Mithraic priest belonging to the "highest rank of all" (draft letter to Jung dated 13 November 1923: *CBA*) demonstrates how very alive and potent this seminal experience of Jung's still was for those around him ten years later. Second, years before the *Red book*'s publication, Gilles Quispel had already concluded that Jung must have been familiar with one crucial passage in a major work by Robert Eisler which identifies this same lion-headed god as the Orphic god Phanes—who just so happens to overshadow Jung's *Red book* as well as *Black books*. See R. Eisler, *Weltenmantel und Himmelszelt* (Munich 1910) ii 398–405 with *Orphicorum et Orphicis similium testimonia et fragmenta* i, ed. A. Bernabé (Munich 2004) 90; G. Quispel in *Gnosis*, ed. B. Aland (Göttingen 1978) 497–507 = his *Gnostica, Judaica, Catholica* (Leiden 2008) 248–60; *RB* 113, 301–2 n.211 "... Phanes is Jung's God ...", 354–5 n.125, 364. And Quispel was right: the precise start of that very same passage he had guessed at is still carefully indicated, with a silk bookmark, inside Jung's own personal copy of the book by Eisler. As far as Jung's library is concerned, it also is worth noting that the marginal markings in his books show how fascinated he was by the ancient Greek phenomenon of immortalization and deification; he was particularly struck by Empedocles' own declaration that he had become a god (H. Leisegang, *Die Gnosis*, Leipzig 1924, 84; compare his copies of A. Dieterich, *Eine Mithrasliturgie*, 2nd ed., Leipzig 1910, 5; R. Reitzenstein, *Die hellenistischen Mysterienreligionen*, Leipzig 1910, 19–20, 25, 44–5; W. Scott, *Hermetica* i, Oxford 1924, 239–49). And as for becoming a god, there is no reason whatever to question the authenticity of a report involving the prominent Jungian Jolande Jacobi (*NL* 165; *JBA*): "On one occasion she had a dream in which Jung appeared to her as a God–figure. On telling him the dream, he replied, 'So now you know who I am!'"

[17] For example Sonu Shamdasani falls straight into this trap when he asserts that, if Jung ever mentions the lived feeling of immortality, he of course doesn't mean immortality in any "literal" sense and is discounting the whole phenomenon as nothing but a projection from the unconscious (*Cult fictions*, London 1998, 52; contrast e.g. *IJP* 153–4). This distorted rationalization by Shamdasani of Jung's ideas would have made even his mentor, Michael Fordham, blush with shame. In fact he is demonstrating exactly what, according to Jung himself, happens when intellectuals impose their "overvalued reason" on a mystery like the experience of immortality—and leave everyone "pauperized" as a result (*MDR* 280/301–2). On Jung's own disdain for reductive attempts at explaining psychological phenomena in terms of "nothing but", cf. e.g. *C.G. Jung: psychological reflections*, ed. J. Jacobi (2nd ed., Princeton 1970) 11, 16–17, 93, 121, 201.

[18] "Psychology is concerned …", "inner vision", and "we cannot understand a thing …": *PA* 13–14 §§14–15. Unfortunately Shamdasani (*Cult fictions*, London 1998, 29) cites Jung's firm opposition to "the construction of new religious truths" without explaining the other half of his equation: the need to help people rediscover the act of seeing by restoring their inner vision. On the crucial importance of learning simply to see without imitating or identifying with what one sees, see *RB* 251a. By temperament Jung was, of course, completely hostile to the construction of new religious truths—but that's only because his own work lay in the reincarnation of ancient religious truths (*FJ* 484 §269J, 29 August 1911; *RB* 311).

[19] For an introduction to Christ as symbol of the self see e.g. *Aion* 36–71 §§68–126. An essential element of symbols is, for Jung, their mystical openness to the mysterious and the unknown (*PT* 474–6 §§815–19, *QPT* 140–1). They are always more, not less, than any physical object or concept they correspond to: are "pregnant" with a special healing and redeeming value which unifies both conscious and unconscious, rational and irrational (*PT* 474–7 §§816–20, *CT* 18 §24, *AS* 28 §44, *Man and his symbols*, New York 1964, 20–1, 55; and compare the exact definition of a symbol at *RB* 311a). On one level the *Red book*, and Jung's work in its entirety, can be seen as a passionate protest against the view that symbols are less real than physical entities—even ourselves. See especially *RB* 233–4 (the physical reality of Jung and of those he loves is no more than a symbol of their souls), 236 (symbols predate and outlive our physical world), 246–9 (Elijah humorously insists that he and any other figures Jung meets in the unconscious are no less real than Jung is, and can only be called symbols if one agrees to call every physical person a symbol; this is completely misunderstood as "Jung's ambivalence about symbolic versus

literal reality" by A. Collins and E. Molchanov, *Spring* 90, 2013, 68 n.45), 250a (the symbol as infallible lord and master), 291a (symbols are the only access to truth), 304a (only symbols have power to save from the worst of acts or deeds), 310–11, 339b. Paul Bishop has pointed to the relevance for Jungian psychology of Goethe's ideas about symbolism, especially his paradoxical insistence that a symbol "is the thing without being the thing, and yet it is the thing" (*Goethes Werke*, Erste Abtheilung, xlix/1, Weimar 1898, 142.7–8; Bishop in *Morphologie und Moderne*, ed. J. Maatsch, Berlin 2014, 160–1). But at the same time, Jung was very familiar with ancient resonances of the word *symbolon* (see e.g. *MDR* 309/335: for some of those resonances compare *APMM* 238, 289–90, 301–3); and that only serves to intensify the similarities between the refusal of most Jung scholars to take his ideas about symbolism seriously and scholars' almost universal refusal to take those beings who appear to Parmenides, during his descent into the underworld, as anything more than simple "allegories" or metaphors. On this major problem in the study of Parmenides see *Reality* 29, 273–4, 583, L. Gemelli Marciano, *Ancient philosophy* 28 (2008) 21–7, *PSIE* 54–8, 257 n.92; for Jung's own explicit differentiation of symbols from mere allegories see *PT* 474 §815, *ST* 77 §114, 222 §329; and on intellectuals' "secret fear" of real symbols because of their living power compare J. Jacobi's comment, *Complex, archetype, symbol in the psychology of C.G. Jung* (London 1959) 87–8. Unfortunately, in this respect many practising Jungians nowadays fall headlong into the category of fearful intellectuals.

[20] "An inner experience, an assimilation of Christ …" and "the 'Christ within'": *Aion* 183 §§285–6. The "immediate and living presence" as opposed to "the idea of the historical Christ": ibid. 68 §123. The inescapably mystical nature of understanding

Christ as symbol of the self is acknowledged with all due clarity by Jung at *PA* 355 §452—where the recognition of oneself "as the equivalent of Christ", and of "Christ as a symbol of the self", is described by him as such a "tremendous conclusion" that even westerners acquainted on a strictly intellectual level with "the spirit of the Upanishads" or other eastern mystical ideas stand no real chance of understanding it. And to remove any possible ambiguity or doubt he takes great care to situate this same reality that he himself refers to as "the 'Christ within'" (*Aion* 183 §285) in the specific context of medieval mysticism, Gnosticism and esoteric Christianity (*SL* 280 §638). Each of these factors helps to explain Cary de Angulo's realization that only through being granted special access to Jung's work on the *Red book* had she been given the clue to uncovering what was really "true" in the world of mystical literature and thought without losing herself, as people always do, in the usual superficial or literal misunderstandings (draft letter to Jung dated 22 October 1922, *CBA*). Needless to say, finding the clue to the true essence of mysticism ignored even by most mystics is the ultimate mystical endeavour. Aside from Jung's own unending frustrations at people's hopelessly confused ideas about what true mysticism is (see e.g. *PR* 184 §274; *FP* 339 §781), note also the remarkable passage he wrote about symbols at a time when he was working on his *Red book*. In the chapter he devoted to definitions near the end of his *Psychological types* he effectively equated the three terms "mystical", "transcendent", and "psychological" ("an as yet unknown and incomprehensible fact of a mystical or transcendent, i.e. psychological, nature": *PT* 474 §815).

[21] Parmenides frs. 2.1, 6.4–7, 1.34–5 and Empedocles frs. 2.1–7, 4.9–13, 17.21 and 25–6, 21.1–3 Diels = Parmenides frs. 11.1, 13.5–8, 14.3–4 and Empedocles frs. 7.8–17, 9.15–19, 26.28 and

32–3, 31.5–8 plus 28.15–24 Gemelli Marciano; *Reality* 79–125, 179–99, 326–559.

[22] Both the words "no longer a struggle …" and the striking statement that it's not the ego but the *alêthinos anthrôpos*, the "true Man" or divine self inside a human, who walks the inner path of transformation come from *Mysterium coniunctionis* (ii, Zurich 1956, 102–3 §157 in the original Swiss edition; cf. *MC* 349 §492). The truth in this statement is something only a mystic can understand: see Llewellyn Vaughan–Lee, *The circle of love* (Inverness, CA 1999) 136–7.

[23] "You are quite right …": letter to P.W. Martin, written by Jung in English and dated 20 August 1945 (*JL* i 377; A. Jaffé, *Was C.G. Jung a mystic?*, Einsiedeln 1989, 16; M. Stein in *The idea of the numinous*, ed. A. Casement and D. Tacey, Hove 2006, 34 = *Minding the self*, Hove 2014, 38; S. Shamdasani, *JAP* 55, 2010, 41; L.S. Owens in A. Ribi, *The search for roots*, Los Angeles 2013, 7). On Martin and Jung see *SL* 606 n.1; W. McGuire, *Bollingen* (Princeton 1982) 136–7; also Emma Jung's letter to Cary Baynes dated 24 October 1944 (*CBA*). For the connection in Jung's mind between the numinous, the unexpected, the inconceivable and the outwardly impossible see e.g. *JP* 324–5; also *ACU* 17 §35, *MDR* 328/356.

[24] For a partial insight into modern strategies for handling the numinous see e.g. *Jung's 'Red book' for our time*, ed. M. Stein and T. Arzt, ii (Asheville 2018) and especially *The idea of the numinous*, ed. A. Casement and D. Tacey (Hove 2006). On Lucy Huskinson's blunt denial that the numinous can have any healing power (ibid. 210) see L. Schlamm, *European journal of psychotherapy and counselling* 9 (2007) 411 n.1; her assertion that "although the numinous cannot be understood on an

objective level, it can be known subjectively" (200: compare the similar remarks by A. Samuels, *Jung and the post-Jungians*, London 1985, 27, 43) undermines the very foundation of Jung's own deepest understanding. As for Samuels' apparently wise statement that with the numinous "there is considerable room for self-deception" (ibid. 77), what he avoids mentioning is the even more considerable room for self-deception which exists in thinking one can avoid the numinous. During her final lecture Marie–Louise von Franz offered an appropriate reminder that "disregard of the numinous powers is, according to Jung, *the* essence of evil" (*JJ* 2/2, 2008, 12); the shocked reaction on the part of prominent modern-day Jungians to this last lecture of hers (e.g. J. Beebe, ibid. 3/4, 2009, 28–38) is an interesting indicator of where many of them might line up along Jung's own moral spectrum. Jung explains the meaning of the word "apotropaic": *TE* 238 n.7; *KY* 33; *SD* 99 §§206–7; *Entretiens* (Paris 2010) 96–7. "You'll think up …": *RB* 291b. On the subject of domesticating the gods, John Dourley is willing to state in clear words what others might prefer not to acknowledge openly (*Psychology and religion at the millennium and beyond*, ed. J.M. Spiegelman, Tempe 1998, 23). "A mere expedient …": *JK* 171; Jung's comment here deserves to be set alongside J.S. Bernstein's poignant observations about the more or less inevitable "one-sidedness" of any psychotherapy when faced with the numinous reality of what Bernstein refers to as borderland persons, or phenomena (*Living in the borderland*, Hove 2005, 78–9).

[25] "Like it or not": *JL* ii 112 (cf. ii 20); P. Bishop, *Jung's 'Answer to Job'* (Hove 2002) 41–4. For the numinous as our tool or the other way around see e.g. *RB* 291b, "You want to employ it, but you are its tool"; *PR* 84 §141; *JL* i 492. Reference to experience of the numinous as "the therapeutic resource that distinguishes

Jungian therapy and theory from other traditions": J. Dourley, *JAP* 47 (2002) 490. For Lucifer in Jung's account of how "every spiritual truth gradually turns into something material, becoming no more than a tool in the hand of man", see *AS* 248–50 §§301–3. Characteristically, prominent Jungians who do comment on this passage make sure to invert the sequence of Jung's own exposition so as to give it all a positive spin (e.g. E.F. Edinger, *Anatomy of the psyche*, LaSalle 1985, 179–80)—which happens to be the identical technique used so effectively by commentators to sanitize Empedocles' cosmic cycle, and with such disastrous results (*ENM* 343, 385–6).

[26] "Wanted God to be alive ...": *PP* 6 (1975) 12. For the indigenous elder known as Mountain Lake, the disastrous effects of "American rationalism", and Jung's own comments about guarding his light because "it is most precious ...", see M. Serrano, *C.G. Jung and Hermann Hesse* (London 1966) 88 = *JL* ii 597. For Jung on the crucial importance of the "religious attitude", and on the absolute indispensability of a true "sense of historical continuity", see e.g. *PPT* 46 §99 with *JL* ii 488; for the decisive question in a person's life, and the life that's wasted, *MDR* 300/325; and for the soul of humanity, the alchemical *opus magnum*, "the whole weight of mankind's problems" and the "supreme responsibility" this involves, *PPT* 235 §449. On Jung's thoughts all circling around the divine see also *JL* ii 235–8. There have been some fine studies of Jung's religious attitude (cf. M. Stein in *Analytical psychology*, ed. J. Cambray and L. Carter, Hove 2004, 204–22), although without an exact understanding of what he meant by historical continuity they can only tell a fragment of the story.

[27] Chrétien de Troyes, *Le roman de Perceval ou le conte du Graal*, ed. K. Busby (Tübingen 1993) 138–40, 271, 504.

[28] The repeated image of Jung during his journey to India as someone constantly withdrawing in search of the inner truth unique to him alone (*MDR* 257/275, 262/280, 265/284) is an obvious reminiscence of the famous words spoken by the ancient Greek philosopher he was most familiar with, Heraclitus: the saying “I searched inside myself” (*edizêsamên emeôuton*) was specially annotated by Jung in his own copy of Heraclitus’ collected Greek fragments (*Die Fragmente der Vorsokratiker*, ed. H. Diels, 3rd ed., Berlin 1912, i 97.14, cf. 86.11–12; J. Olney, *The rhizome and the flower*, Berkeley 1980, 90 n.4, 93). On the paradoxical effects of being so far removed from Europe see *JP* 309. The immensity of the impression made on Jung by his Kolkata dream, although understated in *MDR*, is duly noted at *JP* 306 and 308; it’s also no accident that he compares the special significance of his time in India during 1938, including the sickness and dream, to the crucial importance of his famous illness during 1944 (*JP* 359).

[29] *ETG* 286; cf. *MDR* 263–4/282–3, *MDRC* 287–8. For the dream itself see *MDR* 262–3/280–2, *MDRC* 283–8, *JP* 306–10, 357–9. The utterly inhuman qualities of the dream as emphasized by Jung—metallic, cold, full of horror and terror, inexorably harsh and hard—have a direct bearing on his comment that the intensity of what he experienced while visiting India was something to be measured not in weeks or months, but in centuries (*JP* 358). For the small, nondescript place where what is most precious has been hidden away unnoticed by anyone see *JP* 308; this was a Gnostic and alchemical, as well as biblical, theme very dear to Jung.

[30] Compare, for example, the point where Jung calls salvation “the resolution of the task” and specifically defines this as giving birth to the ancient; as bringing back the old in a time

that is new (*RB* 310a, cf. *RB* 311b). For comments on Jung as healer of his culture see e.g. J. Hillman and S. Shamdasani's impressionistic meanderings in *Lament of the dead* (New York 2013) 145–61, or A. Haaning's more coherent observations at *JAP* 59 (2014) 8–30, plus Jung's own telling comparison of himself to a medicine man—which to him was the simplest way of describing the task he had been "wrestling with" for the whole of his life (*JL* ii 586–9). Joseph Henderson famously came up with the Jungian theory of a "cultural unconscious"; but however satisfying as a concept, it lacks any sense at all of the urgent need or focused duty or very particular obligation that Jung found himself confronted with in regard to the healing of western culture. See e.g. J.L. Henderson in *Proceedings of the second international congress for analytical psychology*, ed. A. Guggenbuhl–Craig (Basel 1964) 3–14 and *Cultural attitudes in psychological perspective* (Toronto 1984); S.L. Kimbles, *SFJI* 22/2 (Summer 2003) 53–8 with *The cultural complex*, ed. T. Singer and Kimbles (Hove 2004); Singer and C. Kaplinsky in *Jungian psychoanalysis*, ed. M. Stein (Chicago 2010) 22–37.

[31] For references to the scholarly literature see e.g. L.O. Gómez in *Curators of the Buddha*, ed. D.S. Lopez (Chicago 1995) 197–250; L. Schlamm, *IJJS* 2 (2010) 32–44 and in *Encyclopedia of psychology and religion* (2nd ed., New York 2014), ed. D.A. Leeming, 956–61. In this context the section of the *Red book* where Jung encounters Izdubar coming from the East is, symbolically, very revealing (*RB* 35–66, 277–86).

[32] I am summarizing and translating the text as first published in *Chinesisch–deutscher Almanach für das Jahr 1931* (Frankfurt 1930) 10–11 and reprinted in Jung's *Über das Phänomen des Geistes in Kunst und Wissenschaft* (2nd ed., Ostfildern 2011) 68–9

§§87–9, with the help of Cary Baynes' magnificent English version (R. Wilhelm and C.G. Jung, *The secret of the golden flower*, London 1931, 145–7); the supposedly authoritative translation offered at *SM* 58–9 §§87–9 is altogether unreliable. Jung refers quite explicitly to Wilhelm's own "cultural task" in the healing of western civilization and of its spiritual need (*Chinesisch–deutscher Almanach* 11; *Über das Phänomen des Geistes* 68 §87; *The secret of the golden flower* 145). As Edward Edinger very nicely put it when asked what Jung thought of westerners embracing eastern religions: "he thought it was an evasion of their own destiny and heritage" (*JJTP* 1/1, 1999, 54). Compare also Jung's own statement about the urgency of the need "to build on our own ground with our own methods. If we snatch these things directly from the East, we have merely indulged our Western acquisitiveness, confirming yet again that 'everything good is outside', whence it has to be fetched and pumped into our barren souls" (in W.Y. Evans–Wentz, *The Tibetan book of the great liberation*, London 1954, xxxviii = *PR* 483 §773); *The secret of the golden flower* 80, "It is not for us to imitate what is organically foreign, or worse still, to send out missionaries to foreign peoples; it is our task to build up our own Western culture, which sickens with a thousand ills"; *ACU* 14–15 §§27–8. On the all-consuming hunger and greed of missionaries, as well as those who stand behind them, see *NZ* i 213. As for Jung's comment about the light of wisdom that "only shines in the dark" (*Chinesisch–deutscher Almanach* 11 = *The secret of the golden flower* 146): this takes us right to the heart of his life, not to mention his work. Already since a child he had felt like an initiate into the realms of darkness, and this inner alignment with darkness guided him in his work for the rest of his life (*MDR* 28/15, 55/45, 92/87; compare *JP* 176, on the "dunkle Substanz" or dark substance that linked him to the alchemists; and see also *JP* 211–14 on Jung, Merlin and the magic of darkness together with S.A. Hoeller, *The Gnostic Jung and the 'Seven sermons to the dead'*, Wheaton, IL 1982, 204 and R. Padel, *In and out of the mind*, Princeton 1992, 72 n.84). He agreed to identifying the essence of his work with the biblical pillar of fire that offers guidance through the night, as opposed to the pillar of cloud that provides guidance through the day (*RB* 213b). And in describing "the primordial light-bringer, who is never himself the light", he was not only defining the role of darkly ambiguous Mercurius. He was also defining, to perfection, his own role in life (*AS* 248 §300: for Jung himself as light-bringer in the depths of darkness see E. Rolfe, *Encounter with Jung*, Boston 1989, 163, 176). That, after all, is why he would give such a special place of honour at Bollingen to the alchemical saying "I give birth to the light even though my nature is darkness" (*Artis auriferae volumen secundum*, Basle 1593, 239; this crucial statement is reduced to gibberish in the English translation at *AS* 125 §161 and in e.g. S. Marlan's *The black sun*, College Station 2005, 99). Very wisely he understood that, while the selfless task of humanity two thousand years ago had been to help the darkness understand the light (John 1:5–10), now our collective attachment to light has become nothing but selfish laziness. Everything changes with time, and the present task is for the light to understand the darkness (*PR* 468 §756). Or as Jung stated the matter very simply, "One doesn't become enlightened by visualizing images of light but by making the darkness conscious" (*Studien über alchemistische Vorstellungen*, 3rd ed., Olten 1988, 286 §335, cf. *AS* 265–6 §335)—although the trick is that we don't make the darkness conscious through our own conscious intentions, but through the intelligence of the darkness itself (*RB* 237a with n.78).

[33] For the "plant-like naïveté" which "is able to express profound things in simple language" see R. Wilhelm and

C.G. Jung, *The secret of the golden flower* (London 1931) 149. “Gnosis should be an experience of your own life ...” is from Constance Long’s transcription—as preserved inside her diary, now held at the Countway Library of Medicine in Boston—of a letter Jung had sent her on 17 December 1921. Apart from the fact that Richard Noll’s published rendering of her transcript is as a whole astonishingly inaccurate, the way he interprets the text in terms of a supposed “German spirituality” is the crudest twisting and distortion of Jung’s own aims and purpose (*The Aryan Christ*, New York 1997, 258–9). In tone, as well as content, this letter is particularly close to the already famous address by Jung to his “friends” at the start of the *Red book* (*RB* 231 with nn.23, 29). “Don’t be greedy ...”: *RB* 231b. On the poison for westerners of “foreign gods” see also *JK* 25 (Indian breathing exercises; cf. 33–5) and *KY* 14, 20; for the crucial importance of tending one’s own garden, *RB* 306a, 316a.

[34] For the masses who “claim in vain that they have found the whole” see Empedocles fr. 2.6 Diels = fr. 7.15 Gemelli Marciano with H. Stein, *Empedoclis Agrigentini fragmenta* (Bonn 1852) 30; *ENM* 360–1 with n.62; *Reality* 326 (cf. 24, 81, 165).

[35] Regarding traditional usage of these expressions, see for example the Gospel of John 4:42—where Christ’s characteristic title in later Greek, *ho sôtêr tou kosmou*, would be translated into Latin as both *salvator mundi* (Vulgate) and the more classically stylish *servator mundi* (Erasmus). It will be noted that in ancient Greek, as well as Latin, saving was an essential part of preserving while protecting or keeping safe was the natural job of a saviour (H. Ebeling, *Lexicon homericum* ii, Leipzig 1880, 269–70; J. Fontenrose, *Didyma*, Berkeley 1988, 140–1). For the praise of Christ by alchemists as *salvator mundi*

see e.g. *Musaeum hermeticum* (Frankfurt 1678) 725 and, on the role of *Christus servator* at the intersection between Latin occult and theological literature, W. Schmidt–Biggemann, *Geschichte der christlichen Kabbala* ii (Stuttgart 2013) 183 with n.114; 348 with n.87. Jung himself was particularly fond of one passage in Khunrath (cf. ibid. 51) that describes the crucified Christ as both saviour of humanity or the microcosm, *salvator mundi minoris*, and preserver of the world or macrocosm, *servator mundi maioris*: *AS* 126–7 §162 with n.43; *MC* 264–5 §355, 580 n.28; reformulated by Jung as *salvator macrocosmi* at *PA* 24 §26. For his use of the words *servator* and *salvator* together compare *Aion* 183 §286; *AS* 235–6 §283, 250 §303, 295–6 §390; and note also *Flying saucers* (London 1959) 28 = *CT* 332 §629 on Mercurius as "a kind of panacea, saviour, and *servator mundi* (preserver of the world). Mercurius is a 'bringer of healing' … as the 'food of immortality' he saves Creation from sickness and corruption, just as Christ saved mankind". Christ or the self as mystical vessel filled with the Holy Spirit which is *servator mundi*: *JL* ii 267. On Christ as *salvator mundi* see esp. *Aion* 127 §194, *AS* 242 §290 and *ETG* 215, where the Latin phrase has been stripped out of the English edition. Interestingly, while the English version of Jung's published biography has his Kolkata dream culminate in the phrase *servator mundi*, the German version here has adopted the more familiar *salvator mundi* (ibid. 286).

[36] Richard Noll famously encountered a savage reaction to his claims that Jung was responsible for creating as well as promoting "a religious movement whose goal is not only the salvation of the individual, but also of the world" and that already right from the start he had considered psychology "the new salvation of the world, with Jung as the prophet". See his *The Jung cult* (2nd ed., New York 1997) 202, 254; *The*

Aryan Christ (New York 1997) 112, 201; P. Homans, *SFJI* 14/2 (Summer 1995) 8–9. But although there is no denying that Noll's books are cesspits of sensationalism and sloppy scholarship, it's only right to note that they occasionally contain some very accurate intuitions—and also to ponder Jung's constant reminder that the rarest of truths is always found in the unlikeliest and dirtiest of places, despised by the high priests as well as academics (cf. e.g. *PA* 80–1 §103, 123 §160, 313 §421, 430 §514).

[37] "Christ in the garden of Gethsemane" and "*servator cosmi* (preserver of the cosmos)": *AS* 295–6 §390. On Jung's identification of his dream companions as members of the Psychological Club see *JP* 306, 307; and for his comparison of himself to Christ at Gethsemane, and the members of the Club to Christ's disciples, ibid. 308. It will be noted that Richard Noll, for all his faults, arrived by a different route and using different texts at precisely the same conclusion: Jung "even drew the analogy between the members of the club and the apostles of Christ" (*The Aryan Christ*, New York 1997, 156). Sightseeing: *JP* 306; D. Bair, *Jung* (Boston 2003) 428.

[38] Jung's attacks on those who set themselves up as world saviours go back to the inaugural dissertation he wrote during his mid-twenties. See e.g. *Psychiatric studies* (2nd ed., London 1970) 16 §34; *RB* 231b, 298b, 309b, 316–17; *Collected papers on analytical psychology* (2nd ed., New York 1917) 462 ("God-Almightiness") and *TE* 169 §260 ("inflation"), 286 §476; *SL* 750 §1699; *JS* 363. For the record, one should add that Freud together with his close circle were very much taken aback by Jung's early aspirations to save the world through becoming "another Christ" (*The complete correspondence of Sigmund Freud and Ernest Jones, 1908–1939*, ed. R.A. Paskauskas, Cambridge,

MA 1993, 180, 182). And good note should also be taken of Jung's own clear hint that the inflationary effects of contact with the unconscious can never be altogether avoided (*TE* 233–4 §§389–90). On the virtues of love and wisdom see his letter to Alice Raphael dated 7 June 1955 (Alice Raphael papers, Beinecke Library, Yale University; *JH* 2/2, 2007, 6); for the "necessary humour", *TE* 170 §262 (where Jung's original "Lächerlichkeit" would be better translated as "laughable absurdity") with *SL* 750 §1699, *JL* ii 324 and E. Rolfe, *Encounter with Jung* (Boston 1989) 179.

[39] *IJP* 107. For a classic example of failure to distinguish between the experience of deification and the inflationary state of god-almightiness see S. Shamdasani, *Cult fictions* (London 1998) 50–1. On deification for Jung as a major "initiation" he had to pass through cf. e.g. M. Stein in *Initiation*, ed. T. Kirsch, V.B. Rutter and T. Singer (Hove 2007) 93; also his comments in *Transformation* (College Station 1998) 44–6. That "the experience of self-deification represents the beginning and not the end of a psychological process" (L. Schlamm, *Religion* 28, 1998, 98) is a truth acknowledged not only by Jung, but by many mystics. The famous Sufi Ibn al–'Arabî demonstrated through his own life the paradox of how, after the state of oneness with God, comes the stage of becoming God's humble servant (C. Addas, *Quest for the red sulphur*, Cambridge 1993)—and, incidentally, also explained that the God I experience is not the Godhead itself but the very personal God–image unique to me (see Corbin, *AWA*). This can be a useful reminder that such distinctions are not unique to Jung and don't require any knowledge of German philosophy. For a vivid account of practical Sufism and its intimate familiarity with the phenomena of inflation see Irina Tweedie's *Daughter of fire* (Nevada City 1986), especially 378–9; ancient Hermetic

texts with which Jung himself was very well acquainted reveal a similar insight into the subtleties of human psychology (P. Kingsley, *Parabola* 22/1, Spring 1997, 21–5 and in *PJB* 17–40); and for the direct links between Hermetic and Sufi traditions see ibid. 29 nn.24 and 26, 38 with 39 nn.45 and 46. On the recognized problem of inflation among Christian mystics cf. e.g. Schlamm in *Encyclopedia of psychology and religion* (2nd ed., New York 2014), ed. D.A. Leeming, 872. "The great psychotherapeutic systems ...": *ST* 356 §553.

[40] Halfway between one's conscious self and the depths of the unconscious: compare, for example, *TE* 221–2 §§364–5. Hidden away inside the human body: *PR* 278 §421; *MC* 477–8 §681, 499 §711, 543 §775. On Jung and his meeting with Mountain Lake—he describes the encounter as so uniquely and profoundly real that it left him at a loss for the right words to explain what happened (*JP* 370)—see e.g. *MDR* 233–8/247–53; M. Serrano, *C.G. Jung and Hermann Hesse* (London 1966) 87–8 = *JL* ii 596–7. But note, also, Jung's own earlier reference to the "saving symbol" of the spoken word that "leads the sun on high" (*RB* 310b: compare the comment by D.G. Barton about Jung's encounter with Mountain Lake mirroring back to him his own experiences while working on the *Red book*, *IJJS* 8, 2016, 82). The deep respect and admiration displayed by Jung for Mountain Lake were reciprocated: the two of them stayed in touch and remained friends for many years (W. McGuire, *Spring* 1978, 43; cf. *JL* i 101–2). "The cosmos would collapse": M.H. Yousef, *Ibn 'Arabî – time and cosmology* (Abingdon 2008) 15, referring specifically to the symbol of the pillar as image of the perfected human being. This image of the perfect human being as a pillar was very familiar to Jung, and he annotated each mention of it carefully in his own copy of the Manichaean *Kephalaia* (ed. H.J. Polotsky and A. Böhlig i,

Stuttgart 1935–7). For the controversial popularizing of similar traditions in Judaism about the hidden few who are needed to keep the world intact see André Schwartz–Bart's *The last of the just* (London 1959) with e.g. B. Wolfsteiner, *Untersuchungen zum französisch–jüdischen Roman nach dem Zweiten Weltkrieg* (Tübingen 2003) 168–80, 350–1; Murray Stein, sensibly enough, cites this material for its relevance to Jungian issues of inflation and identification (*Soul*, Hove 2016, 155).

[41] For Eugene Rolfe's correspondence with Jung—in English—through November and December 1960 see his *Encounter with Jung* (Boston 1989) 157–80, esp. 163, 176. It will be noted that to another Englishman, Sir Herbert Read, Jung in fact makes a very deliberate point at around the same time of comparing himself to a medicine man (*JL* ii 586–9, 2 September 1960). On the other hand Rolfe complains to Jung with more than a little sadness that, although the British Society of Analytical Psychology which had been founded to further his work contained "a number of brilliant names", nobody there was even remotely capable of combining "the roles of Discoverer, Healer, Teacher and Artist" because Jung alone represented a "living embodiment" of his own theories (Rolfe 164, cf. 161–2). On the apparent ordinariness of an individuated human being see e.g. *JL* ii 324; and for Jung's typical association of the phrase "archetypal life" with the legendary life of Christ, *PR* 157 §233. It can be helpful, here, to remember that at the start of the same year Jung had also written to James Kirsch—a particularly influential and thrusting Jungian—to give him the soundest of verbal thrashings for the chaos he was causing through his inflated identification with the archetype of the Anthropos or cosmic Christ (*JK* 259–60: 12 February 1960). This helps to put in its full and true perspective his rare comment almost thirty

years earlier to the effect that, even though to start with there is a constant danger of being swallowed by an archetype, there is also a very long but perfectly natural process which ends at last in the mastership of realizing one's identity as a human with the archetype: of discovering that the archetype "is in a peculiar way man, as man is an archetype" (*NZ* i 318–19). That Rolfe, for his part, was spot on in referring to Jung as a living embodiment of his own teaching is clear from Jung's light-hearted conclusion to the light-hearted interview he gave on his eightieth birthday: "Do you know who already anticipated the whole of my psychology in the eighteenth century? The Hasidic Rabbi Baer from Meseritz, who was called 'the Great Maggid'. He was an extremely remarkable man" (Michael Schabad, "Besuch bei C.G. Jung", *National–Zeitung* 26 July 1955; cf. *JS* 271–2 and, for Jung's lively laughter and humour throughout the interview, ibid. 268–9, 271–2). Sanford Drob has beaten this delightful statement to death in a hundred different ways, taking it as proof that inwardly Jung became a Jew before he died while citing abstruse teachings of Rabbi Baer which Jung himself could never have read or heard about in his lifetime. But, in sober fact, there can be no doubt at all as to what Jung had read inside the comfort of his own library which triggered such a special sense of affinity with the Great Maggid: "The new movements gave birth to a new type of leader, the illuminate, the man whose heart has been touched and changed by God, in a word, the prophet … Rabbi Israel of Koznitz used to say that he had read eight hundred Kabbalistic books before coming to his teacher, the 'Great *Maggid* of Meseritz', but that he had really learned nothing from them … The new element must therefore not be sought on the theoretical and literary plane, but rather in the experience of an inner revival, in the spontaneity of feeling generated in sensitive minds by the encounter with the living incarnations of

Mysticism … Rabbi Baer of Meseritz … gives a new emphasis to psychology, instead of theosophy … the secrets of the Divine realm are presented in the guise of mystical psychology. It is by descending into the depths of his own self that man wanders through all the dimensions of the world … in his own self, finally, he transcends the limits of natural existence and at the end of his way, without, as it were, a single step beyond himself, he discovers that God is 'All in All' and there is 'Nothing but Him' … Hasidism is practical mysticism at its highest. Almost all the Kabbalistic ideas are now placed in relation to values peculiar to the individual life, and those which are not remain empty and ineffective … A tale is told of a famous saint who said: 'I did not go to the Maggid of Meseritz to learn Torah from him but to watch him tie his boot-laces'. This pointed and somewhat extravagant saying … at least throws some light on the complete irrationalization of religious values which set in with the cult of the great religious personality. The new ideal of the religious leader, the Zaddik, differs from the traditional ideal of Rabbinical Judaism, the *Talmid Hakham* or student of the Torah, mainly in that he himself 'has become Torah'. It is no longer his knowledge but his life which lends a religious value to his personality. He is the living incarnation of the Torah" (Gershom Scholem, *Major trends in Jewish mysticism*, Jerusalem 1941, 329–39). One has to remember that Jung didn't call Rabbi Baer from Meseritz a man who held extremely remarkable beliefs: he called him an extremely remarkable man.

[42] On the "irrational and impossible condition" always associated with the appearance of the saviour—which "occurs just when one is least expecting it, and in the most improbable of places"—see *PT* 261 §§438–9, *RB* 229a with n.2, 311. On the relation between the archetype of light-bringer and Christ as *servator mundi*, "the Saviour and Preserver of the world",

see e.g. *AS* 127 §§162–3 (cf. also 247–50 §§299–303). For the Gnostic figure, "suppressed and forgotten", of the cosmic Christ as Saviour and light-bringer "who went forth from the Father ..." and its immediate relevance to Jungian psychology see *SL* 671–2 §§1514–17, 826–9 §§1827–34.

[43] See especially *JP* 113 for Jung's own important unpublished statement; also B. Hannah, *Quadrant* 16 (Spring 1974) 27 with *Jung, his life and work* (New York 1976) 53, 114 and J. Dehing, *JAP* 35 (1990) 379 with G. Quispel in *The rediscovery of Gnosticism*, ed. B. Layton, i (Leiden 1980) 21, 23. I am grateful, as well, to Gilles Quispel for personal comments he made to me on several occasions about things said to him in private by Jung. On the aliveness of the Gnostics compare also the exquisitely profound and funny story told by Jung about his good friend, the famous Gnostic expert G.R.S. Mead (*JP* 195–6). On the Gnostics as psychologists see in particular *Aion* 174 §269 ("for the Gnostics—and this is their real secret—the psyche existed as a source of knowledge"), 222 §347 ("it is clear beyond a doubt that many of the Gnostics were nothing other than psychologists"), 223 §350.

[44] For *gnôsis* as—by definition—a matter of direct knowledge or realization instead of belief see e.g. E. Pagels, *The Gnostic gospels* (New York 1979) xix–xx; W. Barnstone and M. Meyer, *The Gnostic bible* (Boston 2003) 8–9 (on the recent trends towards "de-constructing" ancient Gnosticism as a recognizable phenomenon, cf. ibid. 12–16). With archetypal perversity Robert Segal opens his book on *The Gnostic Jung* by stating that "The belief known as Gnosticism is definable in various ways" (Princeton 1992, 3). On the surprising realities of ancient "heresy" and "orthodoxy" see the foundational work by Walter Bauer, *Rechtgläubigkeit und Ketzerei im ältesten*

Christentum (2nd ed., Tübingen 1964) = *Orthodoxy and heresy in earliest Christianity* (Philadelphia 1971); H. Koester, *Harvard theological review* 58 (1965) 279–318 and D.J. Harrington, ibid. 73 (1980) 289–98; B.A. Pearson, *Gnosticism, Judaism and Egyptian Christianity* (Minneapolis 1990) 194–213; A. Böhlig and C. Markschies, *Gnosis und Manichäismus* (Berlin 1994) 170; P. McKechnie, *Journal of ecclesiastical history* 47 (1996) 413–14. For Jung's own clear statements regarding the matter see e.g. *CS* 14, where he explains that Gnosticism derives directly from the unconscious while Christianity derives in turn from Gnosticism; *PA* 357 §453; J. Dehing, *JAP* 35 (1990) 380. For the Gnostic perspective as the reverse of every ordinary perspective, or the other way around, cf. J.Z. Smith, *Map is not territory* (Leiden 1978) 151–71; *Reality* 417, 588.

45 On the underlying link between the words *gnôstikos*, *gnôsis*, *gignôskein* and the immediacy of sense perception see e.g. Empedocles frs. 5.3 and 89 Diels = frs. 10.6 and 130.2 Gemelli Marciano; *Reality* 551–4, 591. "Psychology is concerned … faculty of seeing": *PA* 13–14 §§14–15. Very significantly, in struggling to answer Martin Buber's accusations that he was a Gnostic, Jung is pulled straight back to the word's original meaning: "What Buber misunderstands as Gnosticism is *psychiatric observation*" (*JL* ii 570, cf. *PR* 307 §460).

46 Letter written by Jung to J.B. Lang on 9 March 1918. The letter as a whole remains unpublished but the central part of the text has been printed, with no comment, at *RBu* 209a; I have added an exact date for it based on the details mentioned by Jung, in the original letter, just above his signature. It will be noted that, although he refers to the "Erkenntnissinhalt der Gnosis und des Neoplatonismus", by Neoplatonism he meant what today would be called Hermetic or occult philosophy (*PA*

83–4 §109 with n.38, *PR* 97 §159, *JL* i 317, *MC* 309 §425; cf. *PJB* 68–9). The language that Jung uses throughout the letter is highly significant. His mention of "the unconscious spirit" is a clear reference to the philosophy of Eduard von Hartmann (*IJP* 4–5; D.N.K. Darnoi, *The unconscious and Eduard von Hartmann*, The Hague 1967, 19, 56 with n.2). But at the same time his conscious or unconscious choice of words here in explaining how he wants to use Gnostic systems to create ("bilden") the foundations for "einer Lehre des Ubw Geistes" is strangely reminiscent of the familiar phrase "Lehre vom Hl. Geist", which instead of "theory" means "teaching" or "doctrine" of the Holy Spirit (cf. Jung himself, *JP* 384, with e.g. H. Leisegang, *Der Heilige Geist* i, Leipzig 1919, 3 on "der Ausbildung einer Lehre vom Heiligen Geiste"). And, if anything, it's even more reminiscent of the standard language used in Jung's time—a language with which he was intimately familiar—for describing the creation of those ancient Gnostic systems themselves. See e.g. W. Schultz, *Dokumente der Gnosis* (Jena 1910) 135 on "das Bild dieser Lehre", referring to the original system created by Simon Magus; 152, on Basilides together with "seine Lehre von der 'großen Unwissenheit'"; and, on the crucial importance of Schultz's book for Jung, L.S. Owens in A. Ribi, *The search for roots* (Los Angeles 2013) 17–20. In short, publicly he might insist that "psychology is concerned with the act of seeing and not with the construction of new religious truths" (*PA* 13–14 §15); in private, though, he may have been sailing a little close to the wind with regard to that bit about not constructing religious truths.

47 "Gnostic coloration": *MDR* 176/182; cf. *JP* 24. On Jung's choice of language to describe the utter terror of encountering his teacher, the total foreignness of the world he found himself plunged in, and his panic when faced "once again" ("wieder

einmal") with the catastrophic prospect of total craziness, see *JP* 175: the words "once again" refer back to the previous page where Jung had just described, using very similar terms, the sheer terror of having to clutch at the table in front of him to prevent himself from falling apart (*JP* 173–4). On his use of the word "Unsinn" here in the Protocols as indicator of a psychotic state compare *ETG* 131–4, 181–2, *Red book* folios ii verso and iv recto (*RBu* 234–5, 240b), and the Grimm brothers' classic entry in their *Deutsches Wörterbuch*. It will be noted that Jaffé does allow an element of fear to remain at this point in Jung's published biography—but safely removed from the saintly guru–figure, Philemon (*MDR* 176–7/183–4). On Philemon's "Egyptian–Gnostic–Hellenistic" background see *JP* 23–4: one of the best pointers to what Jung meant by this term is the subtitle of the work which was his most trusted early guidebook to the *Hermetica*, Richard Reitzenstein's *Poimandres* ("Studien zur griechisch–ägyptischen und frühchristlichen Literatur", Leipzig 1904). For the terror experienced by students, in Hermetic tradition, on first encountering their inner teacher see e.g. *Corpus hermeticum* 1.7–8 (*tremein … en ekplêxei mou ontos*: Reitzenstein 329–30); for the total foreignness or alienness of the situation in which they suddenly find themselves, 13.3 (*allotrios huios*: Reitzenstein 340); for the panic at the prospect of going crazy, 13.4–6 (*eis manian me ouk oligên kai oistrêsin phrenôn eneseisas … memêna ontôs, ô pater*: Reitzenstein 341). On the background to *Corpus hermeticum* 1 and 13 see *PJB* 41–76 and 17–40 respectively; and for the almost perfect interpenetration of Gnostic and Hermetic traditions in Hellenistic Egypt cf. ibid. 22–4, 42 n.1, 48–50 with n.20. As for Aniela Jaffé's motives in stripping such unpleasant features out of Jung's account, one only needs to remember her alleged statement that anything and everything should remain unpublished if "it doesn't throw a good light on Jung" (Jolande

Jacobi interview, *JBA*; R. Noll, *The Jung cult*, 2nd ed., New York 1997, 286 and *The Aryan Christ*, New York 1997, 278).

[48] Philemon a Gnostic: *JP* 174–5 (repeated for emphasis); cf. also 113 (Philemon is one of the Gnostics). Even at *JP* 23–4 Jung repeats himself about Philemon's Gnostic affiliation; a comparison with the revised wording at *MDR* 175–6/182 shows how pointedly, here too, his original emphasis has been watered down. Now of course, since the publication of Jung's own words in the *Red book* identifying Philemon with the famous Gnostic Simon Magus, any lingering uncertainties should already be a thing of the past (*RB* 359b; L.S. Owens in A. Ribi, *The search for roots*, Los Angeles 2013, 17–27). But, as Lance Owens shrewdly observes, there are very strong forces at work in maintaining what he calls the Jungian "amnesis of Gnosis". For the increasingly institutionalized custodians and propagators of Jung's work "there was obviously no professional profit in nominating Jung as a Gnostic prophet" and now, more than ever, "it remains problematic to associate a school of clinical psychology with a widely anathematized heresy intimately entangled in the origins of Christianity" (ibid. 7–8).

[49] "Critical disidentification": *RB* 207a, 218a, 310 n.252; S. Shamdasani, *C.G. Jung: a biography in books* (New York 2012) 104–7; J. Hillman and Shamdasani, *Lament of the dead* (New York 2013) 19–20, 107–9. Interestingly, in this constant talk about critical disidentification there is no real emphasis on the fact that the disidentification was initiated and managed by Philemon himself—as an essential phase of his teaching that every single thought of ours is an independent and intelligent being (*JP* 24–5; *MDR* 176/183). Thought–experiments and ventriloquism: *RB* 223–4, *IJP* xii. Of course one of the biggest problems with the comfortable rational view of Jung as first

and foremost a scientist performing his experiments, magically immune from the danger of falling into a psychosis, is the awkward fact that this is nothing but the convenient narrative offered by his or our egoic no. 1 personality. From a deeper point of view he was never conducting any experiments on the unconscious but, rather, the unconscious was conducting its experiments on him (*MDR* 172/178; *KI* 8, "Jung felt that the unconscious had done an experiment on him"). As Jung repeated consistently until the very end of his life, it's not a question of what we do with the archetypes but of the use that the archetypes make of us; and, at bottom, this brings us back to the way he criticized even his own pupils for being superstitious enough to believe in free will when any such free will is just an illusion (*JL* ii 626). At the same time, his mention of being not so much the experimenter as the one being experimented on is also a crucial nod on Jung's part towards the Hermetic "character of that spirit or thinking which you do not, like an intellectual operation, perform yourself, as the 'little god of this world', but which happens to you as though it came from another, and greater, perhaps the great spirit of the world" (*MC* 233 §313). For the same paradox of being analyzed by "the unconscious guide that dwells within yourself" and is "the analyst in your heart", which Jung saw as the end result of any psychoanalysis, see Shamdasani, *Journal of sandplay therapy* 24/1 (2015) 8–9.

[50] *Protege me protegam te … Ego gigno lumen, tenebrae autem naturae meae sunt. Me igitur et filio meo coniuncto nil melius ac venerabilius in mundo fieri potest.* The Hermetic text was first published, with this precise wording, in the *Rosarium philosophorum* (Frankfurt 1550) and reprinted in the *Artis auriferae volumen secundum*, which was the version most used by Jung (Basle 1593, 239–40: for his purchase of the book see *JP*

175; *MDR* 195–6/204; T. Fischer, *IJJS* 3, 2011, 170–2). He was intimately familiar with every intricacy of this passage (cf. *PA* 109–10 with n.17, 118 with n.29), and it will be noted that on the Bollingen mural he skipped a sentence just before the final announcement about the merging of father and son—obviously because that final statement is what mattered to him most. For very sketchy accounts of the mural see *RB* 317 n.282 and L.S. Owens in A. Ribi, *The search for roots* (Los Angeles 2013) 24 with 286 n.86; for the poorest of reproductions, *Man and his symbols*, ed. C.G. Jung (New York 1964) 198 and D. Bair, *Jung* (Boston 2003) facing p.371. The painting of Philemon in the *Red book*: *RB* 154.

[51] On the subtitle to Jung's final and culminating work about alchemy ("An inquiry into the separation and synthesis of psychic opposites in alchemy") see *MC* v–vi; *JL* ii 469–71. Philemon as father, Jung as son: *RB* 348–56; during their conversations about the *Red book* in 1924, Jung and Cary de Angulo still refer to Philemon as Father (draft letter to Jung dated 26 January 1924, *RB* 213b; *CBA*).

[52] For the BBC interview see H. Purcell, *A very private celebrity* (London 2015) 147–9; *JS* 428 (cf. also 374); *JL* ii 520–3 with n.1, 524–6. Philemon's words to Jung: *RB* 348b. Shamdasani points out that these words of Philemon provide the obvious background for Jung's famous comment in the interview, and even notes that the central emphasis here on direct experience as opposed to creeds or beliefs is in perfect agreement with ancient Gnostic teaching (ibid. 348 n.89)—just as Paul Bishop accurately observes that "analytical psychology is structured at a deep level by the key opposition that characterizes Gnosticism", namely the opposition between direct knowledge and belief (*Jung's 'Answer to Job'*, Hove 2002, 53). But unfortunately

this hasn't prevented either of them from misrepresenting, elsewhere, the crucial nature of the relationship between conventional religions and Jungian psychology (*JAP* 44, 1999, 542–4 and *RB* 212a with n.177; *Morphologie und Moderne*, ed. J. Maatsch, Berlin 2014, 164 with n.30, denying that Jung's "project" was religious on the grounds that Jung denied the importance of belief). For the clearest evidence, which has been available a long time, that Jung's insistent favouring of knowledge or *scio* over belief or *credo* is motivated at root by profoundly mystical considerations see his passionate letter to Bernhard Baur–Celio dated 30 January 1934 (*JL* i 140–2). Here he opens up about the terrifying (141 with n.4) experiences of direct knowing which had overwhelmed him, about the mysteries of initiation, and about the absolute taboo on saying too much.

[53] Good examples of Jung marking up passages about spiritual rebirth, spiritual father and spiritual son can be found in his personal copies of Richard Reitzenstein's *Die hellenistischen Mysterienreligionen* (Leipzig 1910, 25–7, cf. also 44–5) and especially Albrecht Dieterich's *Eine Mithrasliturgie* (2nd ed., Leipzig 1910, 138–56, cf. 5). On the ancient adoption procedures that lie behind these traditions see *IDPW*; and on the equally ancient convention of magician as "father" teaching his "son" cf. *APMM* 221 with n.12, 374. For the passage "I see myself to be the All ..." see *Corpus hermeticum* 13.11, plainly marked by Jung in his edition of Walter Scott's *Hermetica* i (Oxford 1924) 247; for his own experience at Bollingen, *MDR* 213–14/225–6 (note how effortlessly, here, Jung merges and unites with Philemon as both old man and son). On Philemon's copy of the Hermetic texts see *RB* 312a and, on Jung's dedication of Bollingen as sacred to Philemon, *JL* i 49; *JH* 2/2 (2007) 6; *JP* 297; *MDR* 222/235 n.5.

[54] "A typical Goethean answer ...": letter to Alice Raphael dated 7 June 1955 (Alice Raphael papers, Beinecke Library, Yale University). Shamdasani is to be commended for first publishing this letter (*JH* 2/2, 2007, 6–7) but his notes and even transcription are quite unusable; Latin, for instance, is not German and *homo altus* is not an old man. Goethe's own reply can be found in J.P. Eckermann, *Gespräche mit Goethe* (Leipzig 1836) ii 348–9 = *Conversations of Goethe with Eckermann and Soret* (London 1850) ii 399 (6 June 1831): for a much more clearly stated example of Goethe hiding his own vestiges by "enveloping himself in mystery" see ibid. ii 171 = ii 210 (10 January 1830), and for Jung's impression of Goethe as revealed by Eckermann cf. *JL* ii 452–3. On the characters of Philemon and Baucis in the ancient world cf. Ovid, *Metamorphoses* 8.611–724; M. Beller, *Philemon und Baucis in der europäischen Literatur* (Heidelberg 1967); B. Louden, *Homer's 'Odyssey' and the Near East* (Cambridge 2011) 19, 30–56, 280–313; H.S. Versnel, *Coping with the gods* (Leiden 2011) 42–3 with n.71; and N. Schwartz–Salant's observations, *Cahiers jungiens de psychanalyse* 134 (2011) 105. For Jung's comments about being ready to give the whole of the earth just to be able to know what Goethe knew, see *JL* i 310. Regarding ancient traditions about the crucial importance of understanding one's teacher's name, compare especially the issues surrounding the origin and meaning of the name Poimandres in the first of the *Hermetica* (*Corpus hermeticum* 1; *PJB* 41–76; on name as essence cf. *RB* 282b, 315a). Parallels between Jung's Philemon and the Hermetic Poimandres have already been noted, in passing, by others (J. Hubback, *JAP* 11, 1966, 97, 105).

[55] A lot can be learned from comparing the exact expressions Jung uses in his attack on Martin Buber at *SL* 665 §1505 with the beautiful summaries at *JP* 24 or *MDR* 176/183 of that

extraordinary knowledge—about psychological objectivity, about the reality of the psyche, about the complete autonomy of thoughts and fantasies—which he had received as gifts from Philemon. For the teaching Parmenides was given in the underworld about thoughts, perceptions and existence see *Reality* 60–199. And for Parmenides' own affinities with later Gnostic tradition cf. e.g. ibid. 198–9, 576 with J. Mansfeld's crude but well-intentioned efforts in *Studies in Gnosticism and Hellenistic religions*, ed. R. van den Broek and M.J. Vermaseren (Leiden 1981) 261–314.

[56] On Jung's deep sense of the ideas that came to him through the *Seven sermons* as "really quite wonderful things" which caused him no end of struggle "until I could read their [not "this", as mistranscribed at both *JL* i 42 and *RB* 215a] symbolic language, so much superior to my dull conscious mind" see his letter to Henry Murray dated 2 May 1925 (Papers of Henry A. Murray, Harvard University Archives). For their crucial, and continuing, importance to him cf. also *JL* i 33–4; *MDR* 182–4/189–92; *JSB* 100–2; L.S. Owens in A. Ribi, *The search for roots* (Los Angeles 2013) 6–7; A. Yiassemides, *Time and timelessness* (Hove 2014) 4. For the Gnostic elements in the *Seven sermons*, including the fact that Jung ascribed their authorship to the Gnostic Basilides, see e.g. E.M. Brenner, *JAP* 35 (1990) 397–419; Owens 25–7. On Jung's continued immersion in Gnostic literature well into the 1950s see Ribi 130–47. For his public disavowal of the *Seven sermons* at *SL* 663–4 §1501 as "hardly a very candid or courageous statement", as "less than fully candid", see J.P. Dourley in *Jung and the monotheisms*, ed. J. Ryce–Menuhin (London 1994) 129 and *On behalf of the mystical fool* (Hove 2010) 70. Lance Owens has also, very discreetly, pointed out in a note what utter nonsense Jung is speaking when he attacks Buber for drawing unfair attention

"to a sin of my youth": he had written the *Seven sermons* when he was in his forties, authorized an English translation when he was approaching fifty and kept on giving out copies long after (Owens 280 n.17, quoting from *SL* 663 §1501). But there is a far more significant aspect to Jung's characterization of this work as "a sin of my youth" than simple chronology, and the fact that it seems to have been overlooked is no positive testimony to modern Jung scholarship. What appears to have gone completely unnoticed is the way he is quoting an Old Testament psalm that begs the Lord God for love and, above all, forgiveness of every old sin because "my hope is in you all day long"—I ache now to take refuge in you and learn what is right so, please Lord, "do not remember the sins of my youth and my rebellious ways" (*Psalms* 25:4–7). That Jung, whose intimate familiarity with every detail of the Bible amazed even the theologians of his time, was unaware of exactly what is implied in appealing to such an emotive Jewish text while addressing such a prominent Jewish authority as Martin Buber is out of the question. But of course the reality is that, in spite of sending this subtle message of repentance and apology for the error of his Gnostic ways, Jung wasn't repenting of anything: never would. And it would be only too easy to add to that Gnostic sin the additional sins of religious hypocrisy and brazen fraud. For his extraordinary knowledge of the Bible cf. e.g. *JJW* 7 together with his own remarkable statement, about the absolute need for such knowledge, at *JV* i 442. As for the time-honoured practice, forgotten now but still well known to Jung, of quoting a brief word or phrase from a scriptural text to evoke an entire context see *APMM* 42–5, 52–3, *Reality* 64–5, 96–7, 222–8, 332–3, 524–6; and compare his own comment in *JL* i 426.

[57] For Jung lamenting his own moral cowardice, and bourgeois desire for peace and tranquillity, see *JL* ii 155–6. Denouncing his "medieval-minded critics" for denouncing him "as a mystic and Gnostic": J. Dehing, *JAP* 35 (1990) 381. Empedocles and Jung's dual view of the psyche: *ZL* 78–9 §§200–3 (cf. 70 §179, 83 §§217–18).

[58] Hermes' lies: *Homeric hymn to Hermes* 368–9; L. Kahn, *Hermès passe* (Paris 1978); *Reality* 460, 589. Popes: Saint Gregory the Great, *Moralia* 3.28.55 (*sic in facto rem approbat, ut in mysterio contradicat; sic gesta damnat, ut haec mystice gerenda suadeat*); E. Wind, *Pagan mysteries in the Renaissance* (2nd ed., London 1968) 27 n.; *Reality* 417. For such inversions in ancient Gnosticism see e.g. J.Z. Smith, *Map is not territory* (Leiden 1978) 151–71. Jung was not only very familiar with such paradoxical reversals but also practised them himself, for example characterizing the intensely anti-Gnostic Saint Hippolytus "as a secret Gnostic who concealed his allegiance under the guise of opposition" (A. Ribi, *The search for roots*, Los Angeles 2013, 132).

[59] Scholarship, personality no. 1 and the spirit of our time: see e.g. *Red book*, folio ii verso (*RB* 233b); *JP* 300. For the spirit of the time assuming itself to be ever so clever, see *RB* 237a. Scholars as murderers: *RB* 230b. David Miller channels the spirit of our time to perfection when he warns other scholars against presenting Jung in a Gnostic context because this inevitably "lends an esoteric and mystical aura to Jung and his thinking, which makes serious academic thinkers and teachers suspicious" (*Teaching Jung*, ed. K. Bulkeley and C. Weldon, New York 2011, 42). And, from his own angle, Barry Jeromson

is content to cite Jung's very public reply to Martin Buber as reassuringly definitive proof that he never considered himself in any way a Gnostic (*JH* 2/2, 2007, 25–6). But, tellingly, the more that Jeromson tries to maintain this position the deeper he sinks into distortions and misunderstandings: to call symbolic works such as *Seven sermons to the dead* "religious allegories for a psychological process" is to ignore Jung's clear and repeated distinction between allegory and symbol (*PT* 474 §815, *ST* 77 §114, 222 §329, *Aion* 72–3 §127), while to define the ultimate purpose of his entire work as "psychological, not religious" (for this simplistic scholarly parody of Jung cf. e.g. R.A. Segal, *JAP* 40, 1995, 601) is to show the crudest disregard for Jung's own desperate insistence that nothing in the universe is more religious than the study of the human psyche and that people who haven't personally experienced the truth of this are fools to think they have any right at all to talk about religion (*PA* 3–37). For academics' growing love affair with Jung see e.g. D. Tacey, *JAP* 42 (1997) 269–83 and in *Who owns Jung?*, ed. A. Casement (London 2007) 53–71. On his general disaffection with professional scholars compare for example *RB* 264, 312b, *SM* 58 §86, *JL* i 530–1, *JP* 351; E. Rolfe, *Encounter with Jung* (Boston 1989) 213–14. And note his profoundly significant comments in 1952 about how—just as "alchemy is a secret knowledge that collided with the orthodox position and as a result was forced to vegetate in the darkness"—so "we with our psychology would also have to live in the catacombs, as it were, if the academies and other well-intentioned authorities had any power. Oh yes, if that was the case I would already have been burned at the stake long ago. Then I would have been roast beef" (*Bausteine*, ed. A. Schweizer and R. Schweizer–Vüllers, Einsiedeln 2017, 218; the crucial statement here is almost predictably mistranslated in the English edition, *Stone by stone*, ed. Schweizer and Schweizer–Vüllers, Einsiedeln 2017). Ever so often Jung would point to the existence of the occasional "true" scholar, or seeker, but only to make the point that most so-called scholars in their destructive one-sidedness are not true scholars at all (letter to Wilfrid Lay dated 20 April 1946, *CBA* – *JL* i 425). The unnanounced dangers of hearing or seeing our own views reflected back to us: *Reality* 422–9.

[60] For Jung on the Gnostic use of paradoxes and contradictions see e.g. *PR* 275 §§416–18. In his sensitivity to this he is well ahead of his time, and R.A. Segal's clumsy attempt at severing Gnosticism from the use of paradox (*SFJI* 13/2, Summer 1994, 64) could easily have been prevented by referring to the text known as *Thunder, perfect mind* which was discovered at Nag Hammadi (codex 6.2.13.1–21.32; W. Barnstone and M. Meyer, *The Gnostic bible*, Boston 2003, 226–32). True to form, soon after applauding Gnostics for avoiding hubris or inflation through their use of contradictory and paradoxical language, Jung goes on to contradict himself by denouncing them for their "fatal inflation" (*PR* 275 §417, 287 §§438–9: for hubris as inflation cf. e.g. *JL* ii 16, *MDR* 221/234); scholars are quick to note the link between Gnosticism and inflation in the second of these passages while strangely overlooking the contrary statement in the first. Jung is "clear beyond a doubt" that the Gnostics were psychologists (*Aion* 222 §347, cf. 223 §350) but also doubts that they were psychologists (*MDR* 192/201): Segal's feeble effort to "reconcile" these contradictory statements by explaining that, according to Jung, the Gnostics "felt unfulfilled" (*The Gnostic Jung*, Princeton 1992, 34–5) is an insult both to the Gnostics and to Jung. As with the alchemists, Jung was never quite able to decide in which respects the Gnostics were much more primitive than us and in which respects they were far more advanced (*Aion* 190 §297). And he shows similar uncertainty when he admits that it was his

personal experiences which brought him to the Gnostics in the first place, acknowledges that their writings are based without the slightest doubt on their own experiences, but worries about how many metaphysical assumptions they allowed to creep into their teachings and even accuses them of being full-fledged metaphysicians (B. Hannah, *Jung, his life and work*, New York 1976, 114; *JL* i 553, ii 53–5, 245, 290; J. Dehing, *JAP* 35, 1990, 380). Of course this whole issue is greatly complicated, but also vastly simplified, by the fact that behind his brash denials of being a metaphysician he was terrified to come clean about his own unshakeable fascination with metaphysics (*IJP* 12, 50; *JL* ii 344; J. Dourley, *JAP* 47, 2002, 485). For the constant uncertainties of personality no. 1 see e.g. *JP* 302 (also *RB* 254 n.238, on the spirit of this time); for its addiction to lying, *MDR* 55/45.

[61] R.F.C. Hull in A.C. Elms, *Uncovering lives* (New York 1994) 59; cf. D. Bair, *Jung* (Boston 2003) 640, 842–3 n.157. For the dismissal of Hull as an intellectual by Marie–Louise von Franz and Barbara Hannah in particular, see e.g. S. Shamdasani in *Who owns Jung?*, ed. A. Casement (London 2007) 184–5 n.17. M. Saban (*How and why we still read Jung*, ed. J. Kirsch and M. Stein, Hove 2013, 18) is correct to emphasize how eager those around Jung were to dull the sharp edge of his dual personalities by exchanging them for "a more familiar Jungian narrative", and how quickly von Franz in particular was seduced into rationalizing them by trying to make any contradictions disappear; but he seems not to go so far as to recognize the utter absurdity of von Franz's assertion that, while Jung was already a young man, "he once and for all renounced any kind of identification with no. 2" (*C.G. Jung: his myth in our time*, New York 1975, 41).

[62] Jung even cites in support of this the authority of Khidr, the most mysterious of Sufi prophets: *ACU* 144–6 §§253–4; M. Stein in *How and why we still read Jung*, ed. J. Kirsch and Stein (Hove 2013) 38. Of course he openly admits that secrecy had been the most essential component of his whole life ever since earliest childhood (*MDR* 30–65/17–56, 235/249–50). Bollingen and personality no. 2: see especially *JP* 297; *MDR* 214/225. On his profound dislike for talking publicly about the Gnostics, note his awkward comments about being "manoeuvred" during the presentation of the famous Nag Hammadi Jung codex in November 1953 into saying a few truthful words about the relationship between his psychology and ancient Gnosticism (*JW* 223 = *JL* ii 138); Gilles Quispel plausibly reports that before the event "a number of women in his entourage tried to persuade him not to attend" because "they feared Jung would be branded a Gnostic, whereas they wanted to present their hero as a meticulous scholar and scientist" (*Gnostica, Judaica, Catholica*, Leiden 2008, 151–2: compare the Jung household's dedication to stopping him being called a mystic, *JJW* 46). But the most revealing account of Jung's discomfort at the publicity surrounding his involvement with the Gnostic codex, and of the immense relief he felt when the speech he gave about its profound psychological significance was ignored by the press, is his own letter to Cary Baynes dated 30 November 1953 (*CBA*). Here he explains that although he himself was overjoyed at the recovery of such fascinating original material, with its enormous implications for how we understand ancient Gnosticism and its history, there is almost nobody who appreciates the realities involved: very pointedly he adds that even the so-called experts at the event such as Carl Meier or Quispel himself were talking nothing but "hot air", and that he detested the entire performance. On the

aura of secrecy with which he surrounded the *Seven sermons*, in particular, note Michael Fordham's personal reminiscence about only people who had reached "a suitably 'advanced' stage" receiving a copy of the work after being "sworn to secrecy about it" (*RB* 215 n.197); for similar traditions of secrecy in the ancient world cf. *APMM* 289–90, 365–6 n.20. Regarding the "secret knowledge" that Jung was finally forced, as the result of a major illness during his seventies, to deposit inside the only major book in which he ever allowed Gnosticism to take centre stage see M. Ostrowski–Sachs, *From conversations with C.G. Jung* (Zurich 1971) 68; L.S. Owens in A. Ribi, *The search for roots* (Los Angeles 2013) 29–32; for Jung and "secret knowledge" cf. also *JL* i 140–2 with the introductory note at 140. Again there is nothing coincidental about the fact that through the struggle to write this book, called *Aion*, he found himself reunited with Philemon on an even deeper level after a period of over thirty years (*JL* i 480–1, 491–2 = *JW* 103–4, 116–18; Owens, *PP* 54, 2011, 278–9). On Jung's gradual awakening to the personal significance, for him, of Mani's ancient teaching about the central importance of being reunited with one's higher self or celestial twin see Quispel, *SFJI* 13/2 (Summer 1994) 47; and, on this Manichaean teaching about reunion, A. Böhlig and C. Markschies, *Gnosis und Manichäismus* (Berlin 1994) 268 with C.M. Stang, *Our divine double* (Cambridge, MA 2016).

[63] Empedocles' dual spirits: *Reality* 347–473; and for Jung's spirit of the depths as also too powerful for humans to bear cf. e.g. *RB* 238b. On the two halves of Parmenides' poem see *Reality* 55–294 and, for science as belonging to the world of illusion, 212–58; *PSIE* 229–36, 274–5. The inadequacy of Jung's two spirits and the need for balance between their two madnesses: *RB* 238b (and compare, again, *RB* 298a on

the madness that unavoidably attaches itself to every aspect of our daily existence). Empedocles' two madnesses: Caelius Aurelianus, *Chronic diseases* 1.5; *Reality* 438–41. The spirit of this time, with its overwhelming fascinations and seductions, as "the general spirit in which we think and act today": *RB* 240a; compare *Reality* 422–87. "In order to illuminate the stupidity ...": *SL* 671 §§1515, 827 §§1827. "In not expecting the darkness ...": E. Rolfe, *Encounter with Jung* (Boston 1989) 176.

[64] Philemon's appearance: *RB* 312–14. "Jung first goes to him to learn magic, which is an interesting critical theme in the work that doesn't ever really surface in his public writings": S. Shamdasani, *JAP* 55 (2010) 41–2. The *Red book* as seedbed: *JP* 144, 147, 149, 177, 258; *MDR* 184/192, 190–1/199. Philemon as Christ's friend: *BB* vi 85; *RB* 316b with n.280, 359 with n.153.

[65] Jung searches for Philemon the magician: *RB* 311–12, and compare *Reality* 326–41 on the ancient tradition of having to realize one's complete stuckness before setting out in search of the wise magician. For the vital importance to Jung of Goethe's *Faust*, and the devastating impact on him of the scene where Faust's inflated hubris leads to the murder of Philemon and Baucis, see especially *MDR* 221–2/234–5. According to Ovid, as Jung knew very well (*RB* 315a, *PA* 480 §561), Philemon and Baucis' cottage was saved by being transformed into a magnificent temple of the gods; but this, in spite of the Faustian attempt by Wolfgang Giegerich to force an "atheistic" interpretation on Ovid's tale (*Spring* 1984, 63–4), is just another way of removing it completely from our human existence.

[66] Jung's favourite form of respectable denial was to complain that the "funny prejudice" of labelling him an occultist just

because the nature of his work obliged him to study the occult, of course in a purely professional capacity, was as ridiculous as if one were to accuse a criminologist of being a criminal or a medical expert on sexual perversions of being a sexual pervert. This rhetorical argument also became very popular, as a way of defending him against all sorts of accusations, among Jung's family and followers alike. See e.g. *JL* ii 186 (Jung denying he was an occultist); *SL* 730 §1647 (using the same argument to deny he was a Gnostic); *JJW* 46 (others insisting that of course he was no mystic himself because, quite matter-of-factly, "there was a need to know about things mysterious and he was the guy who was doing the research where it had to be done"). And continuing in the same direction he went to even greater lengths to dissociate himself from Paracelsus because, although a direct "forerunner of our modern psychology of the unconscious", the doctor had dabbled so extensively in magic (*AS* 116–22 §§151–6, 189 §§237–8). For a recent addition to the inconclusive, and mostly inconsequential, scholarly debate over Jung's status as a modern esotericist see R. Main in *Sacral revolutions*, ed. G. Heuer (Hove 2010) 167–75.

[67] The sentence he chose was *exaphes ho echeis kai tote lêpsei*, "Let go of what you have and then you will receive". See the heading of his letter to Freud dated 31 August 1910 = *FJ* 387 with Faksimile 8 ("mystische Anweisung aus einem Pariser Zauberpapyrus"), and *IJP* 51 with *MDR* 179/186; S. Shamdasani, *C.G. Jung: a biography in books* (New York 2012) 65–8. Jung came across, and heavily underscored, the saying in his own copy of Albrecht Dieterich's *Eine Mithrasliturgie* (2nd ed., Leipzig 1910, 21.1–2, 84): see also now *Papyri graecae magicae* i (2nd ed., ed. K. Preisendanz and A. Henrichs, Stuttgart 1973) 100–1 (*PGM* IV.828) with M. Meyer in *Mystery and secrecy in the Nag Hammadi collection and other*

ancient literature, ed. C.H. Bull, L.I. Lied and J.D. Turner (Leiden 2012) 449–50. On the Paris magical papyrus (*PGM* IV) and Empedocles see *APMM* 221–3, 238–51, 286–8, 300–14 with nn.37, 64 and 83, 374–5; *ENM* 391 with n.143. *PGM* IV and Parmenides: *IDPW* 129–32; *ENM* 390 n.140. And for the cultural as well as geographical details of how the magical and mystical material that would end up in *PGM* IV came to be transmitted from Sicily or Italy down to Egypt see P. Kingsley, *JWCI* 57 (1994) 1–13; *APMM* 240–7, 268–70, 314–16, 325–34, 339–43, 374. Aside from his numerous errors in matters of detail, Richard Noll makes a commendably passionate effort to underscore the importance for Carl Jung of the ancient Greek magical papyri (*Spring* 53, 1994, 46–8 n.11). "The great Paris magical papyrus" in particular would retain its hallowed status for him to the end of his life (cf. *MC* 196 §§251–2; *JS* 434).

[68] For Jung's analysis of the three possibilities open to a human when confronting the "mana-personality" or magician archetype, see *TE* 227–41 §§374–406. "Assimilate": ibid. 237 §398 ("dissolution of the mana-personality through conscious assimilation of its contents"). Also compare 230 §382, where Jung answers the question of "what happens" during this process to the magical power itself—far from being lost or left behind it's simply transferred, intact, from the grip of the ego into the hands of the higher Self—and contrast his vivid description of how anyone who fails on a conscious level to integrate and assimilate the archetype of the magician is simply gobbled up by it (*JP* 147). For a fine introduction to the mythical theme of swallowing and devouring magical powers as a way of assimilating or integrating them inside oneself, see M. Detienne and J.-P. Vernant, *Les ruses de l'intelligence* (Paris 1974) 61–124. Aside from adding "assimilation" as a key word to his psychological vocabulary (cf. esp. *PPT* 151–6 §§326–38),

Jung himself was perfectly aware of its significance on a mythical level in denoting the absorption of magical power: in fact he often made a very deliberate point of emphasizing the mythical and psychological parallels. See e.g. *TE* 228 §376 with *ST* 183 §268, 339 n.57 ("overpowers the gods in order to assimilate their divine nature and become their lord") and n.58 ("the initiates assimilated the essence of the god"); *PR* 243 §371 ("assimilate the mana"), 275 §418; *MC* 292 §400, 308 §424, 364 §512 with n.394. These examples show beyond any doubt that, when Jung talks in his *Two essays* about "assimilating" the mana–personality or magician archetype, he is at the same time describing a magical process. Compare also *RB* 314–17, where he presents the apparently psychological withdrawal of projections as an essential part of Philemon's magic. As for the widespread view among modern Jungian practitioners that along the path of individuation the archetypal figure of the magician just has to be "seen through and confronted, making possible an exit from this realm" (J. Cambray, *International journal of psychoanalysis* 94, 2013, 417), this is a dangerously irresponsible rationalization of what Jung himself had been trying to convey.

[69] No professors left who know anything about magic: *RB* 312–13. On magic as no longer a matter of outer ceremony or ritual or spells note for example the case of Jung's celebrated predecessor, the Swiss physician Paracelsus: C. Webster, *From Paracelsus to Newton* (Cambridge 1982) 58; D. Burton and D. Grandy, *Magic, mystery and science* (Bloomington, IN 2004) 37. For Philemon the "old magician" see *RB* 312, and note Lance Owens' comments in A. Ribi, *The search for roots* (Los Angeles 2013) 23, 285 n.81: Philemon was an old magician not only because of his age but because he was a reincarnation of the ancient magician Simon Magus (*RB* 359b, cf. 316a).

For Jung himself as "old magician" see Aniela Jaffé, *From the life and work of C.G. Jung* (2nd ed., Einsiedeln 1989) 139 ("the approach of the old magician never lost its excitement in all those years. With my inner ear I still hear it to this day"); compare also Miguel Serrano's personal comments about "Jung, the magician" after meeting him in 1959 (*C.G. Jung and Hermann Hesse*, London 1966, 61–4 and 92–3 = *JS* 464–5: "… I had the feeling that I was facing an incarnation of Abraxas …") as well as his reminiscence of Ruth Bailey telling him how she had helped Jung "perform some rites" at Bollingen (Serrano 98). For Jung as a Gnostic see e.g. *JJW* 25 ("Kerenyi said that he believed Jung thought of himself as a 'kind of Pope … of the Gnostics'": Kerényi said this specifically about a Jung who was already in his eighties). And Gilles Quispel, too, was portraying not a scholar of Gnosticism but a living Gnostic when he described Jung as "the genius of the deep who, time and time again, shocked whoever listened to him with his relentlessly accurate perceptions and plumbed the very depths of Satan" (*Gnostica, Judaica, Catholica*, Leiden 2008, 15). For Jung as alchemist compare his more than humorous retort—again in his eighties, when someone tries to talk about the eclipse and death of alchemy—"But I am an alchemist and I am not dead!" (*JJW* 85). One only needs to add Warren Colman's refreshing admission that, in writing and working so directly from the unconscious, Jung "functions more like a Gnostic or an alchemist than a scientific psychologist" (*JAP* 42, 1997, 342).

[70] Note especially the account of what happened one day when—while drinking wine with Olga Fröbe–Kapteyn, founder of the annual Eranos gatherings—"Jung carried out a ritual" in which he removed the ancient magic ring from his finger, "placed it in a glass filled with wine, uttered some mysterious

formulae, and then slipped the ring onto her finger. The next day Fröbe said to him that he, as a psychologist, had done something grave with this gesture, and she told him: 'You have bound me to you!' Jung, however, is said to have answered: 'It was not I that did it, but the Self'." She was deeply disturbed by the incident and remained troubled by it for years (cited with little understanding by H.T. Hakl: *Eranos*, Sheffield 2013, 45, 307 n.15; cf. also M. Eliade, *Journal* i, Chicago 1990, 161, 165 and R. Bernardini, *Jung a Eranos*, Milan 2011, 184–7). One might be tempted to dismiss this all as just a joke, but it certainly is not: according to Jung's own formal analysis the Self is precisely where, if only our ego can avoid identifying with the archetype of the magician or "mana–personality", the real source and centre of gravity of its magic power will end up (*TE* 230 §382, 237–40 §§398–405). On the intricate issue of Jung's ancient "Gnostic" ring see *JV* i 610–11; M. Serrano, *C.G. Jung and Hermann Hesse* (London 1966) 49, 89 and 101 (cf. *JS* 468); L.S. Owens in A. Ribi, *The search for roots* (Los Angeles 2013) 18–19, 279 n.12, 283 n.59. In 1932 Jung himself describes his special ring as "thoroughly alive and full of mana" (cf. also Serrano 101 = *JS* 468: "absolutely alive within me", spoken almost thirty years later) and significantly adds that to dismiss such statements as "not scientific" would be a mistake, because "science is just a corner of the world in comparison to the real world" (*JV* i 611). C.W. King's *The Gnostics and their remains*, well read by Jung (London 1864; cf. *RB* 349 n.93), has much to say about the magical figures of Agathodaimon and Abraxas on antique gems or rings like his. For the formal consecration of these rings see *Papyri graecae magicae* (2nd ed., ed. K. Preisendanz and A. Henrichs, Stuttgart 1973–74) i 124–7 (*PGM* IV.1596–1715 = H.D. Betz, *The Greek magical papyri in translation*, 2nd ed., Chicago 1992, 68–9) and ii 71–6 (*PGM* XII.201–69 = Betz 161–3) with S. Eitrem, *Symbolae*

Osloenses 19 (1939) 57–85 and J. Dieleman, *Priests, tongues and rites* (Leiden 2005) 147–70: in fact even Jung's modification of his own ring to incorporate elements of Christian symbolism faithfully reflects established ancient practice (Serrano 101 = *JS* 468; Eitrem 82–4). For Greek magical traditions about the "words to whisper over a wine cup" see e.g. J.J. Winkler in *Magika hiera*, ed. C.A. Faraone and D. Obbink (New York 1991) 223 with Faraone, *Classical antiquity* 15 (1996) 77–112 (who repeatedly cites both Empedocles and "Orphic" traditions in passing: 90–1, 103–8, 110, 112). And on the general practice of men "binding" women for friendship, loyalty or love, compare Faraone's *Ancient Greek love magic* (Cambridge, MA 1999); *ENM* 357–8, 395 (referring to Empedocles). It will also be noted that dropping a ring into wine to produce a magical effect would later play a major role in medieval Germanic tradition. See in particular J.B. Sherman, *The magician in medieval German literature* (PhD thesis, University of Illinois at Urbana–Champaign 2008) 83–4, "King Princian also enchants Queen Salme with a magic ring by dipping it into her wine glass: *ein fingerlin er in den win swang, dar nach trang die frauwe wol gethan* ..." (cf. *Salman und Morolf*, ed. A. Karnein, Tübingen 1979, 198 §604).

[71] *RB* 140–4 (cf. 312–14). Although Jung emphasizes that magic and reason have nothing at all to do with each other from a rational point of view, he does add that reason has a certain usefulness for the magician when performing magic (ibid. 314). The soul's warning: *RB* 126, 128, 130 (cf. 307–8); it will be noted that the German word for "comfort" or "solace" ("Trost", "trostlos", "Trösterin", "tröste") occurs in this passage no less than fourteen times. For the ancient teacher's typical job of frustrating the student while destroying every comfortable hope or reassuring expectation, once again the classic and

absolutely crucial text is *Corpus hermeticum* 13 (P. Kingsley, *Parabola* 22/1, Spring 1997, 21–5; *PJB* 17–40; for this same disruptive aspect of training in shamanism see e.g. T. Nathan, *Nouvelle revue d'ethnopsychiatrie* 20, 1993, 47). Now one can begin to understand why, right at the start of the chapter in the *Red book* called "The magician", Jung emphasizes Philemon's familiarity with the wisdom of Hermes Trismegistus (139, cf. 312a). And with his following account of silence as "the best apprenticeship", and of real magic as something that can't be taught (140–8, cf. 313–15), compare specifically *Corpus hermeticum* 13.16: *touto ou didasketai alla kruptetai en sigêi*, "this can't be taught but is hidden in silence" (cf. W.C. Grese, *Corpus hermeticum XIII and early Christian literature*, Leiden 1979, 8–9, 14–15, 20–1, 24–5, 116–17, 157–8).

[72] For Jung comparing the imminent destiny of his own psychology to the institutionalization of early Christianity, with the inevitable loss in both cases of the original spirit and fire, see *CS* 18–21; S. Shamdasani's simplistic comments and contrasts (*JAP* 44, 1999, 541–2) ignore the crucial subtleties in what Jung was clearly trying to convey here. "It is a bewildering thing in human life that the thing that causes the greatest fear is the source of the greatest wisdom": *DA* 329. For Jung's plain and persistent warnings against thinking one can explain any aspect of his psychology—or anything else—in terms of "nothing but", see e.g. *The psychogenesis of mental disease* (2nd ed., London 1972) 192 §423; *TE* 238 §400; *PPT* 46 §98; *CT* 168 §357; *DP* 83 §§156–7, 177 §302; *SL* 274 §627; *PA* 10 §11.

[73] Everyone, without exception, is being eaten away by "the spirit that runs through the masses": *AS* 117–18 §153. For Jung's summary assessment of Jungians—"analysts are not exceptional people", i.e. are no better able to understand what

really matters than anyone else—see *JK* 157. On the academic eradication of Empedocles as magician by either falsifying or turning a blind eye to all the evidence see, for example, the rationalizing achievements of H. Diels, *Sitzungsberichte der Königlich Preussischen Akademie der Wissenschaften zu Berlin* (1898) 407–11 and B.A. van Groningen, *Classica et mediaevalia* 17 (1956) 47–61 with my comments in *APMM*, esp. 217–32; J.–C. Picot, *Revue de philosophie ancienne* 18 (2000) 25–86 with *ENM* 342 n.12, 351–8, 387–99. For the scholarly obliteration of Parmenides as magician see the evidence presented in *IDPW*; *ENM* 379–80 with *Reality* 34–294; L. Gemelli Marciano, *Ancient philosophy* 28 (2008) 21–48 and *PSIE*. "Our time no longer needs magic": *RB* 314a.

[74] The inscription: *JL* i 49; *JP* 297; *MDR* 222/235 n.5; T. Ziolkowski, *The view from the tower* (Princeton 1998) 145; Jung briefly touches on the dynamics of *poenitentia* in *Aion* 191–2 §299. He describes the inscription as "hidden" in his letter to Alice Raphael dated 7 June 1955 ("... in my tower in Bollingen is a hidden inscription: *Philemonis sacrum Fausti poenitentia* ...": Alice Raphael papers, Beinecke Library, Yale University; the published transcription at *JH* 2/2, 2007, 6 is inaccurate). With regard to the element of secrecy, it will be noted that even the Latin word *sacrum* itself had strong overtones of something "secret" (*Lygdamus*, ed. F.N. Antolín, Leiden 1996, 430; L.A. Fisher, *The mystic vision in the Grail legend and in the 'Divine comedy'*, New York 1917, 63–5). For Jung's own association of shrine or sanctuary with secrecy see *JL* i 140–1 plus 140 n.1.

[75] Jung as Faust: *MDR* 221–2/234–5; and cf. *JL* i 309–10. "It's a very long step ... a very different proposition": *SL* 610-11 §1396. "One virtually has to die": *JB* i 385 ("Man muß ja allerdings fast gestorben sein"), cf. *JL* i 310; for Jung's reference

at the beginning of this letter as well as at *JL* i 316 to sitting on the edge of a volcano compare *JP* 149, *APMM* 73–8, 239–40, 280, *IDPW* 68–9, 90 and especially *JV* i 594–7. Descent into hell and recognition of one's "complicity in the act of evil": *RB* 243b, 274b, 288–91; L.S. Owens and S.A. Hoeller in *Encyclopedia of psychology and religion* (2nd ed., New York 2014), ed. D.A. Leeming, 979.

[76] The evil of the new: *MDR* 223–4/235–7; *JP* 212–13. Vicious innovators: *JP* 213; and compare *JL* i 309–10 on Philemon and Baucis alone standing up to the godforsaken ruthlessness of our present age. Faust's "hubris and inflation": *ETG* 238 (cf. *MDR* 221/234); see also *PA* 479–81 §§559–63, *SL* 750 §1699.

[77] *PA* 480–1 §§561–3. Faust's inflation in having Philemon and Baucis killed and their cottage burned to the ground is linked to the collective inflation of Germany not only here but also in *JL* i 310; Jung's letter to Alice Raphael dated 7 June 1955, comparing "the great conflagration of German cities, where all the simple people burned to death" (*JH* 2/2, 2007, 6); *MDR* 221–2/234–5. The veiled but consistent accounts by Jung of his own penance do raise the question of whether the many people who have criticized him for what they believe to be his "moral deficit" (I owe this expression to Paul Bishop: *Jung in contexts*, London 1999, 17) understand anything at all about what he was trying in his life to do.

[78] The magics of Mephistopheles and Merlin: *JP* 212–13. Remedying Faust's actions through "recognition of 'the ancient'" and by ensuring the continuity of history and culture: *MDR* 222/235 = *JP* 233 (although "intellectual history" is hardly satisfactory as a translation of "Geistesgeschichte"; for preservation of cultural traditions cf. *JP* 212–13). Also

mentioned here is genuine respect for humans and their eternal rights—but of course to be able to respect such rights supposes an insight into eternity.

[79] For Jung's many-sidedness see e.g. *PP* 38 (1998) 33, *JSB* 39–42; on the ease of being swallowed up by the past, *IJP* 152. "We are a blinded and deluded race … fail to hear the dead": *RBu* 296b (cf. *RB* 297b). "Annehmen" in Jung's German, for people's failure to "receive" or "honour" the dead, is mistranslated at *RB* 297b as "accept": compare the crucial role played, for Jung, by Philemon and Baucis in both receiving and honouring the gods (ibid. 315; *PA* 480 §§561–2). And more serious is the mistranslation, a few lines later, of "damit die Toten ihn entlassen" as "so that the dead will not let him"—instead of "so that the dead will let him go free".

[80] This is a very rough paraphrase of the magically evocative account by Jung which, together with Jaffé's instructive crossings out and revisions, still remains unpublished: *JP* 113. Throughout his life he kept emphasizing the need to get back, in every aspect of his work, to and beyond the beginnings of Christianity: compare e.g. *PPT* 82 §§188–9, "We are therefore forced to go back to pre-Christian and non-Christian conceptions … Medieval physicians seem to have realized this, for they practised a philosophy whose roots can be traced back to pre-Christian times and whose nature exactly corresponds to our experiences with patients today"; *ST* 3–5 §1. For the "treasure hard to attain" see *ST*; *PA* 117 §155, 158 §205, 170–1 §222, 335–46 §§438–48; *PPT* 82 §187; *MC* 531 §756. On Jung's early fascination with the Grail, note especially *JP* 160–1. And on his passion for archaeology see *FJ* 277 §157J (14 October 1909; cf. 270 §154F, 9 August 1909), 284 §159J (8 November), 307 §170J (25 December); *JL* i 29, 113,

ii 307; *DP* 154 §262; *PPT* 45 §96, 50 §111; *JS* 209, 428, 457; *MDR* 79–90/72–84, 158/162. The name of Jung is strangely missing from recent literature on the topic of philosophical or psychological archaeology (e.g. G. Agamben, *The signature of all things*, New York 2009; J. Thomas in *Contemporary archaeologies*, ed. C. Holtorf and A. Piccini, Frankfurt 2009, 33–45; C. McQuillan, *Parrhesia* 10, 2010, 39–49), although work in progress by Paul Bishop is due to fill that gap.

[81] For alchemy as the crucial bridge back to the Gnostics see especially *JP* 176, 226, 228, *MDR* 192–3/201; for the imagery of the bridge compare e.g. *ST* 4 §1, *JL* i 354, *DP* 145 §250 plus A.C. Lammers, *In God's shadow* (Mahwah 1994) 11–16; when referring to alchemy Jung also enjoyed using the English expression "missing link". The Gnostics who "lived in the first, second and third centuries ...": R.I. Evans, *Jung on elementary psychology* (New York 1976) 232, cf. *JS* 350. The dangers of losing one's head: *MDR* 170/176. The misunderstandings of Jung's statement that the Gnostics were too remote or distant from him (*MDR* 192/201, *JP* 175) have been legion (cf. e.g. R.A. Segal, *The Gnostic Jung*, Princeton 1992, 10; D. Bair, *Jung*, Boston 2003, 370), but it means exactly what he says: they were too deep in the psyche or distant in time, and the link between them and him was missing. For the golden chain or, in Latin, *aurea catena* see especially P. Lévêque's classic work *Aurea catena Homeri* (Paris 1959); Jung refers to the chain at e.g. *PA* 114 n.24; *JL* i 351 with n.3, ii 396; *MC* 254 §344; *MDR* 181/189, 196/205. It will be noted that this important image of a golden chain was transmitted from classical Greek antiquity not only into medieval western alchemy but also into Sufi tradition—where, as the *silsilat adh-dhahab*, it came to play a crucial role for the Naqshbandi Sufi lineage in particular. See for example Mawlânâ 'Alî ibn Husain Safî, *Beads of dew from*

the source of life, trans. M. Holland (Fort Lauderdale 2001) 2, 31, 41–2; H. Algar, *Die Welt des Islams* 13 (1971) 191 with n.3; J.S. Trimingham, *The Sufi orders in Islam* (Oxford 1971) 150. For the devout, but futile attempts at providing an exclusively Islamic explanation of this imagery cf. M.H. Faghfoory in Shaykh Muhammad 'Ali Mu'adhdhin Sabzawârî Khurâsânî, *Tuhfah yi-'Abbâsî* (Lanham 2008) xi; on the ancient "golden chain" or *silsilat adh-dhahab* of Greek philosophers as viewed through the eyes of later Arab alchemists see P. Lory, *Jâbir ibn Hayyân, L'Élaboration de l'élixir suprême* (Damascus 1988) 15; and for the underlying connections between Sufism and alchemy, *APMM* 66 with n.48, 386–91.

[82] On alchemical tradition, for Jung, as fundamentally indistinguishable from Gnosticism see e.g. *PR* 97–102 §160–1, *AS* 204–5 §252, *MC* 243–5 §§327–8, 434–8 §§626–8; and note the relevance of recent attempts to find alchemical ideas in Gnostic literature (D.M. Burns, *Aries* 15, 2015, 81–108). Forever keen as an intellectual to differentiate wherever differentiations are not needed, Robert Segal has claimed that Jung considered alchemy more important than Gnosticism because "he devotes three whole volumes to alchemy but only one essay to Gnosticism, and even this essay deals partly with parallels to alchemy" (*The Gnostic Jung*, Princeton 1992, 8–9). Firstly, though, he fails to notice the irony of the fact that he himself ends up offering such an enormous list of references for passages where Jung refers throughout his writings to Gnosticism (ibid. 9 n.26); secondly he overlooks the significance of the fact that the one major work, *Aion*, where Jung devotes so much space to Gnosticism is also the one in which he claims he deposited his "secret knowledge" (M. Ostrowski–Sachs, *From conversations with C.G. Jung*, Zurich 1971, 68); and third, if Segal had taken the trouble to study

in depth the Gnostic and alchemical texts he claimed to write about, he would have realized that Jung's real reason for not speaking about Gnosticism at greater length was because what is most important and most sacred should only be referred to indirectly. Segal then makes the further mistake of trying to distinguish the supposedly transformative and holistic worldview implicit in alchemy from a supposedly radical, otherworldly or salvational dualism on the part of the Gnostics (*The Gnostic Jung* 31–3, cf. *SFJI* 13/2, Summer 1994, 51–65; this simplistic caricature of the Gnostic outlook is also a crucial flaw in more recent literature such as Sanford Drob's *Kabbalistic visions*, New Orleans 2010, or in summaries such as Ann Casement's *Carl Gustav Jung*, London 2001). But the new mass of Gnostic texts found at Nag Hammadi in 1945, together with a closer examination of other Gnostic literature already known and available for a long time, demonstrates that this view of the Gnostics as world-denying dualists has far more to do with the way orthodox Christians wanted to portray—and attack—them than with any grounded reality. See e.g. I. Dunderberg, *Beyond Gnosticism* (New York 2008); N.D. Lewis, *Cosmology and fate in Gnosticism and Graeco–Roman antiquity* (Leiden 2013); and for the relevance of the Nag Hammadi discoveries to Jung's own understanding of Gnosticism cf. L.S. Owens in A. Ribi, *The search for roots* (Los Angeles 2013) 4–6 with S.A. Hoeller in V. MacDermot, *The fall of Sophia* (Great Barrington 2001) 20. That leaves the final question of the extent to which Jung, himself, could at times be an otherworldly dualist. Many people reading a confession like "it's such a powerful force, this whole unspiritual domination by the earth, that I fear it. It has the ability to push the physical part of me into rebellion against the spirit so that before reaching the highest point of my flight I fall back, crippled, to the earth" might swear these are the words of an ancient Gnostic. In fact they were words written, as part of a personal letter, by Jung (*JB* i 72, cf. *JL* i 49; compare *ST* 396 §615). And, to points like this, one has a natural duty to add that the fundamental structure of two opposing spirits which is already introduced right at the start of the *Red book* owes a very clear debt to the dualistic structures of ancient Gnosticism (Owens 27).

[83] On the depth and persistence of Jung's later involvement with Gnosticism see *AN*, volumes vii–viii; A. Ribi, *Analytische Psychologie* 13 (1982) 210–11 and *The search for roots* (Los Angeles 2013) 130–47. On the other hand, that he had already been alerted to the profound significance of alchemical tradition by 1910 and early 1911 is not only stated without any ambiguity by Jung himself (*JL* i 274). It also is clear from the pencilled markings inside his own copy of Richard Reitzenstein's *Die hellenistischen Mysterienreligionen* (Leipzig 1910, especially 140–1): he devoured its contents as soon as the book was published so that he could refer to it in an important piece he himself would publish the following year (*JPPF* 3/1, 1911, 182 n.2), and his markings at the time show he was particularly fascinated by the alchemical visions of Zosimus. Equally revealing is a comment published by Sabina Spielrein during the same year, in which she notes that for the psychological symbolism of cooking and fire "Jung refers me to the vision of Zosimus" as recorded in Berthelot's *Les alchimistes grecs* (ibid. 353 n.2. Her language when she summarizes what Zosimus saw corresponds, almost exactly, to the wording in Jung's copy of Reitzenstein: for the ongoing relationship between her and Jung see e.g. J. Launer, *IJJS* 7, 2015, 186–9 with L.S. Owens in *Das Rote Buch*, ed. T. Arzt, Würzburg 2015, 234–6). And one year later Jung could hardly contain his continuing enthusiasm about what he had discovered, not only making multiple references in print to the visions of Zosimus

but even referring back to the involvement of Spielrein (*JPPF* 4/1, 1912, 184–5, 250 n.1, 352, 405 n.2, 408, 457 n.1). What this all means is that the traditional account, according to which Jung's interest in alchemy was first sparked or awakened by a Chinese alchemical text he would receive from Richard Wilhelm almost twenty years later, needs major modification. To be sure, he made the very conscious and deliberate decision to postpone plunging into the bewildering world of alchemy for as long as he humanly could. But the crucial fact here is that he had already made his first acquaintance with alchemical literature, and especially with the underworld visions of Zosimus, even before beginning his own formal descent into the underworld or starting work on the *Red book*. So when Andreas Schweizer stands astonished at the amazing similarities between the most terrifying visions in the *Red book* and the equally horrific visions of Zosimus, but makes sure to add "I do not assume that in 1914 Jung already knew the vision of Zosimos" (*JJ* 5/3, 2011, 89), there is no need to be quite so astonished and no need to assume anything. For over a century the evidence has been available that shows Jung not only did know about the visions of Zosimus, but was very actively sharing them with others. And, what's more, clear proof that he had already started teaching the psychological significance of alchemy is also ready to hand. See the note left behind by one of his pupils from a seminar he gave in the summer of 1913, "Alchemy = discovering the secret of rebirth" (notebook titled "*Seminar.* Dr Jung. Summer 1913", Papers of Fanny Bowditch Katz, Countway Library of Medicine, Boston: "Alchemie = das Geheimnis der Wiedergeburt zu finden").

[84] For personality no. 2 as not only the source of "meaning and historical continuity" but also the "region of inner darkness" see *MDR* 92/87. Of course one minor implication of this is that

history and meaning are fundamentally inseparable, which is a position many modern academics will fight to the end (cf. e.g. K. von Stuckrad's chillingly inhuman prohibitions, *Numen* 49, 2002, 215). On the ancient tradition, already prefigured in Parmenides, of outstripping scholars at their own game see *Reality* 221–58. For Jung's understanding of alchemical literature outstripping even the knowledge of Julius Ruska, the greatest expert on alchemical tradition at the time, see e.g. *APMM* 56–8. His original words about the exhaustive and exhausting nature of his own philological method are well worth reading (*JP* 17: the published version in *MDR* 196/205 edits out the most meaningful details); by way of contrast, with few exceptions the work of professional philologists usually left him cold (*FJ* 296 §165J). As for his knowledge of ancient languages, with her usual modesty Marie–Louise von Franz states that later in his life Jung did come to know "Latin and Greek fluently, as well as I do" (*PP* 38, 1998, 15). But although von Franz's own knowledge of Latin and Greek was for the greater part acceptable (see, however, *PB* iv/I 211 with 212 n.4, 233 with 234 n.8; iv/II 121, 385–6), there was often something wooden and almost mechanical about it—whereas Jung's intuitive sensitivity to these languages, which he had already started learning to a high standard as a child (see e.g. J. Sherry, *Carl Gustav Jung*, New York 2010, 21–2; compare also J. Kirsch, *PP* 6, 1975, 60 and testimonials such as *JJW* 7), is the kind that only comes from approaching something with one's whole body and being. Today there are very few people alive who would be able to read Iamblichus' *On the mysteries* in the original Greek as Jung did (see for example the bookmarked note in his personal copy of W. Scott's *Hermetica* iv, Oxford 1936, 36–7); he did his own translations from the difficult Greek written by Zosimus of Panopolis, just consulting von Franz with gratitude on particular philological issues (*PA* x, 360 n.21); and he refused to use the standard published translations of ancient alchemical texts, dismissing them as unreliable because the translators had no real sense of what they were translating (*JP* B31, 19 October 1958). For the scholarly literature denouncing Jung's approach to western alchemy as "unhistorical" because, aside from daring to consider alchemical tradition something essentially spiritual, it also presents a challenge to the simplistic modern creed "that alchemy is not a transhistorical myth but a construct which is culturally produced" (U. Szulakowska, *The alchemy of light*, Leiden 2000, 10) see e.g. W.R. Newman, *Revue d'histoire des sciences* 49 (1996) 159–88; L.M. Principe and Newman in *Secrets of nature*, ed. Newman and A. Grafton (Cambridge, MA 2001) 385–431; plus the kind of references cited by W.J. Hanegraaff, *New age religion and western culture* (Leiden 1996) 509–13 and *Esotericism and the academy* (Cambridge 2012) 195–7, 265, 286–95. Aside from their embarrassingly flimsy rhetoric, such academics would of course need a miracle to get rid of all the evidence showing that western alchemy was a great deal more than glorified laboratory work right from the start: cf. *PA* 78 §99 with n.30, *PR* 97–8 §160; *APMM* 390 n.56 with P. Kingsley in *Crossing religious frontiers*, ed. H. Oldmeadow (Bloomington, IN 2010) 47–8; H. Tilton, *The quest for the phoenix* (Berlin 2003) 1–34; K.A. Fraser, *Dionysius* 25 (2007) 40–51; G.–F. Calian, *Annual of medieval studies at CEU* 16 (2010) 166–90; also D. Boccassini, *Quaderni di studi indo–mediterranei* 5 (2012) 7–8 and A. Cheak in his *Alchemical traditions* (Melbourne 2013) 30–2. As, finally, for the repeated claim by some experts (e.g. Hanegraaff, *New age religion* 503 and *Esotericism* 288–9) that Jung in his unhistorical fantasies invented a fictional Gnostic origin for his vision of a star at the core of every human: if such scholars were to do their own historical job, rather than being so quick to reprimand others for failing to do theirs, they would easily be able to verify that Jung found this very same star imagery in the ancient *Mithras liturgy*. See e.g. G. Quispel, *Gnostica, Judaica, Catholica* (Leiden 2008) 618; the multiple markings in Jung's own edition of the text (A. Dieterich, *Eine Mithrasliturgie*, 2nd ed., Leipzig 1910, 8–9); *JPPF* 3/1 (1911) 200–3 = *ST* 86–90 §§130–5; *BB* v 167–8 with *NZ* ii 1046; *SD* 492 §929; *MDR* 215/227 with n.3; and for the *Mithras liturgy* in its original Gnostic context note the comments by R. van den Broek, *Gnostic religion in antiquity* (Cambridge 2013) 136–50.

[85] For Jung's despair at the impossibility of being understood when he speaks about the dead, see *JP* B26 (13 June 1958). "They still live on": J. Hillman and S. Shamdasani, *Lament of the dead* (New York 2013) 2; cf. *RB* 296–8. On the world of the dead as the reverse of this world see e.g. *APMM* 77 with n.27, 186–7 with n.48. Already by 1918 Jung had become aware that it was the Gnostics who would provide the ultimate "foundations", the "Fundamente", for his own psychology (letter to J.B. Lang dated 9 March 1918, poorly translated at *RB* 207b). But after all his efforts and his work with patients and his scientific discoveries had still left him unrooted, suspended in mid-air, he finally realized it was the alchemists who would provide him with the firm footing and stable foundation he needed because they were the solid bridge deck that could lead him straight back to the Gnostics. Finishing that bridge was a task he was only able to complete with the last major book he ever wrote, and without this firm basis in the past his work would have been nothing but a "phantasmagoria" (*JP* 175–6, 226–8, 233). For the imagery, here, of rootedness and unrootedness see *ST* xxiv–xxv; for being suspended in mid-air compare *PR* 102 §162; and note that Jung's explicit link (*JP* 233) between the completion

of his historical work with *Mysterium coniunctionis* and the completion of his atonement for the crime of Faust has been broken, like so much else, by Aniela Jaffé in her preparation of the published biography. As for his poignant statement here that without the solid historical foundation provided by Gnosticism and alchemy his psychology would have remained a mere phantasmagoria devoid of any substance (*JP* 228), not to mention his anxiety about living no more than a hollow phantom-like existence (ibid. 227; *MDR* 181–2/189), this is a very clear instance of how deeply he had been influenced by Goethe's *Faust*: see D. Luke, *Goethe: Faust part two* (Oxford 1994) xlii and, for the topic in general, M. Warner, *Phantasmagoria* (Oxford 2006). Meanwhile this imagery of both Gnosticism and alchemy as the solid grounding, foothold, foundation not only for his own experiences but for his whole psychology is so crucial that almost predictably it has been either misunderstood or ignored. Trying her best to make sense of it, Jaffé not only rationalizes but trivializes the whole idea by irrelevantly inserting the explanation that alchemy could form a strong bridge back to Gnosticism because it was "grounded" in medieval philosophy—a timely reminder of how little even the people closest to Jung really understood his thoughts and ideas (*MDR* 193/201). In fact Jung's vision of alchemical, and ultimately Gnostic, wisdom as the only true foundation for his work or his life is biblical through and through. I am grateful to the Kant scholar Paula Manchester for pointing me to the seminal imagery of Christ as the one and only true foundation in 1 Corinthians, which just so happened to be Jung's favourite among all the letters of St Paul; and compare, too, the purely biblical "foundation" imagery that keeps recurring throughout the *Red book* (*RB* 230b, 320a, 340a; cf. also 211 n.176 on laying the foundation of one's inner church). For the New Testament imagery of the one and only foundation see J. Pfammatter,

Die Kirche als Bau (Rome 1960), and for its deep influence on German literature as well as philosophy cf. D.L. Purdy, *On the ruins of Babel* (Ithaca, NY 2011), especially 84–6, 92–3.

[86] Jung as an elderly man finds himself, despite all the usual chatter and clichés about his non-dualistic worldview, still positing the firmest dualistic distinction between "this" world and the world of "reality" (*JP* 226)—just as, almost half a century earlier, he had explained that we humans live in two quite separate worlds (*RB* 264a; L.S. Owens, *PP* 54, 2011, 273). How and to what extent he managed to resolve such a dualism by, like the alchemists, finding this world in that and that world in the play of this is a story of its own; but by starting in such a way from a dualistic foundation the tensions will never just vanish. This is the difference between dualism and non-dualism, whether they happen to be ethical or metaphysical; eastern or western. Dualists begin from a position of deep conflict and work towards an inner reconciliation, a hard-earned oneness, whereas monists or non-dualists start from a position of oneness and then have to cheat themselves into making one half of existence disappear. For Jung on our normal, ephemeral existence see e.g. *ST* 3 §1: "A moment ago, and we were completely absorbed in the hectic, ephemeral life of the present; then, the next moment, something very remote and strange flashes upon us, which directs our gaze to a different order of things. We turn away from the vast confusion of the present to glimpse the higher continuity of history". Of course that conflicts profoundly with the modern, eastern-inspired and most often quite rootless attempts at living in the present moment or "now". This is why it can be very important to note that according to Parmenides one first has to make the journey to hell, into the depths of the underworld, before being able to discover the living reality of

the "now" (*Reality* 26–186); and that Empedocles, too, offered a beautiful but very intricate system of practices for learning how to come fully into one's senses (ibid. 318–559). Again, as Jung himself said, we get nowhere when we strip western or eastern teachings from their proper context. On the frequent inability of eastern meditation techniques to give westerners access to their inner nature see also P. Kingsley, *Works & conversations* 22 (2011) 31–3.

[87] "If we seek ...": *SL* 829 §1833, and note the immediately preceding sentence where Jung emphasizes that his professional interest in the Gnostic texts "is not only of a theoretical but also of a practical nature". For the stresses and strains surrounding Jung's delivery of this talk see *JW* 223 = *JL* ii 138 with G. Quispel, *Gnostica, Judaica, Catholica* (Leiden 2008) 151–2. "We are not of today ...": *JS* 433, cf. 337. "We're ancient, incredibly ancient ...": *IDPW* 9. "Supra-personal connections ... obviously wrong": *PPT* 46 §99. For neurosis as a symptom of people's alienation from the world of their ancestors see e.g. *MDR* 142/143–4 and, on neuroses as primarily a general or collective problem rather than a personal or individual phenomenon, compare also ibid. 196–7/205–6, 221/233–4: Jung's trenchant observation that professional therapists in his time were failing to take these collective factors sufficiently into account is still true now and will remain true, as long as the greater cultural issues are not addressed. On the obliteration of the greatest Gnostics by Christianity cf. *JL* i 34 and, for the psychological implications of Gnosticism being not just suppressed but "stamped out completely", *PR* 97 §160 with *SL* 828 §§1829–30. Aristotelianism forcing the western mind to deviate "from its original basis": *JL* i 316–17. For the specific denial that, without history, there can be any psychology see *MDR* 197/205 (compare e.g. *PR* 102 §162, within the immediate

context of 97–102 §§160–1; *FJ* 307 §170J, 25 December 1909). Contemporary literature on Jung is predictably quick to divert such statements into quite different channels of meaning. Note for example Marilyn Nagy's confidently stated belief "that history serves this indispensable purpose, that unless we understand where we came from we can't understand ourselves in the present moment"—which she promptly interprets as pointing to "the urgency of understanding Jung in his own cultural context", i.e. the cultural context of European intellectualism in the nineteenth and twentieth century (*SFJI* 14/2, Summer 1995, 26). On the absolute indispensability of knowing Latin and Greek see *JP* B31 (at Bollingen, 19 October 1958). Of course Jungians can try to claim there is no need for them to learn Latin or Greek because Jung has done all the dirty work for them and they can discover whatever they want about psychology in his published books, or through their trainings. But that's not to understand what Jung was saying, or to take him seriously.

[88] Even when the unpublished Protocols of Jung's interviews with Aniela Jaffé are published, it will be only too easy to miss the remarkable but paradoxical consistency in his crucial account of how initially he had depended on his family and no. 1 personality to serve as the solid ground or foundation which would protect him from the infinite terrors of his inner world—but ultimately found the real ground or foundation for himself, and his work, in the deepest depths of that inner world he had been so scared of (*JP* 226–8). Jaffé unfortunately severed the first part of this account (*MDR* 181–2/189) from the rest, and lost the inner connection. The idea of an "everlasting foundation" stems from Proverbs 10:25 but became a standard part of alchemical language together with any number of other expressions such as foundation of the

apostles and prophets; the foundation of all nature and all that is created; the heavenly foundation stone and cornerstone; the foundations of Zion; the stone of stones or philosophers' stone which is the foundation of this art (*MC* 14–15 §§10–11, 92 n.7, 296 §404, 345 §485, 391 n.53, 437–8 §627, 442 n.288, 444 n.306, 447 §640). Jung, for his own part, called it the "indestructible foundation" of experience which a person or patient can only ever encounter by being left completely alone "to find out what it is that supports him when he can no longer support himself" (*PA* 28 §32; cf. *RB* 323a, *MC* 533 §758). Compare, already, his wild questioning in the *Red book* about whether there is any foundation in chaos or whether the real foundation is the chaos itself (*RB* 298a). For the ancient Orphic speculations about whether or not the abysmal chasm of Tartarus has an ultimate basis or foundation, see *APMM* 126–9.

[89] For Jung no longer belonging to himself but to the "generality", see *MDR* 184/192; *JP* 183, 258. And note also the equally important passage where he has been explaining that there are a few people around the world who understand "the divine cause of my existence" because, thanks to the divine will, he has "unconsciously conveyed" his message to them. Then he says: "Conforming to the divine will I live for mankind, not only for myself, and whoever understands this message contained in and conveyed by my writing will also live for me" (*JW* 71). While the parallelism has been well noted between the first half of this comment and the statement in Jung's biography about him no longer living for himself (cf. e.g. L.S. Owens, *PP* 54, 2011, 266), the second half of the sentence has been strangely neglected—perhaps because his comments about the "message" and living "for me" are so plainly biblical and so clearly modelled on the message of Christ. A valuable insight

into what it means to live, and pray, for Jung is offered by the personal comments of Barbara Robb as preserved at *JW* 74–6.

[90] "For your state ... have built up": *ETG* 286, *MDR* 264/283. A detailed chronology of Jung's visit to Kolkata is offered by A. Ribi, *Analytische Psychologie* 13 (1982) 204–5. "The answer to the spiritual problem ... nowhere save in the symbolism of alchemy": M.–L. von Franz, *C.G. Jung: his myth in our time* (New York 1975) 279; only a few pages earlier von Franz herself had, evidently without grasping its full significance, repeated Jung's own observation that the Grail symbolism reaches back to the Gnostics (ibid. 271–2) just as she often repeated in passing his observation that western alchemy reached back to Gnosticism. But as Lance Owens has very pertinently noted about the subtle marginalization of ancient Gnosticism by later Jungians: "The last disciples to work personally with Jung arrived in a period when his lectures and publications centered on alchemy, and this undoubtedly influenced perceptions about the foundation of his work. Perhaps the most important figure among that final generation was Marie–Louise von Franz, Jung's indispensable collaborator throughout his research into alchemical literature from the late 1930s onwards. After Jung's death, Dr. von Franz naturally became a formative force in the perpetuation of his work ... Her erudition and close association with Jung's alchemical studies also underscored the role of alchemy as an historical focal point for Jungian commentary" (foreword to A. Ribi, *The search for roots*, Los Angeles 2013, 279–80 n.13; on the less theoretical and more personal side of von Franz's identification with the field of alchemy compare D. Bair, *Jung*, Boston 2003, 370–2). For von Franz's schoolteacherly dogmatism, which of course has won her many devoted admirers who without it would feel quite lost, see e.g. *PB* iv/II 196 plus the childishly

innocent portrayal in T.B. Kirsch, *A Jungian life* (Carmel, CA 2014) 19; on her positive pride in her dogmatic rigidity and "fossilizing" of Jung, M. Anthony, *Jung's circle of women* (York Beach 1999) 66–8 with Bair 368, 770 n.69; and for the regrettable consequences of her common tendency to express herself in terms of "always", or "nowhere save", cf. A. Samuels, *Jung and the post-Jungians* (London 1985) 94. Unfortunately the conscious determination of von Franz as well as Edward Edinger to keep Jung's ideas unchanged led on a subtle level to the very opposite result, because to fossilize ideas or laws or teachings brought from another world is already to change them.

[91] As Jung beautifully states this: "The reality is that we have always already known everything all along. All these things are always present for us, but the trouble is that we are not present for these things. The possibility of the deepest insight was there for us all the time, but we were always just too far away from it. What we call evolution or progress is going round and round a central point so as to come gradually closer to it. The truth is that we always remain on the same spot, just a little bit further from or closer to the centre. ... Originally we were all born out of a world of wholeness, and during the first years of our lives are still enclosed completely inside it. There we have all knowledge without knowing it. Later we lose it, and call it progress when we remember again" (*JB* i 345–6, cf. *JL* i 274–5: 22 July 1939; for the recipient of the letter see *JN* 185–7 n.339). Interestingly, and contrary to the usual stereotypes about a woman's intuition, Jung adds that one of the greatest obstacles to understanding or living this perspective is the rigidity of a woman's animus with its "special peculiarity of making false rationalizations about everything" (275). Looking back and into oneself: *RB* 106, 297b.

[92] For some concise comments on the dance of our lives and dreams see *PA* 28 §34, "The way is not straight but appears to go round in circles. More accurate knowledge has proved it to go in spirals: the dream-motifs always return after certain intervals to definite forms, whose characteristic it is to define a centre ..."; and compare 179–80 §§245–6, including n.124, on the specific connection between spirals and the Grail. On the Gnostic and Hermetic origins of the Grail cf. e.g. *PT* 234–42 §§396–409, *IJP* 107, *PA* 180 n.125, *JP* 358. Regarding the Hermetic or Gnostic *kratêr* see *Corpus hermeticum* 4; *Collection des anciens alchimistes grecs*, ed. M. Berthelot (Texte grec, Paris 1887–88) 245.4–7 = *Zosimo di Panopoli: visioni e risvegli*, ed. A. Tonelli (Milan 1988) 120.27–122.2 with R. Reitzenstein, *Poimandres* (Leipzig 1906) 8–9 (as cited by Jung himself, *AS* 73 n.21) and P. Kingsley, *JWCI* 56 (1993) 2–3 = *PJB* 43–4; *DA* 328, *PA* 299 §§408–9, 368 §457, *PR* 91 §150, 101 n.71, 210 §313, 225 §344, 233 §355, *CD* 224–5, *PPT* 312 n.18, *Aion* 191 n.19, *AS* 73 §§96–7, *MC* 240 n.633, 503–4 §717, *MDR* 193/201. Grail as *kratêr* and *kratêr* as Grail: *JV* i 328, *NZ* ii 936; *CD* 225, 295; H. and R. Kahane, *Zeitschrift für deutsches Altertum und deutsche Literatur* 89 (1959) 191–213 and *The krater and the grail* (Urbana 1965); *EII* ii 141–55, 192–8; *APMM* 133–48 with 135 n.9; and for the historians of language who trace the origin of the word "grail" itself all the way back to the ancient Greek word *kratêr* see F. Diez, *Etymologisches Wörterbuch der romanischen Sprachen* (Bonn 1853) 648, W.W. Skeat, *Joseph of Arimathie* (London 1871) xxxvi–xxxvii, W.A. Nitze, *Modern philology* 13 (1916) 185–8 and *American journal of philology* 66 (1945) 279–81. On the *kratêr* in Zurich and Jung, himself, as the *kratêr* see *DA* 328, 419; M. Mather, *The alchemical Mercurius* (Hove 2014) 176, 182. As the editor notes (*DA* 419 with n.9), when Jung talks about someone wanting to "go to the krater at Zurich for analysis—to the *Jungbrunnen*"

or the "fountain of youth", he is punning very obviously on his own name: for the *kratêr* as a living fountain flowing with the magic of its wonder-working waters compare *ST* 431 n.73, *AS* 73 §97, *MC* 503–4 §717. And by comparing the Zurich *kratêr* directly with an ancient "mystical society" (*DA* 328) he is revealing more than a little about how he viewed the group of people who were gathering around him during the 1920s. For *kratêr*, saviour and salvation see, aside from Jung's discussion at *DA* 128, his further comments in *PR* 91 §150. On the *kratêr* as containing the *pharmakon athanasias*, "the medicine of immortality which makes the new man", see *DA* 127–8 and also 108 ("… in which the new being is made …"): Jung's fondness for the expression *pharmakon athanasias*, medicine of immortality, derives from his reading of Richard Reitzenstein's *Die hellenistischen Mysterienreligionen* (*PA* 98 §125 with n.3) although the idea itself goes back all the way to Empedocles (*APMM* 218–23). For the *kratêr* as primordial symbol of Jungian psychology see *MDR* 193/201 with W. Giegerich, *Harvest* 45/1 (1999) 11, "In the account Jung gives of the prehistory of his psychology, it primordially appears as a mixing vessel sent by the higher god"; G. Nicolaus, *C.G. Jung and Nikolai Berdyaev* (Hove 2011) 129.

[93] Already by 1898 Jung had shown his instinctive fascination with the legends of Empedocles' leap into Mount Etna, as well as his curiosity about what the real motive was behind the jump (*ZL* 70 §179). And already by 1912 he was describing Empedocles at Etna as throwing himself into "the *kratêr* of rebirth", "der 'Krater' der Wiedergeburt" (*JPPF* 4/1, 1912, 430 and n.1, cf. 463 with n.1: later modified at *ST* 405 §626, 439 §682 with n.88). This is a theme he will keep coming back to, and discuss at much greater length, later on in his life (*JV* i 487 and 594–7; *NZ* ii 1215–20). Not only Hölderlin but Nietzsche

too, as Jung correctly guessed (ibid. 1217, 1220), had been very much affected by the legend of Empedocles on Etna—so much so that, as we now know, it had provided the original model and backdrop for his *Zarathustra* (D.F. Krell, *Postponements*, Bloomington, IN 1986, and *Lunar voices*, Chicago 1995, 3–23; C. Crawford, *To Nietzsche: Dionysus, I love you! Ariadne*, Albany 1995, 72–5 and in *Nietzsche and depth psychology*, ed. J. Golomb, W. Santaniello and R. Lehrer, Albany 1999, 293–4 n.66). For the stream of volcanic lava out of which all of Jung's later creativity flowed one should consult his words at *JP* 149, rather than the doctored version of them published in *MDR* 190–1/199; for the corresponding crater which, through giving direct access to the underworld, is absolutely central to the dynamics of the *Red book* as a whole see *RB* 247–8, 252a, 366b plus *IJP* 68, 104–5; and note the later, very serious joke that any successful study of Jung's life would have to be a major work of volcanology (letter from Cary Baynes to Jung dated 19 November 1953 and from him to her dated 30 November: *CBA*). That the ultimate purpose behind throwing oneself into the vessel of rebirth is not only to become immortal but to become a god is stated by Jung both in connection with Empedocles (e.g. *JV* i 487, *ST* 405 §626) and elsewhere (*IJP* 107).

[94] For everything falling into place when one has the "historical pattern", see *JP* 16 (a passage excluded from *MDR* 196/205); and compare Jung's well-stated comments on the complete futility of contemplating only the surface of history because, that way, the living reality always "eludes the inquiring eye of the historian" (*CT* 148–9 §315). On the syncretistic nature of Gnosticism see e.g. *Aion* 173 §267 and, for the frequent use he makes of the term "syncretism", *PR* 117 §178, *MC* 410 §591. One typical example of the syncretism running like a thread

through his own life and writings is the dramatic scene inside the *Red book* where his soul hands him the crushing mystery of the magic rod or serpent, soon followed by the seemingly more peaceful scene at Philemon's cottage describing how the old man's magic rod is tucked away in a cupboard alongside the wisdom of Hermes Trismegistus as well as the magical books of Moses (*RB* 307–8, 312a). The significance of these episodes can only be appreciated when one realizes that the magic rod in both cases is not only the famous rod of Moses which turns into a serpent but also the sacred healing wand of Asclepius or Hermes, and that the juxtaposition of mystical texts claiming to be written both by Hermes Trismegistus and by Moses was a constant feature of the ancient syncretistic magic so well known to Jung through the books in his library (cf. e.g. A. Dieterich, *Abraxas*, Leipzig 1891, 70–1, 136–205). The incorporation of Jewish authorities and teachings, sometimes real but sometimes fictional, into late-Hellenistic magical literature was one aspect of an immensely complex cultural phenomenon (*PJB* 69 with n.77, *APMM* 242 with n.29). Richard Reitzenstein wrote a long note about it, which Jung read with his usual attention to detail and made sure to highlight for future reference in his own copy of Reitzenstein's book (*Poimandres*, Leipzig 1904, 14 n.1). Jung himself refers repeatedly in his writings to the complexities of this "Jewish syncretism" (cf. e.g. *CD* 447, *Aion* 58 §105, *JL* ii 90; and for a classic discussion of the phenomenon see E.R. Goodenough's *By light, light*, New Haven 1935, also owned by Jung), where nothing is ever as simple as it seems. Religious and mystical traditions rubbed shoulders with each other, interacted in the subtlest of ways. For example Jews out on the fringes of orthodox Judaism appropriated and absorbed Orphic mystical traditions to create "a superficially Judaized version of the God of the Orphic mystery" (Goodenough 278–97; cf. C.

Riedweg, *Jüdisch–hellenistische Imitation eines orphischen Hieros Logos*, Tübingen 1993), in much the same way that traditions originating with Empedocles would later be absorbed into medieval Jewish Kabbalah (*APMM* 378 n.21, cf. 395). The same infinitely intricate interplay of different elements would also shape the earliest Hellenistic forms of alchemical literature—the complexities are well noted by G.G. Stroumsa, *Another seed* (Leiden 1984) 141 n.20 and K.A. Fraser, *Aries* 4 (2004) 126–7 with n.6—creating a situation where, as Jung points out, "already in Zosimos three sources can be distinguished: Jewish, Christian, and pagan" (*MC* 410 §591). And this triple distinction by Jung himself between Jewish, Christian and pagan brings us straight to his famous three visions of the *hieros gamos* or sacred marriage that came to him with almost ineffable power when he nearly died in 1944. Sanford Drob has rather shamelessly labelled them "Kabbalistic visions" (*JJTP* 7/1, 2005, 33–54; *Kabbalistic visions*, New Orleans 2010) even though only the first, which seems to have been stirred by some Jewish mystical literature he had just been given (S. Shamdasani, *Quadrant* 38/1, 2008, 22), contains any Kabbalistic symbolism at all; the second is Christian through and through, while the third derives straight from the Homeric account of Zeus' sacred union with Hera (*MDR* 274/294). Drob tried to justify his label by claiming that the second and third visions are just worthless straw compared to the Kabbalistic gold of the first, but this is the purest nonsense: Jung's threefold vision "has a kabbalistic, a Christian, and an ancient Greek part … they are all three of equal standing and support each other" (W. Giegerich, *JJTP* 7/1, 2005, 56; note also *JL* i 355–6, which mentions the Christian *hieros gamos* symbolism before the Kabbalistic, and 414–15). One only has to add that even the fact of him experiencing them in this, very particular, triple combination shows what a timeless affinity he had with the old Gnostics and alchemists such as Zosimus. Far more appropriately, Lance Owens has proposed referring to them as Jung's "Gnostic visions" (*PP* 54, 2011, 262).

[95] Gnosticism as a philosophical tradition going back to Greek philosophy: *PT* 11–16 §§14–23, *ACU* 174 §292, *PR* 117 §179, *JW* 119 (cf. *JK* 205), *Aion* 173 §267 (where the contrast in Jung's original German between Greek philosophy and Greek, as well as other, mythologies has been lost), *SL* 730 §1647. In his personal copy of Hans Leisegang's *Die Gnosis* (Leipzig 1924, 3) Jung has carefully underscored the introductory statement that not only early Christians but even classical philosophers, who knew very well what they were talking about, insisted on deriving the religion of the Gnostics "from ancient philosophy"—as well as Leisegang's later statement that Porphyry was perfectly correct when he traced the teachings of the Gnostics back to ancient philosophy, meaning back to the mystical philosophy of the Presocratics (ibid. 185). And in his private alchemy notebooks he also put together, with equal care, a list of references for ancient passages stating that the Gnostics "derive from the old philosophers" (*AN* vii 111). For Jung's letter, dated 22 December 1935, to Erich Neumann see *JN* 170 ("tief in Europa, im christlichen Mittelalter und in letzter Linie in der griechischen Philosophie verwurzelt"), adequately rendered into English at *JL* i 206. But the mistranslation of "in letzter Linie" as "in the last analysis" in the new Philemon Foundation edition of the Jung–Neumann letters is unfortunate (*Analytical psychology in exile*, ed. M. Liebscher, Princeton 2015, 118): Jung is referring not to some process of analysis but to a historical line or lineage. Sanford Drob chooses to override this formal statement by him about his own lineage because he considers that, in it, Jung has "ignored or marginalized" the crucial influence of Judaism

both on his own psychology and on alchemy (*JJTP* 7/1, 2005, 63); Drob seems unaware that, in the process, he has ended up ignoring and marginalizing Jung himself. And his claim that Jung outgrew this affiliation with Greek philosophy after the Second World War or, more crucially, after what Drob mistitles his "Kabbalistic visions" of 1944 is quite empty. Jung was still consistently prioritizing the influence of Greek philosophy on alchemy in his very last works, written after his 1944 visions and published during the 1950s (*Aion* 173 §267, *AS* 102 §134, *MC* 262 §353, cf. *JW* 119); and the passages which according to Drob (*JJ* 6/1, 2012, 40, citing *MC* 24 §19 and 384–5 §551) show that by the 1950s Jung had substituted Jewish Kabbalah for Greek philosophy as the decisive influence on western alchemy show, on the contrary, no more than that Jung continued to view Kabbalah as a parallel development to alchemical tradition and saw the first real impact of Kabbalistic influence on alchemical literature as only occurring late in the sixteenth century. "His explicit confession …": W. Giegerich, *JJTP* 7/1 (2005) 57. For the alchemists referring to themselves, very simply, as philosophers see *JS* 350, *PR* 98–101 §§160–1; P. Kingsley, *JWCI* 57 (1994) 9–13 with n.79, *APMM* 67 with n.49, *ENM* 338 n.7; and note how clearly Jung aligns himself with these alchemist–philosophers in stating that, whenever they claimed to understand something "philosophically", they meant they were understanding it "psychologically" (*Aion* 241 §379). For the "philosophers' vessel" cf. e.g. *PA* 238 n.20 with *Aion* 240–1 §§378–9; for the "philosophical fire", *Flying saucers* (London 1959) 104–5 = *CT* 384–5 §§726–7; for the true alchemical philosophy as opposed to Aristotelian philosophy, *Aion* 161 §248. Being saved and guided onto the right path by Parmenides: Bernard of Treviso in *Theatrum chemicum* i (Oberursel 1602) 795 (cf. *PA* 258 §363; *Aion* 143 §220). "Empedocles circles": *APMM* 376 with n.14; Kingsley in *Crossing religious frontiers*, ed. H. Oldmeadow (Bloomington, IN 2010) 47–8.

[96] Perhaps the most significant statement he does offer is his passing comment that, ever since the time of the ancient Greek mystic Heraclitus, any real sense for the synchronistic principle as so gloriously enshrined in the *I ching* has vanished from western philosophy (R. Wilhelm and C.G. Jung, *The secret of the golden flower*, London 1931, 144 = *SM* 57 §85, cf. *SD* 485 §916). Even more significant than the statement itself, though, is the fact that he never fully develops its historical implications and just leaves it hanging at the edge of his concerns. Jung's attitude to Heraclitus was in fact far more positive than could be guessed from the snapshot evaluation offered by his published biography, which is what most scholars repeat as a matter of course (*MDR* 76/68; cf. e.g. L. Huskinson, *Nietzsche and Jung*, Hove 2004, 81–6). Heraclitus was an immensely important source of inspiration for Jung—he calls him "indeed a very great sage", one of the columns or pillars that support the huge "bridge of the spirit stretching over the morass of world history", "my venerable deceased ancestor"—but precisely because Heraclitus had been so fierce in his independence, so obscure, and stood so far outside of any tradition (*TE* 72 §111, *JB* i 121, 154; cf. *JJW* 24–6, *NZ* ii 1272, *JP* 162 and J. Olney, *The rhizome and the flower*, Berkeley 1980, 89 n.2; the significance of the fact that Jung began his major inscription at Bollingen by faithfully carving out a saying from Heraclitus about *aiôn* is hard to overstate: *MDR* 215/227). For the Aristotelian "deviation" see *JL* i 316–17, and for Jung's almost instinctive aversion to Aristotle cf. e.g. *JS* 211, *JL* ii 501. He was happy, on the other hand, to boast in public of his familiarity with Plato (ibid. 500–1, *FJ* 382 §206J, *ACU* 78–9 §§153–4); but the reality

is that only the *Timaeus*, as well as other places where Plato was obviously transmitting older mythical or Pythagorean traditions (on the *Timaeus*' Pythagorean background see *PR* 118 §179), are what interested him. Otherwise, Plato had never impressed Jung in the least or spoken to him in any truly meaningful way (*JP* 162, 303, and cf. 45 on the neurotic teacher he used to have who identified with Plato in just the same way so many intellectuals still do today). As a matter of fact Jung went to great lengths to describe how Plato never learned to step away from the realm of thought into applying his ideas in the physical world (*PR* 119–27 §§181–92, 164–96 §§243–90). And in spite of comments to the contrary (e.g. Liz Greene, *Jung's studies in astrology*, London 2018, 90–2) he had very little sympathy for the abstract thinking of orthodox later Platonists such as Plotinus, who to him lacked any genuine signs of integration (A. Ribi, *Analytische Psychologie* 13, 1982, 218–19; for Jung's broad use of the term "Neoplatonic" see P. Kingsley, *JWCI* 56, 1993, 19–20 = *PJB* 68–9). Modern philosophy "never says anything ...": *PPT* 122 §250 (cf. ibid. 79 §181, *JL* ii 125, *CT* 284 §550, 456–75 §§858–900). "I am speaking just as a philosopher ... lovers of wisdom": *JS* 98, 255–6; cf. *PPT* 79 §181, 82–3 §§189–90, 122 §250, *JL* i 456 and D. Russell, *The life and ideas of James Hillman* i (New York 2013) 419 (quoting Jung's statement that "my approach is just the contrary from philosophy, at least in the modern sense of the word"). As for the Pythagorean origin of the word "philosophy", in the old sense of "love of wisdom", see *APMM* 157–8, 339 with n.14; *SW* 121. There can be no doubt that, in comparing his own psychology directly to ancient philosophy, Jung had at the back of his mind Gustav Richard Heyer's strategic emphasis on the importance of the role model offered to modern psychologists by the Presocratic philosophers—not only because these primordial philosophers managed so well in their time to grasp and communicate the irrational side of life, to capture "the irrational secrets and powers of the world and of humanity" inside their work, but because they are also pointing the way forward now into the future (*Der Organismus der Seele*, Munich 1932, 5–6; cf. H.T. Hakl, *Eranos*, Sheffield 2013, 65). For the enthusiastic review of Heyer's book by Jung see *SL* 793–4 §1774 and, for his very close friendship with Heyer at the time, Hakl 65–6. On the other hand, the growing academic movement nowadays to start approaching Jung's work from the perspective of classical philosophy has unconsciously stumbled straight into the trap of wanting to present him as a rationalist and an ally of Aristotle (see especially M.H. Barreto, *Spring* 77, 2007, 79–98). The same goes for recent attempts at understanding him in the light of Pierre Hadot's comfortably superficial, although pleasantly fashionable, work on ancient philosophy as a way of life (P. Bishop in *Art, sciences et psychologie*, ed. C. Maillard, Strasbourg 2011, 148; R. Màdera, *Approaching the navel of the darkened soul*, Milan 2013, and *Spring* 92, 2015, 235–54). But at heart Jung was the very opposite of a rationalist; and there is far too little awareness of the extent to which Hadot, for his part, ended up distorting or simply rejecting the earliest of philosophies with which Jung had the deepest affinities so he could create his soporific clichés about philosophy as a rational mode of living (see e.g. *SW* 111, 171). The situation is also identical in the case of the trend now, among Jungians, to present Jung as a modern Platonist (so e.g. J. Weldon, *Platonic Jung*, Asheville 2017). And it's the very same story all over again in the case of Marilyn Nagy's entertaining romp through the pages of western intellectual history (*Philosophical issues in the psychology of C.G. Jung*, Albany 1991), which not only ignores Jung's fundamental distinction between ancient and modern philosophy but also omits any real engagement with the crucial factor that for him separates those who create their sugar-coated versions of historical continuity from those who truly have something to say. This is the factor he himself called the "dunkle Substanz": the dark substance preserved and treasured by the alchemists because it represents the very essence and source of their work, and which completely eludes the grasp of our theorizing minds (*JP* 176). On the historical origins of this phrase see, aside from Jung's comments, my contribution to David Bain's chapter in *The world of ancient magic*, ed. D.R. Jordan, H. Montgomery and E. Thomassen (Bergen 1999) 205–26 = *Magic in the biblical world*, ed. T. Klutz (London 2003) 191–218.

[97] For the intellectualism of western philosophy since the time of Pythagoras and for "the materiality and concreteness of our thinking, as moulded by the Greeks", see *PR* 554–6 §905 with n.42; for Pythagoras' quite different role in alchemy, *PA* 347–50 §§449–50; and on Pythagoras as marking the formal beginnings of philosophy, *APMM* 339 with *SW* 121. "The nature philosophers like Empedocles … marvellous naiveté": *NZ* i 678; on the Presocratics' intensely real concern with consciousness see e.g. *Reality* 77–183 (Parmenides), *ENM* 387–92 (Empedocles) and, regarding their supposed naivety, ibid. 365, 379. Empedocles as "one of the very early Greek philosophers and a sort of saviour": *JV* i 595–6. "No one can claim to be immune to the spirit of his own epoch … the spirit that runs through the masses": *AS* 117–18 §153, and note Jung's comments on the "tremendous tension" that an awareness of this limitation gives rise to; for Empedocles on the unavoidable necessity of conforming to normal conventions see fr. 9.5 Diels (reading *hê sphi themis kaleousi, nomôi d' epiphêmi kai autos*) = fr. 14.5–6 Gemelli Marciano with *ENM* 382–4 and *Reality* 422–5. But Jung also finds himself subtly challenging, in fact even reversing, conventional concepts of cultural progress or

evolution while discussing western alchemy and Gnosticism (e.g. *Aion* 190 §297, *JL* ii 283); or he simply levels the playing field by dismissing any seeming progress at all as only apparent (*JS* 350). It can be interesting to note how bluntly forceful he was in stating that his own deepest experiences were the experiences of the alchemists, and the other way around (*JP* 227, *ETG* 209; the bluntness is arbitrarily softened and qualified at *MDR* 196/205)—and that the solid ground discovered by the alchemists directly corresponded to his own experiences of 1913–1917 (*JP* 227, again subtly diluted at *ETG* 213 and *MDR* 200/209). For the enormity of the task that Jung realized he was faced with in having to solve the riddles of western alchemical tradition, and for his sense of this gruelling labour as a curse or damnation, see especially *JP* 16–17; *MDR* 196/205, *JS* 351, A. Ribi, *Analytische Psychologie* 13 (1982) 202.

[98] The paths leading from Gnostic and Hermetic tradition in Egypt back to Parmenides, Empedocles and Pythagoreans in both Sicily and Italy: *APMM*; *PJB* 18–40; *ENM* 339–56, 382, 386 with 387 n.129, 398 with n.159, 400 n.163, 404; *Reality* 153–5, 198, 324, 383, 416–17, 443; P. Kingsley in *Crossing religious frontiers*, ed. H. Oldmeadow (Bloomington, IN 2010) 43–9. On the continuities between Presocratic philosophy and Gnosticism compare also H. Leisegang, *Die Gnosis* (Leipzig 1924); O. Klíma, *Manis Zeit und Leben* (Prague 1962) 295 n.37, 324 (Empedocles and Pythagoras); U. Bianchi, *Numen* 12 (1965) 161–78 and *Le origini dello Gnosticismo*, ed. Bianchi (Leiden 1967) xxviii, 10–11, 17, 20–3, 27, 320–39, 662, 731, 742 n.; J. Mansfeld in *Studies in Gnosticism and Hellenistic religions*, ed. R. van den Broek and M.J. Vermaseren (Leiden 1981) 261–314 (unreliable on most points of detail although more correct on generalities) and *Heresiography in context* (Leiden 1992); I should add that Gilles Quispel often used

to admit to me that he considered the ultimate influences of Presocratic philosophy and Orphic theology on Gnosticism to be a fundamental baseline for exploring Jewish or other strands of influence. The well-oiled modern industry of treating Gnostic tradition as a debased kind of Platonism (cf. e.g. *Gnosticism and later Platonism*, ed. J.D. Turner and R. Majercik, Atlanta 2000; *Gnosticism, Platonism and the late ancient world*, ed. K. Corrigan and T. Rasimus, Leiden 2013) completely fails to acknowledge the fact that Gnostics were far closer to understanding the spirit, and actual details, of Presocratic philosophy than any Platonists with their fantasies about an "ancient Hellenic tradition" could ever be: see for example *APMM* 38–40, 55–68, 302, 355–6, *ENM* 342–4 with n.12, 384–7, 398. For the major links between Presocratic and alchemical tradition see M. Plessner, *Vorsokratische Philosophie und griechische Alchemie* (Wiesbaden 1975); P. Lory, *Jâbir ibn Hayyân, L'Élaboration de l'élixir suprême* (Damascus 1988) 14–15; Kingsley, *JWCI* 57 (1994) 1–13; C. Viano in *Alchimie: art, histoire et mythes*, ed. D. Kahn and S. Matton (Paris 1995) 95–150; *APMM*. Akhmîm in southern Egypt, called Panopolis by the Greeks, was a particularly significant centre for the transmission of Empedoclean and Pythagorean teachings into western as well as Arab alchemy: *JWCI* 57 (1994) 9–13; *APMM* 10, 58–68, 119 n.26, 365 n.18, 388–91; *ENM* 338 n.7; Kingsley in *Crossing religious frontiers* 47–8. Hebrew and Greek prophetic traditions: C. Grottanelli in *La soteriologia dei culti orientali nell'Impero romano*, ed. U. Bianchi and M.J. Vermaseren (Leiden 1982) 649–70; W. Burkert in *Apocalypticism in the Mediterranean world and the Near East*, ed. D. Hellholm (Tübingen 1983) 235–50 and in *Apollo*, ed. J. Solomon (Tucson 1994) 58. For the origins of the Gnostic and Hermetic *kratêr* in the volcanic craters of Sicily and southern Italy see *APMM*, especially 82–5, 133–48, 159–60, 243–4,

262–3, 282–3. The legends of Empedocles' leap on Etna as coded accounts of his ritual descent into the world of the dead: ibid. 135, 233–56, 272–7, 289–90, 301; J. Bollansée in *Die Fragmente der griechischen Historiker* IVA/3 (Leiden 1999) 455–8. Volcanoes as traditional points of access to the underworld: *APMM* 71–8 with n.10, 82, 84 with n.14, 233–40, 280–3. For Etna as ancient centre of ritual activity, for its temples built out of lava, and for the family of "dream–prophets" see ibid. 278–83. For the connection between Empedocles on Etna and Elijah see Grottanelli 651–62; I.P. Culianu, *Psychanodia* i (Leiden 1983) 35; *APMM* 236 n.14 with 293–4 plus Kingsley, *Journal of the Royal Asiatic Society* 5 (1995) 186–7 on the passage of traditions between the Middle East and Sicily. Jung in the huge crater of the underworld beside "the house of the prophet" Elijah: *RB* 252a, cf. 247–8 and 366b with *IJP* 68–9, 104–5; it will be noted that for Jung the function of both the Gnostic *kratêr* and the later Grail is to give direct access to death, the underworld and the unconscious (*KY* 20, *AS* 73 §96, *CT* 355 §674, cf. also *PT* 242 §410). For the utter futility of the traditional, schizophrenic approach to Empedocles as rational philosopher on the one hand versus religious saviour or prophet on the other see *APMM*; for his philosophy as itself a work of salvation, *ENM* 342–4, *Reality* 322–4.

[99] Jung as psychologist emphasizes the very real risk of insanity for anyone making the ritual descent into a volcano (*JV* i 594–5). Horace too, in a classic passage well known to him, had already linked the myth of Empedocles' leap into Etna with the theme of insanity: see *The art of poetry* 463–72; *ZL* 70 §179, *NZ* ii 1217, *ST* 405 §626; and, on Jung's liking for Horace, *JP* 162 with J.E. Gedo, *Annual of psychoanalysis* 7 (1979) 66. For his powerful description of what happens to whoever descends the whole way into the crater of a volcano—

being completely melted down and recast into a fusion first with one's own primordial beginning and then with the primordial beginning of the entire world—see *Red book*, folio v verso (weakly translated at *RB* 247a). Jung adds straight away that this experience of primordial oneness is only given to the depths of oneself, because our surface consciousness is too rigid and solidly formed to be able to understand it or participate.

[100] "My life is a story ...": *MDR* 17/3; previously worded as a statement that Jung's life was the story of an "act" of self-realization on the part of the unconscious (*MDRC*). "Touch the black bottom ...": *RB* 78; "Landstrassen" are not country roads (ibid. 291b) but highways on—supposedly solid—land (cf. *SM* 83 §131 for those who "cannot endure the broad highway", the "breiten Heerstrassen"). For Jung's imagery of drilling and boring see especially *IJP* 51; *NZ* i 369; L.S. Owens, *The Gnostic* 3 (2010) 28–9; P. Bishop, *Carl Jung* (London 2014) 166.

NOTES TO PART 3

[1] This is of course a constant theme in Jung's life and work. See e.g. M. Serrano, *C.G. Jung and Hermann Hesse* (London 1966) 84–5 = *JL* ii 593–4; G. Adler, *PP* 16 (1985) 23. The howls of angry protest against it on the part of so-called "Traditionalist" thinkers—"As if an archetype … could in some way cast a spell on and vampirize the soul!" (T. Burckhardt, *Mirror of the intellect*, Cambridge 1987, 59)—are a fair indication of how little they understand not only about Jung, but about themselves.

[2] Letter to Emma Jung dated 18 September 1909 (*MDR* 338/368; cf. *ETG* 368). For some context to Jung's first American visit see R. Skues in *After Freud left*, ed. J. Burnham (Chicago 2012) 49–84; S. Shamdasani, ibid. 46–7 and in *Jung contra Freud* (Princeton 2012) vii, xiii.

[3] These, along with many similar, statements about the empire whose capital should go by the name of "Platonopolis" can be found in *The secret destiny of America* (Los Angeles 1944) by Manly Palmer Hall. Heroically he manages to forget that according to Plato's own fictional account, which is the one and only independent account of the place anyone happens to have, Atlantis was the ultimate embodiment of selfishness and

materialism; of brutal expansionism and ruthless imperialism (*Timaeus* 24d–25d, *Critias* 120d–121c; *SW* 128). For the direct influence of Manly Palmer Hall's writings on another Hollywood celebrity, Ronald Reagan, see M. Horowitz in Steven Levingston's "Political bookworm", *The Washington post*, 30 April 2010; R. Perlstein, *The invisible bridge* (New York 2014) 350. And on the "plethora of symbols", all of them "drawn from Greco–Roman and Egyptian civilizations", which since the time of the Founding Fathers have played a much greater role than any Christian imagery or symbolism in shaping American notions about exceptionalism and manifest destiny cf. e.g. P. Mendis, *Commercial providence* (Lanham 2010) 13. On Plato's disastrous failure, due to a combination of impracticality and bad judgement, to imitate the Pythagorean model for creating a kingdom ruled by philosophers see *SW* 156–7 and note also Jung's own comments: *PR* 122 §184. For the Platonopolis which, over five hundred years later, Plotinus unsuccessfully tried creating in southern Italy see Porphyry's *Life of Plotinus* 12; L. Jerphagnon in *Néoplatonisme: Mélanges offerts à Jean Trouillard* (Fontenay-aux-Roses 1981) 215–29; M. Edwards, *Neoplatonic saints* (Liverpool 2000) xxv, 23; D.J. O'Meara, *Platonopolis* (Oxford 2003); and for later attempts cf. e.g. J.H. Billington, *Fire in the minds of men* (2nd ed., New Brunswick 1999) 80, 255 with A. Versluis, *American gurus* (New York 2014) 33–4.

[4] Perhaps the most telling example is Meher Baba, who during the years of his unbroken silence pointed to America's "infinite possibilities"; demonstrated through gestures that America was completely immersed and lost in materialism but explained that a great spiritual master would be able to guide all its misdirected energy "into the right channel"; promised that he himself was the spiritual master who, the moment

he broke his silence and started speaking again, would bring about this instantaneous "spiritual rebirth" by restoring to America its destined role "to lead the world spiritually". He died without speaking. Cf. e.g. J. Ross, *Avatar Meher Baba and the Trail of tears* (Jerome, AZ 2011) vi and 69–71 together with the numerous references to America in *Lord Meher*, ed. Bhau Kalchuri, D. Fenster and L. Reiter (Asheville 1986–2001); J. Adriel, *Avatar* (Santa Barbara 1947) 26; plus the letter by Bhau Kalchuri dated 5 January 2012 and published in *Glow international* (Spring 2012) 3.

[5] *New York Times* Sunday magazine, 29 September 1912, 2; cf. *JS* 11–24. The danger of Americans being turned into machines had already been eloquently portrayed by Henry Thoreau (*Aesthetic papers*, ed. E.P. Peabody, Boston 1849, 191–8 = H.D. Thoreau, *A Yankee in Canada*, Boston 1866, 126–34), and Jung's words would soon find plenty of echoes in the 1920s and 1930s. Note especially the 1923 version of D.H. Lawrence's *Studies in classic American literature* (Cambridge 2003, 28.27–31.3): "And now I, at least, know why I can't stand Benjamin [Franklin]. He tries to take away my wholeness and my dark forest, my freedom ... All this Americanising and mechanising has been for the purpose of overthrowing the past. And now look at America, tangled in her own barbed wire, and mastered by her own machines. Absolutely got down by her own barbed wire of shalt-nots, and shut up fast in her own 'productive' machines like millions of squirrels running in millions of cages." For the Taos–based connections between Jung and Lawrence cf. J.W. Boekhoven, *Genealogies of shamanism* (Groningen 2011) 85–8 together with E. Rolfe's comments, *Encounter with Jung* (Boston 1989) 176–8. By 1931 there was no longer any question of choice or doubt left in

Jung's mind: as a result of our inflation, and blind hubris, "the machines which we have invented ... are now our masters" (*JV* i 502).

[6] For Jung's dismal view of people who come together to help collectively transform the consciousness of the world—which is of course a thousand times more the rage nowadays in America than it was almost a century ago—see *JV* i 201 ("... she is a bit mad, as people who consider how they can help humanity are all a bit mad. For how can you help humanity? Like a woman who came over from America recently, trying to gather all the great men of Europe together, with the idea that something would then be done for the world ...") together with *NZ* ii 828–9. Note also his general scepticism about those who overestimate the power of consciousness ("There are people who believe that the few who are conscious can hold the world against annihilation, but I am afraid of the terrific power of general unconsciousness": *JJW* 93); and for his dismissal of optimism as downright stupid see already *ZL* 86–7 §§228–32. R. Main (*The rupture of time*, Hove 2004, 161–2) naively argues against distinguishing between Jung's own attitudes and the general "new–age" mentality, with its fondness for optimistic utopianism or collective celebration, by noting that the high value Jung ascribed to conscious suffering is also echoed in another key influence on new–age thinking: George Ivanovitch Gurdjieff. But the real question is not who might or might not have influenced the new–age movement; it's how much, or how little, what either Jung or Gurdjieff said has been understood. For Jung's own appreciation of how true work is done ("Neither propaganda nor exhibitionist confessions are needed") see his comments in M. Serrano, *C.G. Jung and Hermann Hesse* (London 1966) 86.

[7] Note especially Jung's words in *JJW* 92–3 about the critical task of becoming conscious—"This is our human work. I am not afraid of communism; I am afraid of unconsciousness and of modern science. I am afraid of America which educates its children away from being individuals into being mass-educated people. These are the Marxists without knowing it ... *This* is today's calamity—the collective shadow, the general unconsciousness while those who are conscious are like a handful of salt in all this" (1955)—together with his cuttingly sharp comments about American life in *JS* 48–9 or ("mass man breeds mass catastrophe") *JL* i 477. And on Jung's fine sense for the fear permeating even the air in America, see his anecdote at *JP* 126. On his high regard for Americans' intuitiveness and openness see e.g. *JP* 351 with *JL* ii 520 = *JK* 250 and D. Bair, *Jung* (Boston 2003) 365. Jung loved showing off his knowledge of American slang (*JJW* 25, cf. *CT* 504–5 §955), although he thanked God that he was able to escape being permanently infected by Americanisms as a young man (*JP* 165). American cars: *JJW* 98; Bair 368. Jung openly admits that the gaudiness of American life offered a perfect image, or caricature, of his no. 1 personality (*JP* 83–4). For Americans' proudly foolish illusions about being able to create a better and brighter future, see e.g. his letter to Wilfrid Lay in Vermont dated 20 April 1946 (*CBA*; *JL* i 426).

[8] See Esther Harding's notebook entry for 13 January 1925: Jung gave a talk at Kristine Mann's New York apartment where he "said many interesting things about the ancestors, how they seem to be in the land ... He said that in America there is a certain lack of reverence, a certain ruthlessness. The ancestors are not considered here, their values not respected ... The American disregards these completely, is, indeed, utterly unconscious of them" (*Quadrant* 8/2, Winter 1975,

10; cf. *JS* 30). Jung's mention of Americans' ruthlessness is already familiar enough (*New York Times* Sunday magazine, 29 September 1912, 2 = *JS* 13–21); but his comments on their "ancestors" are very striking as well as strange, and clearly have to be explained in light of his intense encounter with Mountain Lake at Taos only the week before (for a chronology of Jung's travels see W. McGuire, *Spring*, 1978, 37–48). On Mountain Lake's horror at the ruthlessness and cruelty of white Americans, and the powerful impact it made on Jung, see the published account in *MDR* 233–4/247–9. As for the dramatically uncompromising emphasis that Mountain Lake placed on the importance of the ancestors, and that left an indelible impression on Jung's consciousness, see especially *PA* 131 §171; also *MDR* 234–8/249–53 plus the impassioned words Jung wrote to Miguel Serrano, just a few months before he died, about Mountain Lake's attitude being the one and only possible antidote to "the narrow-mindedness of American rationalism" (M. Serrano, *C.G. Jung and Hermann Hesse*, London 1966, 87–8; cf. *JL* ii 596–7). On the living reality for Jung of the ancestors compare e.g. *RB* 296–8, *JP* B26 (13 June 1958), *MDR* 142/143–4; and for the brutality which at the same time causes, and is the result of, our refusal to "receive" or honour the dead see especially *RBu* 296b = *RB* 106 (ineffectively translated at *RB* 297b).

[9] See Jung's letter to Frances Wickes, written exactly four weeks after the New York event on 10 February 1925, which has been published by W. McGuire in *Spring* (1978) 47: "I can confirm your ideas concerning our New York experiences. Things had to be as they were and you really did most bravely and admirably, what you could and should do under such extraordinary conditions. I felt it like a ceremonial for the Dead. Thus the golden thread has not been injured, the

contrary, it has shown itself in the fact, that the performance of a very dangerous rite has been possible without bad effects. …" This mention of "a ceremonial for the Dead" quite obviously has to be juxtaposed with the evidence for Jung's particular interest in the traditional ceremonials for the dead which were still being practised by Mountain Lake's people at the time of his visit (*JP* 369–70). As for the image here of a "golden thread", this happened to be particularly important to him during the early months of 1925 (M.E. Harding, *Quadrant* 8/2, Winter 1975, 10 = *JS* 31). Frances Wickes played a key role in the evening gathering that took place at Kristine Mann's New York apartment: although most of the people invited were Wickes' personal friends (McGuire 40), her relationship with more formal Jungians such as Kristine Mann or Esther Harding was never easy. Jung had originally been anticipating "an analytical colloquium" in the shape of "an informal meeting"—one that would "give a chance to the people who are *truly interested* in my psychology" and perhaps allow for some discussion of dreams. But as McGuire comments with more than a hint of confusion, Jung's letter to Wickes from back home in Switzerland indicates that things turned out very differently and that the whole affair ended up being "in some sense extraordinary" (40, 44, 47, cf. *Quadrant* 16/1, Spring 1983, 41; note also Jung's mention of the wildly unconscious energies he encountered, both at Taos and on his return to New York, in the letter he wrote to Cary de Angulo dated 19 January 1925: *CBA*). For Frances Wickes' personal role in introducing Jung to Mountain Lake, and the friendship that sprang up between the two men, see *Spring* (1978) 42–3; for the name "Mountain Lake" itself, D.G. Barton, *IJJS* 8 (2016) 77.

[10] For Americans' remote and tenuous connection with their unconscious see e.g. *JL* i 424, ii 432; *Contributions to analytical*

psychology (London 1928) 140 = *CT* 49 §103. "Be careful when you tread on the tiger's tail that is the American unconscious": *JL* i 290; compare, for example, his letter to Cary Baynes dated 28 June 1948 (*CBA*). One can still observe how American intellectuals who were able to visit Jung in Switzerland, far from showing any interest or curiosity when he touched on America's more problematic side, instinctively started feeling they had to turn the tables and criticize him straight away. See especially Joseph Campbell's wife, Jean, in S. and R. Larsen, *A fire in the mind* (New York 1991) 363; the most meaningful comment Joseph himself managed to make about the whole meeting at Bollingen was "That was fun" (*An open life*, ed. J.M. Maher and D. Briggs, Burdett, NY 1988, 122). For Jung on the physician "having to withhold the truth from his patient" and often lie, see e.g. J. Sherry, *Carl Gustav Jung: avant-garde conservative* (New York 2010) 171; on his special talent for charming American audiences, N. Lewin, *Jung on war, politics and Nazi Germany* (London 2009) 51. It will be noted how much more professional—despite their similar initial reactions—Jung remained in his attitude to America than Sigmund Freud, with his undying antipathy towards anything American (cf. E. Falzeder's documentation in *After Freud left*, ed. J. Burnham, Chicago 2012, 85–109). In part this was due to purely practical considerations (ibid. 103), but also to Jung's natural flair for viewing the countries he visited with an ethnographer's impartial eye (M.V. Adams, *The multicultural imagination*, London 1996, 49; B. Burleson, *JAP* 53, 2008, 209; J. Cambray in *Jung and the question of science*, ed. R.A. Jones, Hove 2014, 11–16).

[11] *Forum* 83 (1930) 198–9 = *CT* 511–14 §§972–80. Jung sinisterly notes that these heroic characteristics were absorbed by white Americans from the indigenous people they had

conquered and massacred (ibid. 199 = 513–14 §§977–9: cf. already *Contributions to analytical psychology*, London 1928, 138–40 = *CT* 47–9 §§99–103; M.V. Adams, *The multicultural imagination*, London 1996, 109–110). For the general readership and tenor of the New York magazine *Forum*, Jung's "journalistic flair", and the skilful ability he shows in this essay to "soft-pedal" on sensitive issues, see J. Sherry's astute comments, *Carl Gustav Jung: avant-garde conservative* (New York 2010) 68–9. There is an unfortunate tendency for Jungians, starting from Jung's main editors, to cite this entertaining and flattering 1930 essay as most fully representative of his views on America—even when commenting on passages where Jung explicitly states that his real insights into American psychology came to him in 1912 (*JL* i 532 with n.8).

[12] The quotations are from *MDR* 173–4/179–81, where Jung tells his famous dream of 18 December 1913 about Siegfried's "heroic idealism" and explains this in terms of German national psychology. See also *RB* 242b with n.123; *JP* 98; S.F. Walker, *Jung and the Jungians on myth* (London 2002) 43 (Jung's ideal figure of the hero corresponds to "the militaristic spirit threatening Europe just before the outbreak of World War I … The sinister image of Siegfried represented the ruthless Germanic power drive, a peculiarly German form of bullying heroism"). For the collective attitude of "God-Almightiness" which "does not make man divine, it merely fills him with arrogance and" is bound to "lead to catastrophe", see e.g. *CT* 214–15 §§437–9; and on the disastrous implications of the slogan "Where there is a will there is a way" compare *PR* 534–5 §869, *SL* 241 §555, 705 §1588. For Hitler's eventual identification of himself with the mythological figure of Siegfried see W.E. Grim in *New studies in Richard Wagner's*

'The ring of the Nibelung', ed. H.W. Richardson (Lewiston, NY 1991) 155–75; and on Jung's own, profoundly ambivalent, linking of Siegfried with Nazism during the immediate run-up to the Second World War, *CT* 190 n.16 with A. Samuels, *JAP* 38 (1993) 465–6. For Jung it became almost routine to compare the national psychology of Germans and Americans. Cf. e.g. *CT* 45–6 §§94–5, *JL* i 424, plus passages such as the one where he compares German with American politics before remarkably describing America's decision to go off the gold standard as a downright "crime, highway robbery, just as black as the swastika" (*NZ* i 376–7). American Jungians very naturally tend nowadays to see nothing wrong in the value of money "being hollowed out", and can be only too happy to dismiss these remarks by Jung as betraying the old-world prejudice of "a good Swiss" conservative (J. Sherry, *Carl Gustav Jung: avant-garde conservative*, New York 2010, 161). Otherwise, when not being used to undermine what Jung wanted to convey, the whole tendency to analyze people or countries in terms of national characteristics has become politically very incorrect—because today we live in a single, global world of common oneness. Often, though, no attention is paid to the uncomfortable fact that this irresistible movement towards spiritual as well as material globalization is ever so subtly western-centric: one more manifestation of the western world's, and in particular America's, insidiously missionary dynamic.

[13] *MDR* 174/180–1. Cf. *RB* 241–2 with n.115; *IJP* 53, 61–2. As Jung once explained the matter (ibid. 53), "If you give up this thinking, this hero ideal, you commit a secret murder"—which for any westerner amounts, in a sense, to the murder of that murder already committed thousands of years earlier by Aristotle and Plato. It can be helpful to note that in the *Red book* Jung identifies heroic idealism very squarely with the spirit

he refers to as the spirit of this time: a spirit "bejewelled with the most beautiful heroic virtues" whose constant aim is to keep driving people higher and higher to the "brightest solar heights, in everlasting ascent", at least until the spirit of the depths quietly interferes and "wipes out" any trace of the heroic aspiration inside us (*RBu* 240a with n.101, cf. *RB* 240a with n.100). And there is nothing even remotely accidental about the fact that—when addressing the bravely heroic attitude of "young America" right at the end of a piece about contemporary realities—he does so straight after announcing, as formally and explicitly as possible, that now he is switching over to speak on behalf of "the spirit of the times". See *CT* 93–4 §§195–6 = "die Seele unserer Weltlichkeit" in *Seelenprobleme der Gegenwart* (Zurich 1931) 433; and compare this mention of "Weltlichkeit" or superficial worldliness with the way that, elsewhere, he links the very same word to America (*JP* 83–4).

[14] F.R. Kraus, *Zeitschrift für Assyriologie und verwandte Gebiete* 43 (1936) 96–7.8–9 = B. Böck, *Die babylonisch–assyrische Morphoskopie* (Vienna 2000) 134–5.65–66. See also H.H. Schmid, *Wesen und Geschichte der Weisheit* (Berlin 1966) 127–9; H.D. Galter in *Natur-Bilder*, ed. R.P. Sieferle and H. Breuninger (Frankfurt 1999) 53; N. Veldhuis in *All those nations*, ed. H.L.J. Vanstiphout et al. (Groningen 1999) 170; and, in general, G. Buccellati, *Journal of the American Oriental Society* 101 (1981) 37 with Böck 40–2. For a summary of similar sentiments in Greek prophetic tradition, including the oracular requirement to "bow before the divine" (*proskunei to theion*), see M. McPherran in *Does Socrates have a method?*, ed. G.A. Scott (University Park, PA 2002) 133 n.51.

[15] "Look into the source …": Jalâl al-Dîn Rûmî, *Kitâb-i fîhi mâ fîhi* §38 (ed. B. Furûzânfar, Tehran 1952, 142); of the various

published English translations the most faithful is still A.J. Arberry's, *Discourses of Rûmî* (London 1961) 151–2. Marie-Louise von Franz also has some good words on the subject of human skills and divine revelation (*Creation myths*, Boston 1995, 140–2), although Jung conveys the essence with far more power (*NZ* ii 969–71). For the western traditions of prophecy see e.g. C. Grottanelli in *La soteriologia dei culti orientali nell'Impero romano*, ed. U. Bianchi and M.J. Vermaseren (Leiden 1982) 649–70; W. Burkert in *Apocalypticism in the Mediterranean world and the Near East*, ed. D. Hellholm (Tübingen 1983) 235–54, *The Greek renaissance of the eighth century B.C.*, ed. R. Hägg (Stockholm 1983) 115–19, *The orientalizing revolution* (Cambridge, MA 1992), and *Apollo*, ed. J. Solomon (Tucson 1994) 49–60, 145–7; *APMM* 224–7, 236 n.14, 293–4 and P. Kingsley, *Journal of the Royal Asiatic Society* 5 (1995) 183–91; M.L. West, *The east face of Helicon* (Oxford 1997) 46–54; M.A. Flower, *The seer in ancient Greece* (Berkeley 2008) 24–5, 29–37 with M. Nissinen in *Raising up a faithful exegete*, ed. K.L. Noll and B. Schramm (Winona Lake 2010) 3–29; L. Gemelli Marciano in *La costruzione del discorso filosofico nell'età dei Presocratici*, ed. M.M. Sassi (Pisa 2006) 203–35 and *La filosofia antica*, ed. L. Perilli and D.P. Taormina (Novara 2012) 3–34; O. Levaniouk in *Homeric contexts*, ed. F. Montanari, A. Rengakos and C. Tsagalis (Berlin 2012) 385–6.

[16] "Condescending to lighten ...": K. Dover, *Talanta* 7 (1976) 49. For the standard denunciation by western intellectuals of Empedocles in particular as prophet, charlatan and poseur see e.g. K. Friis Johansen, *A history of ancient philosophy* (London 1998) 64; or Bertrand Russell's far more famous *History of western philosophy* (London 1946) 72. For Parmenides' and Empedocles' portrayals of humanity see *IDPW* 221–3, *Reality* 83–125 and 326–7. With regard to Heraclitus' very

similar comments about everyone being asleep, it somehow never dawns on most modern scholars that he might just be referring—in spite of all their brilliant thoughts and impressive rationality—to them. See e.g. J. Mansfeld, *Mnemosyne* 20 (1967) 1–29; H. Granger, *Classical philology* 95 (2000) 260–81 and in *Doctrine and doxography*, ed. D. Sider and D. Obbink (Berlin 2013) 191; C. Huffman, ibid. 123; E. Hülsz, ibid. 284–91; D.W. Graham, ibid. 306–7.

[17] For Mani's final great shriek, announcing the end of the world, see the passage clearly marked by Jung (both in the margin and by underlining the word "Schrei") inside his copy of Richard Reitzenstein's *Das iranische Erlösungsmysterium* (Bonn 1921) 17; and note also the marking he left in his edition of the Manichaean *Kephalaia* i, Lieferung 7/8, ed. A. Böhlig (Stuttgart 1937) 150.8–12, together with *ST* 44–5 §65 and *MC* 273 n.65. For Merlin as prophet see e.g. *The Didot Perceval*, ed. W. Roach (Philadelphia 1941) 278 ("et si profetiserai çou que nostre Sire me commandera") = *Merlin and the Grail*, trans. N. Bryant (Cambridge 2001) 171; P. Zumthor, *Merlin le prophète* (Geneva 1943); H. Adolf, *Speculum* 21 (1946) 173–85; Emma Jung and M.-L. von Franz, *The Grail legend* (New York 1970) 348, 359, 367, 382; J. Ziolkowski in *Poetry and prophecy*, ed. J.L. Kugel (Ithaca, NY 1990) 151–62, 240–4; B.L. McCauley, *Quondam et futurus* 3/4 (Winter 1993) 41–62; A. Combes in *A companion to the Lancelot–Grail cycle*, ed. C. Dover (Cambridge 2003) 75–6. Merlin as the real meaning of the Grail: *JP* 211–12; von Franz, *C.G. Jung: his myth in our time* (New York 1975) 275, 279 and *PP* 38 (1998) 38–9; D.L. Merritt, *The cry of Merlin* (Carmel, CA 2012) 144, 146. Merlin maddened by people's stupidity and crying from the forest: *MDR* 216/228, *JP* 366; Jung and von Franz, *Grail legend* 359–66; von Franz, *C.G. Jung* 277–8; cf. Ziolkowski 152–61. For Merlin as bird, and for

the ties connecting his cry with bird cries as well as with the lamentations of the "righteous", see Adolf 173–83 with A.C.L. Brown, *Speculum* 20 (1945) 426–32 and McCauley 54–6 n.11; the link between bird–language and language of prophecy is entirely missed by von Franz (*Grail legend* 382–3). For Jung himself as Merlin, and for his own life's work as giving voice again to Merlin's incomprehensible cry, see his comments in *MDR* 216/228 together with his humorous remark as reported by D. Bair, *Jung* (Boston 2003) 758 n.64 ("Merlin disappears in the woods—He goes to Bollingen!": cf. *JP* 211, 223); his direct statement, left out of *Memories*, that something inside him had always profoundly identified with Merlin (*JP* 211); von Franz, *C.G. Jung* 269–87 and *PP* 38 (1998) 38; Merritt 58, 145–6. Onto the final, blank face of the stone beside his tower at Bollingen he had intended to carve "the cry of Merlin"; but, significantly, this was one of the details in his life he left incomplete (*JP* 211, *MDR* 216/228, von Franz 280 with n.29). For his total inability, exactly like Merlin, to be understood see *JP* 366–7. His shock at living out the legend of Merlin and becoming him: von Franz 279; *PP* 38 (1998) 38; Merritt 146. Marie–Louise von Franz is among those Jungians who have most strenuously defended Jung against the unjust accusation of being a prophet (cf. e.g. *C.G. Jung* 41, 121; *PP* 38, 1998, 15) and yet she finishes her famous book on him with a chapter, called "Le cri de Merlin", in which she describes his gradual merging with the prophet Merlin (*C.G. Jung* 269–87): the technical name for this is "having one's cake and eating it".

[18] Hebrew prophets and howling: see especially Isaiah 13:6, 14:31, 16:7, 23:1–14, Jeremiah 4:8, 20:7–9, 48:20 and 31, Ezekiel 21:12, 30:2, Joel 1:5, 1:11 and 13, Micah 1:8, Zephaniah 1:11, Zechariah 11:2–3. Ancient Greek prophets and howling: Empedocles frs. 118 and 121 Diels = frs. 163

and 166 Gemelli Marciano (*klausa te kai kôkusa* ...). *Lallaru*, "howler" or "wailer", as a name for Babylonian prophets: S. Parpola, *Assyrian prophecies* (Helsinki 1997) xlvi, civ n.232; M. Nissinen, *Prophecy in its ancient Near Eastern context* (Atlanta 2000) 93–5, *Prophets and prophecy in the ancient Near East* (Atlanta 2003) 180, 186 (cf. 102, 130) and in *Raising up a faithful exegete*, ed. K.L. Noll and B. Schramm (Winona Lake 2010) 8–12; cf. also M.J. de Jong, *Isaiah among the ancient Near Eastern prophets* (Leiden 2007) 180 n.21, 289 with n.16; there are even scholars willing to suggest that the standard Hebrew and Arabic word for a prophet, *nabî*, really comes from *nabû* meaning to "howl" or "wail" (Parpola xcvii n.141). *Goês*, "howler", as the ancient Greek name for a shaman or medicine man: see especially W. Burkert, *Rheinisches Museum* 105 (1962) 36–55. On the very real connections between Central Asian shamans and Greek prophets, often short-sightedly denied by scholars who are quite incapable of accommodating the evidence, see *SW* together with my earlier comments in *Studia Iranica* 23 (1994) 187–98. And on the issue of analogies between Hebrew or Babylonian prophecy and shamanism see e.g. P.F. Craffert, *The life of a Galilean shaman* (Eugene 2008); L.L. Grabbe in *Prophecy and the prophets in ancient Israel*, ed. J. Day (New York 2010) 117–32; Nissinen in *Raising up a faithful exegete* 28; also Burkert, *Structure and history in Greek mythology and ritual* (Berkeley 1979) 183 n.12. On the intimate association between howling of Hebrew prophets and mourning for the dead see e.g. J.L. Mays, *Micah* (Philadelphia 1976) 50–2, 54, 60. Empedocles' words about crying and howling in fr. 118 Diels = fr. 163 Gemelli Marciano are directly related to the underworld or world of the dead (G. Zuntz, *Persephone*, Oxford 1971, 199–203; L. Gemelli Marciano, *Die Vorsokratiker* ii, 2nd ed., Berlin 2013, 430–2; cf. also R. Janko, *Zeitschrift für Papyrologie und Epigraphik* 150,

2004, 6–8, 20–1). The Babylonian *lallaru* or "howler", too, wails above all for the dead: see the Chicago *Assyrian dictionary* ix (Chicago 1973) 47b–48a; A.-C. Rendu, *Revue de l'histoire des religions* 225 (2008) 209–10; S. Bar, *Biblica* 91 (2010) 270. And, just as with Empedocles, the howling of the *goês* relates especially to the underworld or realms of the dead: aside from Burkert's classic comments (*Rheinisches Museum* 105, 1962, 36–55) see S.I. Johnston's mostly lifeless discussions in *Restless dead* (Berkeley 1999) 100–23 and *The world of ancient magic*, ed. D.R. Jordan, H. Montgomery and E. Thomassen (Bergen 1999) 83–102. Nothing could be less coincidental than the fact that Empedocles, himself, was considered a *goês* (Gorgias in Diogenes Laertius, *Lives and views of famous philosophers* 8.59; the *Suda* s.v. *apnous*; *APMM* 220–1 with n.9). Jung on Nature's outrage: *PR* 344 §531; cf. P. Kingsley, *Works & conversations* 22 (2011) 31–3.

[19] For the dynamic of ancient Hebrew prophets struggling against their mission and trying hard to negotiate, even deny, it cf. e.g. Exodus 3:11, 4:1 and 13, 5:22–3, Jeremiah 20:7–9, Zechariah 13:4–6; A. Laytner, *Arguing with God* (Lanham 1990); M. Dean-Otting in *Encyclopedia of psychology and religion* (2nd ed., New York 2014), ed. D.A. Leeming, 1389. Self-righteous Christian commentators have done a wonderful job of redefining prophets as cheerful and perfectly obliging servants of their Lord—even going so far as to make the absurd claim that Jonah was the only prophet who had a problem with being a prophet. See especially R. Payne, *The expository times* 100 (1989) 131–4, "Jonah is presented as a parody or caricature of a prophet ... He shows a complete lack of understanding of the concerns of God ... inconsistent with a prophet's position ... a prophet who acts in a way completely contrary to his prophetic calling ... a complete reversal of what he should be

... Jonah provides a challenge to all who are called to Christian ministry. This is not the way it should be. ..." And Jungian commentators on Jonah tend to do no better: compare for example J. Park's quite typical discomfort with "the prophet's uncomfortable encounter with God" and his condescending judgement that "while God's command is urgent, Jonah's reaction is contrary to normal expectations" (*Inspired speech*, ed. J. Kaltner and L. Stulman, London 2004, 276–85), as if he could actually know what the normal expectations in such a situation would be. It was with far more humility, and hard experience, that Muhammad supposedly told the people around him: "Let none of you say that I am better than Jonah" (M. Lings, *Muhammad*, London 1983, 212). In other words it takes a prophet to understand a prophet.

[20] For some fine comments on the futility of a prophet's task, and the utter incongruity between the inner vision revealed to a prophet and "the reality of the people's actual condition. The two were often felt to be totally incompatible, even to the extent that the prophet sometimes felt it useless to preach to an audience who were so far away from what their God had intended them to be", see Å. Viberg, *Tyndale bulletin* 47 (1996) 113. For the poignant definition of a prophet as someone who "delivers a message that never arrives", and on the prophetic call as a cry that "howls in a void", cf. J. Wojcik and R.-J. Frontain, *Poetic prophecy in western literature* (Rutherford, NJ 1984) 9–10 with A. Ostriker, *The American poetry review* 26/4 (July–August 1997) 29. And for a very rare modern effort not to ignore or silence the prophets' howl but to understand it, see Rami Shapiro's commentary on Isaiah 13:6: "There is no escape from the ambush of your own cruelty and misdeeds. But there is a response: Howl. Howling is a raw expression of your pain, horror, and fear. It is an inarticulate yet definite blast of

truth. You are reduced to primal emotion, and nothing makes sense. When you howl, you release the energies building up within you. When you howl, you shatter the façade of denial and the delusion that there is rescue waiting. When you howl, you cease all thought and feeling, and reach a level of sheer being that is beneath the foundation of self. When you howl, you exhaust the last remnants of hope ..." (*The Hebrew prophets*, Woodstock, VT 2004, 132).

[21] For some wide-ranging comments on the official suppression of prophecy in the Abrahamic religions see Henry Corbin, *Le monde non chrétien* 51/52 (1960) 135–51 and 70 (1964) 61–85; for its continuation regardless cf. e.g. N. Cohn's *The pursuit of the millennium* (2nd ed., New York 1961), M. Goldish, *The Sabbatean prophets* (Cambridge, MA 2004), M. Baigent, *Racing toward Armageddon* (New York 2009). The standard narratives about the silencing of prophecy in Judaism are brought together and discussed now by L.S. Cook, *On the question of the 'cessation of prophecy' in ancient Judaism* (Tübingen 2011). For the urge of early Christian authorities to reject prophecy as an "abomination" (*ebdelyktai*) see e.g. Eusebius, *Church history* 5.16.4 and 5.19.2 together with Tertullian, *On fasting* 1.3; it will be noted that Carl Jung was particularly taken by the controversial revival of Christian prophecy associated with Joachim of Fiore (*Aion* 82–7 §§137–42 and 149–50 §§232–5; *JL* ii 136–8). In Islam, almost everything came to hang on the Quranic designation of Muhammad as "seal of the prophets": for its specifically Manichaean antecedents, and the dogmatic use of it to claim Muhammad was the last of all the prophets, see C. Colpe, *Orientalia Suecana* 33–5 (1984–86) 71–83 and *Das Siegel der Propheten* (Berlin 1990); G.G. Stroumsa, *Jerusalem studies in Arabic and Islam* 7 (1986) 61–74 = *Savoir et salut* (Paris 1992) 275–88; M.

Gil, *Israel oriental studies* 12 (1992) 38–9; J.C. Reeves, *Heralds of that good realm* (Leiden 1996) 8–11, 22 n.27; C. Robinson in *The cult of saints in late antiquity and the Middle Ages*, ed. J. Howard–Johnston and P.A. Hayward (Oxford 1999) 256–8; J. van Ess, *The flowering of Muslim theology* (Cambridge, MA 2006) 23–4; D.S. Powers, *Muhammad is not the father of any of your men* (Philadelphia 2009) 50–4, 272–3; and U. Rubin's recent, although sadly unbalanced, discussion in *Zeitschrift der Deutschen Morgenländischen Gesellschaft* 164 (2014) 65–96. For the statement attributed to Muhammad's youngest and dearest wife (M. Lings, *Muhammad*, London 1983, 272)—"Say that he is the seal of prophets but do not say that there is no prophet after him"—see Powers 53. It seems not to have been noticed that the same imagery of "sealing", in the ancient sense not of closing or ending anything but of simply validating and endorsing earlier mystical or prophetic teachings, is also used by Numenius of Apamea during the second century AD (fr. 1a des Places = fr. 9a Leemans): for the connection between Apamea, in Syria, and the beginnings of Manichaeism see e.g. C. Elsas, *Neuplatonische und gnostische Weltablehnung in der Schule Plotins* (Berlin 1975) 34–9; G.P. Luttikhuizen, *The revelation of Elchasai* (Tübingen 1985); P. Athanassiadi, *La lutte pour l'orthodoxie dans le platonisme tardif* (Paris 2006) 81–2.

[22] For Ginsberg describing how the forms of "Howl", as well as "Kaddish", "developed out of an extreme rhapsodic wail I once heard in a madhouse" see his comments in *On the poetry of Allen Ginsberg*, ed. L. Hyde (Ann Arbor 1984) 82. It was Jack Kerouac who, catching the essence of the poem, initially proposed the one-word title (*Howl on trial*, ed. B. Morgan and N.J. Peters, San Francisco 2006, 33 and n.4); for the complete text and context see *Howl and other poems* (San Francisco 1956), *Howl* (New York 1986). That all of western culture is mad is a

constant theme in "Howl": cf. also J. Raskin, *American scream* (Berkeley 2004) 119–20 on "the insanity of America" together with the context provided by A. Ostriker in *William Blake and the moderns*, ed. R.J. Bertholf and A.S. Levitt (Albany 1982) 114, 127–8. Exuded from Reason: ibid. 121 and *The American poetry review* 26/4 (July–August 1997) 30; cf. also J.A.W. Heffernan in *On the poetry of Allen Ginsberg* 258. There is more than a little to be learned from comparing Allen Ginsberg's impressions of New York ("So you walk down the city streets in New York for a few blocks, you get this gargantuan feeling of buildings. You walk all day you'll be at the verge of tears. More detail, more attention to the significance of all that robotic detail that impinges on the mind, and you realize through your own body's fears that you are surrounded by a giant robot machine which is crushing and separating people …") with Carl Jung's: "suppose an age when the machine gets on top of us. Then it would become a dragon, the equivalent of the old saurians, and really, when you look at New York, it really is on top of man; he knows that he has done all that and yet it pulls him down … We have ideas about the godlikeness of man and forget about the gods. After a while, when we have invested all our energy in rational forms, they will strangle us. They are the dragons now, they became a sort of nightmare. Slowly and secretly we became their slaves and are devoured. New York has grown to overwhelming proportions and it is due to the machine". See A. Ginsberg in *The craft of poetry*, ed. W. Packard (New York 1974) 73 and *DA* 541–2; also *JS* 48–9, *JV* i 502.

[23] On the healing and magical potencies of Ginsberg's prophetic poetry, and his conscious use of incantatory repetition, see A. Ostriker in *William Blake and the moderns*, ed. R.J. Bertholf and A.S. Levitt (Albany 1982) 125–7; P. Portugés in *Poetic prophecy in western literature*, ed. J. Wojcik and R.-J.

Frontain (Rutherford, NJ 1984) 160–71. On the importance for him of breathing, its cycles and rhythm, in the process of composition as well as recitation cf. ibid. 168–9; and for the equal importance of breathing in the composing, as well as reciting, of ancient Greek poetry see especially D. Cysarz, D. von Bonin, H. Lackner, P. Heusser, M. Moser and H. Bettermann, *American journal of physiology, heart and circulatory physiology* 287 (2004) H579–87, *PSIE* 58–60 with n.37.

[24] "Terrible fucking situation …": *The Paris review* 37 (Spring 1966) 40; cf. P. Portugés in *Poetic prophecy in western literature*, ed. J. Wojcik and R.–J. Frontain (Rutherford, NJ 1984) 161–2, 166, 169–71. For Ginsberg as a Hebrew prophet see especially P. Carroll, *Evergreen review* 5/19 (July–August 1961) 114–16; Portugés 161–73; A. Ostriker, *The American poetry review* 26/4 (July–August 1997) 28–31. On his immersion in the world of the Old Testament see *The letters of Allen Ginsberg*, ed. B. Morgan (Philadelphia 2008) and, for his sense of "Biblical rhetoric", *The Paris review* 37 (Spring 1966) 17. Echoing the howling, as well as the rhythmic and incantatory language, of the Hebrew prophets: Ostriker 29, Portugés 166–71. Presented in court as a Hebrew prophet: *Howl of the censor*, ed. J.W. Ehrlich (San Carlos, CA 1961) 63–4 = *Howl on trial*, ed. B. Morgan and N.J. Peters (San Francisco 2006) 165–6 (Kenneth Rexroth). On Ginsberg's prophetic visions see Portugés 157–73, and for his 1954 vision of Moloch—"Moloch whose mind is pure machinery! … whose name is the Mind!"—that triggered the process of writing "Howl" see J. Raskin's comments, *American scream* (Berkeley 2004) 130–2, 138, with K.M. Stephenson in *John F. Kennedy*, ed. J.D. Williams, R.G. Waite and G.S. Gordon (Grand Forks 2010) 49. For Ginsberg "continuing to prophesy what I really knew despite the drear consciousness of the world" see his own comments in *On the*

poetry of Allen Ginsberg, ed. L. Hyde (Ann Arbor 1984) 80. No escaping from God: Ostriker 29.

[25] "The prophetic image beyond our present strength ...": see Ginsberg, *Gates of wrath* (Bolinas 1972) 16 with the fine commentary by P. Portugés in *Poetic prophecy in western literature*, ed. J. Wojcik and R.-J. Frontain (Rutherford, NJ 1984) 164. And note the final movement of Ginsberg's "Kaddish"—"Caw caw caw crows shriek in the white sun over grave stones in Long Island ... Lord Lord Lord caw caw caw Lord Lord Lord caw caw caw Lord"—with A. Ostriker's comments in *William Blake and the moderns*, ed. R.J. Bertholf and A.S. Levitt (Albany 1982) 124.

[26] Micah 1:8. The common translation "like an ostrich" instead of "like an owl" is simply a mistake, as was already pointed out a long time ago (see e.g. G.R. Driver, *Palestine exploration quarterly* 87, 1955, 12–13; B.K. Waltke, *A commentary on Micah*, Grand Rapids 2007, 66–7). But it seems not to have been noticed that the correctness, here in Micah, of the translation "like an owl" is confirmed by external evidence from ancient Mesopotamia—where one and the same word, *lallaru*, is used both for an owl and for a prophet who wails and howls. See the Chicago *Assyrian dictionary* ix (Chicago 1973) 48a; A.-C. Rendu, *Revue de l'histoire des religions* 225 (2008) 209–10. As far as translations go, it can be reassuring to know that in place of "I will go stripped and naked" one widely distributed English version of the Bible reads "I'll walk around barefoot. I won't have anything on but my underwear."

[27] Jung comes extremely close to a portrayal of prophets' role as the guardians of creation when he describes the relationship between forests, wild animals and how he was made a prophet

(*Red book* folio vi verso, cf. *RB* 251a). For his articulate commentary on the massively disastrous consequences of becoming alienated from nature, in particular from the animal nature inside us, see *JM* 249–53; the desire, in spite of this articulateness, to intellectualize and complicate his intimate relationship to nature (e.g. P. Clarkson in *Sacral revolutions*, ed. G. Heuer, Hove 2010, 97–105) is truly a wonder to behold. "To rely on the birds ...": S.B. Elswit, *The Jewish story finder* (2nd ed., Jefferson, NC 2012) 64 §96. Compare also H. Schwartz, *Leaves from the garden of Eden* (New York 2009) 57 (Solomon as master "of the language of the birds, of the secrets of the wind") and, for Solomon learning the language of the birds, see J. Janssens in *The figure of Solomon in Jewish, Christian and Islamic tradition*, ed. J. Verheyden (Leiden 2013) 250 with A. Asani in *A communion of subjects*, ed. P. Waldau and K. Patton (New York 2006) 170–5. At the extremely ancient Greek oracle of Zeus in Dodona we find the same basic dynamic of birds revealing the language of the winds: the priestesses who interpreted the sound of the winds rustling the leaves of Dodona's great oak tree were called pigeons and traced their lineage back to the first pigeon–priestess who, after she had landed on the tree, gave instructions for founding the oracle by talking in a human voice (Herodotus, *Histories* 2.52–7). For Greek traditions about the time when humans, birds and animals all spoke the same language see e.g. Plato, *Statesman* 272b–d, Iamblichus, *Pythagorean life* 178. As for shamans learning or, rather, remembering the language of the birds see especially M. Eliade in *Conferenze tenute all'Istituto italiano per il Medio ed Estremo Oriente*, ed. G. Tucci, ii (Rome 1955) 57–79. On animals as prophets, and their cries as prophecies, in ancient Egypt compare for instance R. Jasnow and K.-T. Zauzich, *The ancient Egyptian book of Thoth* (Wiesbaden 2005) i 260–2 (B02 10/2–11), 268–9 (B02 11/3); E.P. Butler in *Practicing Gnosis*, ed. A.D. DeConick, G. Shaw and J.D. Turner (Leiden 2013) 237.

[28] For the passage in Porphyry see his *On abstinence from living things* 3.1–6, 186.16–195.5 Nauck = ii 152–160 Bouffartigue–Patillon (... *all' hina tauta parômen dia to xymphyton hêmin pathos tês apistias* ...). For the passage in Plato see his *Statesman* 272b–d (... *homôs d' oun tauta men aphômen* ...) together with the usual, serenely approving comments by scholars about Plato's "explicit manipulation of traditional symbols" (e.g. M.H. Miller, *The philosopher in Plato's 'Statesman'*, The Hague 1980, 37). On the perverse process of "leaving aside" the mythical in myth by reducing everything to what is "reasonably natural", or naturally reasonable, see also Porphyry's *On abstinence from living things* 4.2 = Dicaearchus fr. 49 Wehrli = fr. 56A Mirhady (... *to de lian mythikon aphentas eis to dia tou logou physikon anagein* ...) together with P. Vidal–Naquet, *Journal of Hellenic studies* 98 (1978) 132 and G.E. Sterling in *Reading Philo*, ed. T. Seland (Grand Rapids 2014) 132. Nothing could be more telling than the fact that for Plotinus, Porphyry's teacher and the most famous of Platonists after Plato, nature herself had become completely silent—and would stay silent as long as he kept expecting her to offer the kind of rational explanations for her own existence that he gruesomely tries to put into her mouth (*Enneads* 3.8.4, a passage which completely turns on its head the profound Gnostic awareness of a sacred silence at the root of all creation). It never quite seemed to occur to him that nature might be speaking all the time through every storm and breeze and bird. For Blake on Plato see A.K. Mellor, *Blake's human form divine* (Berkeley 1974) 260, 280–4, 335 n.27; P. Ackroyd, *Blake* (London 1995) 89 with *The complete poetry and prose of William Blake*, ed. D.V. Erdman (2nd ed., Berkeley 1982) 670 ("Wisdom shallow: pompous Ignorance!").

[29] Guénon's essay has been published in the somewhat mistitled *Sword of gnosis*, ed. J. Needleman (London 1986) 299–303 and retranslated in his *Fundamental symbols* (Cambridge 1995) 39–42 = *The underlying religion*, ed. M. Lings and C. Minnaar (Bloomington, IN 2007) 172–5. For the angel–bird in Sufi tradition see especially Rûzbehân al-Baqlî's *Kashf al-asrâr* (*Le dévoilement des secrets et les apparitions des lumières*, trans. P. Ballanfat, Paris 1996, 175, 195, 260 = *The unveiling of secrets*, trans. C.W. Ernst, Chapel Hill 1997, 41, 59, 112). But Guénon neglects to mention that there used to be intense dispute among Islamic mystics or Sufis about how to understand the sacred language of the birds and its relation to physical birdsong: see e.g. Rûmî's *Mathnawî* 1.3355–9, 6.4010–16. Some Sufi scholars are even more extreme, and anthropocentric, in their "symbolic" interpretation than Guénon—formally defining the language of the birds as "the speech of sanctified human spirits" (W.C. Chittick, *The Sufi path of love*, Albany 1983, 16). Psychologically there is something quite remarkable about the perfect ease with which a person nowadays can snatch the language of birds away from mere physical birds and hand it to the angels, even to sanctified human beings.

[30] "Kubrâ begins with these striking words ...": see S. Ruspoli, *Le traité de l'Esprit saint de Rûzbehân de Shîrâz* (Paris 2001) 72–4 with n.9. My thanks to Stéphane Ruspoli for permitting me to translate his words here, with very minor modifications, from the French; the embedded quotations from Kubrâ are from the *Fawâtih al-jamâl wa fawâ'ih al jalâl* = *Les éclosions de la beauté et les parfums de la majesté*, trans. P. Ballanfat (Nîmes 2001) 131, 201. The extra Kubrâ passage that I have added ("I heard these cries ...") is based on *Fawâtih al-jamâl wa fawâ'ih al-jalâl* §150 (Ballanfat 201). For God "who has taught us the language of the birds" see Qur'ân 27:16 ("Oh people, we have

been taught the language of the birds"), spoken by the prophet Solomon; and for the even more explicit claim, famously made by Rûzbehân, that he too was a prophet note C.W. Ernst's very sober comments, *Rûzbihân Baqlî: mysticism and the rhetoric of sainthood in Persian Sufism* (Richmond 1996) 24–6, plus Henry Corbin's contextual observations in *EJ* 26 (1957) 113–37. "Those are the times ...": *Fawâtih al-jamâl wa fawâ'ih al-jalâl* §150 = *Les éclosions de la beauté et les parfums de la majesté* 201.

[31] For Hebrew prophets as mad see Hosea 9:7; 2 Kings 9:11; Jeremiah 29:26; T. Jemielity, *Satire and the Hebrew prophets* (Louisville 1992) 138. And for the same kind of disparaging treatment in Mesopotamia compare M. Nissinen in *Raising up a faithful exegete*, ed. K.L. Noll and B. Schramm (Winona Lake 2010) 14 with n.55. Of course this whole situation was immensely facilitated by the fact that common Akkadian and Greek as well as Hebrew words for "prophet" were, even on an etymological level, directly connected with madness in the technical sense of ecstasy or extraordinary states of consciousness (M.J. de Jong, *Isaiah among the ancient Near Eastern prophets*, Leiden 2007, 340–1; M.A. Flower, *The seer in ancient Greece*, Berkeley 2008, 23; Nissinen 7–8, 27; J. Stökl, *Prophecy in the ancient Near East*, Leiden 2012, 52–3). William Blake is a particularly interesting case of someone who, in addition to being very familiar with the routine dismissal of ancient prophets as just mad, was also dismissed as being not a prophet but mad himself (A. Ostriker in *William Blake and the moderns*, ed. R.J. Bertholf and A.S. Levitt, Albany 1982, 114; P. Portugés in *On the poetry of Allen Ginsberg*, ed. L. Hyde, Ann Arbor 1984, 131–2). Carl Jung, for his part, knew all about Christian prophetic figures being denounced as insane (*Aion* 83 n.55). Among the Greeks, even Aristotle's denunciation of Parmenides and his teaching for leading to

madness has a special significance (*On generation and corruption* 325a13–23; *Reality* 212, 479). For the natural grouping of Empedocles among the mad see Horace, *Art of poetry* 463–72; *Theology of Aristotle* 1.31 with *APMM* 380 and *Reality* 442–3; C. Crawford, *To Nietzsche: Dionysus, I love you! Ariadne* (Albany 1995) 72, 75; A. Thiher, *Revels in madness* (Ann Arbor 1999) 155; J.C. Hampsey, *Paranoia and contentment* (Charlottesville 2004) 50–2. The fact that he dared to speak with the voice of both a scientist and a prophet has also doomed Empedocles to be condemned in the West as a schizophrenic—although, strangely enough, the harder scholars try to rescue him from this "split personality" the less they succeed. See e.g. C.H. Kahn in *Essays in ancient Greek philosophy*, ed. J.P. Anton and G.L. Kustas (Albany 1971) 3–4, 19; F. Jürss, *Geschichte des wissenschaftlichen Denkens im Altertum* (Berlin 1982) 199; V. Vitsaxis, *Thought and faith* (Boston 2009) ii 59–60; S.R.L. Clark in *The Oxford handbook of natural theology*, ed. R. Re Manning (Oxford 2013) 13. For Empedocles' own words about "trusting in mad Strife", as well as his direct insights into the workings of madness, see *Reality* 430–41; and for some general comments on the question of prophetic madness in ancient Greece, H. Lovatt, *The epic gaze* (Cambridge 2013) 122–49.

[32] For 19th-century and 20th-century diagnoses of prophecy see e.g. A. Klostermann, *Theologische Studien und Kritiken* 50 (1877) 391–439 (catalepsy); J. Moses, *Pathological aspects of religions* (Worcester, MA 1906), esp. 125; J.H. Kaplan, *Psychology of prophecy* (Philadelphia 1908: "… these abnormal, pathological phenomena of the soul–life …"); E.C. Broome, *Journal of biblical literature* 65 (1946) 277–92 ("paranoid schizophrenia … a true psychotic"); K. Jaspers, *Aneignung und Polemik* (Munich 1968) 13–21; D.J. Halperin, *Seeking Ezekiel* (University Park, PA 1993); A. Falk, *A psychoanalytic history of the Jews* (Cranbury,

NJ 1996) 184–7; and note Michel Foucault's amusing but appropriate comment on "the classificatory mania of the psychiatrists" (*History of madness*, Abingdon 2006, 393). For prophecy as post-traumatic stress disorder see especially D.M. Daschke, *American imago* 56 (1999) 105–32; D.L. Smith-Christopher, *A biblical theology of exile* (Minneapolis 2002) 75–104; W. Morrow in *Psychology and the Bible*, ed. J.H. Ellens and W.G. Rollins (Westport, CT 2004) i 167–83; D.G. Garber, ibid. ii 220; R. Poser, *Das Ezechielbuch als Trauma-Literatur* (Leiden 2012); and note the resoundingly dogmatic reductionism of the new diagnostic as endorsed by C.J. Sharp, *Old Testament prophets for today* (Louisville 2009) 1, 80, 108 n.1 ("The prophets think they see God—but psychiatrists would tell us that Ezekiel's mystical chariot vision was a hallucination related to psychosis or post-traumatic stress disorder"). Prophets howling is singled out as an obviously pathological phenomenon by Klostermann 430; Halperin 8; E.F. Edinger, *Ego and self* (Toronto 2000) 56, 58, 64; Poser 419–20. Of course there is no consideration whatsoever of the logical probability that the people who really have been traumatized are not the ones who howl, but those who are too scared to howl.

[33] See J.A. Talamo, *A Jungian depth perspective on OCD* (Ann Arbor 2009) 78–81, 107, noting the extent to which his diagnosis has been inspired by Edward Edinger. Rivkah Schärf Kluger, on the other hand, was a somewhat exceptional Jungian who freely admitted that prophets might be able to offer crucial healing to a whole people by helping to counteract and defuse, rather than heighten, collective inflation—provided they could manage to bring their prophetic gift under conscious control (*Psyche in scripture*, Toronto 1995; her idea of a progressive evolution in consciousness on the part of ancient Hebrew prophets is, both psychologically and historically, altogether

questionable). I would be glad to add Marie–Louise von Franz's brief but positive discussion of prophecy in her *Archetypal dimensions of the psyche* (Boston 1997, 12), except that she has done little more than copy out Shärf Kluger's conclusions virtually word for word. For Shärf Kluger see R. Bernardini, G.P. Quaglino and A. Romano, *JAP* 58 (2013) 191–3.

[34] For James Kirsch's diagnoses of Jewish prophets and prophecy in the post-biblical period of exile see especially his *The reluctant prophet* (Los Angeles 1973). His persistently patronizing analysis of Rabbi Wechsler as an altogether inadequate and ineffective figure is no less remarkable than his compensating idealization of the old Hebrew prophets as efficient, hard-working contributors to their communities (e.g. 171–7; on Kirsch's extreme idealizing of pre-exilic Jewish history compare A. Lammers in *Turbulent times, creative minds*, ed. E. Shalit and M. Stein, Asheville 2016, 78–9). To consider the ancient prophets effective and successful at getting their message across is the height of naivety (Å. Viberg, *Tyndale bulletin* 47, 1996, 107–14; A. Ostriker, *The American poetry review* 26/4, July–August 1997, 29) while to judge Rabbi Wechsler a failed prophet, when people far closer to him revered him as a genuine prophet and saint who had saved their lives (*Reluctant prophet* 17, 85), is just a little inappropriate. Regarding Kirsch's notions about the essentially messianic role of both Jung and Jungian psychology see ibid. 186 and 193—for his revealing language in presenting Jung's work as "a turning point in the history of the human spirit" compare e.g. R. Stronstad, *The prophethoood of all believers* (Sheffield 1999) 40—together with his equally revealing assertion that only through Jung is it possible to rediscover what the Jewish people have lost "since the time of the prophets" (*JK* 53). On the problems of his "religious" inflation, as well as Jung's repeated

attempts to confront him with it, see the various materials gathered in *JK* (e.g. xi–xvi, 164, 260); I am also sincerely grateful to Ann Lammers for showing me the text of two unpublished lectures she gave on the subject at St Niklausen in September 2012 and at Berlin in May 2014. As for Kirsch's own inner prophetic calling, ever since he turned 13, to become "like Abraham and Moses" see his comments in *A modern Jew in search of a soul*, ed. J.M. Spiegelman and A. Jacobson (Phoenix 1986) 149, 154; for his view of Jung himself as a prophet "who will lead us back to the Living One" and play a crucial role in "the rebirth of the Jews", *JJ* 6/1 (2012) 25. In the unpublished text of his lecture on "C.G. Jung's individuation as shown especially in *Answer to Job*", which he gave a short while before he died, Kirsch also speaks eloquently as well as explicitly and at length about Jung as one of the greatest prophets humanity has ever known (*KI*). But it seems not to have dawned on him that this, primarily unconscious, elevation of Jung and Jungian psychology to the status of a prophet and prophetic religion has come at the cost of engendering a new religious fundamentalism.

[35] The following quotations are taken from Edinger's *Ego and self* (Toronto 2000) 56–8, which in turn is based on lectures he gave at the Los Angeles Jung Institute in 1986; I am most grateful to Daryl Sharp and Inner City Books for permission to quote the passage at length. Edward Edinger had begun his Jungian analysis with Esther Harding, in New York, during 1951. Often he would comment on what a wonderfully positive experience this analysis had been for him (T.B. Kirsch, *The Jungians*, London 2000, 71, 101; cf. A. Ulanov, *PP* 39, 1999, 42). One has to wonder whether, if it hadn't been quite so "positive", he might have been forced just a little deeper inside himself. For the importance of Edinger's

role as the "pre-eminent interpreter" and representative of Jung at the end of the 20th century see e.g. the obituary of him in the *New York Times* by Ford Burkhart (2 August 1998); D. Sharp in Edinger's *Ego and self* (Toronto 2000) 151; also G.R. Elder, *PP* 39 (1999) 12–16, who even ventures to celebrate him as "the finest example of creative introversion born in America since Emerson". This grandiosely narcissistic nonsense, already anticipated by Jung in his description of how a master's inflated disciples "always stick together, not out of love, but for the very understandable purpose of effortlessly confirming their own convictions" (*TE* 170–1 §263), is par for the course in the lineage of Jungians that Edinger belonged to: compare the quaint lunacy of D. Rothstein's praise for "the philosophy of Marie–Louise von Franz, whose enormous brilliance ... surpassed even the thinking of Emmanuel [sic] Kant" (*PP* 51, 2008, 355). For the view of Jung as, in effect, the second coming compare Elder 13; Edinger's own *The creation of consciousness* (Toronto 1984); W. Colman, *JAP* 42 (1997) 342; T.B. Kirsch, *The Jungians* (London 2000) 101–2, 253; the theological underpinning for Edinger's famous idea that Jungian psychology represents the third dispensation, replacing the first dispensation of the Old Testament and the second of the New, came to him from Esther Harding (*KI* 17). Marie–Louise von Franz not only agreed with Edinger on this but chronologically went one stage further, considering Jung the greatest man since Lao Tzu (*The fountain of the love of wisdom*, ed. E. Kennedy–Xypolitas, Wilmette 2006, 317–19; *PP* 38, 1998, 33). For Jung's own ability to maintain, in the face of everything, an attitude of humility see L. Vaughan–Lee, *Moshkel Gosha* (Inverness, CA 2005) 71–4; and note his very sane insistence that there are Christians, for example, who can help people perfectly well even without any knowledge of modern psychology at all (*JL* ii 226). This quintessential quality of humility is always shared by truly great beings, if not by their disciples. Compare Gurdjieff's comment, "Many man on earth more than me" (E. Wolfe, *Episodes with Gurdjieff*, Millerton 1974, 25).

[36] Edinger states that "the etymology of the word comes from two roots: *pro*, meaning before, in front of, and *phátis*, meaning voice or oracle, so it means 'to speak out before all'" (*Ego and self*, Toronto 2000, 47); David Miller offers a similar explanation (*EJ* 46, 1977, 486 n.98), followed by James Hillman in *Lament of the dead* (New York 2013) 114 ("forth-tellings"). The crucial fact missed by these extravert interpreters is that, etymologically, prophets are not people who "speak in front of" an assembled audience but are those who are made to "speak on behalf of" the divine reality inside them: the focus of the word itself is internal or spiritual, not external and social. For the force of *pro-* see especially Sophocles, *Oedipus the king* 10 and *Oedipus at Colonus* 811 (where *pro tônde phônein* or *erô pro tônde* means not to "speak in front of these" but to "speak on behalf of these") with R.C. Jebb, *Sophocles: the Oedipus tyrannus* (Cambridge 1914) 11. And for the original meaning of *prophêtês* see Aeschylus, *Eumenides* 19 as well as Pindar, *Nemean odes* 1.60 ("*prophêtês* of Zeus"); Bacchylides, *Epinician odes* 9.3 ("*prophêtês* of the Muses") with G. Nagy, *Pindar's Homer* (Baltimore 1990) 163 §34 and *Homeric responses* (Austin 2003) 35–6; C. Frateantonio in *Der neue Pauly* x (Stuttgart 2001) 401 s.v. *promantis* and J.N. Bremmer, ibid. 421 s.v. Prophet; M.A. Flower, *The seer in ancient Greece* (Berkeley 2008) 86; A. Motte, *Kernos* 26 (2013) 13, 17. In Mesopotamian prophecies, too, this fundamental idea of a prophet as someone speaking or crying out on behalf of the sacred is very present (W. Burkert, *The orientalizing revolution*, Cambridge, MA 1992, 80; M. Nissinen, *Prophets and prophecy in the ancient Near*

East, Atlanta 2003, 7, 127; cf. also Deuteronomy 18:16–19). As for who ends up hearing, or understanding, the prophetic call: one could say this is ultimately none of the prophet's business.

[37] Already at the beginning of the *Red book* Jung notes down the taunts of the mocking inner voices who torment him with the accusation that his ambitions to become a prophet are getting the better of him (*RB* 233a). This throws an interesting light on Freud's heavily barbed reference—a few short years later, at a public lecture in 1917—to the early work done by "C.G. Jung, at a time when he was merely a psycho-analyst and had not yet aspired to be a prophet" (*The standard edition of the complete psychological works of Sigmund Freud* xvi, London 1963, 269). It was an accusation that, far from being forgotten, would rankle Jung for the rest of his life (*MDR* 150/154). Freud on Jung as a mystic, and mad: *IJP* 25, *JSB* 72. Since the days of Freud, there has been no end to the list of people wanting to blacken Jung's name by denouncing him as a prophet: see for example E. Fromm, *Scientific American* 209/3 (September 1963) 283–90; P.J. Stern, *C.G. Jung: the haunted prophet* (New York 1976); P. Rieff's *The triumph of the therapeutic* (Chicago 1987); R. Noll, *The Jung cult* (2nd ed., New York 1997); F. McLynn, *Carl Gustav Jung* (New York 1996). For Jung's repeated denials that he was a prophet see e.g. *CT* 91 §190 ("'I do not wish to pass myself off as a prophet, but …', he would write, and after the 'but' would come a stream of prophetic statements!", as David Tacey notes about this passage: *The darkening spirit*, Hove 2013, 40), 514 §980; *JL* i 128 and 203, ii 513; *SL* 637 §1460; *JS* 374; M.T. Kelsey, *Christo–psychology* (New York 1982) 119 (cf. *AS* 113 n.3). Note also his pragmatic comments and references at *CT* 201 §414; *MC* 105 §125. Two prominent examples of those who would dearly love to stamp out any remaining nonsense about Jung being a prophet are M.–L.

von Franz, *C.G. Jung: his myth in our time* (New York 1975) 41, 121 and S. Shamdasani, *Cult fictions* (London 1998); while von Franz insists with her usual dogmatism that he had "definitively renounced" the role of prophet as a young student (*C.G. Jung* 41), publication of the *Red book* shows that her chronology of his life leaves much to be desired. It can also be easy to miss the extent to which Jung's intense and lifelong interest in the subject of prophecy has been more subtly, often unconsciously, suppressed. For example the standard English collection of his letters contains many significant references to the theme—but although the index to the two volumes very generously offers a listing for "prostitution", not a single entry exists for either "prophecy" or "prophets" (*JL* ii 696).

[38] There is a genuine significance in the fact that whenever Jung pondered if Freud could be called a prophet he always intended the term as a compliment and not an insult (*MDR* 163/169; *SM* 36 §51 and 46 §69; P. Bishop, *The Dionysian self*, Berlin 1995, 194–7; cf. D. Tacey, *The darkening spirit*, Hove 2013, 40–1). Freud, on the other hand, only dared to speak positively about Jung as a prophet in the most private and intimate of settings (*FJ* 218 §125F, 17 January 1909)—which must have made his later, public attacks on him for imagining he was a prophet even harder to bear. For Jung's own poignant observation about a "real prophet or saviour" only lasting a few weeks, at the very most, if exposed to our modern world see E. Rolfe, *Encounter with Jung* (Boston 1989) 102–3 = *JL* ii 174.

[39] Jung tells Freud that their psychology has to be a religion, and plainly hints at the need for a saviour: see *FJ* 323–4 §178J (11 February 1910) and compare his passionate announcement, as a young man in his twenties, of the need for "prophets, men sent by God!" (*ZL* 46 §138). Freud's

anxiously negative reply: *FJ* 325 §179F (13 February 1910); J.E. Gedo, *Annual of psychoanalysis* 7 (1979) 66–9. On the need to model psychoanalysis as a modern esoteric institution with its own religious conclave because it "is much too true to be acknowledged ..." see *FJ* 381–2 §206J (11 August 1910). The official English edition of the Freud–Jung correspondence totally destroys the sense of this crucial passage by substituting a geopolitical image for a religious one and mistranslating "nur in einem engsten Konklave" as "only in a very tight enclave"; "Verborgenheit" here does not mean "seclusion" but "secrecy" or "concealment"; Jung's solemn warning that he and Freud need to protect the sacred reality of psychology from their own ambitions for public success and recognition (compare his later criticism of himself for chasing after the ambition to become a prophet, *RB* 233a) is even more horrifically mistranslated as "One should therefore barricade this territory against the ambitions of the public for a long time to come"; and, last but not least, it fails to convey Jung's essential distinction in his original German between the statement that psychoanalysis is "much too true" ("viel zu wahr") to be offered to the public and his very next sentence insisting on the need to saturate the public supply with versions which have deliberately been "falsified" as well as adulterated ("verfälschte"). Ironically, Richard Noll intuited the significance of this passage for an understanding of Jung's aspirations at the time (*The Aryan Christ*, New York 1997, 66). But as he made the mistake of relying on the standard English translation, he had only the poorest idea of what Jung himself really said.

[40] For Jung's original comments on prophecy in 1916 see his *Zwei Schriften über analytische Psychologie* (4th ed., Olten 1989) 302–3 §476 and ("he will not set himself up as a psychoanalytic prophet") 312 §502; *TE* 286 §476, 295 §502.

His warnings here about being overpowered by prophetic ambition ("Ehrgeiz") and yielding to the temptation ("Versuchung") to declare oneself a prophet (*TE* 286 §476, cf. 169 §260) correspond exactly to his own internal struggles as documented, at much the same time, in the *Red book*: compare especially *RB* 233a (Jung's prophetic ambition) and 367b (the temptation to declare himself a prophet). Shamdasani's theory that "the reference to setting oneself up as a 'psychoanalytic prophet' may be an implicit reference to Freud" (*Cult fictions*, London 1998, 51 n.11) shows how little, in spite of his claimed insights into the *Red book* (*JSB* 99–103), he understands of the real situation here. If there is any implicit reference at all, it will be to Jung himself.

[41] For the expanded 1928 version of his comments on prophecy see C.G. Jung, *Zwei Schriften über analytische Psychologie* (4th ed., Olten 1989) 177–9 §§260–5 (*Two essays on analytical psychology*, London 1928, 179–82; *TE* 169–71 §§260–5). His unfailing openness to the possibility of authentic prophets is conveyed by the emphatic use he makes of the words "wirklicher", "echt", "richtige"—"real", "genuine", "true"—while his most revealing statement of all is "Jeder richtige Prophet wehrt sich zunächst mannhaft gegen die unbewußte Zumutung dieser Rolle". Hull's and Shamdasani's mistranslations of "Jeder richtige Prophet" as "every respectable prophet" (*TE* 170 §262) and "every proper prophet" (*Cult fictions*, London 1998, 81) radically distort Jung's intention; only the original version offered by Peter and Cary Baynes conveys his meaning accurately ("every real prophet": *Two essays on analytical psychology*, London 1928, 181). For the quite typical Jungian strategy nowadays of simply equating "prophecy" in Jung with "false prophecy", then waving the whole subject aside as embarrassing and unscientific, see e.g. A. Schweizer, *JJ* 5/3 (2011) 79–81. Elsewhere, too, Jung

repeatedly opens the door for true prophecy as well as for real prophets or prophetesses (*JL* ii 4; ibid. 174 = E. Rolfe, *Encounter with Jung*, Boston 1989, 102–3; *TE* 171 §265); and in the *Red book* he draws the clearest of distinctions between false prophets and true ones (*RB* 153–4, 316–17). In fact his statement here that, "by way of precaution, I would prefer as a very first step to question each individual case" is itself an obvious echo of one biblical passage for which he had the highest regard: "Do not trust every spirit, but test (*dokimazete*) the spirits to see if they come from God because there are many false prophets (*pseudoprophêtai*) who have appeared in the world" (1 John 4:1). On the importance of this passage for Jung see *PR* 416 §659 and 581 §957; the very end of *Mysterium coniunctionis* (*MC* 552 §787); *CT* 444 §839; and compare Shamdasani, *Cult fictions* 82 n.10 (mis-sourcing the passage as John 4:1). Against the true prophet who "valiantly" struggles against identifying with the role of prophet stands, or lies, the would-be prophet who fails the critical tests of ambition and identification. Especially significant in this regard are Jung's unpublished letter to J.B. Lang dated 17 January 1918, on the "delusion of being a prophet" which will always be a primary danger for those working with the unconscious ("Prophetenwahn", misunderstood at *RB* 207a, is not a prophet's delusion but the delusion of being a prophet in just the same way that "Größenwahn" means the delusion of grandeur); *PA* 36 §41, on those who become prophets because they "identify themselves with the archetypal contents of their unconscious"; and his splendidly lurid account of "those terrifying invalids who think they have a prophetic mission" (*ACU* 16 §31). Now, thanks in particular to the *Red book*, we can at last appreciate why throughout the whole of his adult life Jung dedicated so much energy and intensity to this theme.

[42] For what Jung has just been saying, only a moment before, by way of introducing the figure of the true prophet—including the point he makes about the importance of humour—see *TE* 169–70 §§260–2. His repeated emphasis on the critical need, in every possible respect, for time and cautious patience could hardly be plainer ("vorsichtshalber ... zunächst einmal ... leichthin ... ohne weiteres ... im Handumdrehen"; *TE* 170 §262). His own insistence on patiently carrying things around inside himself for a long time before feeling they were ripe enough to be spoken was most unusual: see e.g. *JL* ii 452–3 plus his favourite alchemical saying *Omnis festinatio ex parte diaboli est*, "All haste comes from the devil" (*PPT* 274 n.8, *MDR* 223/236). For Jung's use of prophetic language here, even down to the double negative, compare especially Empedocles fr. 15 Diels = fr. 15B Gemelli Marciano (*ouk ... ouden ...*) together with *APMM* 366 n.21 and my detailed commentary in *Reality* 404–6; the same double negative structure occurs, uncoincidentally, in the climax of the prophetic riddle by Merlin which is placed at the beginning and end of this book (*peu ... nus ...*: *Merlin*, ed. G. Paris and J. Ulrich, Paris 1886, i 32). For prophetic language as used by Parmenides see *ENM* 369–81. Wanting to be deceived: *Reality* 315–559.

[43] For Jung's consistent stance in exempting true prophets from psychological analysis see especially *JL* i 414–15 (on Hosea); *PR* 316–17 §474 (Brother Klaus) and 420 §665 (Ezekiel); also *TE* 45 §66, *SL* 205 §466; and cf. *RB* 295 with *JJW* 94. There were others early in the twentieth century who protested against the widespread, pseudo-scientific practice of psychoanalyzing or "pathologizing" major Biblical figures including the Hebrew prophets: see D.A. Kille's comments in *Psychology and the Bible*, ed. J.H. Ellens and W.G. Rollins

(Westport, CT 2004) i 23. But Carl Jung, as a prominent psychologist himself, was unique in his unambiguous stand on the matter. Notice also how intensely he already expressed his feelings on the same general topic as a young man: *ZL* 43 §134. On any prophet unfortunate enough to have lived "before the time was ready, before analytical psychology was born", as by necessity an unconscious "victim of the process of individuation" see Kirsch's *A reluctant prophet* (Los Angeles 1973) 186. By way of contrast, for prophets as models of individuation according to Jung himself note e.g. *ACU* 145–7 §§254–8 with J.M. Spiegelman in *Sufism, Islam and Jungian psychology*, ed. Spiegelman (Scottsdale 1991) 15; *PR* 294 §448 with L. Beaubien, *L'expérience mystique selon C.G. Jung* (PhD thesis, Université Laval 2009) 63; W.G. Rollins, *Soul and psyche* (Minneapolis 1999) 56. As conscious guides, models of psychological health: C.G. Jung, *Collected papers on analytical psychology* (London 1916) 172–3 = *FP* 320 n.21. Edinger on prophets' failure to adapt: *Ego and self* (Toronto 2000) 58. Jung on the importance of not adapting: *SM* 82–3 §§130–1 with Rollins 55. Prophets as the only defence and protection against inflation: *SL* 109–10 §§245–7 with E. Shalit and N.S. Furlotti in *The dream and its amplification*, ed. Shalit and Furlotti (Skiatook 2013) 2; cf. *ACU* 145–6 §254. For prophets as unique in being able, through their inner vision, to perceive the real needs of their time see *JL* i 60 with e.g. *CD* 142; on the intensity of their struggle to listen to the still small voice within and obey God's will because this sets them so squarely against the ideals of the collective, *JL* ii 85–6. It's important to note that Jung was the last person to be unaware of the prophets' very frequent and very human hesitation, or even refusal, to listen to the inner voice (e.g. *PR* 18 §32).

[44] "We must read the Bible ...": *JV* i 442. On the fundamental importance of the Bible for Jung, and his psychology, see e.g. W.G. Rollins, *Soul and psyche* (Minneapolis 1999) 46–57 and in *Psychology and the Bible*, ed. J.H. Ellens and Rollins (Westport, CT 2004) i 75–95. For his immensely impressive biblical learning in full swing, compare *JJW* 7. "The common man suffers from a hubris of consciousness that borders on the pathological": *PR* 84 §141. For the extremes of religious inflation versus "the rationalistic and political psychosis that is the affliction of our day" see *Aion* 84 §140 ("quasi moderne Menschen die ... eine religiöse Inflation besitzen im Unterschied zum heutigen, dessen Psychose in einer rationalistischen und politischen Affliktion besteht").

[45] The prophet's disciples: *TE* 170–1 §§263–5. On Edinger as "an ordinary man in most respects except for my ability to see Jung's size" see e.g. D.D. Cordic, *PP* 39 (1999) 10; E.F. Edinger, *The Aion lectures* (Toronto 1996) 11 ("Jung's depth and breadth are absolutely awesome. We are all Lilliputians by comparison ... we must begin by accepting our own littleness"); *JJTP* 1/1 (1999) 51 ("Jung is numinous ... Jung's magnitude is such that he dwarfs all of us"); and, for Edinger's "virtual deification" of Jung, W. Colman, *JAP* 42 (1997) 342. Compare also the Swiss Jungian, Andreas Schweizer, very commendably contrasting his littleness and poorness to "Jung's gigantic effort"—while naively affirming the need to hold on to one's "painfully limited reality" as the only available defence against "the danger of inflation" (*JJ* 5/3, 2011, 26 and 79).

[46] For the expert assurances that Jung's portrayal of inflated disciples has no bearing at all on orthodox, as opposed to

"feral", Jungians see especially S. Shamdasani, *Cult fictions* (London 1998) 81–3; D. Tacey, *Jung and the New Age* (Hove 2001) 30–4. "Low-grade": Tacey 33; "feral" is another of Tacey's expressions (23, 28). Theosophists: Shamdasani 83. Shamdasani in particular should have been alerted to the absurdity of his own proposal by Alphonse Maeder's informed report, published while Jung was still alive, about Jungian disciple–psychotherapists competing with devoted Freudians in their fanatical "worship of the Master" (*Schweizerische Zeitschrift für Psychologie* 15, 1956, 121: cf. *JM* 150). For another contemporary perspective, from Wolfgang Hochheimer—"never seen anything like it"—on the "cult of the Master" which was very much alive among "Jung's closest followers" see P. Bishop, *Seminar* 34 (1998) 378–81. One can also compare the criticisms already levelled at both Jungians and Freudians from as early as 1912 for being "devotees of this new cult" who sacrifice any intellectual freedom to their master (J.B. Watson, *Journal of the American Medical Association* 58, 1912, 916; R. Noll, *The Aryan Christ*, New York 1997, 58), not to mention Victor White's horrible discovery in Switzerland that his friend Carl Jung was surrounded by "only sycophants & flatterers" (*JW* 273; cf. D. Bair, *Jung*, Boston 2003, 371). Even insiders from the Jungian community have repeatedly made comments pointing in the same direction (Noll 278). And as one second-generation Jungian, James Kirsch's son, has readily granted in responding to the rabid attacks on both Jung and Jungians by Richard Noll: "there is no question that the early group around Jung formed in cultlike worship ... Any new endeavor that touches individuals so profoundly is bound to have somewhat the characteristics of a cult … the strong personal transferences that were evoked only accentuated a cultlike behavior ... However, the question is not whether there was a Jung cult in the beginning, but whether this was consciously encouraged by Jung, and whether Jung's analytical psychology today is primarily a cult" (T.B. Kirsch, *Psychoanalytic review* 82, 1995, 794–5). As for Kirsch's first question: we soon will see whether Jung encouraged the cultism of his followers, discouraged it, or simply yielded in the face of the inevitable. And, regrettably, Noll's own experiences with the publication of his book on *The Jung cult* only confirmed him in his original answer to the second (*Aryan Christ* 282). But while it can be easy enough now for both Noll and modern-day Jungians to look down from a position of righteous superiority on the cultic inflatedness of those who were close to Jung, the real question is to what extent they themselves are free from that equally insidious inflation: the one Jung referred to as the rationalistic and political psychosis which is the greatest affliction of our age.

[47] For the *Red book*'s palpably impatient and threatening, as much as encouraging, message to find your own path and live your own truth see already *RB* 231 with n.27. For the even darker, and edgier, message to stop imitating Jung or trying to take his secrets for yourself see e.g. 246–7 with n.163. And note also his crucial comments in the section on "The Magician" about Philemon managing to slip away like a serpent out of Jung's own clutching grasp; refusing to surround himself with eager followers ready to devour him by sucking up every word of his, as if it's the elixir of life, before locking the Master in a cage so they can worship him and invent the most fantastic stories about him; resisting the overwhelming temptation to make himself indispensable like all other saviours or prophets; nourishing himself from himself and trying to get others to do the same (315–17). Jung was quite aware of his close followers' servile obsequiousness and learned to tolerate it as gracefully,

and humorously, as possible: see D. Bair, *Jung* (Boston 2003) 371 with 771 n.79, also *JW* 99–100 on the Eranos experience, plus his comment in the *Red book* about leaving people plenty of space to act out their stupidities rather than letting himself be tempted to interfere (*RB* 316a, cf. *JL* i 518). On the habitual imitation of Jung even among those nearest to him see e.g. Bair 535 with D. Russell, *The life and ideas of James Hillman* i (New York 2013) 373 (naming C.A. Meier, Marie–Louise von Franz, Barbara Hannah).

[48] "But in the biography of old Empedocles … ten thousand lovely followers": *NZ* ii 1217. On Empedocles' immense popularity and "tremendous following" compare also *JV* i 596; and note how faithfully the portrayal of Empedocles offered by Jung reflects Empedocles' own description of the ten thousand (*myrioi*) men and women who followed him around begging for prophecies (*mantosuneôn kechrêmenoi*) and desperate to hear his healing word (*euêkea baxin*: fr. 112.7–11 Diels = fr. 157.12–16 Gemelli Marciano; *APMM* 220 n.7, 342–3). Jung's procedure, of first mentioning how a Latin poet had suggested that the real reason why Empedocles made the jump was because he wanted to be thought of as an immortal god before going straight on to offer his own suggestion (*NZ* ii 1217), is no accident: Horace's theory was for Jung purely subjective in origin, an obvious projection of his personal life as a Roman (*ZL* 70 §179), and this sets the scene for Jung's own amusing theory which will be based just as obviously on his own very personal and subjective experience. Sucking up every word as if it's the waters of life: *RB* 148, 315b; and for the entourage of devoted Jungians who typically "hung on Jung's every word" cf. R. Noll, *The Aryan Christ* (New York 1997) 187. "Flocked around him wanting to hear …": B. Hannah, *The archetypal symbolism of animals* (Wilmette 2006) 392.

[49] The passage is *JP* B26 (13 June 1958); see the brief paraphrase by S. Shamdasani, *Quadrant* 38/1 (2008) 25–6, who does well to translate Jung's original German as "repeat parrot–fashion". "The great truth … straight from the Master's hands?": *TE* 170 §263.

[50] For the archetypal saviour or magician forever lamenting, often with more than a touch of inflation, that his "great wisdom is never understood" see especially *TE* 228 §379 (cf. 233–7 §§389–97); *IJP* 95; and for saviour as magician, *PT* 262 §443. For Jung's persistent refrain that no one understands him or his insights, see e.g. *JP* 148, 160, 309; *JJW* 3–4; *JL* ii 32, 299, 424, 453, 516, 530, 584, 586–9, 624; M. Serrano, *C.G. Jung and Hermann Hesse* (London 1966) 60–1; E. Rolfe, *Encounter with Jung* (Boston 1989) 158; E. Falzeder, *JJ* 10/3 (2016) 18, 26. The cry of Merlin as the cry of the prophet whom literally no one understands: *JP* 366–7, *MDR* 216/228. For the golden cage of inflation see *RB* 316b, together with Jung's comment at the end of this same paragraph about the "true one" always having to renounce or disown himself. On his constant concern to prevent "the Master" from being caged, note also Cary de Angulo's draft letter to Jung dated 26 January 1924 (*RB* 213b; *CBA*); and for the Master and the disciple trapping each other, ending up caught "in the same boat", compare *TE* 234 §390. "So humanly understandable … further destination whatever": ibid. 171 §265. "No one should deny … daunts even the gods": *ST* 355–7 §553; the difference in tone as well as content between what Jung says here about the sunset way and his original version of the same text, written forty years earlier, could hardly be more noticeable (*JPPF* 4/1, 1912, 386 = *Psychology of the unconscious*, New York 1916, 390–1; R.D. Scott, *JAP* 2, 1957, 206). For the particular turning point of the sun that Jung is describing, and its visionary implications within the

framework of his own life, compare *RB* 231–2 together with n.32; for the Nietzschean background to the theme of the sun setting, A. Del Caro and R.B. Pippin, *Friedrich Nietzsche: Thus spoke Zarathustra* (Cambridge 2006) 3 n.1; and for the practice of following the sun's path according to Parmenides as well as ancient magical traditions, *IDPW*.

[51] On the *Red book* as source and origin of all Jung's later work see *JP* 144, 147, 149, 177, 258; *MDR* 184/192, 190–1/199; V.W. Odajnyk, *PP* 53 (2010) 441; A. Jung, *JAP* 56 (2011) 665. Assertions by commentators that in their wisdom they understand the logic of his work far better than he did, and that the *Red book* has no practical bearing whatsoever on Jungian or any other "psychology", are predictably already sprouting up like mushrooms (W. Giegerich, *Spring* 83, 2010, 361–411; W.J. Hanegraaff in *Religion und Wahnsinn um 1900*, ed. L. Greisiger, A. van der Haven and S. Schüler, Würzburg 2017, 105–6). For criticisms of the *Red book* as an embarrassment that should never have been published see e.g. R.A. Segal, *IJJS* 6 (2014) 74–9; D. Tacey, ibid. 264–7. On Jung's own embarrassment with its content as well as its style see *JP* 145, 169–70, and especially his crucial comments at 148; *MDR* 171/178. But to echo the words of the *Red book* itself, it's not just grotesquely banal or hackneyed (*RB* 7, 262b; Tacey 265–6). It's hideously simple, ridiculously primitive, indistinguishable from a god of nature—and exactly what we need (*RBu* 337b, cf. *RB* 339b). Or to give a sense of the even simpler language he would use to describe this book of his own unconscious at around the same time as he was working on it, it's not just banal but it's also morbidly sick; it's not only mad but utterly divine (*BB* v 82). For the "disgusting" style of the unconscious and its "very bad taste", which one must learn to accept and allow for and not avoid but simply "observe dispassionately", note also Marie–

Louise von Franz's comments, *Alchemy* (Toronto 1980) 193–4. Ironically she goes straight on to add that, in the alchemical text she is analyzing, she "would like to skip the next chapter for it is very disgusting". It's more than a little interesting that the great mystic and Sufi teacher, Ibn al–'Arabî, was far better able to handle (a word I use advisedly) this problem than von Franz the psychologist. See C. Addas, *Quest for the red sulphur* (Cambridge 1993) 48–9.

[52] For Jungian psychology as a "rejection" of religion see e.g. S. Shamdasani, *RB* 211–12, together with his comment that to consider Jung "a mystic and a visionary" on the basis of his *Red book* would be just as wrong-minded as calling him a charlatan or a psychotic (*JAP* 55, 2010, 47). For the *Red book* as "not a religious work" because instead of leading to God it leads to the soul, see P. Bishop in *Art, sciences et psychologie*, ed. C. Maillard (Strasbourg 2011) 139–40. Compare Murray Stein's view of the *Red book* as demonstrating how "the mind of the psychologist rules in the New Age", a New Age "mentalized by the psychological mind" (*JAP* 57, 2012, 290, 294); or a Jungian's earlier pronouncement that "To be sure, there is no going back to Christianity, or to any other religion for that matter. For these, even while continuing to exist, are now subsumed under psychology" (G. Mogenson, *The dove in the consulting room*, Hove 2003, 172). Alternatively, it could be a little simpler as well as more helpful if one preferred to return to James Kirsch's account of the personal comments Jung made to him on this very same issue. "When I was working with him, the relationship of religion and psychology was a big problem for me. I asked him whether the two were really two different things, since all the holy scriptures were written by men and were based on human experiences of the Divine. He answered, 'they are one'" (*KI* 4).

[53] "Religion can only be replaced by religion": *FJ* 323–4 §178J (11 February 1910: "Religion kann nur durch Religion ersetzt werden"); *JL* i 18; F.X. Charet, *Spiritualism and the foundations of C.G. Jung's psychology* (Albany 1993) 253. I have already documented the crude suppression of any reference to religion in the English-language edition of Jung's crucial comments to Freud during the same year (*FJ* 381–2 §206J, 11 August 1910). And to give just one other example, taken from comments he made almost half a century later: in November 1957 he communicated to his assistant, with the greatest care, that the act of explaining alchemy's essential relationship to psychology is directly equivalent to explaining alchemy as religion. He then goes straight on to describe how as soon as he had come to realize the essentially religious nature of alchemical tradition he found himself back at the very same place, and on the same solid ground, he had arrived at during the years of his underworld experiences that resulted in the *Red book*—because he realized that the alchemists' experiences had also been his experiences and the other way around (*JP* 227). In other words: alchemy's relationship to psychology is alchemy's relationship to religion because psychology and religion are fundamentally the same, while the religious experiences of the alchemists were the same as Jung's own experiences at the time of the *Red book* because these were religious too. Unfortunately his assistant, Aniela Jaffé, in her usual style has interfered again with what he says; trivialized it and jumbled the details, forcing Jung in his published biography to talk confusedly about "religious philosophy" and other such things when he had said nothing of the kind (*MDR* 200/209).

[54] "So long as religion ... Why this fear of psychology?": C.G. Jung, *Psychologie und Alchemie* (2nd ed., Zurich 1952) 25–32; cf. *PA* 12–17 §13–19. To Jung it was an indisputable truth that the

depths of the psyche are divine (compare e.g. *JL* ii 237), and no one happened to be more appreciative than Henry Corbin of the fact that Jungian psychology is concerned by definition with the divine mystery of the soul (*Revue de culture européenne* 5, 1953, 14–15 = *HJ* 267–8). See also *AJ* 89–90, where Corbin cites with full sympathy and approval Jung's protest that "The reproach of 'psychologism' applies only to a fool who thinks he has his soul in his pocket ... Should Meister Eckhart also be reproached with 'psychologism' when he says, 'God must be brought to birth in the soul again and again'?" (R. Wilhelm and C.G. Jung, *The secret of the golden flower*, London 1931, 129–30; *AS* 50 §75). For the soul as Sophia, Sapientia, the hidden wisdom of God, see *RB* 155 (the painting), 317 n.283; *PT* 235 §398 (the "Gnostic" Sophia); L.S. Owens in A. Ribi, *The search for roots* (Los Angeles 2013) 24, 285–6 n.85. "In a church ... as the altar itself": *ACU* 201 §369, 202 §380, and cf. 201 §370 for the crucial element of mysterious ambivalence; *RB* 317 n.283. "I have the feeling that this is a time ...": *FJ* 484 §269J (29 August 1911), to be read in conjunction with Jung's earlier and equally portentious letters about religion and religious secrecy (*FJ* 323–4 §178J, 381–2 §206J). Of course Jung knew very well that the word *sophia* was not just Alexandrian but ancient Greek in origin—which means that when he points very specifically to Alexandrian terminology he is referring, in particular, to Sophia as Gnostic goddess. Presumably the printing of her name as *Sopsia* instead of *Sophia* by the official editors of the Freud–Jung correspondence is designed to illustrate the depths to which wisdom has degenerated in the modern world.

[55] For Cary Fink, known as Cary de Angulo after her first marriage and Cary Baynes after her second, see W. McGuire, *Bollingen* (Princeton 1982), esp. 18–20; *NL* 119–20, 170; D.

Bair, *Jung* (Boston 2003) 334 ("rigorously objective in every aspect of her life"), 359, 371 with 771 n.79, 579–80 with 830 n.51, 606; *JSB* 13–15; *RB* 212b; *IJP* ix–xxi, xxxi–xxxiv. Note in particular her own account of how Jung decided to "turn over" to her all his work on the *Red book* to see what, as an "impartial observer", she would say about it because he trusted so much in her critical sense (draft letter from Cary de Angulo to Jung dated 26 January 1924: *RB* 213b, *CBA*); his strong sense of need for her full collaboration (letter from Jung to de Angulo dated 13 December 1924, *CBA*); and his unconcealed respect for her exceptional forthrightness and honesty (ibid., 18 March 1926), although in later years he could get more than a little irritated with her rationalism (letter from Cary Baynes to Jung dated 23 January 1946 and from him to her dated 25 July 1946: *CBA*). "Every hour I spend with you …": draft letter dated 25 September 1922 (*CBA*). Compare, for example, Tina Keller's emphasis on the potent atmosphere of prayerful mystery into which he helped to initiate her (R. Noll, *The Aryan Christ*, New York 1997, 152; W.K. Swan, *JAP* 51, 2006, 500; *The memoir of Tina Keller-Jenny*, New Orleans 2011, 23 §55) and even Jung's own light-hearted but telling comparison of his morning dream-analysis to "morning worship" (*FJ* 377 §204J, 6 August 1910; J.E. Gedo, *Annual of psychoanalysis* 7, 1979, 78; note also *RB* 204a with n.111, 216a) as well as his striking references to the Christian sacrament (cf. e.g. E.A. Bennet, *Meetings with Jung*, Zurich 1985, 17 for his comment about the woman who burst into tears on hearing him give a lecture: "she got what was there—like the Mass"; and his statement to A. Storr, *JAP* 44, 1999, 535, "Every night you have the chance of the Eucharist"). "You are taking me into the inner dwelling house …": draft letter from de Angulo to Jung dated 26 January 1924 (*CBA*); and compare her note of how, in this situation, so much delicacy is needed that even the weight of a single rose leaf could be a crushing burden (ibid., 28 September 1922). The *Red book* as a personality in its own right, not to be approached aggressively or brusquely: ibid., 28 January 1924. "So full of magic … shadows of past ages": ibid.; and compare her touching description of Jung's library, as home to the *Red book*, one week later (ibid., 5 February 1924).

[56] "Your personality is that 'Kleinod' … why it is so": draft letter from Cary de Angulo to Jung dated 25 September 1922 (*CBA*). She then goes on to repeat a point she had made earlier: that for her he is no longer just an individual human person because he has been transformed, in her eyes, into an impersonal but intensely living symbol. For her use of the word "personality" here in a strictly Jungian sense, compare e.g. *PT* 460 §§789–90; *TE* 230 §382; *DP* 167–86 §§284–323; *JS* 223, 301, 328, 356, 364, 463. Jung's published statements about the jewel, or "Kleinod": *Psychologische Typen* (Zurich 1921) 254–63, 361–80 = *PT* 177–84 §§296–311, 258–72 §§434–60, focussing on Carl Spitteler's *Prometheus and Epimetheus*. Later, it will be noted, Jung will identify "Spitteler's jewel" with the philosophers' stone (*PA* 81 §103, 123 §160, 430 §514). For de Angulo's methodical study of the literature featured by Jung in *Psychological types*, see also her draft note dated 21 May 1924 (on Ernst Barlach's *Der tote Tag*: *CBA*); the English edition of the book, translated by her future husband, would appear in 1923. "The saviour is always a figure … the impossible possible": *PT* 262 §443. Incarnate Bodhisattva, Buddha, jewel in the lotus: ibid. 178 §§297–8, 259 §436. "The saviour–nature of the jewel …": *Psychologische Typen* 374, cf. *PT* 268 §453.

[57] For Jung's multiple quotations from Isaiah while describing the "Kleinod", or redeeming jewel, see *PT* 261–5 §§438–47; for the jewel as cornerstone, *PA* 78 §103. "It is in the Zoroastrian

teaching ... between god and man": *SNZ* 12 (cf. *NZ* i 12). For the Zoroastrian figure of the Saoshyant see e.g. J.R. Hinnells, *Numen* 16 (1969) 161–85; M. Boyce, *Bulletin of the School of Oriental and African Studies* 47 (1984) 57–75; P. Kingsley, *Journal of the Royal Asiatic Society* 5 (1995) 197 with n.153; E. Albrile, *Laurentianum* 39 (1998) 433–53; P.O. Skjærvø in *Zoroastrian rituals in context*, ed. M. Stausberg (Leiden 2004) 272–3; F.M. Kotwal and J.K. Choksy, ibid. 394; and note how uncannily relevant the etymology of the word *Saoshyant*, as meaning "he who will make the world swell again with the vital juices of life" (Skjærvø 273 with n.34), is to Jung's essential intuition in 1914 of his own world mission (*MDR* 170/176; *RB* 231a). "Called out through the need of the time, the emergencies of the actual epoch": *SNZ* 14 (cf. *NZ* i 14); and note Jung's comments here on the various Buddhas and Bodhisattvas (*SNZ* 13, *NZ* i 13). When he also refers here to Nietzsche's experiences of the wise old man archetype as an immensely potent historical figure that carries with it the taste and the flavour of previous centuries, the unmistakeable sense of the actual presence of an ancient past—as a separate identity inside himself which had existed for thousands upon thousands of years since the beginning of eternity, and which brings all our illusions of time to a stop by bringing 5000 BC so close to 2000 AD that it can seem to be in the very next room (*SNZ* 13–14, *NZ* i 13–14)—Jung is of course referring to his own inner experiences as well, following his exact and explicit guidelines in such matters (*ACU* 144–6 §§253–4). "Prophets, appear ... give birth to a new truth": *SNZ* 24 (cf. *NZ* i 24); for revelation always accompanying confusion compare *JL* i 69, and for the supreme saviour figure or Saoshyant as father of all prophets see also *NZ* ii 1033. "Reason must always seek ... from the side it was least expected": *PT* 260–1 §438. The solution only offered by prophecy: ibid. 261–5 §§438–48.

[58] Twisting her bowels: draft note from Cary de Angulo to Jung dated 21 May 1924 (*CBA*); compare Jung's own comments on the spirit of the depths completely burning up his entrails, and on one's bowels being wracked in the process of being crucified (*Red book*, folio i verso = *RB* 230a; 136 = 310a). For the stream of his visions and dreams leading up to the outbreak of war see *RB* 201–2, 226, 231a, 241b, 336b, also 305–6; *IJP* 43–8; *JS* 232–4; *JP* 145–6; *MDR* 169–70/175–6. The quotations from Isaiah: *Red book*, folio i recto = *RB* 229; for Jung's early readings of Isaiah see the comments by James Kirsch, *PP* 6 (1975) 56. "Thus it was presented as a prophetic work": S. Shamdasani, *C.G. Jung: a biography in books* (New York 2012) 117, cf. *RB* 203a; so e.g. J. Beebe, *PP* 53 (2010) 431; V.W. Odajnyk, ibid. 439–51; L.S. Owens in A. Ribi, *The search for roots* (Los Angeles 2013) 30 and, with some puzzlement, in *Jung's 'Red book' for our time*, ed. M. Stein and T. Arzt, i (Asheville 2017) 103–23; S.A. Hoeller, ibid. 92–6.

[59] Isaiah 53:1–4, 9:6, 35:1–2 plus 5–8 are quoted in this particular sequence at *Red book*, folio i recto = *RB* 229; Isaiah 53:1–3, 9:6 and 35:5–8 are quoted in the same sequence at *PT* 261–4 §§439–45. But note also that at *PT* 249 n.159 Jung quotes approvingly from a page in William Blake's *Marriage of heaven and hell* where Blake, himself, has just referred his readers to Isaiah chapter 35. For blindness see Isaiah 35:5; *PT* 172 §285, 185 §313, 190 §320, 263 §445. Unsuitable, unacceptable, inappropriate: ibid. 266 §449. The "Epimethean" retreat into collective rationalism, or rationalistic collectivism: ibid. 184–5 §312; 189–90 §§318–20; 260–1 §§438–40. Similarly, Jeremiah's words about prophecy are not only cited by Jung at the opening to the second book of *Liber novus* but are also quoted by him in *Psychological types*—as part of a sustained argument that fantasy and imagination have been

ruthlessly suppressed along with Gnosticism throughout the course of Christian history, and cast out just like the precious jewel (Jeremiah 23:16 and 25–8, *RB* 1, 259a, *PT* 52–9 §§78–86). If recent commentators (e.g. A. Schweizer, *JJ* 5/3, 2011, 79–80) paid a little attention to the clear reasons given by Jung himself for citing these passages from Jeremiah in *Psychological types*, it would be so much easier for them to understand their real function and purpose in the *Red book*. For the chronology of Jung's work on *Psychological types*, and its relevance to the *Red book*, see *PT* v; *RB* 198b, 215a, 222–3, 255 n.241; B. Hannah, *Jung, his life and work* (New York 1976) 132–4; V.W. Odajnyk, *PP* 56 (2013) 310–28; *QPT*.

[60] "Belongs to the generality … listen to revelations": W. Giegerich, *Spring* 83 (2010) 379–80. Giegerich's "review" has also been criticized by others (e.g. S. Rowland, *Remembering Dionysus*, Abingdon 2017, 44–68); but the psychological significance of the fact, duly underscored by Jung himself (*PT* 260–1 §§437–8), that the most common reaction to the jewel is to welcome it at first with rapturous hymns of excitement before finding very rational ways of rejecting it later seems to have been quite lost on modern interpreters of the *Red book*. For the usual apologies nowadays that the *Red book* is prophetic and yet not prophetic see e.g. M. Stein, *JAP* 55 (2010) 433; A. Schweizer, *JJ* 5/3 (2011) 81; A. Haaning, *JAP* 59 (2014) 26 (Jung finds himself "adopting a certain prophetic mode in these opening passages, but the intention is not to lay claim to being a new prophet or the mouthpiece of a god"); N. Pilard, *Jung and intuition* (London 2015) 92. The denials that Jung's pre-war dreams were prophetic come in a variety of pleasingly rationalistic flavours: *NL* 103–4; N. Lewin, *Jung on war, politics and Nazi Germany* (London 2009) 270–1; W.J. Hanegraaff in *Religion und Wahnsinn um 1900*, ed. L. Greisiger, A. van

der Haven and S. Schüler (Würzburg 2017) 102, 113. The rhetorical flourishes: Stein 433 (in spite of the *Red book*'s "rhetorical flourishes, Jung decisively rejects the role of prophet/avatar"); already the published version of *Memories, dreams, reflections* had strategically replaced Jung's own statements about the *Red book* speaking the language of prophecy with the statement that it spoke the language of rhetoric (*JP* 144–5, 169; *MDRC* 121; *MDR* 171/177–8). On the "tension" between prophetic and anti-prophetic that "runs through" the *Red book* see S. Shamdasani, *C.G. Jung: a biography in books* (New York 2012) 117.

[61] For some time, writers have played with applying Jung's theory of synchronicity to his own prophetic experiences during 1913 and 1914 (cf. e.g. R. Aziz, *C.G. Jung's psychology of religion and synchronicity*, Albany 1990, 206; S. Shamdasani, *RB* 220b). But the clearest statements of the modern, enlightened view that this scientific theory was a very deliberate and focused effort on his part to find an exit from the murky world of prophecy are by Joseph Cambray: *IJJS* 3 (2011) 110–24, *International journal of psychoanalysis* 94 (2013) 418 and in *The Red book*, ed. T. Kirsch and G. Hogenson (London 2014) 47–51; George Bright has shrewdly noted that the one person most "relieved to have found an exit from *The Red Book*'s challenging world of non-rational Divine power and magic" is not so much Jung as Cambray himself (*JAP* 59, 2014, 287). The new, politically correct tendency to remove the word "prophetic" and substitute the much more proper term "synchronistic" when discussing those visions and dreams that led Jung to start his work on the *Red book*—because "otherwise it gets a little bit too magical, forecasting the future and things"—is also quite evident in Murray Stein's *The red book: a global seminar* (Asheville Jung Center DVD: Asheville 2010) 1:16:29–1:18:40.

But Jung himself had no problem whatsoever, at least in the right circumstances, admitting quite unashamedly that he had the ability to forecast the future because there was something inside him which just knew such things (*JP* 205, cf. 278).

[62] Jung had already spoken out articulately, as well as passionately, in defence of prophetic dreams and visions years before meeting Freud: see *ZL* 42–3 §§131–4 (1897), where he cites Old Testament prophets as examples, and compare e.g. *SL* 298–9 §§710–13 (1905, again citing Old Testament prophets), *JM* 101–2 (1935), *JL* ii 536 (1960). He evidently failed to receive any bulletin or update about synchronicity because up until the time of his death he was still describing his pre-war dreams and visions of 1913 and 1914 as examples of precognition, genuine precognition, seeing into the future, premonition. See especially *JP* 145–6 (30 September 1957), where his language of miraculous prescience or foresight has not changed an iota from the language he used during his earliest work on the *Red book* almost half a century earlier (folio iv recto = *RB* 241b); M. Serrano, *C.G. Jung and Hermann Hesse* (London 1966) 88–9 = *JS* 462–3. On the fundamental, and non-negotiable, importance of prophetic visions or dreams for Jung's worldview see e.g. *MDR* 313–14/340–1; M.-L. von Franz in *ZL* xviii; J.E. Gedo, *Annual of psychoanalysis* 7 (1979) 80–1. Three older writers who helped to buttress his sympathies in this regard were Swedenborg (*SL* 296–9 §§705–14; P. Bishop, *Carl Jung*, London 2014, 75; S. Shamdasani, *History of psychiatry* 27, 2016, 384), Schopenhauer (*JM* 103, 110) and von Schubert (ibid. 103, 147); and for his very self-conscious determination to get back even beyond these predecessors so he could revive the "antique science" of ancient Greek dream interpretation see ibid. 104. "The palm of honour … existence of prophetic dreams": W.V. Harris, *Dreams and*

experience in classical antiquity (Cambridge, MA 2009) 233. On the grassroots respect for the prophetic value of dreams which continued, regardless of Aristotle, both among people in general and among ancient physicians in particular see S.R.F. Price, *Past and present* 113 (1986) 11–12, 23. As for Freud: although he sometimes is presented as moderately open to the possibility of prophetic dreams, this can be misleading. In his earlier work he did try at least to create an appearance of being non-judgemental, before invariably allowing his cynicism to have the last word (cf. e.g. *The standard edition of the complete psychological works of Sigmund Freud* vi, London 1960, 261–3); and later, even after he had started warming towards the reality of telepathy, his explicitly Aristotelian rejection of prophetic dreams only hardened (R. Aziz, *C.G. Jung's psychology of religion and synchronicity*, Albany 1990, 106–7; K. Frieden, *Freud's dream of interpretation*, Albany 1990, 95–107, 130).

63 "To avoid the task ... when you accepted it": draft letter from Cary de Angulo to Jung dated 5 February 1924 (*CBA*). Her mention of the grace or "Gnade"—to follow her own faithful use of Jung's original German word for it—that at last descended on him is a reference to *Red book* folio i verso, which has been very poorly translated at *RB* 230b as "mercy". For the traditional scenario of Hebrew prophets questioning and challenging as well as fighting and even denying the role of prophet I already cited earlier some of the most typical passages from Exodus, Jeremiah, Zechariah, not to mention the book of Jonah; Anson Laytner's book *Arguing with God* (Lanham 1990); and one emphatic recent reminder of the ancient prophet's characteristic "*reluctance to accept the role.* Even so, a prophet is *compelled to speak* ... Finally, a prophet most often *rejects the designation*" (M. Dean–Otting in *Encyclopedia of psychology and religion*, 2nd ed., New York 2014, ed. D.A.

Leeming, 1389). Also essential reading for any commentator on Jung is the extensive modern literature about the prophet Jeremiah's "Confessions" of his disputes and struggles with God (cf. J.A. Thompson, *The book of Jeremiah*, Grand Rapids 1980, 88–92; A.R. Diamond, *The confessions of Jeremiah in context*, Sheffield 1987; R.R. Laha, *Jeremiah*, Louisville 2002, 40–9). For Jung's own awareness of the constant conflicts and tensions traditionally endured by prophets, together with his gruesome emphasis on the unavoidable need to face crushing and unbearable tension along the way of individuation, see e.g. *PR* 18–19 §32 with *RB* 308–18. In ancient Greek tradition, too, such conflicts of course reach their tragic height with the prophetic figure of Cassandra. On the other hand, there are those who seem to find direct support for claiming "Jung decisively rejects the role of prophet/avatar" in the fact that he argumentatively "asks questions of his inner teachers" throughout the *Red book* "and raises objections to what they are asking him to take aboard" (M. Stein, *JAP* 55, 2010, 433); and even stranger is the notion that Jung refused to be a prophet because, far from representing a "whole human being" who has become ready to carry the ethical burdens of humanity, the archetypal figure of the prophet is a "winged solar hero who escapes the gravity of the earth" (A. Schweizer, *JJ* 5/3, 2011, 81). But perhaps the most unfortunate example of misunderstanding inside Jungian circles is the case of James Kirsch, who in his book-length study of prophecy decided to disqualify the nineteenth-century rabbi Hile Wechsler from being a "true prophet" precisely because of his inner reluctance and conflicts about accepting the prophetic role (*The reluctant prophet*, Los Angeles 1973, 190–2). With striking inconsistency, although in line with his naïve idealization of the ancient Hebrew prophets, Kirsch also explained that when Isaiah expresses horror as well as reluctance at the prospect of his own prophetic mission this is because psychologically and very commendably "he remains differentiated from what is happening within him" (*JK* 273). It would be nice to assume that Kirsch might have been logical enough to apply the same explanation not only to Isaiah, but also to Rabbi Wechsler as well as to Carl Jung.

[64] "No religious experience please ... 2,000 years ago": letter from Jung to Eugene Rolfe dated 14 July 1959 and published in Rolfe's *Encounter with Jung* (Boston 1989) 132. On the direct relationship between orthodox Christianity's crushing of Gnosticism and its suppression of religious experience see especially *PT* 52–9 §§80–81; also *PR* 97 §160, *Aion* 178–81 §§276–81, *SL* 826–9 §§1827–33; and for Jung's long-held conviction that the essential purpose of the Christian Church has always been to block all direct, personal experience compare e.g. *PR* 553 §903. For prophets as the writers of the books produced by God see in particular 2 Peter 1:20–1, "First and foremost you need to understand that all scriptural prophecy which has been written is not the prophet's own explanation, because no prophecy has ever been fetched by any human's will. On the contrary, the human speaks straight from God while being carried by the Holy Spirit"; Jung was of course intimately familiar with the Christian doctrines surrounding this prophetic role (*PR* 144 §217). "Above all, write exactly (*getreu*) what you see": *RB* 252b, cf. L.S. Owens, *The Gnostic* 3 (2010) 31–2; Jung himself has just (*RB* 251a) described the experience of becoming a prophet. The unfortunate notion (L. Corbett, *JJ* 5/3, 2011, 67) that for Jung the figure of Elijah "was fiercely antagonistic" to any religious innovation and so "would be a figure with whom Jung has to deal" could hardly be more mistaken (*ACU* 141 §247, 145 §253; *SL* 673–8 §§1518–31). On the traditional need to report "exactly what you have

seen" after descending to the underworld, see especially the Zoroastrian *Ardâ Vîrâz nâmag*, ed. P. Gignoux (Paris 1984) 101.3–4, "convey exactly (*râstîhâ*) what you have seen"; 3.5–7, "tell us exactly (*râstîhâ*) everything you have seen"; 1.20, "I will go to fetch this message accurately (*drustîhâ*) and convey it exactly (*râstîhâ*)"; 3.14, "and everything he said was written down accurately (*drust*), clearly and in detail". Compare also Parmenides fr. 4.1 Diels = fr. 9.1 Gemelli Marciano, together with *Reality* 55–9; Plato, *Republic* 614d (*angelon anthrôpois genesthai tôn ekei kai … theasthai panta ta en tôi topôi*) and 619b; Dante, *Inferno* 32.7–12 together with *RB* 252 n.213. For the antiquity of the traditions contained in the *Ardâ Vîrâz nâmag* see P. Kingsley, *Studia iranica* 23 (1994) 193 and n.25. For its connections with Parmenides note e.g. *Reality* 563; and with Dante's *Divine comedy*, E. Yarshater in *Persian presence in the Islamic world*, R.G. Hovannisian and G. Sabagh (Cambridge 1998) 32 plus the references at n.130.

[65] Without even trying to document all the features of prophetic language and style in the *Red book* from the very first pages onwards, I will just note the irony in Shamdasani's assertion that although the book is certainly presented as a prophetic work "Yet at the same time, Jung eschewed presenting himself as a prophet: 'There is only one way and that is your way … May each go his own way …'" (*C.G. Jung: a biography in books*, New York 2012, 117). First, Shamdasani seems not to have noticed that simply for Jung to announce the existence of one single way (*RB* 231b, 308b) is already for him to speak as a prophet; the same prophetic language continues throughout (compare e.g. 297 n.187, reading "tittle", which is a blatant echo of Matthew 5:17–18) and the closest parallel to his particular announcement here is to be found, very significantly, in Parmenides ("There is only one tale of a path left to tell":

fr. 8.1–2 Diels = fr. 14B.7–8 Gemelli Marciano, cf. *Reality* 157–60 with the Zoroastrian parallel cited at 563). Second, it also has escaped him that this paradoxical declaration about only one way existing but everyone having to go their own way is a deliberate riddle and that prophets in general—as well as the Jung of the *Red book*—very deliberately speak in riddles. Shamdasani appears, in short, not to have realized that a true classical prophet is no modern guru but is made to play a totally different game. For the whole of humanity as "ein verblendetes Geschlecht", a blinded and deluded race behaving like brutes, see *RBu* 296b (cf. *RB* 297b). The theme of blindness is already present on the first page of the *Red book*, in the form of Isaiah's announcement that "the eyes of the blind shall be opened"; and is immediately taken up on the second page in the form of Jung's confession that he, like everyone, had been blinded by the spirit of his time before being unblinded by the spirit of the depths (*Red book*, folio i recto and verso; *RB* 229). But it also should be noted that Jung's language in describing humanity as a "verblendetes Geschlecht", such a blinded and deluded race, belongs to the standard prophetic language of his own time: see e.g. Samuel Hirsch, *Die Messiaslehre der Juden in Kanzelvorträgen* (Leipzig 1843) 243 ("du, verblendetes Geschlecht!"); Saul Kaatz, *Das Wesen des prophetischen Judentums* (Berlin 1907) 88 ("ein sündiges, verblendetes Geschlecht"). For Parmenides' powerful portrayal, after his own return from the underworld, of the whole human race as blind and deluded and deaf (*brotoi eidotes ouden … kôphoi homôs tuphloi te tethêpotes akrita phula*) see fr. 6.4–7 Diels = fr. 13.5–8 Gemelli Marciano; also fr. 1.34–6 Diels = fr. 14.3–5 Gemelli Marciano; *IDPW* 221–3, *Reality* 83–8, 105–7, 120–5; for Empedocles' prophetic language see e.g. E. Norden, *Agnostos theos* (Leipzig 1913) 132–3, 198–200 with *ENM* 351 and *APMM* 370 with *ENM* 348 n.31. "The masses

… strike it dead": *PA* 480–1 §563, a passage that deserves close comparison with *RB* 297b. For similar expressions compare e.g. *PT* 185 §313; *SL* 316 §754, 571 §1316; *JL* ii 209.

[66] In *Psychological types* Jung brings his chapter on the "Kleinod" or precious jewel to a close by quoting a few words from William Blake and then emphasizing, with unusual formality, how simply and effectively they summarize his entire discussion (*PT* 272 §460, cf. 332 §559 "Blake's intuition did not err …"; he also quotes Blake at 249 n.159). As the *Red book*'s editor has well noted, considering the overlap in time between Jung's work on *Psychological types* and his most intense involvement with the *Red book* this is hardly insignificant—especially in view of the extent to which the *Red book*'s extraordinary "combination of text and image recalls the illuminated works of William Blake" (S. Shamdasani, *C.G. Jung: a biography in books*, New York 2012, 110–20, cf. *RB* 203b). But what hasn't yet been noticed is the equally extraordinary extent to which the text of the *Red book* is modelled on Blake's prophetic writings. To mention just one example here, because its implications are so rich: the *Red book* opens with a peculiarly enigmatic scene. In the middle of Jung's confrontation with the duelling claims being made on him by the spirit of his time and the spirit of the depths, suddenly the spirit of the time approaches him holding huge books that he lays before him. The books contain all of Jung's knowledge; their leaves are made of brass, and adamantine words have been carved into their metal pages by an iron pen (*Red book*, folio i verso; cf. *RB* 230b). Why this spirit of our time should be carrying such books will seem a complete mystery until one remembers Blake's most famous character, Urizen, carrying his books that contain all the knowledge of our world: "But still his books he bore in his strong hands and his iron pen / … the books remaind still

unconsumd / Still to be written & interleavd with brass & iron & gold / Time after time for such a journey none but iron pens / Can write & adamantine leaves recieve ..." (*The complete poetry and prose of William Blake*, ed. D.V. Erdman, 2nd ed., Berkeley 1982, 348–9; cf. M.O. Percival, *William Blake's circle of destiny*, New York 1938, 23–4, a book Jung would devour as soon as it was published). This passage, from the section of Blake's *Four Zoas* called "Night the sixth" (a title which will sound rather familiar to anyone acquainted with Jung's *Red book*), almost says it all about Urizen or "your reason": the deceptive, blind, proud, stern, inexorable demiurge who does everything in his dwindling power to pretend he is the supreme authority although he is just the feeblest reflection of the real divine spirit or even of the primordial reason which Urizen was originally meant to be. And to help fill out the bigger picture I will simply add that for Blake the opposite pole to Urizen, or Reason, is Imagination: the spirit of prophecy. Of course the true significance of the *Red book* for Jung himself lay in the very specific fact that its contents derive from the myth-making imagination completely banished by the principle of reason which is the proud, blind, deceptive spirit of our time (cf. Shamdasani, *RB* 208a). What this means is that here in the work of Blake, not to mention other figures such as Paracelsus or Jacob Boehme, the mythical underpinning of Jung's entire *Red book* is openly presented and revealed. But then the interesting reaction begins of Jung slowly distancing himself from Blake: gradually, inevitably concealing his vestiges. In 1930 he would still be willing to speak charitably about Blake's access, through his mythological imagery, to the primordial experience of the unconscious; then, anything positive he had to say about him would almost absurdly be delegated to a little footnote; and twenty years later he could hardly wait to discredit him in the very same way that his no. 1 personality couldn't wait to discredit the Gnostics (*SM* 91 §142, 96–7 §151; *PR* 555 with n.41; *JL* i 513–14, ii 17). Some things, though, are not so easy to conceal. In his personal copy of *The writings of William Blake* there is a single bookmark that he inserted at a very particular place, beside a full-page reproduction of one of Blake's most powerful drawings. It's called "The Sun of Reason" and shows a man kneeling submissively in the worship of a monstrous decaying sun: a sun which symbolizes not just the secular religion that humanity under the influence of Urizen has created out of reason but the hollow rational creeds that orthodox priests, also thanks to Urizen, have created out of religion (*The writings of William Blake*, ed. G. Keynes, London 1925, i, plate xxvi: compare Blake's verbal reference to "the dark globe of Urizen" in his *Book of Urizen*; D.W. Dörrbecker, *Huntington library quarterly* 52, 1989, 56–9, 71 n.54, 72–3 n.67). Needless to say, this harmonizes perfectly with Jung's own narrative about the high priests whose rationality obliges them to banish the "Kleinod" or precious jewel as a disgusting sacrilege (*PT* 260–1 §§437–8, 266–9 §§451–5). It also harmonizes perfectly with his fury at the rationalism and rigidity of a Church that denounces even the possibility of a "new book" as blasphemy (E. Rolfe, *Encounter with Jung*, Boston 1989, 132). But far more important, it shows why commentators on Jung have been so terrified to draw attention to his constant denigrating and even demonizing of reason throughout his published writings—because this attitude of his, just like Blake's own visions of Urizen, derives from the world of prophecy. For general comments on Blake's "demonizing" of reason see K. Raine, *William Blake* (London 1970) 146–52; P. Cantor, *Creature and creator* (Cambridge 1984) 29–30; P. Ackroyd, *Blake* (New York 1995) 23, 325. Reason, in Blake, as the opposite pole of both imagination and prophecy: Percival 36–9, 69; S.F. Damon, *A Blake dictionary* (2nd ed., Hanover,

NH 2013) 195, 322, 419–20, 426; Raine 57; A. Ostriker in *William Blake and the moderns*, ed. R.J. Bertholf and A.S. Levitt (Albany 1982) 115–16. Urizen as blinding and blinded (cf. *RB* 229b): Percival 22–3, 69, 182. As king of pride (cf. *RB* 229–30): Damon 419–21; Cantor 31–2. As deceptive (cf. *ACU* 93 §173): Percival 23–4. For Urizen's books of brass and iron see Damon 424.

[67] In the Bible see especially John 4:16–19, where the woman tells Jesus "I see you are a prophet" (*theôrô hoti prophêtês ei su*) not because he has just told the future but because he has just shown that he knows her past. For ancient Mesopotamia see e.g. M. Neujahr's *Predicting the past in the ancient Near East* (Providence 2012) and, for the familiar expression "The future will be like the past", S. Parpola's *Assyrian prophecies* (Helsinki 1997) xlix, lxvi, 6, 14. Empedocles, prophecy and the past: J.–P. Vernant, *Journal de psychologie normale et pathologique* 56 (1959) 14–18; *ENM* 339–43, 350 n.37. "Ancient crimes": Plato, *Phaedrus* 244d–e; Vernant 14; W. Burkert, *The orientalizing revolution* (Cambridge, MA 1992) 125–6. Cassandra: Aeschylus, *Agamemnon* 1178–1201. Epimenides: Aristotle, *Rhetoric* 1418a23–5 (*peri tôn esomenôn ouk emanteueto alla peri tôn gegonotôn men adêlôn de*) = *Poetae epici graeci*, ed. A. Bernabé, ii/3 (Berlin 2007) 145; but even in conveying this valid, and important, point Aristotle is unable to hide his cynicism or sarcasm about Epimenides and prophecy as a whole (E.M. Cope and J.E. Sandys, *Aristotle: Rhetoric*, Cambridge 1877, iii 202). For Epimenides' *katabasis* see e.g. G.G. Stroumsa, *Hidden wisdom* (2nd ed., Leiden 2005) 172; *IDPW* 102, 214–16. On Aristotle's rationalizing of memory and devaluing of the past see Vernant 28–9. The state which is neither sleep nor waking: *IDPW* 79–80, 110–11, 245.

[68] "And so I became a prophet ... the wild animals": *RBu* 251a (cf. *RB* 251a). The *Red book* repeatedly ties a knowledge of the future to a knowledge of the primordial past—in perfect agreement with the ancient notion of prophets as those who know *ta t' eonta ta t' essomena pro t' eonta*, "the things that are and that shall be and that have been" (Homer, *Iliad* 1.70). This is the "panoptic vision" both of the gods and of humans initiated into the ways of the gods (on the "simultaneous 'sight' of past, present and future; divine omniscience stems precisely from the possession of panoptic vision" cf. G. Manetti, *Theories of the sign in classical antiquity*, Bloomington, IN 1993, 15) which is well known to classical scholars but frighteningly alien to students of Jung. It was also very familiar to Goethe in his overtly prophetic texts, as a form of vision altogether alien to our "verblendete Welt" or blinded world ("... Whoever knows the past understands what is to come ...": *Weissagungen des Bakis* 16 = *Göthe's neue Schriften* vii, Berlin 1800, 318–19, cf. H.S. Jantz, *The soothsayings of Bakis*, Baltimore 1966, 33). And it was even given a characteristically pragmatic twist by Winston Churchill during the war years ("The longer you can look back, the farther you can look forward. This is not a philosophical or political argument—any oculist will tell you this is true": *The Lancet* 243, 11 March 1944, 349 = W.S. Churchill, *The dawn of liberation*, London 1945, 24, cf. R.M. Langworth, *Churchill by himself*, London 2008, 25, 576). For Jung's intimate familiarity with this perspective see *RB* 247b, 250a, 253b, 304a, 305a, and especially 306a (gifts of ancient things which are indicative of the future), 316a (Philemon's knowledge of the future is linked to his immeasurable past), 357 (Elijah's knowledge of the future is linked by Jung to his connection with what is primordially old), 358a (Elijah sees the future by looking into the past); also *PT* 400–1 §§659–60. Ironically, many years before the *Red book*'s publication James Olney already realized

that "Jung read the future, as did Yeats, out of the past" thanks to the care with which he traced this prophetic ability of both Yeats and Jung straight back to Empedocles (*The rhizome and the flower*, Berkeley 1980, 172–3); but now it's a sign of the times we live in that Christine Maillard can write a supposedly authoritative paper on the *Red book* and its "obsession" with the future without pointing, even once, to the fundamental importance of the past (*Cahiers jungiens de psychanalyse* 134, 2011, 119–31). Jung's constant linkage of the primordial past with "das Kommende", or what is to come, is faithfully preserved in the record of the extraordinary attempts made by his colleague Josef Lang during October 1917 to enter the psyche of Hermann Hesse and engrave inside it "the primordial scripture of humanity" which is preserved on "the tablets of the law of what is to come" ("die Urschrift der Menschen, die Du sie lehren mußt, die Gesetzestafeln des Kommenden": H. Ball, *Hermann Hesse*, Berlin 1927, 159). Fortunately we still happen to have the text of Jung's solemn warning to Lang, written less than three months later, that the only way to avoid the inflation of identifying with the role of prophet is if we refuse ever to forget that "in the first place we have to do the work on the unconscious *for ourselves*" rather than anybody else (letter to J.B. Lang dated 17 January 1918, cf. *RB* 207a; the words "for ourselves" are underlined in the original). Richard Noll deserves all due credit for noting the remarkable significance of Lang's psychological experiments with Hesse (*The Jung cult*, 2nd ed., New York 1997, 233–5, 367–8 n.53); but he had no access to Jung's warning letter and probably, in his determination to present Jung as the deliberate founder of a religious cult, would have ignored it anyway. As for Jung's own visions of the future in the *Red book*: far from being utopian (Maillard 122, 131), almost all of them are visions of sheer horror at the terrors lying ahead (cf. e.g. *RB* 198–9 with n.45, 274b, 306a,

335a, 345b). Leaving the future alone: *RB* 306b. One of the most desperate sections in the *Red book*: ibid. 306–12. It will be noted that the poignant injunction to hold the incomprehensible riddles in one's heart and become pregnant with them (308b) is pure Pythagoreanism: *APMM* 230–1 with n.48, 299 with n.35, 363 with n.12, 366 with n.20; *IDPW* 28, 120. Suspension of the will and stopping of the mind: *RB* 311b; cf. 238a and *JV* ii 1125 ("whatever one thinks is an expectation; it is trying to force God; one is whining about something and trying to squeeze something out of him; therefore, think of nothing"). For the excruciating process of being transformed, not into what one will be but into what one always has been, compare also Jung's account of the individual who has experienced the inner *katabasis* and *nekyia* of descending into the underworld only to return as a complete human being: "This man stands opposed to the man of the present, because he is the one who ever is as he was, whereas the other is what he is only for the moment" (*SM* 139–40 §213). The salvation that comes from the place you would least have expected: *RB* 311b (compare *PT* 260–2 §§438–43, *ACU* 157–8 §267). "Always it's something primordially ancient … in a new time": *RBu* 310a (cf. *RB* 311b). The accompanying image in the *Red book* of the charioteer with his celestial horses (*RBu* 309–10 = *RB* 311, cf. e.g. *JPPF* 4/1, 1912, 321 = *ST* 279 §423) derives from ancient sources; but Jung's criticism of the chariot–driver who, through his noble will and intention, interferes with the future is primarily a rejection of the rational charioteer as portrayed by Plato (*Phaedrus* 246a–256b, cf. *PT* 544 §963, *NZ* ii 846). His uniquely pragmatic valuation here of the "primordially ancient" is of course the exact opposite of the naïve aspiration to "return to antiquity" (*PT* 187–8 §§315–16). Note also Wolfgang Pauli's favourite expression during the early 1950s, "das noch Ältere ist immer das Neue", "the even older is always the new" (*PB* iv/I 386–7, 389 n.3, 400; iv/II 343; S. Gieser, *The innermost kernel*, Berlin 2005, 195) as well as Henry Corbin's equally fine account of psychological integration in his *Philosophie iranienne et philosophie comparée* (Paris 1985) 79: "It's not a question of going off and making oneself at home in a fictitious past. It's a question of preparing inside oneself a home for the future of that past. This is a process of integration in the most fundamental sense."

[69] Jung to Freud on reincarnating the Gnostic Sophia: *FJ* 484 §269J (29 August 1911). For the act of giving birth to the ancient in the new as, itself, a Gnostic or alchemical process cf. e.g. *Aion* 181 §281. The image of the jewel in the marketplace: *PT* 267–9 §§452–5. Philemon and Jung as father and son: *RB* 348–56. *Prophêtôn patêr polyphilos Philêmôn*: *RB* 154; the official edition of the *Red book* mistranslates *prophêtôn patêr* as "Father of the Prophet" (ibid. 317 n.282). I should add that Jung's phrase "father of the prophets" is an obvious echo of the biblical expression "sons of the prophets", which referred to the prophets gathered under the leadership of Elijah: for the ancient biblical language about fathers of prophets and sons of prophets, with both the fathers and the sons being quite naturally prophets themselves, see J.G. Williams, *Journal of biblical literature* 85 (1966) 344–8; and for Jung, himself, as son of Elijah cf. e.g. *RB* 368a. *Philêmôn tôn prophêtôn propatôr*: L.S. Owens in A. Ribi, *The search for roots* (Los Angeles 2013) 24 with 286 n.86; *Man and his symbols*, ed. C.G. Jung (New York 1964) 198. The ancient Gnostic *Propatôr*, or primordial father of the depths, was a figure of the most obvious significance for Jung. See for example the pencil markings in his copy of E. Klebba's *Des heiligen Irenäus fünf Bücher gegen die Häresien* (Munich 1912) i 3–4 and note that here, at the very start of Irenaeus' famous attack on the Gnostics, *Propatôr* is presented

as the alternative title for *Bythos* or the unspeakable spirit of the Deep (*Against the heresies* 1.1.1, cf. e.g. *JL* ii 132 with n.2); even without this confirmation, there could never be any doubting that the *Red book*'s crucial contest between "the spirit of this time" and "the spirit of the depths" has been directly inspired by Gnosticism (Owens 27–8). For general literature on, and references to, the Gnostic *Propatôr* see also Irenaeus 1.6.3 (crucially stating that the most secret and mysterious name of *Propatôr* is *Anthrôpos*, or "Man") and 1.12 (citing Isaiah); Hippolytus, *Refutation of all heresies* 6.43.5, 6.48.3; F.–M.–M. Sagnard, *La gnose valentinienne et le témoignage de Saint Irénée* (Paris 1947) 653 s.v. *Propatôr*; C.A. Baynes, *A Coptic Gnostic treatise contained in the Codex Brucianus* (Cambridge 1933) 209 s.vv. "Forefather", *"Forefather"* and "Forefather Deep"; V. Macdermot, *The books of Jeu and the untitled text in the Bruce codex* (Leiden 1978) 218–23, 258–79, 304–5 (228–30, 248–58, 271 Schmidt) with 219 n.3; J.D. Turner in *Nag Hammadi codices XI, XII, XIII*, ed. C.W. Hedrick (Leiden 1990) 248; *Corpus hermeticum*, ed. A.D. Nock and A.–J. Festugière (Paris 1946–54) iii 7, 11 n.19, 14, iv 4, 10; *Papyri graecae magicae* (2nd ed., ed. K. Preisendanz and A. Henrichs, Stuttgart 1973–74) i 132–3 (*PGM* IV.1988–9) and ii 74 (*PGM* XII.236–7) with A. Dieterich, *Kleine Schriften* (Leipzig 1911) 18–19; Iamblichus, *On the mysteries* 8.4 with G. Shaw, *Theurgy and the soul* (University Park, PA 1995) 113 n.9; R.M. van den Berg, *Proclus' hymns* (Leiden 2001) 264. The Latin alchemical text quoted on the mural at Bollingen: *Artis auriferae volumen secundum* (Basle 1593) 239–40; cf. *PA* 109–10 §140.

[70] On the archetypal prophet who "neither speaks nor hides but offers a sign" see the famous saying by Jung's favourite author Heraclitus, fr. 7 Gemelli Marciano = C.H. Kahn, *The art and thought of Heraclitus* (Cambridge 1979) 42–3, 123–4; and for the

ancient tradition of speaking to those who have eyes to see and ears to hear cf. *APMM* 370, *Reality* 433. Zarathustra, Buddha, Christ, Mani, Muhammad: *NZ* i 12–14, 45, 492–3, ii 852, 1296, 1531; draft letter from Cary de Angulo to Jung dated 26 January 1924 (*CBA*), cf. *RB* 213b; L.S. Owens and S.A. Hoeller in *Encyclopedia of psychology and religion* (2nd ed., New York 2014), ed. D.A. Leeming, 979. For the historical dating of Zarathustra see P. Kingsley, *Bulletin of the School of Oriental and African Studies* 53 (1990) 245–65 and *Journal of the Royal Asiatic Society* 5 (1995) 173–209 with e.g. F. Grenet in *The Wiley Blackwell companion to Zoroastrianism*, ed. M. Stausberg and Y.S-D. Vevaina (Chichester 2015) 21–2; the return by Martin West to dating him as late as the seventh century BC is contradicted by both the Greek and Iranian evidence (*Hellenica* iii, Oxford 2013, 89–109). "He has been Christ ... born again": *NZ* i 45. "The one that goes and the one that comes": ibid. 44. "Only now and then": draft letter from de Angulo to Jung dated 25 September 1922 (*CBA*); for the periodic reappearances cf. also *RB* 149 = 316a. "Rare phenomenon": *PT* 268 §453. Naturally this all brings Jung very close to the teachings of the Theosophists (*IJP* 101). "Whenever there is a decline ...": *RB* 154 left margin, citing an English version of *Bhagavad gîtâ* 4.7–8; for Jung's acquaintance at the time with the *Gîtâ* as well as related literature see *JPPF* 4/1 (1912) 209 n.2, 219 n.1 = *ST* 166 §241, 174 n.4 and *Psychological types* (London 1923) 242–57 with 244 n.5. Buddhas and Bodhisattvas: *NZ* i 13, 97, 264. It will be noted that, for Jung, the boundary between prophet and saviour was completely porous (*TE* 169 §260, *ACU* 157 §267, *JL* ii 174 = E. Rolfe, *Encounter with Jung*, Boston 1989, 102–3).

[71] For the standard view that by "1919, Jung had gone through his major period of psychological distress", see e.g. A.C. Elms, *Uncovering lives* (New York 1994) 68; P. Homans, *Jung in*

context (2nd ed., Chicago 1995) 80 ("by August 1914 Jung had entered the most conflicted phase of his critical years, which terminated only toward the end of the decade"); *MDR* 197–8/206–7. Discussions with his soul: *BB* vii 92 sheet "c"; *RB* 211 (5 January 1922). For the narrative of Jung's uniquely sound sleep see Aniela Jaffé, *From the life and work of C.G. Jung* (2nd ed., Einsiedeln 1989) 121–2; for his shame at having to induce sleep artificially (ibid. 121), which has more than a little to do with his lingering fears of becoming a second Nietzsche, see his own comments at *NZ* ii 1470–1. Most of Jung's original work on the material that emerged in the *Red book* was done at night (*RB* 223a, 238b with n.91; L.S. Owens, *The Gnostic* 3, July 2010, 23–36), and sleeplessness recurs as a constant issue throughout the *Red book* itself (*RB* 262a, 264b, 296, 306a; cf. *BB* ii 41, 65). Only to people close to him such as Victor White or, ironically, Aniela Jaffé did he say a word about the "severe" insomnia that haunted him again with a vengeance while in the process of writing *Aion* and *Answer to Job* (*JL* i 480, 492 = *JW* 103, 118; *JL* ii 18; cf. ibid. 125, *JK* 203). During the 1930s he also makes some interesting observations about the archetypes never sleeping, about the sleeplessness that inevitably derives from any human contact with them, and about the futility of trying to turn back the clock for the sake of a good night's sleep by pretending such contact never happened (*NZ* i 283–5).

[72] Draft letter from Cary de Angulo to Jung dated 26 January 1924 and documenting the conversation that took place between them on Monday the 21st: *RB* 213b (*CBA*; this passage is absurdly misunderstood by Liz Greene in her astrological ramblings, *The astrological world of Jung's 'Liber novus'*, London 2018, 95). I have made some very minor corrections to Shamdasani's transcript, based on comparison with the original manuscript.

[73] The most meaningful introductions to Mani and Manichaeism are still, in spite of their age, *Le Manichéisme: son fondateur, sa doctrine* (Paris 1949) by Henry Corbin's friend Henri–Charles Puech as well as the extraordinary paper on "The concept of redemption in Manichaeism" which Puech presented at Eranos during the summer of 1936 (*The mystic vision*, ed. J. Campbell, Princeton 1968, 247–314); *Mani and Manichaeism* by Geo Widengren (London 1965); and *Mani*, by L.J.R. Ort (Leiden 1967). For Mani, his relationship to Empedocles, and the whole question of science as salvation, see also *ENM* 342–4, 386–7. On Jung's vital appreciation for Mani and the work he inspired—which he freely describes as "most important", "marvellous", "most gorgeous"—cf. e.g. *JV* i 461, ii 659–60, 840, 1004–5, 1028, *NZ* i 45, 305–8, 492–3, 668, ii 852–3, 1086–7, 1116, 1526. The English text of *Mysterium coniunctionis* contains a very unfortunate mistranslation: far from stating as his own assessment that "Mani concocted his pernicious heresy which poisoned the nations" (*MC* 38 §31) Jung is simply reporting the fact that, "according to Christian tradition, Mani is said to have concocted his pernicious heresy with which he poisoned the nations." Of course lingering behind all these details lies one endlessly delicate question. That's the question of the extent to which in spite of his ardent denials, and especially through his constant assault on the doctrine of evil as *privatio boni* or simple absence of the good which had been shaped by orthodox Christians for the sake of combatting Manichaean dualism, Jung considered it his role to help bring an updated form of Manichaean heresy back into the modern world (cf. e.g. *Aion* 61 n.74; L. Oglesby, *C.G. Jung and Hans Urs von Balthasar*, Hove 2014, 85–6, 110–11).

[74] The master who transcends the universe: draft letter from Cary de Angulo to Jung dated 28 January 1924 (*CBA*). For

Jung's instinctive horror at the tendency to "concretize" (cf. *JL* ii 203) the infinitely subtle quintessence of the saviour in the form of a single human being rather than allowing the saving principle to operate freely, beyond and contrary to all our reasonable expectations, see e.g. *RB* 311b, *PT* 260–2 §§438–43, *ACU* 157–8 §267. On the cage in which Master and disciple so easily trap each other cf. *RB* 316b; *TE* 234 §390. For the biblical pillar of fire which guides through the night, as opposed to the pillar of cloud that guides in the daytime, see Exodus 13:21–2, 14:24, Numbers 14:14, Nehemiah 9:12 and 19. On the pillar of fire or light as a specifically Manichaean—and, later, Sufi—symbol cf. e.g. C. Schmidt and H.J. Polotsky, *Ein Mani-Fund in Ägypten* (Berlin 1933) 66 with S.N.C. Lieu, *Manichaeism in the later Roman Empire and medieval China* (2nd ed., Tübingen 1992) 139; H. Corbin, *Cyclical time and Ismaili gnosis* (London 1983) 109–15, 140–1, 181 with G. Böwering, *The mystical vision of existence in classical Islam* (Berlin 1980) 149–54; F. Kazemi in *Lights of 'Irfán*, ed. I. Ayman, xiv (Darmstadt 2013) 60–6. For the prophet as a pillar see also W. Bousset, *Hauptprobleme der Gnosis* (Göttingen 1907) 173 (cf. 193 with *AN* vii 142) and, on the broader historical context, C.-M. Edsman, *Le baptême de feu* (Uppsala 1940) 154–74 (especially 166–72 for both Christ and Mani as pillars of fire); M. Idel, *Ascensions on high in Jewish mysticism* (Budapest 2005) 123–7; M. Popović, *Reading the human body* (Leiden 2007) 248–9. Jung himself was intimately familiar with the various roles played by the pillar of fire or light in Manichaean tradition: *JV* ii 1004–5; *NZ* ii 853; *MC* 76 n.219, 395 §567. For his own observations on its psychological meaning see also *IJP* 147, 154; *NZ* ii 1420; *PPT* 220 n.17; *AS* 62, 310 with n.20.

[75] *NZ* ii 852. Jung is primarily talking here about the archetypal "distortion" that was caused as soon as Nietzsche

started identifying with Zarathustra; but the very same principle applies in the case of Zarathustra or any other prophets identifying with their own prophetic role. Compare *PR* 345–6 §534, where Jung describes the infinite blessings that spontaneously arise as a result of "the archetypes awaking to independent life"; and note also his advice to Barbara Robb ("I hope she won't be tempted to identify herself with that greater personality owing to which she knows myself") at *JW* 71, where the point is that any identification would simply interfere with the ability of this greater being to do its mysterious work around the world in conformity "to the divine will" (ibid. 70–6). On the other hand, as a vivid example of the devil's face that appears when someone personally identifies with the archetype of the saviour see *JK* 259–60, 261–2.

[76] Jung on doubt: *RB* 301b; C. MacKenna in *Insanity and divinity*, ed. J. Gale, M. Robson and G. Rapsomatioti (Hove 2014) 68; and on "the importance of doubting our doubt" compare *APMM* 13. For Corbin and the *Ishrâqî* tradition see e.g. *AE* xvi; on *Ishrâqî* mysticism and the Presocratics, *APMM* 371–91.

[77] On the inevitable "corruption" caused by the misunderstandings—and misunderstandings of misunderstandings—of apostles, followers and disciples see W.B. Henning, *Journal of the Royal Asiatic Society* 2 (1944) 136–7 = *Selected papers* (Tehran 1977) ii 142–3. For Mani's innovation of both painting and writing see e.g. L.J.R. Ort, *Mani* (Leiden 1967) 106–17 plus, on the whole question of Manichaean art, A. von Le Coq, *Die buddhistische Spätantike in Mittelasien* ii (Die manichäischen Miniaturen, Berlin 1923) and v (Neue Bildwerke, Berlin 1926); H.-J. Klimkeit, *Manichäische Kunst an der Seidenstrasse* (Opladen 1996); Z. Gulácsi, *Mani's pictures* (Leiden 2015);

and note also Henry Corbin's comments, *L'homme de lumière dans le soufisme iranien* (Paris 1971) 194–201 = *The man of light in Iranian Sufism* (Boulder 1978) 133–8. For the dynamic in Manichaeism of essential continuity with, as well as superiority to and divergence from, one's prophetic predecessors see Ort 115–27. For the crucial emphasis on one's own source of inspiration being identical to the source that inspired every single predecessor, compare Henning's formal summary of "Manichaean prophetology" (in Mani's particular case "the object of the divine inspirations he had received was to make known the true state of the world to mankind" but the essence "of all revelations, whether received by Mani or by his predecessors, was the same: they emanated from the same source and were given for the same purpose"; *Journal of the Royal Asiatic Society* 2, 1944, 136 = *Selected papers* ii 142) as well as Ort 118: "when we listen carefully to his words, we do not hear the voice of a syncretist. Mani only wants to say that his forerunners and he were sent and inspired by the same sender. This means that Buddha, Zarathustra and Jesus received their inspiration from the very same source as Mani did … Instead of syncretism we should call this phenomenon 'common source' or 'same inspiration'". On the standard Gnostic and Manichaean as well as Islamic procedure of listing prophetic predecessors by name, with a notable fondness for the number four, see e.g. H. Jonas, *Gnosis und spätantiker Geist* i (3rd ed., Göttingen 1964) 285 n.1; E. Rose, *Die manichäische Christologie* (Wiesbaden 1979) 33; C. Colpe, *Das Siegel der Propheten* (Berlin 1990) 228–9; J.C. Reeves, *Heralds of that good realm* (Leiden 1996). Jung's addition of Muhammad to the list of prophets is simply an acknowledgement of the well-known fact that Muhammad succeeded Mani as the next major figure in history to become the "Seal of Prophets", and took over many Manichaean traditions in the process: see e.g. Colpe 227–47;

M. Frenschkowski, *Offenbarung und Epiphanie* i (Tübingen 1995) 208–9.

[78] *MDRC* 224–30; *MDR* 228–32/242–6; cf. *JP* 31–4 (8 November 1957). Note that at *MDR* 228/242, where Jung is describing his arrangements for sailing back to Europe, "from Marseilles" should read "for Marseilles". Although a reference to the Uigurian script and Turfan Manichaean fragments is missing in the unpublished Protocols (see also *BB* vii 92 sheet "d"), there is no way that Aniela Jaffé would have invented such details; and of course in such a case she had access not only to various kinds of additional written material (cf. e.g. her *From the life and work of C.G. Jung*, 2nd ed., Einsiedeln 1989, 134; *JSB* 25) but to Jung himself. The omission of the reference in his own 1957 rendering is significant as an indicator of how, on a certain conscious or unconscious level, Jung came to review and even revise the meaning of his older dreams.

[79] Sad to say, Sonu Shamdasani prefaces the first-ever publication of this potent dialogue by forcefully insisting that Jung's role as a psychologist demanded the outright "rejection" of anything relating to religion which his anima or soul might suggest to him (*RB* 211–12). But such an idea of "rejection" involves the most fundamental misunderstanding, and distortion, of Jungian psychology—and guarantees an instant return to that "rational standpoint" which, Jung himself warns, will always find ways to dismiss the soul's promptings as worthless (*PT* 251–2 §426). This particular dialogue between him and his soul is of course a classic example of the inner dialogue between conscious and unconscious which aims at producing what he came to call the transcendent function; and the transcendent function involves no rejection of anything at all, except on the surface. Underneath the warring of

opposites, it's nothing but a matter of constant refinement and collaboration working towards the mystery of integration on a deeper level (*SD* 87–90 §§181–9). This is why Jung liked to cite the tempting of Christ in the desert as a perfect instance of the transcendent function at work: on the surface it could seem that Christ is simply rejecting the devil's attempts to seduce him with power. But ultimately he is rejecting nothing because, thanks to the devil, he is brought straight to the realization of his spiritual or invisible power (*JL* i 267–8, cf. *PT* 53 §80). As for the popular idea nowadays that Jung couldn't wait to reject the cunning and seductive suggestions of his soul, it can be helpful to consider how attentive and respectful he was towards her prophecies about his own destiny (*JP* 258). The fact is that his quotation in *Psychological types* of Spitteler's words to the soul contains, like the opening to the *Red book*, more than a touch of the autobiographical: "And though I be stripped of all, yet am I rich beyond all measure so long as you alone remain with me, and name me 'my friend' with your sweet mouth" (cf. *PT* 174 §290).

[80] "Secret church": Jung to Esther Harding on 5 July 1922, *Quadrant* 8/2 (Winter 1975) 9 ("He said that if we belong to the secret church, then we belong, and we need not worry about it, but can go our own way") = *JS* 29; L.S. Owens in *Das 'Rote Buch'*, ed. T. Arzt (Würzburg 2015) 250, 252. "Invisible church": *CS* 19–20, *RB* 211 n.176; it will be noted that the idea of an "invisible church" has closer ties with orthodox Christianity than the notion of a "secret church" (cf. e.g. A. Gamman, *Church invisible*, Whangaparaoa 2013). Later Jung would also often refer to the *ecclesia spiritualis* or "spiritual church", in harmony with the traditions deriving from Joachim of Fiore, and encounter significant resistance for doing so (L. Oglesby, *C.G. Jung and Hans Urs von Balthasar*,

Hove 2014, 73; for the history of the idea see e.g. M. Reeves, *The influence of prophecy in the later Middle Ages*, Oxford 1969, 203, 272). Richard Noll usefully cites Harold McCormick's formal description in 1916 of the Psychological Club as "the Visible Church", by way of contrast with the invisible church he calls the "School of Zurich"—but gratuitously adds that "Harold's reference to the club as the 'Visible Church' reveals that he had been reading the works of Arthur Edward Waite, particularly his 1909 book *The Hidden Church of the Holy Grail*" (*The Aryan Christ*, New York 1997, 229). Clearly all it reveals is that McCormick, no less than Esther Harding and others, has been listening to Jung. For Waite's research into the mystical path "which, according to western traditions centred on the Holy Grail, has been called the path of the 'Secret Church' in the sense of the church that lies hidden inside the 'secret' of every human soul", see Henry Corbin's comments: *Temple et contemplation* (2nd ed., Paris 2006) 315, 456.

[81] Right at the start of the *Red book*: *RBu* 229b (folio i verso; *RB* 229b). Jung's opening announcement here about what he needs to proclaim ("euch verkünden") is just as unmistakably biblical as his statement, a little later on the same folio page, about being overpowered by divine grace. The single passage he is echoing most closely and most obviously is John 16:13–15 ("was zukünfftig ist wirt er euch verkünden … euch verkünden … euch verkünden" in the Zürcher Bibel), which is no accident at all considering that he has already started the *Red book* by inserting a quotation from the Gospel of John alongside his three quotations from Isaiah (folio i recto, *RB* 229a). But the language at Isaiah 61:1 of proclaiming ("verkünden") the prophetic message ("Botschaft") is equally relevant in light of the importance that, even many years later, Jung will continue ascribing to his own prophetic message or "Botschaft" to the

world (*JP* 144); see also Exodus 19:3, John 4:19–26, Acts of the Apostles 26:22–24. For his explicit introductory statements about being forced to speak on behalf of the spirit of the depths and being given the divine grace or "Gnade" which is needed for him not to resist, see *Red book* folio i verso (*RB* 230b) and compare e.g. Isaiah 6:5–8. The spirit of the depths takes everything away from him including his attachment to science, robs him of joy and life and the ability to speak about anything else: *RB* 229–30; cf. V.W. Odajnyk, *PP* 53 (2010) 447–8. Having no choice: *RB* 229–30; *JP* 145 (softened for the published biography: *MDRC* 122, *MDR* 171/178). "Glad to have escaped from death": Homer, *Odyssey* 9.63, 9.566, 10.134; *ZL* 23 §69; *JP* 147; *MDRC* 120 with n.1 = *ETG* 180 with n.4. Keeping Odysseus, or Ulysses, in mind: *RB* 245b, 246 n.159, 247b with n.176, 304 n.223, 366a, 367a; *NZ* i 462 with n.3, ii 1191 with n.2; *ETG* 103–4. When Jung told Aniela Jaffé during October 1957 that by writing the *Red book* he had been obeying exactly and faithfully ("getreu") the divine obligation imposed on him, he was referring straight back to Elijah's command—over forty years earlier—to write down exactly and faithfully ("getreu") whatever he had been shown: *RB* 252b, *JP* 148 (cf. 144–5 and also *RB* 190, written in 1959). His disappointed hope of being freed: *JP* 148. The part of him that couldn't stand the grand prophetic style, the overpowering language of "Prophetentum": *JP* 144–5, 169; Jaffé has caused no end of harm, and dragged down any number of Jungian commentators in the process, by removing what Jung had said about prophetic language and replacing it with her pretty nonsense about him abandoning the *Red book* because he felt it was too "aesthetic" (*MDR* 180–1/188). For Jung's awareness of the need to translate the "Botschaft", the message or mission to the world which had forcibly been imposed on him, into another language which is the language of science see his crystal-clear statement at *JP* 144.

[82] Parmenides and Empedocles on the need to re-adapt to human conventions, and to the acceptable language of science in their time: Parmenides frs. 1.28–32, 8.50–2 and 60–1 Diels = frs. 8A.35–7 and 8B, 14B.76–8 and 15C.11–12 Gemelli Marciano; Empedocles frs. 4, 8 and 9 Diels = frs. 9, 13 and 14 Gemelli Marciano; *ENM* 382–4; *Reality* 27, 205–58, 422–9. Jung on returning to the "human side", and science: *RB* 219b, cf. *JP* 148; it should be remembered how acutely conscious Jung was, not least through his intimate familiarity with ancient Greek and Latin literature, of the huge difficulties involved in returning to the world of the living from the world of the dead (*PA* 39; S. Shamdasani, *C.G. Jung: a biography in books*, New York 2012, 201–2). The divinity and the perils of *mêtis*: M. Detienne and J.–P. Vernant, *Les ruses de l'intelligence* (Paris 1974); and for the crucial role of *mêtis* in the life as well as the teachings of both Parmenides and Empedocles see *Reality*. The divine takes care of everything: *IDPW*; *Reality* 26–284. Hopefully there is no need to give references for Odysseus' famous return at the end of the Homeric *Odyssey*. With manifest scorn, as if even to mention such absurd notions is already to discredit them, Sonu Shamdasani refers to the work of Paul Stern—"In his view, Jung was a 'seer' disguised as a scientist"—and not only notes that Frank McLynn similarly "regarded Jung as a prophet masquerading as a scientist" but also cites McLynn's hilarious comment about how "acres of print could have been saved if Jung had come clean and admitted that he was a prophet" (P.J. Stern, *C.G. Jung: the haunted prophet*, New York 1976; F. McLynn, *Carl Gustav Jung*, New York 1996, 316; *JSB* 72, 83). For descriptions of Jungian

psychology as simply Gnosticism or Theosophy in disguise see already H. Ellenberger, *L'évolution psychiatrique* 17 (1952) 151. Jung bluntly states that the task imposed on him was to translate his mission and message to the world out from the language of prophecy into the language of science: *JP* 144 (September 1957); cf. 145, 169. "Today the voice of one crying ...": *SM* 38 §55 (1934), citing Isaiah 40:3; cf. *ZL* 35 §108. On the futility of appearing openly as a prophet in the modern world see *JL* ii 174 = E. Rolfe, *Encounter with Jung* (Boston 1989) 102–3 (1954); and note, as well, Rolfe's later comment to Jung that in this age "of spiritual collapse without a parallel in human history" nobody believes what mystics or medicine men or saviours say "because they lack a scientific foundation, and the Scientist is the Medicine Man of the modern age" (ibid. 163–4: for scientists as modern prophets in fact and deed, compare Lynda Walsh's recent study *Scientists as prophets*, New York 2013). Of course this brings Jung himself breathtakingly close to what he describes as the "attempts at concealment" by people like Rudolf Steiner or Mary Baker Eddy, whose movements "have a genuinely religious character even when they pretend to be scientific"; but that simply helps to explain why he was so conscious of the need to emphasize his scientific credentials. And besides, as he goes straight on to add: the fact that all these movements "give themselves a scientific veneer is not just a grotesque caricature or a masquerade, but a positive sign that they are actually pursuing 'science', i.e., *knowledge*, instead of *faith*, which ... modern man abhors ... He wants to *know*—to experience for himself" (*CT* 84 §§170–1). For the situation of the mystic putting on the garment of science see also P. Kingsley, *Black zinnias* 1 (2003–4) 21–6.

[83] Worth mentioning twice: Empedocles fr. 25 Diels; cf. fr. 35.1–3 Diels = fr. 38.1–3 Gemelli Marciano with *ENM* 395–6.

1st October 1957: *JP* 149. With Jung's contrast between fiery lava and the ordered rigidity of his published books compare Cary de Angulo's contrast, over thirty years earlier, between the fire that burns through his spoken words as well as through the written words of the *Red book* and the "doctoring" of his published books so as to make them come from the head rather than the heart (*RB* 214a; *CBA*). For Aniela Jaffé's misunderstandings and distortions of this particular passage in the Protocols, including her replacement of Jung's cosmological image of transforming the oozing primordial substance "into an orderly world" with the trivial idea of him wanting to incorporate it "into the contemporary picture of the world", see *MDRC* 145, *ETG* 203, *MDR* 190/199; for Sonu Shamdasani's, *JM* 22 ("… and then had to classify everything …"). "The ordinary language … before man had the thought": *NZ* ii 970–1. As a mythological example of "the revelation of the thought that existed before man had the thought" Jung cites the Babylonian fish–god Oannes, who delivers his primordial wisdom to humanity from the sea of the unconscious (ibid. 971). This is no accident, because elsewhere Jung describes a dream he had in which Oannes was identical to his own teacher Philemon (letter to Cary de Angulo dated 17 August 1925: *CBA*)—and the discovery that not even one's thoughts are one's own was, of course, Philemon's greatest gift to Jung. See *JP* 24; *MDR* 176/183; and note also *TE* 201 §323 on the danger of falling so deeply into "the habit of identifying ourselves with the thoughts that come to us that we invariably assume we have made them".

[84] Empedocles fr. 9.5 Diels = fr. 14.5–6 Gemelli Marciano; *ENM* 382–4 with n.120; *Reality* 422–5; Gemelli Marciano, *Die Vorsokratiker* ii (2nd ed., Berlin 2013) 374–5.

[85] "I'm the damnedest dilettante ...": *JP* 149; the passage has already been showcased, with the most unfortunate results, at *JM* 22. Aside from his grotesque mistranslation of the words "der hat dann alles angeordnet" as meaning that Jung himself "then had to classify everything", Sonu Shamdasani lurches from disaster to disaster by also mistranslating "ich bin der verfluchteste Dilettant" as "I am the most cursed dilettante"—and using this image of a cursed but noble dilettante as the basis for an entire book about how Jung the struggling scientist made it his life's goal to unite all the scientific disciplines of his time under a single, psychological banner (*JM* 1, 22). But Jung is simply swearing here ("I'm the damnedest dilettante who ever lived"), as he often did; and although he sometimes talked elsewhere about the value of trying "to counter the fragmentation of the sciences" (ibid. 22), anyone caring to continue reading this particular passage in the unpublished Protocols will soon realize that his real meaning and the true focus of his interest lay somewhere else entirely. Unfortunately, the almost complete absence of discrimination being demonstrated in such matters by the Jungian community means that all these misunderstandings are already percolating into the literature about Jung (so e.g. J.R. Haule, *Jung in the 21st century*, Hove 2011, i 2, 258, 262 n.6); and while Shamdasani has made a crusade out of denouncing the fanciful "myth-making" (*JM* 1–2, 24, etc.) enveloping the figure of Jung, it seems to have escaped him that to over-rationalize Jung's words and work is just another form of myth-making. The one point where Shamdasani is at least close to correct about Jung's confession here to being a dilettante is when he notes how it was excluded by Aniela Jaffé from the published version of Jung's biography, and how "it is not surprising that it was omitted, being so far away from prevalent images of Jung" (ibid. 22). In fact Jaffé's surviving

typescript of the Protocols still shows how desperate she was, at the point where Jung opens up quite honestly about his dilettantism, to insert into the text a handwritten addition of her own praising him for the unquestioned excellence and exactness of his science (*JP* 149). This is the same story which has just repeated itself all over again with the recent editors of a collection of his letters: at the point where Jung describes both himself and the person he is writing to as "mere dilettantes", "bloße Dilettanten", his editors are quick to insist that the word "dilettante" is here being used by him "in a nonpejorative sense" (*QPT* 40 with n.44; the fact that Jung goes on to refer to both himself and his correspondent as amateurs, in the literal sense of lovers, changes nothing). For Jung as dilettante compare also Sonja Marjasch's portrayal of him as "like a magpie, picking everything up and taking it home" (D. Bair, *Jung*, Boston 2003, 826 n.102); his own confession, in 1957, to being "utterly *amathematikos*" (*JL* ii 404, cf. *SD* 419 §816); his descriptions of himself as a dilettante at *JL* i 114 and *MDR* 91/86; and the strikingly lifeless foreword he wrote for a projected American Eranos volume which, it just so happens, was never published (*Spring* 92, 2015, 83). It's more than a little ironic that Shamdasani should make the mistake of using this uniquely superficial foreword, with its hollow-sounding call for specialists from various fields to bring their talents together at Eranos, to try and throw light on Jung's uniquely profound explanation of his dilettantism here in the Protocols (*JM* 21–2): forcing the exoteric to explain the esoteric is never a good idea. As it happens, Cary Baynes was not only intelligent but courageous enough to tell Jung that the foreword he had written was so pathetically feeble it didn't deserve printing. He wholeheartedly agreed, but refused to rewrite it as she was urging. He had only written the piece to get the organizer of the Eranos gatherings, Olga Fröbe–Kapteyn, off his back and wasn't going to waste any more of his precious time or effort on something he considered so unimportant (Bair 472; R. Bernardini, *Jung a Eranos*, Milan 2011, 296–7).

[86] *JP* 149. In the original, the fundamental contrast is plain and clear between the "Urstoff" or "primordial material" of the unconscious—what he also refers to as the "raw material" or "Rohstoff" which is the spontaneously flowing substance of prophecy (*JP* 169)—and the "Bekleidungsstoff" or cloaking material that he uses to cover and hide it. Due to obvious legal restrictions, and also out of respect for the unpublished nature of the material, I have limited myself to faithfully paraphrasing rather than translating what Jung says in this crucial passage. Anything more will have to wait until the Protocols of his interviews with Aniela Jaffé are published and officially mistranslated.

[87] For Jung's straightforward and unqualified statement that the alchemists' experiences were his own experiences see *JP* 227 (22 November 1957; dismembered, as well as watered down, in *MDR* 196/205, 200/209). For his complaining, evidently to Marie–Louise von Franz, about the ordeal imposed on him by his researches into alchemy cf. A. Ribi, *Analytische Psychologie* 13 (1982) 202 ("Er soll gesagt haben, diese Arbeit habe ihn noch viel mehr Mühe gekostet als die Auseinandersetzung mit dem Unbewussten"). Regarding the psychological significance implicit, for Jung, in such imagery of clothing and unclothing see F.X. Charet, *Spiritualism and the foundations of C.G. Jung's psychology* (Albany 1993) 253. On alchemical tradition as itself prophetic, note for example the magical hymn to Hermes as *thnêtoisi prophêta* or "prophet to mortals" with which Jung introduces his major study on "The spirit Mercurius" (*AS* 192); and compare the statement he quotes, in his last major work,

from Nicholas Barnaud about "the entire Law and Prophecy of alchemy" (*tota Lex et Prophetia chemica*: *MC* 61 §59 with 566 n.140. To understand what lies behind this combination of "Law and Prophecy" see e.g. P. Lory, *Jâbir ibn Hayyân, L'Élaboration de l'élixir suprême*, Damascus 1988, 15 with n.33 and *IDPW* 204–19). For alchemy as a prophetic tradition right from the start see, in general, R. Reitzenstein, *Poimandres* (Leipzig 1904), especially 215 n. ("Der vollkommene Alchemist hat die *gnôsis* und ist der wahre Prophet"); S.L. Grimes, *Zosimus of Panopolis* (PhD thesis, Syracuse University 2006) 37 with n.64, 38, 42; K.A. Fraser, *Dionysius* 25 (2007) 37, 47–9; M. Martelli, *Nuncius* 26 (2011) 289–90; R. Patai, *The Jewish alchemists* (Princeton 1994) 18, 21, 29–30, 49, 70; Lory 15; L. DeVun, *Prophecy, alchemy and the end of time* (New York 2009). And for the later expression "alchemy is the sister of prophecy" compare *SB* xi, 205–6, 301 n.72, 324 nn.54–5.

[88] For the very respectable idea that Jung finally managed to "find his true life's work" in the world of science by slamming the door shut on the world of prophecy see e.g. Joseph Cambray, *IJJS* 3 (2011) 110–24. When I happened to meet one of the leading authorities on Jung's relationship to science during February 2016, I asked why he never mentioned how profoundly ambiguous Jung was about science throughout his life and how eager he had been in practice to keep "turning a blind eye to scientific knowledge" (*CT* 251 §496). The answer I was given is quite indicative of how much attention one should be paying to a lot of the Jungian literature on the subject being published nowadays: "Of course I'm aware of what you are referring to but I am not able to mention it when I speak or teach or write because, if I did, I'd immediately lose my funding and no one would invite me to speak at conferences any more." As for the idea, more popular now than

ever since the *Red book* has been published, that Jung simply abandoned the world of prophecy for the world of science: this is mostly presented as a sophisticated modern account of his intellectual evolution and development. What seems to have gone unnoticed is that it's just a tired reproduction of all the schizophrenic attempts already made for almost two centuries by rationalistic historians to dispose of the unbearable tensions, the intolerable conflicts and contradictions, between the figure of Empedocles the scientist and the reality of Empedocles the prophet. Supposedly everything could be solved by arguing that Empedocles played the role of irrational prophet while he was still a hot-headed youth only to abandon such utter nonsense, later, for the sober life of a scientist (so e.g. J. Bidez, *La biographie d'Empédocle*, Ghent 1894, 159–74; W. Kranz, *Hermes* 70, 1935, 111–119); it has taken the better part of two hundred years to discredit such childish ideas once and for all by proving that Empedocles the prophet was also a scientist while Empedocles the scientist, doctor, philosopher, never stopped inwardly being a prophet (A. Martin and O. Primavesi, *L'Empédocle de Strasbourg*, Berlin 1999, 114–19; *ENM* 339–41). As for Jung's own early days of initially wanting to achieve something through science before, in 1913, he ended up bumping into the fateful stream of lava (*JP* 149): he had thrown himself into the world of science as fully as he could (*MDR* 79–92/72–86; E. Taylor, *Psychoanalytic review* 83, 1996, 547–68) even though he was already filled with horror at the cold, robotic heartlessness of most science as well as most scientists (see e.g. M.–L. von Franz, *ZL* xvi–xviii for 1896 and 1897; A. Jaffé, *Word and image*, Princeton 1979, 26–7 for his diary entries in 1898). The lava then takes away his belief in science: *RB* 229b (cf. 336b with n.18). And as for his later dilettantism: one of the more obvious examples is the saga of P.W. Martin's attempts, initially under the aegis of UNESCO, to establish a solid scientific basis for the study of individuation. Jung began by offering the most ambiguous as well as half-hearted assistance and, after years of expensive funding from the Bollingen Foundation, Martin's projects effectively came to nothing (*SL* 606–13; *JL* ii 219; W. McGuire, *Bollingen*, Princeton 1982, 136–7; P. Pietikainen, *Alchemists of human nature*, London 2007, 125–6). Or there is the earlier case of his involvement with the journal called *Weltanschauung*, which very ambitiously aimed "to bring about a synthesis of the sciences"; but rather than describing in glowing terms how the scale of this project "indicates the enormous scope of Jung's undertaking" and "provides a good illustration of his encyclopedic conception of psychology", it would be better simply to note that "the project came to nothing" (*JM* 19–21). As for the immensely successful Eranos conferences, on the other hand: rather than suggesting Jung was the guiding force behind them (ibid. 21–2) it would be far more accurate to explain that the real guiding force and inspiration was Olga Fröbe–Kapteyn, who not only struggled constantly with Jung's influence but most often experienced him as a force that "worked against Eranos" (H.T. Hakl, *Eranos*, Sheffield 2013, 45, 104–5, 165–6; R. Bernardini, *Historia religionum* 5, 2013, 98). And with regard to his most famous scientific publication, on synchronicity, it helps to remember how quickly the friends who read what he had written turned into ex-friends as soon as they dared to point out how flawed it was from a scientific point of view; how eventually he had to let the physicist Wolfgang Pauli rewrite the text, before it was ever published, to bring it up to scientific standards; and how Pauli himself later broke off any formal ties with Jung's work because of the utter disregard among Jungians for scientific method or principles (D. Bair, *Jung*, Boston 2003, 551–4; *PB* iv/II 75–8, iv/III 536, 620–2, 627–30, 647, 710–11, iv/IV 254, 317, 420–1).

[89] "To strip off the fantasy … simply 'meaningful coincidences'": M. Fordham's preface to C.G. Jung, *Synchronicity* (Princeton 1973). For the idea of synchronicity viewed as a very welcome exit from the "world of non-rational Divine power and magic" compare G. Bright's comments, *JAP* 59 (2014) 287; M. Stein, *The red book: a global seminar* (Asheville Jung Center DVD: Asheville 2010) 1:16:29–1:18:40. In fact Jung's collaborator Wolfgang Pauli was far better positioned to understand the real factors involved when, on the contrary, he described their collaboration as meant to provoke a head-on "collision" ("Zusammenprall") between the "magical–alchemical attitude" and the attitude of modern science (*Wolfgang Pauli und C.G. Jung: ein Briefwechsel*, ed. C.A. Meier, Berlin 1992, 37; D. Bair, *Jung*, Boston 2003, 553). On the intimate links between synchronicity and the magical doctrine of *sympatheia* see *SD* 489–503 §§924–44 (cf. *JL* ii 45, 82, 175, 409), especially Jung's quaint but very ironic account of synchronicity itself as "an archaic assumption that ought at all costs to be avoided" (*SD* 502 §944); *PB* iv/I 186, 319, iv/II 363, 745; *AWA* 303 n.27. Regarding *sympatheia* and the magic-based teachings of Empedocles see *APMM* 296–300, 335–41: it's no coincidence that the one magical technique which Philemon mentions by name to Jung in the *Red book* is, precisely, this technique of sympathies or sympathetic magic (*RB* 140, 312b). For a particularly helpful perspective on the ancient view of synchronicities as indicating not only miraculous intervention but also "divine responsibility", and on their very close association with both prophecy and dreams, see D. Wardle, *Cicero: on divination, book 1* (Oxford 2006) 227–8, 287–8, 296; for Jung's own association of synchronicity with miracles, R. Main, *The rupture of time* (Hove 2004) 146. On his firm intention to make sure that his synchronicity theory "shakes

the security of our scientific foundations" as precisely the goal he was aiming at, see *JL* ii 217; and compare his statement, two years later to Wolfgang Pauli, about "the infinitesimal psychological factors which, overlooked by everybody, shake the foundations of our world" (*PB* iv/IV 514; S. Gieser, *The innermost kernel*, Berlin 2005, 328). Synchronicity as the "rupture of time": Jung in *Combat* (9 October 1952) 7 = *JS* 230; Main 181–3. For synchronicities as "border" phenomena see *SD* 487 §921; M.-L. von Franz, *C.G. Jung: his myth in our time* (New York 1975) 239; Bair 553. On Jung's instinctive impatience with any theorizing about synchronicity that failed to return to "die Erfahrung der Fülle des Seins", the immediate experience of the fullness of being, see G. Quispel in *The rediscovery of Gnosticism*, ed. B. Layton, i (Leiden 1980) 26; for Quispel's explicit equation here of fullness with the Gnostic *plêrôma* see Jung himself, *RB* 347 with n.82. Compare also A. Ribi's important comments (*Analytische Psychologie* 13, 1982, 219) on synchronicity, for Jung, as both first and last a matter of experience; and note *JM* 265–6 on Jung's highly unscientific disdain, even at Eranos, for "possibilities of interdisciplinary research" because of his exclusive concern with the primacy of direct experience. On his "theory" of synchronicity as essentially a matter of redirecting people to the reality of the numinous cf. Main 131–46; for his own presentation of it as an attempt to reintroduce the "ensouling" of matter into the soulless world of science, see e.g. *Pauli und Jung: ein Briefwechsel* 100 = *Atom and archetype*, ed. Meier (London 2001) 98; and on his "concern for the depersonalizing effects of excessive rationalization and the resulting mass-mindedness in society as 'the reason and the motive'" for him publishing anything at all on the subject of synchronicity, *JL* ii 216 with Main, *IJJS* 3 (2011) 147.

[90] Aside from *JP* 149, the word "Uroffenbarung" also occurs with a neatly double sense at *ETG* 24 (cf. *MDR* 31/17): the dream Jung is referring to is primordial not only because of its strikingly pagan and pre-Christian content but also because it's the earliest dream he remembers having, a dream more ancient and therefore more prophetic (*CD* 1, *JM* 157) than any other. His markings in the copy he owned of Wilhelm Bousset's *Hauptprobleme der Gnosis* (Göttingen 1907, 273–6) prove that Jung was familiar with the language of "Uroffenbarung" as applied, very specifically, to ancient Gnostic and Manichaean traditions; see now also E. Rose, *Die manichäische Christologie* (Wiesbaden 1979) 42 ("Botschaft ... Uroffenbarung ... Propheten der Wahrheit" in connection with the lineage of Zarathustra, Buddha, Christ and Mani) and e.g. G. Quispel, *Gnostica, Judaica, Catholica* (Leiden 2008) 33. It should be mentioned that these pencilled markings in Bousset's work date back to the time when Jung first read and studied the book soon after buying it (the list of comments about it which made their way into his alchemy notebooks at *AN* vii 134–47 dates from much later): compare the very similar annotations in his copy of Richard Reitzenstein's *Die hellenistischen Mysterienreligionen* (Leipzig 1910) 18–20 where Reitzenstein is discussing at length the words "Uroffenbarung ... Botschaft ... Prophet" and where, among his other markings, Jung highlights Reitzenstein's memorable assertion that "revelation sets free" ("Offenbarung macht frei"). For the history and meaning of this word "Uroffenbarung" see e.g. F.W.J. von Schelling, *Sämmtliche Werke* i/2 (Stuttgart 1856) 87–92 with W.A. von Schmidt, *Zeitschrift für Religions- und Geistesgeschichte* 25 (1973) 43; E. Troeltsch, *Kritische Gesamtausgabe* ii (Berlin 2007) 575; J.H. Sailhamer, *The meaning of the Pentateuch* (Downers Grove 2009) 566–9. It also will be noted that the idea of an "Uroffenbarung" came to be closely associated with

the work of Friedrich Schleiermacher (Sailhamer 135–45)—whom Jung, as he confided to Henry Corbin, considered one of his "spiritual ancestors" (*HC* 328 = *AJ* 156–7, cf. *JL* ii 115). For the essential link between the word "Uroffenbarung" and the world of prophecy see e.g. Sailhamer's comments (196) on "the prophetic notion of primeval revelation"; G.B. Gerlach, *Ammon und Schleiermacher* (Berlin 1821) 80–2; H.W.J. Thiersch, *Vorlesungen über Katholicismus und Protestantismus* (Erlangen 1846) ii 9; Bousset, *Hauptprobleme* 275–6 and *Religionsgeschichtliche Studien* (Leiden 1979) 95; Reitzenstein 18–20; *Christen und Muslime*, ed. A. Guthmann et al. (Bielefeld 2010) 2.25.

[91] The "Uroffenbarung" that Jung couldn't master, and that he had to cloak in science: *JP* 149 (1 October 1957); the "Botschaft" that overwhelmed him with its power, and that he had to translate into science: ibid. 144 (30 September 1957). For his formal and final statement that he had to give up his work on the *Red book* to start working on alchemy see *RB* 190 = 360: his comments here, in 1959, about almost being overpowered and driven mad by the force of his original experiences agree perfectly with what he had said to Aniela Jaffé about the very same situation just a couple of years earlier (*JP* 149). The dream of the Manichaean book: *MDR* 228–32/242–6. For some comments on the subtleties of change in ancient prophetic traditions see *PJB* 41–76; as Jung himself knew very well from his readings in Hermetic literature (cf. e.g. R. Reitzenstein, *Poimandres*, Leipzig 1904, 214–50), the mystery of rebirth which he so often wrote and talked about was a mystery reserved for prophets. On the need for dissimulation see *ACU* 144–6 §§253–4; on concealing one's vestiges, Jung's letter to Alice Raphael dated 7 June 1955 (Alice Raphael papers, Beinecke Library, Yale University). The

talk with his soul: *BB* v 79–80, where "sich lossagen" means not just "dissociate oneself" but "renounce"; *RBu* 334b. As one example of the dilettantish passion for an evolutionary or "diachronic reading of Jung. The various terms and conceptions as well as shifts to other conceptions can be assigned to particular phases of Jung's scholarly life. The illusion that there is a monolithic psychological theory of Jung's is thoroughly destroyed", see W. Giegerich, *Spring* 71 (2004) 201. With much more subtlety, Sonu Shamdasani points out that Jung's "theories—I'm not the first to point out—are massively inconsistent right throughout. And also they're a makeshift, post 1915–1916. The theories are not the core of Jung's work; they're simply an approximation by which he's attempting to translate his insights into a language for a scientific and medical audience. It's a compromise. Hence the contradictions." But as for what the core is, the best Shamdasani is able to say is that through his science Jung was "trying to construct a new science that redeems or provides new access to the ancient" (*JAP* 57, 2012, 375). Jung's "many unfinished beginnings": *JM* 345–7, portraying the Jung Institute in Zurich as one of the more striking examples of his dilettantism.

[92] "A path of blood and suffering … proved to be stronger than all my science": letter written by Jung in 1926 and published by Gerhard Adler, *PP* 6 (1975) 12; Lionel Corbett's dating of the letter to 1936 is incorrect (*The religious function of the psyche*, London 1996, 134). For the compensatory role of Jung's own life and writings see *SL* 704 §1585; *JP* 383–4; *MDR* 211/222; A. Jaffé, *From the life and work of C.G. Jung* (2nd ed., Einsiedeln 1989) 140; *JM* 351. He was of course very aware of the dangers, to him, of overcompensating by identifying exclusively with the unconscious (cf. e.g. *AS* 119–21 §155, on Paracelsus; *MC* 234–5 §314, an extraordinarily dense passage about apparent hostility

and defensiveness, on Michael Maier; *SL* 704–5 §§1586–8; *JP* 169–70). "The same compensatory role … commercial worldliness": C.G. Jung in H.R. Zimmer, *Der Weg zum Selbst* (Zurich 1944) 22; cf. *PR* 584 §962. For the compensatory role of prophets compare e.g. *SM* 98 §153, 122–3 §184, *JL* ii 4, *JN* 101–2. Jung's crucial task of helping westerners to remember their own cultural continuity and spiritual past: *JP* 212–13, 233, *ETG* 239 = *MDR* 222/235 (wrongly rendering "Geistesgeschichte" as "intellectual history"). The "lunatic asylum" of collective western rationalism: *Aion* 181 §282. On the enormous problem of not just material but spiritual acquisitiveness see e.g. *RB* 231b, 315–16, *SM* 58 §88, and especially *PR* 483 §773. With Jung's statement in his letter about submitting to the deliberate practice of suffering because he "wanted God to be alive and free" compare especially his question in the *Red book* as to whether any suffering could exist which would be too great to want to experience for the sake of God, a question soon followed by his confession that he has submitted to doing deliberate penance for the sake of restoring God to wholeness and health (*RB* 112): both the question and the confession are sprinkled with references to Isaiah, including chapter 53 which Jung had already quoted right at the start of the *Red book* (300a with n.204, 300b with n.206). The growing tendency nowadays to dispose of these opening passages from Isaiah with a quick wave of the hand as just some "series of preliminary biblical quotes" before moving straight on to the supposed substance, the real meat, of the *Red book* (so e.g. J. Cambray, *International journal of psychoanalysis* 94, 2013, 416) echoes exactly the disastrous tendency of modern critics to ignore Parmenides' crucial "proem" or introduction to his own teaching and rush straight on to the supposed core of what he had to say—without noticing how the essential clues to understanding everything that comes later are already contained in those opening lines (*Reality* 9–306). As for the correspondences between Jung's letter, written in 1926, and the text of the *Red book*: they should be enough, by themselves, to dispose once and for all of the claims sometimes made nowadays that the *Red book* was little more than a literary exercise or some detached and impersonal experiment in ventriloquism. "Truly, he himself has borne …": Isaiah 53:4; I have translated from the Latin text used by Jung (*Red book*, folio i recto = *RB* 229a) while keeping an eye on the Zürcher Bibel version he was also familiar with (cf. *MC* 123 n.161). As a few wise commentators have already been forced to realize just on the basis of this opening quotation, Jung is identifying himself directly with that being who according to Isaiah "has borne our sicknesses and carried our pains" (V.W. Odajnyk, *PP* 53, 2010, 441–2; R.J. Woolger, *Scientific and medical network review*, Summer 2011, 4–5). Presciently, because he didn't have direct access to the *Red book*, Edward Edinger had also connected the statement made by Jung in his letter about wanting to take God's suffering on himself with Isaiah 53: "I think we could say that that remark comes from the archetype of the Suffering Servant of Yahweh." But although Edinger makes sure to admit that this whole subject is "a mysterious business", "quite astonishing", he is a little too scrupulous about surgically removing what he calls "the archetype of the Suffering Servant" from the context of prophecy and salvation which gives it life (*Ego and self*, Toronto 2000, 40–6). For an eloquent account of the difference between true prophets or saviours and false ones, see *RB* 315–17; for prophet as saviour and saviour as prophet cf. e.g. *NZ* i 12–13, 24 (Saoshyant); on the compensating factor from the unconscious as precisely what we don't expect, *PA* 44 §48; and on the saviour not as an impossibly "concrete" person (cf. *JL* ii 203) but as the saving principle always operating beyond, and contrary to, our reasonable expectations see e.g. *RB* 311b, *PT* 260–2 §§438–43, *ACU* 157–8 §267. For the Gnostic saviour as embodying the gnosis or true knowledge of life cf. *NZ* i 569; *PR* 513–14 §841; and E.S. Drower's classic, as well as irreplaceable, study *The secret Adam* (Oxford 1960). As for the problems faced by modern rationalists and would-be psychologists when confronting the voluntary suffering of prophets, see e.g. Carolyn Sharp's discussion of Ezekiel in *Old Testament prophets for today* (Louisville 2009) 80 ("… It is possible that Ezekiel struggles with a dissociative illness or seizure disorder …"); D.J. Halperin, *Seeking Ezekiel* (University Park, PA 1993). For the prophetic acceptance of suffering see also R.E. Averbeck's observations in *The gospel according to Isaiah 53*, ed. D.L. Bock and M. Glaser (Grand Rapids 2012) 40–5, together with Jung's far more tender words on the role of the "true" or genuine prophet at *NZ* i 496.

[93] On Jung's need to compensate for humanity's collective rationalism, compare e.g. *SL* 704 §1585. For the outrage experienced by vengeful nature at "the individual and his rationally ordered world" because of "the violence his reason has done to her", see especially *PR* 344 §531: the language here is notably close to the language in Jung's letter about God and "the suffering man has put on him by loving his own reason …". On the role played according to William Blake by reason, or Urizen, in "the agony of Nature herself" see S.F. Damon, *A Blake dictionary* (2nd ed., Hanover, NH 2013) 311; on the "revenge" of Nature in her "howling melancholy", ibid. 429–31; and note also Allen Ginsberg's comments, *The Paris review* 37 (Spring 1966) 38–9. On "mystical fool" as Jung's formulaic expression for a prophet who is mocked and unacknowledged, see *ACU* 48 §98. Referring to this passage, John Dourley describes Jung as not only someone who made a

point of writing about the mystical fool but "as one himself"—although his book, titled *On behalf of the mystical fool* (Hove 2010, esp. vi–vii), would have been far richer if he had noticed the letter where Jung applies the same expression directly to himself. Jung's rationale for using such a phrase to evoke the figure of the unwelcome and unrecognized prophet could, to anyone who knew the Bible as well as he did, hardly be easier to understand. It was simply a matter of echoing the famous words of Hosea 9:7: "The prophet is a fool, the man of the spirit is insane, because of the enormity of your iniquity and the enormity of your hostility." See for this verse T. Jemielity, *Satire and the Hebrew prophets* (Louisville 1992) 138; also Rivkah Schärf Kluger's comments (*Psyche in scripture*, Toronto 1995, 37), later repeated by Marie–Louise von Franz (*Archetypal dimensions of the psyche*, Boston 1997, 12 = *Archetypische Dimensionen der Seele*, 2nd ed., Einsiedeln 2005, 23); compare *MC* 549 §783; and note Jung's description of himself at *MDR* 328/356 as a "fool" because no one could perceive or understand his vision, together with D. Tacey's comments, *The darkening spirit* (Hove 2013) 41. On the forgotten but time-honoured art of evoking and echoing such phrases or images from sacred scripture, which until recently played such a central role in western culture and literature and communication, cf. *APMM* 42–3.

[94] Trying to finish the *Red book* and complete the last painting: *ETG* 387 ("… Er konnte oder wollte es jedoch auch jetzt nicht vollenden. Es habe, so sagte er, mit dem Tod zu tun"); *RB* 221a. The last painting: *RB* 169. Jung's visions of people who soon would die: *MDR* 42/30. For the deletion of the original passage by his family because it was too explicit in documenting Jung's prophetic powers, see A.C. Elms, *Uncovering lives* (New York 1994) 64. The deleted passage can

still be found and read in the typescript of *Memories, dreams, reflections* held at the Countway Library of Medicine in Boston (*MDRC* 23): Jung himself had made a point of emphasizing in it that such visions of faces are nowhere near as insignificant, or innocuous, as most people usually assume them to be. The quest for the impossible: F. McCormick in *Carl Gustav Jung, 1875–1961: a memorial meeting* (New York 1962) 13. Magically making the impossible possible: *PT* 262 §443.

[95] The "unsayable": *JP* 359–60, reworked for publication as *MDR* 211/222; D. Bair, *Jung* (Boston 2003) 597. For the mystical implications, in such a context, of the unspeakable or "unsagbar" see e.g. D. Hell, *Soul hunger* (Einsiedeln 2010) 52 with n.2; the language in referring to a completely different reality from ours is, also, not mine but Jung's (*JP* 359). *Mysterium coniunctionis* and the transcendent: *JP* 233, to be read in preference to the dressed-up version at *MDR* 210–11/221; and, for the transcendent, compare the final pages of the book itself (*MC* 547–53 §§781–9). For the modern mantra that, far from being a religious person or prophet, Jung was simply a detached psychologist engaged in studying the "religion–making process" see e.g. S. Shamdasani, *JAP* 44 (1999) 543 and *RB* 212a ("religious–making process", ibid., is presumably a misprint). Jung on his psychology as "a movement of the spirit which took possession of me and which I had to and was allowed to serve all my life": *JK* 157 (cf. *JL* ii 104; January 1953). This of course, like pretty much everything else he says about himself during the last ten years of his life, is very different from the contemporary idea of Jung as an independent and freewheeling player never willing for a moment to let the archetypal reality of the unconscious "dictate to him as a servile mortal who must obey or face doom" (M. Stein, *JAP* 56, 2011, 603).

[96] Illness and the experience of ecstatic mystical union in 1944: *MDR* 270–7/289–97; the inner reality of the experience remained with him to the end of his life (M. Serrano, *C.G. Jung and Hermann Hesse*, London 1966, 60). Unspeakable: *MDR* 274–5/294–5. For the immediacy of Jung's closeness to death after 1944 see the material gathered by Sonu Shamdasani in *Quadrant* 38/1 (2008) 21–4, although to describe this natural development as "a critical shift in Jung's perspective on life" (23) is to risk underestimating the extent to which it represented a return to the intense familiarity with death that was already guiding Jung at the time of his work on the *Red book* (cf. e.g. *RB* 266–7, 273–5, 323a; *BB* v 168–75; S.L. Drob, *Kabbalistic visions*, New Orleans 2010, 219). *Aion* as something he was forced to write: *JW* 103 = *JL* i 480. For the direct connection between it and his experience of deification through becoming the lion-headed god Aion almost forty years earlier, compare the frontispiece of the book with *RB* 252; *IJP* 103–8; *JPPF* 4/1 (1912) 322–3 and *ST* 108 n.72, 279 n.21, 280–1 §§425–6 plus plate XLIV; *SL* 121 §266; *CD* 63–4, 205, 225, 249; R. Noll, *Spring* 53 (1994) 12–60; E.F. Edinger, *The Aion lectures* (Toronto 1996) 17–18, 190–2; L.S. Owens, *PP* 54 (2011) 281. Similarly, it was the work of writing *Aion* that would plunge Jung back into the direct presence of his spiritual teacher and father Philemon (*JL* i 480–1, 491–2 = *JW* 103–4, 116–18; Owens 278–9). On Aion as both god and concept see e.g. C. Lackeit, *Aion* i (Königsberg 1916); G. Zuntz, *Aion, Gott des Römerreichs* (Heidelberg 1989) and *Aion in der Literatur der Kaiserzeit* (Vienna 1992); G. Casadio in *Religion im Wandel der Kosmologien*, ed. D. Zeller (Frankfurt 1999) 175–90. "Before my illness … everything was perfect": M. Ostrowski-Sachs, *From conversations with C.G. Jung* (Zurich 1971) 68. For Joachim of Fiore see Jung himself, *Aion* 82–7 §§137–42, 149–50 §§232–5, 253 §399 with plate II; Joachim's teaching

of world ages is, very significantly, already present in Jung's *Black books* (*BB* v 163; *RB* 370a; C. Maillard, *Cahiers jungiens de psychanalyse* 134, 2011, 127–8). Joachim's "vision": *JW* 220 = *JL* ii 136, cf. M. Reeves, *Joachim of Fiore and the prophetic future* (London 1976) 3–5, 19 with L. DeVun, *Prophecy, alchemy and the end of time* (New York 2009) 47 as well as J.V. Fleming in *Joachim of Fiore and the influence of inspiration*, ed. J.E. Wannenmacher (Farnham 2013) 75–98; and for Joachim's own "secret" knowledge, M. Goldish, *The Sabbatean prophets* (Cambridge, MA 2004) 12–13. Of course other prophets also figure prominently in *Aion*—for Ezekiel see *JK* 171 = *JL* ii 118; for Gnostics and prophecy, *Aion* 184 §287; for Nostradamus, ibid. 95–102 and 125–6 with Owens 280—but none of them plays as crucial a role as Joachim. "Path of blood and suffering": *PP* 6 (1975) 12. "The vast majority … splitting of the world": *JW* 222, cf. *JL* ii 137–8 (November 1953). Jung's "remarkable leap": P. Bishop, *Jung's 'Answer to Job'* (Hove 2002) 154. "As a modern Joachim di Fiore …": J.P. Dourley, *JJTP* 8/1 (2006) 44, cf. his *On behalf of the mystical fool* (Hove 2010) 56, 120–1, 175. On Merlin as "taken up again" by Jung in his psychology see *MDR* 216/228; for the phrase's karmic implications, ibid. 295/319. For the intertwining of prophetic traditions derived from Joachim of Fiore with prophetic traditions ascribed to Merlin, cf. Reeves, *The influence of prophecy in the later Middle Ages* (Oxford 1969) 47, 52–3, 56 with n.4, 57 with n.3, 93–6, 222, 253 n., 434, 537–40; D.L. Hoffman in *Culture and the king*, ed. M.B. Shichtman and J.P. Carley (Albany 1994) 113–28; Wannenmacher, *Hermeneutik der Heilsgeschichte* (Leiden 2005) 272–305.

[97] Jung's identification with Merlin: *JP* 211, 223. For Hebrew prophets already denying that they are prophets see especially the classic example of Amos 7:14 ("I am not a prophet");

Å. Viberg, *Tyndale bulletin* 47 (1996) 91–114, who in effect explains Amos' archetypal denial as a deliberately ironic and self-disparaging way of avoiding inflation (111–13); M.J. de Jong, *Isaiah among the ancient Near Eastern prophets* (Leiden 2007) 323–8; also M. Dean–Otting's comments in *Encyclopedia of psychology and religion* (2nd ed., New York 2014), ed. D.A. Leeming, 1389. For Joachim of Fiore's notorious denials that he was a prophet see e.g. M. Reeves, *The influence of prophecy in the later Middle Ages* (Oxford 1969) 13–16, 42; B. McGinn, *Apocalyptic spirituality* (Mahwah 1979) 100; K.–V. Selge, *Deutsches Archiv für Erforschung des Mittelalters* 46 (1990) 92 with n.21. Other prophetic figures denying that they were prophets: Reeves 226; R.E. Lerner, *The powers of prophecy* (Berkeley 1983) 184; L. DeVun, *Prophecy, alchemy and the end of time* (New York 2009) 47. For the particular case of John of Rupescissa, whose work was well known to Jung (*Aion* 146 §226 with n.87, 241 §379, 265 §420, *MC* 192 §244, etc.), see DeVun 44–8 and 183 n.75: on one hand, at times he openly compared himself to the Old Testament prophets but on the other hand his "claim to visionary authority was certainly not without risk. Prophetic visions were thought to have been common before the incarnation and during the time of the early Church, but thereafter miracles and visions increasingly aroused suspicion" which could easily lead to imprisonment or death. Jung on the indispensability of knowing the Bible: *JV* i 442. On the almost universal ignorance nowadays about biblical prophecy and prophetic tradition see Mitch Glaser's recent comment: "I can safely say that, in the United States, most Jewish people would recognize Isaiah as the first name of a professional athlete sooner than they would recognize the prophet of biblical literature" (*The gospel according to Isaiah 53*, ed. D.L. Bock and Glaser, Grand Rapids 2012, 239). The best introduction to the interests and studies of Jung's father is still J. Ryce–Menuhin in *Jung and the monotheisms*, ed. Ryce–Menuhin (London 1994) 233–40 (for references to Isaiah and Jeremiah see 236, 239, 240) with Nicholas Battye's comments on the importance of these same interests to the son, ibid. 168–70, 184, 190 n.131; see now also B.D. Walfish and M. Kizilov, *Bibliographia karaitica* (Leiden 2011) 408. For Jung's unconscious acknowledgement of his father's inner immersion in Old Testament wisdom and learning, which is clearly much more than a compensation for his conscious attitude towards him, cf. *MDR* 203–10/213–20; David Tacey's superficial portrayal of the relationship between son and father as a conflict between prophet and priest ignores the many subtleties of the situation, just as Tacey's unwittingly new–age misuse of the word "prophet" dilutes it to the point of meaninglessness (*The darkening spirit*, Hove 2013, 45–6, 51–2). It will be noted that, in Jung's family, not only his father but also his maternal grandfather Samuel Preiswerk was a biblical expert and Hebrew scholar too (*ETG* 405–6; H.F. Ellenberger, *The discovery of the unconscious*, New York 1970, 661; A. Jung, *JAP* 56, 2011, 657).

[98] *Answer to Job* as damnable, Jung himself as bourgeois coward alongside the "unspeakable fool": *JL* ii 155. Landing the whale: ibid. 17–18. The magnificent music: ibid. 116 (*HC* 328 = *AJ* 157). The one book he would never want to rewrite or change: M.–L. von Franz, *C.G. Jung: his myth in our time* (New York 1975) 161; but this isn't to say he didn't initially spend a huge amount of energy revising the text that had just come through him, and removing its more obvious crudities (*KI* 1; D. Bair, *Jung*, Boston 2003, 528; S. Shamdasani in C.G. Jung, *Answer to Job*, Princeton 2010, viii). *Answer to Job* as a necessary compensation for the "man-made" politeness of *Aion*: *JL* ii 155; on the relationship between the two books see also *PR* 357, *JL*

ii 281–2, *MDR* 206/216. For the thread connecting *Answer to Job* back to the *Red book* see Jung in *Combat* (9 October 1952) 7 ("I waited for forty years to write it ... for almost forty years"), cf. *JS* 225, 234; Shamdasani in Jung, *Answer to Job* ix–x and *JAP* 55 (2010) 41; L.S. Owens, *PP* 54 (2011) 273 and in A. Ribi, *The search for roots* (Los Angeles 2013) 31. On the links between *Answer to Job* and the *Seven sermons to the dead*, in particular, see e.g. *JN* 299 (5 December 1951); letter from Cary Baynes to Carl Jung dated 31 March 1952 (*CBA*); Henry Corbin, *EJ* 31 (1962) 11–12 = *AJ* 175–6 and in C.G. Jung, *Réponse à Job* (Paris 1964) 260–1 = *AJ* 158–9; L. Schlamm in *Dreaming the myth onwards*, ed. L. Huskinson (Hove 2008) 118 n.3. It came through sickness: *JL* ii 18, 34 (*JN* 309), 112, 116 ("pendant une maladie, dans la fièvre": *HC* 328 = *AJ* 157), 155; von Franz 161; P. Bishop, *Jung's 'Answer to Job'* (Hove 2002) 41. Repeatedly when describing the onset of *Answer to Job* Jung emphasizes how helpless and choiceless he was, swept along by its arrival and unable to stop it: *JL* ii 18 ("*tour de force* of the unconscious"), 20 (its arrival was just "like the spirit seizing one by the scruff of the neck"), 39–40, 112 ("not mine to control ... like it or not"), 116 ("Le livre 'm'est venu'": *HC* 328 = *AJ* 157); also *JP* 302. For the comments from people near to him about the experience of living through the time when he was working on *Answer to Job*, and for his gardener as "closer to reality. Jung lived now in another world", see Bair 528. On his earlier sleeplessness while writing *Aion* see especially *JW* 118 = *JL* i 492 (also *JW* 103 = *JL* i 480, or ii 18 for *Answer to Job*); and note that in many ways this took him back to the sleepless nights he had experienced during, as well as after, the height of his work on the *Red book* (*RB* 211, 223a, 237 n.81, 238b, cf. 262a, 264b, 296a and, later, *MDR* 273–4/293). Compare also his telling observations about the sleeplessness that comes with entering the world of archetypes (*NZ* i 283–5)—as well as his general philosophy that, "when one could not sleep", this meant "the unconscious had something to say and one should get up and write to find out what was waiting for expression" (T. Keller, *Inward light* 35, 1972, 11 = *The memoir of Tina Keller-Jenny*, ed. W.K. Swan, New Orleans 2011, 20–1 §48, cf. 35 §94).

[99] Arguing not about God but directly, without keeping any distance, with God: *JN* 309 = *JL* ii 34. Thanked by his father for writing *Answer to Job*: S. Shamdasani in C.G. Jung, *Answer to Job* (Princeton 2010) ix n.5; Cary Baynes, for her part, was not impressed (*NL* 170). Compare with this Jung's comments on the inability of his father, while still alive, to quarrel with God (*MDR* 96–7/92–3) as well as the crucial dream he had of his father which anticipated the task of writing *Answer to Job* (*JP* 80–2; *MDR* 206–10/216–20; M. Stein, *JAP* 52, 2007, 312). Job and Christ as suffering servants: *MDR* 206/216. For Jung on the "deceptive light" of reason see e.g. *ACU* 93 §173. "I live in my deepest hell ...": M.-L. von Franz, *C.G. Jung: his myth in our time* (New York 1975) 174; compare *JN* 309 = *JL* ii 34, "I have to be everywhere *beneath* and not *above*". On the "tragic self-contradiction" of God see *ETG* 220 ("tragische Gegensätzlichkeit"; cf. *MDR* 206/216). Jung finds himself accused of anti-Semitism or, at the very least, anti-Judaism because of *Answer to Job*: note e.g. A. Jaffé's comments, *Was C.G. Jung a mystic?* (Einsiedeln 1989) 74–5 together with the observations by R. Valois, *Laval théologique et philosophique* 48 (1992) 293; S.M. Wasserstrom, *Religion after religion* (Princeton 1999) 177, 232–4 with *Journal of the American Academy of Religion* 69 (2001) 461; and writers such as J.A. Pople (*To speak well of God*, Fair Oak 2009, 81–2) who accuses both book, and author, of satanic folly. Such critics show no awareness of the extent to which radical questioning of God and arguing with the divine are essential aspects of Jewish piety (F. Rosenzweig,

Gesammelte Schriften i/1, The Hague 1979, 694; C.E.M. Struyker Boudier in *Questions and questioning*, ed. M. Meyer, Berlin 1988, 13–14; D.A. Frank, *Argumentation and advocacy* 41, 2004, 74, 79) or of the very particular recent tendency in Judaism to revive the ancient prophetic privilege of arguing with God as "a form of post–holocaust Jewish theology" (D.R. Blumenthal, *Modern Judaism* 12, 1992, 105–110). Jewish traditions in *Answer to Job*: L. Schlamm in *Dreaming the myth onwards*, ed. L. Huskinson (Hove 2008) 115, 117, 118 n.9; S.L. Drob, *Kabbalistic visions* (New Orleans 2010) 213, 290 n.28; and compare also Henry Corbin's comments in *HJ* 264 = *AJ* 107; there is more than a little irony in the way that certain Jewish authors have taken issue with Jung's *Answer to Job* for not being Jewish enough (É.A. Lévy–Valensi, *Job: réponse à Jung*, Paris 1991: cf. Valois 291–5). For the specifics of Jewish prophets challenging and arguing with God see e.g. A. Laytner, *Arguing with God* (Lanham 1990); Frank 71–86. "In a very real sense it's an argument with God ..." ("In gewissem Sinne ist es ein Streitgespräch mit Gott, ein Anliegen ähnlich dem Abrahams, als er mit Gott rechtete ..."): *JN* 298 (5 December 1951), cf. *JL* ii 33 n.1. I have translated "in gewissem Sinne" here, coming straight after "eigentlich", as "in a very real sense" because "in a certain sense" fails to convey the force or strength of the German original. Neumann is referring in particular to Abraham's argument with God about the fate of Sodom: Genesis 18:22–33. Abraham described as a prophet: ibid. 20:7; Neumann's comparison of Jung to Abraham of course has extra poignancy because ever since Jung was a boy he had, instinctively, been compared to Abraham (*JP* 49, *MDR* 74/66). On Habakkuk as archetypal arguer with God see e.g. Laytner 29, 180–2, 252 n.14, 270 n.19; for some extended comments on the closeness between the biblical Book of Habakkuk and the Book of Job see D.E. Gowan, *The triumph of faith in Habakkuk* (Atlanta 1976); and note that Jung himself interprets Job's predicament not only in the light of Abraham's argument over Sodom but also with the help of Habakkuk (*Aion* 58–60 §§105–111). The cry of Habakkuk: Habakkuk 1:2, 2:11.

[100] For Jung's awareness of the most apparently ordinary objects as living and conscious beings see e.g. *IJP* 28; *JS* 147; *JL* ii 344; M. Serrano, *C.G. Jung and Hermann Hesse* (London 1966) 98. Philemon, "beloved father of prophets" (*RB* 154), as giver of the awareness that even one's most ordinary thoughts are conscious living entities: *JP* 24, *MDR* 176/183. This same awareness of everything, even one's own thoughts or words, as living and conscious beings is included—according to the "Gnostic–Hellenistic" world Philemon belonged to (*JP* 23–4, cf. *MDR* 176/182)—in the gift traditionally given to prophets. See e.g. Theophrastus, *On the senses* 4 = A.H. Coxon, *The fragments of Parmenides* (2nd ed., Las Vegas 2009) 142–3 §45 for the case of Parmenides (*pan to on echein tina gnôsin*); Empedocles fr. 110.8–10 Diels = fr. 156.10–13 Gemelli Marciano with *ENM* 399–404, *Reality* 518–33; *Corpus hermeticum* 13.11 (a passage well known to Jung) and the Hermetic *Asclepius* 19 with R. Reitzenstein, *Poimandres* (Leipzig 1904) 214–50 plus *ENM* 351 and n.39, 353. Marie–Louise von Franz is a fine example of the disciple who takes turns at transforming the unmediated experience of everything as alive into an item of dogma, dutifully learning certain of its signs and symptoms by rote, and nervously trying to dismiss it as a joke (*FRJ* i 51:01–55:26; *MH* 1:13:55–1:16:03; *PP* 38, 1998, 16, 26–7). On the crucial importance for Jung of his pipe smoking see e.g. *JL* ii 105; B. Hannah, *Jung, his life and work* (New York 1976) 281 (through his near–death experience in 1944 he left everything as well as everybody behind until "the

only earthly thought that crossed his mind was that he hoped no one would disturb his pipes, as if somewhere he knew he was going to need them again"); D. Bair, *Jung* (Boston 2003) 564 (after Emma Jung's death in 1955 he sat "staring into a distance that only he could see. He even forgot to fuss with his many pipes, which alarmed his children most of all"). Habakkuk as the name of Jung's tobacco pot: A. Jaffé, *From the life and work of C.G. Jung* (2nd ed., Einsiedeln 1989) 145 (his tobacco was kept by him "in a dark bronze box, which for some unaccountable reason bore the name 'Habakkuk'"); R. Hayman, *A life of Jung* (London 1999) 309–10; G. Lachman, *Jung the mystic* (New York 2010) 146–7; I am very grateful to Jung's grandson Andreas for giving me a photo of Habakkuk. Handed down from his grandfather: *MDR* 329/358.

NOTES TO PART 4

[1] "Effort of spiritual struggle ... one might even say that they are frankly hostile to them": 'Abd al-Razzâq Lâhîjî in H. Corbin, *Spiritual body and celestial earth* (Princeton 1977) 171; cf. *APMM* 381, 387. For Corbin's use of the term "prophetic philosophy" see especially *EJ* 31 (1962) 49–116; *Histoire de la philosophie islamique* (Paris 1964 and 1986: *History of Islamic philosophy*, London 1993); *L'Iran et la philosophie* (Paris 1990: *The voyage and the messenger*, Berkeley 1998); *EII* i 12–13, 43–53, 235, iii 222–3, 249–50 and iv 68–83, 418–24; *Corps spirituel et terre céleste* (2nd ed., Paris 1979) 12–13 (*SB* xii–xiii); and note in particular his emphasis on the tradition that, without this unbroken chain of prophetic philosophy, humanity would be totally deaf and blind and lost (*EII* iv 419 = *L'homme et son ange*, Paris 1983, 251; cf. Parmenides fr. 6.4–7 Diels = fr. 13.5–8 Gemelli Marciano). On the great Presocratics, most notably Empedocles, as links in the chain of prophetic philosophers see e.g. *EII* i 225 n.194, ii 70 n.88; *Corps spirituel* (2nd ed.) 12 (*SB* xii); P. Lory, *Jâbir ibn Hayyân, L'Élaboration de l'élixir suprême* (Damascus 1988) 14–16; *APMM* 371–91. There even happened to be Persian Sufis who were perfectly aware of the crucial role Aristotle played in distorting and corrupting this tradition of prophetic philosophy by trying to make sure

that "the traces of the paths of the ancient sages disappeared" (Shahrazûrî in *OMM* ii 5.19–6.6 = *SSO* 80–1; J. Walbridge and H. Ziai, *Suhrawardî: The philosophy of illumination*, Provo 1999, xl–xli; *APMM* 387). It perhaps should be noted that modern academics who make a specialty of venturing into the field of esotericism have taken Corbin, as well as me (K. von Stuckrad, *Numen* 49, 2002, 214–15), to task for the apparent mistake of finding meaning in the subjects we write about: "the moment a scholar leaves the position of impartiality or 'methodological agnosticism'" and highlights certain "claims and opinions as more true or valuable than others, he starts practicing what I have been referring to as 'eclectic historiography' on the basis of some philosophical or theological *a priori*" (W.J. Hanegraaff, *Esotericism and the academy*, Cambridge 2012, 310). Of course what these academics conveniently fail to mention is the elephant in the room—the huge philosophical and theological assumptions, collective as well as unspoken, under which they themselves labour. If such a rumoured "position of impartiality" exists, as a genuine objectivity, it lies far beyond the reach of such scholars.

[2] "One colleague from a distant country … 'the mouth speaks from the fullness of the heart'": *HC* 51 (June 1978); cf. A. Schimmel in H. Corbin, *Die smaragdene Vision* (Munich 1989) 16–17, H.T. Hakl, *Eranos* (Sheffield 2013) 165. *Secretum meum mihi* (*to mystêrion mou emoi* in Greek: R.R. Ottley, *The book of Isaiah according to the Septuagint* ii, Cambridge 1906, 223) is quoted by Corbin from the Latin Vulgate version of Isaiah 24:16. *Ummah* is the specific term in Islam for any group of loyal people who gather around a prophet and, of course, around Muhammad in particular. "The mouth speaks from the fullness of the heart": Matthew 12:34, Luke 6:45.

[3] "Absolute spiritual freedom": *Revue de culture européenne* 5 (1953) 12 = *HJ* 265; cf. *HC* 48 ("integral spiritual freedom"). Jung "said that if we belong to the secret church … can bring us there": Esther Harding's note of her conversation with Jung at his home in Küsnacht on 5 July 1922, *Quadrant* 8/2 (Winter 1975) 9; cf. *JS* 29. Jung here cites in particular the alternative manuscript tradition of Luke 6:4, "If thou knowest what thou doest, blessed art thou …" (A. Resch, *Agrapha*, 2nd ed., Leipzig 1906, 45–8). For Jung on the invisible or spiritual church see e.g. *CS* 19–20 with *RB* 211 n.176, *MC* 12–61 §§9–12, *JL* ii 215; for Corbin on the "secret church" compare passages such as his *Temple et contemplation* (2nd ed., Paris 2006) 315, 456.

[4] *HC* 46 (June 1978). Significantly, for anyone who understands these things, Corbin goes on to suggest that the only people he could talk with in Istanbul about his experiences were Bektashi Sufis. From a strictly historical perspective, it will be noted that he had first been introduced to Suhrawardî's work by Louis Massignon ten years earlier (ibid. 16, 40–1). For the meaning of *ketmân* compare Corbin's comments in *EJ* 30 (1961) 74, 93; ibid. 39 (1970) 126 = *L'homme et son ange* (Paris 1983) 187; *EII* iii 177, 297, iv 244. This cryptic account of the crucial encounter with his inner teacher was not brief enough to prevent some modern scholars from twisting and misusing it to further their own foolish ends by finding support in it either for their allegation that Corbin was a fascist (S.M. Wasserstrom, *Religion after religion*, Princeton 1999, 146–7, cf. *Journal of the American Academy of Religion* 69, 2001, 461) or for their naïve attempt to portray him as a "rational gnostic" (J.J. Kripal, *The serpent's gift*, Chicago 2007, 109–10). On the other hand, it was too brief to prevent Daniel Proulx from describing Corbin's famous experience at a Swedish lake in 1932 as

"the only spiritual experience he ever spoke of": a mystical experience which is "extremely important because in the life of Corbin it represents the one moment when he touched the divine mystery" (*Os trabalhos da imaginação: abordagens teóricas e modelizações*, ed. J.–J. Wunenburger, A.F. Araújo and R. de Almeida, João Pessoa 2018; for the experience in Sweden see *HC* 62–3). This sadly misguided attempt to reduce the mystical component of Corbin's life to a single if formative experience is an unfortunate by-product of the modern academic insistence on promoting Corbin the philosopher at the cost of suppressing, as much as possible, Corbin the mystic. But Corbin, on his own public admission and as confirmed to me in private on numerous occasions by his wife, was an *Ishrâqî*; for any *Ishrâqî* in the lineage of Suhrawardî, the direct experience of a mystic and the clear thinking of a philosopher were equally indispensable (see e.g. *AE* xvi–xx with *EII* ii 68–72 as well as iii 223, where Corbin emphatically appeals to the Jungian concept of individuation); and, if for some reason a choice ever had to be made between them, the mystical would instantly take priority and precedence over the philosophical (ibid. ii 71). As Daryoush Shayegan observes, what distinguished Corbin from his colleagues wasn't the fact that he understood and explained the materials he commented on better than anyone else. It was the fact that he had lived, and personally experienced, everything he wrote about (*Mélanges offerts à Henry Corbin*. ed. S.H. Nasr, Tehran 1977, 29).

[5] With regard to the meaning of *ishrâq*: the majority of scholars have strangely lost touch with the basic reality that, for Suhrawardî himself, the sense of the word will have been determined above all by the famous passage in the Qur'an where it refers to the glorious moment of the sun rising over the mountains at dawn (38:18; compare *IDPW* 89–90).

Corbin became perfectly aware of this reality and stated it with increasing clarity as he got older. See for example his immensely quotable summary at *SB* 110: in the teaching of Suhrawardî the word *ishrâq* "takes on a technical meaning. In the literal sense, it is at one and the same time the geographic East ... and the hour when the horizon is lighted by the fires of dawn. In the true sense—that is to say, in the spiritual sense—the Orient is the world of the beings of Light, from which the dawn of knowledge and ecstasy rises in the pilgrim of the spirit. There is no true philosophy which does not reach completion in a metaphysic of ecstasy, nor mystical experience which does not demand a serious philosophical preparation. And such precisely was the *dawning* wisdom ..." Also compare e.g. *Les motifs zoroastriens dans la philosophie de Sohrawardî* (Tehran 1946) 27–31; *Histoire de la philosophie islamique* (2nd ed., Paris 1986) 290–3; *AE* xiv–xv (" ... On ne doit donc pas se contenter de traduire le mot *Ishrâq* par 'illumination' ..."); *L'Iran et la philosophie* (Paris 1990) 131. It will be noted that not only his reference in every single one of these texts to the Latin expression *cognitio matutina* or "dawn consciousness" (cf. *AS* 247–50 §§299–303), but also his later tendency to translate *ishrâq* as *aurora consurgens* (e.g. *AE* xiv, *SB* 110–11), are eloquent witnesses to the interests he would come to share with Carl Jung. To be sure, when Corbin published his first ever piece about Suhrawardî in 1933, he started by reciting the opinion that the word *ishrâqî* simply meant "illuminative" (*Recherches philosophiques* 2, 1932–33, 371–3); but this is only because, at that early stage, he was still heavily under the influence of older western scholarship on Suhrawardî such as Max Horten's *Die Philosophie der Erleuchtung nach Suhrawardi* (cited ibid. 372 n.1). Corbin's own private copy of the Horten book, which came into his possession at Berlin in June 1936 (for his stay at Berlin see S. Camilleri and D. Proulx, *Bulletin heideggérien* 4, 2014,

21–2 with nn.42, 46; Proulx, *De la hiérohistoire*, PhD thesis, Université catholique de Louvain 2017, 211–14) and which the tram tickets still tucked away inside the book show he took with him to Turkey in 1939, was given to me in 1995 by Stella Corbin. The marginal notes inside it eloquently express his growing criticisms of Horten and his progressive departure from Horten's intellectual positions.

[6] "I was drawn … National Library": *Problèmes et méthodes d'histoire des religions: Mélanges publiés par la Section des Sciences religieuses à l'occasion du centenaire de l'École pratique des Hautes Études* (Paris 1968) 130 = *L'Iran et la philosophie* (Paris 1990) 99. The English translation destroys the deliberate repetition ("I was drawn … Then Suhrawardi took me …": *The voyage and the messenger*, Berkeley 1998, 91), which is all the more significant in its deliberateness because the French verb "entraîner" also means "to train" someone: Corbin is in effect, on another level, describing the inner training that Suhrawardî put him through. For Jung's highly stylized repetitions at the start of the *Red book*—"forces … took … robbed … forced … took … robbed …"—describing how he was held fast by the spirit of the depths, see folio i verso = *RB* 229b and the continuation into 230a. For Parmenides' incantatory repetition of the verb "carry", four times in the first four verses of his poem, see fr. 1.1–4 Diels = fr. 8A.7–10 Gemelli Marciano; *IDPW* 53–4, 119–20, *ENM* 370–80, *Reality* 26–7, 34–6, *SW* 90, 103–7. Our "superiors": Empedocles fr. 5.1 Diels = fr. 10.4 Gemelli Marciano; *Reality* 544–56.

[7] "Eternal leaven" (*al-hamîrat al-azaliyyah*) and "leaven of the Pythagoreans" (*hamîrat al-faithâghûriyyîn*): *OMM* i xli–xlii (Corbin emphasizes, xlii with n.61, that this eternal leaven

serves the purpose of constant "revivification"), 502–3; G. Böwering, *The mystical vision of existence in classical Islam* (Berlin 1980) 52; *APMM* 388–9; P. Kingsley in *Crossing religious frontiers*, ed. H. Oldmeadow (Bloomington, IN 2010) 43; and note the similarities with Jung's awareness of himself as a naturally leavening force ("if life had led you to take up an artificial attitude, then you wouldn't be able to stand me, because I am a natural being. By my very presence I crystalize; I am a ferment. The unconscious of people who live in an artificial manner senses me as a danger. Everything about me irritates them, my way of speaking, my way of laughing. They sense nature": *JJW* 51–2). On the factors contributing to Suhrawardî's execution for heresy see e.g. Corbin, *L'homme et son ange* (Paris 1983) 194; H. Landolt, *Journal of the American Oriental Society* 107 (1987) 481 and 119 (1999) 485; H. Ziai in *The political aspects of Islamic philosophy*, ed. C.E. Butterworth (Cambridge, MA 1992) 336–43 with nn.104, 108; A.-M. Eddé in *La religion civique à l'époque médiévale et moderne*, ed. A. Vauchez (Rome 1995) 236–41. Suhrawardî and Empedocles: Corbin, *Recherches philosophiques* 2 (1932–33) 377–8; *Les motifs zoroastriens dans la philosophie de Sohrawardî* (Tehran 1946) 23; *OMM* ii 24; *SSO* 80, 88, 150–1 (cf. J. Walbridge and H. Ziai, *Suhrawardî: The philosophy of illumination*, Provo 1999, xl, 2, 107–8), 242–4, 253; *APMM* 375 n.12, 380–90; Walbridge, *The leaven of the ancients* (Albany 2000) 29–54.

[8] For the subterranean but potent influence of Mani and Manichaean Gnostic tradition on Suhrawardî see e.g. Corbin's *Les motifs zoroastriens dans la philosophie de Sohrawardî* (Tehran 1946) 49 n.47 with *AE* 27 n.20, 40, 87 n.115, 268 plus the further references in 280 n.c, 281 n.6, 400 plus 409 n.17 (on

Mani's reputation as a painter), 475; *OMM* ii 51–5; *EII* ii 57–8; *SSO* 408 n.a; also *APMM* 380–4 with n.38; and for a few general observations on Manichaean influences in Islam cf. M. Gil, *Israel oriental studies* 12 (1992) 38–41 with A. Esmailpour, *Manichaean gnosis and creation myth* (Sino–Platonic papers 156, Philadelphia 2005). It will be noted that, in private, Corbin talked of himself as not only an *Ishrâqî* but a Gnostic: see, for example, his letter to Gershom Scholem dated 2 November 1973 and reproduced by Paul Fenton in *Henry Corbin: philosophies et sagesses des religions du Livre*, ed. M.A. Amir-Moezzi, C. Jambet and P. Lory (Turnhout 2005) 163–4. For his published comments on the wisdom embedded in oriental traditions of spiritual chivalry, and their links to the western Grail legends, see e.g. his foreword to *Traités des compagnons-chevaliers*, ed. M. Sarraf (Tehran 1973) 5–12; *EII* iv 410–30 and *L'homme et son ange* (Paris 1983) 202–60 with C.-H. de Fouchécour in *Henry Corbin: philosophies et sagesses* 137–9; cf. also *IDPW* 217–19. "My Iranian friends … ulterior motive": *HC* 51 ("c'est là, je crois, ce qui mit parfaitement à l'aise mes amis iraniens pour me témoigner … une amitié libre de toute arrière-pensée").

[9] On the blunt criticisms of Corbin by both Seyyed Hossein Nasr and 'Allâmah Tabâtabâ'î for failing to take a physical teacher or, by implication, convert to Islam see S.H. Nasr and R. Jahanbegloo, *In search of the sacred* (Santa Barbara 2010) 105; also ibid. 93, where a false etymology of the word "orthodoxy" is used by Seyyed Hossein Nasr to press his religious concerns ("The main point of difference that I had with Corbin concerned the question of orthodoxy, which … means to possess the truth"). Nasr not only permitted but clearly encouraged one of his closest disciples to contrast

Nasr's own "authentically Sufi" voice with the writings on Sufism by Corbin which, because he had never converted to Islam and so was not "a Sufi in a tenable sense of the term", are devoid of any fundamental legitimacy or authority (ibid. xxix); he also implies as much, himself, by insisting that the sacred teachings of Suhrawardî can only be "fully assimilated" through participation in "an orthodox tradition" (*The Islamic intellectual tradition in Persia*, ed. M.A. Razavi, Richmond, Surrey 1996, 169). On Corbin's refusal to become a Muslim, or accept a physical teacher, cf. also Nasr, *Temenos Academy review* 2 (1999) 35 = *Ésotérisme, gnoses et imaginaire symbolique*, ed. R. Caron, J. Godwin, W.J. Hanegraaff and J.–L. Vieillard–Baron (Leuven 2001) 785; H.T. Hakl, *Eranos* (Sheffield 2013) 356 n.113. Nasr appeals in the context of Corbin's inner spirituality to the Uwaisîs, Khidr and Elijah: *In search of the sacred* 105; Corbin for his part, far from considering the attachment to an inner teacher as opposed to an outer *sheikh* unusual or questionable in Islam, even judged it the most primordial and least decadent form of Islamic spirituality (X. Accart, *Politica hermetica* 16, 2002, 185). For the romantic cliché of Suhrawardî stretching out his hand and taking the hand of his disciple see Nasr, *Traditional Islam in the modern world* (London 1987) 277 ("almost literally"), 284; *Temenos Academy review* 2 (1999) 37, 40 = *Ésotérisme, gnoses et imaginaire symbolique* 787, 790. Nasr was willing to take much more seriously al–Hallâj's "visitation" of Louis Massignon, who had been the formal teacher and predecessor of Corbin in Paris (*Traditional Islam* 254–6); but this is simply because he had particular uses for Massignon which were quite separate from the ways that, on his own candid admission, he "made use" of Corbin (*In search of the sacred* 93). To him Henry Corbin would always be someone who had a special imaginative "ability to fly into the world of traditional philosophical and spiritual speculation and meditation" (*Traditional Islam* 274) while his experience of Suhrawardî, far from being choiceless or imposed on him, was ultimately just the result of his own human wanting and choosing ("Corbin wanted to have a spiritual guide but did not want to have a human guide": *In search of the sacred* 105).

[10] For the quintessential mistranslation of Suhrawardî's "eternal leaven", *al–hamîrat al–azaliyyah*, as "eternal dough" see S.H. Nasr, *Islamic philosophy from its origin to the present* (Albany 2006) 159; subsequently reprinted in *The essential Seyyed Hossein Nasr*, ed. W.C. Chittick (Bloomington, IN 2007) 112. Ironically, Nasr had introduced his book by summarizing my work on Parmenides and Empedocles "in order to demonstrate that the relation between philosophy and prophecy … is of great significance not only for the understanding of Islamic philosophy but also for a deeper comprehension of the origins of Western philosophy itself" (*Islamic philosophy* 1–5; compare Nasr's reviews of my books in *Journal of Islamic studies* 8, 1997, 242–4 and *Parabola* 29/2, Summer 2004, 106–11). Perhaps even more ironic in the light of such a blatant mistranslation is the enthusiastic praise Nasr had showered on Louis Massignon, Corbin's academic teacher, for stressing the importance of arriving at a precise appreciation of the technical vocabulary used by Sufis if one wants to understand what they mean (*Traditional Islam in the modern world*, London 1987, 260–1). That this mistranslation is no accident but a deliberate and doctrinaire alteration of Suhrawardî's teachings is quite clear from the fixed set of beliefs Nasr, as a "Traditionalist" Muslim, was labouring under. Whereas Corbin had a fine appreciation for Suhrawardî's vision of sacred history in which "every exoteric opposition between Greek sages and 'oriental' sages disappears", and according to which spiritual traditions

naturally jump between East and West and then back again (*EII* ii 35–6; cf. e.g. *OMM* i xlii and *SSO* 245 with, on the historical accuracy of these movements, P. Kingsley, *JWCI* 57, 1994, 1–13), for Nasr the only true end point or starting point can be the religion of Islam ("the primordial religion, a return to the original religion of oneness, and the final religion": *The heart of Islam*, New York 2002, 18 = *The essential Seyyed Hossein Nasr* 54). To him, all previous revealed or prophetic traditions were only truly activated and brought to their "full glory" in the protective fold of Islam (*Islamic philosophy* 159 = *The essential Seyyed Hossein Nasr* 112; compare *The heart of Islam* 18). As for Nasr's assertion that Suhrawardî, in tracing his lineage back to figures such as Empedocles, was talking not historically but only symbolically: this has to be understood in the light of his theological claim that prophets owe nothing to the past or to history because they receive all their wisdom straight from God (Islam rejects the idea that it has inherited older prophets' teachings "through temporal and historical transmission, for a prophet owes nothing to anyone and receives everything from Heaven": ibid. 18). That Suhrawardî was not establishing a historical link between himself and earlier, pre-Islamic figures (Suhrawardî "never mentions historical chains connecting him to this long tradition of wisdom", *Islamic philosophy* 159; aside from choosing to use pre-Islamic symbols "his spiritual affiliation was certainly completely Islamic", *An introduction to Islamic cosmological doctrines*, 2nd ed., London 1978, 191) is palpably untrue: see e.g. G. Böwering, *The mystical vision of existence in classical Islam* (Berlin 1980) 52–5, *APMM* 386–90. And to insist that Suhrawardî saw the link to his predecessors as not historical but just symbolic (see now also H. Ziai in *The political aspects of Islamic philosophy*, ed. C.E. Butterworth, Cambridge, MA 1992, 344; A. Hartmann in *Biographical encyclopaedia of Sufis: Central Asia and Middle East*, ed. N.

Hanif, New Delhi 2002, 465) is, if nothing else, ridiculously disrespectful; not many people go to their deaths for "only" a symbol. Besides, to formulate such a simplistic contrast between the historic and the symbolic is to rationalize and also trivialize the meaning of the word "symbol" itself—which for both Suhrawardî (*OMM* ii 24; *SSO* 88–9 with 89 n.a, 243) and Corbin (see e.g. *AWA* 13–14 on the importance of healing the split "between symbol and history"), as well as Jung, includes and embraces physical reality because it's so much greater. These are all examples of what happens when a little bit of spiritual truth is trapped inside intelligent but rigid minds, only to be changed into something piously false. And at the same time the apparently simple mistake of translating "leaven" as "dough" is a vivid reminder of how, through one strategic mistranslation, an entire worldview can be distorted and destroyed.

[11] "Extraordinary joy ... intellectual vacuum": letter from Jung to Corbin dated 4 May 1953 (*FC*); *HC* 328 = *AJ* 156, cf. *JL* ii 115. Jung went on to describe the "avalanche of prejudice, misunderstandings and, above all, atrocious stupidity" he had been buried under and Corbin himself, in later reflecting on these words of his, would shrewdly talk about the "vigilant incomprehension" that was surrounding Jung (C.G. Jung, *Réponse à Job*, Paris 1964, 248 = *AJ* 150; compare Jung's own repeated reference to those things that are "assiduously overlooked": e.g. *Aion* 173 §268, *MC* xvii). The mystical theme of horses recognizing each other by their smell is appropriate, and traditional: "Those who in this world live in joy and agreement with one another must have been akin to one another in yonder place. Here they love one another and are called the friends of God, and they are brethren who

love one another for God's sake. These souls know each other by the smell, like horses. Though one be in the East and the other in the West, yet they feel joy and comfort in each other's talk" (R.A. Nicholson, *Studies in Islamic mysticism*, Cambridge 1921, 56; Mohammad Ebn-e Monavvar, *The secrets of God's mystical oneness*, Costa Mesa 1992, 466). For the gross misrepresentations in Tom Cheetham's now–standard account of the relationship between Corbin and Jung, see e.g. his *All the world an icon* (Berkeley 2012) 130–89. Corbin's thrills and excitement: ibid. 137, 158. His failure to carve in stone: ibid. 140. Most of Cheetham's bizarre examples of "why Corbin had such trouble with Jung" (158)—such as the contradiction he claims to find between Corbin's rejection of the collective and Jung's acceptance of it (147–9, 152: "Here again is Corbin's protest against the authority of the Church, any church … Here he makes his differentiation from Jung clear once more")—show that even though he may have taken some trouble to read Jung's words, he had little success at understanding them. Ironically it was Corbin himself who warned against the great dangers of misunderstanding the word "collective" in Jung's notion of a "collective unconscious" (*HC* 48); but in vain. For the infinite complexity of the real relationships, on an esoteric level, between what outwardly can appear to be quite different individuals or groups see my comments in *Journal of the Royal Asiatic Society* 3 (1992) 339–46; *IDPW* 160–92; *Reality* 477–99.

[12] For the first meeting between Corbin and Jung, "si cordial, si communicatif et plein de promesses", see Corbin's letter to Olga Fröbe–Kapteyn dated 6 September 1949 (*FC*; *AJ* 163). Corbin had already referred to the *cognitio matutina* or "consciousness of dawn" in *Les motifs zoroastriens dans la philosophie de*

Sohrawardî (Tehran 1946) 28; compare his later elaborations on the theme in e.g. *L'homme de lumière dans le soufisme iranien* (Paris 1971) 91–2 = *The man of light in Iranian Sufism* (Boulder 1978) 59. Jung had published an important piece about the *cognitio matutina* during the year before their meeting: *Symbolik des Geistes* (Zurich 1948) 144–8; cf. *AS* 247–50 §§299–303. This "synchronicity" of converging interests, as Jung would have called it, was referred to by Corbin as "homophonie": *HC* 262 ("... une 'homophonie', dont le sentiment nous a chaque fois bouleversés ..."); H.T. Hakl, *Eranos* (Sheffield 2013) 165; and for the general sentiment compare R. Bernardini, *Historia religionum* 5 (2013) 100.

[13] Corbin would describe his encounter with Jung over *Answer to Job*, and over his own review of it, as "a great encounter which took place between us, our previous encounters had only been its prelude" (letter to Carl Jung dated 14 August 1953, *FC*). He had already hailed Jung's *Aion* as a magnificent piece of work (letter to Olga Fröbe–Kapteyn dated 22 November 1951, *FC*; R. Bernardini, *Historia religionum* 5, 2013, 101). "The rarest of experiences ... completely understood": letter from Jung to Corbin dated 4 May 1953 (*FC*); *HC* 328 = *AJ* 156, cf. *JL* ii 115. For *Answer to Job* as music see Corbin's review in *Revue de culture européenne* 5 (1953) 37 = *HJ* 285, Jung's response in his letter dated 4 May 1953 (*FC*; *HC* 328 = *AJ* 157, cf. *JL* ii 116) and Corbin's later comments in C.G. Jung, *Réponse à Job* (Paris 1964) 255–6 = *AJ* 155. Murray Stein offers a useful sketch of the extent to which "*Answer to Job* occupies a unique place in Jung's published oeuvre" (*JAP* 52, 2007, 311–13). But by presenting Father Victor White as the decisive trigger that initiated the entire creative process he is simply contributing to the progressive, and degenerative, tendency in Jungian psychology to personalize and also trivialize the

numinous. It's not Victor White who was the piece of sand in the oyster that gave rise to this literary pearl (ibid. 310). The irritating piece of sand was called Carl Jung.

[14] On *Answer to Job* as embodying the most essential aspect of Jung's work and task see *MDR* 206/216. The stupidity of the medical profession, together with its attitude of mockery towards everything that *Answer to Job* represents—as well as the intense awareness that this collective rationalistic attitude had become his own idiocy, a part of his own shadow—is beautifully encapsulated by Jung in the account he gives of the related dream he had about the two Brunner doctors (*JP* 80–1, *MDR* 207–8/217–18). As he would sum up the same situation in 1953: "the clinical practice of psychotherapy is a mere expedient, which prevents numinous experiences as much as possible" (*JK* 171). For Jung's painful confrontation with the stupidity and stubbornness of his own "dull conscious mind" see the letter he wrote to Henry Murray on 2 May 1925 (Papers of Henry A. Murray, Harvard University Archives; cf. *JL* i 42, *RB* 215a).

[15] On the incomprehension Jung encountered even among his most trusted Jungian analysts in Zurich, when he solicited their reactions to *Answer to Job* before the book was ready to be released, see *KI* 1; *JK* 157 n.4. His own considered response could hardly have been more to the point: very few people anywhere will be able to understand the book "and analysts are not exceptional people" (*JK* 157, 29 January 1953). By no means is it insignificant that even James Kirsch, who prided himself on his uniquely sympathetic appraisal of *Answer to Job*, was reprimanded by Jung for approaching the book in a way that was "too rational" (ibid. 149). Jung's followers and Christ's disciples at Gethsemane: *JP* 306–8.

[16] For Henry Corbin on Jung as a prophet, and on *Answer to Job* as a work of prophecy, see especially *Revue de culture européenne* 5 (1953) 16 ("ce même livre ... n'est plus simplement de la psychologie, mais ressortit à la philosophie prophétique"), 23, 33 ("ce qui est proprement la perspective prophétique et eschatologique chez Jung"), 37 ("prophète de la Sophia éternelle"), 38 = *HJ* 269, 274, 282, 285, 286. Aniela Jaffé was quick here to catch the essential and, at the Eranos gathering in 1974, was only too happy to ascribe to Corbin the idea of Jung as a prophet which she would hardly dare attribute to herself (*Was C.G. Jung a mystic?*, Einsiedeln 1989, 94 = *EJ* 43, 1974, 358); it will be noted that Henry Corbin was physically present as a participant in this Eranos gathering and spoke at length on the theme of visionary prophecy (ibid. 183–254). Recently, English-speaking commentators have taken it upon themselves to claim that in his review of *Answer to Job* Corbin committed some major mistakes of interpretation and that Jung made an even bigger mistake in imagining Corbin had understood him (so L. Schlamm, *Harvest* 50/2, 2004, 189 followed by T. Cheetham, *All the world an icon*, Berkeley 2012, 146–7). These commentators should not be blamed too much for their own confused and mistaken impression that everyone else was mistaken and confused, because they unwisely were basing their judgements on the appalling "translation" of Corbin's review into English which has been published by Molly Tuby (*Harvest* 31, 1985, 7–22). Aside from being riddled with inaccuracies (for example her "Darkness has received Light which has vanquished it", ibid. 18, fails completely to convey the multiple resonances in Corbin's account of how according to Christian dogma "les Ténèbres aient enfin reçu la Lumière et que la Lumière les ait prises et captivées": he is commenting here on *PR* 468 §756), Tuby's version is rendered worse than useless by the way that she chopped up Corbin's

words and—supposedly for the sake of saving space—gouged out most of the essential connecting passages in his review. The fine thread of logic running through his text is repeatedly snapped, statements are torn out of their context, and the original sense is turned into nonsense. As for the disaster of hacking such a delicate and extended piece of argument to bits: Corbin himself already said everything that needs to be said when, apologizing to the original French publisher for the length of his review, he explained how he'd tried in vain to reduce its size only to realize that to cut anything out "would be a massacre ... one has to have the whole of it available in front of one's eyes" ("ce serait un massacre ... Il faut qu'on ait tout sous les yeux à la fois": letter to Sten Melry dated 19 March 1953, *FC*). And there are far larger issues at stake here, as well. To take the naïve theoretical position that in Jung's own eyes light and darkness were simple equals waiting to be integrated with each other psychologically is to ignore what Corbin himself, when referring to Jung's psychology, described with such appropriateness as "the lived situation" ("la situation vécue": *La table ronde* 97, 1956, 37 = *L'Iran et la philosophie*, Paris 1990, 235). We forget everything of any real importance when we fail to remember that Jung viewed his essential task as being "to illuminate the stupidity, darkness, and unconsciousness of mankind" (*SL* 671–2 §§1515–17, 827–9 §§1827–33); or fail to remember his very dualistic grief on seeing, just before he died, how naïve he had been "in not expecting the darkness to be so dense" (E. Rolfe, *Encounter with Jung*, Boston 1989, 176). As Corbin so rightly says, with Jung we are dealing not just with psychology but also with prophecy. Aside from Corbin's own important comments on the subject (*Revue de culture européenne* 5, 1953, 16; *HJ* 269) compare also James Kirsch's account of how "in *Answer to Job*, and in some letters written after *Answer to Job*," Jung very clearly states that "he, as a psychologist, is, in fact, the prophet of the direct experience of God" (*KI* 5). And for Corbin's way of defining a prophet see e.g. *HC* 131 (also *SB* xii), "Le prophète, ce n'est pas quelqu'un qui prédit l'avenir, mais l'inspiré qui profère le verbe de l'invisible, le surhumain que l'inspiration divine instaure en médiateur entre la divinité inconnaissable et l'ignorance ou l'impuissance des hommes": far from being a fortune-teller, the prophet is someone who has been "put in place by divine inspiration as mediator between the unknowable divine and the ignorance or impotence of mankind".

[17] Erich Neumann on Jung and Abraham: *JN* 298 (5 December 1951), cf. *JL* ii 33 n.1. For James Kirsch on Jung as prophet and *Answer to Job* as a prophetic work see his lecture, which significantly has never been published, on "C.G. Jung's individuation as shown especially in *Answer to Job*"; the references in the text of this lecture (*KI* 15) to his own piece on Jung and Freud which was published by *American imago* in 1984, as well as to Alfred Ribi's paper on Jung and Elijah which was published in the 1984 issue of *Harvest*, show that he composed it during the very last years of his life. "He, himself, told me ... afraid to look at him": *KI* 8. This closeness of Jung to Moses fits very well with the 1924 dialogue between Jung and Cary de Angulo about his very privileged relationship to the biblical pillar of fire (draft letter from Cary de Angulo to Jung dated 26 January 1924 = *RB* 213b; cf. Exodus 13:21–2, 14:24, Numbers 14:14, Nehemiah 9:12–14) as well as with the powerful dream, so intimately linked to the creation of *Answer to Job*, in which the part of himself represented by his father is reading straight from the Books of Moses only to be greeted by the utter incomprehension of everyone listening (*JP* 80, *ETG* 221). Also worth noting, in this context, is Jung's comment to Tina Keller about his hair turning grey as a result

of the overwhelming visions and experiences he had during the time of his work on the *Red book* (R. Noll, *The Aryan Christ*, New York 1997, 152): on the strong tradition of prophets' hair turning grey as a direct result of their visions and revelations compare, for instance, the famous case of Muhammad (*Tafsîr ibn Kathîr*, abridged edition, Riyadh 2003, v 17, cf. Qur'an 73:17).

[18] For the continuing conversation about *Answer to Job* after both the book, and Corbin's review of it, had been published see *HJ* 264 (the review "fut le point de départ de longs entretiens amicaux sur tous les points soulevés à propos du livre …") with his letter to Olga Fröbe–Kapteyn dated 5 September 1953 (*FC*; R. Bernardini, *Historia religionum* 5, 2013, 105); for the meetings first at Ascona, then at Küsnacht and Bollingen, *HC* 48. "Alas!": Corbin in C.G. Jung, *Réponse à Job* (Paris 1964) 255; the specific memories he offers here of "ce qui fut, hélas! notre dernier entretien" make it clear that he is referring to their discussion in September 1955. The handwritten notes which he left behind of that discussion, dated "2 September 1955—Küsnacht", have been preserved in Paris together with Stella Corbin's typed transcript (*FC*). With characteristic disregard for detail, Michel Cazenave offers the vaguest reminiscence of Stella Corbin once showing him some notes from her husband about a discussion between him and Jung which had led Corbin to "complain" that Jung misinterpreted what he was saying by understanding it on a psychological level (*Carl Gustav Jung*, Escalquens 2011, 103; cf. Bernardini 95): this, too, almost certainly goes back to Corbin's notes of their discussion in September 1955 (Cazenave's memory of it taking place at Ascona rather than Küsnacht is in line with his usual, sometimes even self-conscious, confusions over points of fact). To be sure, a couple of important errors in Stella Corbin's typed

transcript made such misinterpretations of what happened between Jung and Corbin only too easy. First, she ends her record of their interaction on a note of discord—with Corbin appearing to complain that Jung was only considering the case of someone who is mentally ill whereas he, Corbin, was considering the ideal case of a mystic. But it's quite plain from his original handwritten notes that he had wanted to bracket these words in parentheses as an issue of subordinate, rather than primary, importance. And, even more significantly, she omitted Corbin's three crucial final words which he had written in Greek on a line of their own: *monos pros monon*, "alone to alone".

[19] For *sohbet* see e.g. Coleman Barks' *Rumi: the book of love* (New York 2005) 12 ("Sufis say there are three ways of being with the mystery: prayer, then a step up from that, meditation, and a step up from that, conversation, the mystical exchange they call *sohbet*"), 102 ("The *sohbet* of Friendship is … an encounter with 'a person like the dawn'"). On the tradition of mystical dialogue among Bektashi Sufis in particular, whom Corbin became intimately familiar with during his wartime years at Istanbul (*HC* 46), compare F. Trix, *Spiritual discourse* (Philadelphia 1993). To experience exactly what one is saying, and say just what one is doing, is standard procedure in the context of Bektashi *sohbet* (ibid. 145: "what Baba did by singing of muhabbet during a time of muhabbet was name the closeness and pleasure and joy we were having in each other's company"); James Hillman has well noted Corbin's uncanny ability to be what he said and become the physical embodiment of his words (*The thought of the heart*, Dallas 1981, 1–2).

[20] For the history of the expression *monos pros monon* see e.g. A.F. Segal in *Studies in Gnosticism and Hellenistic religions*

presented to Gilles Quispel on the occasion of his 65th birthday, ed. R. van den Broek and M.J. Vermaseren (Leiden 1981) 371–2 with n.53; K. Corrigan, *Journal of religion* 76 (1996) 28–32; Z. Mazur in *Gnosticism, Platonism and the late ancient world*, ed. Corrigan and T. Rasimus (Leiden 2013) 346 n.65; P. Kalligas, *The 'Enneads' of Plotinus* i (Princeton 2014) 210. On the phrase as a decisive marker, in Corbin's writings, for the process of individuation see especially *ARV* ii 94–107, 142 (*Avicenna and the visionary recital*, London 1960, 81–92, 121). For those who live the inner reality of *monos pros monon* as "solitary, authentically alone, freed from every collective norm" see Corbin in C.G. Jung, *Réponse à Job* (Paris 1964) 252 = *AJ* 153, but note also the strong contrast he draws in his original review between Jung "*seul*, fort de la seule force de son âme", and more or less everyone else ("Car combien d'hommes, aujourd'hui, peuvent prétendre être vraiment les 'représentants' d'*eux-mêmes*, alors qu'ils ne représentent que les normes collectives, les dogmes officiels, les opinions toutes faites?": *Revue de culture européenne* 5, 1953, 13–14 = *HJ* 267). For the language here, of aloneness and being authentically oneself, compare Corbin's own translation of Martin Heidegger (*Qu'est-ce que la métaphysique?*, Paris 1951, 160–4); in Sufi tradition these "solitary ones" are known as the *afrâd* (C. Addas, *Quest for the red sulphur*, Cambridge 1993, 71–8). "In the sense that no one else is present to such intimacy": Corrigan 32. For the old meaning of *monos pros monon* in the context of human conversation cf. e.g. ibid. 31 with J.–M. Narbonne, *Plotinus in dialogue with the Gnostics* (Leiden 2011) 98; Corbin always retained an awareness that the formula implies some kind of actual dialogue ("dialogue seul à seul", *L'imagination créatrice dans le soufisme d'Ibn Arabî*, 2nd ed., Paris 1977, 210: the detail is lost in the English translation). His use of the formula in introducing Jung's *Answer to Job*: *Revue de culture européenne* 5

(1953) 12–14 = *HJ* 265–7. "It's because we find ourselves, here, ...": ibid. 14 = *HJ* 267. Jung on the process of individuation as becoming a solitary star: *BB* v 167–9 (the absolutely critical word "Einzelsein", "singleness" or "uniqueness", is mistranslated at *RB* 370b as "individuality"); compare also *MDR* (New York 1973) 388 = *RB* 352–3, where "Einzelsein" is already translated as it should be ("singleness", directly corresponding in sense to Greek *monos*). For Corbin describing, just before he died, the inevitability of his "separation" from Jung see *HC* 48–9; for Jung on the secret of individuation as the highest mystery of the Grail, *JP* 308–9; and for Corbin on the ultimate aloneness of God cf. e.g. *AWA* 184. "The ultimate, the unforgivable, truth ...": *Revue de culture européenne* 5 (1953) 23 = *HJ* 274; Corbin's comments here about the pages of *Answer to Job* coming to life as a prophetic hymn are repeated by him, word for word, in C.G. Jung, *Réponse à Job* (Paris 1964) 255 = *AJ* 155.

[21] "Music only has any purificatory virtue ...": C.G. Jung, *Réponse à Job* (Paris 1964) 255–6 = *AJ* 155 ("la musique n'a vertu de *katharsis* que si elle nous conduit à une expérience *visionnaire* intérieure, au sens fort et prophétique de ce mot").

[22] Jung was already discussing Khidr, together with Elijah, at length in 1912 (*JPPF* 4/1, 1912, 236–45, 275 = *Psychology of the unconscious*, New York 1916, 216–27, 261; cf. *ST* 193–202 §§282–96). Compare also passages in his later writings such as *SL* 556 §1290, 675–7 §§1525–9, 738 §1672; *JV* ii 1285–6, 1312; *ACU* 122 §219, 133 §238, 135–47 §§240–58; *CD* 444–54; *JL* i 346 and ii 40, 571; and cf. N. Battye in *Jung and the monotheisms*, ed. J. Ryce–Menuhin (London 1994) 166–91. It should never be forgotten that for Jung the real goal of psychotherapy is to find "the unconscious guide that dwells within yourself" (S. Shamdasani, *Journal of sandplay therapy*

24/1, 2015, 8–9, 15), what Corbin typically describes as "the Khidr of your being" (*AWA* 61). Corbin, for his part, would refer with full approval to Jung's most celebrated treatment of Khidr while discussing Suhrawardî in his first-ever lecture at Eranos (*EJ* 17, 1949, 150–1 with n.45). The place where he himself talks most potently, as well as famously, about Khidr is *AWA* 32–93; on the major significance of Khidr for Ibn al–'Arabî see now C. Addas, *Quest for the red sulphur* (Cambridge 1993). To Corbin, it will be noted, the infinitely elusive and intimate experience of encountering Khidr is inseparable from the inner experience of *monos pros monon* or "the alone to the alone" (*AWA* 6). That Corbin was influenced by Louis Massignon's empathy for Khidr, and especially by Massignon's extraordinary paper on Khidr and Elijah (in *Élie le prophète*, ed. C. Baudouin, Paris 1956, ii 269–90 = *Opera minora*, Beirut 1963, i 142–61), is beyond question (*AWA* 55–7 with nn.18, 21). On the other hand, H.T. Hakl's suggestion (*Eranos*, Sheffield 2013, 120) that Jung was indebted to Massignon not only for much of what he knew about Islam in general but also for much of his knowledge about Khidr is chronologically impossible and more than a little wide of the mark.

[23] For the intensity of Corbin's involvement with Joachim of Fiore see e.g. *EII* i 167–70, iii 197–8, iv 443–9; *L'homme et son ange* (Paris 1983) 196–200, 231, 240; also his emphasis at *AE* 40 on Joachim's "primordial significance" for the history of western spirituality. With regard to the remarkable idea of "a true instead of a fantastical imagination", *vera imaginatio et non phantastica*: Carl Jung cites as his main source for this notion the *Rosarium philosophorum* (Frankfurt 1550, 12 = *Artis auriferae volumen secundum*, Basle 1593, 215; *PA* 167 §§218–19, 252 §355, 257 §360 with n.36, 276 §393). But compare also ibid. 250 §350, where he quotes another alchemical statement

that ordinary people are completely blind to what "the eyes of the intellect and of the imagination are able to perceive through true, through truest, vision" (*& vulgarium hominum oculi ista non vident, sed oculi intellectus & imaginationis percipiunt, visu vero, verissimo*: *Musaeum hermeticum*, Frankfurt 1678, 574). For Jung these statements offered the most perfect confirmation, from alchemy, of the initiatory teaching he had been given by his inner teacher Philemon: the teaching that the psyche, together with everything inside it, is real. See especially *MDR* 176/183; *SL* 665 §1505 and 775 §1740; and his personal account of the terror he experienced when encountering this reality for the first time, just like some man who entered his workshop "and found all the tools flying about doing things independently of his will" (*IJP* 28). "The real is what works": *TE* 217 §353. For this "reality" of imagination, or true fantasy, see also Jung's letter to Kurt Plachte dated 10 January 1929 in which he describes creative imagination as the only primordial reality which is immediately available to us (*JL* i 60); R. Bernardini, *Jung a Eranos* (Milan 2011) 138; and compare P. Bishop, *Analytical psychology and German classical aesthetics* i (Hove 2008) 111–16, who unfortunately omits any reference to Hermetic tradition. Very significantly Henry Corbin refers straight to Jung's discussion of *imaginatio vera* when touching on the subject during his first appearance at Eranos (*EJ* 17, 1949, 146 with n.33, 148 with n.39), just as he will continue to do later on (e.g. *SB* 11 with 274 n.24); his extremely casual use of the expression when writing, only a few weeks after the gathering, to the organizer of Eranos also shows how familiar it must have been at the time in Jung's immediate circle (letter to Olga Fröbe–Kapteyn dated 10 October 1949, *FC*; *AJ* 165). Needless to say, this idea of "true imagination" or the "imaginal" was to become a fundamental concern for Corbin throughout the rest of his life: note the urgency of the comments he wrote just a few months before he died (*SB* ix–xii, xviii). And it's impossible to overstate the importance of the fact (well understood by Bernardini 139) that, whatever may have been done by later Jungians to muddy the waters, on this central point Jung and Corbin were in full agreement. Hopefully there is no need to say too much about the continuity of the thread running all the way from Jung's dramatic initiation into the mysteries of "true imagination" by Philemon, father of prophets, right through to Corbin's constant reminder that the forgotten faculty of true imagination is the property of prophets. As far as Philemon is concerned: it can be helpful to note how exactly the ambiguity of his status as not only a prophet but also "the father of prophets" is reflected in the ambiguous situation of Khidr, who not only is a prophet but also has a unique status and "charisma superior to that of the prophets" (*SB* 314 n.25, cf. *EII* i 250 n.233, iii 25). And regarding Corbin's awareness of the essential link between *imaginatio vera* and prophecy, see for instance *Nouvelles de l'Institut catholique de Paris* (February 1977) 189–91 = *L'Iran et la philosophie* (Paris 1990) 135–9 (cf. *Temenos Academy review* 8, 1987, 229–32: "… the *Imaginatio vera* of the visionary contemplatives in the true sense of the word … all the visions of the prophets …"); *SB* ix–xiii. But the crucial point to remember here is that this connection between imagination and prophecy, which can seem so bizarre to us, has a vibrantly meaningful history extending back in time for two thousand years. See G. O'Daly, *Augustine's philosophy of mind* (London 1987) 120–7; E.C. Clarke, *Iamblichus' 'De mysteriis'* (Aldershot 2001) 98 n.112; A. Sheppard, *The poetics of phantasia* (London 2014) 77–88, 102 and in *On prophecy, dreams and human imagination*, ed. D.A. Russell and H.–G. Nesselrath (Tübingen 2014) 97–110; and compare also P. Kraus, *Jâbir ibn Hayyân* ii (Cairo 1942) 105 ("le prophète … possède …

une imagination parfaite"), a passage highlighted as specially important by Henry Corbin inside his own copy of Kraus' book which is in my possession. This broad historical background makes it all the more reassuring that even the occasional Jungian has been drawn to an awareness of the "prophetic capacity" inherent in what Jung described, so specifically, as true imagination (S. Salman, *Spring* 74, 2006, 180).

[24] To cite one example of the problems Henry Corbin already encountered during his lifetime, and that only intensified after he died: the usual grandiose narratives about the Université Saint Jean de Jérusalem which, in 1974, he helped to establish as a continuation of the work already done at Eranos (so e.g. R. Bernardini, *Historia religionum* 5, 2013, 107–8; W.J. Hanegraaff, *Esotericism and the academy*, Cambridge 2012, 341–3) need to be corrected and balanced by the humble fact that Stella Corbin finally had to close the entire affair down because the clash of egos among the major protagonists had become unbearable. "In matters of the spirit", as she said to me every time she went over what happened, "one does not compromise!" As for Corbin's striking diplomacy or chivalry when colleagues infuriated him and let him down, the clearest and most explicit example of his policy can be found in his correspondence with the Russian scholar Vladimir Ivanow. "Certainly there is more than one point on which we disagree ... but I made the very deliberate effort to slide over the fact so discreetly that no one, aside from you and me, would be able to notice ... I have always wished to avoid even the slightest hint or shadow of any polemic against you ... Alas, I fear that our inability to understand each other is beyond any remedy; but is it really necessary to make it public? ... Wouldn't it be better simply to agree? ... my dear Colleague ... From my side I have always adopted the same policy with your books of throwing

the spotlight on those points where you and I agree, while using the discreetest hints to skip past any point on which I take issue with you … All the best to you, my dear Colleague and Friend" (*Correspondance Corbin–Ivanow*, ed. S. Schmidtke, Paris 1999, 126–8). Corbin's closeness to the prophets towards the end of his life was mostly a matter of personal discussion between him and Stella—but it appropriately is reflected in some of the last words he ever wrote (*Cahiers de l'Université Saint Jean de Jérusalem* 5, 1978, 141, 169) and also echoed in the commemorative comments made by the friend he instructed to take care of ceremonies for his funeral ("Au sens le plus authentique de ce verbe, il 'prophétisait' …": R. Stauffer, ibid. 10; H.T. Hakl, *Eranos*, Sheffield 2013, 163).

[25] For Jung and Corbin as the two "immediate fathers" of James Hillman's psychology see in particular his *Archetypal psychology* (Dallas 1983) 2–3, where of course he mentions nothing of what actually happened. After the explosive episode in Paris which Stella Corbin remembered so clearly, her husband not only followed his normal operating procedure of treating Hillman as his dear colleague and friend (e.g. *HC* 49). Apotropaically he also went to the extent of inventing points of consensus where no real agreement existed, describing the metaphysical existence of the Persian Sufis' "imaginal world" as "my great meeting-point with our dear James Hillman"—even though, just one month later, he would warn that Hillman along with other Jungians hadn't understood this metaphysical reality at all (letter from Corbin to David Miller dated 9 February 1978, *FC*; cf. D.L. Miller, *The new polytheism*, 2nd ed., Dallas 1981, 4). And, interestingly, a similar sequence of events unfolded in Corbin's relationship with David Miller. Miller related to me during a long conversation in April 2014 how Corbin exploded into a furious outburst at their first encounter

because of a lecture Miller had just given about polytheism, with Corbin shouting that Miller didn't have a clue what he was saying. From then on, every year they met at Eranos, the Corbins were extra nice towards him and made sure to have a meal with him. But, as Miller himself agreed with me, even the famous congratulatory letter that Corbin wrote to him in February 1978 (reproduced at Miller's *New polytheism* 1–6, although Stella Corbin made sure to prevent him from publishing one paragraph which is vital for understanding the letter as a whole) has nothing straightforward or obvious about it. He pretends to agree with Miller about polytheism while, in fact, leading him on far beyond the positions with which Corbin is claiming to agree. Using a standard Sufi ruse, or teacher's trick, he appears to praise the pupil whereas all the time he is pointing straight past the pupil's concepts to something quite different. It's only too easy to see in the language of this letter Corbin's wholehearted "approbation" of Miller, or James Hillman (G. Shaw, *Dionysius* 21, 2003, 78 n.12), except that here too nothing is what it seems. Even the way in which Corbin dismisses the profanity and "frivolity" of Renaissance art (*New polytheism* 3) is, not only subtly but also obviously, a coded criticism of Hillman's whole approach.

[26] Aside from the pressing need Stella Corbin felt to describe what happened at her and her husband's Paris home, she also told me with the greatest intensity and suffering that the words he would go on to publish in March of 1978 just a few months before his death were aimed directly at Hillman even though for the sake of discretion he avoided mentioning Hillman by name. These were Corbin's words of solemn "warning" about the "great danger" of misusing the word "imaginal" and abusing the realities of true imagination by tearing them away from their mystical context as preserved in Sufi teaching

(*Corps spirituel et terre céleste*, 2nd ed., Paris 1979, 18; cf. *SB* xviii–xix). But that was more than enough to trouble a number of people. The popular American literary expert Harold Bloom, famous for his view that the whole of literature is nothing but a "weak" or "strong" misreading of older authors, confessed to his uneasiness at hearing a great man like Henry Corbin issuing such generic warnings (*AWA* xvi). And Tom Cheetham, after I relayed to him that Corbin had his sights set on James Hillman, decided to offer a public retelling of the "story" so he could point out how unacceptably rigid and old-fashioned Corbin was in getting "upset" with Hillman or bothering to issue any such warning (*Imaginal love*, Thompson, CT 2015, 23–31, 186–95). Even so, Hillman is still much better known for disregarding the warnings of that other "father" he found in Carl Jung; and there is more than a little truth in the argument that he only wanted fathers he could kill through a good old-fashioned patricide (D. Tacey, *JAP* 59, 2014, 472; for Hillman's admittedly "schizoid" relationship to Jung see D. Russell, *The life and ideas of James Hillman* i, New York 2013, 386–7). Jung himself had warned very solemnly that his psychology, and in particular the method of active imagination, "is not a plaything for children" (*SD* 68: "almost like a label on a modern-day consumer product", as noted by J.C. Miller, *The transcendent function*, Albany 2004, 13). But Hillman, as eternal child or *puer*, was determined to the end to make a plaything of them—always misunderstanding both Jung's and Corbin's simple warning that the only true *puer aeternus* is not the child who wants to remain a child but the young boy who has been born directly "from the maturity of the adult man" (*PR* 457 §742; *Revue de culture européenne* 5, 1953, 33 = *HJ* 282; C.G. Jung, *Réponse à Job*, Paris 1964, 251 = *AJ* 152). On Zoroastrian prophecies relating to disrespect for elders and contempt for their warnings, see e.g. *Zand–î vohûman yasn* 4.13–15 (ed. B.T.

Anklesaria, Bombay 1957, 20–1, 107); F. Cumont, *Revue de l'histoire des religions* 103 (1931) 81 with J. Bidez and Cumont, *Les mages hellénisés* (Paris 1938) i 215–22, ii 370–3. In Jewish tradition compare especially Isaiah 3:4–5 and, for the same theme in ancient Greece and Rome, Hesiod, *Works and days* 182–201; *The conflict of generations in ancient Greece and Rome*, ed. S. Bertman (Amsterdam 1976); J. Bremmer, *Zeitschrift für Papyrologie und Epigraphik* 39 (1980) 31.

[27] For Corbin's earlier encounters with Jungians see *HC* 48–9, where he makes it very clear that his need to differentiate between his work and Jung's was provoked to a large extent by the collective pressure from Jungians to make him one of their own. This is also where he significantly describes how, during the intimate discussions he and Jung held together, Jung in effect washed his hands of the so-called Jungians and their unconscious behaviour (ibid. 48). "With all the consequences this entails": *JL* ii 77 = *Jung on Christianity*, ed. M. Stein (Princeton 1999) 170.

[28] For Corbin's heartfelt feelings of fondness, love and gratitude towards Jung see e.g. the letter he wrote to Olga Fröbe–Kapteyn dated 4 January 1950 (*FC*, *AJ* 165, R. Bernardini, *Historia religionum* 5, 2013, 101); *Du* 15/4 (April 1955) 29 = *HC* 262; his letter to Fröbe–Kapteyn dated 11 June 1961 (*FC*, Bernardini 107); C.G. Jung, *Réponse à Job* (Paris 1964) 255 = *AJ* 155. But one plain sign of how tired he had become of the whole Jung business towards the end of his life, and how jarred his sensibilities had become due to the constant abuse of his term "imaginal" by Hillman in particular, is the complaint Corbin made just before dying that Jungian psychologists are totally incapable of distinguishing as needed between the true visionary nature of the imaginal and the

worthless self-indulgence of the imaginary (*HC* 49, repeated for example by C. Jambet, *La logique des Orientaux*, Paris 1983, 40–4). The great irony here is that the person who, with his rediscovery of the fundamental difference between true and false imagination, gave the most powerful impetus to Corbin's own distinction between the imaginal and the imaginary was none other than Carl Jung. Corbin himself had for years been perfectly well aware of this (see e.g. *EJ* 17, 1949, 146 with n.33, 148 with n.39; *ARV* iii 74 n.48; *SB* 11 with 274 n.24)—although it has become only too easy, thanks to the directions in which Jungian psychology ended up forging ahead, to forget that "in actual fact both Jung and Corbin distinguished between a 'genuine' form of imagination and an 'illusory' form" (Bernardini, *Jung a Eranos*, Milan 2011, 139). And just how close Jung and Corbin were to each other in their inner understanding of this matter can be shown by simply taking one from a number of different possible examples. So, for instance, nothing might sound more alien to Carl Jung's own interests or style than the emphasis placed by Henry Corbin on the traditional idea that only through linking up with the pure consciousness known to ancient Greeks as *nous* can *imaginatio vera* or true imagination offer full access to the prophetic realities (*Nouvelles de l'Institut catholique de Paris*, February 1977, 189–91 = *L'Iran et la philosophie*, Paris 1990, 135–9). But while Corbin was busy reading his Persian texts, Jung was busy reading ancient Greek texts; and that includes the extremely difficult text of Iamblichus' *On the mysteries*. In fact he was able to read parts of it in the original Greek, which is something very few people nowadays are even remotely capable of, and there was one specific passage that caught his attention. He carefully bookmarked the place where Iamblichus touches on the subject of ordinary human fantasy or imagination only to add that "none of this fantasizing is aroused when the life of consciousness inside us is fully activated" (*phantasia d' oudemia egeiretai tês noeras zôês teleiôs energousês*: *De mysteriis* 10.2). At the top of his paper bookmark, plainly inserted to remind him of this particular paragraph where Iamblichus is distinguishing between the normal human faculty of imagination and the state of pure consciousness or *nous* that exists far beyond it, Jung wrote the two words *imaginatio vera*. And he also slipped another bookmark further on into the same volume, at a point where the English editor has added a few words of explanatory commentary on this same passage: "The rites of initiation culminate in a vision of 'great things' (i.e. of gods and things divine). Porphyry has suggested that the things which men see in such visions are not realities, but are merely phantasms produced by their own imagination. Abammon denies this. In the men who see these visions, it is not *phantasia* or ordinary imagination, he says, but *nous* or pure consciousness, that is at work; and *nous* does not produce phantasms, but apprehends 'the realities that truly are'." The first bookmark was placed by Jung in his own copy of Walter Scott's *Hermetica* (iv, Oxford 1936) at pages 36–7 (I am very grateful to Vreni Jung for confirming that the two words at the top of it are indeed in Carl Jung's handwriting); the second was inserted at pages 88–9. Gregory Shaw's comments (*Dionysius* 21, 2003, 75–6) on the almost identical dichotomies between true and false imagination as presented both by Iamblichus and by Jungian psychology need some significant updating in light of the fact that Jung himself was, not just probably but demonstrably, reading Iamblichus.

[29] On Corbin's persistent defence of Jung in the face of Nasr's provocations, see Nasr himself: *Temenos Academy review* 2 (1999) 38 = *Ésotérisme, gnoses et imaginaire symbolique*, ed. R. Caron, J. Godwin, W.J. Hanegraaff and J.–L. Vieillard–Baron

(Leuven 2001) 788; also *The philosophy of Seyyed Hossein Nasr*, ed. L.E. Hahn, R.E. Auxier and L.W. Stone (Chicago 2001) 50. This isn't to say that, in the inevitable give-and-take, Nasr was above presenting himself as the injured party (*In search of the sacred*, Santa Barbara 2010, 92–3): on Corbin's own tendency to be just as provocative, in conversation, as his tone was mild in his published works see the personal letter from Stella Corbin to David Miller dated 2 June 1980 (*FC*: "Dans la conversation, Henry aimait parfois provoquer, jamais dans un livre"). For the constant onslaught of "Traditionalists" against Jung's psychology see e.g. René Guénon, *Symbols of sacred science* (Hillsdale NY 2004) 38–42 ("... 'inverse spirituality' ... 'reign of the Antichrist' ...") and *Le théosophisme* (2nd ed., Paris 1965) 425–6 with J. Biès in *René Guénon*, ed. J.–P. Laurant and P. Barbanegra (Paris 1985) 38 and X. Accart, *Politica hermetica* 16 (2002) 187; Julius Evola in *Sezession* 11 (October 2005) 5; Titus Burckhardt, *Mirror of the intellect* (Cambridge 1987) 45–67; Frithjof Schuon, ibid. 66–7 n.64 ("... the almost universal refusal of people to see the devil and to call him by his name ..."); Martin Lings in *The underlying religion*, ed. Lings and C. Minnaar (Bloomington, IN 2007) 113 n.7; Whitall Perry, *The widening breach* (Cambridge 1995) and *Challenges to a secular society* (Oakton, VA 1996); Philip Sherrard, *Studies in comparative religion* 3/1 (Winter 1969) 33–49; Wolfgang Smith, *Cosmos and transcendence* (2nd ed., San Rafael 2008); Jacob Needleman, *A sense of the cosmos* (Garden City, NY 1975); Harry Oldmeadow, *Journeys east* (Bloomington, IN 2004); Charles Upton, *The science of the greater jihad* (San Rafael 2011) with Samuel Bendeck Sotillos, *Sacred web* 33 (Summer 2014) 181–3; *Psychology and the perennial philosophy*, ed. Bendeck Sotillos (Bloomington, IN 2013). The general level of sustained incomprehension fuelling these criticisms is well captured by Seyyed Hossein Nasr's mocking dismissal of Jungian psychology as a "dead end" due to "the limitations of the ultimately agnostic views of Jung" (Nasr and R. Jahanbegloo, *In search of the sacred*, Santa Barbara 2010, 196). But it probably is worth offering one very characteristic example of the wilful twisting or skewing which is needed to create, then maintain, this collective and psychologically quite fascinating demonization of Jung. Recently he has been attacked, in the name of the Traditionalist cause, for claiming that the "concept of the 'transcendent'" is completely relative and points to nothing real beyond it (Bendeck Sotillos, *Sacred web* 31, Summer 2013, 147 n.7). One only has to look at the passage this author is citing, though, to see how crudely he has misquoted and distorted what Jung himself was saying—which is not that the philosophical "concept of the 'transcendent'" corresponds to no reality but that the concept "transcendent", as bandied around by people so happily, has no real meaning because they don't have a clue what they are talking about. And if one cares to read on in the same passage and see what Jung himself continues to say, nothing could be clearer than that he is not denying the existence of a transcendent reality. He is just pointing out the foolishness of people who get dangerously inflated by their fanatical absolutism because in the absence of any direct experience they turn their hollow beliefs, like many Traditionalists, into assertions of absolute truth so they can fill the emptiness they feel inside (*JL* ii 378–9). As for the author who is so bent on making Jung say what he didn't say: the only thing traditional about this Traditionalist is his adherence to the time-honoured ways of early Christian authorities who disposed of their enemies by twisting whatever they said, misleadingly inserting words of their own into passages they pretended to be quoting, then abruptly cutting off their opponents' statements to deprive them of their proper context (A. Busine, *Paroles d'Apollon*, Leiden 2005, 341–9; cf. e.g.

C.D. Stanley, *Paul and the language of scripture*, Cambridge 1992, 337). The truth is that Jung in his published writings often refers to the existence of a transcendent reality, only questioning our ability as fallible humans to access it or the ability of scientists to know it: see for example *PR* 363 §558, *MDR* 323–4/351–3, *JL* ii 352 and 368, also the unpublished letter from Jung to R.F.C. Hull dated 23 February 1954 (Library of Congress), plus his comments at *PR* 275 §417 on the crucial need to keep the transcendent reality a mystery even from oneself so as to stop the human intellect getting inflated by greedily grabbing hold of what doesn't belong to it. And note in particular the striking example of an Englishman who towards the end of Jung's life sent him a text he had written on alchemy that opens by quoting some words from Henry Corbin about the need for an "explosion" of all earthly limitations, even including one's human hopes, into a "*transcendence*" where every human limit is abolished. Jung's reply was equally affirmative and direct: "The fact is that the figures behind the epistemological curtain, i.e. the archetypes, are 'impossible' unions of opposites, transcendental beings … the *coniunctio* is an essentially transcendental, i.e. archetypal process … because it belongs inevitably to the transcendental, archetypal reality" (J. Trinick, *The fire-tried stone*, Marazion 1967, 13, 10, cf. *JL* ii 394–5; this correspondence between Trinick and Jung should be enough by itself to put paid to the gratuitous claim that Jung's views on transcendence were not only hopelessly confused but also diametrically opposed to Corbin's: see the profoundly confused account by T. Cheetham, *All the world an icon*, Berkeley 2012, 142–5). As a matter of fact, he even states that to deprive people of any transcendent reality is psychologically to destroy them (*MDR* 301/326). And, if one searches carefully, it's possible to find Jung describing his own experiences of such a transcendent reality. See the draft letter from Cary de Angulo to Jung dated 28 January 1924 (*CBA*) which records their shared experiences of the Master who transcends the universe: this passage also has to be set alongside their discussions about the absolute need to disidentify from the Master by leaving him free, completely uncaged, which she had noted down two days earlier in her draft letter dated 26 January (*CBA*; *RB* 213b). But most significant of all is Jung's account of what happened to him with the writing and completion of his last major work, *Mysterium coniunctionis*. In finishing it, he explains, he also acquitted himself of the task he had been born to perform by finally placing the whole of his work on its true foundation. And in that moment he arrived at the furthest boundaries of existence, coming face to face with the transcendent reality about which no statements can possibly ever be made (*JP* 233, subtly rationalized in *MDR* 210–11/221; at *JJ* 5/3, 2011, 70 Lionel Corbett acknowledges that "in Jung's later work" he "does, in fact, introduce a transcendent level to his theorizing", but fails to note the essential point that such "theorizing" was based on Jung's own experiences). This statement by Jung about his final book, and about at last arriving at the transcendent, needs to be placed side by side with what he says in the closing pages of the book itself. Right at the end of *Mysterium coniunctionis* he arrives, appropriately enough, at the theme of transcendent reality: after all, what he wrote is what he experienced because what he experienced is what he wrote. And the last ten pages can more or less be summed up in the following quotation. "The existence of a transcendental reality is, indeed, self-evident … That the world inside and outside us rests on a transcendental background is as certain as our own existence; but it is equally certain that the accuracy of our direct conception of the archetypal world inside us is just as questionable as the accuracy of the way we view the physical world outside us. If we are convinced we know the ultimate truth about metaphysical things, this means nothing more than that archetypal images have taken possession of our powers of thought and feeling ... The object about which we claim to have an opinion then becomes absolute and indisputable and surrounds itself with such an emotional taboo that anyone who dares reflect on it is automatically branded a heretic and blasphemer ..." (*Mysterium coniunctionis* ii, Zurich 1956, 324–34 §§431–44, especially 332 §442; cf. *MC* 544–53 §§776–89, esp. 551–2 §787). Jung goes straight on to illustrate this paradoxical reality of possession by the very same transcendent reality one is attempting to talk about: what he means by it is irrational "possession" in the strongest possible sense. In effect he is vividly describing all the symptoms of mental, as well as emotional, inflation from which Traditionalists have been suffering; and it's interesting to see how, by continuing to engage in their attacks on Jung, they are not only entering a one-sided debate. They are also walking right into the trap life has laid for them. To appreciate just what Jung means when he refers to the unconscious state of possession by the transcendent, all we have to do is read to the end of this same author's assault on Jung where he announces that of course there are "absolute criteria by which we can know the Supreme Reality with all certitude as the saints and sages of the plenary revelations have, such as Shankara, Ibn 'Arabî and Meister Eckhart" (*Sacred web* 31, 2013, 147 n.7; compare the even more grandiose statements about Meister Eckhart, Ibn al-'Arabî and Shankara by C. Upton, *Vectors of the counter–initiation*, San Rafael 2012, 56). In other words, by sitting at home and thinking the right thoughts we can delude ourselves that we "know" the supreme reality just as well as the greatest mystics who ever lived even though such a reality is totally beyond the grasp of our human intellects. Of course the only real question is whether it's wiser to trust those who merrily write about what they haven't experienced and would die of shock if they happened to come face to face with it; or someone who, by digging down through his whole life as deep as possible into himself, finally arrived at the transcendent reality beyond himself.

[30] For the ancient Platonic attacks on Gnostics see especially Plotinus, *Enneads* 2.9, Porphyry's *Life of Plotinus* 16 and *On abstinence from living things* 1.42, with e.g. J. Bernays, *Theophrastos' Schrift 'Über Frömmigkeit'* (Berlin 1866) 14–16, 143–5; H.-C. Puech in *Les sources de Plotin* (Entretiens Hardt; Vandœvres 1960) 161–90; J. Zandee, *The terminology of Plotinus and of some Gnostic writings, mainly the fourth treatise of the Jung codex* (Istanbul 1961); V. Cilento, *Paideia antignostica* (Florence 1971); C. Elsas, *Neuplatonische und gnostische Weltablehnung in der Schule Plotins* (Berlin 1975); Z. Mazur in *History of Platonism*, ed. R. Berchman and J. Finamore (New Orleans 2005) 95–112; *Gnosticism, Platonism and the late ancient world*, ed. K. Corrigan and T. Rasimus (Leiden 2013). On the rebirth of this invective against Gnosticism in modern times cf. Arthur Versluis, *The esoteric origins of the American renaissance* (New York 2001) 79–80; but to see how uncannily these archetypal conflicts reincarnate one only has to compare Titus Burckhardt's onslaught on Jung in his *Mirror of the intellect* (Cambridge 1987, 45–67) with Plotinus' onslaught on the Gnostics in *Enneads* 2.9. Just like Traditionalists nowadays, the Platonists of almost two thousand years ago claimed privileged access to an ancient or primordial tradition (Plotinus, *Enneads* 2.9.6; Porphyry, *Life of Plotinus* 16): a claim that, just as in the case of modern Traditionalism, is based on a total illusion. In fact it was the Gnostics who paradoxically had far greater access to what could be called a primordial or ancient tradition

than most Platonic thinkers (*ENM* 342 n.12, cf. ibid. 342–51, 382–6, 387 n.129, 398; *Reality* 198–9, 324, 375, 383, 417, 442–3, 552–3), and for the illusoriness of Platonists' general historical understanding see e.g. *APMM* 38–40, 302. Similarly the greatest hallmark of the Traditionalists, which has become their constant appeal to what they refer to as "intellect", is just one among many examples of how unprimordial their theories are. Henry Corbin strongly criticized them, from a Sufi point of view, for elevating this single term to a position of such isolated importance (*Revue de métaphysique et de morale* 68, 1963, 235–6, cf. *Histoire de la philosophie islamique*, 2nd ed., Paris 1986, 86–9); but from a western perspective its distance from any genuinely ancient or primordial tradition is even more striking. The notion of "intellect", Latin *intellectus*, derives above all from the world of medieval scholastic philosophy which just so happens to be the intellectual environment where contemporary Traditionalist thought is most at home. And in that world it had already become no more than a dim, pathetically distorted reflection of the Greek word *nous*—which originally meant not "intellect" but consciousness, immediate perception, the purest awareness, the organ of direct and lived experience (see *Reality* 77–82 with the further references in *SW* 124). It was this tortuous egoic process, which led via Plato and Aristotle from consciousness to all our notions of intellect, that ended up creating "one of the greatest absurdities, and tragedies, in the history of western culture" (ibid. 124, cf. 53–5); and the modern Traditionalist school, far from representing anything even close to primordial, is simply another small part of that tragic absurdity. Needless to say, the psychological paradox which comes into play as soon as people start over-emphasizing what they imagine the intellect to be is that they usually find themselves getting up to the strangest and bizarrest of tricks: on Frithjof Schuon as divine Avatar, quite unmoored, playing the role for his disciples of primordially naked Native American see M. Sedgwick, *Against the modern world* (New York 2004) 9, 170–7. For the Face of God in the Qur'an see especially 28:88 ("Everything will perish except His Face") and 55:26–7 ("Everyone on earth perishes; all that remains is the Face of your Lord").

[31] Although Henry Corbin's relationship to the so-called Traditionalist school and to René Guénon in particular has been described as "complex" (W.J. Hanegraaff, *Esotericism and the academy*, Cambridge 2012, 301 n.155), that complexity is largely an illusion. While still a young man in his early twenties he published, under a pseudonym, some brief but enthusiastic comments about Guénon's work. It will be noted, though, that even here he prefaced his positive assessment with strong reservations alongside some equally strong warnings against the perils of dogmatism (Trong–Ni, *Tribune indochinoise*, 15 August 1927, 4). But the situation changed radically after Guénon wrote a savage review of Corbin's first book on Suhrawardî, denouncing him as a gullible academic who failed to realize that Suhrawardî was just a philosophical thinker and not a genuine Sufi (*Études traditionnelles* 258, March 1947, 92; compare Martin Lings' later suspicions regarding Suhrawardî and concerns over his orthodoxy, ibid. 387, January–February 1965, 45–6). In other words, it was the symbolic re-enactment of Suhrawardî's trial and execution all over again. From this point onwards, Corbin's silence about the supposedly "esoteric" work of Guénon spoke volumes; but when he did choose to speak about Guénon in private, or write about him confidentially, or on one occasion publicly address the issue of Guénon's work after being provoked, his criticisms of its rigid "dogmatism" and "systematic rationalism" and "intellectualizing of the spiritual quest" were damning.

See *Revue de métaphysique et de morale* 68 (1963) 234–7, where Corbin replies in print to the Traditionalist attack by Muhammad Askari (cf. ibid. 5–6); Frédérick Tristan's report of his conversation with Corbin in June 1976 (*René Guénon*, ed. P.–M. Sigaud, Lausanne 1984, 205–6); the unpublished letter from Corbin to Richard Pickrell dated 28 September 1976 (*FC*); D. Bisson, *René Guénon* (Paris 2013) 403–6; D. Proulx in *Os trabalhos da imaginação: abordagens teóricas e modelizações*, ed. J.–J. Wunenburger, A.F. Araújo and R. de Almeida (João Pessoa 2018). And here one also needs to consider Corbin's warnings "against the illusory pretensions" of those intellectuals who allow themselves to get inflated with "an overweening and absurd spiritual pride" (*AWA* 131; X. Accart, *Politica hermetica* 16, 2002, 194). To be sure, there was a time when he would feel glad to find in Frithjof Schuon someone willing to take a stand against the evolutionary popularism of Teilhard de Chardin (*EII* iv 121 with n.154: cf. S.H. Nasr and R. Jahanbegloo, *In search of the sacred*, Santa Barbara 2010, 92–3); but to pretend that Corbin was ever tempted to side with the Traditionalists in attacking Carl Jung (as proposed by Ali Lakhani, *Sacred web* 23, Summer 2009, 162–3) means having to rely on the most hopelessly unreliable of sources combined, if one happens to be a Traditionalist, with sheer wishful thinking. "Really hit the roof" is Jung's expression, colourful but altogether appropriate where the Traditionalists are concerned, for what happened according to the Qur'an when a very stuffy and self-righteous Moses came face to face with Khidr: "Now Khidr is also someone who can appear in many different forms; in particular he appears as a wanderer in various places, appears all of a sudden and causes all kinds of situations. For you can imagine that good old Moses really hit the roof when Khidr played such tricks. All that approximately describes the peculiar psychological factor represented by Khidr. For obviously he is an unconscious figure that causes all kinds of frightening things, that makes you think: 'Now this goes awry, this goes all wrong,' but then it turns out to have been exactly the right thing ... All this expresses a sudden appearance from the unconscious, not understood at first, but then revealing itself as something of the highest value" (*CD* 451; compare John Dourley's comments on the "rage" experienced by "fundamentalist believers" when confronted with the work of Jung, *JAP* 47, 2002, 481). "So alien to our normal modern consciousness ... a lived experience": Corbin, *La table ronde* 97 (1956) 37 = *L'Iran et la philosophie* (Paris 1990) 235 (cf. *The voyage and the messenger*, Berkeley 1998, 221). "It was at Eranos that the pilgrim ... the eternal Sophia": *Du* 15/4 (April 1955) 29 = *HC* 262. For Jung on the mystery of the eternal Sophia or Sapientia see *RB* 155, 317 n.283; L.S. Owens in A. Ribi, *The search for roots* (Los Angeles 2013) 24, 285–6 n.85.

[32] For Corbin's text about Jung—already planned in 1953 and completed, in its present form, by 1955 but only published in 2014—see *AJ* 21–101 together with the original manuscript and paginated typescript both titled "C.G. Jung et le bouddhisme" (*FC*). Right at the start of this text, Corbin determines its tone as well as its purpose by citing Jung's own words about the near-impossibility in the West of finding one's way back to the kind of "primordial experience" or *Urerfahrung* encountered traditionally through Tibetan teachings or Zen. Not only does the Christian Church offer no help, Jung explains, but the main reason for the Church's existence is precisely to block any such experience; on the other hand, trying to import eastern methods and techniques without any understanding of westerners' psychology is a recipe for disaster and the only real hope lies in the psychological process of individuation (Jung in D.T. Suzuki, *Die grosse Befreiung*, Leipzig 1939, 31–2,

cf. *PR* 553–4 §903; Corbin, "C.G. Jung et le bouddhisme" iii–iv, cf. *AJ* 23). In fact this one word *Urerfahrung*, primordial experience, locates with exquisite precision the real meeting-place between Corbin and Jung. For Jung it was a word that had the deepest meaning (see e.g. *FP* 339 §780 with P. Bishop, *Carl Jung*, London 2014, 16; *CT* 85 §173, 92 §192; *PR* 320–1 §§480–3, 346 §535; *SM* 90–7 §§141–51; *ETG* 196 and 278 with S.A. Hoeller, *The Gnostic Jung and the 'Seven sermons to the dead'*, Wheaton, IL 1982, xxv). And, significantly, Corbin too was fond of embedding the German word in his own writings not only here but elsewhere (e.g. *Étude préliminaire pour 'Le livre réunissant les deux sagesses' de Nâsir–e Khosraw*, Tehran 1953, 70; *ARV* iii 79 n.64; *AJ* 23). It should hardly need adding that Jung's preference for direct experience and immediate perception over intellectual theories and generalizations is the essential reason why Corbin aligned himself with Jung against the school of so-called Traditionalists who, like so many other dedicated "non-dualists", think they can put aside the subtle and infinitely mysterious modalities of human experiencing. See X. Accart, *Politica hermetica* 16 (2002) 190, 196; also A. Daniélou in *René Guénon*, ed. P.–M. Sigaud (Lausanne 1984) 139.

[33] For Corbin as a westerner, doing his work to help in redeeming and saving the West, see e.g. *HC* 51 which he wrote shortly before he died: "Of course I am and I remain a westerner (in the terrestrial sense of the word), because it's as a westerner that I have perhaps been able to succeed in doing what it was given to me to succeed at." Compare also Christian Jambet's emphasis on the fact that "the journey to the East isn't an expatriation but a return, meant to shower us with a light we already possess but have forgotten … Far from rejecting the West, its culture, its horizon, Corbin dedicated himself

instead to its salvation and preservation" (ibid. 14); Daryoush Shayegan's observation that Henry Corbin brought to bear "all the immense resources of western culture, of which he is one of the most legitimate representatives" (*Mélanges offerts à Henry Corbin*, ed. S.H. Nasr, Tehran 1977, 29–30); Xavier Accart's clear contrast between René Guénon, who considered himself an "easterner" free from any debts or connections to the West, and Henry Corbin who considered himself the opposite in every respect (*Politica hermetica* 16, 2002, 178 n.7, 180, 199) together with David Bisson's further comments, *René Guénon* (Paris 2013) 402; and Daniel Proulx's account of how for Corbin, as opposed to Guénon, "it was a question of presenting Iranian spirituality as a model which will allow the West to rediscover in its own roots the traces of the great spiritual and mystical traditions" (*Os trabalhos da imaginação: abordagens teóricas e modelizações*, ed. J.-J. Wunenburger, A.F. Araújo and R. de Almeida, João Pessoa 2018). As usual, with his claim that Corbin "declared war on *us*" because "he declared war on the West", the American scholar Steven Wasserstrom shows himself tragically clueless about what matters most (*Religion after religion*, Princeton 1999, 156).

[34] For Corbin on Jung's psychology—his "exegesis of the soul"—as the arrival of dawn, the inner East inside us, and his direct comparison of Suhrawardî see "C.G. Jung et le bouddhisme" 88–9 (*FC*) = *AJ* 90–1. When he states here that "To wish to reject the premises of our own culture, and assimilate the East through a purely literal exegesis, would be the surest way of causing yet another uprooting of consciousness" he is simply quoting, as he himself acknowledges, Jung's own solemn words of warning (*The secret of the golden flower*, London 1931, 128, cf. *AS* 49 §72); for the gobbling of foreign fruits compare *RB* 231b. It should always be remembered that although Corbin

distinguished himself as a metaphysician or philosopher from Jung as a psychologist, and by nature was eager to free himself from what he often perceived to be the limitations of any psychology, this is far from being the only place where he made a point of emphasizing how Jung's "psychology" was first and foremost the true study or science of the soul (compare, most famously, *Revue de culture européenne* 5, 1953, 14–15 = *HJ* 267–8). Here is the basic reason, as Corbin understood but Traditionalists couldn't, why Jung knew how to talk alongside Meister Eckhart about the possibility of God being born in the human soul (*The secret of the golden flower* 129–30 = *AS* 50 §75; *AJ* 89–90; *Sacred web* 31, Summer 2013, 146–7).

[35] For Corbin on descent into the darkness see especially *ARV* ii 184 (*Avicenna and the visionary recital*, London 1960, 159). "The wound is only healed by the lance that made it": *Question de* 1/4 (1973) 107; in this piece, which he appropriately titled "Pour une nouvelle chevalerie", Corbin is quoting from the final act of Richard Wagner's *Parsifal* ("Nur eine Waffe taugt: die Wunde schließt der Speer nur, der sie schlug"). See further *EII* i 9, "There is a mysterious law: 'The wound is only healed by the weapon that made it'. Perhaps, if the West has secreted the poison, then the West is in a position to secrete the antidote. But it's far from clear that, as of yet, it has become aware of this responsibility"; Corbin's *Philosophie iranienne et philosophie comparée* (Paris 1985) 47, "There has been deception and trickery. The science that was meant to free us has created an instrument of death. But it's my conviction that this despair carries inside itself the redemption of the West. Only what secretes the poison can secrete the remedy. 'The wound is only healed by the weapon that made it'"; X. Accart, *Politica hermetica* 16 (2002) 199, "And so" for Corbin "the antidote to the crisis of civilization needs to come not from the East, as

Guénon had maintained, but from the West which had caused it. This is the sense in which he had interpreted a saying from *Parsifal*: 'Seule guérit la blessure, la lance qui la fît'"; and D. Proulx in *Femme, 'erôs' et philosophie*, ed. E.D. Diotte Besnou, Proulx and J.–M. Counet (Louvain-la-Neuve 2016) 306–7. Jung on the mystery of the Grail and the Saoshyant who returns as saviour to heal the wound he originally caused: *NZ* ii 1364; for the relation of the Saoshyant figure to the Grail legends compare A. Schult, *Die Weltsendung des heiligen Gral im Parzifal des Wolfram von Eschenbach* (Beitingheim 1975) 20. The importance of not filling the hole: P. Kingsley, *Works and conversations* 22 (2011) 31–2.

[36] The prophecy by Jung's soul: *JP* 258; this detail was judiciously omitted from the corresponding sections of his published biography (*MDR* 18–19/5, 184/192). A prominent Jungian analyst once confided to me in Zurich that whoever makes a career or living from Jung's work is living off the corpse of Jung: the unusual language and imagery he used were clear indicators that he was relating a visionary experience. For Jung's reaction when people announced the creation of some new training institute see e.g. J.B. Wheelwright, *PP* 6 (1975) 68 ("He looked as though he'd been struck by a heavy object") and *JM* 345 ("looked as if 'he had been hit by a Mack truck'"), ibid. 344–5 ("He was really very much against these societies starting at all", "hated the idea of promoting a school" and, on hearing that someone in Texas had attached Jung's name to the title of an educational centre, was naturally inclined to dismiss the whole business as "a mere advertising bluff"), and for his general objections and resistance cf. Wheelwright 67; M. Fordham, *JAP* 24 (1979) 280; E. Rolfe, *Encounter with Jung* (Boston 1989) 161–2; D. Bair, *Jung* (Boston 2003) 819 n.36. The ordeal of manipulating him into accepting the

creation of a C.G. Jung Institute in Zurich: B. Hannah, *Jung, his life and work* (New York 1976) 286, 295–6; Bair 530. For "My grandfather, Carl Gustav Jung ..." see *NL* 170–1: "... an institution in his name which he did *not* think was a good idea. He disliked institutions of any sort, and felt, 'If people want to know my work, they can read my books.' His opening words at the Institute may prove prophetic ... 'My grandfather, Carl Gustav Jung ...'"; *JM* 345. For Jung directing people to his own books if they want to understand him see also *JL* i 519, ii 574. Would sometimes go to the Institute, "but not very often": Wheelwright 68. On his policy of standing back and allowing people to make a mess of things see e.g. *JL* i 518 (for his habit of not interfering with pupils); *RB* 316a (admiring Philemon's principle of leaving people the space they need for acting out their stupidities).

[37] For Jung's clear stipulations that the C.G. Jung Institute dedicate itself professionally to in-depth research and interdisciplinary partnerships see *SL* 471–6 §§1129–41; P. Bishop in *Jung in contexts*, ed. Bishop (London 1999) 6–7; *JM* 345–7; M. Stein in *Teaching Jung*, ed. K. Bulkeley and C. Weldon (New York 2011) 65–6; J. Hillman and S. Shamdasani, *Lament of the dead* (New York 2013) 144. On the absurdity of a training institute because everyone's path of individuation is so unique see C.A. Meier in *JM* 347. Characteristic of the later, revisionist disregard for Jung's own intentions is the strikingly unreflective account by Mario Jacoby: "On April 24, 1948, there was the official inauguration to celebrate the founding of the Institute. Jung gave an address at this occasion and it is remarkable that he never mentions one of the main purposes of the Institute, namely the training of new Jungian analysts. He seems mainly interested in research and ... also announced directions, which future researches conducted by the Institute

might be expected to take ... Although Jung, in his inaugural speech, had said hardly anything concerning the training of new analysts, this endeavour became the main activity of the Institute from the beginning" (*Who owns Jung?*, ed. A. Casement, London 2007, 138).

[38] For Wolfgang Pauli as scientific patron of the C.G. Jung Institute see e.g. *PB* iv/I 146, 245, iv/II 74, iv/III 620, 622, 634, 647, 711, iv/IV 317, 325, 421; for his comments on the institute's betrayal of its principles, ibid. iv/III 620–2, 627–30, iv/IV 420–1 = *Atom and archetype*, ed. C.A. Meier (Princeton 2001) 212–17. On Pauli's horror at the institute becoming a "conveyor belt" or "assembly line" see especially his letter to Meier dated 22 July 1956: *PB* iv/III 621 ("Massenbetrieb ... Massenbetrieb ... Massenbetriebes") = *Atom and archetype* 213 ("conveyor-belt system ... assembly-line system ... assembly-line industry"). The accusation clearly made an impression on Meier because, years later, he too would use the identical imagery to describe the institute's activities ("a conveyor belt for turning out ready-made analysts", *JM* 347). Significantly, whereas Pauli had chosen this image of a conveyor belt to describe the mechanical treatment by Jungian therapists of their patients, Meier transferred the same image to describe the training of the Jungians themselves; Meier was quicker than Pauli to carry through with resigning from his position at the institute (*PB* iv/IV 317, 325, 421, *JM* 347 with n.138). For Pauli's view of Jungian therapists as ruining their patients' dreams see the letter that Cary Baynes wrote to Carl Jung on 9 March 1959 (*CBA*, cf. *JM* 348); she tellingly mentions this in the context of stating that, if only Pauli had been able to read the text of Jung's biography which was being prepared for publication at the time, he would have recognized it as the *Book of Living Fire.*

[39] On Henry Corbin's denunciation of the Jungians for essentially undermining and destroying Jung's great discoveries with their little mechanical devices see *HC* 48–9 ("… pour valoriser ce que Jung fut le premier à discerner et à exprimer par les concepts d'*Animus* et *Anima*, bien que malheureusement l'usage que l'on en fit ensuite ressemblât un peu trop à celui d'un petit appareil automatique que l'on applique, vaille que vaille, à n'importe quel cas"). There is a very obvious resonance between Corbin's comments here and Wolfgang Pauli's constant complaints about how the discoveries made by Jung had, in complete violation of Jung's own wishes as well as his example, degenerated at the hands of Jungians into dogmatic clichés (*PB* iv/II 75, 78, cf. 196) and almost meaningless trivialities (iv/III 673, cf. 375). Alongside his biting criticism of the Jungians, Corbin also makes a special point of emphasizing the full extent to which Jung himself in private "forcefully and humorously denied that he was a 'Jungian'" (*HC* 48). Compare Alan Watts' reminiscence—Jung "was careful to explain that he himself was not a Jungian and that he had had no intention of promulgating a particular system of psychotherapy. He had simply followed his intuition and written down his findings as they came along" (*In my own way*, New York 1972, 338)—as well as Laurens van der Post's: "Above all, he had a profound horror of 'isms', and the adjective 'Jungian', which could so easily be a doorstep to 'Jungianism', was ruled out in his own discipline of psychology. 'I do not want anybody to be a Jungian', he told me. 'I want people above all to be themselves'" (*Jung and the story of our time*, New York 1975, 4; for the same sentiment of wanting to discourage people from becoming Jungians cf. *JL* i 405).

[40] For Jung's story about the old man meditating in a cave who used to draw on its walls with a piece of red chalk until his

greedy disciples "all imitated the diagrams" and "in so doing they turned the whole process upside down", see *ACU* 129–30 §233. For his strongly worded regret about "so many pupils of mine who have fabricated all sorts of garbage out of what they took from me" see *JB* ii 143–4 (cf. *JL* i 518); note also his quickness, especially towards the end of his life, to denounce his pupils for their laziness in failing to come to grips with the depths of the unconscious (*JL* ii 626); and compare P.J. Stern's equally depreciative comments about the chief students of Jung who "not only disseminated his ideas, but distorted them in the process. Not content to act as his mouthpiece, they used the mantle of his authority to smuggle their own shallow ideas into the public arena" (*C.G. Jung: the haunted prophet*, New York 1976, 247) as well as H. Ellenberger's earlier remarks about the absurdly tragic contrast between the profundity and subtlety of Jung's own ideas and the over-simplifications published by "certain of his pupils" (*L'évolution psychiatrique* 17, 1952, 154). On Jung's grim realization "that those who mouth my name basically don't have a clue what it's all about" see *JB* iii 279 (*JL* ii 530); certain members of his family who, to my surprise, knew these words by heart have emphasized to me that he was referring not to outsiders but to the most orthodox or mainstream Jungians. "The Jungian gang": see C.A. Meier in *JM* 347. Jungians as neither better nor wiser than ordinary people: *JK* 157; and on the perception of just how little it took to turn Jungians into monsters see e.g. S. Shamdasani, *Cult fictions* (London 1998) 80 n.7.

[41] General knowledge of the famous statement "Thank God I am Jung and not a Jungian" goes back to Barbara Hannah's report that he happened to say it "once in exasperation" (*Jung, his life and work*, New York 1976, 78). The various elaborations and interpretations of this damning comment read as a

terrifying testimony to the self-absorbed mentality of Jungians and post-Jungians alike. See e.g. J. Kroth, *Psyche's exile* (Austin 2010) 67 (when Jung said "Thank God I'm Jung and not a Jungian", in fact "what he meant was that the individuation process uncovers one's own essence and uniqueness") and M.V. Adams, *For love of the imagination* (Hove 2014) 73 ("What would Jungian Studies be without Hillman? What if Hillman had never existed? Would Jungians have had to invent him? Would Jungians have had to imagine him? Jung may have said: 'Thank God I am Jung and not a Jungian.' I might reverse that and say: 'Thank God I am a Jungian and not Jung.' Or, I might say: 'Thank God I am a Hillmanian'"). Murray Stein tries, very diplomatically, to downplay the seriousness of Jung's poor regard for Jungians by reducing it in the first instance to personal factors: "Jung's strong aversion to 'Jungians' around himself had its roots in large measure in his personal need to remain free to think as he wished and to change his mind or to set out in new directions. Any sort of fixed doctrine cobbled together from his previous writings and teachings would have hindered his own freedom to think ..." (*Teaching Jung*, ed. K. Bulkeley and C. Weldon, New York 2011, 65). But this is to overlook the most fundamental issues and understate the scale of the problem enormously.

[42] On the intimate link between Jungians, "Jungianism" and the C.G. Jung Institute in Zurich see e.g. L. van der Post, *Jung and the story of our time* (New York 1975) 4. On the dangers of professional teaching, the best-case scenario of being able to keep the institute "afloat for a while", and the impossibility of any real truth ever being destroyed see the letter from Carl Jung to Cary Baynes dated 9 May 1949 (*JM* 348, giving a wrong date; *CBA*). "The Institute would be lucky if it did not outlive its creative uses within a generation": van der Post

4. For Jung's very explicit, and detailed, comparison of the process that led to the institutionalizing and deadening of Christ's teaching by the Christian Church with the process which would lead to the institutionalizing and deadening of his own psychology see especially *CS* 18–20 (spoken in 1923). And on the inevitable reduction, straight after his coming death, of its original fire and spirit to nothing but lifeless specimens see Jung's equally explicit and completely consistent forecast at *JB* iii 211 (mistranslated in *JL* ii 469)—a prediction made by him over thirty-five years later. "Their first disciples already had misunderstood them ... from the path of the truth": W.B. Henning, *Journal of the Royal Asiatic Society* 2 (1944) 136–7 = *Selected papers* (Tehran 1977) ii 142–3.

[43] For the idea of needing to find an "exit" from the world of the *Red book* into the realms of modern science I am indebted especially to Joseph Cambray (*IJJS* 3, 2011, 110–24, *International journal of psychoanalysis* 94, 2013, 417–18 and in *The Red book*, ed. T. Kirsch and G. Hogenson, London 2014, 36–51). Each of Jung's books as an inner command or commission: *JP* 359–60, cf. *MDR* 211/222. "Grace ... the divine cause of my existence ... will also live for me": letter, dated 23 January 1947, from Carl Jung to Victor White regarding Barbara Robb (*JW* 70–1; for Jung's physical meeting with her, almost five years later, see ibid. 168–72).

[44] The trope of heralding Jung as pioneer "of a new aeon", of the age of Aquarius, goes back already to his immediate disciples: cf. e.g. G. Adler, *PP* 6 (1975) 21. The fact that, aside from copying everything he knows about the age of Aquarius from Jung, Adler distorts and completely misunderstands Jung's writings in the process (so e.g. in his comments on Jung's letter to Erich Neumann dated 5 January 1952: ibid. 20) is a little

disconcerting. For the remarks made by Jung himself about the "Christification of many" see his *Answer to Job* (London 1954) 180 = *PR* 470 §758 as well as Paul Bishop's surgically accurate commentary, *Jung's 'Answer to Job'* (Hove 2002) 161–2. With true American flair, along with disastrous consequences thanks to his influence, Edward Edinger totally neglected the small print containing Jung's accompanying warnings and crucial qualifications (*PP* 25, 1991, 44, *The creation of consciousness*, Toronto 1984, 113): of course, in such matters, people far prefer to follow Edinger rather than Jung because he is so "much easier to read" (T.B. Kirsch, *The Jungians*, London 2000, 71, 101). For the new trope that the *Red book* has been published during our lifetimes because only now are we humans evolved enough in consciousness to receive it, see e.g. L.S. Owens in A. Ribi, *The search for roots* (Los Angeles 2013) 1–2, 33. The fallacy of imagining that fresh texts will, thanks to some miracle, allow one to understand authors never quite understood before is amply demonstrated by the discovery of the famous Empedocles papyrus at Strasbourg in the 1990s: the hype surrounding its publication was that at last it revealed the "real" Empedocles for the first time, and it certainly contains some wonderful new material. But, in practice, all it did was give students even more rope to hang themselves by—offering plenty of extra Empedoclean material onto which they could project their old rationalizing points of view while extinguishing every remaining trace of Empedocles' magic (*ENM* 333–413). Jung's modesty in facing his idiocy: *JP* 80–1, *MDR* 207–8/217–18. Jung is forced to learn how to laugh and say yes at the prospect of total destruction: see *RB* 230b with V.W. Odajnyk, *PP* 53 (2010) 450–1 and, years later, *JJW* 77–8, 81. For our god-almighty power to destroy ourselves as the only authentic or tangible manifestation of humanity's new divine status see e.g. *PR* 460–1 §§746–7; *JW* 237 = *JL* ii 167–8;

JL ii 225; on Jung's poor opinion of those who fantasize about becoming creative little gods, *NZ* ii 936–7.

[45] "New religion … and all over the world": see Jung's response to the famous dream of Max Zeller as published in *PP* 6 (1975) 75, Zeller's *The dream: the vision of the night* (2nd ed., Boston 1990) 2–3, *JJW* 109. Marie–Louise von Franz explained the dream as meaning "there are thousands of Jungians who have never heard the name 'Jung'" (*FRJ* iii 56:42–9)—marking, with her subtle but egotistic comment, the vast inner gulf separating Jung from his closest collaborator. For Jung's own passing comments about other people in the world who perhaps are working, or being worked on, in ways similar to him but whom he doesn't know about see *RB* 250 n.194. "Barbarian disintegration … God knows where" and sharing the fate of Meister Eckhart: *FRJ* ii 42:46–43:35 = *PP* 38 (1998) 39. The statement here by von Franz about Meister Eckhart being "forgotten for four hundred years" is a mistake on her part for "six hundred years": cf. *CS* 20, *Aion* 87 §143 and 194 §302, *JL* ii 586. As for Jung's repeated emphasis on a delay of six hundred years, this is far from accidental and closely corresponds to the fallow periods of "incubation" between ages according to the system put forward by Joachim of Fiore (N. Cohn, *The pursuit of the millennium*, 2nd ed., New York 1970, 109–10). With regard to Meister Eckhart in particular: it will be noted that Jung spoke about the group of people who immediately gathered around him, and proudly misinterpreted him, as creating "the open way to Hell" (*CS* 20).

[46] For the overwhelming darkness Jung sees ahead, cf. e.g. *JL* ii 136, 225–6, 229–30. One could describe much of the subsequent Jungian literature as a discreet sterilization, or bowdlerizing, of this vision; and the desperate attempt at

finding "a more hopeful side" to Jung in the occasional hint he dropped about how, contrary to our own ideals of domination, "the afternoon of humanity, in a distant future, may yet evolve a different ideal. In time, even conquest will cease to be the dream" overlooks the crucial fact that some distant future is altogether different from the immediate future we and the next few generations are faced with (W.Y. Evans–Wentz, *The Tibetan book of the great liberation*, London 1954, xlix, cf. *PR* 493 §787; J. Dourley in *Psychology and religion at the millennium and beyond*, ed. J.M. Spiegelman, Tempe 1998, 33). On the future as so entirely different from the present as to be incomprehensible, and on the futility of speculating about it, see especially *RB* 306 with n.236; *JW* 222 = *JL* ii 137–8; *JL* ii 225. Regarding the idea of seeds being sown in the present for the future see e.g. *JL* ii 225 together with Jung's unpublished notes on secret Gnostic teachings about the "ends of the aeons", or *telê tôn aiônôn*, at *AN* vii 115. This type of imagery, as well as the notion that somewhere and somehow some tiny essence always manages to survive, is deeply embedded in western traditions about the different cycles of humanity (*SW* 172–3). For ancient Gnostics on sowing and harvest see also *Gospel according to Philip* 7, 52.25–35 (*Nag Hammadi codex II,2–7*, ed. B. Layton, Leiden 1989, i 144–5 = *L'Évangile selon Philippe*, ed. J.É. Ménard, Paris 1967, 48–9, 126–7); Origen, *Commentaries on the gospel according to John*, ed. E. Preuschen (Leipzig 1903) 276.18–277.1, 278.33–279.8 = *The fragments of Heracleon*, ed. A.E. Brooke (Cambridge 1891) 87–9 §§35–6; W. Foerster, *Gnosis* (Oxford 1972–74) i 175–6, ii 78–9. Jung on the crucial need for a thorough knowledge of Latin and Greek if one is to have any hope of understanding western psychology: *JP* B31 (at Bollingen, 19 October 1958). Because we have entered the darkness which still belongs to the Christian aeon "we shall need Christian virtues *to the utmost*": *JW* 220–2 = *JL* ii 136–7;

and for the Christian virtues of conscious suffering or voluntary sacrifice see, aside from the *Red book*, Jung's testimonial in *PP* 6 (1975) 12. For the transitions between ages as times of particular melancholy and despair, Jung's words "now we are coming to Aquarius ... and we are standing only at the very beginning of this apocalyptic development!", plus his Latin quotation, see *JB* ii 463 (cf. *JL* ii 229). For the sake of completeness it should be noted that among supporters of the popular new–age views about a coming dawn of Aquarius, the celebratory optimism is mostly only skin-deep and little more than a distraction from their underlying fears as well as despair (W.J. Hanegraaff, *New age religion and western culture*, Leiden 1996, 339, 344–8, 355–6): even the most obvious founders of the new–age movement have been quick to denounce its narcissism (ibid. 358–60). The words *Luciferi vires accendit Aquarius acres* come at the culmination to book 5 of the *Sibylline oracles*, and well deserve to be read in their original context. See the Latin edition used by Jung, *Sibyllina oracula*, ed. Servatius Gallaeus (Amsterdam 1689) 647; for the original Greek text, ibid. with *Die Oracula Sibyllina*, ed. J. Geffcken (Leipzig 1902) 129; and for an English translation, *The Sibylline oracles, books III–V*, trans. H.N. Bate (London 1918) 118. Jung also quotes the same Latin text in *Answer to Job* to evoke the "dark end" to the age of Pisces "which we have still to experience, and before whose—without exaggeration—truly apocalyptic possibilities mankind shudders" because it threatens to "eclipse even the horrors described in the Apocalypse" (*Answer to Job*, London 1954, 146; cf. *PR* 450–1 §733).

[47] "To understand, that I was unable ... continue to exist?": see the letter, dated 13 November 1960, from Jung to Eugene Rolfe published in Rolfe's *Encounter with Jung* (Boston 1989) 158 and reproduced ibid., plates VII–VIII; Jung wrote, as always

to Rolfe, in English. The disease that he refers to was a deep infection (*JL* ii 620–1). For his language of understanding this or that but not seeing "the whole", compare Empedocles fr. 2.5–8 Diels = fr. 7.13–19 Gemelli Marciano; *ENM* 360–1 with n.62; and note, also, Cary Baynes' comments on the failure even of those closest to Jung to understand him "as a whole" (*JSB* 64).

[48] The voluntary responders to Jung's letter include Gerhard Adler, *PP* 6 (1975) 14 = *Dynamics of the self* (London 1979) 92: "in a short and uncharacteristic bout of depression ... Jung's words express clearly how he experienced and suffered from the incompleteness and faultiness of the world's condition. But it is just out of such realizations that the creative spirit helps to shape the character of a new generation"; Adler then goes rattling on (*PP* 6, 1975, 14) about the need to look not at the present but towards a vision of some better future, suffering from the exact same ailment that Jung himself had diagnosed as "the disease of our time" or as "Happy Neurosis Island, where the great thing is still ahead" to which one can eagerly keep looking forward (*JV* ii 759–60). For other responders compare e.g. Edward Edinger, *Ego and self* (Toronto 2000) 148–9 ("Jung speaks of his depression ... His spirits picked up again, but I think it is important for us lesser mortals to know that Jung had such experiences to the end", cf. *PP* 48, 2005, 46), L.S. Owens in A. Ribi, *The search for roots* (Los Angeles 2013) 1–2 and Anne Baring, *The dream of the cosmos* (Shaftesbury 2013) 257 ("But he did not fail. The seeds sown by him are beginning to bear fruit, not only in the branch of psychology which has taken his name but in the culture as a whole ..."). "I cannot tell you often enough that we are definitely the leaders we have been waiting for, and that we have been raised, since childhood, for this time precisely":

Clarissa Pinkola Estés in *A clear and present danger: narcissism in the era of President Trump*, ed. L. Cruz and S. Buser (Asheville 2017) 275; there is more than a touch of irony about the way this statement is made in a book on narcissism, and more than a little tragedy about the fact that modern spirituality has become just as narcissistic as the politicians.

[49] For the characteristically new–age sentiment that, thanks to Freud and Jung but "especially since the 1960s and the radical increase in psychological self-consciousness which that era helped mediate, … what individuals and psychologists have long been doing has now become the collective responsibility of our culture: to make the unconscious conscious" see Richard Tarnas in *The vision thing*, ed. T. Singer (London 2000) 251. But Jung was adamant that the focus on "making the unconscious conscious" is a concern much more of Freud's psychology than of his own and represents only one aspect of a far more intricate process, for which few people have the time or the inclination. See *JS* 39–40 with K.A. Connidis in *The variables of moral capacity*, ed. D.C. Thomasma and D.N. Weisstub (Dordrecht 2004) 104, *MC* 355–9 §§498–505, and for his often ambiguous assessment of consciousness cf. e.g. *JS* 210–11 (flatly contradicting his usual account of individuation as an increase in consciousness) together with *JL* ii 626 (criticizing the tendency even among Jungians to overvalue the importance of making the unconscious conscious); L. Schlamm, *European journal of psychotherapy and counselling* 9 (2007) 411; C. Doran, *IJJS* 8 (2016) 171–2. For the report about Jung's extended experiences before he died leading him to acknowledge that "he does not trust consciousness in the usual sense any more" see the letter, dated 10 December 1960, to James Hillman from his wife Kate: D. Russell, *The life and ideas of James Hillman* i (New York 2013) 468–9.

[50] Jung's statement on 13 November 1960 that he had "picked up again" was clearly a reference to his physical recovery from the infection, rather than to any psychological improvement ("I was caught by a disease … a serious disease in my age! However I have picked up again": E. Rolfe, *Encounter with Jung*, Boston 1989, 158). In fact when he went down to Lugano later that month, he was still feeling too miserable even to see colleagues or friends (letter from Carl Jung to R.F.C. Hull dated 6 January 1961, Library of Congress; for Jung's visit to Lugano see the letterhead in Rolfe, plate IX). And as Sonu Shamdasani has noted, his depressed words and feelings during November were far from just a "passing" phenomenon "because there were a number of statements towards the end of his life of a similar sort" (*PP* 53, 2010, 433; cf. *NL* 175, *JM* 351–2). For a classic example of Jung as diplomat, note his masterfully controlled behaviour towards James Kirsch even when he was feeling "at wits' end" and "could hardly touch" the letters Kirsch was sending (A. Lammers in *Turbulent times, creative minds*, ed. E. Shalit and M. Stein, Asheville 2016, 76–7). In general it was only too tempting to mistake what he said for what he felt: the history of Jung as trickster, and the ways in which the people around him allowed themselves to be tricked, still remains to be written. Smiling for a photograph on his last birthday: A. Jaffé, *Word and image* (Princeton 1979) 145, cf. *NL* 169, 174–5; for his last days, M. Serrano, *C.G. Jung and Hermann Hesse* (London 1966) 104. The last bottle of wine: D. Bair, *Jung* (Boston 2003) 623; D. Russell, *The life and ideas of James Hillman* i (New York 2013) 469. For the comparison explicitly drawn by Jung between the superficiality of his worldly personality no. 1, drowning out the mysterious silence or stillness of another world, and the flamboyant gaudiness of a loud brass band blaring in some hotel lobby see *MDR* 204/214. But note especially the original version of his account at *JP*

83–4—where he explains that the specific hotels which had given rise to this striking image were the Blackstone Hotel he had visited in Chicago, with its ostentatious sumptiousness and luxury, and the Plaza Hotel he had also visited in New York with all its showy grandeur. For Jung's unfortunate experience at the Plaza Hotel see *JS* 94–5. For the music on offer at the Blackstone Hotel, "a venerable edifice that played host to many American presidents" and "had been a gathering place for the city's rich and famous from its opening in 1910", cf. C.A. Sengstock, *That toddlin' town* (Urbana 2004) 95.

[51] For Europe as a "rotting carcass" and the comparison with the final years of the Roman Empire, see Jung's letter to Esther Harding dated 8 July 1947 (*JM* 349). "The precincts of hell … a remnant and that its days are counted": letter from Jung to Cary Baynes dated 2 November 1945 (S. Shamdasani, *Quadrant* 38/1, 2008, 24; *CBA*), and compare for example the letter he would write to Eugene Rolfe at the end of 1960 ("… the fires of Hell, which have broken through in Europe since 20 years now": E. Rolfe, *Encounter with Jung*, Boston 1989, 170 = plates IX–X). Very significantly Jung had already expressed similar prophetic views back in 1942 while, as he put it, sitting on the edge of a volcano (*JL* i 316, cf. 309): for him the image of a volcanic crater was one of the most intensely meaningful and potent symbols conceivable, because at the bottom of the crater stands "the house of the prophet" (*RB* 252a; cf. 247–8, 366b, *IJP* 68–9, 104–5).

[52] Jung on being able to prophesy war because he carried it inside him: *RB* 241b with n.106. Alchemists on the inner "fighting and violence and war": Olympiodorus, *On the sacred art* 28 in *Collection des anciens alchimistes grecs*, ed. M. Berthelot (Texte grec, Paris 1887–88) 86.4 (*machê kai bia kai polemos*);

MC 350–1 §493 (cited in the context of the alchemist's despair, depression, and *katabasis* or descent into the underworld); *Reality* 345. For Jung's most important work disturbing his sleep and the tranquillity of his mind "in its deepest layers" see e.g. *JW* 118 – *JL* i 492; and on the final struggle, against dangerous odds, to complete his last piece of work cf. D. Bair, *Jung* (Boston 2003) 619.

[53] Jung's mystical experiences in 1944, and what happened afterwards: *MDR* 270–7/289–98. His intense initial irritation (ibid. 275/295) didn't simply disappear (D. Bair, *Jung*, Boston 2003, 528). The fact that the real *mysterium coniunctionis* paradoxically takes place on another level of existence offers a direct parallel to Jung's statement that the true path of psychological transformation is walked not by our conscious human ego, but by the divine Self inside us (*MC* 349 §492). As Edward Edinger indicates with a fair degree of accuracy, although without exploring any of the practical or existential implications, "There is reason to believe that the *coniunctio* is only experienced in its complete form in physical death" (*PP* 25, 1991, 50–1). For physical existence as a prison compare Jung's explicit remarks (*MDR* 273/292, 275/295; cf. *JL* i 358) with e.g. Hans Jonas' *The Gnostic religion* (2nd ed., Boston 1963), *AE* and Henry Corbin's *L'homme de lumière dans le soufisme iranien* (Paris 1971) = *The man of light in Iranian Sufism* (Boulder 1978); also Plato, *Phaedo* 62b (Pythagorean tradition), *Cratylus* 400c (Orphic); and on the unbearable crampedness of being confined in the physical world note already Empedocles frs. 2.1 (*steinôpoi*) and 126 Diels = frs. 7.8 and 170 Gemelli Marciano. For Jung living "in another world" while he was writing see Bair 528. His final book and the experience of transcendence: *JP* 233. For his last few months of living "in an 'in between' state … leaving the ego and the mind out" with

"another kind of awareness, on a very deep level ... that Jung has always known about" without "until now really taking it on", see D. Russell, *The life and ideas of James Hillman* i (New York 2013) 468–9; and compare with this his comments to Kristine Mann in 1945 on the process of voiding oneself of the whole world, along with "the ego–will", as a preparation for death (*JL* i 357–8; S. Shamdasani, *Quadrant* 38/1, 2008, 23).

[54] For Fordham and Hillman as arguably the "two major original figures following in the wake of Jung" see S. Shamdasani in D. Russell, *The life and ideas of James Hillman* i (New York 2013) xi. "I believe that I was ... made him feel a failure": M. Fordham, *The making of an analyst* (London 1993) 119–20; cf. J. Astor, *Michael Fordham: innovations in analytical psychology* (London 1995) 33–4, W. Colman, *JAP* 42 (1997) 342, *JM* 351. The disturbing image of Jung as world saviour was obviously a discussion point among the London Jungians (E. Rolfe, *Encounter with Jung*, Boston 1989, 163, cf. also *JL* ii 586–9)—a strange reversion to what had troubled Freud half a century earlier (*The complete correspondence of Sigmund Freud and Ernest Jones, 1908–1939*, ed. R.A. Paskauskas, Cambridge, MA 1993, 182).

[55] For Marie–Louise von Franz's comments during her interview with Suzanne Wagner in March 1977, at her own Bollingen tower, see *FRJ* i 41:33–45:40. The comments have also been edited, for film, at *MH* 1:36:09–1:39:56 and, for the printed word, at *PP* 38 (1998) 24–5. I am most grateful to Suzanne Wagner for sending me her unedited transcript of von Franz's words, based on the original film footage, and I have followed her in editing von Franz's English very slightly here or there where the sense isn't altogether clear. For Barbara Hannah's statement that von Franz saw Jung for the last time

eight days before he died see her *Jung, his life and work* (New York 1976) 347: "His last visions were largely concerned with the future of the world after his death. He told Marie–Louise, the last time she saw him, eight days before his death, that he had had a vision in which a large part of the world was destroyed, but he added, 'Thank God not all of it'." It should be noted that throughout this final stage of Jung's life he had the greatest difficulty speaking (Aniela Jaffé in J. Trinick, *The fire-tried stone*, Marazion 1967, 12; D. Bair, *Jung*, Boston 2003, 622–3). For the primarily oral phenomenon of "ring composition" compare e.g. W.A.A. van Otterlo, *Untersuchungen über Begriff, Anwendung und Entstehung der griechischen Ringkomposition* (Amsterdam 1944); M.L. West, *Zeitschrift für Papyrologie und Epigraphik* 98 (1993) 10–11; *ENM* 387; Mary Douglas' *Thinking in circles* (New Haven 2007); and the many further references offered by R. Barney in *Plato's 'Republic': a critical guide*, ed. M.L. McPherran (Cambridge 2010) 32–51. Marie–Louise von Franz's own unconscious, as well as conscious, resistance to openly discussing Jung's final visions has had the unfortunate effect of making other people's references to them even more confused. See for example A. Baring, *The dream of the cosmos* (Shaftesbury 2013) 262: "towards the end of his life Jung had a vision of enormous stretches of the Earth devastated, and another just before he died of which he said, 'Thank God, it wasn't the whole planet'." For the standard western traditions about the end of a cycle of humanity being marked by unimaginable devastation—"terrifying, infinite desolation; enormous wastes of land without limit; almost all living creatures made utterly extinct"—out of which the seeds or embers of a future cycle will miraculously emerge, see e.g. Plato's *Laws* 677a–e with *SW* 172. For the earliest traditions about Noah see now I. Finkel, *The ark before Noah* (London 2014).

[56] On the removal from his published biography of "a number of Jung's more mystical or superstitious statements", including his own original statement that his "visions at times actually foresaw the deaths" of people he knew, because family members evidently found such "foreboding" prophecies unacceptable for public consumption see A.C. Elms' comments, *Uncovering lives* (New York 1994) 64; also ibid. 60–1 on the general background to this "ideological censorship". As for von Franz: Jung himself with every justification considered her his most talented and scholarly pupil, his intellectual "hound" (A. Ribi, *Analytische Psychologie* 13, 1982, 210). But this is not to say that, especially where the realities of prophecy and mysticism are concerned, she had the greatest appreciation for the subtleties of the unconscious. And she was so determined to dispose of all the nonsense about Jung being a prophet that she ended up writing utter nonsense herself—famously stating that, as the result of a dream he had at around the age of twenty, he "once and for all renounced any kind of identification with" the world of personality no. 2 and from then onwards maintained an attitude of the purest scientific detachment from any inner reality (*C.G. Jung: his myth in our time*, New York 1975, 41). In this caricature of Jung's development she completely ignores the contrary or compensatory pull of the soul which, during his thirties and the time of his work on the *Red book*, dragged him back from the onesidedness of his fictitious scientific detachment into the inner world he for a brief while had been able to abandon (M. Stein, *JAP* 57, 2012, 282–3 with n.5); she just sweeps aside the intensity of his later immersion, particularly when alone on retreat at Bollingen, in the prophetic wisdom of his personality no. 2 (*MDR* 213–16/225–8, cf. 224/237); and quite unlike Jung, who often emphasized that he was forced against every conscious intention to do the

bidding of his personality no. 2, she very revealingly associates the experience of this no. 2 personality with the terrifying experience of taking hallucinogenic drugs and insists that for young people the "ego-consciousness" of their personality no. 1 is "the only thing they have which can guide them forward into the future" (*C.G. Jung* 41). Ironically, almost humorously in its inevitability, this same paradoxical reluctance to plumb the depths of the inner reality which she appears to navigate with such eloquence and skill emerges again at the time of Jung's final visions. Without any doubt von Franz's greatest and most learned work of collaboration with Jung was her major study of the medieval *Aurora consurgens*. In it she spent enormous effort as well as passion presenting to the public her arguments for supposing this alchemical text was dictated by Thomas Aquinas, on his deathbed, as the direct result of a powerful vision that erupted from his unconscious and blew away all his scholarly learning just before he died (*Aurora consurgens*, London 1966). But when confronted with the final prophetic visions of the man she was actually closest to, she finds them so disturbing that she doesn't want to speak about them. It's always nice to talk knowledgeably about eruptions of the unconscious when they are sweet, or happened a few centuries ago, or fit into a preconceived design. But the unconscious itself always tricks us by coming up in the way our conscious minds least expect. As, finally, for the positive pride that von Franz took in "fossilizing" Jung's psychology by insisting all his ideas were quite "final and fixed at his death" (see M. Anthony, *Jung's circle of women*, York Beach 1999, 66–8 with D. Bair, *Jung*, Boston 2003, 368, 770 n.69): one can now be a little more specific. As a matter of fact she made sure to fossilize and freeze them not at the moment of his death but already before it, because that was the only way she could manage to put his last prophetic visions aside and forget them. And just how successful she was at forgetting them is demonstrated by the comment she made, a few years before she died, about why Jung had liked to paint "such a gloomy picture" of the fate lying ahead for the world. He used to present such a terrifying picture, she explained, not because he believed in it or had seen it for himself but because he made the strategic decision to frighten us all as if we are children by consciously exaggerating the seriousness of the dangers we face—hoping he might be able to shock people out of their normal state in which everyone manages to find ways to push the real facts aside "and then takes a cup of tea and does nothing" (*Harvest* 48/2, 2002, 147).

[57] One of the most memorable results of Aniela Jaffé dressing up Jung's memoirs for publication is the portrayal of the *Red book* as a purely "aesthetic" piece of work that he decided to give up on because its artful "aestheticizing" needed translating into another medium. But it just so happens that this portrayal of the *Red book* as aesthetic or aestheticizing, as an "aesthetic elaboration" of his experiences in the underworld, has nothing to do with Jung. It's purely Jaffé's own artistic elaboration and invention: a pastiche of several passages in the unpublished Protocols where Jung was making the entirely different point that he had realized the essential message of the *Red book* needed translating out from the rough and raw language of prophecy (with *MDR* 180–1/188 contrast his own statements at *JP* 144–8, 169; the word "elaboration" comes at *JP* 148 but in the context of revelation, not aesthetics). In other words she has turned his meaning completely on its head, substituting her own criticism of the *Red book* as too "aesthetic" for what had been his very specific concerns about the excruciating crudeness of its overwhelming bluster and prophetic wildness.

The first irony here is that, in spite of its beautiful calligraphy and extraordinary paintings, few things would have been more absurdly inappropriate than for Jung himself to describe his *Red book* as "aesthetic". He could hardly have been clearer about how he understood the word: "Aestheticism is the literary original sin. One doesn't let the whole person speak, one doesn't participate, one shoves it away. Thus everything is only aesthetic" (C.G. Jung, *On psychological and visionary art*, ed. C.E. Stephenson, Princeton 2015, 83). The second irony in this bizarre situation is that Jung had protested as strongly as possible, while he still had the chance, against the way he saw Jaffé interfering with his memoirs by introducing her own style which was "too feminine" and turning them into something "too aesthetic". Quite characteristically, rather than taking his protest as a sign that she should go back and revise what she had written, the attitude she adopted was just to wait instead: either until he ran out of energy to keep complaining or perhaps until he simply died (letter from Jaffé to Kurt Wolff dated 19 October 1958, Helen and Kurt Wolff papers, Beinecke Library, Yale University; cf. *JSB* 32–3). And by managing to transform the *Red book* itself into an aesthetic piece of work she deserves all due credit for her wonderfully successful creation; at the same time, though, she couldn't possibly have demonstrated better what he was warning about. Then there is the greatest irony of all. In the pages of *Memories, dreams, reflections* leading straight up to this paragraph where Aniela Jaffé demotes the *Red book* to a simple piece of art, she had included the lengthy passage documenting Jung's fierce struggle not only with a certain woman he bluntly described as "aesthetic" but also with his own internal feminine anima—both of whom were determined at all costs to convince him that in labouring on the *Red book* he was producing nothing but an aesthetic piece of art (*MDR* 178–80/185–8; for the "aesthetic" woman cf. 187/195). Jung had managed to silence this seductive voice. Jaffé plainly didn't and instead, through her closeness to Jung, was unconscious enough as a woman to fall into a total identification with his anima: on some of the strange complexities of her working relationship with Jung, see M. Saban in *How and why we still read Jung*, ed. J. Kirsch and M. Stein (Hove 2013) 13. Countless people have been tricked by her characterization of the *Red book* as an "aesthetic elaboration", even including members of Jung's family (*RB* viii) and the editor of the *Red book* itself (S. Shamdasani, *Journal of sandplay therapy* 24/1, 2015, 13). Both Wolfgang Giegerich (*Spring* 83, 2010, 380) and David Tacey (*JAP* 59, 2014, 470–81) have, only too predictably, made it a major plank in their arguments that the *Red book* is unworthy of serious consideration by any self-respecting Jungian. But to get from these completely illusory assessments to the truth lying hidden behind them would mean having to travel a long, and painful, road.

[58] I have already mentioned the only too typical example of how—in terms strangely evocative of a medieval heresy–hunter, which is what on an unconscious level we moderns have become—Andreas Schweizer collapses the broad category of "prophecy" into the single category of "false prophecy" so he can propose a saving remedy for rescuing us from the pernicious dangers of the *Red book* (*JJ* 5/3, 2011, 79–81). Then there are other Jungians who, apparently unaware of their own rationalistic inflation, denounce the prophetic tone of the *Red book* as proof of Jung's narcissistic inflatedness at the time ("Il se peut tout à fait que ses visions aient été prophétiques. Mais sa réponse le montre identifié à la source archétypique, condition du narcissisme … Il semble en proie à l'inflation": N.

Schwartz–Salant, *Cahiers jungiens de psychanalyse* 134, 2011, 97–8). These rejections of the prophetic element inside the *Red book* ultimately go back, it should be added, to Jungian literature dating from well before that particular work was ever published. Compare for example J.W. Heisig, *Imago Dei* (Lewisburg 1979) 106, on the "certain tone of *prophetic authority* in Jung's mature style" which demonstrates how "tainted" he was by antagonism towards other schools of psychology; or M. Welland, *Studies in religion* 26 (1997) 307–8, who cites Jung's prophetic tone in *Answer to Job* as showing how dangerous psychological inflation can be. Quite similarly, in recent comments by Jungians about Jung it's not unusual to find the word "prophetic" grouped together with other terms such as "angry, intemperate, aggressive" (M. Stein, *JAP* 52, 2007, 312) when touching on the subject of his *Answer to Job*: the temptation to compare such comments with Jung's own dream, which he linked straight to his work on *Answer to Job*, about those psychologists who are quite incapable of understanding the inspired and biblically prophetic figure of his father (*ETG* 219–22, *MDR* 206–8/216–18) can seem overwhelming. Here, it will be noted, we have arrived at the uniquely special point where both Jung's fiercest defenders and his fiercest critics (e.g. R. Noll, *The Jung cult*, 2nd ed., New York 1997, 14–15) can see eye to eye. The idea of having prophetic powers belongs, everyone can agree, to the outdated realms of magic and myth; is self-evident proof of narcissistic inflation; and is totally unacceptable in our modern rational world. I should just add one honourable exception, in the form of John Beebe's openness and willingness to accept that Jung had visions which were genuinely prophetic ("The problems of World War I were presented to Jung from within, in the form of visions that he interpreted as prophetic. And I personally would agree: They convince me that they are prophetic", *PP* 53, 2010, 431). In fact he even refers to Jung's deathbed vision and the profound challenges it poses, although without saying anything specific about how such challenges could possibly be met: "on his deathbed Jung supposedly told von Franz about a vision—something about 'the last 50 years of the human race'. And of course that was in 1961. We're in 2010, so next year is 2011, which would be 50 years after that vision on his deathbed. We have been going right on, many of us, neglecting the spirit of the depths. And at just this time", he notes, the *Red book* "comes out. The world today is not unlike the lead-up to World War I. The book is a reminder of the dangers of neglecting the depths—and the possibility of taking them up in an individual way" (ibid. 432).

[59] *Malista anthrôpoi chrêsmôidousin, hotan mellôsin apothaneisthai*: Plato, *Apology* 39c; J. Bussanich in *The Bloomsbury companion to Socrates*, ed. Bussanich and N.D. Smith (London 2013) 290–1. *Divinare morientes*: Posidonius fr. 108 Edelstein–Kidd = Cicero, *On divination* 1.64. For the importance attached, throughout the history of western culture, to the prophetic words and visions of a dying person note also Aristotle fr. 10 Rose = *Aristotele: della filosofia*, ed. M. Untersteiner (Rome 1963) 22–3 §12a; Cicero, *On divination* 1.63–5 with A.S. Pease's comments in *M. Tulli Ciceronis de divinatione liber primus* (Urbana 1920) 204–9 on the persistence of this idea from Homer through to modern rural traditions as well as D. Wardle, *Cicero: on divination, book 1* (Oxford 2006) 66, 264–9; Diodorus Siculus, *Historical library* 18.1.1 (Pythagorean tradition); J.D.P. Bolton, *Aristeas of Proconnesus* (Oxford 1962) 154–5, 202 n.16; E.R. Dodds, *The ancient concept of progress* (Oxford 1973) 180 with n.5; K.S. Guthke, *Last words* (Princeton 1992) 38–42, 157, 165, 184, 193 n.21, 220 n.6; T. Döring, *Performances of mourning*

in Shakespearean theatre and early modern culture (Basingstoke 2006) 44–6; and in Judaism, S.L. Drob, *Kabbalistic visions* (New Orleans 2010) 219. As for the particular case of Socrates: aside from his famous words in Plato's *Apology* about the tradition of prophesying at the point of death, we also have his even more famous final words which he speaks to a friend just before dying at the very end of Plato's *Phaedo*: "Crito, we owe a cock to Asclepius so do make sure to pay him and don't forget" (118a). Although Plato was a notorious fiction–writer, Socrates had been far too well known a figure in Athens for him simply to invent such a statement. And as for what it means: while Jung's final attempt to communicate before dying has been virtually ignored, the opposite fate has been reserved for Socrates' last words. Scholars themselves have obsessively counted up over twenty-five different interpretations of this reference by Socrates to the healing god Asclepius, each new one even more ridiculous and far-fetched than the one that came before (for some recent listings see S. Peterson in *Desire, identity and existence*, ed. N. Reshotko, Kelowna 2003, 33–5; M.L. McPherran, *Ancient philosophy* 23, 2003, 73–5 with n.8). Still the only remotely plausible interpretation is the one often attributed to Friedrich Nietzsche, even though in fact it goes back one and a half thousand years before Nietzsche to the philosopher Damascius—who has a remarkably good record for being spot on in his explanations of passages from Plato's *Phaedo* (*APMM* 120–6, 181–2, 193–4). That interpretation is as simple, and meaningful, as it's elegant: a cock is traditionally offered to Asclepius when someone has just been healed and Socrates, on the point of dying, is asking his friend to offer a cock to the god because he sees his own death as the ultimate healing (Damascius, *Commentary on Plato's 'Phaedo'*, ed. L.G. Westerink, Amsterdam 1977, 284–5 §561, 370–1 §157;

for Socrates' use of the plural "we" in referring primarily to himself compare e.g. *Phaedo* 116d and A. Nehamas, *The art of living*, Berkeley 1998, 247). But to most modern philosophers and thinkers this obvious explanation is far too gloomy, not to mention too mystical, as if being mystical or gloomy automatically makes something untrue. Angrily they protest that Socrates would never have endorsed the view of physical existence as a sickness, and in the process they miss what he actually says throughout the course of Plato's *Phaedo*: that philosophy, real philosophy, is a process of purification from the contaminating physical world which ends in complete separation of soul from body (114c; M. Anderson, *Plato and Nietzsche*, London 2014, 131–3). Add to this what we happen to know about the historical thinker called Phaedo, which is that he too understood philosophical purification and healing as being one and the same (Julian, *Letters* 82, 445a Bidez, *ouden aniaton einai têi philosophiai, pantas de ek pantôn hyp' autês kathairesthai biôn*; G. Boys–Stones, *Phronesis* 49, 2004, 22 n.36), and the picture could hardly be more complete. Throughout this entire Platonic dialogue Socrates has been insisting that the soul has to be purified by being separated from the body and, at the very end, he offers thanks for the ultimate healing or purification which is physical death. That leaves the only other real objection to this "Nietzschean" way of interpreting Socrates' final words which critics have been able to raise: that it would have been unacceptably presumptuous, sacrilegious, downright inconceivable even to think about owing thanks to the god Asclepius for an act of healing which hasn't yet taken place. "To utter thanks beforehand would be impertinent, if not impious" (G.W. Most, *Classical quarterly* 43, 1993, 104); "Socrates cannot owe a past debt for something that has not yet happened" and "cannot be at all sure that he is about to take a vacation in the Isles of the Blest" (McPherran 76). And here we encounter the utter foolishness of scholars who, aside from being the murderers Jung accused them of being, can never quite manage to see the obvious. These are Socrates' last words at the moment of dying; Socrates himself states in Plato's *Apology* that the last words spoken at the moment of dying are traditionally visionary, prophetic; and through the visionary grace of prophecy he is now being allowed to see how, after his life of purificatory efforts to die before he dies, the final healing is what lies just ahead. In fact even the smallest of descriptive details at the end of Plato's *Phaedo* confirm this. In lying down after drinking the poison to die, he is lying down to incubate just like people lying down for ritual incubation at the temples of Asclepius because they are hoping to be healed (117e, cf. *Reality* 31–46). In requesting *hêsychia*, silence and stillness, of everyone present (117d–e, cf. *IDPW* 82–3, 162, 176–82) he is invoking the ritual stillness and silence needed for the healing to take place. And even in covering himself with his cloak, he is hiding himself from this world just as people used to do during the practice of incubation while waiting to be healed (118a, cf. Elizabeth Belfiore in Peterson 50 n.44; Anderson 133–7). As always in the tradition of *iatromanteia*, or prophetic healing, the healing and the prophecy go hand in hand. But to anyone unwilling to die before dying, that will always be a complete mystery.

[60] For the humanistic aspects of the *ars moriendi*, the moment of death as stripping away a person's mask, the *hora mortis* as "a condensed biography" in its own right, and the crucial role of a trusted friend as "the essential intermediary between a dying speaker and the public" see Lisa Neal's fine study in *Reading the Renaissance*, ed. J. Hart (New York 1996) 45–61. "There is

no more pretending … at the bottom of the pot": Michel de Montaigne, *Essays* 1.19; Neal 47; A. Calhoun, *Montaigne and the lives of the philosophers* (Newark 2015) 118–20.

[61] Paul Bishop has pointed repeatedly to Jung's familiarity with the long-standing traditions of *ars vivendi* and *ars moriendi*: see e.g. *Carl Gustav Jung (1875–1961): pour une réévaluation de l'œuvre*, ed. C. Maillard and V. Liard (Strasbourg 2014) 112–13 with n.41; G. Bright, *JAP* 59 (2014) 286. For the high value Jung always attached, ever since his early twenties, to prophetic visions see already *ZL* 41–3 §§129–33, *SL* 296–9 §§705–14 with *Psychology and the occult* (Princeton 1977). "Mouth my name … what it's all about": *JB* iii 279 (cf. *JL* ii 530). For death as the ultimate goal of Jung's psychology see *RB* 266–7, 273–5; the letter from him to Cary Baynes dated 2 November 1945 (*CBA*: cf. S. Shamdasani, *Quadrant* 38/1, 2008, 24); *JP* 309; *Spring* (1970) 178 = *JS* 360 ("Man goes through analysis so that he can die. I have analyzed to the end with the end in sight—to accompany the individual in order that he may die"); and compare the central function of dying before death in both Sufism and Buddhism (T.L. Perreira, *The Muslim world* 100, 2010, 247–67). The western philosophical teaching about dying before one dies goes back well before the Socrates of Plato's *Phaedo* to ancient Pythagoreanism (M. Detienne, *La notion de 'daïmôn' dans le pythagorisme ancien*, Paris 1963, 60–92; *IDPW* 61–76; *Reality* 29–43): one more sign among many of Socrates' indebtedness to Pythagorean tradition. Jung's psychology as preparation for the end of our culture, and the choice between killing our "infantile psychology" or killing ourselves: letter from Jung to Cary Baynes dated 12 April 1959 (*JM* 352, cf. *CBA*). His reference, immediately before making these remarks, to the darkest of clouds hanging over the horizon of western civilization makes it altogether clear that he is talking

not just about preparing for one's own end as an individual but about preparing for the end of a culture: earlier in this same letter he also comments very pointedly on men's primitive habit of hoping that by not acknowledging a danger, and acting as if it doesn't exist, the danger will somehow disappear. And anyone who finds it strange that Jung should be describing his psychology as a preparation not only for our end as individuals, but for the ending of our entire culture—as the direct manifestation of his concern "for all those who are caught unprepared" because he considers it his inescapable duty to "undertake this thankless task in the expectation that my chisel will make no impression on the hard stone it encounters"—would be well advised to read the opening to one of his final pieces of work (*Flying saucers*, London 1959, xi–xii; cf. *CT* 311–12 §§589–90 and, for his writing of this text, *JP* 302).

[62] For the spiral movements of Empedocles' cosmic cycles see *ENM* 384–90 with nn.124–5, 138, and *Reality* 347–83. Plato takes over these Empedoclean and Pythagorean teachings, embellishing them with the usual brilliant sillinesses, for his myth in the *Statesman* (268d–274e). He describes there how at a certain point the watchful god "let go" of the cosmos and withdrew, together with the other divinities, which is when everything started moving backwards; and, one day at the beginning of 2011, I saw the great Masters who hold the thread linking this physical existence to the world of reality suddenly drop it and withdraw.

[63] As Martin Heidegger already hinted in 1935: "The spiritual decline of the earth is so far advanced that people are in danger of losing their last spiritual strength, the strength that makes it possible even to see the disintegration and to recognize it as such" (*Einführung in die Metaphysik*, Tübingen 1953, 29 =

Introduction to metaphysics, New Haven 2000, 40). For Jung himself on the infinite difficulties involved in convincing people they are only animals and that they need to make incomprehensible efforts to become, or remain, human see e.g. *JL* ii xxxix.

[64] For Joachim's periods of incubation see N. Cohn, *The pursuit of the millennium* (2nd ed., New York 1970) 109–10 ("... each age must be preceded by a period of incubation ..."); H.G. Koenigsberger, G.L. Mosse and G.Q. Bowler, *Europe in the sixteenth century* (2nd ed., London 1989) 131; R.G. Kyle, *Apocalyptic fever* (Eugene 2012) 32. Jung was aware of them, too: *Aion* 83 §139. For an introduction to the ancient practice of incubation see *IDPW* and *Reality*, as well as the standard texts like L. Deubner's *De incubatione* (Leipzig 1900) and M. Hamilton's *Incubation* (London 1906); E.J. and L. Edelstein, *Asclepius* (2 vols., Baltimore 1945); C.A. Meier, *Ancient incubation and modern psychotherapy* (Evanston 1967) = *Healing dream and ritual* (Einsiedeln 1989), originally published as the first study of the C.G. Jung Institute (cf. *SL* 487–8). On the role of incubation in the ancient Near East and rest of Asia see e.g. K. Bulkeley, *Dreaming in the world's religions* (New York 2008) and K. Kim, *Incubation as a type-scene in the 'Aqhatu, Kirta and Hannah stories* (Leiden 2011).

[65] "I am refuted ... open only in the night": *Seelenprobleme der Gegenwart* (Zurich 1931) 432–3; cf. *CT* 93 §194. On the situation—both personally and for a whole age—where "all the methods that seem appropriate have already been tried out with no success whatever" but no one has the courage to admit there is nothing to be done because everybody is so "busy hatching out clever plans to meet the situation" see ibid. 148 §§313–14. For the Sufi who insisted that "This is no time for

prayer, it is the time for resignation. When doom descends, prayer profits not", see 'Umar ibn Wâsil in D.S. Margoliouth, *The table–talk of a Mesopotamian judge* (London 1921–22) i 215, ii 226 and G. Böwering, *The mystical vision of existence in classical Islam* (Berlin 1980) 88: through his connection to Sahl al–Tustarî, Ibn Wâsil was a part of the secret Gnostic lineage responsible for bringing the "Pythagorean leaven" along with the essence of Empedocles' teaching into Islam (*APMM* 388–90). On the alchemical, as well as Hermetic, doctrine of total submission to fate see e.g. *Collection des anciens alchimistes grecs*, ed. M. Berthelot (Texte grec, Paris 1887–88) 229.3–230.16 (*Zosimos of Panopolis on the letter omega*, ed. H.M. Jackson, Missoula 1978, 20–5 = *Zosime de Panopolis, 'Mémoires authentiques'*, ed. M. Mertens, Paris 1995, 2–4); G. Fowden, *The Egyptian Hermes* (2nd ed., Princeton 1993) 109, 124. For Jung on the "small and fragmentary people" who always need to be doing something see *Asia* 39 (1939) 97 = *CT* 526 §1006. On psychological work as nothing but the initial, preliminary steps along the path towards death compare S. Shamdasani, *Quadrant* 38/1 (2008) 24, citing Jung's letter to Cary Baynes dated 2 November 1945 (*CBA*); *Spring* (1970) 178 = *JS* 360; also *JP* 309 where he emphasizes how rare it is for people to arrive consciously at being able to endure the final stage. For his language when he describes death as the process of being stripped of everything, see *MDR* 271/290–1 along with the well-thought-out rationalizations offered by Edward Edinger in his *Archetype of the apocalypse* (Chicago 1999) 154–5. For the language of shedding, note especially Jung's comments in 1959 to the effect that "All the riches I seem to possess are also my poverty, my lonesomeness in the world. The more I seem to possess, the more I stand to lose, when I get ready to approach the dark gate … Whatever I have acquired serves a purpose I have not foreseen. Everything has to be shed and nothing remains my own. I quite agree with you: it is not easy to reach utmost poverty and simplicity. But it meets you, unbidden, on the way to the end of this existence" (*JW* 298, cf. *JL* ii 516). "The future should be left ...": *RBu* 305a (cf. *RB* 306b); for the connection between this "way of what is to come" and the terrors of death, the destruction of civilizations, the collapses and ends of empires, see *RB* 235b, 236b.

7
INDEX

INDEX

A

Abraham 357, 378, 645, 720–1, 740
Abraxas 509, 579–80, 604
adaptation 217, 255, 265, 318–19, 325–6, 401, 415, 423, 654, 695
Adler, Gerhard 507, 512, 520, 526, 774, 779
adoption 46, 52, 152, 156, 489, 565
aestheticism 424, 694, 788–90
afrâd 743
Agathodaimon 580
aiôn 347, 537–8, 608, 714, 777
Aion 347–8, 353–4, 574, 587, 686, 714–18, 736
alchemical tradition 35, 75, 89, 103, 108–9, 117, 122, 133–4, 150–1, 171, 181–205, 302, 328–33, 413, 443, 475, 478–9, 500, 505, 510, 545–50, 564, 570–1, 579, 586–99, 605–13, 653, 661–2, 683–4, 700–7, 745–6, 757, 782–3, 787, 799
aloneness and the alone 45, 66, 71, 86, 102, 108, 110, 125, 134, 141, 145, 181, 213, 231, 235, 264, 269–70, 294, 319, 326, 329, 340, 350, 358, 364, 367, 372, 378, 382–4, 389, 408, 443, 497, 533, 598, 742–5, 786, 799
ambiguity 34, 50, 63, 76–8, 278, 323, 410, 426, 479, 497, 511–13
America 218–27, 239–40, 467, 512, 522, 530, 616–26, 635
Amos 351, 357, 715–16
ancestors 16–17, 53, 182, 191, 203, 215, 223–4, 272, 300, 444, 480–2, 489, 527, 596, 608, 620–1, 707

anima and animus 23, 600, 691–2, 771, 789–90
animals 153, 156, 234, 242–4, 298, 430, 436, 480, 497, 637–8, 680, 734–5, 798
Answer to Job 353–6, 376–85, 391, 419, 535, 686, 717–20, 736–44, 775, 778, 791
Anthropos 19, 143, 468, 543, 555, 684
anti-Semitism 356, 719
Apamea 634
Aphrodite 19, 502
apocalypse 69, 407, 494, 505, 778
Apollo 31–2, 476
apostles 312, 400, 552, 598, 689
Aquarius, age of 402–7, 774, 778
Aquinas, St Thomas 787
archaeology 45–6, 185, 213, 307, 485, 585–6
archetypes and the archetypal 18–24, 30, 86, 89, 103, 107–110, 118, 135, 140–4, 170, 186, 253–4, 309–13, 319, 323, 408, 468, 488, 518, 530, 555–6, 563, 577–80, 616, 666, 686, 688–9, 718, 757–60
Ardâ Vîrâz nâmag 674
arguing with God 290–2, 354–7, 631, 671–2, 719–21
Aristotle 28, 35, 47–8, 51, 57–8, 77, 85, 87, 191, 200–3, 219, 229, 291, 298, 364, 476, 484–7, 491, 503, 513, 521, 596, 607–10, 641–2, 671, 679, 723, 761, 792
ars moriendi and *ars vivendi* 426, 795–6
Ascona 7, 741
Asclepius 529, 604, 793–5
assimilation 115, 170, 541, 577–8
Atlantis 220, 478, 616
Aurobindo, Sri 483
aurora consurgens 727
Aurora consurgens 787

B

Babylonian traditions (*see also* Mesopotamia) 227, 235, 306, 422, 630–1, 697
balance 12, 26, 39, 60, 66, 87, 166, 173, 249, 262, 265, 291, 304, 325, 341, 353–4, 410, 494, 502, 574
Barnaud, Nicholas 701
Basilides 560, 567
Baynes, Cary (*see also* de Angulo, Cary) 529, 548, 603, 651, 663–5, 699, 718–19, 770, 779, 796
Baynes, Peter 651
begging 35, 129, 131, 320–1, 488, 658
Bektashis 725, 742
Bernard of Treviso 607

Bhagavad gîtâ 303, 685
Bible, the 265–6, 293, 343, 351–2, 568, 655, 716
biblical literature and traditions 141, 204, 239, 241, 248, 254–5, 287, 292, 297, 308, 323, 338, 351, 354, 357, 366, 484, 509, 536, 546, 549, 568, 594, 598, 629–32, 636–7, 641–6, 652–4, 667–75, 679, 683, 688, 693–4, 709, 711–12, 716–21, 740, 791
birds 37, 147–8, 156, 182, 232–4, 240–8, 254–5, 275, 310, 430, 433, 519, 628–9, 637–41
Black books 169, 538, 708, 715
Blake, William 244, 296, 343, 639, 641, 667, 676–9, 711
blindness 34–5, 46, 56, 59, 103, 129, 166, 181, 183, 286, 288, 295–6, 433, 475, 585, 619, 667, 675–80, 723, 746
Bodhisattvas 282, 303, 665–6, 685
Boehme, Jacob 677
Bollingen 81–3, 97–104, 150, 153, 164, 177, 206–8, 232, 302, 321, 328, 380, 517, 525–9, 549, 564–5, 573, 579, 583, 597, 608, 623, 629, 684, 741, 777, 784, 786
breath and breathing 25, 47–8, 84, 208, 239, 485–6, 550, 636
bridges and bridging 125, 186–9, 192, 479, 586, 593–4, 608
Brunton, Paul 501, 507
Buber, Martin 157–9, 165, 559, 566–70
Buddha 39, 282–3, 303, 306–11, 665–6, 685, 690, 706
Buddhism 129, 229, 306, 392, 796

C

C.G. Jung Institute in Zurich 395–400, 708, 768–70, 773, 798
calligraphy 313–14, 789
Cambridge University 45
Campbell, Joseph and Jean 623
Cassandra 297–8, 672, 679
China 129, 306, 404, 590
chivalry 110, 371, 384, 387–8, 527, 730, 748, 767
choicelessness and choice 13, 25, 38, 41, 55, 82, 85, 98, 107–110, 120, 221–2, 226–8, 240, 275, 316–27, 353–6, 369, 372–3, 411–14, 423–8, 445, 504, 515, 563, 694, 714, 718, 726, 728, 732, 786–7, 796
Christ 29, 40, 63, 115, 121,

132–4, 141–4, 166–7, 174, 179, 194, 252–4, 283, 299, 303, 306–11, 314, 323, 355, 366, 378, 399–403, 482, 499, 540–2, 550–8, 575, 594, 598, 685, 688, 692, 706, 719, 737, 774
Christianity 29, 32, 40, 127–9, 145–6, 174, 185, 191, 199, 237–8, 248, 278–9, 287, 293, 306, 314, 331, 348–9, 392, 399–400, 406, 505, 542, 554, 559, 582–8, 596, 605–6, 631–3, 641, 646, 661, 664, 668, 673, 687, 692, 756, 764, 774, 777–8
"Christification of many" 111, 402–3, 535, 775
church, secret or invisible 314, 365–6, 372, 594, 692–3, 725
circles and circling 7–8, 44, 47, 76–7, 86, 196, 510, 513, 600–1
cognitio matutina 376, 727, 735–6
comfort 9, 17, 24, 53, 132, 172–4, 181, 273, 276, 290, 299, 581, 632, 735
compensation 39, 60, 71, 182, 338–42, 355, 439, 494, 708–11, 717, 786
concealment 65, 70–1, 156–9, 164–5, 177, 183–4, 259–64, 279, 296, 301, 319–21, 325–9, 333–4, 350–1, 424–8, 501, 566, 569, 582–3, 650, 677–8, 696, 700, 707, 795
consciousness and unconsciousness 33–6, 42–6, 60, 81–8, 109–112, 135–7, 143–8, 201–2, 206–8, 217–26, 261–6, 275–6, 299–301, 313, 323–6, 333–4, 337–43, 349, 355–7, 409–10, 419–23, 467–8, 479, 486–7, 515–17, 530–2, 540, 549, 554, 563, 611, 615, 619–23, 643–5, 654–5, 660, 691, 708, 710, 719, 721, 744, 753–4, 761, 780, 783, 799
contamination 140, 164, 309, 352, 376, 794
contradiction 113, 135, 160–6, 356, 479, 501, 571–2, 702, 708, 719, 780
contrary, the 17, 423
conversion 129, 365, 372, 390–2, 730–1
Corbin, Henry 8–9, 25, 188, 246, 310, 363–94, 397–8, 465–7, 474, 527, 553, 633, 641, 663, 683, 687–93, 707, 718, 720, 723–67, 771, 783
Corbin, Stella 364–5, 367–8, 372, 388, 398, 726, 728,

741–2, 748–50, 755
cosmic cycles 371, 429–31, 545, 797
coyote 17, 249
cries and crying 108, 195, 214, 232–49, 257, 264, 274–5, 321, 350, 537, 628–32, 635, 647, 659, 664, 696, 721
crucifixion 133, 299, 337, 400, 482, 551, 667
"cultural unconscious" 547

D

daimon or daimonic 86–90, 107, 305, 313, 333, 354, 502, 520–3
Damascius 484, 793
danger 18–20, 23–4, 60, 84, 89–90, 99, 113, 119, 126–9, 135, 142, 164, 195, 220–4, 255, 260–8, 275, 296, 323, 369, 399, 466, 470, 490–2, 495, 508, 512, 516, 556, 571, 586, 618, 622, 655, 697, 708, 729, 750, 756, 773, 788–92, 797
Dante Alighieri 294, 674
darkness 43–50, 59–61, 66–7, 107–8, 121, 129–30, 140–4, 150, 181–8, 208, 230–1, 270, 314, 354–5, 393–4, 403–8, 440, 487, 492, 496–7, 509, 519, 529–30, 548–9, 590, 611, 678, 738–9, 767, 776–8, 796
Darwin, Charles 481
dawn 49–50, 121, 368–81, 393, 439, 487, 726–7, 735, 742, 766
de Angulo, Cary (*see also* Baynes, Cary) 280–8, 292, 301, 305–14, 502–3, 518–19, 529, 538, 542, 564, 659, 663–7, 671, 685–7, 697, 740, 758
de Angulo Roelli, Ximena 514
dead, the 17, 43, 54, 58, 62–3, 73–4, 85–6, 104, 156, 182–4, 189, 193–4, 204, 223–4, 236, 264, 272–3, 294–5, 299, 318, 320, 355, 369, 384, 434, 437–9, 444, 529, 585, 593, 614, 621–2, 630–1, 695
death and dying 20, 53–5, 63, 79, 123, 173, 179, 204–6, 236, 270, 272, 296, 317, 323, 344–7, 370–1, 383, 387–9, 408, 414–28, 442, 469, 498, 533, 583–4, 614, 694, 714, 721–2, 783–8, 792–7, 799–800
deception and lies 20, 35, 77, 85, 108, 155, 158, 162–5, 184, 259–60, 264, 319–20, 325, 355, 496, 517, 530, 544, 569, 572, 623,

650, 653, 677–9, 719, 767
deification 114, 136, 268, 278, 294, 347, 537–9, 553, 655, 714
Delphi 31–2, 478
depression 237, 243, 408–10, 779–83
Derrida, Jacques 492
devastation 31, 419–22, 785
devil 61, 70, 168, 182, 310, 380, 495, 653, 689, 692, 755
dhikr 246
Dieterich, Albrecht 493, 509, 539, 565, 576, 593, 684
dilettantism 83, 327–35, 698–9, 702–3, 708
disciples 20, 63–4, 90, 113, 134, 195, 203, 252, 267–75, 312, 357, 378, 397–400, 469, 500, 552, 646–7, 655–9, 688–9, 772–4
disgust 128, 276, 282, 285, 317, 660–1, 678
divinare morientes 425, 792
Dodona 638
dogma and dogmatism 9, 34, 104, 114, 146, 152, 191, 195, 200, 217, 238, 250, 278, 293, 314, 357, 370, 374, 392, 397–8, 466, 599–600, 633, 643, 649, 721, 743, 762, 771
domestication 9, 21, 30, 78, 120, 213–14, 234, 544
double negative 263, 653
doubt 162, 181, 253–4, 257, 290–2, 311, 330, 348, 480, 519–20, 571–2, 689
dreams and dreaming 12–13, 35–6, 44–8, 54, 79–82, 100–1, 124–6, 131–4, 141, 182, 194–6, 204, 213–16, 286–91, 305, 313, 321, 333, 397, 411, 427, 433, 441, 487, 502, 526–9, 539, 546, 551–2, 601, 614, 622, 624, 664, 667–71, 691, 697, 704, 706–7, 719, 737, 740, 770, 776, 786, 791, 798
dualism 66–7, 160, 165–6, 468–9, 501–2, 569–75, 588–9, 595, 687, 739

E

Eckhart, Meister 404–5, 663, 759, 767, 776
ecstasy 45–6, 58, 239, 297, 347, 414, 641, 714, 727
Eddy, Mary Baker 696
Edinger, Edward 251–5, 264–5, 268, 512, 535–6, 545, 548, 600, 643–7, 654–5, 710, 775, 779, 783, 799
Egypt 149, 196, 199–203, 219, 561, 577, 612–13, 617, 638
Eisler, Robert 538–9
Elijah 204, 294, 305–6, 372, 540, 614, 673, 680, 683,

694, 731, 740, 744–5
Eliot, T.S. 466
Ellenberger, Henri 696, 772
Empedocles 41–3, 61, 67–8, 75–8, 85–7, 103, 110, 116, 132, 160, 165–6, 169, 176, 197–205, 231, 235, 264, 270–4, 297, 307, 310, 315, 318–21, 325, 331, 335, 363, 369–70, 421, 429, 466, 474, 481–2, 486, 502–4, 508–13, 521, 526, 533–4, 539, 542, 545, 550, 559, 569, 574–7, 581–3, 596, 602–14, 627–31, 642, 653, 658, 675, 679, 681, 687, 695–7, 702, 704, 721–3, 728–9, 732–3, 775, 779, 783, 797, 799
empiricism 65, 75, 158, 468, 510
entrails 36, 246–7, 286, 667
Epimenides 298, 679
Eranos 7–9, 366, 376, 391, 465–7, 579–80, 658, 687, 699–700, 703–5, 738, 745–50, 764
esotericism and the esoteric 44, 51, 116, 152, 245, 259, 365, 376, 381, 390, 532, 542, 569, 576, 650, 699, 724, 735, 762
eternity 162, 179, 193–6, 245, 306–9, 324–5, 336, 347, 353, 369–73, 382, 391, 437–9, 469, 531, 537, 585, 666
Etna, Mount 197, 204, 270, 602–3, 614
evil 179–82, 303, 544, 584, 687
evolution 33–6, 44, 74, 103, 111, 202, 220, 249, 335, 337, 427, 475, 478–83, 505, 526, 533, 600, 612, 643, 702, 708, 763, 775–7
Ezekiel 629, 642–3, 653, 711, 715

F

failure 119–20, 255–6, 265, 284, 292, 383–4, 406–9, 416–17, 511, 779
faith 443, 696
father, spiritual 43, 46, 52–3, 58, 150–3, 157, 171, 302–5, 311, 388, 489, 564–5, 683, 714
“father of prophets” 283–4, 288, 301–3, 306–7, 357, 394, 666, 683, 721, 747
Faust and the Faustian 168, 177–81, 192, 195, 299, 335, 397, 528, 575, 583–4, 594
fear and terror 23–6, 53, 58, 62, 70, 82, 86–9, 115–16, 133, 145, 148–9, 153, 164–5, 173–4, 181, 197, 219, 222, 243, 254, 278, 282, 287,

296, 299, 311, 354, 378, 421, 427, 429, 431, 471–2, 492, 505, 518–19, 541, 546, 560–1, 565, 573, 582, 588, 590, 597, 619–20, 632, 635, 662, 678, 681, 686, 740, 746, 764, 778, 785, 788, 800
fire 57, 82, 174, 197, 200, 293, 306, 308, 322, 399, 403, 407, 516, 549, 582, 589, 607, 688, 697, 727, 740, 770, 774, 782
Fordham, Michael 330, 415–17, 472–3, 574, 704, 784
foundations 42, 129, 147, 189–93, 305, 346, 404, 430, 495, 560, 593–8, 705, 758
free association 79, 514–15
freedom 9, 27, 32, 35–7, 71, 121, 140, 164, 180, 191, 282, 308–9, 314, 317, 333, 337–42, 366–7, 382, 415, 419, 431, 445, 466, 475, 494, 563, 585, 618, 688, 694, 706, 709, 725, 743, 758, 767, 773
Freud, Sigmund 22, 74, 87, 147, 169, 219, 257–60, 277, 279, 291, 301, 314, 410, 471–2, 502, 506, 508, 512, 514, 521, 552, 576, 623, 648–51, 656, 662–3, 670–1, 683, 780, 784
Fröbe–Kapteyn, Olga 579–80, 699, 703, 735–6, 741, 746, 752

G

George, Stefan 493
Gethsemane 134, 378, 552, 737
Giegerich, Wolfgang 486, 525–6, 530, 575, 605, 607, 660, 668, 708, 790
Ginsberg, Allen 238–40, 634–7, 711
gnôsis 130, 146, 528, 550, 558–9, 701, 711, 721
Gnostics and Gnosticism 19, 35, 104, 144–66, 171, 186–205, 232, 259, 279, 293–4, 301–2, 306, 311–14, 331–2, 371, 390, 400, 406, 414–15, 421, 468–9, 478–9, 494, 504, 510, 523, 528, 535, 542, 546, 558–80, 586–606, 612–14, 639, 663, 668, 673, 678, 683–4, 690, 696, 705–6, 711, 715, 721, 729–30, 760, 777, 799
god-almightiness 135–6, 225, 552–3, 624, 775
goês 235, 630–1
Goethe, Johann Wolfgang von 155–8, 165, 168, 178, 495, 504, 528–9, 541, 566, 575,

594, 680
golden chain 187, 586–7
golden thread 621–2
grace 292, 317, 401, 405, 671, 693–4, 774, 795
Grail 110, 123–6, 133–4, 140–1, 185, 194–8, 232, 384, 393–4, 508, 526–7, 533, 585, 599–601, 614, 628–9, 693, 730, 744, 768
greed, spiritual 130–1, 222, 338–9, 393, 548, 709, 757, 772
Greek, ancient language and literature 10, 19, 28, 63, 89, 101, 146, 150, 152–3, 169, 192, 196–7, 200, 235, 278, 297–8, 301–2, 347, 382, 406, 498, 503–4, 516, 546, 550, 581, 591–2, 597, 601, 630, 663, 742–4, 753–4, 761, 777
Guénon, René 245, 640, 755, 762–3, 766–8
Gurdjieff, George Ivanovitch 619, 647

H

Habakkuk 357–8, 720–2
Hadot, Pierre 533, 610
Hannah, Barbara 271, 421, 480, 572, 658, 772, 784–5
Harding, Esther 523, 620, 622, 645–6, 692–3, 725, 782
Hasidism 556–7
Heidegger, Martin 44, 483, 743, 797
hell 56, 61–3, 130, 179–80, 218, 270, 279, 355, 411, 499, 533, 584, 595, 719, 776, 782
Henderson, Joseph 547
Heraclitus 101, 483, 546, 608, 627–8, 684
heresy and heretics 140, 146, 205, 309, 313–14, 348, 371, 392, 400, 558–9, 687, 729, 759, 790
Hermes 150, 161, 370, 529, 569, 604, 700
Hermetic tradition 113, 149–53, 161, 187, 196–204, 370, 386, 479, 537, 553–4, 559–66, 581–2, 601, 604, 612–13, 707, 721, 746, 799
heroism 50, 81, 127, 140–1, 178, 221, 225–7, 262, 521, 573, 623–6, 672
Hesse, Hermann 147, 681
Heyer, Gustav Richard 500, 609–10
Hillman, James 388, 416, 465, 470, 476, 522, 531, 647, 742, 749–52, 773, 784
historical continuity 122, 182, 188–91, 301, 545, 584, 590, 595, 611

Hitler, Adolf 467, 624
Hoerni, Ulrich 528
Hölderlin, Friedrich 470, 519, 602
Homer 63, 79, 87, 101, 297, 498, 521, 529, 605, 680, 694–5, 792
hope 34, 119–20, 221–2, 234–5, 271, 333, 337, 398, 431, 442–3, 505–6, 519, 581–2, 633, 757, 764, 777, 797
hora mortis 426, 795
Horace 614, 642, 658
howling 17, 195, 214, 234–55, 343, 432, 629–37, 643, 711
Hull, R.F.C. (Jung's English translator) 23, 163–4, 473, 572, 651, 781

I

Iamblichus 513, 591, 638, 684, 753–4
iatromantis 76, 511, 513, 795
Ibn al-'Arabî, Muhyî al-Dîn 380, 553–4, 661, 745, 759
Ibn Wâsil, 'Umar 799
identification and disidentification 18–20, 24, 89, 135–42, 149–51, 161, 166, 170, 178, 225, 251, 262, 274, 306–11, 315, 319, 342, 350, 444, 469–70, 507, 516, 540, 555, 562, 572, 580, 599, 609, 624, 629, 652, 681, 689, 697, 708, 710, 715, 758, 786, 790
imaginatio vera 386, 745–7, 753–4
imagination 53–4, 62, 156–7, 385–6, 388, 414, 667, 677–8, 745–54
imitatio Christi 349
imitation 23, 114–16, 129, 153, 157, 269–73, 357, 389, 400, 466, 540, 548, 657–8, 771–2
immortality 114, 196–7, 537–9, 551, 602–3, 658
impersonal, the 107–110, 118, 143, 191, 194, 207, 334, 415, 531, 665
impossible, the 10, 61, 89, 104, 119–20, 130–1, 140, 143, 153, 173–6, 206, 248, 282, 288, 309, 319, 325–6, 342, 345, 394, 406, 443, 519, 527–8, 543, 557, 593, 665, 713, 757
incantation 43–6, 56, 68, 76, 239, 503–4, 508, 635–6, 728
incubation 45–6, 79, 298, 437, 440, 484–5, 490, 493, 776, 795, 798
India 124–7, 133, 194–6, 404, 546, 550–1, 599
individualism 84, 108–9, 142,

222, 531
individuation 89, 109–113, 123–4, 140–2, 169, 197, 251, 264–6, 380–3, 389, 392, 396–7, 467, 523, 527, 531–7, 555, 578, 654, 672, 703, 726, 743–4, 764, 769, 780
inflation 19–20, 24, 111–12, 122, 127, 135–44, 162, 180–1, 202, 251, 261, 265–74, 295, 309–10, 319, 324, 343–4, 352, 469, 514, 535, 552–5, 571, 575, 584, 619, 643–6, 654–9, 681, 716, 756–9, 763, 790–1
initiation 43, 51–3, 62, 136, 152, 196, 245, 365–72, 488, 492, 512, 533, 536–8, 548, 553, 565, 578, 664, 680, 746–7, 754
insanity: *see* madness
inscriptions 46, 100–1, 104, 177, 208, 213, 216, 478, 517, 527–9, 583, 608
institutions and institutionalizing 174, 314, 395–402, 562, 582, 650, 708, 768–74
integration 66, 74, 125, 170, 260, 304, 353–4, 380, 414, 444, 501, 535, 577, 609, 683, 692, 739
intellect 380, 746, 757, 759–61
interference 80, 84, 109, 139, 147, 216, 293, 299, 304, 396, 443, 478, 658, 662, 689, 769, 789
intuition 11, 16, 34, 36, 60, 75, 106, 131, 146, 201, 222, 230, 298, 431, 478, 483–4, 509, 591, 600, 620, 676
inversion and reversal 82, 115, 146, 161, 175, 189–90, 241–2, 331, 377, 396, 421, 429–31, 477, 499, 516, 545, 559, 569, 593
Irenaeus 683–4
Isaiah 283, 287–8, 321, 339–40, 357, 365, 382, 629, 632, 665, 667, 672–3, 675, 684, 693–4, 696, 709–11, 716–17, 724, 752
ishrâq 368, 393, 726–7
Ishrâqî 368–71, 689, 726–7, 730
Islam 238, 242, 247, 365, 370, 372–4, 390–2, 587, 633–4, 640, 690, 724, 730–3, 745, 799
Istanbul 367, 725, 742
Ivanow, Vladimir 748–9

J

Jacobi, Jolande 539, 541, 561–2
Jaffé, Aniela 424, 530, 579, 686, 719, 722, 738, 788–90
Jeremiah 254–5, 629, 631, 641, 667–8, 671–2, 717

jewel, precious 281–4, 288, 301, 309, 394, 665, 668, 676, 678, 683
Jewish traditions 199, 203–4, 231, 235–43, 248–9, 265–6, 292–4, 323, 338, 351–8, 378, 422, 556–7, 568, 604–7, 612–14, 636–8, 641–5, 671–3, 716–21, 740, 752
Joachim of Fiore 348–51, 385, 440, 633, 692, 714–16, 745, 776, 798
Job 354–5, 719–21
John of Rupescissa 716
Jonah 236, 250, 631–2, 671
joy 182, 246, 317, 375, 381, 465, 529, 573, 694, 734–5, 742
Jung, Andreas 722
Jung, Carl Gustav 7–9, 18–24, 27, 34–5, 58–208, 219–27, 232–5, 239, 250–358, 366, 369, 373–429, 434, 438, 443–5, 465–722, 725–9, 734–800
Jung, Carl Gustav (Jung's paternal grandfather) 358, 395, 722, 769
Jung, Emma 107, 219, 530, 543, 722
Jung, Franz 507
Jung, Johann Paul Achilles (Jung's father) 352–5, 358, 716–19, 722, 740, 791
Jung, Vreni 754

K

Kabbalah 556–7, 605–7
katabasis 493, 522, 679, 682, 783
Keller, Tina 471, 501, 664, 719, 740
Kerényi, Karl 579
Kerouac, Jack 634
ketmân 367, 725
Khidr 372, 385, 391, 573, 731, 744–5, 747, 763
Khunrath, Heinrich 551
Kirsch, James 250–1, 264, 378–9, 555, 644–5, 654, 661, 667, 672–3, 737, 739–40, 781
Klages, Ludwig 493
Klaus, Brother 525, 653
Kleinod (*see also* jewel, precious) 281, 284, 288, 665, 676, 678
knight 99, 103, 110, 120, 124, 134, 185, 196, 371, 384, 508, 526–7
kratêr 196–8, 204, 601–2, 613–14
Kubrâ, Najm al-Dîn 246–7, 640
Küsnacht 380, 416, 507, 725, 741

L

Lâhîjî, 'Abd al-Razzâq 364, 723
Laing, R.D. 22
Lang, Josef 146–7, 495, 559–60, 593, 652, 681
language 23, 34, 43, 54, 76, 90, 157, 188, 192, 242–7, 263–5, 294–5, 313, 317–26, 332–5, 435, 567, 571, 629, 636, 638, 640–1, 653, 674–5, 693–7
Lao Tzu 646
Latin language and literature 104, 132–3, 150, 192, 200, 278, 301–2, 386, 406–7, 522, 527–8, 550–1, 566, 583, 586, 591, 597, 658, 684, 695, 710, 724, 727, 761, 777–8
laughter and humour 35, 78, 129, 135, 171, 196, 262, 270, 396, 398, 403, 473, 478, 506, 540, 553, 556, 579, 603, 629, 653, 658, 729, 771, 775
lava: *see* volcanic craters and lava
Lawrence, D.H. 618
laws and lawgiving 42, 45, 49–50, 55–6, 72, 110, 141, 194, 215–18, 227, 229, 240, 284, 297, 303, 323, 371, 410, 435, 484, 487–91, 600, 681, 701, 767
leaven 369–70, 373, 728–9, 732, 734, 799
Leisegang, Hans 504, 523, 539, 560, 606, 612
Liber novus or "new book" 287–302, 339, 667, 678
library, Corbin's 727–8, 748
library, Jung's 74, 152–4, 281, 328, 332, 493, 504, 523, 525, 528–9, 538–9, 546, 554, 556, 576, 589, 591, 593, 604, 606, 628, 665, 678, 683, 706, 753–4
light-bringer 141, 143–4, 549, 557–8
logic 42–9, 54–7, 62, 72, 77–9, 156, 182, 193, 213, 229, 343, 364, 421, 438, 483–4, 490–1, 513
logos 483, 526
Lucifer 108, 121, 175, 407, 530, 545, 778

M

madness 12, 19, 21–6, 57–61, 66–7, 145, 166, 183–4, 205–6, 214, 230–2, 235, 238–9, 247–57, 287, 305, 339, 470–4, 489, 491–3, 502, 519, 574–5, 614, 619, 628, 634–5, 641–3, 648,

660, 707, 709, 712
Maeder, Alphonse 506, 656
magic 7, 43, 49, 68, 75–6, 88–90, 99, 106–7, 123, 137, 145, 152, 168–84, 196, 213–14, 232, 239, 259, 262–3, 273, 280, 282, 299, 308, 319, 325, 330–1, 344–5, 382, 503–4, 509–10, 522–3, 548–9, 565, 575–85, 602, 604, 635, 657, 659–60, 665, 669, 700, 704, 713, 775, 791
Maier, Michael 709
mana-personality 577–8, 580
Mani and Manichaeism 232, 303, 306–15, 332–4, 371, 400, 415, 554, 574, 628, 633–4, 685–91, 706–7, 729–30
Mann, Kristine 620, 622, 784
Martin, P.W. 543, 702–3
Massignon, Louis 725, 731–2, 745
master, the 20, 79, 163, 267–8, 271–3, 305–8, 311, 541, 656–9, 687–8, 758, 797
mastery 46, 88–9, 200, 221, 313, 328, 332–4, 473, 513, 519–20, 556, 618–19, 638, 707
McCormick, Fowler 527
McCormick, Harold 693
Mead, G.R.S. 558
medicine women and men 13–17, 23, 141, 467, 547, 555, 630, 696
meditation 38, 45, 130, 190, 229, 234, 381, 383, 410, 437, 490, 596, 742, 771
Meher Baba 617–18
Meier, C.A. 573, 658, 769–70, 772, 798
Memories, dreams, reflections 124–7, 207–8, 466, 770
Mephistopheles 495, 584
Mercurius 549, 551, 700
Merlin 1, 182, 232–3, 274, 350, 548, 584, 628–9, 653, 659, 715, 829
Mesopotamia (*see also* Babylonian traditions) 199, 235, 637, 641, 647, 679
metaphysics 114–15, 162, 382, 510, 572, 749, 759, 766–7
mêtis 319–20, 325–6, 695
Micah 241, 629–30, 637
Miller, David LeRoy 569, 647, 749–50, 755
missionaries 129, 200, 252, 260, 340, 548, 625
Mithraic mysteries 537–8
Mithras liturgy 565, 576, 593
monos pros monon 382–4, 742–5
Montaigne, Michel de 426–8, 795–6
moon 99–101, 137

Moses 323, 378, 604, 645, 740, 763
Mountain Lake 138, 223–4, 545, 554, 621–2
Muhammad 200, 238, 303, 306, 309, 370, 632–4, 685, 690, 724, 741
music 353, 377, 380, 385, 387, 717, 736, 744, 781–2
mysterium coniunctionis 414, 757, 783
Mysterium coniunctionis 151, 346, 543, 594, 652, 687, 713, 758–9
mystery and mysteries 51, 59, 62, 84, 104–5, 110–12, 123–4, 127, 132, 139–40, 152–3, 156–61, 169–70, 183–4, 196–7, 270, 275–9, 294, 308, 342, 347, 350, 369–74, 381–7, 401–2, 414–15, 488, 492, 512, 522–3, 527, 529, 533, 537–40, 565–6, 569, 604–5, 663–4, 684, 689, 692, 707, 742–7, 757–8, 764–8, 795
mystical union 347, 381, 414–15, 420, 714
mystics and mysticism 8, 20, 23, 27, 29, 42, 49, 68, 70–2, 110, 116–17, 121, 136–7, 152, 160, 191, 200, 207, 246, 257–9, 310–11, 314–15, 337, 343–8, 363–4, 368, 373, 380–2, 386, 400, 404, 414, 487–90, 500, 503, 506–7, 525, 532, 540–3, 551, 553–7, 565, 569, 573, 576–7, 602–8, 634, 640, 643, 648, 661, 689, 693, 696, 711–14, 726–7, 734–5, 742, 750, 759, 783, 786, 794
myth 34, 50–5, 62, 110–11, 126, 170, 182, 185–7, 230, 243–4, 272, 433, 478, 488, 509, 526, 533, 577–8, 624, 639, 677, 697–8, 791

N

Nag Hammadi 571, 573, 588
Naqshbandis 586
Nasr, Seyyed Hossein 372–4, 389–91, 730–4, 754–6
Native American traditions 13–17, 39, 121, 138–9, 223–4, 249, 409, 444, 623–4, 762
nature and naturalness 38–40, 43, 47, 60, 66, 74, 76–7, 82, 89, 103, 109, 114–16, 120, 146, 190, 197–8, 201–2, 214–16, 228–30, 235–6, 241–6, 253–5, 298, 322, 327, 342–3, 355, 413, 423–4, 429–31, 440, 468,

494, 508, 516, 522, 531, 556–7, 596, 598, 611, 631, 637–9, 660, 711, 729
nekyia 493, 497–8, 682
Neoplatonism 559, 609, 617
Neumann, Erich 199, 356, 378, 606, 720, 740, 774
neurosis 118–19, 191, 596, 779
new age 127, 222, 237, 299–301, 307, 350, 402, 407, 439, 478, 516, 619, 661, 717, 778, 780
New York 224, 238, 252–3, 410, 620–2, 635, 645, 782
Nietzsche, Friedrich 44, 483, 519, 602–3, 660, 666, 686, 688–9, 793
night 45, 49, 126, 304–5, 308, 376, 429, 443, 486–7, 548–9, 664, 677, 686, 688
Noah 422, 785
non-duality 595, 765
Nostradamus 715
"nothing but" 174, 539, 582
nous 753–4, 761
"now", the 595–6
Numenius 634
numinous 71, 107, 118–22, 125, 377, 521, 543–4, 655, 705, 736–7

O

Oannes 697
objectivity 107–9, 117, 143, 156–7, 310, 346, 394, 414–15, 531, 543–4, 567, 724
occultism 169, 171, 219, 330, 521, 551, 559, 575–6
Odysseus 317, 319, 497–8, 694–5
omniscience 217, 483, 680
optimism 221–2, 411, 418–24, 442–3, 480, 505, 619–20, 777–8
oracles 31–3, 219, 243, 407, 477–8, 626, 638, 647, 778
original instructions 444
Orpheus and Orphic tradition 503–4, 529, 538, 581, 598, 604–5, 613, 783
orthodoxy 191, 290, 374, 390, 558–9, 570, 588, 604, 609, 655, 673, 678, 692, 730–1, 762, 772
Ovid 566, 575
Oxford University 46

P

paintings 63, 150–1, 278–9, 302–7, 312, 344–5, 391, 442, 499, 564, 663, 689–90, 712, 730, 789
panoptic vision 680
Paracelsus 576, 578, 677, 708
paradox 25, 61–2, 67, 77, 79, 82, 88, 122, 124, 158, 162–3, 188, 310, 323–5,

333, 364, 386, 392, 415, 444, 468, 492, 497, 503, 513, 541, 546, 553, 563, 569, 571, 597, 675, 759–61, 783
Paris magical papyrus 169, 576–7
Parmenides 43–62, 67–8, 75–9, 85, 87, 110, 116, 156, 165, 176, 193, 200, 203–4, 208, 213–15, 231, 264, 294–5, 318–20, 335, 369, 474–5, 481–91, 502, 504, 509–18, 521, 533, 541–2, 567, 574, 577, 583, 591, 595–6, 607, 611–12, 627, 641, 653, 660, 674–5, 695, 709, 721, 723, 728, 732
Pauli, Wolfgang 397, 682, 703–5, 770–1
penitence and penance 177–84, 192, 583–4, 709
Persephone 43, 54, 104, 502, 528–9
personalities no. 1 and no. 2 66–7, 72, 81, 160–4, 167, 175, 188, 351, 353, 376, 410, 501–2, 507–8, 563, 569, 572–3, 590, 597, 620, 677, 781, 786–7
Phaedo 794
phantasia 747, 754
phantasmagoria 190, 593–4
pharmakon 196, 503–4, 602
Philemon 148–57, 164, 167–82, 186, 302–6, 357, 518, 561–7, 574–5, 578, 582–5, 604, 657, 680, 683, 697, 704, 714, 721, 746–7, 769
philosopher-kings 219, 488, 534, 617
philosophy, ancient 41–5, 124, 198–201, 363–4, 427, 606, 609–10
philosophy, modern 200, 408, 609–11
philosophy, prophetic 364, 723, 738
physikos 75, 509
pillar 306, 308, 549, 554–5, 608, 688, 740
plants and planting 14, 43, 50, 130–1, 153
Plato and Platonism 28–35, 48–58, 79, 85, 201–3, 219–20, 229, 243–4, 294, 390, 476, 484, 486–92, 512–13, 533–4, 608–10, 613, 616–17, 625, 638–9, 674, 679, 682, 760–1, 783, 785, 792–7
plêrôma 331, 468, 705
Plotinus 609, 617, 639, 760
Plutarch 31, 477
Poimandres 566
poison 59–60, 68, 130–1, 493, 503–5, 508, 550, 687, 767, 795
Porphyry 31, 243–4, 290, 477, 606, 617, 639, 754, 760

prayer 246, 381, 443, 559, 664, 742, 798–9
Preiswerk, Samuel 717
primordial experience 331, 392, 509, 677, 764–5
primordial origin 198, 205, 216, 298–300, 440, 444, 508–9, 615
primordial revelation 324, 328, 331–3, 336, 706–7
primordial tradition 390, 484, 760–1
prison, existence as a 414–15, 783
privatio boni 687
proclamation 135, 268, 304, 307, 314, 316, 693–4
progress 21, 24, 29, 33–5, 39–40, 44, 51, 117, 168, 175–6, 179–80, 195, 228–30, 250, 289–90, 299, 402–3, 409–10, 427, 479–81, 483, 600, 611–12, 643
projection 170, 178, 201, 263, 273, 383, 539, 578, 775
propatôr 302, 683–4
prophecy and prophets 18–19, 31, 45–77, 85, 102, 119, 126, 129, 200–4, 213–19, 227–427, 433–44, 477, 484–7, 492, 495, 513, 517, 528–9, 551, 556, 562, 573, 598, 613–14, 626–59, 666–724, 732–53, 768–9, 782, 786–96
prophet–healers (*see also iatromantis*) 46, 67, 76–7, 213, 239
prophêtês 647, 679
prostitution 649
Psychological Club in Zurich 133–4, 552, 693
Psychological types 281–3, 287–8, 542, 665, 667–8, 676, 685, 692
Puech, Henri–Charles 687
purity and purification 385, 744, 753–4, 794–5
Pythagoras and Pythagoreans 50–1, 55, 62–4, 116, 152, 201, 203, 370, 486, 488, 498–9, 534, 609, 611–13, 617, 682, 728, 783, 792, 796–7, 799

Q

Quispel, Gilles 538, 558, 573–4, 579, 612–13, 705
Qur'an 390, 633, 640–1, 726, 741, 762–3

R

Rank, Otto 508
Raphael, Alice 155, 553, 566, 583–4, 707
rationality and reason 26–33, 40–5, 48–51, 55–62, 66–71, 77–85, 102–4, 121,

131, 139, 150, 173–83, 201–3, 214–16, 220–3, 228–30, 234–9, 243–5, 266, 282–5, 288–301, 309–10, 326–7, 331, 337–9, 342–4, 355–6, 363–4, 373, 377, 380, 396, 414, 424–6, 433, 438, 443, 472, 475–6, 482–8, 492–501, 508, 513, 518, 521–2, 526, 530, 533, 538–40, 545, 557, 562, 572, 578, 581–3, 594, 600, 610, 614, 621, 628, 635, 639, 655–7, 664–9, 677–9, 682, 688, 691, 698, 702–5, 709–11, 719, 737, 762, 775, 790–1

reality, another 190, 346–7, 414–15, 595, 713

rebirth (*see also* reincarnation) 110, 152–3, 191, 196–7, 284, 333, 350, 439, 565, 590, 602–3, 618, 645, 707, 760

Red book 22, 58, 63, 66–72, 102, 108–9, 114, 130, 147, 150–3, 158, 165–83, 198, 204, 260, 269–70, 276–80, 286–353, 369, 378, 383, 391, 395, 401–3, 411–13, 424–6, 444, 470–4, 492–5, 500–4, 507–11, 515, 518, 531, 538–42, 547, 550, 554, 561–4, 569, 575, 589–90, 594, 598, 603–4, 615, 625, 638, 648–52, 657–86, 692–718, 728, 741, 774–8, 786–92

reincarnation (*see also* rebirth) 279, 300–1, 303, 314, 330, 540, 578–9, 683

Reitzenstein, Richard 539, 561, 565, 589, 601–4, 628, 701, 706–7, 721

religion 114–16, 122, 128, 133, 136, 152, 191, 199–202, 237, 248, 259, 276–9, 283, 289, 293, 304–7, 312–14, 323–4, 346–7, 365, 372, 400, 403–4, 408, 540, 545, 548, 557, 560, 564–5, 570, 633, 645, 649–50, 661–3, 673, 678, 681, 691–2, 696

repetition 43–6, 76, 239, 369, 398, 510–11, 513, 635, 728

responsibility 10–11, 123, 127, 178, 189, 229–31, 341, 393, 443, 545, 767

revelation 44, 165, 200, 230–1, 283–4, 289, 295, 307, 312, 315, 323–36, 378, 380, 394, 627, 666, 668, 690, 697, 706–7, 741, 759, 788

rhetoric 26, 273, 289–95, 483, 492, 576, 636, 669

riddles 77, 177, 186, 200, 225–6, 326, 512, 612, 653, 675, 682

ring composition 422, 785

ritual and ceremonies 153, 171–2, 176, 204–5, 224, 422, 442, 578–81, 614, 621–2, 795
Robb, Barbara 599, 689, 774
Rolfe, Eugene 140–4, 408–9, 416, 549, 553, 555–6, 570, 575, 618, 649, 652, 659, 673, 678, 685, 696, 739, 768, 778–9, 781–2, 784
Rosa, Salvator 63–4, 499
Rûmî, Jalâl al-Dîn 230, 626–7, 640, 742
Ruska, Julius 591
Ruspoli, Stéphane 246, 640
Rûzbehân al-Baqlî 640–1

S

Sahl al-Tustarî 799
salvator mundi 132, 550–1
Saoshyant 283–4, 288, 301, 303, 394, 666, 710, 768
Sapientia 278, 663, 764
saviours and salvation 20, 127, 132–44, 172, 195–6, 202–5, 232, 251–2, 258–9, 263, 271, 273, 282–4, 288, 300–3, 307–15, 321, 340, 394, 406, 411, 417, 470, 546, 550–2, 554, 557–8, 588, 602, 611, 614, 649, 657, 659, 665–6, 682, 685, 687–9, 696, 710–11, 765–8, 784, 790
scepticism 310–11
Schärf Kluger, Rivkah 643–4, 712
Schleiermacher, Friedrich 707
scholars and scholarship 36, 44–8, 53, 58–9, 62, 161–2, 170–1, 176, 188–9, 241, 276–85, 338, 342, 364, 368, 482, 489–90, 494–6, 499–50, 503, 511–12, 515, 518, 533, 541, 552, 569–71, 582–3, 591–2, 610, 627–8, 639–40, 724, 786–7, 795
Scholem, Gershom 556–7, 730
Schopenhauer, Arthur 670
Schultz, Wolfgang 504, 560
Schuon, Frithjof 483–4, 755, 761–3
science 34–5, 42–3, 47, 59, 61, 65–75, 79, 83–4, 90, 116, 134, 139, 150–4, 157–9, 165, 169–71, 180, 189, 202, 207, 213, 218, 222, 228–9, 278, 289–96, 299, 307–11, 315–37, 342–7, 364, 392, 397–9, 404, 480–1, 495, 500–3, 505–8, 533, 562–3, 573–4, 579–80, 593, 620, 642, 669–70, 687, 694–708, 757, 767, 770, 786
Seal of prophets 307, 312, 371, 633–4, 690
secrets and secrecy 18–19, 27,

32, 39, 58, 70–1, 102, 105–6, 110, 116, 119, 121, 124, 127, 136, 140, 159, 165, 168, 177, 182, 184, 195, 197, 207, 218, 230–2, 259, 262, 270–1, 279, 288, 301–3, 311, 314, 337, 342, 348, 363–6, 368–9, 380–4, 402, 412, 414, 431, 433, 475, 494, 507, 525–30, 541, 557–8, 569–70, 573–4, 583, 587, 590, 610, 625, 635, 638, 650, 657, 663, 684, 692–3, 715, 724–5, 744, 777, 799
self, true 66, 109, 115, 117, 153, 185–8, 221, 382, 393, 468, 501, 531–2, 537, 540–3, 551, 565, 574, 577, 580, 615, 689, 783–4
Serrano, Miguel 90, 506, 523, 534, 545, 554, 579–81, 616, 619, 621, 659, 670, 714, 721, 781
servator mundi 126, 132–4, 140, 144, 195–6, 550–2, 557–8
Seven sermons to the dead 158–9, 165, 567–8, 570, 574, 718
shadow 18, 119, 136, 157, 170, 224, 257, 306, 309, 620, 737
shamans 23, 229, 235, 242, 395, 473, 482, 582, 630, 638
Sibylline oracles 407, 778
Sicily 50, 197, 203–4, 577, 612–14
sickness 118-19, 124, 127, 131, 225, 249, 297, 305, 339–40, 347–8, 353, 382, 408, 420, 474, 476, 546, 548, 551, 574, 660, 710–11, 714, 718, 779, 781, 794
silence 12–14, 25, 31–2, 36, 41, 47, 55–6, 67, 84–5, 100, 109, 111, 115, 122, 148, 152, 167, 173–6, 181, 188, 232, 237–8, 245, 248, 256, 260, 267, 277, 285, 302, 334, 340, 343–6, 363, 367–9, 377, 424, 430–1, 474, 485, 582, 617–18, 632–3, 639, 762, 781, 795
Simon Magus 523, 560, 562, 578
singleness 383, 537, 744
six hundred years 403–5, 440, 776
sleep 47, 49, 108, 125, 134, 140, 231, 237, 298, 304–5, 344, 354, 378, 413–14, 430, 439, 441, 486–7, 628, 679, 686, 718–19, 783
Socrates 202, 425, 476, 487–8, 792–6
sohbet 381, 742
Sophia 278–9, 301, 391, 663, 683, 738, 764
soul 51, 66, 114–19, 122, 128, 172, 277–80, 304, 314,

334–5, 338, 365, 380, 391–2, 395, 408, 443, 476, 486–7, 503, 540, 545, 548, 581, 604, 661, 663, 686, 691–3, 705, 708, 735, 766–8, 786, 794
Spielrein, Sabina 589–90
spirit of the depths and spirit of this time 58–9, 66–7, 72, 79–80, 84, 161, 165–9, 175–6, 178, 188, 202, 252, 289, 292, 302, 316–17, 321, 335, 343, 347, 369, 373, 390–1, 474, 492, 497, 501–2, 507–8, 515, 522, 525, 569, 572, 574–5, 582, 589, 611, 625–6, 667, 675–7, 684, 694, 728, 792
Spitteler, Carl 665, 692
Steiner, Rudolf 478, 483, 696
stillness 55, 100, 188, 190, 237, 429–31, 781, 795
stone 38, 46, 81–2, 99–101, 103–4, 126, 143, 200, 206–8, 213, 216, 283, 322, 517, 598, 629, 637, 665, 797
stripping, inner 44, 62, 109–110, 125, 241, 329, 426, 444–5, 692, 795, 799
suffering 26–7, 29–30, 60, 71, 100, 106, 108–9, 118, 121, 144, 191, 231–2, 237, 266, 281, 297, 303, 319, 328–9, 337–43, 349, 354–5, 406, 414, 475, 494, 535–6, 619, 655, 708–11, 715, 719, 778–9
Sufis and Sufism 8, 33, 137, 139, 230, 246–7, 310, 364–7, 372, 379, 381, 388, 391, 393, 415, 443, 553–4, 573, 586–7, 640–1, 661, 688, 723–5, 731–3, 742–3, 749–50, 761–2, 796, 798–9
Suhrawardî, Shihâb al-Dîn Yahyâ 367–74, 393, 415, 725–34, 745, 762, 766
sun 43–9, 101, 125, 130, 137–8, 275, 393, 487, 529, 554, 637, 659–60, 678, 726
superiors 369, 728
surrender, mystical 110, 120, 310, 532
Swedenborg, Emanuel 670
symbol 115, 182, 193, 196–8, 538–42, 554, 567, 570, 665, 733–4
sympatheia 330, 704
synchronicity 154, 290, 330–1, 397, 402–3, 608, 669–70, 703–5, 736
syncretism 199, 603–4, 690
Syria 137, 634

T

Tartarus 598
teacher, inner 148–57, 164–77,

186–7, 357, 364–8, 372, 385, 474, 560–3, 714, 725, 730–2, 744–6
technology 40, 69–70, 180, 218–21, 228–9, 338–9, 432, 439, 481, 506
Teilhard de Chardin, Pierre 763
telê tôn aiônôn 777
Tertullian 528, 633
Theosophists 269, 272, 656, 685, 696
therapeia 28, 310, 476
therapy 27–30, 118–23, 222, 310, 380, 397, 534, 544, 563, 596, 737, 744, 770–1
thought and thinking 10, 43–4, 49–50, 54–6, 79, 82, 89, 100, 116, 122, 135, 156–7, 173, 180, 183, 299, 324, 386, 394, 431, 490–1, 562–3, 567, 609, 628, 682, 697, 759
Tibetan traditions 229, 392, 405, 764
"Traditionalists" 245, 390–2, 479, 483–4, 616, 730–4, 754–63, 765–7
transcendence 308, 346, 415, 467–8, 542, 557, 687, 713, 756–60, 783
transcendent function 691–2
translation and mistranslation 41, 83–5, 157, 188, 192, 259–60, 318–22, 326–35, 368, 374, 516–18, 591–3, 637, 650–1, 687, 694–8, 707–8, 728, 732–4, 738–9, 788
treasure 121, 132, 185, 262, 276, 405, 408, 585, 611
trickery 18–20, 30, 36, 41, 43, 55, 58, 77, 108, 139, 165, 180, 215, 238, 276, 289, 296, 310, 319–20, 337, 368, 395, 432, 444, 750, 763, 767, 781, 787, 790
truth 9–11, 30–7, 45, 62, 108–9, 121, 155, 165, 179, 181, 267–9, 273, 283, 301, 323–7, 369, 376, 384, 399–400, 466, 484, 494, 540–2, 545–6, 552, 623, 650, 657–9, 666, 734, 744, 759, 773–4
Tunisia 32, 313, 333
Turfan 307, 313, 691

U

ummah 365, 724
underworld 43, 53–64, 67, 72, 76, 79, 85–6, 101, 104, 108, 110, 148, 156, 165, 194, 198, 204–5, 218, 269–70, 276–7, 291, 294, 298, 304, 318–19, 328, 438, 470, 490, 492–3, 497–9, 512, 515, 522, 528–9, 541, 567, 590, 595,

603, 614, 630–1, 662, 674–5, 682, 783, 788
UNESCO 702
unexpected, the 14, 27, 61, 98, 142–4, 163, 166, 183, 189, 284, 288, 300–1, 340, 349, 370, 543, 557, 575, 581–2, 632, 666, 682, 688, 710–11, 739, 764, 787
United Nations 178
United States: *see* America
unspeakable, the 346–7, 489, 684, 713–14
Upanishads 129, 542
Urerfahrung: *see* primordial experience
urgency 10, 21, 126–7, 132, 137, 165, 190, 194, 220, 264, 295, 317, 364, 424, 547–8, 747
Urizen 676–9, 711
Uroffenbarung: *see* primordial revelation

V

van der Post, Laurens 771, 773
Velia 46, 52–8, 213–16, 234–5, 485, 489–92
ventriloquism 150, 562, 710
vision and visions 44–7, 79, 81–2, 115–16, 146–7, 182, 194, 198, 236, 240, 265, 286, 289–91, 324, 344, 348–51, 373–4, 380, 385, 403–4, 407, 411, 418–29, 443, 471, 540, 559–60, 589–90, 592, 594, 605–7, 632, 636, 643, 654, 659, 661, 667, 669–70, 678, 680–1, 685, 712–13, 715–16, 732, 738, 741, 744, 746–7, 753–4, 768, 776, 779, 785–92, 795–6
volcanic craters and lava 82–3, 88, 197–8, 204–5, 270–1, 276, 294, 321–2, 326–30, 374, 516–19, 584, 603, 613–15, 697, 702, 782
von Franz, Marie-Louise 418–25, 469, 475, 507, 544, 572, 591, 599–600, 627–9, 644, 646, 648–9, 658, 660–1, 700, 721, 776, 784–8
von Hartmann, Eduard 560
von Schubert, Gotthilf Heinrich 670

W

Wagner, Richard 624–5, 767
Wagner, Suzanne 420–1, 784
Waite, Arthur Edward 693
war 181, 202, 225, 286–90, 367, 404–5, 411–13, 415, 505–6, 624–5, 667–70, 680, 742, 782, 791–2
warnings 19, 24, 55–6, 73, 84, 108, 111–13, 119–20,

129–30, 142, 172, 174, 195, 219–21, 248, 251, 259–61, 265–6, 288, 338–40, 388–9, 424, 466, 472, 480, 495, 511, 516, 581–2, 650–1, 681, 691, 735, 749–52, 762–3, 766, 775, 789
Watts, Alan 771
Wechsler, Rabbi Hile 644, 672–3
White, Victor 528, 656, 686, 736–7, 774
whole, the 132, 408–9, 550, 779
Wickes, Frances 621–2
wildness 77, 120, 156, 213–15, 247, 298, 326, 332–3, 353, 424, 598, 622, 637–8, 680, 788
Wilhelm, Richard 129, 548, 590
will, divine 401–2, 598, 689
Wolff, Toni 518–19, 529
Woolf, Virginia 519
world ages 347–50, 389, 406, 437–40, 714–15, 777–8

Y

Yeats, W.B. 681

Z

Zarathustra 303, 307, 309–10, 685, 689–90, 706
Zeller, Max 776
Zen Buddhism 229, 392, 764
Zeno 485, 489
Zeus 605, 638, 647
Zoroastrianism (*see also* Zarathustra) 283, 294, 306, 665–6, 674–5, 751–2
Zosimus of Panopolis 589–91, 601, 605–6, 799

And just as I'm dark, and also will be towards those
to whom I have no intention of revealing myself,
so the whole of this book will remain incomprehensible;
and not much will happen without anyone receiving its gifts

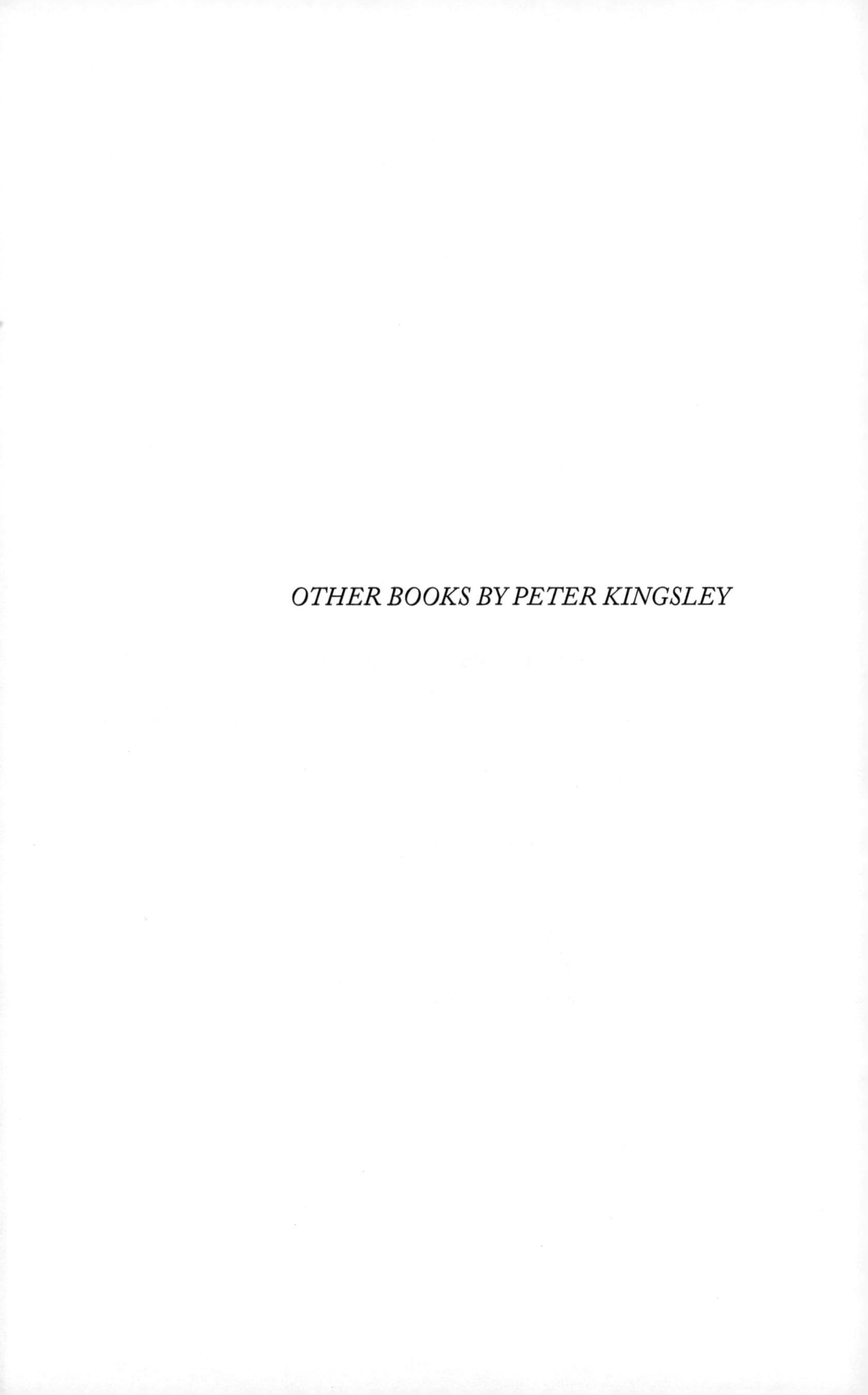

OTHER BOOKS BY PETER KINGSLEY

ANCIENT PHILOSOPHY, MYSTERY AND MAGIC

"A masterpiece, gripping, urgent and important: a unique pioneering work."

European Review of History

"Every scholar dreams of writing a truly original book, but in reality hardly anyone ever does. A truly original book, one that can transform a whole discipline, appears at the most once in a generation. In the field of ancient philosophy, Peter Kingsley's *Ancient Philosophy, Mystery and Magic* is such a book."

Prof. Anthony Long, author of *Greek Models of Mind and Self* and
editor of *The Cambridge Companion to Early Greek Philosophy*

IN THE DARK PLACES OF WISDOM

"This remarkable book speaks with equal power to the scholar and the seeker alike. To absorb what it says is to encounter a completely new vision of the ancient world that lies at the root of our own civilization. Right there, at our own feet, lies a forgotten tradition that has the power to transform all our views about our culture and our life."

Jacob Needleman, author of *Lost Christianity,*
The Heart of Philosophy and *I am not I*

"Quite simply a masterpiece: a work of immaculate, luminous scholarship which recovers for Western civilization the treasures of wisdom discarded by Plato over 2000 years ago. No-one could fail to respond to this story or be moved by the poetic prose which takes us 'as far as longing can reach' and opens a door into depths which have never been recognized, let alone explored by our culture."

Anne Baring, author of *The Dream of the Cosmos* and
co-author of *The Myth of the Goddess*

REALITY

"Reality contains the purest and most powerful writing I have ever read."

Michael Baigent, author of *Ancient Traces* and *The Holy Blood and the Holy Grail*

"Peter Kingsley is a successor to Carl Jung and Joseph Campbell. He is a transformative and life-changing force in our world. Never have we needed such a message as now."

Larry Dossey, M.D., author of *Reinventing Medicine* and *Healing Words*

"Dr. Kingsley's remarkable new book, *Reality*, is extraordinarily valuable. It would be difficult not to conclude that, through his research into our past, he has found the key to the modern world impasse."

Robert Johnson, author of *He, She, Inner Work*, and *Balancing Heaven and Earth*

A STORY WAITING TO PIERCE YOU

"This is the real thing. In each paragraph of the book, the Spirit is there. This is what the native people of the Americas have been trying to say, but were never permitted to. This song is the song of wisdom that we native people have not been allowed to sing."

Joseph Rael (Beautiful Painted Arrow), from the Foreword

"The rich and dense scholarship in this book is admirable, nay incredible, with worldwide scope. Scholarly discussion depends on evidence—of which *A Story Waiting to Pierce You* offers the most surprising riches combined with overwhelming expertise."

Prof. Walter Burkert, author of *Greek Religion* and *Babylon, Memphis, Persepolis*

"In this profoundly erudite and eloquent book is a startling ancient secret that will forever alter the way we think about the origins of western civilization."

Pir Zia Inayat Khan, Sufi sheikh and spiritual leader of the Inayati Order

To learn more about Peter Kingsley's work visit

www.peterkingsley.org